THE HANDBOOK
OF ADDICTION TREATMENT
FOR WOMEN

THE HANDBOOK
OF ADDICTION
TREATMENT
FOR WOMEN

Shulamith Lala Ashenberg Straussner
and
Stephanie Brown,
Editors

JOSSEY-BASS
A Wiley Company
www.josseybass.com

Published by

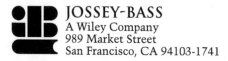

JOSSEY-BASS
A Wiley Company
989 Market Street
San Francisco, CA 94103-1741

www.josseybass.com

Jossey-Bass books and products are available through most bookstores. To contact Jossey-Bass
directly, call (888) 378-2537, fax to (800) 605-2665, or visit our website at www.josseybass.com.

Substantial discounts on bulk quantities of Jossey-Bass books are available to corporations,
professional associations, and other organizations. For details and discount information, contact
the special sales department at Jossey-Bass.

Library of Congress Cataloging-in-Publication Data

The handbook of addiction treatment for women/Shulamith Lala
Ashenberg Straussner and Stephanie Brown, editors.
       p. ; cm.
Includes bibliographical references and index.
   ISBN 0-7879-5355-5 (alk. paper)
   1. Women—Substance use—Handbooks, manuals, etc.   2. Substance
abuse—Sex differences—Handbooks, manuals, etc.   3. Compulsive
behavior—Handbooks, manuals, etc.
   [DNLM: 1. Substance-Related Disorders—therapy.   2. Behavior,
Addictive—therapy.   3. Substance-Related Disorders—psychology.
4. Women's Health.· WM   270   H2355   2002]   I. Straussner, Shulamith
Lala Ashenberg.   II. Brown, Stephanie, date.
   RC564.5.W65   H36   2002
   616.86'0082—dc21   2001006949

FIRST EDITION
HB Printing   10 9 8 7 6 5 4 3 2 1

CONTENTS

To all women struggling to overcome their addictions and
to those helping them in their struggles

PREFACE

This is a book about women and addiction—all kinds of women and all kinds of addiction. We look at women who are in the throes of active addiction and women who are in recovery, women who are young and women who are old, women who are Black and women who are White, women who use drugs and women who spend. Often the same woman will fit many of these categories and the many others that we address. This is a book about all women and, especially, this particular woman—this one woman in our office, treatment center, homeless shelter, or prison. This book is about the individual woman needing help, seeking help, or being forced to seek help, and how we help her.

This is a book for therapists of all disciplines, from experienced addiction specialists to those with minimal or no knowledge about this population. The book is both general and specific. We start with the general in Part One, reviewing what is known about women and addiction both historically and in the present. We next explore the paradoxes and challenges that a women's point of view raises and, finally, outline the theoretical and clinical perspectives that we believe offer the greatest strengths for diagnosing addictions and treating women addicts today.

This is not a one-size-fits-all book. Quite the contrary. We emphasize the great diversity and complexity of all women and the importance of including multiple perspectives in assessment and treatment. We have organized this book to emphasize different points of view—that is, the multiple meanings and organizing principles that must inform treatment for women with addictions. Our authors do not have a party line, nor do they necessarily see addiction, or addiction treatment, in the same way. They are here to tell us what we need to think about, including modifications to our own individualized theories and practice, when we work with women who have a special concern—and in our view, every woman has a special concern. So there is no typical woman and no typical best treatment. There are no "right" answers. Instead, you will find a cultural-social-psychological map with widely varied terrain. The therapist's job is to know the whole and its parts, to be able to listen carefully to the client and consider all factors as relevant to her treatment.

Following our general introduction, we move to the specific. Part Two tackles different kinds of addictions, with chapters focused on the women abusing alcohol and other drugs, smoking, or exhibiting other out-of-control behaviors, such as eating disorders or addictions to gambling, spending, relationships, or sex. The authors explore the organizing role of the substance or behavior in the woman's inner and outer world, and guide us in how to think about working with a woman with a particular addiction.

In Part Three we shift the organizing lens to age; the authors consider addiction in relation to the adolescent, middle-aged, and older woman. What are the major biopsychosocial issues for the young or older woman? What are the major addictions? What are the roles and meanings of addiction at different stages of the life cycle? How does the therapist think about assessment and treatment in relation to the age of the female client?

The authors in Part Four show us how to think about women from the perspective of race or ethnic heritage and culture. What is the impact on our view of the woman addict when we consider her racial and cultural background? How much do these factors influence her choice of drug or particular addiction, and how do race and culture affect our thinking about treatment? What should we know about a Latina adolescent? About an elderly immigrant from China? Or about a Black, lesbian, middle-aged woman who has come from Jamaica?

And so our point of view grows in breadth and complexity. Next we explore other issues that will have an organizing role for the woman and her addiction and for us, as clinicians, in our efforts to help her. Part Five explores additional groups or contexts that have an important impact on women addicts, such as lesbians, homeless women, the workplace, women in the criminal justice system, and women with dual diagnoses. Again, how does the therapist think about the influence of each of these factors on this particular woman now seeking help?

Finally, what and how do we think about treatment? Although all the authors have addressed treatment issues in their chapters, in Part Six we look at two specific treatment approaches: group psychotherapy and the self-help, or mutual-help, groups. Why and how do these modalities serve addicted women?

◆ ◆ ◆

Is this a book about gender? Yes and no. It is a book about women. But it is not a book about women compared to men. It is much more about women in relation to other women: What are general guiding principles in thinking about women as a group, and what are the differences between women? This book is about variability, diversity, and complexity; it is a theoretical and practical map to guide the therapist in determining the most therapeutic next step for a particular woman. We hope this book offers some of the essential guideposts that will help clinicians provide better help to the many addicted women who are struggling to cope in this increasingly complex world.

January 2002   Shulamith Lala Ashenberg Straussner
                                                                              New York, New York

                                                                                Stephanie Brown
                                                                          Menlo Park, California

ACKNOWLEDGMENTS

This book is all about women and addiction. The creation and writing of this book is also all about women: the thirty-six authors who are themselves all kinds of women—women of different ages, from different ethnic cultures and different professional backgrounds, and with a wide range of experiences. We say an enormous thank you to all of them for their generosity of time and tremendous effort in crafting their chapters to fit the overall broad and comprehensive design of this book, while also offering their unique and sophisticated perspectives. We asked a great deal of them, and we are grateful for their willingness and commitment to this huge project. We believe that the whole far surpasses our original hopes for this book.

We thought we had a fertile project from day one. Apparently, so did some of the authors. Three gave birth to babies as well as their chapters. All the other authors juggled the demands of writing with their accomplished and busy professional and personal lives. We end the construction of this book with a wonderful spirit of teamwork, dedication, goodwill, and gratitude.

These feelings extend to our editors and production people at Jossey-Bass. Alan Rinzler has been a supportive, thoughtful, and rigorous boss as he has guided and prodded us throughout. Amy Scott has also been extremely helpful with production and management issues, and Rachel Anderson has directed the final production with enormous skill and concern in a difficult time. We thank them all.

We also thank the women who are represented in all the chapters: women struggling with addiction—their own or someone else's—in clinics, shelters, prisons, treatment centers, outpatient therapies, AA, and all other meeting grounds where help is offered. Their voices and experiences are invaluable in teaching us what we need to know.

Most of all, we want to thank each other. This project came together through odd circumstances, so it very well might not have happened. We are so grateful that it did.

The Editors

Working on a book is a very intimate endeavor. It requires trust, mutual respect, cooperation, support, and constant encouragement. I feel lucky to have found this in my coeditor, a woman whose books I've read over the years, but whose world, both professional and physical, seemed far away from mine. To have worked with Stephanie, whom I met only once for a few minutes prior to beginning this project, has been an incredibly gratifying experience. Thank you, Stephanie, for being there and for being you.

I'm grateful to have had the pleasure of "meeting" the many authors around the country whose willingness to edit and re-edit their work has made this enormous task seem *almost* painless. Thank you all. I look forward to *really* meeting you one of these days. Special thanks are due to my friends and colleagues who may not have known what they were getting into when they agreed to be talked into contributing a chapter: Trish, Linda, Liz, Jeannine, Carol, Katherine, Diana, and Muriel.

This book would not have been possible without the work of my administrative assistant, Samantha Freire, whose always-cheerful demeanor and general helpfulness is appreciated. I would like to thank my dean, Tom Meenaghan, for his support of all my work, and my many friends and colleagues at New York University and particularly at the Ehrenkranz School of Social Work for being there when I felt overwhelmed and needed a supportive "fix." My deep appreciation to my friend, Norma Phillips, who willingly did more than her share on "our" book when I was busy with this one. Finally, my everlasting gratitude to my husband, Joel, who provided constant support, picked up the slack when needed, and tolerated the tons of books all over the house; and to my children, Adam and Sarina, who probably thought that I'd never again leave the chair by the computer, and whose growing independence and maturity are a pleasure to see.

S.L.A.S.

I did not start out to be part of this book, yet that is where I ended up, and it couldn't have been better. Joining this project offered me an opportunity to propose a challenging point of view in thinking about women, which I wanted to do. And it offered me the opportunity to work as a coeditor with Lala Straussner, also an appealing idea. How lucky I have been. Working with Lala has been a highlight of my writing and professional life. I am grateful for her point of view, her organizing and management skills, her creativity, boundless energy, and support. I have reaped the benefits of this partnership and of working with all the extraordinary authors on this team. Their commitment, professionalism, and endurance have been wonderful. Many feel like friends after so much hard work together and such goodwill. Special thanks to my colleagues and friends who agreed so readily to write chapters: Lynn, Susan, Renee, and Joyce.

I also thank all the people who have supported me for nearly thirty years in my thinking, writing, teaching, and clinical work—professionals, recovering friends, volunteer research participants and donors, and patients. I also extend a special thanks to all my associates at the Addictions Institute, who enrich my thinking and offer so much support. In that group, I wish to especially thank Joanne Stultz for her help in editing and clarifying my thinking in my own chapter, and Jim Hutt and Joanne for their support in the process of finding my way. I give another thanks to Alan Rinzler for his terrific editing and support of my creative labors. Always, I am grateful to my husband, Bob Harris, and our daughter, Makenzie, for our loving family.

I have loved this project. Thank you to Lala, and to all.

S.B.

THE HANDBOOK
OF ADDICTION TREATMENT
FOR WOMEN

PART ONE

UNDERSTANDING
ADDICTED WOMEN

CHAPTER ONE

WOMEN'S ADDICTION AND TREATMENT THROUGH A HISTORICAL LENS

Shulamith Lala Ashenberg Straussner and Patricia Rose Attia

Women's addictions span a wide scope—from alcohol and other drug dependence to smoking, gambling, sex, eating disorders, and shopping. Nonetheless, it is the use of alcohol and other drugs that has been, and remains, the most pervasive and most stigmatizing of all addictions for women. According to the National Center on Addiction and Substance Abuse, 4.5 million women in the United States are alcohol abusers or alcoholics, 3.5 million misuse prescription drugs, and 3.1 million regularly use illicit drugs.

It is instructive to look at the history of women's use of alcohol and other drugs in the United States, because such a historical perspective helps us understand women's substance abuse problems in the context of their role in society. It also helps us understand society's responses to women's problems with these substances, and consequently the treatment offered them.

This chapter examines the history of women's use and abuse of alcohol and other drugs and points out how women's substance abuse and treatment in the United States has been affected by gender and racial bias, economic factors, and ignorance by treatment providers. The emphasis is on the history of alcohol and other drug problems among White, heterosexual women. Although there are some current data regarding substance abuse and treatment of African American and other women of color and of lesbians, their historical relationship to these issues has yet to be fully explored.

A Historical View of Women and Alcohol Use

Women have used alcohol from ancient times and frequently have been condemned for its use. The Old Testament talks about Hannah, the mother of the prophet Samuel, as being falsely accused of being "drunken" (1 Sam. 1:13–15), and during the early Roman era a woman who was caught drinking, or even suspected of it, was treated the same way as one who was adulterous—with a prompt execution by her husband or another man in the family (Sandmaier, 1980). The availability of cheap gin in eighteenth-century England led to its widespread use by poverty-stricken women in London and to widespread disgust toward those who became addicted to it. This so-called gin epidemic also led to a growing concern about the impact of women's drinking on their offspring (Fielding, 1751, cited in Hornik, 1977), a dynamic first noted by ancient Greeks.

The history of women's use and abuse of alcohol in the United States is intertwined with the political movements of temperance, prohibition, and suffrage and with the ever-changing role of women in political and family life.

Alcohol has been part of White America since the arrival of the Pilgrims and was a constant presence in colonial life. As indicated by White (1998), "what is striking about early colonial history is the utter pervasiveness of alcohol. It was consumed throughout the day by men, women and children and integrated into nearly every ritual of social and political discourse" (p. 1). Despite its widespread acceptance, as early as 1780 Dr. Benjamin Rush, a signer of the Declaration of Independence and the "father" of American psychiatry, voiced concern about abusive drinking habits of both men and women. He was the first person in the new republic to view chronic drunkenness as a "disease of the will" (O'Dwyer, 1993). Moreover, according to White (1998), Rush anticipated the self-medication theory of women's substance abuse when he pointed out that women "were sometimes drawn into drunkenness in the use of ardent spirits to seek relief from what was then called 'breeding sickness' (menstrual distress)" (p. 3).

In the 1830s, Harriet Martineau, the author of *Society in America* (1837), toured the United States and wrote critically of women's excessive drinking habits. She determined that there were four reasons why privileged women in a country of peace and prosperity would turn to inebriety: cultural oppression, "vacuity of mind," desire to stop using prescription medication, and physicians' prescription of cordials (pp. 159–160). Physicians prescribed alcohol for a variety of medical ills specific to women: "to alleviate discomfort during pregnancy and delivery, as well as a relaxant in premenstrual tension, and for preventing infection after childbirth. Beer was thought to fortify a woman for breast feeding" (Hornik, 1977, p. 20). Women, of course, followed the advice of their male doctors. By the end of the

1800s, there was another reason for women's increasing reliance on alcohol: the liquor industry's advertising campaigns. "As narcotics became increasingly stigmatized, liquor sellers stepped into the breach, socializing women to the benefits of drinking" (Murdock, 1998, p. 49).

The Victorian values of the nineteenth century led to the formulation of the "ideal" American family, and public inebriety, violence, and family disruption related to excessive drinking were increasingly frowned on. Thus, unlike the generally tolerant attitude at that time toward women's use of opium, which, as we will discuss shortly, was viewed as more "genteel" and "feminine" (Murdock, 1998, p. 49), alcohol use was associated with male inebriety, especially with the drinking of poor Irish and German immigrants. Consequently, women's drinking was strongly condemned. As pointed out by Sandmaier (1980, p. 41),

> drunkenness among both sexes was often punished by imprisonment; however, Victorian morality may have imposed an even harsher fate on some chronically drunk or alcoholic women. In an address before the Medico-Legal Society in 1897, a Brooklyn physician recommended that the alcoholic woman "be desexualized . . . whether maid or matron" if she failed to respond to routine treatment. As "desexualization"—removal of a woman's uterus and ovaries— was a fairly common procedure performed on sexually active or otherwise unruly women in the late 1800s, it is likely that this operation was carried out on at least some alcoholic women during this period.

Such severe treatment of alcoholic women was also reflected in the growing eugenics movement during the early part of the twentieth century, with its emphasis on the sterilization of "the unfit." Sterilization of alcoholic women continued as late as the 1950s. White (1998) describes interviewing a number of alcoholic women who had been committed to state psychiatric facilities in the 1940s and 1950s and whose medical records confirmed that they were able to obtain discharge only after "voluntarily" agreeing to be sterilized.

An interesting profile of nineteenth-century alcoholic women is provided by Dr. Lucy Hall (1888), who served as the physician in charge of the Reformatory Prison in Sherborn, Massachusetts. In a study of 204 inebriate women under her care, Hall found that the majority of them started drinking excessively before they were twenty-one years old. Their first drink was usually alcohol-laced tonics, and gradually they switched to beer and then distilled spirits. Half of these women had a history of multiple imprisonments for drunkenness-related offenses, and they tended to drink with other women, not alone. Of interest is her observation that more than one-third of the married women had been so beaten by their drunken husbands that they had scars on their heads.

Women and the Temperance Movement

The early nineteenth-century temperance movement, which, as reflected by its name, was initially conceived as a movement that sought to temper excessive drinking with moderate, socially approved levels of drinking, soon attracted the attention of women who suffered significantly from men's drinking: "Barred by law or custom from divorcing inebriate husbands, unable to earn a living wage themselves, isolated in a society with few mechanisms to reform drinkers or their families, drunkards' wives faced brutality, poverty and abandonment" (Murdock, 1998, p. 16). These women, as exemplified by the well-known saloon-wrecker Carrie Nation, whose first husband was an extremely abusive alcoholic man, knew that religious-led efforts to "convert whisky-drinking drunkards into temperate beer-drinkers" (White, 1998, p. 5) were futile. Consequently, they became staunch advocates of shifting the philosophy from temperance as moderation to temperance as abstinence. As early as 1805, women had formed their own temperance societies, and by 1848, the Daughters of Temperance had thirty thousand members (Murdock, 1998).

The temperance movement gained momentum toward the end of the nineteenth century. The so-called Women's Crusade of 1873–1874 was a culmination of many years of women's taking action against saloons and the widespread availability of liquor. Because at this time they had no direct political power, women used petitions, prayer vigils, and demonstrations to persuade saloonkeepers to close their doors. By 1874, local antisaloon crusades were widespread, and they united to form the Women's Christian Temperance Movement (Murdock, 1998; Sandmaier, 1980; White, 1998).

One of the most politically influential movements of the late 1800s, the Women's Christian Temperance Movement (WCTU) initially focused on endorsing prohibition, temperance education, and dry government facilities. However, under the leadership of Frances Willard, president from 1879 to 1898, the WCTU expanded its agenda significantly and "soon considered woman's suffrage the catalyst for prohibition's victory" (Murdock, 1998, p. 25). Willard, a brilliant strategist, recognized that even though women were not allowed into the political sphere, they were allowed to perform "good works." Consequently, she was able to build on the virtuous work of women on behalf of the prohibition movement as an entrée to gain voting rights for women. It is thus not surprising that the eighteenth amendment, which established Prohibition, and the nineteenth amendment, which gave women voting rights, were ratified within one year of each other.

Yet the relationship between the suffrage and prohibition movements in the late nineteenth and early twentieth centuries was complicated. Although at times the groups seemed to work toward common goals, each also viewed the other as compromising the goals and values of its cause (Murdock, 1998). While the suffragettes worked toward the establishment of the moral and legal right of women not only to vote but also to be viewed as independent women with their own rights apart from their fathers and husbands, the underlying assumption of the temperance movement was that a woman's role was to *moderate* the potential excesses and immorality of her husband's drinking. This role called for a "virtuous" abstinent woman. The idea that women also could drink alcohol would have threatened the status quo; thus women drinkers were stigmatized and typically depicted as prostitutes (Murdock, 1998).

Women's Alcohol Use During the Nineteenth Century

In her book *Domesticating Drink,* Catherine Gilbert Murdock (1998) offers exhaustive research regarding women's use of alcohol during the nineteenth and early twentieth centuries. Murdock documents the growing concern about women's drinking and what was viewed as " 'masculinization' and the perceived unwomanly, nonmaternal qualities of women drinkers" (p. 51). She goes on to state that "women alcoholics, barred from treatment or sympathy by their own denial and others' prejudices, are one of the greatest tragedies of the period" (p. 51).

Thus, at the turn of the century, many women are involved in a vigorous campaign against all drinking, while other women are clearly drinking quite liberally. Sandmaier (1980, p. 40) makes reference to an 1899 article in *Catholic World* that estimated that eight thousand women were arrested in New York City for drunkenness the previous year. Murdock (1998) delineates regional differences in women's drinking: in the rural Midwest—home of the WCTU—women did not drink or even serve wine, but they did do so in many urban communities.

Ironically, the majority of *all* women used over-the-counter patent medications that promised relief from whatever ailed them. Some of these patent medicines contained 50 percent alcohol or opium. According to Sandmaier (1980, p. 45), "Edward Bok, editor of the *Ladies Home Journal* in the late 1800s and a leading opponent of the patent medicine business, surveyed fifty members of the WCTU and found that three out of four used patent medicines with an alcohol content of one-eighth to one-half spirits." By the end of the nineteenth century, Americans were spending $100 million on patent medicines per year, and, as will be discussed later, the majority of the users were women (Wood, 1906).

Women's Alcohol Use During the Twentieth Century

During the early part of the twentieth century, as women's use of opiates and patent medicines began to decline, it was not uncommon for women in the larger cities to be seen in cabarets and public dining areas drinking with men. And even when the Volstead Act of 1919 prohibited the sale or use of alcohol, "millions of women began drinking openly, sometimes defiantly, at cocktail parties, in speakeasies, at women's luncheons and bridge parties, at country club dinners, in cars with their dates" (Sandmaier, 1980, p. 48). This change in drinking patterns reflected the changing role of women in society.

As a result of World War I, women entered the workforce in unprecedented numbers. At the same time, Sigmund Freud's message about the appropriateness of sexual expression had reached the United States—and alcohol helped with this expression. The 1920s and 1930s also saw a political split: some women remained true to the prohibition movement, while others joined the Women's Organization for National Prohibition Reform. The debate between the "wets" and the "drys" was vociferous, with the "drys" continuing to portray the "wets" as sexually promiscuous drunkards (Sandmaier, 1980).

During the Great Depression of the 1930s, however, many of the "modern" liberated "wet" women retreated home, and although Prohibition was repealed in 1933, women's drinking once again became unacceptable. A *Ladies Home Journal* survey in 1938 found that the majority of women disapproved of women's drinking: "More than fifty percent of all the respondents thought it was wrong for women to drink at all, while fully two-thirds believed that women should not be seen imbibing in public" (Sandmaier, 1980, p. 55). The unknown number of women who not only drank but also were unfortunate enough to become addicted to alcohol remained well hidden.

World War II shook up things again and provided new opportunities for women. Women's independence and greater economic freedom also increased their rates of alcohol use. According to the Gallup Poll, from 1939 to 1978 the percentage of women in the United States who drank jumped from 45 to 66 percent (Sandmaier, 1980, p. 56). The multibillion-dollar alcohol industry was quick to recognize a new clientele. "Until 1958, the liquor industry code forbade portrayal of women in its advertising. And even through the 1960s, the only alcohol advertising likely found in most women's magazines was an occasional ad for sherry, possibly accompanied by a recipe for chicken a la king" (Sandmaier, 1980, p. 66). But by 1978, *Cosmopolitan* and *Better Homes and Gardens* became the top magazine targets for the liquor and wine industries, and ads depicting attractive women with a drink in their hands filled the pages of these and other women-oriented magazines.

These changing social mores were paralleled by the growing public and professional recognition of alcohol problems among women. A literature review by Marc Schuckit (1972) found that between 1929 and 1970, only twenty-nine studies on women alcoholics were published in the English language. Such literature grew rapidly during the 1970s and 1980s (for example, Beckman, 1984; Blume, 1978; Corrigan, 1980; Gomberg, 1986; Greenblatt & Schuckit, 1976; Hornik,

1977; Sandmaier, 1980; Straussner, 1985). A new journal, *Focus on Women: Journal of Addictions and Health,* began (and folded) in 1980.

Unfortunately, whereas there has been a virtual explosion of research on women and illicit drugs, such as crack cocaine, during the 1990s, research on women and alcohol seems to have disappeared once again, reflecting federal funding priorities.

According to Edith Gomberg's review (1986) of survey data and treatment reports published during the 1970s, alcohol problems among females remained steady, with a male-to-female ratio of 3:1 to 4:1, depending on the criteria used to define problem drinking, but were higher than the 5:1 male-to-female ratio indicated by government data put out by the National Institute on Alcohol Abuse and Alcoholism during the 1960s. Moreover, a study by Straussner, Kitman, Straussner, and Demos (1980) of alcoholic housewives who were in an alcoholism treatment facility during the early 1970s found a 3:1 ratio of alcoholic fathers to mothers among these middle-age housewives. Based on their findings, the authors point out that the ratio of alcoholic women to men in the previous generation may have been higher than officially acknowledged; the 3:1 alcoholic male-to-female ratio may not have changed much from the 1940s to the 1970s, and even today.

Women's Drug Use During the Nineteenth and Twentieth Centuries

The documented history of women's addiction to drugs in the United States begins during the 1800s, when physicians (almost exclusively male) exhorted women to take medications for every ache and pain. Laudanum, "a liquid form of opium dissolved in alcohol" (Jonnes, 1999, p. 15), was prescribed for all kinds of physical complaints presented by women; opium itself was prescribed for what was diagnosed as "neurasthenia" or "nervous weakness," a set of vague symptoms that were seen as being directly connected to the female gender (Kandall, 1996).

The use of opium became widespread during the Civil War as treatment for soldiers dealing with pain from their wounds and for those suffering from dysentery (Friedman, 1993). In 1856, the hypodermic needle, invented in Europe in 1843, was brought to the United States. The availability of the syringe made it even easier to alleviate pain, and America's huge appetite for opium imports grew from twelve grains per capita in the 1840s to fifty-two grains by the 1890s (Jonnes, 1999, p. 17). Although both men and women used opium to deal with pain, women were especially vulnerable to addiction because they were often advised to take opium for longer periods of time (Kandall, 1996). Unlike men, women were more likely to eat or smoke opium than to inject it. (Women's greater dislike of injection may account, in part, for the rapid spread of smokable crack cocaine among women 130 years later.)

Women's addiction to drugs was largely iatrogenic, as existing medical customs contributed to the use of drugs (Aldrich, 1994). For example, in 1879, Dr. T. Gaillard Thomas (1879, p. 316), president of the American Gynecological Society, advised his fellow doctors that "for the relief of pain, the treatment is all summed up in one word, and that is opium. This divine drug overshadows all other anodynes. . . . You can easily educate her to become an opium eater, and nothing short of this should be aimed at by the medical attendant."

Due to the limited state of formal training, the medical community largely ignored concerns about the addictive qualities of opium despite some warnings, such as the widely read book *Confessions of an English Opium Eater*, written by Thomas DeQuincy in 1821. DeQuincy, an Oxford-educated writer, began his use of laudanum for medical purposes and subsequently chronicled his devastating "habituation" to this drug (Jonnes, 1999). Many doctors in the United States and Europe, including Freud, experimented on themselves with new drugs, and it was not unusual for doctors themselves to become addicted.

By the end of the nineteenth century, the majority of morphine and opium addicts in the United States were women (Kandall, 1996). J. M. Hull of the Iowa Board of Health observed in 1885 that most of the addicted women were well educated, and they had both access to physicians who prescribed their drugs and the means to afford long-term opiate use (Jonnes, 1999). A description of the genteel, abrasive Mrs. Dubose in Harper Lee's *To Kill a Mockingbird* (1960) stands out as the prototypical upper-class Southern lady of the 1800s. She is described as a bigoted woman whose tortured personality was complicated by opium addiction. Her greatest accomplishment was her ability to wean herself from the drug during an excruciating process. Another literary example can be seen in Eugene O'Neill's autobiographical play *Long Day's Journey into Night*, which takes place from 1912 to 1940 and describes Mary Tyrone's decompensation as a result of her long-term opium addiction, and her hatred of the medical profession: "He deliberately humiliates you! He makes you beg and plead! He treats you like a criminal and understands nothing! And yet it was exactly the same type of cheap quack who first gave you the medication—and you never knew what it was until too late!" (1956/1989, p. 74).

The use of opium was not limited to women in higher socioeconomic classes, however. In his book *Substance and Shadow*, Stephan Kandall (1996) describes how rural women resorted to opium to relieve boredom and social isolation. Other women, forced through economic necessity to work in the mills and sewing factories, also were frequent users of opium to relieve pain and physical exhaustion. And, of course, opium was frequently used by prostitutes and sold in many brothels (Jonnes, 1999).

Nineteenth-century women were also heavy users of cocaine. By the end of the 1800s, the American Pharmaceutical Association estimated that 1 in every 375 Americans was a cocaine addict and 1 in every 300 was an opiate addict; the majority were women: "Assuming there was some overlap in these two groups of addicts, one might guess that at the turn of the [twentieth] century, *one American in two hundred was a drug addict. And the bulk of these were genteel, middle-class women*" (Jonnes, 1999, p. 25, italics added).

The extensive long-term use of opiates and cocaine by women was "to some degree responsible for the growth of an entire branch of the American pharmaceutical industry at the turn of the century" (Kandall, 1996, p. 3). For example, the pharmaceutical company Parke-Davis was promoting coca to physicians, and hundreds of coca tonics were marketed by the patent medicine industry as "enterprising Americans formulated the logical alternative for a temperance-minded society: coca-based soft drinks that promised to pep you up" (Jonnes, 1999, pp. 20–21). At the same time in Germany, the pharmaceutical company Bayer launched a cough sedative derived from morphine that they called Heroin, "a play on the German word *heroisch,* meaning powerful" (Jonnes, 1999, p. 36). This was marketed in America as a safe, powerful, and nonaddictive substitute for the addictive opium derivatives morphine and codeine (Abadinsky, 1997). Not until the 1920s would the use of heroin be recognized as a serious problem itself.

Women's Use of Opiates During the Twentieth Century

By the end of the 1800s, the widespread use of patent medicines and the harmful effects of drugs were beginning to be widely recognized. Special attention centered on the search for a cure and on the impact of women's drug use on their infants and children. Although women were initially advised to use opium derivatives to soothe their infants—a practice known as infant doping (Aldrich, 1994)—by the turn of the century, this practice became abhorred, and mothers were held to blame for their and their babies' addictions. For example, Kandall cites an article titled "The Opium Habit in Children," published in a medical journal in 1894, in which the author, Louis Fischer, warns about "ignorant mothers, stupid nurses and careless women, who in order to get sleep at night feed their nurslings with soothing syrups, teething cordials, and other soothing liquids, not to mention the most common and also the most easily obtainable paregoric" (quoted in Kandall, 1996, p. 56). It is obvious that Dr. Fischer, as was true of many other men at that time, did not have to worry about lack of sleep due to crying, teething infants; tending to the child was a responsibility that fell solely to "ignorant" mothers and other women. As will be discussed later in this chapter, such "mother blaming" reared its ugly head again during the 1990s as the federal and state governments turned toward the criminalization of drug-using mothers and away from the provision of treatment for their addictions.

Women's use of narcotics decreased dramatically following the passage of the Harrison Act in 1914, which outlawed the prescribing of drugs by physicians. The Harrison Act and subsequent court cases effectively criminalized the use of opiates and reduced the life options of their users. From then on, drug users were viewed as members of a deviant criminal class and treated accordingly. Now, instead of obtaining drugs over the counter or by prescriptions from their male doctors, women were introduced to drugs as a result of contact with other addicts and male drug dealers (Dai, 1937/1970). Overall, while the use of opiates among women decreased, use of alcohol increased, and other drugs took their place in the medicine cabinets of women throughout the country.

Women's Use of Other Drugs

Originally touted as safe and nonaddictive, barbiturates were one of the major drugs of abuse in the 1950s (Abadinsky, 1997), and, once again, women became addicted through the help of their male doctors. In addition to prescribing amphetamines for weight loss and barbiturates for sleep, many physicians in the 1960s prescribed addictive tranquilizers or sedatives to reduce anxiety. These substances were heavily promoted by advertisers as a way of helping women get through the day and achieve ideal slenderness (Abadinsky, 1997; Kandall, 1996). Statistics also revealed that the vast majority of prescriptions filled for Valium and Librium were for women, and they were prescribed to counter the effects of other, allegedly nonaddictive stimulants they were taking (Kandall, 1996).

The medicinal use of marijuana dates back to ancient China, and during the nineteenth century it was recommended for use as an analgesic, a hypnotic, and a treatment for migraine headaches (Doweiko, 1999). Basing their statements on stories told by their African American grandmothers, a number of students of coauthor Straussner indicated that marijuana was widely used by rural Black women as folk medicine in many Southern communities during the first half of the twentieth century. While the medical use of marijuana within the White community disappeared with the development of more effective medications and growing legal constraints, its use as a psychoactive substance spread during the 1920s and 1930s as a substitute for alcohol. The antimarijuana hysteria during the 1950s—fed by the Federal Bureau of Narcotics, which kept referring to marijuana as a narcotic—diminished its use by women until the rise of the hippie movement in the 1960s (Kandall, 1996).

Use of all kinds of illicit drugs by female baby boomers was widespread during the 1960s and 1970s; during the 1980s, women's use of cocaine increased, both for its stimulant and appetite-suppressant effects. Crack cocaine, which hit inner-city communities during the mid-1980s, had a particularly devastating impact on Black and Latina women and their families (Straussner, 1994) and brought a renewed focus on the impact of women's drug use on their children (Kandall, 1996). Although some of the concern was justified, much of it was fueled by public hysteria reminiscent of public reaction to the gin epidemic in eighteenth-century London. The concern was directed less toward the addicted women than toward the impact on their children.

A major current issue for women, especially women of color, is the spread of HIV-AIDS. Between 1991 and 1997, the rates of HIV-AIDS in women increased by 364 percent (American Psychiatric Association, 2000). Since the epidemic began, 58 percent of all AIDS cases among women have been attributed to sex with infected partners who inject drugs and, to a lesser extent, to their own injection drug use, often in the company of men (Centers for Disease Control and Prevention, 1998). Thus women's dependence on drug-abusing men can be deadly. Moreover, whereas males financed their drug use through criminal activities, such as theft and drug dealing, women turned to prostitution. As Straussner (1997) indicates, "men sell drugs, while women sell themselves" (p. 21), further increasing their sense of shame and guilt.

Treatment of Women with Drug and Alcohol Problems

As seen previously, women's addiction to alcohol and other drugs was often the unintended outcome of the latest well-meaning treatment approaches. For example, morphine was recommended as a cure for alcoholism, and coca syrup was touted as a cure for morphine addiction (Murdock, 1998; White, 1998). Across the Atlantic, Sigmund Freud recommended the use of cocaine as

> a panacea for pain, exhaustion, low spirits and morphine addictions. . . . He recommended it recklessly, even sending moderate quantities to Martha Bernays [his fiancée] when he thought her indispositions warranted it. In June 1885—this was not the only time—he mailed to Wandsbek [Martha's home] a vial of cocaine holding about half a gram and suggested that she "make for yourself 8 small (or 5 large) doses from it." She acknowledged the shipment promptly, thanked him warmly, and told him that, even though she did not

need any, she would divide up the shipment and take some of the drug [Gay, 1988, p. 44].

Heroin, as indicated earlier, was widely marketed as a cure for addictions to morphine and codeine, which themselves were recommended originally as cures for opium addiction. And during the mid-1960s, methadone maintenance clinics were established as another "magic bullet" cure for heroin addicts, despite methadone's greater addictability than the substance it replaced. It is worth noting that Bill Wilson (known as Bill W.), one of the cofounders of AA, took LSD during the 1950s and 1960s under medical supervision as a possible cure for his depression and in line with then widely proclaimed benefits of LSD in the treatment of alcoholism (Abramson, 1967). Moreover, Bill W. even persuaded his spiritual mentor Father Dowling and the two important women in his life, his wife, Lois, and his secretary, Nell Wing, to try LSD (White, 1998).

Growth of Asylums

In *Slaying the Dragon,* his fascinating history of addictions treatment in the United States, William White (1998) notes that although the idea of provision of care for people who were "mad from wine or beer" has been identified in Egyptian records dating back approximately five thousand years ago, "in America, the idea of creating special institutions and special professional roles for the care of inebriates began in the late eighteenth century and blossomed in the mid-nineteenth century" (p. 22). According to Murdock (1998), "institutions to cure, or at least dry out, problem drinkers were a common feature of the late Victorian landscape. Between the Civil War and the turn of the century, more than a hundred inebriates' hospitals opened in the United States" (p. 46). Awareness of the special needs of women was evident.

The first institutional programs for inebriate women were started in 1841, when "industrial homes" for women were established by temperance programs (White, 1998). In Chicago, the home of the wealthy Charles Hull served as a residence for the care of alcoholic women. In June 1869, the women moved to the Martha Washington Home, a new institution that was built for them. Hull's house then became the first settlement house in the United States under the leadership of Jane Addams, one of the "mothers" of social work, who, by the way, also experimented with opium "as a seventeen-year-old seminary student" (Kandall, 1996, p. 18), although she later became an important advocate for prohibition of alcohol and against the sale of pure cocaine (as opposed to the then commonly used cocaine catarrh powders) (Jonnes, 1999; Murdock, 1998).

The fees for treatment at the Washington Home ranged from $5 to $15 a week for those who could afford them; treatment was free for the indigent. It is interesting to note that the length of treatment for women ranged from two to four months, in contrast to only two to four weeks for men who were treated in a sister institution. Thus it is evident that from early on, women were seen as needing longer treatment than men.

At a time when many alcoholic women were imprisoned or locked in insane asylums, an increasing number sought voluntary admission to the rapidly growing asylums for inebriates that were being established in the mid- and late 1800s. Although some of the new asylums, such as Kings Country Home in Brooklyn, admitted both men and women, others opened special women's units within their existing programs, and still others were built specifically for women only. The male-to-female ratio of admissions to treatment institutions in the years 1884 to 1912 ranged from 3:1 to 9:1, reflecting a surprisingly large number of women in many of these programs (Lender, 1981). Despite women's great use of treatment services, "stigma and shame . . . shaped the nature of treatment for women. Inebriate asylums that catered to women made special note of the separate quarters and entrances for women whereby the secrecy of their presence could be guaranteed" (White, 1998, p. 44).

The Cure Industry

Inebriate asylums, whose general success rate was low, gradually disappeared and were replaced by psychiatric asylums and by a tremendous rise in quack "miracle cures." The "cure industry" of the late 1800s and early 1900s included sanitariums, exercise, steam and heat treatments, and special diets. The most famous were the Keeley Institutes, whose use of recovering doctors to provide treatment and other innovative approaches presaged many aspects of modern treatment for addictions. (For a detailed description of the treatment, see White, 1998.) Advertisements for miracle cures were plastered in newspapers and magazines. Although numerous "testimonials" as to the efficacy of these cures and treatment regimens were offered, few data were available regarding outcome or efficacy, and most of them went out of business following the passage of the 1906 Pure Food and Drug Act, although some continued as late as the 1940s (White, 1998); their modern manifestations can be seen in today's herbal medicines that claim to relieve many of life's problems.

Despite the passage of the Harrison Act in 1914, drug maintenance clinics flourished in the 1920s and early 1930s in New York, Memphis, New Orleans, New Haven, Cleveland, and Los Angeles, and statistics show that about 30 percent of those seeking treatment were women. These women came from diverse backgrounds and included nurses, doctors' wives, and prostitutes (Abadinsky, 1997). As the country moved away from treatment and toward criminalization, these clinics were closed. Women of means could generally still obtain small amounts of drugs from sympathetic doctors, but others were forced to commit illegal acts to support their addiction. As law enforcement sought to cut off the supply, the shame of being addicted increased and drove many women further underground.

In 1940, the singer Billie Holiday was quoted as saying, "There was no cure. They don't cut you down slow, weaning you off the stuff gradually. They just throw you in the hospital by yourself, take you off cold turkey and watch you suffer" (quoted in Kandall, 1996, p. 103). As criminalization took hold, the only treatment that was available was in federal treatment centers that were part of the criminal justice system. Facilities like the Clinical Research Center, a component of the U.S. Public Health Service Hospital in Lexington, opened in 1935 with voluntary and involuntary male clients and began admitting women in 1941 (Dai, 1937/1970). By 1955, over 40 percent of the Demerol addicts at the Lexington treatment facility were women, the majority of whom were registered nurses (Kandall, 1996).

Modern Treatment for Alcoholic Women

Alcohol and drug treatment programs began to operate widely once again during the 1950s and 1960s. One of the earliest of modern programs established exclusively for the treatment of alcoholic women was Dia Linn, which opened its doors in 1956. It started as a fifteen-bed women's offshoot of Hazelden on a three-hundred-acre estate near White Bear Lake, Minnesota, and was based on a twelve-step abstinence philosophy pioneered at Willmar State Hospital in Minnesota and expanded later at Hazelden. According to Damian McElrath (1981), who chronicled the establishment of Dia Linn (Gaelic for "God be with us—a term expressing polite concern for the status of another person's health," p. 7) on its twenty-fifth anniversary, there were few alternatives for women alcoholics at that time. "Throughout the United States, the female alcoholic had a problem finding suitable and dignified help in the 1950s. It was very much a male-dominated field and the idea of female counselors was hardly conceivable. . . women, for the most part, were still viewed as moral degenerates. Women had few choices: a state institution like Willmar State Hospital in Minnesota, where alcoholic treatment was changing, but the institutional environment was not; or a psychiatric ward where alcoholism was treated as a secondary problem" (p. 3). The author goes on to state, "Local rumors of immorality at Dia Linn, although not rampant, were not uncommon. During the initial years, people would drive by on Sundays actually looking for the wild women drinkers" (p. 11). The women suffered additional discrimination: local hospitals would not accept them when they required emergency treatment during withdrawal from alcohol, and they had to be transported for many miles to a medical clinic in St. Croix Falls, Wisconsin.

From the beginning, female alcoholics at Dia Linn were acknowledged as needing a longer period of treatment than the three weeks provided to men at Hazelden; in recognition of their connection to their loved ones, a family component was established in 1962. By 1963, the program grew to twenty-three patients who were treated by a multidisciplinary staff consisting of a psychologist, nurse, counselor, clergy member, and social worker. In 1966, the women's program was moved to Hazelden in Center City; the merged program served as a model for the many alcoholism inpatient treatment facilities, or rehab units, that opened throughout the United States and abroad during the 1970s and 1980s— what has been termed "the golden age of alcoholism treatment" (O'Dwyer, 1993, p. 121).

Modern Treatment Approaches for Drug-Abusing Women

Treatment options for drug-abusing women, particularly those using opiates and cocaine, have increased since the 1950s. The two most influential approaches have been the use of methadone maintenance and the development of drug-free therapeutic communities.

Although women were excluded from the original methadone trials (Dole & Nyswander, 1965), the growing numbers of heroin-addicted women in the 1960s and 1970s readily flocked to the new methadone maintenance treatment programs. Reminiscent of the narcotic clinics of the early 1920s, women once again sought "to free themselves from their quest for illegal drugs and their dependence on men as pimps, protectors or sexual partners" (Kandall, 1996, p. 221). From 1969 to 1973, almost one-fourth of the forty thousand patients treated in federally funded drug treatment programs were women, and their proportion quickly increased. In 1973, over a third of all New York City patients on methadone were women (Kandall, 1996). Yet "their specific needs usually remained unaddressed. Early programs were male-oriented and male-dominated. . . . Women in these programs felt pressured to conform to sexual stereotypes, and endured exploitation, voyeurism and psychological abuse" (Kandall, 1996, p. 224). Although some women found methadone treatment to be "life saving," many others continued to abuse other drugs. Moreover, unlike heroin, "methadone restored women's normal menstrual function, sexual function, and fertility" (Kandall, 1996). Consequently, women on methadone were more likely to become pregnant than those on heroin, resulting in the birth of numerous babies addicted to methadone.

Although most experts felt that it is better to maintain a pregnant woman on methadone and then to detoxify the baby after birth rather than to have the pregnant woman use adulterated street drugs or even to detoxify from heroin while pregnant, the long-term developmental consequences of being born addicted to methadone are unknown (Kandall, 1996).

The term *therapeutic community* (TC) typically refers to a residential, self-help, drug-free treatment program (Abadinsky, 1997). Originated in 1958 by a recovered alcoholic, Charles Dederich, TCs grew in importance during the 1960s and 1970s. Although women were part of TCs from the beginning, the TC's historically highly structured, confrontational, group-centered approach has been seen as "inappropriate for female addicts, who were often guilt-ridden, ashamed of their addiction, involved in debasing and abusive relationships, and in great need of supportive interventions" (Kandall, 1996, p. 204). Coauthor Straussner remembers hearing from one of the earliest women committed to treatment at a TC in lieu of legal action for drug theft at a medical setting in which she worked. As official "punishment" for her perceived "bad attitude" and misbehavior while in treatment, she was gang-raped during her long-term stay in a TC during the 1960s. Although she went on to recover from her drug addiction, the trauma of her rape has stayed with her for years.

TCs became more "women friendly" over the years, and today there are numerous women-only and women-child TCs providing supportive and truly therapeutic communities to thousands of substance-abusing women with no place else to go and without the ability to care for themselves. However, the destructive potential of such programs for vulnerable women needs to be kept in mind.

Women and Mutual Aid

Mutual-aid, or self-help, programs for alcoholic women can be traced to the Martha Washington Society, organized in 1841 in New York as a companion to the male-based Washingtonian Total Abstinence Society, which was first established in Baltimore in 1840. In line with their social role at the time, members of the Martha Washington Society encouraged women to abstain from drinking and to banish alcohol from their house. Women members provided food, clothing, and shelter to male "reforming inebriates" (White, 1998, p. 10). However, they also provided "special support to female inebriates and to the wives and children of inebriates. . . . The Martha Washington Societies were the first organizations in the temperance movement in which women assumed leadership roles. They were also the first organized effort to focus on the needs of inebriate women, who were recruited, restored to health, and embraced as full members of the Martha Washington Societies" (White, 1998, p. 10). For a variety of reasons, the Washingtonian Societies were short lived and few of them remained after 1845.

At the beginning of the 1890s, another mutual-aid group, the Women's Keeley League, was established (White, 1998). Like the Washingtonian Societies, this league was started as a companion to a men's organization, the Keeley League, which grew rapidly during the 1890s to form 370 chapters in over ten eastern and midwestern states. The mission of the league, which originated as a club for Keeley Institute patients, included treatment, prevention, and public education. According to White (1998), the league's constitution listed the following purposes: (1) "curing the drunkard of the disease of intemperance," (2) "preventing the youth of the country, by education and example, from contracting it," (3) binding "together in one fraternal bond all who have taken the Keeley treatment," and (4) "extending public knowledge of the Keeley cure" (quoted in White, 1998, p. 57). The Women's Keeley League included not only the wives, mothers, and other female relatives of Keeley graduates but also those women who "have themselves been delivered from slavery of drunkenness, or opium" as well (quoted in White, 1998, p. 57). With the demise of the Keeley Institutes, the league declined; the last Keeley League National Convention was held in 1897 in Minneapolis, Minnesota.

It was not until the formation of Alcoholics Anonymous (AA) in 1935 that women once again become part of a mutual-aid movement for alcoholics. AA was started by two men, Bill Wilson and Dr. Bob Smith, and initially was seen as aiming at alcoholic men only: "The founding fathers of AA . . . adhered to rather traditional family values and to conservative gender roles. Dr. Bob, for example, was not happy about letting women into AA" (Makela et al., 1996, p. 170). The first women in AA did not do well: "Florence R., whose story appeared in the first edition of the Big Book, and who objected to one of the book's proposed titles, 'One Hundred Men' . . . later returned to drinking and died of alcoholism. Lil, the very first woman to seek help from A.A., got loaded with Victor, another prospect, pioneering what would come to be christened 'thirteenth stepping' (sexual or romantic involvement with someone whose sobriety is relatively new and therefore potentially unstable)" (White, 1998, p. 158). Sponsorship of women was a problem. Initially, nonalcoholic wives of recovering men attended meetings with their husbands, and alcoholic women were turned over to them for help (Coker, 1997). During the early years, AA wives attempted to start a women-only group, which would include both alcoholic women and wives of alcoholic men: "This can be interpreted as support for alcoholic women, but also as a means of protecting wives' relationships with their husbands" (Makela et al., 1996, p. 170). From the beginning, the relationships between the wives and the women attempting to recover in AA were strained, and eventually the wives left to form their own group, which became known as Al-Anon. It is worth noting that initially the goal of Al-Anon was very much in line with the traditional role of wives: to help women adjust to their husbands' alcoholism and recoveries. Only later did the emphasis shift to focusing on the wives' own needs, a move that allowed the inclusion of a growing number of husbands of alcoholic wives (Makela et al., 1996).

Marty Mann, who joined AA in 1937, became the first documented alcoholic woman to remain sober through AA (Robertson, 1988). She went on to make a major contribution to the field of alcoholism as the founder of what was initially called the National Committee for Education on Alcoholism and more recently renamed the National Council on Alcoholism and Drug Dependence.

The membership of women in AA has increased over the years. AA surveys indicate that the proportion of women rose from 22 percent in 1968 to 32 percent in 1977 (Coker, 1997; Makela et al., 1996) to 34 percent in 1998 (Alcoholics Anonymous, 1999). Although women-only AA groups increased rapidly during the 1970s and 1980s, they seem much less popular today.

In 1975, Jean Kirkpatrick, believing that AA's focus on powerlessness was not appropriate to meet the needs of the already powerless alcoholic woman, founded Women for Sobriety (WFS). The goal of WFS was to increase women's self-esteem, empowerment, and self-reliance and to reduce their sense of guilt and shame. WFS meetings, similar to the women-only AA meetings, grew rapidly during the late 1970s and 1980s. However, by the end of the 1990s, few WFS groups remained in existence.

Thus, despite the increasing recognition of the need for women to connect to other women (Byington, 1997; Miller, 1976), the history of self-help groups for women reveals that most tend to be offshoots of men's self-help movements and that women-only groups, as well as women-only treatment facilities, appear to have a limited life span. Clearly, these dynamics need to be understood better.

Societal Responses to Users of Alcohol and Other Drugs

The historical legislative response to the widespread use of alcohol and drugs in the United States has always been strongly influenced by the social forces of racism and economic profiteering, and laws were frequently passed in the guise of saving American women. For example, antiopium legislation was fostered by stories of women being seduced by Chinese white slavers and sex-crazed dope fiends and by the fear that women would become targets of sexually predatory racial groups (Abadinsky, 1997; Kandall, 1996). During the 1930s, anti-Mexican feelings in the Southwest became centered on Mexicans' use of marijuana, resulting in hysterical concerns about how "marijuana has led to some of the most revolting cases of sadistic rape and murder of modern time" (Earle & Rowell, 1939, quoted in Abadinsky, 1997, pp. 51–52).

Similarly, discussion of alcohol usage during the end of the nineteenth century remained inseparable from "discussion of women's sexuality, oppression, and physical danger" (Murdock, 1998, p. 78). Fears were rampant about "men who reputedly lured girls into movie houses or saloons, administered a drugged drink or injection, and then entrapped their victims in a life of prostitution" (Murdock, 1998, p. 78). These fears were fueled in great part by anti-immigrant sentiment of the 1840s and 1850s and by "rural, white Protestants antagonistic to urban Roman Catholics, particularly the Irish, who used the social world of the saloon to gain political power in large cities" (Abadinsky, 1997, pp. 24–25).

Recent federal laws reflect our current racial fears and our changing views of women: sentencings for the possession of cocaine show a dramatic disparity between the possession of powdered cocaine, which is more likely to be used by White men and women, and crack cocaine, which is commonly used in Black communities: "In 1988, Congress, responding to the fast-spreading crack epidemic, decided to make the possession of five grams of crack in federal cases punishable by a mandatory sentence of five years in prison. To get a comparable sentence for powdered cocaine, you would have to be caught with five hundred grams, *or one hundred times as much*" (Jonnes, 1999, p. 433, emphasis added).

Consequently, a disproportionate number of young Black men and women are imprisoned "because 88.3 percent of those arrested in federal crack cases are black" (Jonnes, 1999, p. 433). Although the great majority of those arrested are men, it is important to note that since the start of the crack epidemic, the rate of increase in the female prison population has exceeded the male rate (Bureau of Justice Statistics, 1999). Thus women—particularly poor, Black women—are no longer seen as needing protection; rather, as we will discuss shortly, they are seen as part of the problem of the War on Drugs.

History Revisited

Women in the United States have come a long way: they not only can vote but also have access to unprecedented political power and economic independence. They also can, and do, use drugs to a degree unseen since the nineteenth century, and drink more than ever before and at a younger age. According to government reports (Substance Abuse and Mental Health Services Administration, 1998), whereas in the 1960s only 7 percent of new alcohol users were girls between the ages of ten and fourteen, by the early 1990s the figure had risen to 31 percent.

Moreover, during the early 1960s, girls were likely to begin drinking later than boys, but by the 1990s such gender difference became negligible. Nonetheless, although alcohol- and drug-abusing women are no longer "invisible," they continue to be stigmatized, and insurance coverage and treatment resources for addicted women remain woefully inadequate. The early life traumas of today's substance-abusing women, as well as their inadequate housing and child care, lack of transportation, health and medical problems, low self-esteem, and experiences of discrimination, are just some of the issues that are not being addressed even by those lucky enough to get into treatment (Straussner & Zelvin, 1997; Woolis, 1998).

As was true for many of the women in the temperance movement, and for countless others before and since, women today continue to suffer from domestic violence and physical and sexual assaults. The treatment needs of these women are unlikely to be supported by their abusive husbands and boyfriends (Straussner, 1997). Despite these realities, at the beginning of the twenty-first century, women with drug and alcohol problems are once again facing increasing criminalization of their addictions, as states intervene in the lives of pregnant substance abusers in an effort to protect the fetus (Gustavsson & MacEachron, 1997). Health care professionals in many states are now required to report cases of pregnant drug- and alcohol-abusing women. Among the consequences are imprisonment, mandatory treatment, and foster care placement of the child after birth. There is abundant evidence that the laws requiring mandatory reporting are applied unfairly toward poor women and women of color. For example, a Florida study demonstrated that despite equal percentages of Black and White mothers testing positive for cocaine in obstetrical offices, Black women were ten times more likely to be reported to state officials than were White women (Gustavsson & MacEachron, 1997). Moreover, as states struggle to keep up with the federal mandates of the Temporary Assistance for Needy Families Act, women with a history of substance abuse are pushed into the workplace, and the magnitude and severity of their needs are becoming more evident (Bush & Kraft, 2001).

Unfortunately, only a very small percentage of all women—regardless of race, ethnic background, and socioeconomic class—are offered appropriate treatment. Managed care, an industry whose top leadership is overwhelmingly male, has put severe restrictions on treatment access for working- and middle-class substance-abusing women (and men, for that matter, although they are much more likely to have greater resources for treatment and fewer family obstacles). Many communities have long waiting lists for publicly funded treatment for low-income women. Moreover, few facilities, and even fewer appropriately trained clinicians, are available to address the high rates of co-occurring mental disorders common to women of all classes. Thus, at the start of the twenty-first century, and despite the fact that women have "come a long way" and achieved much, many women continue to struggle alone in their search for an effective solution to their painful addictions to alcohol and other drugs.

Conclusion

The history of women and addiction presents an opportunity to glimpse the world of American women for the last two hundred years. Women's use of and addiction to alcohol and other drugs is closely related to their dependence on men—including their doctors.

The close connection between the temperance movement, prohibition, and the suffrage movement highlights the linkage between substance use and women's role in society. It is obvious that the treatment of substance-abusing women cannot be viewed without taking into account the social context in which they live. Entire communities, such as inner-city Black neighborhoods, fell apart once women started using crack cocaine—which was supplied by men. Today women pay a high price for the War on Drugs—conducted by men. Yet women are not necessarily helpless victims; they also wield power, which they can use either to save or to destroy themselves. It is our job as clinicians to help addicted women get in touch with this power and use it on their own behalf.

References

Abadinsky, H. (1997). *Drug abuse: An introduction.* Chicago: Nelson-Hall.

Abramson, H. (1967). *The use of LSD in psychotherapy and alcoholism.* New York: Bobbs-Merrill.

Alcoholics Anonymous. (1999). *1998 Membership Survey.* New York: Alcoholics Anonymous World Services.

Aldrich, M. R. (1994). Historical notes on women addicts. *Journal of Psychoactive Drugs, 26,* 61–64.

American Psychiatric Association. (2000). *Practice guidelines for the treatment of patients with HIV/AIDS.* Washington, DC: Author.

Beckman, L. (1984). Treatment needs of women alcoholics. *Alcoholism Treatment Quarterly, 1*(2), 101–115.

Blume, S. (1978). Diagnosis, casefinding and treatment of alcohol problems in women. *Alcohol Health and Research World, 2*(3).

Bureau of Justice Statistics. (1999). *Women offenders.* Washington, DC: U.S. Department of Justice.

Bush, I. R., & Kraft, M. K. (2001). Self-sufficiency and sobriety: Substance-abusing women and welfare reform. *Journal of Social Work Practice in the Addictions, 1*(1), 41–65.

Byington, D. B. (1997). Applying relational theory to addiction treatment. In S.L.A. Straussner & E. Zelvin (Eds.), *Gender and addictions: Men and women in treatment* (pp. 33–46). Northvale, NJ: Aronson.

Centers for Disease Control and Prevention. (1998). *HIV/AIDS Surveillance Report 19*(2), 1–43 [Special issue].

Coker, M. (1997). Overcoming sexism in AA: How women cope. In S.L.A. Straussner & E. Zelvin (Eds.), *Gender and addictions: Men and women in treatment* (pp. 263–281). Northvale, NJ: Aronson.

Corrigan, E. M. (1980). *Alcoholic women in treatment.* New York: Oxford University Press.

Dai, B. (1970). *Opium addiction in Chicago.* Montclair, NJ: Patterson Smith. (Original work published 1937)

Dole, V. P., & Nyswander, M. (1965). Medical treatment for diacetylmorphine (heroin) addiction. *Journal of the American Medical Association, 193,* 645–656.

Doweiko, H. E. (1999). *Concepts of chemical dependency* (4th ed.). Pacific Grove, CA: Brooks/Cole.

Friedman, E. G. (1993). Methadone maintenance in the treatment of addiction. In S.L.A. Straussner (Ed.), *Clinical work with substance abusing clients* (pp. 135–152). New York: Guilford Press.

Gay, P. (1988). *Freud: A life for our time.* New York: Norton.

Gomberg, E.S.L. (1986). Women with alcohol problems. In N. J. Estes & M. E. Heinemann (Eds.), *Alcoholism: Development, consequences and interventions* (pp. 241–256). St. Louis, MO: Mosby-Year Book.

Greenblatt, M., & Schuckit, M. A. (Eds.). (1976). *Alcoholism problems in women and children.* New York: Grune & Stratton.

Gustavsson, N. S., & MacEachron, A. E. (1997). Criminalizing women's behavior. *Journal of Drug Issues, 27,* 673–687.

Hall, L. (1888). Inebriety in women: Its causes and results. *Quarterly Journal of Inebriety, 5,* 223–224.

Hornik, E. L. (1977). *The drinking woman.* New York: Association Press.

Jonnes, J. (1999). *Hep-cats, narcs and pipe dreams.* Baltimore, MD: Johns Hopkins University Press.

Kandall, S. R. (1996). *Substance and shadow.* Cambridge, MA: Harvard University Press.

Lee, H. (1960). *To kill a mockingbird.* New York: Warner Books.

Lender, M. (1981). Women alcoholics: Prevalence estimates and their problems as reflected in turn of the century institutional data. *International Journal of the Addictions, 16*(3), 443–448.

Makela, K., et al. (1996). *Alcoholics Anonymous as a mutual-help movement: A study in eight societies.* Madison: University of Wisconsin Press.

Martineau, H. (1837). *Society in America.* London: Sander and Ottley.

McElrath, D. (1981). *Roses of Dia Linn.* Center City, MN: Hazelden.

Miller, J. B. (1976). *Toward a new psychology of women.* Boston: Beacon Press.

Murdock, C. G. (1998). *Domesticating drink: Women, men and alcohol in America, 1870–1940.* Baltimore, MD: Johns Hopkins University Press.

O'Dwyer, P. (1993). Alcoholism treatment facilities. In S.L.A. Straussner (Ed.), *Clinical work with substance abusing clients* (pp. 119–134). New York: Guilford Press.

O'Neill, E. (1956/1989). *Long day's journey into night.* New Haven, CT: Yale University Press.

Robertson, N. (1988). *Getting better: Inside Alcoholics Anonymous.* New York: Morrow.

Sandmaier, M. (1980). *The invisible alcoholics: Women and alcohol abuse in America.* New York: McGraw-Hill.

Schuckit, M. (1972). The alcoholic woman: A literature review. *Psychiatry in Medicine, 3,* 37–43.

Straussner, S.L.A. (1985). Alcoholism in women: Current knowledge and implications for treatment. *Alcoholism Treatment Quarterly, 2*(1), 61–77.

Straussner, S.L.A. (1994). The impact of alcohol and other drug abuse on the American family. *Drug and Alcohol Review, 13,* 393–399.

Straussner, S.L.A. (1997). Gender and substance abuse. In S.L.A. Straussner & E. Zelvin (Eds.), *Gender and addictions: Men and women in treatment* (pp. 3–27). Northvale, NJ: Aronson.

Straussner, S.L.A., Kitman, C., Straussner, J., & Demos, E. S. (1980). The alcoholic housewife: A psychosocial analysis of fifty self-defined housewives treated at an alcoholism rehabilitation center. *Focus on Women, 1,* 5–31.

Straussner, S.L.A., & Zelvin, E. (Eds.). (1997). *Gender and addictions: Men and women in treatment.* Northvale, NJ: Aronson.

Substance Abuse and Mental Health Services Administration. (1998, January/February). Substance use among women. *Public Health Reports, 113*(1), 13. Washington, DC: Author.

Thomas, T. G. (1879). Clinical lecture on diseases of women. *Medical Record, 16.*

White, W. (1998). *Slaying the dragon: The history of addiction treatment and recovery in America.* Bloomington, IL: Chestnut Health Systems/Lighthouse Institute.

Wood, H. C. (1906). On the medical activity of the hemp plant as grown in North America. *Proceedings of the American Philosophical Society, 11,* 226–232.

Woolis, D. D. (1998). Family works: Substance abuse treatment and welfare reform. *Public Welfare, 56,* 24–31.

CHAPTER TWO

WOMEN AND ADDICTION

Expanding Theoretical Points of View

Stephanie Brown

For many years, even centuries, it was a commonly held belief that women did not become alcoholics or addicts. Thus there was no need for a women's perspective regarding becoming addicted, needing treatment, or understanding recovery. This absence of acknowledgment and resultant absence of theory of addiction and recovery existed until the birth of the women's movement in the 1960s and 1970s. This political and social revolution defined women as different and separate from men, and, feminists hoped, as equal. As a reflection of these changes, women were recognized as alcoholics and addicts, and a field of gender-based addiction research evolved. Today there is an extensive, influential literature that addresses women and addiction, and treatment designed especially for women. So what's left to do?

A lot. The gains women have made in visibility and acknowledgment of their addictions have come with new social, political, and psychological paradox and conflict. Women's focused need for differentiation and separation from men, so necessary in the sociopolitical struggle for gender recognition and equality, has a hidden and paradoxical downside when it comes to understanding and treating addiction. The often oppositional framework of gender comparison may keep women in a competitive, adversarial stance against men, whereby women maintain a focus on achieving power that limits their ability to embrace the fundamental human experience of loss of control, or powerlessness, that is essential to recovery.

This chapter proposes a way of thinking about women and addiction that broadens a gender point of view: a developmental, process model of active addiction and recovery. The first part of the chapter explores important paradoxes women face; for example, how can women fight against men for differentiation and share a fundamental identification with them at the same time? This is followed by a review of the history of women and addiction, leading to a discussion of current gender perspectives that inform addiction treatment for women. Finally, the chapter presents an outline of the developmental model of addiction, with a suggestion that this framework is essential to understanding women's complex experience and, particularly, to understanding differences between women.

This chapter looks at women and addiction from a developmental perspective organized around the core experience of loss of control. It demonstrates that women and men are similar in the process of losing control, becoming and being addicted, and being in recovery. It also elaborates significant differences between men and women in what it means to be addicted and to be in recovery. There are also great differences among women in the meanings attached to being addicted.

The purpose of this chapter is to expand ways of thinking about women and to open up more questions, more conflicts, and more issues for therapists to consider in understanding and treating women.

Paradoxes of a Women's Perspective

The experiences of being addicted and identifying oneself as an addict often seem at odds with many sociopolitical views of key issues related to women's long-term fight for equality with men. These seeming contradictions in point of view can cause conflicts for women, which can then become barriers to acceptance of their addiction and treatment. These issues include (1) different meanings of the concept of empowerment, (2) continuing stigma, and (3) viewing women within a minority, gender frame.

Empowerment

The idea of empowerment for women in relation to the sociopolitical-economic establishment involves opposing what has existed, specifically male dominance and inequality, and aggressively pressing for change and equal status. This challenge involves much comparison of past to present, gender to gender, and minority to majority with regard to power and who has how much. The fight for equality involves vigilance and analysis of whatever might be unequal or unjust and therefore disempowering. The focus on the need for equal power and status can imply that increasing the power of the woman, in relation to men, is the only route to empowerment.

A woman's empowerment and recovery in relation to addiction are very different from the empowerment process in the sociopolitical-economic arena. There is a surrender process that is a hallmark of effective recovery for the individual—a time when the addicted woman fully accepts her complete inability to control her use of drugs or alcohol (or both), or other addictive behavior. This acknowledgment of powerlessness over the substance involves concepts and language of openness and vulnerability—hardly the way to empowerment at the sociopolitical-economic level.

Women working toward empowerment in the world are involved in conflicts in which they want to be winners of skirmishes that will incrementally lead to greater power. Women working toward recovery from addiction are dealing with an internal conflict that cannot be resolved by a drive for more power, but rather requires a restructuring of their relationship with themselves; first, by acknowledging powerlessness over the substance, then, by building their lives around personal honesty and responsibility that culminates in a different kind of victory: freedom from domination by a cruel substance.

These differences in paths toward empowerment can be problematic for women in recovery. For some, entering into recovery can initially feel like disempowerment and abandonment of the larger women's movement. Understanding the differences can ease this conflict: women can engage in the developmental process of recovery and maintain their commitment to the women's movement and the gains achieved by it.

Stigma

Historically, alcoholism in women has been viewed as a moral failure, a view that persists today. This stigma paradoxically reinforces denial of addiction. Women have come from being invisible alcoholics with negative stigma to visible and acknowledged alcoholics with continuing negative stigma, a new recognition that some might say is a dubious victory. The growing acceptance, visibility, and legitimacy of women as addicts parallel and reflect the growth of the sociopolitical women's movement. Feminists, striving to achieve separate and equal status with men, have made enormous gains for women in recognition, visibility, and equal rights. In terms of addiction, however, it is an ironic victory: women have gained the right to be acknowledged alcoholics and drug addicts, an attribution that still carries severe negative moral connotation and stigma for females. Women have paradoxically gained the right to acknowledge moral failure.

The disease concept of addiction (Jellinek, 1960) helped ease this stigma somewhat by expanding theories of addiction beyond a moral frame. There would be less shame, and therefore less need for denial, if addiction could be viewed as a disease. The disease concept also emphasized equality; men and women both have a disease, the same disease. Still, a key dilemma in thinking about women and addiction remains: how to acknowledge addiction in women and explain it in a way that will be freeing and growth enhancing rather than demoralizing.

Women as Minority: A Gender Perspective

Side by side with the challenge of stigma is another: how to reconcile the political struggle for gender equality—with its dichotomous, comparative framework and a language emphasizing power and control—with the broader, fundamental human experience of loss of control and its paradoxically liberating language centered on powerlessness and defeat rather than on victory. Anthropologist Gregory Bateson addressed this apparent contradiction. According to Bateson (1971), coming to terms with addiction is fundamentally about the self; it is always, ultimately, an individual issue. Bateson outlined a crucial framework for understanding alcoholism as a struggle within the self. He suggested that the alcoholic is caught in what he termed a competitive, symmetric internal war. One part of the self believes in the omnipotence of control over drinking. Another part of the self is victim to the reality of loss of control. This is a dichotomous, either-or frame that places the alcoholic at war with himself or herself, defying the existence of limits while breaking these limits at the same time. The individual says, "I can control my drinking," while repeatedly losing control. The dominating and winning part of the individual (the belief in the possibility of control) alternates with the submissive and losing side (the submission to the reality of loss of control).

This terrible bind is not solvable until the individual acknowledges defeat, which is the reality of loss of control and the inability to regain it. The alcoholic comes face-to-face with human limits and the key experience of powerlessness. At a point of "hitting bottom" and "surrender" (Tiebout, 1949, 1953), the alcoholic gives up the idea of "getting control" and reaches outside the self for help. This relinquishment of the belief in the power of self to control alcohol frees the individual from the internal, polarized struggle.

A framework of gender comparison can operate on this same symmetrical structure, particularly in the sociopolitical gender "wars." Women have fought for power "over" and "against" men—power to become visible and equal.

Comparative gender theories tend to reinforce a dichotomous structure that emphasizes polarization and differentiation. This structure can lead to rigid thinking and either-or conclusions, freezing an exploration of women into a position "against" men. This either-or frame also contributes to denial and defensiveness because it requires a winner and a loser, an aggressor and a victim. Women will fight hard to deny aspects of their experience if acknowledgment means they must accept failure or fault—and somebody has to accept failure or fault in this rigid frame.

In a political context, the gender frame emphasizes women as a minority, always secondary and submissive to the dominance of the male majority. From this perspective, women have been repeatedly identified as victims of male dominance and privilege. The win-lose gender battleground replicates the core of addictive pathology within the self, as described by Bateson: the struggle for control against the reality of loss of control. In this dichotomous, competitive frame, with its emphasis on "power over self and other," it is difficult for women to acknowledge loss of control while claiming self-power and denying helplessness at the same time. There is also a danger in defining women's addiction through a comparative gender lens because such a view can paradoxically take women away from a focus on the self. The political gender war places the enemy in the "other." With addiction, the woman is at war with herself. But it is difficult for her to recognize and accept personal responsibility for her loss of control—that is, to accept that she is an active agent in her addiction—if she keeps her focus on strengthening her own power and control.

The difficulty of a gender view comes not from gender comparison itself but from the competitive organizing perspective inherent in a minority view. Women have always occupied a minority position in the comparative gender frame. Historically, the role and goal of any minority in a sociopolitical context has been to define and differentiate itself from a dominant majority. Sometimes, basic survival is the only goal. To be visible and separate requires opposition—the minority holding its own against a dominant majority.

Though important in the sociopolitical realm, this continuing focus as a minority fighting against a dominating majority also works against women's freedom to focus on themselves and their addiction as an internal struggle. The minority view requires an external focus (the dominance of the majority) and an attitude of defense and vigilance. It is not a framework of self-definition that allows for inward focus and development from within.

The move to a broader concept of human process—away from the dichotomous, comparative gender frame—removes women from an automatic position of "minority" and frees them for autonomous self-exploration and development. The broader view of human process requires an acceptance of personal responsibility for one's addiction, a responsibility that is solely individual and solely one's own. Paradoxically, the acceptance of personal responsibility requires an acceptance of self and an acceptance of agency (an acknowledgment of being an active participant in one's addiction), which become the route to freedom and equality. Women are often caught between maintaining an oppositional stance against a male majority with a goal of freedom and equality, versus identifying with a larger, shared human experience that implicitly requires an acceptance of self. In accepting personal responsibility for their loss of control, women gain the separate, equal self that they have been fighting so hard to achieve through the struggle against men. But it is still hard for women to do both: maintain their differentiated female selves and identify with the larger experience they share with men. In the gender framework, they may feel they are betraying their loyalties to the women's movement; they may perceive the acceptance of loss of control—the defining experience of addiction—as bringing with it a loss of self, rather than the opposite: the existence of self and personal freedom.

This dilemma is intensified by a competitive, aggressive language. In the political context, the fight for equality is often conceived of as a fight for power and control; fighting for and winning equality is equal to empowerment.

Although important to women's social and political rights, the notion of empowerment can hinder and confuse a woman who is coming to terms with her addictive loss of control. In this context, the idea of empowerment may reinforce a competitive, dichotomous frame and the pathology of the addictive struggle for control. In order to win this so-called empowerment, the woman must reject the submissive, losing position implied by accepting the loss of control. This "losing" is often incorrectly interpreted as "personal fault": "If I accept that I am responsible for my addiction and my loss of control, I will be accepting failure as a woman, or failure in the fight for equality." Coming full circle, the woman may then tell herself again to claim "self-power" and "self-control" in the service of rejecting this conclusion.

Becoming "empowered" is a victory "over"—the illusion of success in the addictive struggle for control: I have to gain "power over" or "control over" my drinking, eating, spending. The political view that women need "power" and that this is "power over," solidifies the divided, warring self. In order to free women from this view, it is essential to understand the differences between the sociopolitical concepts and language described earlier and the concepts and language of addiction recovery. In the pathology of the internal alcoholic "system," the woman is both abuser and victim, of herself. The woman is the perpetrator of her own addiction, and she is her own victim. Women need a model that allows them to be responsible, to identify as sole agents in the development of their addiction, and to identify as sole agents responsible for their recovery.

The same paradox of meaning exists for the idea of loss of control. In the developmental model, a woman's loss of control is not equated with failure, nor with victimization by another, male or female. The acceptance of loss of control is not a passive resignation but a paradoxical path to autonomy. Women and men may drink and develop other addictions to cope with experiences of victimization, but loss of control of oneself to an addiction and in an addictive process is ultimately individual. The key for both sexes is to accept personal responsibility and agency in becoming and being addicted, regardless of cause—be it physical, relational, social, cultural.

The developmental perspective on addiction and recovery releases women from the paradoxes of stigma and of the dichotomous, minority position. Recovery from addiction is the development of autonomy from within. It is not an autonomy achieved by winning power over anybody or anything. Empowerment is the acquisition of self and self-development, achieved as a direct result of acknowledging loss of control and of engaging in a process of recovery.

History

The history of women's use and abuse of alcohol and other substances is a chronicle of blatant denial or of distorted explanations for what could not be denied. The "history" of women and addiction has been an absence of history, with some exceptions.

There have always been women alcoholics and addicts; they just weren't acknowledged. In the late 1800s, women were regular consumers of Lydia Pinkham's Vegetable Compound, an elixir advertised to put a "blush in milady's cheek"—a promise easily fulfilled by the 30 percent alcohol content. Although "milady" could nip at her medicine, she was not welcome as a drinker with the men.

Nor was she accepted as having an addiction. It was neither ladylike nor morally defensible. Women could have illnesses and take medication routinely for every conceivable ache and pain, but drinking was not yet recommended as a medicine, and alcoholism was not yet accepted as a disease. It was a moral failure and a sign of masculine weakness, outside the bounds of idealized female experience. Drinking was a social and cultural ritual for men. It was associated with aggression, autonomy, and dominance. Men were supposed to be able to "hold their liquor" and to "control" their drinking, a view and a vocabulary that have long been associated with masculine beliefs about power, dominance, aggression, and agency. Women were historically seen as homebodies and caretakers, a view that valued passivity, subjugation, and submission. There was no social or close relational position in which a woman could exist as a drinker, so women had to be "hidden" drinkers and "hidden" alcoholics, as Sandmaier (1980) described.

The history of women and addiction has been colored, like most contemporary thinking in any age, by the sociocultural, political, and psychological conflicts and "truths" of the time. Until the latter part of the twentieth century, women were viewed as secondary and ancillary to men and to the dominance of a male point of view. Thus women's use of substances was acknowledged only to the extent that explanations fit within this secondary role. Women were invisible and anonymous in any context that might view them as agents in their own right, autonomous and free to make choices—a perspective that carries an implicit equality with men and one that is still controversial.

A history of women and addiction parallels this historical tundra of invisibility and anonymity. Women have always been addicts, but neither openly nor with agency. Their use of substances, if acknowledged, had to be explained in a way that maintained their idealized, noncompetitive, unequal status. Substance use was acknowledged for fallen, sexually promiscuous women. Substance use was also permissible in disguised form as medicine, such as Lydia Pinkham's. But acknowledgment of use, recognition of problems with use, and provision for treatment did not exist until the last few decades.

The dilemmas of language and meaning, denial, stigma, and the minority position must have faced people in Alcoholics Anonymous from its inception: If women were not alcoholic, what were they doing in AA? AA, founded by men in 1935, was based on the experience of men. Women were accepted members from the beginning, but they always had minority status, based on their smaller numbers and, probably, the history of denial. The view that women were not supposed to be addicted could be maintained if those who identified themselves as alcoholics were viewed as exceptions—the fallen women. Thus, initially, women were incorporated into AA as a subpopulation, with special needs perhaps, but whose experience of addiction should fit in with the dominant male perspective. In fact, it did. Loss of control is the defining experience of addiction and the core identification for both men and women in AA. But drinking at all, and loss of control, were not part of anyone's view of women.

For years, women occupied minority status in AA. There was one women's story in the first edition of the *Big Book,* then more as time passed. By 1998, an AA survey estimated that women made up 34 percent of the total membership and 38 percent of the membership under thirty years old (Alcoholics Anonymous, 1999).

Because AA meetings and much of the literature of early AA were focused on male experience, it is not surprising that early research and clinical references to women also viewed them as a "subcategory" of the dominant male. In an important text published in 1962 (Hirsch, 1962), women occupied six pages, as a "special problem." Women were either subsumed within the male experience or viewed as an aberration of the "normal" pathology and course of male addiction.

A huge part of the gender emphasis in recent years has been to break denial about women and addiction. Though the challenge to denial has been successful, the idea of a woman alcoholic still threatens the cherished, idealized view of women, and though women are clearly recognized today as addicts, a moral stigma remains. The woman suffering with addiction continues to be regarded, by herself and others, as having failed in a way that does not apply to men. Women's failure is a challenge of the ideal, the contamination of a portrait of woman as selfless, giving, and without aggression.

The great paradox is that by accepting the reality of loss of control, a woman is stepping out of the shadow of comparison to anyone and is taking personal responsibility for having lost control. This is real, tangible, painful equality. She is claiming her sense of agency and selfhood.

Loss of control is the great equalizer, a universal experience of human nature. Yet, for centuries, losing control to alcohol or other drugs was the distinct province of men. Women, idealized as supporters, containers, and nurturers, could not lose control.

Over the last twenty-five years, the acknowledgment of women addicts has increased dramatically. Today, entire books about theory (Bepko, 1991; Van Den Bergh, 1991; Wilsnack & Wilsnack, 1998) and treatment (Straussner & Zelvin, 1997) are focused on women. Similarities and differences with men in the etiology, meaning, course of addiction, and treatment have been well documented (Brown, 1977; Straussner & Zelvin, 1997), and a women-sensitive treatment has been outlined (Bloom & Covington, 1999). A unique women's perspective now informs theory and treatment.

Current Thinking

Parallel to the women's movement of the last quarter-century, theories about women addicts have been organized around gender. Women have been defined "against" men, "in relation to" men, and "different from" men with the vital goal of viewing women as separate from men. The gender perspective illuminates and facilitates differentiation and separation.

The gender perspective has been and continues to be extremely important. It has been well defined in theories of psychology and development (Chodorow, 1978; Gilligan, 1982; Miller, 1976), in relation to a variety of psychopathologies (Gilligan, 1982; Herman, 1992; Turnbull & Gomberg, 1988), and with regard to the criminal justice system (Covington, 1998); these theories have been applied to an understanding of addiction. As Covington points out, understanding differences between men and women is a source of strength. She also stresses the important fact that equality is not sameness. Women may have different treatment needs than men. She also emphasizes the importance of individualized treatment for women, a consideration that the developmental model stresses and facilitates.

Excellent research and texts abound defining women's particular experience and treatment needs. Although historically women had always been seen as a subpopulation of male addiction, this appendage point of view no longer prevails. Most treatment centers acknowledge differences between men and women, and many have separate programs. Some authors continue to criticize AA for failing to rewrite its texts in gender-neutral language. But some AA literature, and many popular books, are directed at women, legitimizing their separate status.

Today researchers, clinicians, and authors agree to the importance of a "gender-sensitized" treatment frame. It is important not to confuse this view with a gender-organizing frame. The latter often dictates the competitive, adversarial perspective. This chapter proposes a broader, more in-depth and complex portrait of women. This view must include a multitude of factors and an appreciation for differences among women. The developmental model accomplishes this task.

The Current Gender Focus

There is little or no denial left today: women can be and are addicts in alarming numbers. Many authors, as exemplified by Straussner (1997), have outlined the common denominators of the female addict's etiology and experience. Straussner includes a review of Freud's theory of gender differences compared to recent feminist views of gender development, emphasizing biological and sociocultural differences. Central to the current feminist view is the relational model of self (Byington, 1997), established in 1981 through research at the Stone Center for Developmental Studies at Wellesley College and credited to Miller (1976), Gilligan (1982), and Chodorow (1978). This theory differentiates women and men on the basis of attachment: women are seen to seek attachment and connection as a way of finding self and female identity, whereas men are seen to seek separation and individuation as their route to self and male identity. By identifying different paths of normal, healthy development, theorists moved women from the status of a deviant subpopulation, failing in its development, to a separate, distinct group, with a different developmental path and goal.

Within this widely accepted view of gender development, Straussner (1997) summarizes current understanding of women and addiction. She identifies epidemiological differences in choice of substance and frequency of use. For example, men continue to be more likely to use alcohol and illegal drugs, whereas women use more legal drugs, including alcohol and prescription medications. This pattern is changing, however, as women are becoming more comfortable using such illicit drugs as cocaine and amphetamines. Women nevertheless still rationalize these drugs as tools to overcome problems, such as weight or depression (Straussner, 1997).

Straussner (1997) also summarizes research on differences in patterns of dual diagnoses, or co-occurring disorders. In general, men are more likely to have antisocial and other impulse disorders, whereas women are more likely to have depression, panic, and eating disorders. There is also widespread agreement (Brown, 1994; Covington & Surrey, 1998) that many women have experienced acute and chronic traumas in the past and present, which may intensify their addictions and add to difficulties in treatment and recovery.

Straussner also includes etiological differences, including why and how women use substances, and biophysiological differences, particularly in relation to reproductive function and problems with pregnancy and birth. She also outlines different "styles of pathology" for men and women. According to Robbins (1989), substance-abusing women have a greater incidence of depression, anxiety, and guilt than men. All these differences are now considered in the design and provision of what is specified as gender-sensitive treatment.

Beyond Gender

Straussner and Zelvin (1997) define and describe differences between men and women, but without a standard, or norm of comparison. They have established theoretical differences between the sexes that have an impact on assessment and treatment. In their view, men and women are separate, equal, and different.

This chapter follows their lead in not using the male experience as a standard, but it also emphasizes similarities and differences between men and women, and among women. It is important to understand women in their own right and not make the overgeneralizing error of assuming sameness among them. It is essential to individualize assessment and treatment for women and to recognize that multiple factors contribute to a woman's particular, individual perspective. The developmental frame accents the woman in relation to herself and to others. It emphasizes the individual: how to think about and treat this particular woman, in this setting, at this age, with these issues.

What Is Addiction?

This chapter defines addiction as a developmental process that is organized by the deep experience of loss of control during active addiction, and by the acceptance of loss of control as the foundation of new self-development in recovery. It is important, though perhaps shocking, to note that loss of control, as a definition and as an experience, is exactly the same for men and women. Addiction is the inability to predictably and consistently stop using a substance or acting out a behavior, once started.

In the developmental model of addiction, both sexes have a pathological relationship to (dependence on) the addictive object and the process of addiction. People experience a painful need, or craving, for alcohol, sex, gambling, or food, for example, and once they act on the need, they experience an inability to stop. Being addicted is the repetitive process of acting on impulse to satisfy or quiet an internal experience that usually includes an emotional or concrete threat to the security of self. Both women and men need to separate from their pathological dependence in order to be able to grow as healthy individuals.

The separation from an unhealthy dependence does not occur in a vacuum. Instead, there is a transfer of dependence through forging a new connection to a healthier object. For many, the new object of attachment is AA, NA, OA, or other twelve-step program that invites people to rely on the elements of "the program" to achieve and maintain abstinence. People are encouraged to substitute a dependence on meetings, literature, contacts by phone, and "working the steps" for the behaviors and thinking of active addiction. Newly recovering people also use other kinds of support, including treatment programs, therapy, religion, or a combination of these.

In a culture that values self-control and self-sufficiency, people typically see the idea of dependence as negative and distasteful. The idea of dependence—especially lifelong dependence—is viewed by many people, clients and clinicians alike, as a bad thing. This negative view of dependence undermines the ability of men and women to accept their loss of control, because its acceptance implicitly means dependence.

Acceptance of loss of control also is complicated by current gender theories. Men are supposed to "separate" from dependency relationships and become "independent," which often means that they deny having any needs at all. Acknowledging a dependence on alcohol or any other substance or process, automatically means failure.

Dependency needs have been legitimized for women in the relational model, which emphasizes the importance of "connection" for women. Still, the sociopolitical emphasis on achieving power tends to nullify women's acceptance of their dependence or, at least, the power emphasis creates conflicts for women.

Both men and women have an unhealthy dependence from which they need to separate, and both will require a healthy dependence to enable their growth in recovery. The AA concepts of surrender and detachment—that is, accepting the loss of control and detaching from an investment in regaining it—are based on separation. The individual "lets go" of the active attachment to addiction, moving to abstinence. People who continue to believe in their own "self-control" and "self-power" often "let go" of the active addiction but vest their new abstinent dependence within the self, claiming will power as the source of strength in maintaining abstinence. Those who accept the permanent loss of control often vest their new emotional attachment in AA and the belief in a "Higher Power" as the objects of substitute, healthy dependence.

Both men and women require a "holding" "other," a source of help and safety outside themselves as they shift from the pathological dependence of active addiction to a healthy dependence in recovery. AA and Al-Anon are relational holding objects, used by both men and women in the service of containing and building on the deep emotional experience of loss of control.

This view complicates a gender-focused understanding of "relational female development," which suggests that women do not experience a natural separation from attachment figures as part of their normal growth. In cases of an ideal experience of healthy attachment and identification, this might certainly be so. But in the developmental model, men and women both have a pathological dependence—an attachment or "connection" from which they must separate, behaviorally, cognitively, and affectively. Both sexes require connection, a substitute dependence, as an essential aspect of healthy growth in recovery. The importance of healthy human dependence to replace the unhealthy addiction, rather than some form of ultimate "separation," is fundamental. This model challenges the either-or categories of much gender thinking. Separation and connection (dependence) are essential to recovery for both sexes.

The developmental frame outlines how people resolve these conflicts in meaning about dependency and control through the stages of recovery.

The Four Stages of Addiction and Recovery

In the 1970s, Brown (1977, 1985, 1995) worked with eighty members of Alcoholics Anonymous (forty women and forty men) to define a process of recovery from alcoholism by asking the question, What happens over time when an individual stops drinking? The developmental model that defines stages of active addiction and recovery is the result of that research. It is a model of change based on the experiences of people who identified themselves as alcoholics and who belonged to AA. It is also a model of change for individuals who identify themselves as "addicts" with many other kinds of addictions who also seek help at AA, Al-Anon, addiction-specific twelve-step groups, and professional and nonprofessional treatment programs.

The four stages of the developmental model—drinking, transition, early re-covery, and ongoing recovery—apply to people who identify themselves as alco-holic or addicted, who accept the belief in loss of control, and who have reached outside themselves for a new source of support in recovery.

Stage One: Drinking

Active alcoholism is characterized by subtle or dramatic changes in drinking be-havior and changes in thinking. In its behavioral manifestation, the individual needs to drink more and more alcohol and at the same time maintains that she has no problem with drinking.

As the drinking progresses, the woman is guided in her behavior, percep-tion, and explanations of reality by a belief in control. She must maintain two core beliefs: (1) I am not an alcoholic, and (2) I can control my drinking. Evidence to the contrary must be denied, rationalized, or explained as something else. The faulty belief in the power to control her drinking serves as an organizing belief system about the self, others, and the world.

As alcoholism progresses, the woman becomes increasingly influenced by the need to deny the reality of her drinking behavior and to maintain that behavior at the same time. The need for alcohol and the denial of that need become the central organizing principles in her life. The core of this faulty logic and denial system rests on the following premise: "I am not drinking too much. I have not lost control, and I need to drink this much because. . . ." The reason, of course, is something else that becomes identified as the "real" problem: "I need alcohol to cope with the kids," "to regulate my mood swings," "to bind my anger at my hus-band," "to compete with men for power or prestige," "to enhance my self-esteem," "to provide insulation for my nerves," "to get to sleep," or "to treat my depres-sion." Although all these issues can be valid and difficult, they serve as rational-izations for continued drinking when a woman uses them in the context of defending her addiction. It is a complicated task for the therapist and her female client to simultaneously validate the multitude of issues with which the client is trying to cope, and target responsibility for the drinking back to her as well.

Stage Two: Transition

The transition stage includes the end of drinking and the beginning of abstinence. Cracks in the rigid system of logic, rationalization, and behavior signal its onset. The disadvantages and problems of drinking begin to outweigh the advantages. The woman begins to doubt her airtight logic or is faced with stark evidence that she cannot deny. The breakdown of denial, central to the task of therapy with the drinking alcoholic, moves the client toward a point of despair referred to by AA members as "hitting bottom" or "surrender."

The task of transition is to move toward this point of despair, which, if successful, leads the woman from active addiction into abstinence. A corresponding change must take place in her core identity as well. The woman now comes to hold these beliefs: (1) I am an alcoholic, and (2) I cannot control my drinking.

The process of transition is difficult, painful, and frightening. Movement is often characterized by fits and starts—shifts back and forth between drinking (with the belief in self-control reinstated) and abstinence (with the acceptance of loss of control).

In transition, the alcoholic woman begins to be "cornered" by the tension of the double bind, namely, needing more alcohol but denying that need at the same time or explaining it as something else. She also begins to experience consequences related directly to her drinking or to her denial and distorted thinking.

Surrender is the point when the tension breaks and reality wins. Surrender is the acceptance of reality on the unconscious level (Tiebout, 1949, 1953), the giving up of one's belief in self-power or control. Reality is the loss of control, the powerlessness over alcohol. Individuals are supported in sustaining this new belief in loss of control by reaching out for help. This belief is central to treatment and to establishing a process of recovery.

Bateson (1971) saw that a belief in a Higher Power, central to AA philosophy, facilitated the breakdown of the myth of self-power. The alcoholic, accepting defeat, reaches outward to rely on an external authority for help. In the transition stage, this power outside the self may be a counselor, an AA member, an AA group, a friend, or a family member who can accept the reality of alcoholism and offer guidance and support for abstinence. Much later, the external authority will become a more abstract Higher Power. Relinquishing a belief in self-power and acquiring a belief in a Higher Power are central tasks in the process of change for individuals within AA (Brown, 1993).

Most critical in this change is the acceptance of defeat and the end of efforts to "solve" alone the struggle for control. Reaching out and accepting help enable the individual to embrace a new framework of behavioral and cognitive change that heralds the beginning of an active recovery process.

As noted earlier, women's emphasis on a competitive fight against men for social, economic, and political power can interfere with this externalization of the source of personal power. Women may maintain a belief that they should not need help and that they should work on building up self-sufficiency, which they equate with self-power. The developmental perspective recognizes dependence as necessary for all human beings and legitimizes new healthy sources of support.

Stage Three: Early Recovery

Early recovery is defined by a marked reduction in impulses that demand an immediate behavioral response. The new actions and beliefs of abstinence are familiar, if not yet secure, and are practiced routinely. The alcoholic now learns to pause and think before responding immediately to an impulse to drink. This delay, achieved with the addition of cognition, is one of the developmental building blocks of recovery. Women are instructed by helpers to remind themselves that they are alcoholic and cannot control their drinking. These reminders are important to counter the return of the illusion of control, the idea that maybe one drink wouldn't hurt, that all the work in recovery will lead to a reinstatement of control.

Of course, this is not the case. Loss of control is a permanent organizing principle of self-development in recovery. When a woman's new behavior and cognition are stabilized, she can focus on the intensive learning of early recovery, which involves constructing a story of her own drinking and incorporating emotional exploration and expression.

Early recovery involves an expansion in a woman's awareness and feelings of both the past and the present—an opening up that can feel like a loss of control. When this growth in feeling and awareness does feel out of control, it can threaten her newfound sense of safety and awaken a need for defense. In an attempt to reduce her anxiety, she may reject loss of control—or well-meaning others may counsel her to reject loss of control—and its "losing" implications, in favor of "seizing" power and control or "asserting" her will to gain control of her feelings. Such injunctions can send a woman back to a belief in control that can derail the developmental process and perhaps lead to relapse.

Stage Four: Ongoing Recovery

Ongoing recovery is defined by the stabilization of all the dramatic changes in behavior, thinking, and affect that characterized the work of the early stages. Women in ongoing recovery maintain a concrete behavioral and cognitive focus, usually through a maintenance program of AA meetings and regular contact with AA friends. In this stage, they incorporate deeper self-exploration, which occurs through the structure of the twelve steps and, often, the process of psychotherapy as well. Many women speak of their ongoing recovery as spiritual development, anchored by the belief in a power greater than the self.

Women may also be tackling other difficult and painful issues from the past—growing up with addicted parents, abuse, neglect, and all kinds of other traumas—and the present, as well as the intricacies of close interpersonal relationship. At this time, many women combine participation in twelve-step recovery programs with individual, group, couple, or family therapy (or a combination of these) to maintain and deepen recovery. Yet, seeking help may be difficult. It is ironic that many women believe they must be doing something wrong if they experience difficulties in ongoing sobriety. In fact, it is just the opposite (Brown & Lewis, 1999): the stability of abstinence, often beginning in early recovery, frees them to open up other difficult and painful issues. But it's hard to see the onset of anxiety, depression, and interpersonal struggles as a marker of progress. It is even harder if a woman believes she is failing in recovery because she is supposed to have solved her problems. Even at this point, a view that urges her to assert her will and power can unwittingly interfere and hold her back. It is a great paradox of recovery that the woman accepts responsibility for her loss of control, courageously works on self-development, and gets to feel not only the pain of being addicted but also the pain of everything else.

The Developmental Frame

The developmental model presents a different way of thinking than most mental health models, because it focuses on normal growth rather than on pathology. The developmental model also supports a continuum of care, recognizing that women have different needs at different times and that treatment and recovery are long term—a view that contrasts sharply with the current mental health emphasis on short-term cures. An extended perspective illuminates the natural course of addiction and recovery, highlighting how particular roles and settings; the kind of addiction; and a woman's age, stage in the life cycle, and ethnicity affect her at different stages. In addition, the developmental model offers a broad, holistic perspective that frees women from the adversarial difficulties of defining themselves as different from or "against" men. In the developmental model, men and women are equal. There is no dominance and no submission, no privilege and denial of privilege to be addressed between the sexes. There is only the focus on the woman's relationship with herself and the fundamental deep human experience of loss of control.

The stages and tasks—the process of being addicted and of being in recovery— are the same for men and women. Differences abound, however, in the meanings attached to these processes, and to other issues and conflicts that people face, which may greatly influence their experience of addiction and recovery (Brown, 1977, 1985; Brown & Lewis, 1999). The meanings attached to being addicted and to being in recovery are also different among women. So are decisions regarding intervention, best treatment options, and timing.

For example, many women develop multiple addictions to cope with unnamed and unresolved traumas from the past, such as sexual molestation, physical violence, and emotional abuse. Although the woman usually must deal with these issues at some point, there is no formula for a particular intervention or for timing. One woman may be unable to stay sober until she has opened the past, whereas another can't open the past until long into recovery. The challenge for the therapist is to tell the difference. The therapist does this by listening to and understanding this particular woman as well as possible, rather than by imposing a formula based on an idea or an image of what should be right. Although it is not practically possible to provide individual therapy to all women everywhere, it is not at all impractical to hold the attitude that there is no right answer and no single way of seeing things. There are few interventions or interpretations that will be right for all women.

The Process of Being Addicted

Addiction can be viewed variously as

> A disease, with physiological, biological, neurological, and metabolic properties
>
> A behavioral disorder
>
> A cognitive disturbance of faulty logic and false premises
>
> An expression of, or way of coping with, internal and interpersonal conflict and trauma

All these points of view are valid, and all may be applicable to any one person. Nevertheless, the fundamental and most profound experience of addiction is loss of control.

The process of being addicted, therefore, includes the physical realities, behaviors, and cognitive-emotional experience of losing control, and the cognitive-affective changes required to defend against awareness of the reality of loss of control. Men and women create the same internal addictive system: becoming obsessive and compulsive, needing the substance or the behavior more and more, and simultaneously denying and rationalizing that need. The individual becomes dominated by the double-bind need to deny any problem with alcohol and to explain why drinking is necessary in a way that allows her to maintain the behavior.

Shirley illustrates the thinking, described earlier, that sets the process of addiction in place:

I liked alcohol. I liked the taste, and I liked what it did for me. I did not want to have problems with it. So, as I drank more and began to think about it more, to crave it, I got scared. I told myself and others that I was under a lot of stress and drinking helped me cope. I could work harder, longer, take care of the kids, and never complain—as long as I knew I could drink. Drinking wasn't a luxury; it wasn't an option I could easily discard. It was a necessity.

Addiction is a painful experience of increasing debilitation, from subtle to extreme, from temporary to permanent. Loss of control is a primary experience of utter helplessness, which involves a threat to, and a loss of, capacity to function. The experience of losing control is similar to other states of trauma in which the safety of self is overwhelmed, and it has been likened to death (Brown, 1994). Shirley continues,

At first I loved the high. I loved being out of control. Then it got scary when I couldn't remember whole conversations or even whole evenings, and when I did shameful and embarrassing things. Eventually, I was drunk a lot of the time, and I no longer felt in charge of being high. Being out of control had become terrifying. It felt like it was happening to me and there was nothing I could do. Yet, there I was—the one picking up the drink. Then I got into other trouble that went along with my drinking. I used every kind of pill to try to get the feeling of control I no longer got from alcohol. And then I started gambling to pay for it all.

In the developmental frame, addiction is perceived as a systems conflict—Bateson's war within the self—that complicates simple interventions. A woman experiences a conscious wish to do well, to stop using, and an unconscious need to continue to drink or an inability to stop. As noted earlier, the individual is pitted against the self and against the other. The woman is in a divided, polarized struggle within the self as she holds onto the belief "I am not an alcoholic; I can control my drinking" while, in fact, her drinking is out of control. The same internal struggle exists for other addictions: the fight for control against the reality of loss of control.

In the developmental model—for the individual, the couple, and the family—both men and women sacrifice themselves, losing control to the greater power of their own addiction *and* to the greater power of the addicted couple and family system they establish. Addiction becomes a chronic adaptation to pathology.

This kind of system is extreme. It is also logically backwards and counterintuitive. The individual becomes locked in a polarized internal battle: there must be a winner and a loser. Winning involves the fight to maintain drinking as well as the defenses that deny loss of control. Losing is the recognition of loss of control, the acceptance of defeat. Paradoxically, in this schema, winning means maintaining pathology: the belief in self-power and the ability to control her drinking. Never mind that this kind of "win" is killing her. The woman tightens her defenses in response to a threat of recognizing the loss of control.

The polarized system is based on a dichotomy of dominance-submission, aggressor-victim. In this system—the individual in relation to self or other—the alcoholic or addicted person, whether male or female, is dominant. Others in this system become submissive to the dominance of the alcoholic and to the rules of the pathological system. All members of this system, including the woman in relation to herself, sacrifice autonomy to maintain the dominant organizing principle of addiction: to deny that any problem with control exists and to explain why the behavior is necessary in a way that allows the abuse and reality of loss of control to continue. Within the authoritarian, dichotomous structure of self and of self and other, the individual establishes and changes definitions and meanings as well as systemic roles, rules, boundaries, and hierarchies at will, in order to preserve the pathology of his or her dominant view. These systemic elements are not static, nor are they necessarily defined by gender. Dominance begins as a need for control over one's point of view about the self—"I am in control of my drinking"—and usually extends to a need to control the other's point of view and position in interpersonal relationships.

Recent research (Brown & Lewis, 1995, 1999; Brown, Lewis, & Liotta, 2000) on the alcoholic couple and family in recovery confirms that the alcoholic, male or female, is dominant in organizing the system. The addicted person, male or female, may also be the most overtly out of control, a combination that reduces people in the system to the lowest level of health and function. Everyone submits to and is shaped by the pathology of addiction. In recovery, this pattern continues, with more differences between alcoholics and coalcoholics than between men and women (D. Petroni, personal communication, December 2000). The dominance of addiction organizes the system more than gender.

The key to the dynamics of the alcoholic system—the individual in relation to self and other—is the struggle for willful self-control and for the power to disprove and defy the reality of loss of control. Men and women are the same in their relation to self-power and alcohol. Both are fighting for their belief in control and rejecting the reality of loss of control.

Maria, a compulsive shopper, and her husband, a drug addict and alcoholic, recall the way they saw things:

Maria: No way I was out of control. You were out of control, for sure, with your pot and booze, and that was our problem. It wasn't going to be about me.

Juan: Yea, I was out of control, but I was convinced you drove me to it. You were spending all this money, all the time, and eating, day and night. Wasn't that out of control?

Maria and Juan illustrate the angry, defensive struggle for power in the relationship, described earlier as the paradox of an adversarial, competitive view: which partner gets to say who is out of control? In this "war," both are focused outward, attributing fault to the other. This battle for control over point of view— who will be the winner and who will be the loser, the one at fault—makes it more difficult for either partner to acknowledge personal responsibility and to shift attention from the intense couple battle to a necessary focus on the self. Although it is inherent to the sociopolitical gender battle, this dichotomous structure can exist for other relationships as well—lesbian, friendships, working relationships—any dyad or system that operates within a symmetrical, competitive structure. (Maria and Juan both experienced the devastating consequences of their separate addictions. Today, both identify as addicts, and both are in recovery.)

The acceptance of loss of control signals the end of the dichotomous struggle within the self and against the other. In conjunction with abstinence, the belief in loss of control becomes the cornerstone of an individual developmental process of recovery. Again, the process is the same for men and women. Recovery is launched with separation from the addictive object and a transfer of dependence to a new object, such as AA, Al-Anon, books, meetings, a therapist, a treatment or recovery community—something that represents a new, healthier dependence.

The Meanings of Being Addicted

In the research of the 1970s (Brown, 1977), men and women who belonged to Alcoholics Anonymous defined themselves as alcoholics on the basis of having lost control of their drinking. Yet what it meant to lose control, how and why they came to lose control, and what it meant to be alcoholic were different for men and women. Understanding these differences is important to individualizing women's treatment.

Men described the experience of having lost control as an issue of masculinity, a competitive failure in relation to other men who can drink without losing control. There are winners and losers; male winners have control.

Women demonstrated greater variability in the meanings they attached to the loss of control. For some women it was a competitive failure in relation to men, as it was for males. In these cases, women were caught in a struggle for power "against" or "over" men, or simply to prove that they were strong winners, just like the men. This is the power frame that was then, and is now, structured around the pursuit of self-power in relation to a dominant or superior "other"—that is, the other who is seen as successful. Women also experience this power battle as the fight against the loss of control within the self—drinking, using other drugs, eating, spending, gambling. One woman emphasized this internal war: "I wanted to win; You couldn't have trouble with drinking and be number one."

A larger group of women identified "being alcoholic" as a failure in their relationship to men, particularly their husbands. These women saw themselves as having failed not in "self-power" but rather in the performance of their roles as wives and mothers, a view that underscores the significance of the relational theory of women's development. Some women also experienced a sense of competitive failure with other women whom they perceived as successful wives and mothers or, at the least, as satisfied and accepting in these traditional roles. Sharifa said, "I was always feeling inadequate as a wife and mother when I looked at my friends or the good TV mothers. I was angry that I had to be a wife and mother, but that was so hard to see."

This woman has an understanding of internal conflict, which is an important part of addiction and recovery, especially in relation to the meanings attached to loss of control. Conflict involves holding mixed feelings, wishes, or motives that likely contradict deep beliefs. Jenny illustrates: "I was a sweet girl, a good student and a member of my church choir. In my mind, I was not supposed to need anything else. I was certainly not supposed to be addicted. Well, I struggled with an eating disorder, and I loved drinking. I felt like such a failure because I couldn't control myself."

All kinds of interpersonal and internal conflicts can interfere with treatment and recovery if the woman does not recognize these conflicts and accept responsibility for them. Sharifa felt conflicted about being a mother. She added that alcohol and pot helped her quiet her feelings of inadequacy and anger, though she also felt conflicted about her use. "At first, alcohol and pot worked to mellow me out. Then I began to feel guilty about using, thinking I needed these drugs to cope but also realizing on some level that I was abusing them. Eventually, I could see the conflict in me, but nothing changed until I took responsibility: I had to do something about my problem. No one could fix it for me."

Women can accept and understand conflict, but it is not easy as long as they maintain a black-and-white view. The dichotomous gender position leaves little room for the "gray"—mixed feelings and ambivalence, conscious and unconscious, which are part of healthy growth. An adversarial frame leaves little room for differences among women or for conflict, both internal and interpersonal, and leads to chronic guilt, self-blame, or anger at self and other. The win-lose nature of the majority-minority, dominant-submissive political view underscores the necessity of a "united" women's front and reinforces an externalized adversarial stance.

The political view makes it more difficult for women to accept conflict, contradictory motives and feelings in themselves, and anything that is outright negative, because experiencing ambivalence and problems so automatically implies failure. This can lead to a defensive emphasis on the positives about women— their motivation and natural caring, for example. There is no room in this context for the woman to accept that she wants children and at the same time doesn't want children, for example. And there may be difficulty for the woman who has mixed feelings about close relationship. Tula said she fought with the treatment staff about her desire for "connection." "No," Tula said, "they wanted me to identify with these other women, to share and be close. I used to be disconnected, to be able to feel myself and shut others out. I couldn't do it any other way. Now, I'm supposed to be close?"

It is also hard within the adversarial political context to see that women can be self-sabotaging. There is a tendency to believe that women want the best for themselves and others and will behave accordingly to achieve it. But defining what is "best" is full of conflict for the woman and full of controversy in the culture. At the manifest level of real life and real relationship, women are struggling with a multitude of mixed needs and motives that they cannot make conscious, nor sort out, without a culture and a treatment community that can accept the reality and normality of conflict.

For example, Tina, a woman with several young children, kept using and selling drugs, despite knowing that it meant an automatic return to jail. She ached with the knowledge that her children were suffering and the certainty that she would eventually lose them. Treatment professionals felt sure that the threatened loss of her children would be a strong incentive for Tina to stop her drug use, and they were baffled and angry with her when she did not stop. She felt deep guilt about her behavior, and terror that she couldn't stop using. After ultimately being clean and sober for many years, however, she had an insight she could not recognize before: she grew up with an absent alcoholic mother who was "always in the bars." Tina lived with a nagging fear that she would abuse her children. Going to jail was both her unconscious identification with her mother's absence and her effort to protect her children.

In the research that defined the developmental model, women in recovery reported that they drank for many different reasons. The meanings they attached to their drinking and to being alcoholic were also varied, and often full of ambivalence. For most women in that research, drinking was initially seen as goal-directed and positive. There was a purpose to drinking: it was part of coping, and it was adaptive. There was a problem to solve, and drinking did the job.

In all cases, drinking gave these women the illusion that they could control some problematic aspect of themselves. For example, Helen never liked drinking much, but believed she should not miss the Friday afternoon kegs at her fast-paced high-tech job, because "team players" showed up. "Friday afternoons sometimes felt like the Olympics—who could drink the most and the fastest. You didn't want to opt out of this event. Drinking took away my anxiety, and I felt like I belonged. I was finally on the inside." Moira also problem-solved with alcohol: "I used alcohol and then pills to quiet the chronic pain I felt about everything. When I drank, I could change my mood—get a breather from the awful state of my life."

Some women drank to be able to be mothers, and others stopped drinking for the same reason. Hildy explained: "I stopped drinking with my first pregnancy so I could be a 'good mother.' Never thought too much about it as the kids grew up. During this time, I turned to food as a tranquilizer, I smoked, and did a little pot now and then. When my youngest moved away from home, I turned back to alcohol, like a horse headed for the barn. I picked up that drink as if I had never put it aside."

Tula explained that alcohol and tranquilizers had given her the "strength" and "stamina" to be able to be a decent mother to four children under five. "The promise of a drink or a pill got me through the worst moments. With that first taste, I felt a wave of relief." After years of sobriety she noted that the alcohol and pills helped her control her moods and the extremes of emotion she always felt. She was very afraid she'd blow up at her children, and she knew she was capable of hitting them. She lived in terror of herself. In her view, drugs stood between her rages and her kids. Tula could not see the very negative consequences of her addiction until she fell asleep with a cigarette and set the house on fire.

The range of meanings and examples is infinite. Some women become addicted in order to feel and be different, some to treat anxiety and depression; some want desperately to fit in, to open up, whereas others want to shut down. Finding the "perfect" amount of alcohol, the "perfect" dose of an amphetamine, or the "perfect" fix from food is the elusive goal of most addicts. Becoming addicted almost always is adaptive—it usually solves a conscious or unconscious problem. And then it becomes the problem.

The key to pathology is the sacrifice of a healthy self and a healthy relationship to self in the service of maintaining an addiction and an addictive system. The key to recovery is the opposite, as emphasized throughout this chapter. The focus shifts from the pathology of addiction with its central struggle for power and control, to an acceptance of loss of control, which becomes the cornerstone for a new developmental process focused on autonomy and healthy self-development.

Sharifa illustrates the key to recovery, an acceptance of personal responsibility: "I was angry and I was hell-bent on destroying myself. I didn't need any help, and nobody better offer it. Then I got it. I just got it. I was kiddin' myself and for what? The world wasn't gonna miss me and I wasn't showin' 'em one thing. I was all by myself, sluggin' at the air. Time to stop. It took awhile, but I finally could look at myself and see that nothin' was gonna come my way if I didn't show up. That's me now—I show up, and I don't drink or use."

Conclusion

Women have come a long way, gaining the "right" to be acknowledged as addicts and the right to treatment for their addictions. Yet this new visibility brings complications that require an understanding of paradox.

The developmental model of addiction and recovery helps resolve these dilemmas and further an understanding of the process of addiction. Women are the same in their fundamental experience of loss of control. The meanings and circumstances of their addictions are not the same, however. It is important to understand differences among women, to individualize their treatment, and to hold a long-term perspective.

References

Alcoholics Anonymous. (1955). *Alcoholics Anonymous*. New York: Alcoholics Anonymous World Services.

Alcoholics Anonymous. (1999). *1998 membership survey*. New York: Alcoholics Anonymous World Services.

Bateson, G. (1971). The cybernetics of self: A theory of alcoholism. *Psychiatry, 34*(1), 1–18.

Bepko, C. (Ed.). (1991). *Feminism and addiction*. Binghamton, NY: Haworth Press.

Bloom, B., & Covington, S. (1999, December 13–15). *Gender-responsivity: An essential element in women's programming*. Paper presented at the National Symposium on Women Offenders, Office of Justice Programs.

Brown, S. (1977). *Defining a process of recovery in alcoholism*. Unpublished doctoral dissertation, California School of Professional Psychology, Berkeley.

Brown, S. (1985). *Treating the alcoholic: A developmental model of recovery*. New York: Wiley.

Brown, S. (1993). Therapeutic processes in Alcoholics Anonymous. In B. McCrady & W. Miller (Eds.), *Research on Alcoholics Anonymous* (pp. 137–152). New Brunswick, NJ: Rutgers Center of Alcohol Studies.

Brown, S. (1994). Alcoholism and trauma: A theoretical comparison and overview. *Journal of Psychoactive Drugs, 26*, 345–355.

Brown, S. (Ed.). (1995). *Treating alcoholism*. San Francisco: Jossey-Bass.

Brown, S., & Lewis, V. (1995). The alcoholic family: A developmental model of recovery. In S. Brown (Ed.), *Treating alcoholism* (pp. 279–315). San Francisco: Jossey-Bass.

Brown, S., & Lewis, V. (1999). *The alcoholic family in recovery: A developmental model.* New York: Guilford Press.

Brown, S., Lewis, V., & Liotta, A. (2000). *The family guide to recovery: A map for healthy growth.* Oakland, CA: New Harbinger Press.

Byington, D. (1997). Applying relational theory to addiction treatment. In S.L.A. Straussner & E. Zelvin (Eds.), *Gender and addiction: Men and women in treatment* (pp. 33–46). New York: Guilford Press.

Chodorow, N. (1978). *The reproduction of mothering.* Berkeley: University of California Press.

Covington, S. (1998). The relational theory of women's psychological development: Implications for the criminal justice system. In R. Zaplin (Ed.), *Female offenders: Critical perspectives and effective interventions* (pp. 113–131). Gaithersburg, MD: Aspen.

Covington, S., & Surrey, J. (1998). The relational model of women's psychological development: Implications for substance abuse. In S. Wilsnack & R. Wilsnack (Eds.), *Gender and alcohol: Individual and social perspectives* (pp. 335–351). Piscataway, NJ: Rutgers University Press.

Gilligan, C. (1982). *In a different voice: Psychological theory and women's development.* Cambridge: Harvard University Press.

Herman, J. (1992). *Trauma and recovery.* New York: HarperCollins/Basic Books.

Hirsch, J. (1962). Women and alcoholism. In W. C. Bier (Ed.), *Problems in addiction: Alcoholism and narcotics* (pp. 108–115). New York: Fordham University Press.

Jellinek, E. M. (1960). *The disease concept of alcoholism.* New Haven: College and Universities Press.

Miller, J. B. (1976). *Towards a new psychology of women.* Boston: Beacon Press.

Robbins, C. (1989). Sex differences in psychosocial consequences of alcohol and drug abuse. *Journal of Health and Social Behavior, 30,* 117–130.

Sandmaier, M. (1980). *The invisible alcoholics: Women and alcohol abuse in America.* New York: McGraw-Hill.

Straussner, S.L.A. (1997). Gender and substance abuse. In S.L.A. Straussner & E. Zelvin (Eds.), *Gender and addictions: Men and women in treatment* (pp. 5–27). Northvale, NY: Aronson.

Straussner, S.L.A., & Zelvin, E. (Eds.). (1997). *Gender and addictions: Men and women in treatment.* New York: Guilford Press.

Tiebout, H. (1949). The act of surrender in the psychotherapeutic process with special reference to alcoholism. *Quarterly Journal of Studies on Alcohol, 10,* 48–58.

Tiebout, H. (1953). Surrender vs. compliance in therapy with special reference to alcoholism. *Journal of Studies on Alcohol, 14,* 58–68.

Turnbull, J. E., & Gomberg, E.S.L. (1988). Structure of depression in alcoholic women. *Journal of Studies on Alcohol, 51,* 148–155.

Van Den Bergh, N. (Ed.). (1991). *Feminist perspectives on addiction.* New York: Springer.

Wilsnack, S., & Wilsnack, R. (Eds.). (1998). *Gender and alcohol: Individual and social perspectives.* Piscataway, NJ: Rutgers University Press.

CHAPTER THREE

HELPING WOMEN RECOVER

Creating Gender-Responsive Treatment

Stephanie S. Covington

In the last two decades, clinicians and researchers have developed a solid body of knowledge in best practices for the treatment of addicted women. Research indicates that clinical services for addiction treatment that address women's specific issues are more effective for women than are traditional programs, originally designed for men (Abbott & Kerr, 1995; Carten, 1996; Center for Substance Abuse Treatment, 1994; Covington, 1998a; Finkelstein, 1993). However, many of the services that women encounter in the public and private sectors are not designed for women. In addition, they often lack cohesion and consistency because they are constructed from a variety of resources that are not consistent in their theoretical bases.

This chapter presents a new, integrated approach to women's treatment, based on theory, research, and clinical experience. The treatment philosophy and guiding principles discussed are designed to create a foundation for clinical thought and practice. These principles can be applied in any setting (inpatient, outpatient, private practice, therapeutic community, criminal justice, and so on) and to any modality (individual, group, or family therapy). A key concept is that if we are to develop effective treatment for women, we must include the experience and impact of living as a woman in a male-based society—in other words, gender—as part of the clinical perspective. The definition of the term *gender-responsive* used in this chapter is as follows: *creating an environment through site selection, staff selection, program development, content, and material that reflects an understanding of the realities of women's lives, and is responsive to the issues of the clients* (Covington, 2001). Therefore, this chapter focuses on both the content and context of women's treatment.

Underlying Theory and Research

A basic principle of clinical work is to know who the client is and what she brings into the treatment setting. Until recently, this in-depth knowledge about the woman addict was missing. However, recent research provides important information for understanding both the development of addiction in women and the critical issues that must be considered in the design and process of treatment.

Research demonstrates that addiction is rarely, if ever, a single-dimension issue for women. Addiction is always a part of a larger portrait that includes a woman's individual history and the social, economic, and cultural factors that create the context of her life. Therefore, in thinking about treatment for addicted women, it is essential to start from the premise that theory and practice should be based on a multidimensional perspective. As Abbott and Kerr (1995) suggest, "If treatment is to be effective, it must . . . take the context of women's lives into account" (p. 3).

In examining the life histories of addicted women, we can see two elements that many women share in addition to their dependence on chemicals: the lack of healthy relationships and the experience of trauma (for example, physical abuse, sexual abuse, poverty, racism) (Covington, 1999). These elements create multiple issues that are interrelated in women's lives and need to be considered when assisting a woman into recovery. Therefore, we will discuss three theoretical formulations that will provide a framework of thought (the foundation) for clinical services: theory of addiction, theory of women's psychological development, and theory of trauma.

Theory of Addiction

It is important to have a theoretical model to work from when treating addicted women.

Disorder Versus Disease

Historically, addiction was viewed as a sign of lapsed morals. In the 1950s, mental health professionals began to view addiction as a sign of an underlying psychological disorder. The belief was that if one could resolve the underlying disorder, the addiction would disappear. As the chemical dependency field was born, its practitioners viewed addiction not as a symptom but as a primary condition with its own symptoms. The condition could not be managed through will power; instead, the afflicted person needed to make lifestyle changes to achieve emotional and physical stability, just as in the case of a disease such as diabetes. The concept of addiction as a disease gained wide acceptance. However, the analogy to diabetes still saw the disease as rooted in the physical aspects of the individual. As health professionals in many disciplines began revising their concepts of all disease, a more holistic view of health came to acknowledge not only the physical aspects of disease but also the emotional, psychological, and spiritual aspects (Northrup, 1994). Alcoholics Anonymous (AA) was one of the first proponents of a holistic health model of the disease of addiction, encompassing the physical, emotional, psychological, and spiritual aspects.

In addition to this broader view, we have learned also to consider the environmental and sociopolitical aspects of addiction and other diseases. Cancer can be used as an analogy. Like addiction, cancer has physical, emotional, psychological, spiritual, and environmental dimensions. B. Siegel (personal communication, Oct. 1996) reports that 80 percent of doctors link cancer to lifestyle choices (diet and exercise) and the environment (pesticides, emissions, nuclear waste, and so on). Cancer also has sociopolitical aspects, especially when one considers the huge profits made by the producers of carcinogenic products. Even though cancer and addictions share a number of characteristics, cancer is universally acknowledged as a disease; addiction is not. Moreover, addiction is often treated as a crime. This has resulted in a huge population increase in our prisons, where few inmates receive adequate treatment.

Although the debate over models will probably continue, the disease perspective offers a more helpful approach to the treatment of addiction because it is more comprehensive and thus meets the requirements for a multidimensional framework. The disorder model focuses on social learning theory and a cognitive-behavioral approach (Parks, 1997), thereby minimizing the importance of genetic studies, the affective aspects of the problem and its solution (Brown, 1985), and its sociocultural and environmental elements. The holistic health model allows clinicians to treat addiction as the primary problem while also addressing the complexity of issues that women bring to treatment: genetic predisposition, health consequences, shame, isolation, a history of abuse, or a combination of these. For example, though some women may have a genetic predisposition to addiction, it is important in treatment to acknowledge that many of them have grown up in environments in which drug dealing and addiction are ways of life. When addiction has been a core part of multiple aspects of a woman's life, the treatment process requires a holistic multidimensional approach.

Research Studies on Males Versus Females

Because research studies on male addicts have focused on different topics from those conducted on female addicts, research has yielded different types of data and suffered from information gaps. For example, many studies have examined alcoholism in fathers and sons, clearly indicating a genetic link in men. Few studies, however, have focused on the genetic link in women.

Environmental and psychosocial factors in women's addictions have been studied more thoroughly, however (Finkelstein, Kennedy, Thomas, & Kearns, 1997). *Stigma* (severe social disapproval) is the main psychosocial issue differentiating the substance abuse of females from that of males. Although drinking alcohol is often seen as "macho" in men, it conflicts with society's view of femininity and the roles of wife and mother. The words still associated with female addicts are *slut, lush,* and *bad mother.* Women often internalize this stigma and feel guilt, shame, despair, and fear when they are addicted to alcohol or other drugs. Mothers also know that addiction may cause them to lose their children. Stigma and the threat of severe consequences often lead women and their families to minimize the impact of substance abuse by using denial.

The Spiral of Addiction and Recovery

In addition to seeing addiction holistically, we can envision the process of addiction and recovery as a spiral (Brown, 1985; Covington, 1999), as illustrated in Figure 3.1. The downward spiral of addiction revolves around the drug of choice. Addiction pulls the addict into ever-tightening circles, constricting her life until she is completely focused on the drug. The object of her addiction becomes the organizing principle of her life. Using alcohol or other drugs, protecting her supply, hiding her addiction from others, and cultivating her love-hate relationship with her drug begin to dominate her world.

When a woman is in this downward phase of constriction, the therapist's task is to break through her denial. The woman must come to a point of transition, in which she shifts her perceptions in two ways. She must shift from believing "I am in control" to admitting, "I am not in control." She must stop believing "I am not an addict" and admit, "I am an addict" (Brown, 1985, p. 34).

Both shifts can feel humiliating. Our society's double standard inflicts far more shame on a woman who has an addiction than on a man who does. Although society may stigmatize a male addict as a "bum," it rarely attacks his sexuality or his competence as a parent. We must understand that a woman who enters treatment may come with a heavy burden of shame. She does not need to be shamed further; rather, she needs to be offered the hope that she can heal.

FIGURE 3.1. THE SPIRAL OF ADDICTION AND RECOVERY.

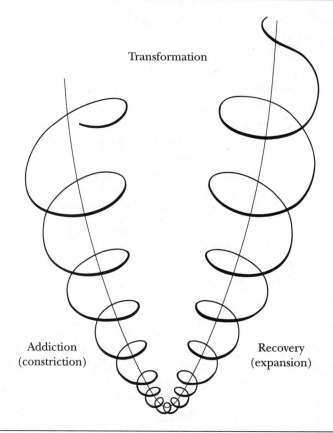

Transformation

Addiction
(constriction)

Recovery
(expansion)

Source: Helping Women Recover: A Program for Treating Addiction, Stephanie S. Covington, copyright © 1999 by Stephanie S. Covington. Reprinted by permission of Jossey-Bass, Inc., a subsidiary of John Wiley & Sons, Inc.

The upward spiral of recovery revolves around the drug in ever-widening circles, as the addiction loosens its grip and the woman's world expands away from the drug. Her world grows to include healthy relationships, an expanded self-concept, and a richer sexual and spiritual life.

Notice that the process is not merely one of turning around and ascending the same spiral but one of profound change, so that the woman ascends a different spiral. When women speak of recovery, they speak of a fundamental transformation: "I'm not the same person. I'm different than I was."

Addiction as a Neglect of Self

The generic definition of the word *addiction* used in this chapter is a *chronic neglect of self in favor of something or someone else.* This neglect of self includes patterns of repetition and compulsion that reinforce self-destructive behavior, cognition, and affect.

Many practitioners who have studied men see addicts as self-focused, and they perceive their task as breaking that obsession with self. Men who are addicted typically build up grandiose false selves that must be challenged before they can discover and cultivate their true selves. The descriptive terms used in AA include *king baby, inflated self ego,* and *grandiosity* (Alcoholics Anonymous, 1976). The confrontation used in traditional therapeutic communities and early treatment programs was designed to break through this false, grandiose self of men. Addicted women, however, generally have a diminished sense of self. They have learned to negate and neglect their true selves in favor of other people and their drug(s) of choice. Female addicts may appear self-obsessed because their lives are constricted around their drugs, while healthy give-and-take with others recedes into the background. However, their obsession with their drugs hides their true selves.

Questions then arise: How does a woman shift from a chronic neglect of self to a healthy care of self? How does a woman shift from constriction to expansion and growth? How does a woman grow and recover? These questions alert clinicians to the importance of understanding women's psychological development.

Theory of Women's Psychological Development

The spiral shown in Figure 3.1 shows recovery as an upward spiral of growth and expansion. In order to assist women in the transition from addiction to recovery, it is important to understand how women grow and develop.

Growth-Fostering Relationships

Traditional theories of psychology have described human development as a progression from childlike dependence to mature independence through a process of separation and individuation. Only when the individual was self-sufficient and autonomous was that person perceived to be capable of adult intimacy.

In her groundbreaking book *Toward a New Psychology of Women,* Miller (1976) challenged the assumption that separation is the route to intimacy. She said that connection, not separation, is the guiding principle of growth for women. Her work led to the creation of the Stone Center at Wellesley College, established to explore the qualities of relationships that foster healthy growth in women. According to the relational model, the primary motivation for women throughout life is to establish a strong sense of connection. Women develop a sense of self and self-worth when their actions arise from and lead back to connections with others. Healthy, growth-fostering relationships create increased vitality, empowerment, self-knowledge, and self-worth, and a desire for more connection. Such relationships are mutual, empathic, creative, and empowering for all participants.

Mutuality means that each person in a relationship can reveal his or her feelings and perceptions and can be moved by the feelings and perceptions of the other. Each person and the relationship itself can change and move forward because there is mutual influence and responsiveness. *Empathy* is a highly developed ability to join with another at a cognitive and affective level without losing connection with one's own experience (Covington & Surrey, 1997, 2000). An empathic person feels authentic in the relationship and feels that he or she knows the other. Mutuality and empathy empower women, not with power *over* others but with power that is used *with* others. As a result, they feel more able to share power for constructive, creative ends.

Healthy connections are crucial for women; their psychological problems can be traced to disconnection or violations within relationships—in families, with personal acquaintances, or in society at large (Miller, 1986). When a woman is disconnected from others or involved in abusive relationships, she experiences disempowerment, confusion, and diminished vitality and self-worth—fertile ground for addiction.

When clinicians are trying to help women change, grow, and heal from addictions, it is critical that they place women in environments in which they can experience mutual, empathic, healthy relationships with their counselors and with one another.

Addiction and Relationships

From the perspective of the relational model, women often use drugs in order to make or keep connections. Finkelstein (1993) states that clinicians need to consider past and current family relationships, relationships with friends and partners, and relationships developed within the treatment context.

Researchers have identified five ways in which relationships with male partners can contribute to women's substance abuse and hinder their recovery. First, male partners often introduce women to alcohol or other drugs. Second, whether or not a male partner first encouraged a woman's drug use, he often is her supplier once she is addicted. Third, addicted women's lives are full of men who disappoint them, do not provide for their children, and go to jail. These women long for the men to provide emotional support (and financial support for any children). Their disappointment often leads to seeking solace in drug use. Fourth, many addicted women report physical abuse from men. Drugs help numb the pain of abusive relationships that also lack mutuality and empathy. Fifth, studies indicate that women receive less support from their partners for entering treatment than men receive from theirs (Amaro & Hardy-Fanta, 1995).

Women also may use drugs in order to fit into their relationships. For example, a sexually dysfunctional woman may use alcohol to become willing to engage in sex. In addition, nonmutual or abusive relationships produce what Miller (1990) calls a "depressive spiral": diminished vitality, inability to act, confusion, diminished self-worth, and abandonment of relationships. Women may then turn to substances to provide what their relationships are not providing, such as energy or a sense of power.

Addicted women often speak of their addictions as relationships—for example, "Alcohol was my true love," or "Food was my source of comfort." However, as the addiction progresses, a woman finds that this friend becomes lethal: "I turned to Valium, but Valium turned on me" (Covington & Surrey, 1997, 2000). Addiction is a relationship that constricts a woman's life. The task in helping a woman recover is to help her transfer her attachments from addictive "relationships" (with substances, people, or both) to sources of growth-fostering connections, such as her therapist, her mutual-help group, or members of her recovery group.

Theory of Trauma

A history of abuse drastically increases the likelihood that a woman will abuse alcohol and other drugs. In a comparison study of women who were addicts and women who were not (Covington & Kohen, 1984), 74 percent of the addicted women reported sexual abuse, 52 percent reported physical abuse, and 72 percent reported emotional abuse. In contrast, 50 percent of the women who were not addicts reported sexual abuse, 34 percent reported physical abuse, and 44 percent reported emotional abuse. "Moreover, the addicted women were found to have been abused sexually, physically, and emotionally by more perpetrators, more frequently and for longer periods of time than their non-addicted counterparts. The addicted women also reported more incidents of incest and rape" (Covington & Surrey, 1997, p. 342).

The connection between addiction and interpersonal violence is complex and multifaceted; for example, substance-abusing men are often violent toward women and children, substance-abusing women are particularly vulnerable targets for violence, and childhood and current abuse increase a woman's risk of substance abuse (Miller, 1991). There are also gender differences in terms of abuse. "While both male and female children are at risk for abuse, females continue to be at risk for interpersonal violence in their adolescence and adult lives. The risk for males to be abused in their teenage and adult relationships is far less than for females" (Covington & Surrey, 1997, p. 341).

Consequently, the treatment of substance-abusing women must take into account the likelihood that most clients will have suffered abuse (Covington, 1998a, 1998b). Moreover, trauma is not limited to suffering violence; it includes witnessing violence as well as stigmatization because of gender, race, poverty, incarceration, or sexual orientation. Trauma also increases the likelihood of interaction with the criminal justice system (Covington, 1998b). Thus, in treating the woman with an addiction, clinicians need to understand that they also are probably treating a trauma survivor. Many women who used to be considered "treatment failures" because they relapsed may now be understood as trauma survivors who returned to alcohol or other drugs in order to medicate the pain of trauma. Our increased understanding of trauma offers new treatment possibilities for substance-abusing trauma survivors (Barrett & Trepper, 1991). By integrating trauma treatment with addiction treatment, there is less risk of trauma-based relapse.

Traditional addiction treatment often does not deal with abuse issues in early recovery, even though they are primary triggers for relapse among women (Covington & Surrey, 1997, 2000). Although clinicians do not need to be experts in trauma recovery, it is important to have an understanding of trauma theory and a conceptual framework for clinical practice. In *Trauma and Recovery,* Judith Herman (1992) offers a framework that considers trauma a disease of disconnection and presents a three-stage model of trauma recovery: safety, remembrance and mourning, and reconnection. It is important to maintain support for addiction recovery throughout the three stages of trauma treatment.

Stage 1, *safety,* focuses on caring for oneself in the present. On entering addiction treatment, a woman typically is in Stage 1, and her primary need is safety. "Survivors feel unsafe in their bodies. They also feel unsafe in relation to other people" (Herman, 1992, p. 160). Clinicians can help women feel safe by ensuring as much as possible that the environment is free of physical and sexual harassment and by assessing each woman's risk of domestic violence. Clinicians also can help women feel safe *internally* by teaching them to use self-soothing techniques, rather than drugs, to alleviate depression and anxiety.

Herman emphasizes that a trauma survivor who is working on safety issues needs to be in a homogenous recovery group (including the facilitator). Until they are in Stage 3, women may not want to talk about physical or sexual abuse in groups that include men.

Herman cites twelve-step groups as the type appropriate for Stage 1 recovery because of their focus on present-tense issues of self-care in a supportive, structured environment. This stage focuses on issues that are congruent with the issues of beginning recovery.

Stage 2, *remembrance and mourning,* focuses on the trauma that occurred in the past. For example, in a survivors' group, participants tell their stories of trauma and mourn their old selves, which the trauma destroyed. Typically, a woman who is stabilized in her addiction treatment may be ready to begin Stage 2 trauma work. Although the risk of relapse can be high during this phase of work, this risk can be minimized through anticipation, planning, and the development of self-soothing mechanisms.

Stage 3, *reconnection,* focuses on developing a new self and creating a new future. Stage 3 groups are traditionally unstructured and heterogeneous (as in a psychodynamically focused psychotherapy group). This phase of trauma recovery corresponds to the ongoing recovery phase of addiction treatment. For some women, this work can only occur after several years of recovery.

◆ ◆ ◆

We have looked at three theoretical perspectives: theory of addiction, theory of women's psychological development, and theory of trauma. Women often have been expected to seek help for addiction, psychological disorders, and trauma from separate sources and to put together for themselves what they learned from a recovery group and from a clinician. This expectation that women do the integration for themselves places an unnecessary additional burden on recovering women (Brown, Huba, & Melchior, 1995). It is important that clinicians use a comprehensive, gender-responsive model that integrates all three theoretical models so as to remove that burden from women and increase their potential for recovery and healing.

Guiding Principles of Women's Treatment

In addition to a comprehensive theoretical framework for women's treatment, there are six key principles to consider in creating the therapeutic process and milieu. These core principles are based on the theories already presented (theory of addiction, theory of women's psychological development, and theory of trauma) and on clinical experience.

1. *Develop and use women's groups.* Research (Aries, 1976; Bernardez, 1978, 1983; Graham & Linehan, 1987) indicates that group dynamics differ between all-female

groups and mixed female-male groups. Fedele and Harrington (1990) conclude that single- and mixed-sex groups are appropriate for women at different stages of their lives at different stages of their recovery. Women-only groups are the modality of choice for women in the early stage of addiction recovery and for sexual abuse survivors. When a woman needs to share and integrate her experiences, ideas, and feelings and to create a sense of self (as in early recovery), a single-sex group is preferable. When the woman's experience has been validated, when she has more empathy for herself and is more empowered (as in later recovery), a mixed group may take her to the next stage of development. So although mixed groups may have their place in later recovery, it is important that treatment for early addiction recovery use all-female groups (with a female facilitator).

2. *Recognize the multiple issues involved, and establish a comprehensive, integrated, and collaborative system of care.* The Center for Substance Abuse Treatment (1994), a federal agency, identifies seventeen critical areas of focus for women's treatment. These issues underscore the complexity of women's treatment, the need for a comprehensive perspective, and the importance of theoretical integration and collaboration in clinical practice.

1. The causes of addiction, especially gender-specific issues related to addiction (for example, factors related to onset of addiction, and the social, physiological, and psychological consequences of addiction)
2. Low self-esteem
3. Race, ethnicity, and cultural issues
4. Gender discrimination and harassment
5. Disability-related issues
6. Relationships with family members and significant others
7. Attachments to unhealthy interpersonal relationships
8. Interpersonal violence, including incest, rape, battering, and other abuse
9. Eating disorders
10. Sexuality, including sexual functioning and sexual orientation
11. Parenting
12. Grief related to the loss of children, family members, partners, and alcohol and other drugs
13. Work
14. Appearance and overall health and hygiene
15. Isolation related to a lack of support systems (which may or may not include family members and partners) and other resources
16. Development of life plans
17. Child care and child custody

The list takes into account the physical, psychological, emotional, spiritual, and sociopolitical aspects of the holistic health model of addiction. It also reflects the need for a collaborative approach. These seventeen issues may also be grouped into four major areas: self, relationships, sexuality, and spirituality. Interviews with women in recovery indicate that these four areas represent both the major aspects of life that change during recovery and the most common triggers for relapse if not addressed (Covington, 1994).

3. *Create an environment that fosters safety, respect, and dignity.* The treatment setting has a profound impact on a woman's recovery. Both relational theory and trauma theory take this impact into account, emphasizing the context of treatment and providing guidelines for developing a therapeutic environment and culture. Women recover in an environment that facilitates healing—one that is characterized by the elements of safety, mutuality, and empowerment discussed in the section on relational theory. *Safety* means that there are appropriate boundaries between the client and the clinician (that is, the environment is free of physical, emotional, and sexual harassment). Although it may be possible for a clinician to guarantee absolute safety only in a private practice setting, participants in treatment programs need to know that the environment is likely to be safe for them.

In this context, *mutuality* means that exchanges between the treatment provider and the client are mutual rather than authoritarian. Women sense when a therapist wants to understand their experiences, is fully present with them when they recall painful experiences, allows their stories to affect her, and is not overwhelmed by their stories. The clinician respects each woman's uniqueness while affirming ways in which she and the woman are alike. As this kind of mutual, empathic, compassionate, and respectful connection is modeled in group settings, similar connections grow among participants.

Empowerment means that the clinician models how to use power *with* and *for* others rather than *over* them. She sets limits that are firm but respectful rather than blaming. She encourages women to believe in and exercise their abilities, and in group settings she enables them to practice and observe one another using power appropriately. Empowerment also encourages women to find their inner sources of power.

4. *Develop and use a variety of therapeutic approaches.* To fully address the needs of addicted women, it is important to work on multiple levels, using behavioral, cognitive, affective-dynamic, and systems perspectives. At this time, cognitive-behavioral therapy is often touted as the best treatment approach, although research does not support the assumption of cognitive-behavioral programming models as the sole basis of treatment for females. Attention to affect and, often, to early childhood experiences of trauma is frequently missing in women's treatment.

Cognitive-behavioral theory assumes that affect (the feeling function) can be addressed through cognitive process (thinking). This therapeutic approach is too narrowly focused for women at any stage, but especially at the points of active addiction and of movement into abstinence and early recovery. Women's treatment needs to be based on the premise of the whole person, incorporating the holistic model of addiction and emphasizing affective, cognitive, and behavioral change. The affective aspect is especially important for females because their substance-abusing behavior needs to be understood in the context of their emotional lives.

Miller and Stiver (1997, p. 212) offer the following analysis of the current emphasis on cognitive functioning: "This separation of thought and feeling seems clearly linked to a long-standing gender division in Western culture. Thinking has been linked with men and is the valued capacity; feeling has been linked with women and is disparaged. In contrast, we believe that all thoughts are accompanied by emotions and all emotions have thought content. Attempting to focus on one to the neglect of the other diminishes people's ability to understand and act on their experiences."

For many women, the absence of feeling or reduced feeling is common in early recovery (Brown, 1985). For others, it is just the opposite; the beginning of abstinence may open up a flood of painful affect and memory. Either way—no feeling, or overwhelming emotion—women need to learn how to express their feelings appropriately and to contain them in healthy ways. Females frequently become dependent on drugs in order to seek relief from painful emotions. In recovery they must come to terms with the feelings and the drive to cope with them in self-destructive ways. Recovery involves a shift from acting out destructive behaviors in order to displace feeling or rid oneself of feeling, to accepting and integrating feeling, a process that involves learning to calm oneself through self-soothing techniques and sharing with others.

Women may experience this opening-up process as a bind. Because females are often raised to suppress their feelings and to be compliant, a treatment program that is unable or unwilling to work with women's emotions can feel like the abusive environment in which they learned to keep silent and turn to alcohol or other drugs and addictive behaviors. Such silence encourages them to avoid dealing with issues that can lead to relapse (Pepi, 1998). As feelings emerge in early recovery, women may feel confused unless they have a context that encourages awareness and expression of feeling in contained and healthy ways.

5. *Focus on women's competence and strength.* In a traditional treatment model, the therapist typically approaches assessment with a problem focus: What is missing in the client? or What is wrong with the client? Many women already are struggling with a poor sense of self because of the stigma attached to their addictions, their parenting histories, their trauma, or their prison records, for example.

It is difficult and often antitherapeutic to add another problem to the woman's list of perceived failures.

A strength-based (asset) model of treatment shifts the focus from targeting problems to identifying the multiple issues a woman must contend with and the strategies she has adopted to cope. This has been referred to as assessing a woman's "level of burden" (Brown et al., 1995). The focus is on support, rather than on confrontation to break the woman's defenses (Fedele & Miller, 1988).

In using an asset model, the therapist helps the client see the strengths and skills she already has that will aid her healing. The clinician looks for the seeds of health and strength, even in the woman's symptoms. For example, the clinician portrays a woman's relational difficulties as efforts to connect, rather than as failures to separate or disconnect. The counselor repeatedly affirms the woman's abilities to care, empathize, use her intuition, and build relationships. "As a woman feels more valued, her need for alcohol, tobacco, and other drugs might diminish and her resilience increase" (Finkelstein et al., 1997, p. 6).

6. *Individualize treatment plans, and match treatment to identified strengths and issues.* Just as women's lives are different from men's, all women's lives are not the same. Although there are common threads because of gender, it is important to be sensitive to differences and to acknowledge both similarities and differences. For example, there are differences in the lives of African American women, Hispanic women, and Asian women. There are differences among heterosexual women, bisexual women, and lesbian women. There are differences among older women and younger women. There are differences resulting from privilege and oppression.

It has become evident that treatment needs to be individualized in order to be effective. The Project on Women, Addiction, and Recovery (POWAR) chart, shown in Figure 3.2, is an assessment tool that was developed in one of the author's research projects on women and addiction (Covington, 1990). It illustrates one way to individualize treatment for women by integrating women's treatment issues with a developmental model of recovery. On the left side of the chart are some of the major issues that can affect women's recovery. These are some of the major areas of focus in treatment. Across the top of the chart, a timeline represents the stages in a developmental model of recovery. For each individual woman, there are issues in the foreground of her life and issues in the background at any particular time. Depending on where she is in recovery, an issue may shift from background to foreground and vice versa. In each recovery stage, the issues that are in the foreground need to be addressed most directly at that time.

As a woman moves out of the limitations and constrictions of addiction toward discovery and growth (see Figure 3.1), she may find that certain themes recur. As she deals with them, she confronts them at increasingly higher levels of self-awareness and strength. When women speak of recovery, they speak of a fundamental

FIGURE 3.2. MODEL FOR INDIVIDUALIZED TREATMENT.

	Stages			
	Active Addiction	Transition	Early Recovery	Ongoing Recovery
Aspects of Addiction				
• Physical				
• Behavioral				
• Cognitive				
• Affective				
• Other addictions				
Self				
• Sense of self (self-image)				
• Self-care				
• Race, ethnicity, cultural issues				
• Disability-related issues				
Relationships				
• Attachment issues				
• Interpersonal violence				
• Parenting, child care, custody				
• Support system				
Sexuality				
• Sexual dysfunctions				
• Body image				
• Sexual identity				
• Sexual abuse				
Spirituality				
• Creating connection				
• Grief work				
• Prayer, meditation				
• Vision (development of life plan)				

Source: Unpublished research by Stephanie S. Covington, 1990. Reprinted with permission.

transformation: "I'm not the same person." It is important to see recovery as a lifelong process of increasing consciousness and growth, accompanied by shifts in focus and issues. This is true for recovery from both addiction and trauma.

A Model Treatment Program for Women

Helping Women Recover (Covington, 1999) is a program curriculum for creating gender-responsive addiction treatment based on the theories and principles outlined in this chapter. The Facilitator's Guide for the program is a step-by-step manual containing the theory, structure, and content needed for running groups. A Woman's Journal, the participant's workbook, allows women to process and record the therapeutic experience. The materials can be used in a variety of settings, and the exercises can be adapted for work with individuals. The program is organized into four modules: self, relationships, sexuality, and spirituality. These reflect the four areas that women say are the triggers for relapse and the areas of greatest change in recovery (Covington, 1994). The modules incorporate the seventeen issues outlined by the Center for Substance Abuse Treatment (listed earlier). The following paragraphs briefly describe the specific topics covered within each module:

1. *Self module.* Women discover what the "self" is; learn that addiction can be understood as a disorder of the self; learn the sources of self-esteem; consider the effects of sexism, racism, and stigma on a sense of self; and learn that recovery includes the expansion and growth of the self. They begin to develop their own sense of themselves. This module enables them to integrate their outer self (their roles) with their inner self (their feelings, thoughts, and attitudes).

2. *Relationship module.* Women explore their roles in their families of origin (Covington & Beckett, 1988); discuss myths about motherhood and their relationships with their mothers; review their relationship histories, including any interpersonal violence; and consider how they can build healthy support systems. To assist the participants' growth, the counselors in group settings model healthy relationships among themselves and with the participants.

3. *Sexuality module.* Women explore the connections between addiction and sexuality: body image, sexual identity, sexual abuse, and the fear of sex when clean and sober. Sexuality often is neglected in addiction treatment, although it is a major cause of relapse (Covington, 1997, 2000). Healthy sexuality is essential to a woman's sense of self-worth. Women may enter recovery with arrested sexual development, because substance abuse often interrupts the process of healthy sexual development. Many also struggle with sexual dysfunction, shame, fear, and trauma that must be addressed so that they do not return to addiction to manage the pain of these difficulties.

4. *Spirituality module.* Women are introduced to the concepts of spirituality, prayer, and meditation. Spirituality deals with transformation, connection, meaning, and wholeness—important elements in recovery. Connecting to her own definition of spirituality is essential to a woman's recovery, so each woman is given an opportunity to experience aspects of spirituality and to create a vision for her future in recovery.

Mutual-Help Groups for Women

For centuries women have sought to teach and support themselves and each other by meeting in groups and sharing information and experiences. In traditional and modern societies alike, women continue to meet to wash clothes and sew quilts together, share stories around a coffee pot, meet for lunch during a busy workday, play cards and watch children. These activities have always and will always involve offers of solace and support that come in casual conversation with dependable and cherished women friends.

Today, women who meet in mutual-help groups do so for many of the same reasons that their forbears gathered together. Few developments of recent years have become so widespread as the use of mutual-help groups to aid people in recovering from alcohol and other drug addiction. The phenomenon is most obviously measured by the growth in the sheer numbers of such groups. These include AA, Al-Anon, and Narcotics Anonymous, which are the predominant examples of mutual-help groups concerned with addiction. Moreover, the so-called twelve-step model, which originated in AA, is now used by over 126 "anonymous" groups to deal with a host of other problems (Alcoholics Anonymous, 1993). People use them to cope with a spectrum of substances, behaviors, and processes. Overeating, gambling, workaholism, sexual and incest issues, and other relationship topics are now addressed in mutual-help groups modeled after AA. Quite clearly these are people with problems to which complete solutions have not been found in traditional approaches offered by established helping professionals (Fiorentine, 1999).

A major advantage of mutual-help groups for women is that they are free and, in most urban communities, readily available throughout most parts of the day. It is in this respect that they are most unlike conventional problem-solving techniques, whereby help is provided only on occasion, almost exclusively as a response to a specific request from a particular individual.

In recent years, twelve-step programs have been critiqued in various ways and, as some feminists have pointed out, the language used is simplistic, sexist, and reductionist (Berenson, 1991; Rapping, 1996). Feminists are particularly concerned about the twelve steps' emphasis on powerlessness as liberating. In contrasting the recovery movement with the women's movement, Marianne Walters (1990) points out that "one movement encourages individuals to surrender to a spiritual higher power, where the other encourages people to join together to challenge and restructure power arrangements in the larger society" (p. 55). What is often missed in feminist analysis is that masculine power *over* is what is being relinquished in order to experience the feminine power *with*, power *to be able*—in other words, a sense of empowerment (Miller, 1982). "The process of recovery from addiction is a process of recovering a different, more feminine, sense of power and will" (Berenson, 1991, p. 74). There is also a confusion between surrender and submission. "When we submit, we give in to a force that's trying to control us. When we surrender, we let go of our need to control" (Covington, 1994, p. 48). Recovery encourages surrender and giving up the illusion of control. Feminist writer Marilyn French (1985) states that "life is the highest value for 'feminine' people; whereas control is the highest value for 'masculine' people" (p. 93).

If we look at the underpinnings of Alcoholics Anonymous, we can see that it was actually very radical for the 1930s, when it was founded, and that this continues to be true even today. Twelve-step programs are free, a radical concept in a capitalistic society; they are nonhierarchical, a radical idea in a patriarchal society; and they are spiritual, a radical stance in a nonspiritual society. As previously stated, women grow and develop in relationship, and twelve-step programs can provide a growth-fostering relational context and can offer their members social support through the creation of a caring community (Covington, 1991; Covington & Surrey, 1997, 2000). These programs can also create a safe environment, an essential element for recovery from trauma (Herman, 1992). Although some critics have focused on the sexist language in which the twelve steps are couched, many women are able to interpret the steps in ways that are distinctly personal, meaningful, and useful to them (Covington, 1994).

Conclusion

The reasons that the majority of addiction treatment is still based on the male experience are complex. Some of the reasons are related to stereotypical views of women and men. Others relate to a lack of acknowledgment of gender differences as well as gender-based needs. It is important to understand and acknowledge some of the dynamics inherent in a gendered society; for example, when something is declared gender-neutral or genderless, it is essentially male (Kaschak, 1992). In addition, researchers, theorists, and policymakers are still predominantly men, as are the majority of those who direct addiction treatment programs. In most cases, this means they view and experience the world through a different lens that often excludes women's reality. Therefore, the primary barriers to providing gender-responsive treatment are multilayered: they are theoretical, administrative, and structural, and involve policy and funding decisions.

This chapter has presented an integrated theoretical philosophy with guiding principles, which focuses on both the content and the context of women's treatment in hopes of being a resource to those who seek to eliminate these barriers.

Just as it is essential to look at each woman's addiction from a multidimensional perspective and acknowledge the interconnectedness of her life issues, it is essential that the systemic barriers to gender-responsive services for women be seen from a multidimensional and interconnected perspective.

References

Abbott, B., & Kerr, D. (1995). *Substance abuse program for federally sentenced women*. Ottawa, Ontario: Correctional Services of Canada.

Alcoholics Anonymous. (1976). *Alcoholics Anonymous*. New York: Alcoholics Anonymous World Services.

Alcoholics Anonymous. (1993). *Analysis of the 1991 membership survey*. New York: Alcoholics Anonymous World Services.

Amaro, H., & Hardy-Fanta, C. (1995). Gender relations in addiction and recovery. *Journal of Psychoactive Drugs, 27*, 325–337.

Aries, E. (1976). Interaction patterns and themes of males, females, and mixed groups. *Small Group Behavior, 7*(1), 7–18.

Barrett, M., & Trepper, T. (1991). Treating women drug abusers who were victims of childhood sexual abuse. In C. Bepko (Ed.), *Feminism and addiction* (pp. 127–146). Binghamton, NY: Haworth Press.

Berenson, D. (1991). Powerlessness—liberation or enslaving? Responding to the feminist critique of the twelve steps. In C. Bepko (Ed.), *Feminism and addiction* (pp. 67–80). Binghamton, NY: Haworth Press.

Bernardez, T. (1978). Women's groups: A feminist perspective on the treatment of women. In H. H. Grayson & C. Loew (Eds.), *Changing approaches to the psychotherapies*. New York: Spectrum.

Bernardez, T. (1983). Women's groups. In M. Rosenbaum (Ed.), *Handbook of short-term therapy groups*. New York: McGraw-Hill.

Brown, S. (1985). *Treating the alcoholic: A developmental model*. New York: Wiley.

Brown, V., Huba, G., & Melchior, L. (1995). Level of burden: Women with more than one co-occurring disorder. *Journal of Psychoactive Drugs, 27*, 339–345.

Carten, A. F. (1996). Mothers in recovery: Rebuilding families in the aftermath of addiction. *Social Work, 41*, 214–223.

Center for Substance Abuse Treatment. (1994). *Practical approaches in the treatment of women who abuse alcohol and other drugs*. Rockville, MD: Department of Health and Human Services.

Covington, S. (1990). *Project on women, addiction, and recovery*. Unpublished research.

Covington, S. (1991). Sororities of helping and healing: Women and mutual help groups. In P. Roth (Ed.), *Alcohol and drugs are women's issues* (pp. 85–92). Metuchen, NJ: Scarecrow Press.

Covington, S. (1994). *A woman's way through the twelve steps*. Center City, MN: Hazelden.

Covington, S. (1997). Women, addiction, and sexuality. In S.L.A. Straussner & E. Zelvin (Eds.), *Gender issues in addiction: Men and women in treatment* (pp. 73–95). Northvale, NJ: Aronson.

Covington, S. (1998a). The relational theory of women's psychological development: Implications for the criminal justice system. In R. Zaplin (Ed.), *Female offenders: Critical perspectives and effective interventions* (pp. 113–131). Gaithersburg, MD: Aspen.

Covington, S. (1998b). Women in prison: Approaches in the treatment of our most invisible population. *Women in Therapy, 21*(1), 141–155.

Covington, S. (1999). *Helping women recover: A program for treating addiction* (with a special edition for the criminal justice system). San Francisco: Jossey-Bass.

Covington, S. (2000). *Awakening your sexuality: A guide for recovering women.* Center City, MN: Hazelden.

Covington, S. (2001, February). Creating gender-responsive programs: The next step for women's services. *Corrections Today, 63,* 85–87.

Covington, S., & Beckett, L. (1988). *Leaving the enchanted forest: The path from relationship addiction to intimacy.* San Francisco: Harper San Francisco.

Covington, S., & Kohen, J. (1984). Women, alcohol and sexuality. *Advances in Alcohol and Substance Abuse, 4*(1), 41–56.

Covington, S., & Surrey, J. (1997). The relational model of women's psychological development: Implications for substance abuse. In S. Wilsnack & R. Wilsnack (Eds.), *Gender and alcohol: Individual and social perspectives* (pp. 335–351). New Brunswick, NJ: Rutgers University Press.

Covington, S., & Surrey, J. (2000). *The relational model of women's psychological development: Implications for substance abuse.* (Work in Progress No. 91). Wellesley, MA: Stone Center.

Fedele, N., & Harrington, E. (1990). *Women's groups: How connections heal.* (Work in Progress No. 47). Wellesley, MA: Stone Center.

Fedele, N., & Miller, J. (1988). *Putting theory into practice: Creating mental health programs for women.* (Work in Progress No. 32). Wellesley, MA: Stone Center.

Finkelstein, N. (1993, July). The relational model. In D. Kronstadt, P. F. Green, & C. Marcus (Eds.), *Pregnancy and exposure to alcohol and other drug use* (pp. 126–163). Washington, DC: Center for Substance Abuse Prevention.

Finkelstein, N., Kennedy, C., Thomas, K., & Kearns, M. (1997, March). *Gender-specific substance abuse treatment* [Draft]. Washington, DC: Center for Substance Abuse Prevention.

Fiorentine, R. (1999). After drug treatment: Are 12-step programs effective in maintaining abstinence? *American Journal of Drug and Alcohol Abuse, 25*(1), 93–116.

French, M. (1985). *Beyond power: On women, men, and morals.* New York: Ballantine.

Graham, B., & Linehan, N. (1987). Group treatment for the homeless and chronic alcoholic woman. In C. Brody (Ed.), *Women's therapy groups: Paradigms of feminist treatment* (pp. 177–197). New York: Springer.

Herman, J. (1992). *Trauma and recovery.* New York: HarperCollins.

Kaschak, E. (1992). *Engendered lives: A new psychology of women's experience.* New York: Basic Books.

Miller, D. (1991). Are we keeping up with Oprah: A treatment and training model for addictions and interpersonal violence. In C. Bepko (Ed.), *Feminism and addiction* (pp. 103–126). Binghamton, NY: Haworth Press.

Miller, J. B. (1976). *Toward a new psychology of women.* Boston: Beacon Press.

Miller, J. B. (1982). *Women and power.* (Work in Progress No. 82-01). Wellesley, MA: Stone Center.

Miller, J. B. (1986). *What do we mean by relationships?* (Work in Progress No. 22). Wellesley, MA: Stone Center.

Miller, J. B. (1990). *Connections, disconnections, and violations.* (Work in Progress No. 33). Wellesley, MA: Stone Center.

Miller, J. B., & Stiver, I. P. (1997). *The healing connection: How women form relationships in therapy and in life.* Boston: Beacon Press.

Northrup, C. (1994). *Women's bodies, women's wisdom.* New York: Bantam Books.

Parks, G. (1997). *What works in relapse prevention?* Paper presented at Fifth Annual Research Conference of the International Community Corrections Association, Cleveland, OH.

Pepi, C. (1998). Children without childhoods: A feminist intervention strategy utilizing systems theory and restorative justice in treating female adolescent offenders. In J. Harden & M. Hill (Eds.), *Breaking the rules: Women in prison and feminist therapy* (pp. 85–101). Binghamton, NY: Haworth Press.

Rapping, E. (1996). *The culture of recovery.* Boston: Beacon Press.

Walters, M. (1990, July-August). The co-dependent Cinderella who loves too much . . . fights back. *Family Therapy Networker,* pp. 53–57.

PART TWO

MAJOR ADDICTIONS AMONG WOMEN

CHAPTER FOUR

DRUG- AND ALCOHOL-ABUSING WOMEN

Lynn E. O'Connor, Milena Esherick, and Cassandra Vieten

Substance abuse is one of the most common psychiatric problems affecting women. There are millions of adult women in the United States addicted to mind-altering substances, including legal and prescription drugs such as alcohol, Valium, and other sedating benzodiazepines and opiate-type pain relievers; and illegal substances such as marijuana, heroin, cocaine, amphetamines, PCP, and the contemporary "rave drugs" such as ecstasy. According to the National Comorbidity Survey (Kandel, 1998), 6 percent of women ages fifteen to fifty-four meet the lifetime criteria for illicit drug dependence. Among pregnant women, sixty-two thousand (2.3 percent) used an illicit drug during the last month, 584,000 used alcohol (20 percent), and 591,000 (21.5 percent) used cigarettes. Millions of women are addicted to nicotine. "Thirty-one percent of women who have ever smoked meet the criteria for dependence" (Kandel, 1998, p. 25).

The impact of drug addiction is enormous. Under the influence of drugs, women lose their spouses, their jobs, their children, and their lives. Women are being incarcerated at increasing rates for drug-related offenses (Snell & Morton, 1991); alcohol and drugs are implicated in the crimes of 80 percent of incarcerated women (National Center on Addiction and Substance Abuse at Columbia University, 1998). In addition, the rate of women's driving under the influence of alcohol is increasing (Lex, Goldberg, Mendelson, Lawler, & Bower, 1994), and there are more drug-related cases of child abuse and neglect (Bays, 1990).

Addiction to alcohol and other drugs (AOD) affects a broad spectrum of women from all socioeconomic and cultural backgrounds. The results of several national surveys demonstrate that across class and ethnicity, women outside traditional social roles, such as marriage or employment, have significantly higher rates of female drinking (Wilsnack & Cheloha, 1987). Surveys of ethnic differences in drinking reveal that among three major ethnic groups, White women are most likely to drink, African American women are least likely, and Hispanic women are in between (Caetano, 1991; Herd, 1998). In this chapter, we discuss factors that lead women to drug addiction, and we describe the immediate and long-term effects of various substances. This chapter also presents issues related to the assessment and treatment of women addicted to AOD.

Etiology of Addiction

Many women experiment with alcohol and drugs during their high school and college years, although some, particularly those women who grew up with AOD-addicted parents or siblings, begin sooner. A period of experimentation is considered normal, and there is some indication that adolescents who abstain from all substances are more likely to suffer from emotional problems (Shedler & Block, 1990). Most adolescent girls limit their experimentation with drugs to occasional recreational events. However, for a variety of reasons, some young women are particularly vulnerable to the effects of AOD, to escalating substance use, and to addiction. Some women who are able to limit their adolescent drug experimentation may develop serious drug problems at middle or older ages, frequently in response to marital or family difficulties, illness, or other stressful life events. Often this later-onset drug abuse involves prescription drugs, legally obtained through physicians or psychiatrists. Iatrogenic addiction—that is, addiction caused by medical practice—is an enormous problem for women (Hughs, 1976). However, the full extent of iatrogenic addiction is well hidden, and reliable statistics are not available. Women suffering from prescription drug addiction are often at risk for alcohol abuse. For example, a woman who has become addicted to benzodiazepines may need to increase her dosage in order to avoid withdrawal symptoms. Unable to obtain more of her legal prescription, she may resort to alcohol as a substitute. As is true of adolescents, middle-aged or elderly women vary in their vulnerability to addiction.

Biological and Genetic Factors

Vulnerability to addiction begins with a woman's biology. Biological differences among women affect their response to drugs; women may differ in drug metabolism, how pleasant they find the drugged state to be, and how quickly they get addicted. For example, when prescribed an addictive medication (for example, Valium, Xanax, Ativan, Klonipin, Vicodin, or Percodan), a woman with a family history of substance abuse is likely, as a result of a genetic vulnerability, to rapidly develop tissue tolerance (the need to take more of the medication to achieve the same effect) and addiction. In contrast, a woman with no family history of substance abuse may be able to take an addictive drug for several months before becoming addicted. Thus, biological factors may be the primary cause of some women's addiction.

A discussion of the genetics of addiction necessarily focuses on the drug alcohol, as most of the research to date has been on alcohol dependence. Since the time of ancient Greece, the observation that alcoholism tends to run in families led observers to suspect that it was inherited. Family studies have confirmed this observation by noting that first-degree relatives of alcoholics are three to five times more likely to develop alcoholism than the general population (Schuckit, 1999). However, this fact alone does not prove that genetics play a role, as families share environment as well as genes. One way to address the question of nature versus nurture in the development of addiction has been through twin and adoption studies. Identical twins adopted apart at birth provide the best situation for studying the relative contributions of genetics and environment, because they share all of their genes and none of their environment. This situation is rare, however, so twin studies often use the behavioral genetic method of comparing identical twins and fraternal twins. Identical twins share all of their DNA, whereas fraternal twins share an average of 50 percent of their genes. If a trait is genetically influenced, identical twins should share it more often than fraternal twins. This is the case in alcoholism: identical twins are more likely to share drinking patterns than fraternal twins. Adoption studies allow researchers to look at individuals born to alcoholic parents but adopted into nonalcoholic households. Children of alcoholics have a higher risk for alcoholism, even when adopted into a nonalcoholic family (Goodwin, Schulsinger, Hermansen, Guve, & Winokur, 1973; Goodwin et al., 1974; Hesselbrock, 1995; Cadoret, O'Gorman, Troughton, & Heywood, 1985).

The extent to which genetics influence women's vulnerability to alcoholism has been questioned. As is the case in other areas of medical research, women are underrepresented in studies on the genetics of addiction, but this is gradually being rectified. Reviews of the literature have suggested that across twin and adoption studies, support for the genetic influence on alcoholism is strong in men and variable in women (George, 1997; McGue, 1993). In early family studies of alcoholism, Cotton (1979) reported that 20 to 25 percent of sons and brothers of alcoholics become alcoholics, but only 5 percent of daughters and sisters. However, there are not sufficient data to rule out equal influence of genetics in women's vulnerability to addiction (Hill & Smith, 1991). In fact, Hill (1993, 1995) reported that rates of alcoholism in relatives of female alcoholics were higher than for those of male alcoholics.

Analyzing Swedish adoption study data, Cloninger, Bohman, and Sigvardsson (1981) contributed to the view that alcoholism in women is less influenced by genetics. These researchers classified alcoholics as one of two types. Type II alcoholism was termed *male-limited* or familial alcoholism, and was characterized by a higher severity, earlier age of onset, and comorbid antisocial personality traits. Type I alcoholism affected both men and women, had a weaker familial component, and was characterized by a later onset and comorbid depressive and anxious traits. More recent research has proposed that these subgroups exist among women: an early-onset, high-severity group and a later-onset, lower-severity group, with the former exhibiting a higher influence of genetics (Hill, 1993).

The lower rate of alcoholism in women, as well as difficulties with the definition of the disorder, may have confounded earlier studies. Recent studies have provided evidence that similarly for men and women, genetics seem to account for about half of the vulnerability to addiction, and environment the other half (Kendler, Heath, Neale, Kessler, & Eaves, 1992; Pickens et al., 1991).

The vast majority of studies on the genetics of addiction have focused on alcoholism, but a few recent studies have examined other drugs of abuse. Kendler and Prescott (1998) studied cocaine and marijuana use in 1,934 pairs of female twins. They concluded that family and environmental factors were more influential in determining whether a woman began using drugs, but genes were largely responsible for whether she progressed to abuse or dependence. They estimate that genetic factors account for 60 to 80 percent of the difference in abuse of and dependence on marijuana and cocaine between fraternal and identical twin pairs, suggesting that abuse and dependence are in large part heritable. Similarly, when examining the genetic and environmental factors influencing women's use and abuse of hallucinogens, opiates, sedatives, and stimulants, Kendler, Karkowski, and Prescott (1999) found that genetic factors alone accounted for twin resemblances in the use of opiates, sedatives, and the abuse of stimulants, while both genetic and familial factors contribute to twin resemblances in the use of hallucinogens and the nonabusive use of stimulants. As for the drug nicotine, a recent National Institute on Drug Abuse report (Zickler, 2000) suggests that for women, the genetic contribution is significantly greater than for men.

The fact that both genetics and environment contribute to the development of addiction in women has significant clinical implications. Women most often come into treatment blaming themselves for everything, including their addiction (Inaba, Cohen, & Holstein, 1997; O'Connor, Berry, Inaba, Weiss, & Morrison, 1994; Straussner, 1997). These clients find education about the genetic component of addiction reassuring: it helps explain both the power addiction has over their lives and their continued use of drugs despite grave consequences. Similarly, psychoeducation about the role of genetics in addictions and other mental disorders can help women come to terms with dysfunction in their families. Knowing that there is a biological basis to addictive patterns in their families helps women understand some of the underlying reasons for abusive or neglectful behavior from their family members, and it mediates the feeling that they did something wrong to deserve the abuse or neglect they experienced.

In the future, genetics and neuroscience may play a more direct role in treating drug addiction in women. By identifying the particular biological abnormalities that underlie craving, tolerance, and withdrawal, there may be problem-specific medical or psychosocial treatments that ease the process of withdrawal and recovery. It is possible that these medical interventions will be particularly useful for that portion of the population with whom our best efforts fail: women who have tried many avenues to recovery yet continue to have difficulty maintaining a drug-free state.

In addition, genetic testing may someday be available to estimate addiction risk. Although testing carries with it a host of ethical problems, it may be useful in assessing the risk for vulnerability, and contribute to prevention efforts.

Sociocultural Factors

In addition to having a possible biological vulnerability, some women may also have sociocultural predisposing factors. Young women who are unable to pursue age-appropriate developmental goals and ambitions (such as successful work) because of poverty, racism, sexism, or other factors that limit opportunities may find the drugged state attractive. Limited by social and economic conditions, they may find hanging out with their peers, taking drugs, and socializing their only pleasurable structured and social option. At an age when more fortunate young women are studying for careers and carefully planning for future families, women who grow up in settings with limited horizons may use drugs as a kind of occupation. Some women may turn to illegal activities to support themselves, including drug dealing and prostitution, which in turn may lead to drug addiction. A lack of voice or power in the society can lead disenfranchised women to seek out men with social power in their neighborhood, often drug dealers and pimps. Single mothers living in dangerous areas may connect with drug-using circles in order to protect themselves and their children. In addition, drug use allows a woman to change her own physical and mental state, temporarily affording her a feeling of power to control her situation.

Drug preference, sometimes referred to as the *drug-of-choice phenomenon,* is also influenced by sociocultural factors (Inaba et al., 1997; O'Connor & Berry, 1990; O'Connor, Berry, Morrison, & Brown, 1995). Different drugs are popular in different sectors of society at different times. For example, cocaine was popular with middle-class White women in the late nineteenth and early twentieth centuries until it fell out of favor when it became illegal in 1914. Women in the 1950s who were trying to lose weight commonly became addicted to legally prescribed stimulants, and women who were trying to control anxiety often became addicted to sedative tranquilizers. Young women in the 1960s, trying to fit into a "hippie" social group and alternative lifestyle, commonly abused marijuana and psychedelics. In the individualistic 1970s and 1980s, women were more likely to abuse cocaine and alcohol. Recently cocaine, in the less expensive smokable form known as crack, has become a significant drug problem for disadvantaged African American women. Heroin use, while frowned upon by middle-class users in the 1980s, has gained in popularity in recent years and is increasingly seen in adolescents and upwardly mobile young women. Currently, middle-aged and older women are often afflicted with an iatrogenic opiate addiction, the result of physician-prescribed pain medication. Alcohol, the legal drug of our culture, remains the drug of choice for many women, although it too goes through periods in which it is more or less fashionable.

Although drug preference may vary according to the historical period and a woman's particular social group, the majority of women who are addicted suffer from feelings of shame and guilt as a result of the strong cultural bias against inebriated and drug-addicted women. Addicted women are regarded as failures as partners, mothers, and workers even when the addiction is iatrogenic or part of the culture (Gomberg, 1988; Straussner, 1997). However, societal responses to addiction in women tend to differ according to the woman's social class and drug preference. Poor women who suffer from addiction are often threatened with the loss of their children. In contrast, pregnant middle-class women addicted to cocaine or marijuana are often counseled with no threats of losing custody of their children (Marwick, 1998). In some states, disadvantaged pregnant women addicted to opiates are forced to take methadone or are threatened with the loss of their children. Calls for criminalization of addiction in pregnant women reflect a continuing societal bias against drug-addicted women. Despite advances in addiction medicine, many still perceive drug addiction as a manifestation of poor moral standards and a lack of will power.

Psychological Factors

A woman's psychological vulnerability is another factor critical to the development of addiction. Women who for psychological reasons are unable to pursue age-appropriate ambitions may find the effects and experience of daily drug use attractive, and may quickly develop the disease of addiction. Psychological vulnerability often stems from maladaptive beliefs that a woman develops in childhood, in relation to her parents, siblings, other caretakers, or members of her social group. Beliefs that lead to the inhibition of ambitions (such as the desire to have rewarding work, to have intimate relationships, to be successful and happy, to be a good mother) are sometimes called pathogenic beliefs, because they directly lead to psychological problems and psychopathology (O'Connor & Weiss, 1993; Weiss, Sampson, & the Mount Zion Psychotherapy Research Group, 1986; Weiss, 1993). According to Weiss's theory (often referred to as Control Mastery theory), many psychological problems are associated with pathogenic beliefs derived from aversive childhood experiences. These beliefs may warn a woman that if she pursues age-appropriate developmental goals, she will hurt someone she loves. For example, a woman who grows up with a depressed mother may believe it is her responsibility to ease her mother's pain—a task often doomed to failure. She grows up with the belief that she has harmed her mother, because she couldn't make her mother happy. She believes that to be happy and successful herself would be unfair to her mother. She may think, "I couldn't make my mother happy, so what right do I have to be happy?" As a result, she may be unable to develop a successful work or family life. Similarly, a child who grows up with a physically or cognitively disabled sibling may suffer from "survivor guilt" and believe that she doesn't have the right to be better off than her sister or brother. Thus she may hold herself back from success because she believes her success would make her sibling feel inadequate by comparison. Survivor guilt—that is, guilt derived from the belief that one is harming others by surpassing them, being better off, being successful or happy—is a normal psychological mechanism that, when exaggerated, is often connected to psychological problems, including addiction (Bush, 1989; Meehan et al., 1996; O'Connor & Weiss, 1993).

Women who grow up in drug-addicted families may develop the belief that to be loyal to their addicted mother, father, or sibling, they too must use drugs. Thus women from drug-using or otherwise dysfunctional families may begin using drugs out of an identification with and loyalty to their loved ones. They may believe that in order to avoid harming family members, they must inhibit their ambitions. They then become vulnerable to psychopathology, including depression and addiction.

In some cases, when a woman suffers from psychological problems derived from pathogenic beliefs or from a biologically based dysfunction such as bipolar illness or obsessive-compulsive disorder, she seeks and uses drugs regularly in an effort to overcome symptoms, such as guilt, shame, anxiety, depression, or an exaggerated sense of responsibility. In fact, most pathogenic beliefs, including the beliefs associated with addiction, lead to guilt, shame, anxiety, and depression. Despite the varying nature and effects of different drugs of abuse, most drugs function initially to reduce guilt and shame and other negative affects. Over time, however, drugs that initially serve to alleviate these symptoms stop working and instead cause the symptoms to escalate.

Effects and Ramifications of Commonly Abused Drugs

This section discusses the use of and withdrawal from specific drugs of abuse. Addictive drug use over time mimics a variety of psychiatric disorders, and it is important to recognize that many symptoms may not be premorbid and should be reassessed after acute and protracted withdrawal has subsided (O'Connor et al., 1992, 1995). In the initial phases of treatment, the drug-addicted woman often creates a confusing clinical picture. It may take many months of abstinence from drugs before the clinician is able to determine how many of the patient's problems are neurochemical, temporary drug effects derived from use and how many are truly "psychological" in nature. The experience of drug abuse and addiction itself leads to massive social and psychological disruption (Bean, 1981). Many women who have been addicted have experienced painful and depressing losses in addition to the emotional, physical, and sexual trauma connected to their addiction. Many women have participated in the destruction of their physical and mental health, their relationships and families, and their jobs and means of livelihood. Women suffering from addiction are not gratified by their condition, and no addicted woman wants to be addicted.

All drug abuse will eventually cause both biologically and psychologically based guilt, shame, anxiety, and depression (O'Connor et al., 1992; O'Connor et al., 1994; Meehan et al., 1996). Women in the grip of drug addiction commonly present with these unpleasant feelings and may not know that the feelings are directly caused by the pharmacological and neurochemical effects of drug use and withdrawal. When first seeking help, addicted women may deny or minimize the extent of their drug use, and on the face of it they may appear to want to continue using. However, this denial is usually a manifestation of hopelessness (O'Connor & Weiss, 1993) and is, in essence, a defense against it. Women addicted to drugs most often try to stop using and fail. They interpret their failure as a sign of psychological weakness or moral deficiency rather than as the result of the disease of addiction. As a defense against this pessimistic perspective, they deny the extent of their addiction. Thus a drug-addicted woman may enter treatment denying the extent of her addiction, complaining instead of depression, worry, insomnia, and anxiety. Nevertheless eager to recover, however, the woman in denial will manage, often early in treatment, to coach the therapist to take note of her problem with substances (Bugas & Silberschatz, 2000).

Alcohol, Antianxiety, and Sedative Medications

Although alcohol and sedating medications are legal, they are often abused and may lead to dysfunctional behavior. In 1994, 2.6 percent of women reported heavy alcohol use (U.S. Department of Health and Human Services, 1997), and in 1998, 2.1 percent of women reported nonmedical use of prescription drugs (U.S. Department of Health and Human Services, 1998). Alcohol and sedating substances such as the benzodiazepines (Valium, Xanax, Ativan, Klonopin) initially cause a mixture of an anxiolytic and sedating effect, elevating mood and lowering anxiety and inhibitions. After a short while, sedation increases, accompanied by loss of muscle coordination and depression. Withdrawal from these drugs causes the opposite effect: excessive anxiety and fear, insomnia, restlessness, the "shakes," and potentially life-threatening seizures. Thus treatment providers will encounter a different clinical picture depending on whether the addicted woman is intoxicated or in withdrawal at the time of assessment. Although alcohol and antianxiety medications are legal and often considered less harmful than opiates or amphetamines, in fact the withdrawal from these substances is the most life threatening. A medically supervised withdrawal and detoxification from alcohol and sedative drugs is indicated. Often medications are prescribed to control seizure activity, anxiety, and insomnia.

Marijuana

Marijuana is a deceptive and pernicious drug, and its use is difficult to assess. Although marijuana was promoted in the late 1960s and 1970s as a benign and non-addictive high, regular use of the drug has been shown to lead to physical dependence and a distinct withdrawal syndrome. Marijuana use often causes loss of ambition, interference in goal-directed behavior, and a degree of disorganization frequently called *amotivational syndrome.* A woman who has been regularly using marijuana is unlikely to be highly functional, although the degree of impairment may be less striking than that seen with other drugs. If the woman has used marijuana within the last few hours, her eyes may be red (although she may conceal this with eye drops), but otherwise there may be no obvious signs or symptoms. During the course of treatment, however, it will soon be evident that the woman is unable to achieve her full potential and is often mired in complicated relationships and family problems. For some women, marijuana use increases irritability except immediately after use. Marijuana, like other drugs, impedes development and leads to depression. In addition, as marijuana use progresses, it tends to induce feelings of anxiety and paranoia. It also affects a woman's hormone production, immune system, pulmonary function, and reproductive system. (For a summary of specific effects on the body, see Doweiko, 1993; Inaba et al., 1997.)

Withdrawal from marijuana may be subtle and drawn out as a result of marijuana's long half-life in the body. It ordinarily sets in about three to six weeks after cessation of drug use and may include irritability, copious crying, a severe depression, anxiety, insomnia, excessive rumination, guilt, and shame. In addition, people have also reported physical symptoms, such as nausea or vomiting, lack of appetite, sweating, and a general flu-like condition (Haney, Ward, Comer, Foltin, & Fischman, 1999). Marijuana addiction is difficult to overcome. Despite its reputation as a "lighter" drug, the amotivational syndrome, depression, and accompanying drug craving may persist for over a year, diminishing slowly over time.

Stimulant Drugs

The stimulant drugs, cocaine and amphetamines, have a long history in the saga of women's addiction. Cocaine was an ingredient (along with heroin) in the "tonics" popular with women in the late 1800s and early 1900s (Fields, 1995; Inaba et al., 1997). In the 1950s and 1960s, amphetamines were frequently prescribed to women for weight control and the "housewife blues." Stimulants result in decreased appetite, wakefulness, agitation, feelings of euphoria, and, after prolonged use, paranoid ideation and psychotic symptoms such as auditory hallucinations. For a time in the 1960s and 1970s, cocaine was considered to be nonaddictive. This myth was quickly dispelled by animal experiments in which it was demonstrated that cocaine was the most reinforcing drug known: if given the opportunity, primates would self-inject cocaine, forgoing food and sleep, until they died.

Stimulants may decrease depression when first ingested. After the initial "high," however, the user quickly becomes depressed unless she uses more of the drug. Stimulant use is often accompanied by alcohol or other sedative abuse, as the user attempts to minimize the agitating effects of the drug. Stimulant abuse may mimic bipolar illness, the woman appearing to be in a manic state while using, and depressed when the high is subsiding. Withdrawal from cocaine and amphetamines causes anhedonia (inability to feel pleasure), and a woman in early recovery can be expected to suffer from anxiety, excessive sleep, and depression.

Opiate Drugs

Narcotic drugs or opiates also play a part in the history of women's addiction, as they too were included in the popular tonics of the late nineteenth and early twentieth centuries (Doweiko, 1993; Inaba et al., 1997). In recent years, opiate abuse common to women has included illegal use of heroin as well as both legal (prescribed) and illegal use of pain medication such as codeine, Percodan, Vicodin, and other analgesic drugs. Opiates, similar to other "downers" such as alcohol and sedatives, initially decrease anxiety, decrease guilt and shame, and cause muscle relaxation and feelings of euphoria. In addition, opiate use causes constipation, cough suppression, pupil constriction, and hormonal and other physiological changes. Withdrawal from opiates may cause anxiety, restlessness, diarrhea, cramps, chills and flushes, intense craving, and depression. Although opiate withdrawal is often likened to a bad case of the flu and is highly unpleasant, it is not life threatening in most cases, unlike withdrawal from alcohol and sedatives.

Assessment

Pathways to addiction are highly individual and case specific, and case specificity is an underlying principle of assessment and treatment (Lieb & Young, 1994; O'Connor & Weiss, 1993). Because of the shame surrounding addiction, many women will not directly seek help for this problem, but instead will visit a therapist or physician with complaints of anxiety, depression, or insomnia (Straussner, 1997). The initial process of assessment is crucial to recovery (Brown, 1985): a misdiagnosed case may lead to years of further drug use; psychiatric problems; and loss of family, health, freedom, and life itself. For example, Susan was a young polydrug abuser who came to a low-fee clinic for psychotherapy, presenting with insomnia, anxiety, and depression. Her first two therapists, inexperienced psychology trainees, failed to ask about her drug history and current use, and diagnosed her with generalized anxiety disorder, depression, and borderline personality disorder. Even after Susan had attended several therapy sessions inebriated, the second therapist continued to focus on what she perceived as Susan's "underlying conflicts." The therapy was unsuccessful, and Susan endured two more years of escalating addiction and turmoil in her life. Susan's third therapist, who had prior experience with substance-abusing clients, focused the treatment on Susan's drug use and her desire to get into recovery. Within three months, Susan was abstinent and overcoming the many other problems that had been precipitated by her addiction. Susan, like many drug-addicted women, was highly motivated to recover and kept trying therapy until she found a therapist who was able to help her. Brown (1985) offers many examples of psychotherapists failing to identify alcohol or other drugs as their client's primary problem. In reporting on several studies of alcoholics recovering in Alcoholics Anonymous (AA), Brown (1985) notes this failure as "the primary [source] of hostility" (p. 4) between AA members and their therapists. In many cases, the window of opportunity for treatment may be short, and it is in the treatment provider's hands to make an accurate assessment and case-specific treatment plan.

Many women seeking help for addiction, even when the addiction is initially disguised as some other emotional problem, will coach the therapist or physician by noting something related to drug use, either their own or someone else's (Bugas & Silberschatz, 2000; O'Connor & Weiss, 1993). They may mention drinking, or taking prescription drugs for anxiety, or using drugs with friends or their partner (Brown, 1985). In the absence of direct comments about drug use in the initial interview, the therapist should ask women about their use of drugs, including alcohol and prescription medications. Without knowledge of the client's drug use, a therapist is unable to properly diagnose a woman's presenting symptoms. Drugs affect brain chemistry, and a woman who appears to be clinically depressed or suffering from an anxiety disorder may in fact be suffering from addiction to alcohol, sedatives, marijuana, opiates, or stimulants. Women who do not come forward with information about drug use will most often be willing to answer direct questions, although they may minimize the extent of their drug involvement in fear of social disapproval or a demand that they stop using drugs before they feel able. Despite some women's initial reluctance, denial, or minimization, all addicts want to stop using drugs and want to overcome their problems (Brown, 1985; O'Connor & Weiss, 1993; Weiss et al., 1986).

In some cases a woman may appear "resistant" to treatment: she may minimize the extent of her drug use or continue to use despite obvious and concrete problems caused by her addiction. She may insist that drugs are not a problem and that her use is recreational. Or she may persistently suggest that her children, her parents, her marriage, or her job are the source of her difficulties. This "resistance" is ordinarily due to fear, guilt, and hopelessness. A woman may be terrified of drug withdrawal, particularly if she has tried repeatedly to withdraw from drugs and found herself unable to do so. In cases where the woman is from a family in which drinking or drug use is part of the family culture, she may fear losing her family (Brown, 1985; O'Connor & Weiss, 1993). She may suffer from survivor guilt toward family members: she may believe that if she gets off drugs, she will make her addicted mother or father feel bad by comparison. A woman with children may believe she will be abandoning her children should she need to enter a residential or hospital-based program due to the severity of her physical dependency. She may believe involvement in recovery will mean she is failing her partner and children. She may believe she is an inherently flawed person, unable to live without drugs. Many women believe they do not deserve recovery; in compliance with critical or disapproving parents, they believe it is their lot in life to be addicted and unsuccessful. Thus a major goal of early therapy is to systematically counter the beliefs that underlie or fuel the "resistance." Wanting recovery, a woman carefully and deliberately works with her therapist to try to change the maladaptive beliefs that are warning her against recovery (Brown, 1985; O'Connor & Weiss, 1993; Lieb & Young, 1994).

Treatment

There are many varieties of treatment for drug-addicted women, and the selection of a particular kind of treatment is based on a woman's particular needs and situation, her unique psychology and chemistry, and the severity of her addiction. In many cases, a medical detoxification is required, particularly when there are sedatives, alcohol, or tranquilizers involved. Sometimes a period of hospitalization is needed. In some cases, when a woman is living alone, isolated, or without social support, treatment that follows a residential social model is recommended. In many cases, self-help programs like AA, Narcotics Anonymous (NA), or other drug-specific programs modeled on AA (Cocaine Anonymous, Marijuana Anonymous, Nicotine Anonymous) are the primary mode of treatment, sometimes used alone and sometimes in conjunction with psychotherapy. Other self-help groups, such as Rational Recovery (RR) and Secular Organization for Sobriety (SOS) are helpful in cases where any reference to religious language is intolerable. Women-centered groups such as Women for Sobriety (WFS) and women-only AA meetings may be extremely useful for women.

In some cases, pharmaceutical intervention in early recovery includes the use of medications that are presumed to make drug use either unattractive or less desired. For example, Antabuse works to make an alcohol-addicted person sick if she drinks. Naltrexone, which counteracts the effects of opiates, is sometimes used in conjunction with psychosocial treatment of opiate addiction and is currently also being used in alcohol addiction, as it appears to reduce the craving for alcohol.

Methadone, a synthetic long-acting opiate, is often used to detoxify from heroin, although its use is controversial. Advocates of methadone detoxification report the following benefits: it is effective in reducing the craving for heroin; it prevents the addict from achieving a heroin "high" should she use; it removes the addict from illegal drug-related activity; and it does not require injection (it is administered once daily in liquid form), thus lowering the risk for transmission of HIV and Hepatitis C. Furthermore, methadone detoxification brings the addicted woman into daily contact with the treatment program, as she is required to come every day to get her methadone dose. Proponents of methadone claim that addicts who participate in a methadone program don't continue to use heroin and other drugs. Methadone advocates also suggest that methadone allows for an easier detoxification from heroin. However, many heroin addicts who begin methadone in a detoxification program end up staying on methadone indefinitely. Treatment providers justify this with the argument that opiate addicts suffer a chronic deficiency in the endorphin system in the brain and therefore need methadone maintenance to compensate for this deficiency (Dole, 1988).

Critics of methadone detoxification object to this perspective, believing that opiate addicts are capable of full and abstinent recovery. They point to studies demonstrating that addicts on methadone continue to use other drugs, such as cocaine, alcohol, and heroin at the same time as using methadone (see Wasserman, Korcha, Havassy, & Hall, 1999). They further support their critique by referring to the many abstinent recovering heroin and methadone addicts who have reported they were able to get high on heroin while using methadone (Inaba et al., 1997). In addition, withdrawal from methadone is far more long lasting, painful, and severe than heroin withdrawal. Furthermore, recovering heroin addicts report that the experience of methadone addiction is humiliating, and it keeps them from participating in an abstinence-model recovery program such as Narcotics Anonymous. Methadone maintenance, usually started in an effort to withdraw from heroin, has been called a "chemical prison" by recovering opiate addicts.

Other medications sometimes used in early recovery include antianxiety drugs, although most treatment specialists believe there is too high a risk of dependence, and limit antianxiety medications to a few days. Sedating antidepressants are sometimes used to help a woman sleep while undergoing withdrawal. Antiseizure medications may be necessary for women withdrawing from alcohol, sedatives, or tranquilizers. Clonidine, a blood pressure medication, has been found effective in countering some of the effects of opiate and nicotine withdrawal. Antidepressants may be used to reduce the depression and anxiety frequently associated with withdrawal.

The use of medications by substance-abusing women is controversial in some recovery circles. The abstinence model of recovery (refraining from all mind-altering drug use), has been effective for many addicts, and to some, any drug affecting the brain is considered dangerous to one's sobriety. Complete abstinence is often a particularly successful model of treatment for a variety of reasons. Addiction is often referred to as a chronic and relapsing brain disorder, and the abstinence model appears to provide protection against relapse (Margolis & Zweben, 1998; Rawson, 1994). In many cases, people who believe they only need to stop using their drug of choice find that continuing their use of other drugs leads them back to their preferred drug or that they become dependent on a new drug. For example, a woman who had successfully overcome her addiction to heroin in a residential drug treatment program developed a serious addiction to alcohol when she resumed drinking. She thought she could drink because, she said, "Alcohol was never my problem." Many drugs of abuse have the effect of lowering inhibitions, and when drug-dependent women are uninhibited they are more likely to resume use of their preferred drug. The abstinence model also avoids the effects of state-dependent learning: when using any substances, women are more likely to remember the drug euphoria they first experienced when they began using drugs and to suffer from drug craving. Abstinence is further justified by the escalating nature of the disease of addiction: studies of addiction in rats show that with repeated administration of an addictive drug there is an increased reward threshold, meaning that it takes more of the drug to have a rewarding effect (Koob & LeMoal, 1997). Other studies have demonstrated that when rats are addicted to alcohol, then withdrawn and subsequently addicted again, each successive withdrawal syndrome is more severe. This is known as the *kindling effect* (Becker, 1998; Maier & Pohorecky, 1989). These study results are in accordance with an AA principle: addiction escalates in severity, and each time a woman relapses, her illness becomes more severe.

A currently popular, though controversial, treatment approach is known as *harm reduction*. This treatment modality acknowledges that many addicts are unable to achieve abstinence and that making a drug-free life a goal of treatment leads to disappointment and a sense of failure. Instead, advocates recommend that the goal of treatment be a reduction in drug use. Although harm reduction may be an effective model for some women in recovery, for many women it is a high-risk strategy. For example, Audrey Kishline, a leader in the controlled drinking model of treatment, killed two people in an automobile collision as the result of driving with a blood alcohol level of .26. Facing arrest, Kishline stated that Moderation Management is a "program for alcoholics covering up their own alcoholism" (Rivera, 2000, p. 47). Dr. Ernest Nobel, director of UCLA's Alcohol Research Center, notes that "attempts at moderation, such as Controlled Drinking, Drink Watchers, and Rational Recovery, have a long history of failure" (Rivera, 2000, p. 47).

Social Model Programs

In treatment following the social model programs, recovering addicts live and work together, usually under the supervision of longer-term recovering addicts. In some social model programs such as Delancey Street Foundation in San Francisco, recovering people work in the program. In other programs, residents find employment in the broader community while living at the program facility. Social model programs emphasize the development of social skills, vocational skills, and a sense of personal responsibility—including taking responsibility for one's addiction and recovery. Based on programs initially designed for drug-addicted men, some social model programs tend to put great emphasis on taking responsibility, which can be overinterpreted by women, creating an additional burden of guilt and shame. This may be counterproductive for drug-addicted women, who tend to blame themselves for everything prior to and during their addiction (Meehan et al., 1996; O'Connor & Weiss, 1993) and whose self-loathing and self-criticism are relapse triggers. Some social model programs, in the wake of increasing numbers of women seeking treatment, have revised their program design to be more appropriate for women. Such programs try directly to reduce women's feelings of exaggerated shame and guilt. Many women who otherwise might not be able to afford treatment (other than in self-help programs) find support, access to resources, psychoeducation, and a protected drug-free environment in social model programs. In addition, social model programs often are able to meet the relational needs of recovering women. For the increasing numbers of women arrested for drug-related crimes, social model programs may provide a more viable, more effective, and less expensive solution than imprisonment. Furthermore, drug treatment is more likely to prevent recidivism. The use of social model programs instead of prison may be especially relevant to minority women, who are being incarcerated at a much higher rate than European American women (Henderson, 1998).

Individual and Group Psychotherapy

Group or individual psychotherapy (or both) is often a necessary component of the addicted woman's treatment plan. In some cases, women are unable to stop using drugs until they have been in intensive psychotherapy long enough to disconfirm the pathogenic beliefs warning them against abstinence and recovery. For example, a woman may need to address the belief that if she pursues a successful life without drugs she will be betraying, deserting, or sneering at her alcoholic or drug-addicted parent(s) or sibling(s). Or a woman may need to address the inhibiting belief that if she stops using drugs she will be defying a parental dictate that she is supposed to be inadequate and out of control.

Clients deliberately—though often unconsciously—test their therapists. Consequently, a woman may need to test the therapist many times before sticking with AA and getting sober. In an effort to change the inhibiting beliefs derived from traumatic childhood experiences, clients take specific actions so as to find out how the therapist will react (O'Connor & Weiss, 1993; Silberschatz & Curtis, 1993; Weiss, 1993; Weiss et al., 1986). For example, a woman who believes she will harm her actively alcoholic mother by getting sober (perhaps she fears she will make her mother feel inadequate or inferior by comparison) will test this belief with her therapist. She may do this by saying she doesn't want to stop drinking, by saying she hates AA and that she doesn't have a problem or that the people at meetings are "much sicker than I am." Or the client may appear at a therapy session after drinking to see if the therapist will notice, care, or feel hopeless about her. These activities are carefully designed tests of the therapist to see if the therapist supports the woman's abstinence and recovery. When the therapist consistently responds with a calm support for recovery, and treats her client optimistically, the client will be able to change the beliefs that prevent her from getting into recovery.

A therapist's countertransference, or internal emotional reaction to a client, helps the therapist understand the client's feelings. In general, it is likely that a patient is testing if the therapist experiences a strong emotional response to her or feels a strong pull to make an intervention. Therapists are able to understand the specific nature of their clients' tests by carefully noting exactly what they feel pulled to do or what emotion they are experiencing. For example, a client may test by treating the therapist as an authority figure or as a parent. In this scenario, the client has transferred her experience with her parents onto the therapist in order to test the pathogenic beliefs she developed as a child in relation to her parents. The client is acting with her therapist the way she did with her parents in the hope of attaining an experience different from the one she had as a child. For example, a woman who grew up with highly critical or neglecting parents—parents who perhaps were unable to acknowledge her achievements—may have the expectation that all authorities will treat her as she was treated by her parents and that she deserves their poor treatment. She may test this belief in relation to her therapist by describing a recent success of hers. The therapist, by responding to the client in a different way than her parents responded to her, may be able to help the client change some of her maladaptive beliefs, such as that she deserves to be criticized or neglected.

At other times, therapists will find themselves feeling guilty, inadequate, hopeless, or fearful in reaction to the client. In these instances, clients are most often actively imitating behaviors that they had to endure passively as children. For example, another client who was also unfairly criticized as a child may test her therapist by becoming harshly critical of her (playing the role of the parent instead of the child). Her therapist, in response, may find herself feeling like a "bad child" who can't do anything right. In this case, there may be several purposes to the client's test. One purpose is to unconsciously demonstrate what she had to endure as a child. This is particularly likely to occur if the client feels too guilty to verbally describe her parents' behavior or if she is not able to remember their behavior. Another purpose is to learn how to respond to criticism without believing that she is deserving of it. (By adulthood, the client has often internalized her parent's criticisms and, as a result, is constantly criticizing herself, usually in the tone her parents used with her when she was a child.) In order to provide a corrective experience and to pass the client's test in this situation, the therapist needs to accept or tolerate the client's behavior and understand it as information about the client's childhood. In addition, the therapist needs to model a different response to the experience of being criticized. The therapist needs to let herself experience the test, to endure feeling like "a bad child" without actually believing that she is bad and deserves criticism. The client will then be able to imitate the therapist's response to criticism when she herself is faced with her internal parental criticisms.

Developing skill at noting and interpreting countertransference reactions is particularly important in working with women addicted to AOD. Many women with chemical dependency problems come from AOD-dependent families and have therefore experienced significant childhood trauma. While in treatment, they will need to test the beliefs they developed in their dysfunctional families, and the therapist must rely on his or her countertransference reactions in order to help the client.

Psychoeducation

The period of withdrawal from drugs is often very difficult and filled with physiologically based anxiety, depression, restlessness, insomnia or hypersomnia, fear, guilt, and sometimes hallucinations and psychosis. Understanding this process from a biopsychosocial perspective is most helpful. Most women in early recovery—whether they are in individual or group therapy, in a residential, inpatient, or outpatient treatment program, in AA, or in some combination of programs—are well served by obtaining education about addiction, through films, lectures, literature, and group discussions. Becoming an expert on their own addiction helps empower women to understand that even though they may be powerless over their disease, they are not helpless. The individual or group psychotherapist working with clients in early recovery can help by recommending educational materials, books, and videos and by being knowledgeable enough themselves to engage in in-depth discussions about addiction as a biopsychosocial disease. By learning about the biomedical and hereditary basis of addiction, the client builds a rationale—beyond an unquestioning belief in the treatment provider or program—for stopping drug use. Understanding protracted withdrawal—that is, the recurrence of withdrawal symptoms and accompanying craving long after abstinence—helps demystify the experience. For example, when a woman in recovery from alcohol addiction experiences a wave of severe anxiety and shaking, perhaps triggered by a drug cue such as a smell or sight, she may find herself thinking that she is a hopeless case and so may as well drink. However, if she understands the protracted withdrawal phenomenon and knows the reaction will pass, she is far less likely to relapse. Education about addiction and about the case-specific vulnerabilities of a client is a helpful weapon in the fight against relapse. Addiction is a relapsing disease, and many addicted women find themselves using again. Education about the facts of addiction is helpful in getting a woman back into recovery. Countering the perspective that addiction is a moral weakness or a sign that the client is psychologically flawed and hopeless, the biopsychosocial viewpoint is far more accurate and helpful.

The Twelve-Step Model of Recovery

Over the past fifty years, AA (and, more recently, NA, Marijuana Anonymous, Cocaine Anonymous, and other twelve-step programs) has been a central part of many women's recovery, despite some male-derived aspects of the program. Twelve-step programs, like other self-help groups and group therapy, are often helpful because they give women the opportunity to hear about the experiences of other recovering women (Brown, 1985; Lieb & Young, 1994; O'Connor & Weiss, 1993). This breaks their sense of isolation and uniqueness and validates and normalizes their experience. Women in AA and NA are particularly helped by hearing women's stories in speaker meetings and in women-only meetings. Although twelve-step programs do not work for everyone, they work for many. Women who are not successful with the program alone may find that it works when combined with other treatment, such as residential treatment, transitional halfway houses, hospital inpatient or outpatient programs, group or individual psychotherapy (or both), and, in some cases, medical detoxification or psychiatric medications.

AA and NA, like other helpful treatments, help counter women's pervasive sense of shame and guilt and their exaggerated sense of responsibility for others. The often-criticized "spiritual" component to the twelve-step program is particularly effective in this process. The first step of the program, sometimes considered controversial by feminist women, suggests accepting that "We are powerless over drugs and alcohol and our lives have become unmanageable." Objections to this step relate to the declaration of powerlessness, with the assertion that women already feel too powerless and that in order to recover they need to feel powerful. In fact many, if not most, drug-addicted women suffer from an exaggerated sense of power, the persistent fear that they are harming others, and the belief that if they are successful and sober they will harm a loved one. The first step helps counter this belief in their omnipotence. The second and third steps, calling on a belief in a "power greater than ourselves," also help women put into perspective their omnipotent sense of responsibility for others. These steps ask the addicted person to put control into the hands of a "Higher Power." A Higher Power may be viewed as God or Buddha or some other spiritual entity, or it may be a belief in nature or the twelve-step group or some other entity of the woman's choosing. Belief in a Higher Power offers guilt-ridden women a more realistic sense of their power over others for whom they feel an omnipotent sense of responsibility.

Some women are unable to make use of AA or NA until they have been in psychotherapy for a while, and others are never able to connect to a twelve-step program. Twelve-step and other self-help programs may be less immediately useful for some women with particular kinds of problems, such as intense shyness, severe psychopathology, or employment in a public position in which it would be detrimental to their work to appear in a public treatment setting. Some professionals have formed professional AA and NA groups to work around this problem. There are AA and NA groups for doctors, lawyers, and mental health professionals in many communities. Women who have recently immigrated from another country, or women who are contending with physical disabilities and illness, may also find themselves unable to make good use of twelve-steps programs. Women who are from a culture in which it is considered highly inappropriate to discuss personal issues in public may likewise find it difficult to make use of these programs. Case-specific treatment planning is essential in designing the optimal program for any woman. Often, when a woman finds that AA or NA is authentically not helpful, the therapist or counselor should try to find other resources in the community that will better suit her client's particular situation.

Additional Issues Affecting Treatment

As mentioned earlier, it is difficult to diagnose other mental disorders until a woman has a period of time abstinent from drugs; the length of time needed to make that assessment varies. Most women in early recovery will have at least some symptoms of a mood or anxiety disorder, and to treat these symptoms as indicators of a non-drug-related depression or anxiety disorder is controversial (O'Connor et al., 1992).

Historically, many clinicians, influenced by a traditional psychodynamic perspective on addiction, have assumed that drug-addicted women are suffering from a personality disorder, a mood disorder, or some other underlying psychiatric problem or manifestation of unconscious conflict. This perspective resulted in clinicians' denying or minimizing the importance of drug use and led to treatment failures. Many chemical dependency specialists concluded that psychotherapy was harmful to drug-addicted women.

As a result of this history, some HMOs currently deny psychotherapy to drug- and alcohol-abusing women. This is problematic for women who need therapy in order to overcome inhibitions against recovery and for women who are suffering from mental disorders independent of their drug use. There are women in recovery who have been using drugs to control the symptoms of severe psychiatric illnesses. This includes problems such as the mania and depression of bipolar illness; the ruminations, anhedonia, and sleep disturbance of major depression; the obsessions and compulsions of obsessive-compulsive disorder; and the self-destructive behaviors of a severe personality disorder. The dually diagnosed woman requires a comprehensive treatment plan that includes a highly supported withdrawal and early recovery period, early or continuous trials and use of medications, and on-going psychotherapy. Women suffering from psychotic or other illnesses that result in unusual social behaviors may have a hard time fitting into AA or social model programs until they have their more overt symptoms under control.

Conclusion

The need to provide AOD-dependent women with appropriate gender-sensitive assessment and treatment remains a significant issue for the mental health system as a whole and for psychotherapists working with this population, be they in HMOs, community mental health settings, or private practice. Drug and alcohol dependence causes many of the mental health problems affecting our society and has a widely felt destructive impact. Not only are AOD-addicted women themselves suffering, but so are their families and their social and work groups. The cost of drug and alcohol addiction spreads exponentially as it ripples throughout whole communities. However, treatment for even one drug-dependent woman has the potential to save numerous lives. There are many kinds of treatment for addiction; the urgent issue is to make treatment more accessible and sensitive to the particular needs of women, and to educate psychotherapists working with AOD-addicted women and their families.

References

Bays, J. (1990). Substance abuse and child abuse: Impact of addiction on the child. *Pediatric Clinics of North America, 37,* 881–904.

Bean, M. (1981). Denial and the psychological complications of alcoholism. In M. H. Bean & N. E. Zimberg (Eds.), *Dynamic approaches to the understanding and treatment of alcoholism* (pp. 55–96). New York: Free Press.

Becker, H. C. (1998). Kindling in alcohol withdrawal. *Alcohol Health and Research World, 22*(1), 25–33.

Brim, G. (1992). Our drive for growth and mastery. In G. Brim (Ed.), *Ambition* (pp. 9–27). New York: Basic Books.

Brown, S. (1985). *Treating the alcoholic: A developmental model of recovery.* New York: Wiley.

Brown, S., & Lewis, V. (1999). *The alcoholic family in recovery: A developmental model.* New York: Guilford Press.

Bugas, J., & Silberschatz, G. (2000). How patients coach their therapists in psychotherapy. *Psychotherapy, 37*(1), 64–70.

Bush, M. (1989). The role of unconscious guilt in psychopathology and psychotherapy. *Bulletin of the Menninger Clinic, 52,* 97–103.

Cadoret, R. J., O'Gorman, T. W., Troughton, E., & Heywood, E. (1985). Alcoholism and antisocial personality: Interrelationships, genetic, and environmental factors. *Archives of General Psychiatry, 42,* 161–167.

Caetano, R. (1991). Findings from the 1984 National Survey of Alcohol Use Among U.S. Hispanics. In W. B. Clark & M. E. Hinton (Eds.), *Alcohol in America: Drinking practices and problems* (pp. 291–307). Albany: State University of New York Press.

Cloninger, C. R., Bohman, M., & Sigvardsson, S. (1981). Inheritance of alcohol abuse: Cross-fostering analysis of adopted men. *Archives of General Psychiatry, 36,* 861–868.

Cotton, N. S. (1979). The familial incidence of alcoholism: A review. *Journal of Studies on Alcohol, 40,* 89–116.

Dole, V. (1988). Implication of methadone maintenance for theories of narcotic addiction. *Journal of the American Medical Association, 260,* 3025–3029.

Doweiko, H. E. (1993). *Concepts of chemical dependency* (2nd ed.). Pacific Grove, CA: Brooks/Cole.

Fields, R. (1995). *Drugs in perspective* (2nd ed.). Madison, WI: Brown & Benchmark.

George, F. R. (1997). Behavioral genetics of addiction. In B. A. Johnson & J. D. Roache (Eds.), *Drug addiction and its treatment: Nexus of neuroscience and behavior.* Philadelphia: Lippincott-Raven.

Gomberg, E.S.L. (1988). Alcoholic women in treatment: The question of stigma and age. *Alcohol and Alcoholism, 23,* 507–514.

Goodwin, D. W., Schulsinger, F., Hermansen, L., Guve, S. B., & Winokur, G. (1973). Alcohol problems in adoptees raised apart from alcoholic biological parents. *Archives of General Psychiatry, 28,* 238–243.

Goodwin, D. W., Schulsinger, F., Moller, N., Hermansen, L., Winokur, G., & Guve, S. B. (1974). Drinking problems in adopted and non adopted sons of alcoholics. *Archives of General Psychiatry, 31,* 164–169.

Haney, M., Ward, A. S., Comer, S. D., Foltin, R. W., & Fischman, M. W. (1999). Abstinence symptoms following smoked marijuana in humans. *Psychopharmacology, 141,* 395–404.

Henderson, D. J. (1998). Drug abuse in incarcerated women. *Journal of Substance Abuse Treatment, 15,* 579–587.

Herd, D. (1998). Drinking by black and white women. *Social Problems, 35,* 493–505.

Hesselbrock, B. (1995). The genetic epidemiology of alcoholism. In H. Begleiter & B. Kissin (Eds.), *The genetics of alcoholism* (pp. 17–39). New York: Oxford University Press.

Hill, S. Y. (1993). Genetic vulnerability to alcoholism in women. In E.S.L. Gomberg & T. D. Nirenberg (Eds.), *Women and substance abuse* (pp. 42–61). Norwood, NJ: Ablex.

Hill, S. Y. (1995). Vulnerability to alcoholism in women: Genetic and cultural factors. In M. Gallanter (Ed.), *Recent developments in alcoholism: Vol. 12. Women and alcoholism* (pp. 9–28). New York: Plenum Press.

Hill, S. Y., & Smith, T. R. (1991). Evidence for genetic mediation of alcoholism in women. *Journal of Substance Abuse, 3,* 159–174.

Hughs, R. (1976). *The tranquilizing of America.* Orlando: Harcourt Brace.

Inaba, D., Cohen, W. E., & Holstein, M. E. (1997). *Uppers downers all arounders: Physical and mental effects of psychoactive drugs* (3rd ed.). Ashland, OR: CNS Publications.

Kandel, D. B. (1998). Epidemiology of drug use and abuse among women. In C. L. Wetherington & A. B. Roman (Eds.), *Drug addiction research and the health of women.* Rockville, MD: National Institute of Drug Abuse.

Kendler, K. S., Heath, A. C., Neale, M. C., Kessler, R. C., & Eaves, L. J. (1992). A population-based twin study of alcoholism in women. *Journal of the American Medical Association, 268,* 1877–1882.

Kendler, K. S., Karkowski, L., & Prescott, C. A. (1999). Hallucinogen, opiate, sedative and stimulant use and abuse in a population-based sample of female twins. *Acta Psychiatrica Scandinavica, 99,* 368–376.

Kendler, K. S., & Prescott, C. A. (1998). Cannabis use, abuse, and dependence in a population-based sample of female twins. *American Journal of Psychiatry, 155,* 1016–1022.

Koob, G. F., & LeMoal. (1997, October 3). Drug abuse: Hedonic homeostatic dysregulation. *Science, 278,* 52–58.

Lerman, C., Caporaso, N. E., Audrain, J., Main, D., Bowman, E. D., Lockshin, B., Boyd, N. R., & Shields, P. G. (1999). Evidence suggesting the role of specific genetic factors in cigarette smoking. *Health Psychology, 18*(1), 14–20.

Lex, B. W., Goldberg, M. E., Mendelson, J. H., Lawler, N. S., & Bower, T. (1994). Components of antisocial personality disorder among women convicted for drunken driving. *Annals of the New York Academy of Sciences, 708,* 49–58.

Lieb, R. J., & Young, N. P. (1994). A case-specific approach to the treatment of alcoholism: The application of Control Mastery Theory to Alcoholics Anonymous and professional practice. *Journal of Substance Abuse Treatment, 11,* 35–44.

Maier, D. M., & Pohorecky, L. A. (1989). The effect of repeated withdrawal episodes on subsequent withdrawal severity in ethanol-treated rats. *Drug and Alcohol Dependence, 23,* 103–110.

Margolis, R. D., & Zweben, J. E. (1998). *Treating patients with alcohol and other drug problems: An integrated approach.* Washington, DC: American Psychological Association.

Marwick, C. (1998). Challenging report on pregnancy and drug abuse. *Journal of the American Medical Association, 280,* 1039.

McGue, M. (1993). From proteins to cognitions: The behavioral genetics of alcoholism. In R. Plomin & G. E. McClearn (Eds.), *Nature, nurture and psychology* (pp. 245–268). Washington, DC: American Psychological Association.

Meehan, W., O'Connor, L. E., Berry, J. W., Weiss, J., Morrison, A., & Acampora, A. (1996). Guilt, shame, and depression in clients in recovery from addiction. *Journal of Psychoactive Drugs, 28,* 125–133.

National Center on Addiction and Substance Abuse at Columbia University. (1998). Behind bars. *CASA Newsletter* 1457. Available: www.casacolumbia.org/newsletter 1457/ newsletter_show.htm?doc_id3567.

O'Connor, L. E., & Berry, J. W. (1990). The drug-of-choice phenomenon: Why addicts start using their preferred drug. *Journal of Psychoactive Drugs, 22,* 305–311.

O'Connor, L. E., & Berry, J. W. (1997). Interpersonal guilt: The development of a scale. *Journal of Clinical Psychology, 53,* 73–89.

O'Connor, L. E., Berry, J. W., Inaba, D., Weiss, J., & Morrison, A. (1994). Shame, guilt and depression in men and women in recovery from addiction. *Journal of Substance Abuse Treatment, 11,* 503–510.

O'Connor, L. E., Berry, J. W., Morrison, A., & Brown, S. (1992). Retrospective reports of psychiatric symptoms before, during, and after drug use in a recovering population. *Journal of Psychoactive Drugs, 24,* 65–68.

O'Connor, L. E., Berry, J. W., Morrison, A., & Brown, S. (1995). The drug-of-choice phenomenon: Psychological differences among drug users who preferred different drugs. *Interpersonal Journal of the Addictions, 30,* 541–555.

O'Connor, L. E., & Weiss, J. (1993). Individual psychotherapy for addicted clients: An application of Control Mastery Theory. *Journal of Psychoactive Drugs, 25,* 283–291.

Pickens, R. W., Svikis, D. S., McGue, M., Lykken, D. T., Heston, L. L., & Clayton, P. J. (1991). Heterogeneity in the inheritance of alcoholism: A study of male and female twins. *Archives of General Psychiatry, 48,* 19–28.

Rawson, R. (1994, April). Relapse prevention models. In J. E. Zweben & R. Rawson (Cochairs), *Psychological models of outpatient substance abuse treatment: Recovery oriented psychotherapy and relapse prevention models.* Workshop conducted at the 25th Annual Medical-Scientific Conference of the American Society of Addiction Medicine, New York.

Rivera, E. (2000). License to drink. *Time, 156*(5), 47.

Schuckit, M. A. (1999). New findings in the genetics of alcoholism. *Journal of the American Medical Association, 281,* 1875–1876.

Shedler, J., & Block, J. (1990). Adolescent drug use and psychological health: A longitudinal inquiry. *American Psychologist, 45,* 612–630.

Silberschatz, G., & Curtis, J. (1993). Measuring the therapist's impact on the patient's therapeutic progress. *Journal of Consulting and Clinical Psychology, 61,* 403–411.

Snell, T. L., & Morton, D. C. (1991). *Women in prison: Survey of state prison inmates* (Bureau of Justice Statistics Special Report NCJ-145321). Washington, DC: U.S. Government Printing Office.

Straussner, S.L.A. (1997). Gender and substance abuse. In S.L.A. Straussner & E. Zelvin (Eds.), *Gender and addictions: Men and women in treatment* (pp. 3–27). Northvale, NJ: Aronson.

True, W. R., Xian, H., Scherrer, J. F., Madden, P. A., Bucholz, K. K., Heath, A. C., Eisen, S. A., Lyons, M. J., Goldberg, J., & Tsuang, M. (1999). Common genetic vulnerability for nicotine and alcohol dependence in men. *Archives of General Psychiatry, 56,* 655–661.

U.S. Department of Health and Human Services, Office of Applied Studies, Substance Abuse and Mental Health Services Administration. (1997). *Substance use among women in the United States.* Washington DC: U.S. Government Printing Office.

U.S. Department of Health and Human Services, Office of Applied Studies, Substance Abuse and Mental Health Services Administration. (1998). *National Household Survey of Drug Abuse: Main findings.* Washington DC: U.S. Government Printing Office.

Wasserman, D. A., Korcha, R., Havassy, B. E., & Hall, S. M. (1999). Detection of illicit opioid and cocaine use in methadone maintenance treatment. *American Journal of Drug and Alcohol Abuse, 25,* 561–571.

Weiss, J. (1993). *How psychotherapy works: Process and technique.* New York: Guilford Press.

Weiss, J., Sampson, H., & the Mount Zion Psychotherapy Research Group. (1986). *The psychoanalytic process: Theory, clinical observation, and empirical research.* New York: Guilford Press.

Wilsnack, R. W., & Cheloha, R. (1987). Women's roles and problem drinking across the lifespan. *Social Problems, 34,* 231–248.

Zickler, P. (2000). Evidence builds that genes influence cigarette smoking. *NIDA Notes, 15*(2), 1–5.

CHAPTER FIVE

THE QUEEN OF DIAMONDS

Women and Compulsive Gambling

Diane Rae Davis

Women who gamble compulsively in this country are almost invisible in their
misery. You cannot tell by looking at a woman that she is craving to be at
the video poker machine or that she has spent all of her last paycheck on gambling the night before. Even those closest to her are easily deceived. You cannot
smell gambling on her breath, and her eyes do not dilate no matter how big her
problem is. You won't see her much in the research studies on gambling, and you
will see very little of her in formal treatment programs. In a very few areas of the
country, you may see her with a roomful of recovering women at a Gamblers
Anonymous (GA) meeting, but in most states she will be greatly outnumbered by
White males. She may show up at your health clinic with gastrointestinal problems related to uncontrolled gambling, or at a family service agency with her family in disarray, but it is very unlikely she will receive any professional recognition
of what's really wrong unless she specifically admits her gambling problems. Even
if she does, there is little in the way of organized treatment, social policy, or research that focuses directly on helping women avoid or address compulsive gambling problems.

This dismal state of affairs, reminiscent of the status of women in the alcohol and drug field thirty years ago, is beginning to change. As some form of gambling has become legal in every state except three (Utah, Hawaii, and Tennessee),
and casino or casino-style gambling is available in twenty-one states, gambling

has become much more socially acceptable and accessible for both women and men (National Research Council, 1999). Consequently, many more women suffering the consequences of excessive gambling are surfacing and asking for help. Helping professionals are noticing the devastating effects of compulsive gambling on women and their families, and want answers. To help in this endeavor, this chapter will provide a badly needed focus on women compulsive gamblers, an explanation of theories that attempt to explain a woman's out-of-control gambling, a review of current assessment and diagnostic practices, and models for treatment and recovery.

Women Problem Gamblers: A Growth Industry?

Although many professionals have never considered "women" and "problem gambling" in the same sentence, there is mounting evidence from state helplines for problem gamblers that the number of women seeking help with gambling problems is increasing. In New Jersey, calls about women have doubled since 1990. In Texas, calls about women problem gamblers have increased from 34 percent in 1992 to 40 percent in 1999 (Texas Council on Problem and Compulsive Gambling, 2000). In Minnesota, 30 percent of the calls to the Minnesota Compulsive Gambling Hotline were about women in 1992, but by 1996, that percentage had risen to 42 percent (Minnesota Institute of Public Health, 1998). In 1997, women made up 41.6 percent of the gambling treatment population in Minnesota and were more likely than men to receive a more serious score on the South Oaks Gambling Screen (SOGS) (Rhodes, Norman, Langenbahn, Harmon, & Deal, 1997).

To date, prevalence studies have not caught up with this phenomenon; they consistently report that men are more likely to be pathological or problem gamblers than women. The National Research Council analysis (1999) of general population studies (not clinical or institutional) from eighteen states conducted during the last ten years reveals that the proportion of women among pathological and problem gamblers ranged from 20 to 55 percent, with a median of 38 percent. Overall, the National Gambling Impact Study Commission ([NGISC], 1999) estimates that there were 125 million American adults who gambled in the last year, about half of whom were women. Most of them experienced no negative consequences; approximately 7.5 million were either problem or pathological gamblers. The National Research Council's estimate (1999) is that between 3 and 7 percent of those who gambled in the past year reported some symptoms of problem or pathological gambling.

Problem Versus Pathological Gambling

What is the difference between problem and pathological gambling (or, in lay terms, "compulsive" gambling)? As defined by the National Research Council (1999), *pathological gambling* is a "mental disorder characterized by a continuous or periodic loss of control over gambling, a preoccupation with gambling, and with obtaining money with which to gamble, irrational thinking, and a continuation of the behavior despite adverse consequences" (chap. 2, p. 4). A clinical diagnosis is reached when a person meets five or more *DSM-IV* criteria (American Psychiatric Association, 1994). In short, "pathological gamblers engage in destructive behaviors: they commit crimes, they run up large debts, they damage relationships with family and friends, and they kill themselves" (National Research Council, 1999, p. Exec-2).

Problem gambling is a category used in research studies to indicate that the person has developed some family, work, or financial problems because of his or her gambling but has not met at least five of the *DSM-IV* criteria. It is also applied to adolescents, regardless of their scores on various assessment instruments, because of a reluctance to label them as pathological while they are in the midst of fluctuating and experimental behavior patterns. Many times the general term *problem gamblers* is used inclusively to indicate both pathological (compulsive) and problem gamblers (Pavalko, 1999). In this chapter, the lay term *compulsive gambler* will be used to designate women who by diagnosis, self-report, or research findings fall into the category of pathological gambling.

Escape Versus Action Gamblers

A common designation of many women is that they are "escape" gamblers. The designation of *escape gambler* has been almost exclusively applied to women until very recently. Escape gamblers tend to become compulsive in their gambling in a very short span of six months to three years; play "luck" games such as bingo, slots, video poker; and start playing as a recreation but quickly move into using gambling to escape from problems (Arizona Council on Compulsive Gambling, 2000; Lesieur & Blume, 1991b). The lure of the escape is characterized by a feeling of being "hypnotized," "in a trance," or even "out of body," or of "having tunnel vision where nothing else mattered." As one woman put it, "It's not whether I'm winning or losing, it's how long do I have until my money runs out and I have to come back to myself and face the ride home. Winning only counts because it delays the terrible, humiliating ride home" (personal communication, September 2000).

In contrast, men have historically been characterized as "action" gamblers: gambling began early in life; has been a long-term problem of ten to thirty years; focuses on "skill" games such as poker, horses, and sports; and provides action as well as escape. While men continue to outnumber women in actional types of gambling, they also make up a substantial portion of "escape" types of gambling. For example, in Mississippi, 75 percent of female problem gamblers identify casino gambling as their favorite type of gambling, whereas only 47 percent of male problem gamblers prefer casinos (Volberg, 1997). A gender comparison of a large treatment sample in Australia (Crisp et al., 2000) revealed from the assessment data (male = 696, female = 583) that women were one-and-a-half times more likely than men to gamble as a way of escaping from other problems. In addition, the women were more likely to be older, married, and living with family, and to have dependent children. The women reported average debts that were less than half what was owed by the male gamblers. Women were more likely than males to report using electronic gambling machines (91.1 percent versus 61.4 percent) and more likely to play bingo (4.8 percent versus 1.0 percent).

Although the descriptions of action and escape gamblers are commonly used in the literature to describe gender differences, new information suggests that we use caution in applying them to a specific gender. The Arizona Council on Compulsive Gambling noted that in 1999, 73 percent of all calls to the Arizona Crisis Helpline were from or about escape gamblers, and that 94 percent of the women and 49 percent of the men who called identified themselves as an escape gambler (Arizona Council on Compulsive Gambling, 2000). This led Don Hulen and Paula Burns of the Arizona Council to reframe the designations *escape* or *action* gambler to relate to a *type of gambler* and not to the gender of the gambler. They point to the growing accessibility of casino-type gambling as the major cause of increasing escape gambling, regardless of gender. This phenomenon "is affecting men who had no previous history of gambling or compulsive gambling in the same way it affects women" (Hulen & Burns, 2001, p. 7).

In addition, there is some evidence that women participate equally in all types of betting; for example, in a recent research study by Steel and Blaszcynski (1998), a gender breakout of subjects entering treatment ($n = 82$) revealed no differences in the types of gambling and no differences in the severity as indicated by the SOGS.

There could be an edge of dominant-culture patronizing in designating women as preferring "nonskill" gambling games and consequently not living up to the popular culture's idea of "real" gambling. Discounting out-of-control gambling behavior because it involves games like bingo only adds to the difficulties of these women in recognizing their own problems and getting help.

A Woman's Path to Compulsive Gambling

Mary began visiting the riverboat casinos in Kansas City, Missouri, shortly after her husband of 40 years died. "It was something to do. The lights, the music, there were people around. You could forget where you were at," she said. March 9, 1997 marked the one-year anniversary of her husband's death. She decided to stay out that night to help forget the pain. She won several jackpots, including one of $28,000. From then on, Mary became a regular. Casino workers knew her by name, and treated her as a VIP. In 1997, she received 14 W-2 forms from the casino, each representing a jackpot of over $1,200.

But behind the wins were many, many losses. The money from her husband's life insurance, his $50,000 annual pension, and Mary's monthly social security payment all went to the casinos. She then racked up $85,000 in debt on her 14 credit cards. She was forced to file for bankruptcy. Not once did anyone in the casinos ever ask this 60-year-old grandmother if she had a problem with gambling. Instead, besides the free rooms and meals at the casino, she was also bombarded with marketing mailings. "They know you have no control," she said. "They do everything they can to lure you in" [NGISC, 1999, chap. 4, p. 9].

Women get started down the path to compulsive gambling in a variety of ways. Escape from emotional pain, as in Mary's story, appears to be a dominant motivator. In a pioneering study of women in GA, Lesieur (1987) found that two major reasons for escape reported by over half the women interviewed (*n* = 50) were "escape from memories of parental upbringing and escape from troubled husbands and loneliness" (p. 234). In this sample, 40 percent of the women grew up in homes where one or both parents were addicted to alcohol or gambling. Having "troubled husbands" was a reality for 60 percent of the women, who were married to alcoholics (35 percent), drug abusers (10 percent), and compulsive gamblers (15 percent).

Another motivation for women to gamble compulsively may be desire to escape the social stereotypes and economic limitations that are still imposed on many women. As noted in the Queen of Hearts research project (Brown & Coventry, 1997), gambling provides an opportunity to escape the humdrum and pain of daily existence within prescribed "women's roles" and a place where women can participate in decision making (even if it relates only to how to play a nickel slot machine); it also "offers momentary hope . . . and can enhance women's sense of control over their lives" (p. 13). When women feel helpless or overwhelmed, they may understandably turn to a gambling environment that is reasonably safe to enter without a man and that provides social contact, fun (at least initially), excitement, control, and hope for material success.

In the preliminary results from an on-line survey of women in recovery from compulsive gambling (Davis, 2000), many women reported that they started gambling as a way of dealing with the death or loss of a significant family member— for example, a divorce or the death of a parent. Other factors found to be predictive of problem gambling for women in an Iowa sample ($n = 1,011$) included childhood exposure to gambling, frequent marriages and residential moves, lack of religious affiliation, lack of integration into a "conventional community," and service in the armed forces (Hraba & Lee, 1996).

Women report that their experience of gambling dramatically changes over time, frequently in just a few years. Initially, women who become problem gamblers gamble just like everyone else, that is, recreationally. Over time, and particularly after a win, the gambling becomes more intense; the bets are higher; and trips to casinos, card rooms, and horse races begin to be made alone. "I found my friends just didn't want to stay as long or go as often as I did, and besides, I didn't want anyone else to see how much I was betting" (personal communication, August 2000). Women who are escaping through gambling start spending more and more time relying on the action and the adrenaline high to get away from their troubles (Lesieur & Blume, 1991b). Irrationally chasing the inevitable losses by increasing her gambling leads to progressive deterioration in all areas of a woman's life. Instead of having just the original problems to deal with, women problem gamblers have compounded their troubles. A final "hopeless" stage occurs when the woman knows she can't retrieve her losses and may recognize that she is out of control, but has given up caring, so continues to gamble. As Lesieur and Rosenthal put it in their chilling description of this final stage, "like laboratory animals with electrodes planted in their pleasure center, they gamble to the point of exhaustion" (1991, pp. 14–15).

Costs and Consequences of Women's Compulsive Gambling

Compulsive gambling incurs financial, social, emotional, health, and spiritual costs. Financial debt is the cost that usually comes to mind with compulsive gambling, and although it is likely to be staggering, other costs may be even more devastating. By learning about these typical costs, clinicians will be more alert to areas of their client's life that may need attention, and a woman problem gambler will be better able to "universalize" her predicament. To the extent possible, the information presented here applies specifically to women; unfortunately, many of the research findings are not broken down by gender.

Financial Costs

Financially, the average amount of gambling-related debt for women entering GA was $24,883, but lifetime gambling-related debts for both genders averaged $61,000 ($25,000 median) in Wisconsin and $215,406 ($45,000 median) in Illinois (Lesieur, 1998a). Although there is no gender breakdown of results in Lesieur's report (1998b) of 394 GA members (78 percent male, 22 percent female) from Illinois, Wisconsin, and Connecticut, 223 out of the 394 admitted stealing to finance gambling, for a total of over $30 million, or an average of $76,309 (four stole over $1 million). An earlier study of fifty women in GA (Lesieur, 1987) found that 68 percent of the women used illegal means to finance their gambling, most commonly check forgery, embezzlement, running illegal gambling operations, passing bad checks, and prostitution.

It is not surprising that financial problems lead to legal problems and bankruptcy. The NGISC (1999) found that 19.2 percent of the pathological gamblers, both genders combined, reported filing bankruptcy, compared to a rate of 4.2 percent for nongamblers. Other typical problems that develop include using the family's resources to finance gambling; not paying rent, mortgage, or other bills; borrowing from family, friends, and their own children; pawning anything and everything of value; spending entire paychecks; and being locked into the extremely high interest rates of ready-loan companies. Not surprisingly, an array of social problems accompanies this state of affairs.

Social Costs

Social costs usually start with the gradual ripping apart of the fabric of family life, eventually to leave only a few threads of mistrust, isolation, and guilt. This is the inevitable cost for women who are out of control with their gambling and for women who have a partner who is out of control with his or her gambling. A compelling description of what happens to families who have a compulsive gambler can be gleaned from the Gam-Anon checklist, Are You Living with a Compulsive Gambler? (see Exhibit 5.1).

The following is an account from GA that describes the costs to gamblers and their families in the late stages: "They are physically and psychologically exhausted with a feeling of hopelessness and helplessness. They are heavily in debt, alienated from everyone, on the verge of divorce, and welcome nowhere. One-fourth of them are about to be arrested. Depression and suicidal thoughts and attempts are fairly common at this time. It is not known how many complete suicide. It is

EXHIBIT 5.1. GAM-ANON QUESTIONNAIRE:
ARE YOU LIVING WITH A COMPULSIVE GAMBLER?

1. Do you find yourself haunted by bill collectors?
2. Is the person in question often away from home for long unexplained periods of time?
3. Do you feel that he or she cannot be trusted with money?
3. Does he or she promise faithfully to stop gambling; beg, plead for another chance, yet gamble again and again?
4. Does he or she borrow money to gamble with or to pay gambling debts?
5. Have you noticed a personality change in the gambler as his or her gambling progresses?
6. Have you come to the point of hiding money needed for living expenses, knowing that you and the rest of the family may go without food and clothing if you do not?
7. Do you search the gambler's clothing or go through his wallet when the opportunity presents itself, or otherwise check on his or her activities?
8. Does the gambler hide his or her money?
9. Does the gambler lie sometimes compulsively, avoid any discussion of his or her debts, or refuse to face realities of the situation?
10. Does the gambler use guilt induction as a method of shifting responsibility for his or her gambling upon you?
11. Do you attempt to anticipate the gambler's moods, or try to control his or her life?
12. Do you feel that your life together is a nightmare?

Source: From *Sharing Recovery Through Gamblers Anonymous* (p. 86), by Gamblers Anonymous, 1999, Los Angeles: Author. Reprinted with permission.

at this time they see only four options: suicide, imprisonment (others controlling), running or seeking help. They still have the urge to gamble" (Gamblers Anonymous [GA], 1999a, p. 108).

Women compulsive gamblers in GA are more likely than men to be single, separated, or divorced. Like alcoholic or drug-addicted women, they are less likely than men to receive familial pressure to get help and have fewer social supports during recovery (Davis, 1996; Lesieur & Blume, 1991b). For both genders, the divorce rate is extremely high: 53.5 percent of identified pathological gamblers report having been divorced, compared to 18.2 percent of nongamblers and to 29.8 percent of low-risk gamblers (NGISC, 1999). Other social costs include demonstrated links between expanded gambling and homelessness, increases in domestic violence, and abuse and neglect of children. The NGISC (1999) reports that leaving children in the parking lot in the Foxwoods casino (the Mashantucket Pequots facility in Connecticut, which is the largest casino in the world) became so commonplace that management posted signs warning that such incidents would be reported to police.

Social costs to the women of specific racial-ethnic groups and cultural communities are difficult to assess because of the lack of empirical research relating specifically to compulsive gambling in minority communities (Blaszczynski, Huynh, Dumlao, & Farrell, 1998; Cozzetto & Larocque, 1996; NGISC, 1999). For example, although tribal gambling in the United States accounted for $6.7 billion in revenues in 1997, information about the social costs of gambling to Native American women is nonexistent to date. While noting the importance of casinos to the economic development of reservations, Cozzetto (1995) (one of the few writers on this topic) implores Indian leaders to address what he deems a significant and alarming increase in pathological gambling behavior in Minnesota's Native American population.

Health Costs

There is very little documentation of health costs due to gambling, although there are indications that this may be an important issue. Neither the constant stress of problem gambling nor the diminished resources for food and health care promote physical health (Brown & Coventry, 1997). In a recent Australian study of a large treatment population (Crisp et al., 2000), women were 1.47 times more likely than men to report having physical symptoms associated with gambling. The NGISC (1999) reports that 29.6 percent of the pathological gamblers surveyed state that their health was poor or fair in the past year compared to 21 percent of nongamblers and 12.3 percent of low-risk gamblers.

Although no research was found to address spiritual health and well-being, anecdotal evidence indicates that a woman's spiritual life suffers as much as all the other areas; attendance at organized religious services and other spiritual practices tends to drop dramatically as the focus of the problem gambler narrows to the next bet.

Concurrent Disorders

Which comes first, problem gambling or a concurrent disorder associated with problem gambling (such as substance misuse, antisocial personality disorder, anxiety disorders, mood disorders, and attention deficit disorders)? More and better gender-specific research is needed to answer that question. From the few studies available, it appears that women who are compulsive gamblers have concurrent problems with depression, boredom, anxiety, stress, and escapism (Brown & Coventry, 1997; Lesieur & Blume, 1991b).

According to the National Research Council (1999), substance use disorders are associated with both progression to problem gambling and subsequent pathological gambling (without regard to gender). The rate of lifetime substance use disorders among pathological gamblers ranges from 25 percent to 63 percent. In a general population study in St. Louis, problem gamblers were three times more likely than nongamblers to meet criteria for depression, schizophrenia, alcoholism, and antisocial personality disorder.

Attempted suicide and suicide may be a real threat. Although not gender specific, various studies indicate that up to 75 percent of compulsive gamblers in treatment populations suffer from depression; 61 percent report suicidal ideation, and over 22 percent have made actual suicide attempts (Blaszczynski, 1995). According to the National Council on Problem Gambling, the suicide rate for pathological gamblers is higher than for any other addictive disorder (NGISC, 1999). At a minimum, shame, guilt, and remorse are constant companions, making it even more difficult for a woman problem gambler to seek help.

Obtaining Help

Unfortunately, needing help and getting help are often two different things when it comes to problem gambling. As the National Research Council reports, "the need to provide treatment for pathological gambling has not been widely recognized" (1999, chap. 6, p. 12). Most health insurers and managed care providers do not reimburse for treatment of pathological gambling. State helplines are now operating in only thirty-five of the forty-seven states that have some type of legalized gambling. About half of these states support some type of treatment with public funding, but the level of funding is miniscule compared to the amount of income the state receives from gambling enterprises. For example, in Minnesota in 1997, treatment allocations for gambling made up .5 percent of the state's income from gambling; in New York in 1998, treatment allocations were .1 percent of the state's income from gambling (National Research Council, 1999). The majority of states do not receive even this paltry level of funding for treatment. It is no wonder that Lesieur (1998a) concludes that "legislatures and the gaming industry are paying lip service to the problem" (p. 165).

Given this current state of affairs, it becomes even more important that helping professionals become knowledgeable about compulsive gambling and be willing to address gambling problems that may exist within the client population they are serving.

Conceptual Models of Gambling Problems

The question "Why can't she just stop?" haunts every woman who is trying unsuccessfully to stop gambling and every family member who cannot understand her inability to stop. Researchers, academics, and helping professionals have answered this question with a variety of explanatory models that are often the subject of heated debate and controversy.

Addiction or Disease Model

By far the most popular explanation in the United States is that compulsive gambling is an addiction or disease, and that is why a woman in the throes of compulsive gambling has trouble quitting. The *DSM-IV* uses dependence criteria (tolerance, withdrawal, loss of control, and preoccupation) to describe the typical damage or disruption caused by excessive gambling. However, this explanation is controversial, because pathological gambling is classified under impulse-control disorders in the *DSM-IV* even though impulsivity is not directly addressed in the criteria (Steel & Blaszczynski, 1998).

Biogenetic Model

Howard Shaffer (1999) from the Harvard Medical School's Division on Addictions and other scientists are looking for a "gold standard" such as neurogenetic or biobehavioral markers that are independent of a woman's behavior to explain why she cannot seem to stop gambling. He cites encouraging recent research indicating that dopaminergic and serotinergic brain functions are altered in pathological gamblers (Berg, Sodersten, & Nordin, 1997; DeCaria, Begaz, & Hollander, 1998) and that biogenetic vulnerabilities have been identified among pathological gamblers (Comings, 1998). Alan Leshner, director of the National Institute for Drug Abuse, declares that "addiction is, at its core, a consequence of fundamental changes in brain function" (Leshner, 1997, p. 46). However, until a gold standard is established as to what these changes are that qualify as addiction, Shaffer (1999) invites us to approach the issue "with a substantial dose of scientific skepticism and uncertainty" (p. 1448).

Feminist Model

A feminist explanation of "why she can't just stop" incorporates a wider social context of analysis, one which recognizes that the gender and economic disadvantage of women plays a part in structuring the potential gambling problem.

Using a feminist methodology and analysis, Sarah Brown and Louise Coventry (1997) launched a community-based research project in Victoria, Australia, called Queen of Hearts, the results of which led them to conclude that women compulsive gamblers may be the victims of social stereotypes and the economic and gender limitations imposed on women.

Behavioral Model

Behavioral approaches explain gambling as a learned maladaptive behavior with accompanying distorted thoughts, which can be unlearned through techniques derived from learning theory (Blaszczynski, 1995). Behaviorists would note that when women gamble it produces states of excitement, dissociation, and increased heart rate, and occasionally a win. According to Blaszczynski (2000, p. 4), "wins, delivered at variable ratios that are resistant to the effects of extinctions, produce states of excitement described as equivalent to a 'drug-induced high' . . . and through second order conditioning, gambling cues elicit an urge to gamble, which results in a habitual pattern of gambling." In effect, the gambler has been on a partial reinforcement schedule just as in a classical conditioning experiment. Thus a woman who "can't just stop" would be viewed as being in the conditioned grip of repeated pairings between the arousal of the "high" and the gambling environment.

Cognitive Model

Cognitive models would explain "why she can't just stop" as the result of developing irrational cognitive schemas in response to early and repeated wins in gambling. These include illusions of control, biased thinking, the attribution of human qualities to gambling devices, and erroneous beliefs about the nature of randomness (Blaszczynski, 2000; Turner, 2000). For example, in Delfabbro and Winefield's Australian study (2000) of regular slot machine gamblers ($n = 20$) drawn from the general community, 75 percent of the gambling-related cognitions were found to be irrational.

Implications of the Conceptual Models

Perhaps each of these conceptual frameworks can give us a clue to understanding why a woman "can't just stop." However, other than the feminist explanation, the models are not based on studying women specifically. Mark and Lesieur (1992) point out the dramatic exclusion of women and other populations (Asians, Blacks, Hispanics, gay, lesbian) from the existing literature on pathological and problem gambling, concluding that "it is time for professionals in the field to rethink their conceptualization of problem gambling in terms of the various subgroups within the population-at-large, and *not* just the dominant culture" (p. 561). Regardless of this issue and the differences in these conceptual frameworks, all would agree that women who are out of control with their gambling behavior are at major risk for an array of devastating problems, and need help.

Assessment and Treatment Issues

To find out if a woman is experiencing gambling problems, helping professionals must be prepared to ask a few questions. This sounds simple, but there may be barriers that interfere with actually asking those questions: denial that gambling can even be a problem, a belief that screening interferes with building a therapeutic relationship, and a reluctance to delve into an area where the counselor may not feel adequately trained (Sheperd, 1996). The National Research Council (1999) identifies additional barriers as (1) the unwillingness of clients to get help in this area, (2) lack of health insurance coverage and lack of insurance recognition of professionals as qualified providers of gambling treatment, (3) lack of state funding, and (4) a perception that treatment is or may be ineffective. Finally, negative attitudes about a person who "throws her money away" or "puts her family in jeopardy" may prevent even the beginning of a therapeutic alliance.

In order for a clinician to be helpful, he or she must first become knowledgeable about all facets of problem gambling. Next comes a growing conviction that it's important to establish a therapeutic environment in which a woman's gambling problems can be brought into the light of day. Staff training is essential for overcoming these barriers. For training and resource materials, state problem gambling councils may be able to provide assistance and the names of the closest certified gambling counselor. The GA website lists meetings available in each state, and the Internet has a wealth of gambling resources and information. (To find your closest state council, contact the National Council on Problem Gambling at 800-522-4700, or see their website at http://www.ncpgambling.org/.)

"Resistance" Versus Self-Determination

It is important to keep in mind that in the case of gambling, the main source of information about the behavior is self-report from the woman herself. There is no urine drug screen or even typical patterns of withdrawal symptoms that might confirm recent use or indicate the severity of the problem. Many sources in the literature focus on the gambler's "uncanny ability to deceive relatives and clinicians, at least in the short run" (Blanco, Ibanez, Saiz-Ruiz, Blanco-Jerez, & Nunes,

2000, p. 401). In the alcohol and drug field as practiced in the addiction or medical model in the United States, this behavior is commonly interpreted as resistance and denial. Gathering collateral information from friends, spouses, partners, and relatives is recommended in order to confront the person with their behavior and "break down" the denial.

In contrast, a motivational interviewing model or a solution-focused therapy model would interpret the "resistance" of the gambler (alcoholic, addict) as a natural product of a confrontational environment (Berg & Miller, 1992; Miller & Rollnick, 1991). Advocates of these models prefer interviewing strategies that engage the client in formulating her own goals for change and that stay congruent with the client's process of change. In these models, the therapist is allied with the goals the client thinks will be helpful, even if these goals don't initially include stopping gambling.

Initial Questions

This section will focus on initial questions the clinician can ask so as to open up the therapeutic conversation to include problem gambling. To help build trust and increase candidness, clinicians would do well to conduct an assessment that is collaborative in nature, and in the spirit of concerned curiosity.

It is helpful to ask permission from the client to explore the area of gambling; for example, "I'm wondering how gambling activities or the gambling of someone in your family may play into what we've been discussing. Could I ask you a few questions about that?" If the woman states she does not gamble and no one in her family gambles, then fine, go on to another area of inquiry. If she does gamble problematically or has a problem with someone in her family around gambling but is not ready to discuss it, this opening question signals that you are ready when she is.

If the woman agrees to discuss her gambling, there are several questions that have aided clinicians in identifying gambling problems (Minnesota Institute of Public Health, 2000):

1. Have you ever borrowed money in order to gamble or cover lost money?
2. Have you ever thought you might have a gambling problem, or been told that you might?
3. Have you ever been untruthful about the extent of your gambling, or hid it from another?
4. Have you ever tried to stop or cut back on how much or how often you gamble?

Answering yes to any one of these questions suggests a problem and indicates further exploration. Although each yes indicates increased likelihood of a gambling problem, no one or two questions can diagnose the majority of those who experience gambling problems.

There are two other questions, developed from the *DSM-IV* criteria, that have high sensitivity (.99, the proportion of pathological gamblers who test positive) and high specificity (.91, the proportion of nonproblem gamblers who test negatively) (Johnson et al., 1997). These are as follows:

1. When you gamble, have you ever felt the need to bet more and more money?
2. Have you ever had to lie to people important to you about how much you gambled?

According to Johnson et al. (1997), answering yes to one or both of these questions classifies the respondent as a pathological gambler. Considering that most gambling screens do better at classifying nonpathological gamblers than pathological gamblers ("Screening for Pathological Gambling," 1997), it seems more reasonable to assume that a yes answer to either of these two questions is an indication that there may be a problem and that more needs to be explored.

Clinicians can give clients the opportunity to participate in a self-diagnosis by employing the user-friendly Gamblers Anonymous Twenty Questions (shown in Exhibit 5.2) or Gam-Anon's Are You Living with a Compulsive Gambler? (Exhibit 5.1) or by converting the *DSM-IV* criteria into questions.

Screening and Diagnosis

Once it appears that the client is having problems with gambling, it may be helpful to identify a certified gambling counselor or a treatment program that could further assess the situation and make recommendations for specific gambling treatment. Most state problem gambling councils have lists of the certified counselors and treatment facilities that are available in each state.

Many treatment professionals use the SOGS (Lesieur & Blume, 1991b) to screen women and men for pathological gambling. The SOGS is a twenty-item screen that is widely used in research and epidemiological studies and has good reliability and validity in clinical work. The clinical cutoff score for "probable pathological gambler" is five. The severity of the gambling problem is commonly assessed by the number of SOGS questions answered yes and by considering the time spent and the money lost on gambling. Questions include such items as "Have people criticized your betting or told you that you had a gambling problem?" and "Have you ever hidden betting slips, lottery tickets, gambling money, IOUs, or other signs of betting or gambling from your spouse, children or other important people in your life?"

EXHIBIT 5.2. GAMBLERS ANONYMOUS
TWENTY QUESTIONS FOR SELF-DIAGNOSIS.

1. Did you ever lose time from work or school due to gambling?
2. Has gambling ever made your home life unhappy?
3. Did gambling affect your reputation?
4. Have you ever felt remorse after gambling?
5. Did you ever gamble to get money with which to pay debts or otherwise solve financial difficulties?
6. Did gambling cause a decrease in your ambition or efficiency?
7. After losing did you feel you must return as soon as possible and win back your losses?
8. After a win did you have a strong urge to return and win more?
9. Did you often gamble until your last dollar was gone?
10. Did you ever borrow to finance your gambling?
11. Have you ever sold anything to finance gambling?
12. Were you reluctant to use "gambling money" for normal expenditures?
13. Did gambling make you careless of the welfare of yourself or your family?
14. Did you ever gamble longer than you had planned?
15. Have you ever gambled to escape worry or trouble?
16. Have you ever committed, or considered committing, an illegal act to finance gambling?
17. Did gambling cause you to have difficulty in sleeping?
18. Do arguments, disappointments or frustrations create within you an urge to gamble?
19. Did you ever have an urge to celebrate any good fortune by a few hours of gambling?
20. Have you ever considered self-destruction or suicide as a result of your gambling?

Source: Gamblers Anonymous. (September 1999). [*Combo Book*] (pp. 15–16). Los Angeles: Author.

Once screening and clinical questions indicate probable pathological gambling, the next step in the addiction or medical model is a formal diagnosis. Although there is no standard way of doing this, most clinicians rely on the *DSM-IV* criteria. It is important to note that the only exclusionary criterion for the diagnosis of pathological gambling in the *DSM-IV* is the presence of a manic episode. According to Blanco et al. (2000), there are new semistructured clinical interviews (based on *DSM-IV* criteria) that are being developed.

In other models (solution focused, feminist, GA), the gambling problem is best assessed and diagnosed by individuals themselves. For example, GA (2000, p. 1) states that "people seek help when they have reached a personal low in their lives, and only the individual sufferer knows when that point has been reached." In the feminist approach as outlined in the Queen of Hearts research project (Brown &

Coventry, 1997), it is important for women to be permitted to "make their own evaluation about where their behavior could be placed on a continuum, based on their perceived level of control" (p. 9). The solution-focused method of assessing addictions is "atheoretical and client-centered," which roughly translates to helping the client conceptualize her unique complaints and needs rather than rely on a formal screening or diagnostic tool (Berg & Miller, 1992, p. 8).

Referral to Gamblers Anonymous

In many areas, there are no readily available certified gambling counselors or formal treatment programs for gambling. Or, even if there are, the woman may refuse this resource. Clinicians may have to rely on their own knowledge and skills to help the problem gambler. When that is the situation, it is especially important to introduce the client to GA as a potential resource.

GA is a twelve-step mutual-help program of men and women "who share their experience, strength and hope with each other that they may solve their common problem and help others to recover from a gambling problem" (GA, 2000, p. 2). The GA program acknowledges Alcoholics Anonymous (AA) as a guide and foundation, and its organizational principles and twelve steps of recovery are very similar. As is customary in twelve-step groups, the final "diagnosis" is left up to the person. The criteria for membership is not a diagnosis but "a desire to stop gambling" (GA, 2000, p. 2). When a person has reached that point, abstinence from all gambling is deemed a necessary goal.

GA is run entirely by recovering compulsive gamblers who volunteer their time to be sponsors, chair meetings, arrange for meeting places, secure GA literature, and respond to requests for help day and night. Helping professionals need to know the following facts about GA: (1) there are no dues or fees; (2) GA meetings are available in all fifty states, and there are on-line meetings on the Internet; (3) a fundamental principle is that the help offered by GA "can be effective only when it is asked for and open-mindedly accepted by the newcomer" (GA, 2000, p. 1); and (4) GA is run by recovering compulsive gamblers, not paid professionals.

Although GA is "probably the most popular intervention for pathological gambling" (Blanco et al., 2000, p. 402), like its counterpart AA it is not without its critics. (See Davis & Jansen, 1998, for an analysis of the criticisms aimed at AA.) Some of the criticism stems from helping professionals' viewing GA as an alternative treatment model, which implies that there is "service delivery" through regular meetings in the same place at the same time. To the contrary, GA is a mutual-help organization that is run by recovering gamblers, takes place in various hospitable locales (which can change), and may be implemented a little differently across groups. Like AA, it is fundamentally a spiritual program, not a service delivery program. Eliminating gambling is only the first step to recovery; the rest of the twelve steps involve addressing "character defects," such as "lying, stealing, avoiding reality and escaping into a dream world, or sometimes indulging in all three," and building a life based on spiritual principles (GA, 1999b, p. 3).

GA is sometimes perceived as a White, middle-class male organization that is not friendly to women. This may still be the case in some areas, but it appears that the landscape is changing rapidly as more women seek help for gambling problems. For example, even though GA started in Arizona in 1973, "For the first 18 years, a few women walked through the doors . . . and left. By their own admission, the men didn't quite know what to do with them. The women were told they hadn't gambled long enough; they hadn't lost enough to be real gamblers. They didn't play real games. Their tears and their stories were ridiculed. They were 'hit' on, 'let's go for coffee . . . at my place, baby. . . .' They didn't stay. The men said, 'Women just don't seem to have what it takes to stay in recovery'" (Arizona Council on Compulsive Gambling, 2000).

The year 1992 marked a change in Arizona, when one woman (Marilyn L.) started a "women preferred" GA meeting in her home. Although the meeting struggled in the beginning, by 1999 there were three "women preferred" meetings out of the nineteen GA meetings in the Phoenix area. The Arizona Council estimates that women now make up about 40 percent of the GA meeting attendance.

Preliminary responses to an on-line survey of recovering women (Davis, 2000) support the idea that "times are changing," but a gender barrier can still exist. Some survey respondents noted barriers: "When I came into GA in 1991, the men didn't think slot players were real gamblers," and "I'm a woman, so they ignored me the first three months." In contrast, many of the women reported that they felt welcomed: "Although I was the only woman, I felt welcomed," "I did not feel alone," "They understood my problem as no one who is not a compulsive gambler ever will," "When I finally began attending regularly, I felt welcomed in every way. . . . Mostly, I felt that I belonged somewhere."

How well does GA work? Members of GA will readily admit that "attending GA ruins your gambling," but whether participating in meetings makes a significant impact on long-term abstinence is not known (National Research Council, 1999). As is true of studies of AA, serious methodological problems arise from the voluntary, anonymous self-selection of GA membership. One study (Stewart & Brown, 1988) indicates that total abstinence from gambling was reported by only 8 percent of the GA members studied one year after their first attendance, and by only 7 percent after two years. In contrast, Taber, McCormick, Russo, Adkins, and Ramirez (1987) found that attending GA was helpful in maintaining abstinence: 74 percent of the abstinent gamblers in their sample attended at least three GA meetings in the prior month, compared with only 42 percent of those who continued to gamble. There is some evidence that GA attendance combined with professional help may improve outcomes (Blackman, Simone, & Thoms, 1989; Lesieur & Blume, 1991a). Clearly, more research, particularly gender-specific research, is needed.

Gam-Anon is a mutual-help twelve-step program for spouses, family, and friends of compulsive gamblers. The purpose of Gam-Anon is to help individuals involved with a compulsive gambler find help for the devastation, bitterness, resentment, stress, and tensions that come with that relationship while the gambler is "out practicing." The members offer practical suggestions for living with or without the compulsive gambler, and guides for building and maintaining a more satisfying, spiritual life. The 1999 edition of *Sharing Recovery Through Gamblers Anonymous,* states that "the majority of Gam-Anon members are wives of compulsive gamblers, since most members of GA are married males" (GA, 1999a, p. 85). Because the number of female GA members is increasing, the balance may change in Gam-Anon as well.

At a minimum, the members of these mutual-help programs can offer acceptance on a deep level to persons who are usually isolated from their families and shamed by their inability to stop gambling. GA offers hope of recovery to a person who is most likely hopeless. For these reasons alone, it is helpful for the clinician to make a referral to GA, giving the client a brief summary of the purpose of the meetings and some preparation as to how to locate the meetings and how they are conducted.

Models of Treatment and Recovery

Although women are known to seek professional help at twice the rate of males, this is not the case for women problem gamblers. Volberg (1997) found that treatment programs in five states had between 86 to 93 percent male patients, despite data that at least one-third of all problem gamblers are women. Based on a review of the literature, Crisp et al. (2000) suggest several reasons for this discrepancy: women are less likely to be routinely assessed for gambling problems by health or welfare professionals; existing programs have failed to consider important issues for women, such as child care, sexual assault, and domestic violence; and treatment programs designed for men may not have the expertise or resources to treat women effectively. Unfortunately, much of the research into treating problem gamblers is based on all-male samples or has failed to analyze gender differences. The treatment and intervention strategies that have been developed for problem gamblers are largely untested, have not been subjected to any kind of rigorous empirical research, and may not generalize to the specific needs of women.

As noted by the National Research Council (1999, chap. 6, p. 1), "given the lack of national attention to the treatment of pathological gambling, it is difficult to estimate the scope of intervention services available in the United States."

Most approaches to gambling treatment in the United States borrow strategies from the treatment of substance use disorders utilizing the addiction or disease model. Consequently, abstinence is favored as a goal, in spite of recent findings that indicate long-term controlled gambling is "not an uncommon outcome nor one that is necessarily associated with an increased probability of relapse" (Blaszczynski & Silove, 1995, p. 195). It is also important to recognize that recovery from compulsive gambling can take place without any formal treatment—that is, there can be natural "spontaneous" recovery, or recovery attained solely from participating in a mutual-help group such as GA.

The following sections will describe several models that have been used to help compulsive gamblers and what is known about their treatment effectiveness. Although these models are separated for the purpose of clarity in this text, there is a movement toward a more eclectic approach that combines many different strategies. For example, Blaszczynski and Silove (1995) recommend behavioral desensitization, identification of cognitive distortions, antidepressant medication as needed, marital therapy, addiction counseling with relapse prevention training, and attendance at GA.

Addiction or Disease Model of Treatment

Addiction or disease treatment is by far the most popular model in the United States and has a long tradition of acceptance from the general public and from helping professionals. The first gambling inpatient program began in 1972 at the VA hospital in Brecksville, Ohio, and was modeled on the existing program for alcoholics.

Addiction or disease treatment is an abstinence-based model that follows the traditional multimodal strategies used in treatment of addiction to alcohol and other drugs, including the use of recovering gamblers as peer counselors, emphasis on GA and "working" the steps, education about addiction, family involvement and therapy, exploration of family-of-origin issues, training in coping and problem-solving skills and relapse prevention, and aftercare planning. Having each patient write an autobiography of the significant events in her life and then read it to the group is another frequently used component that was borrowed from alcohol and drug treatment (National Research Council, 1999).

A current example of a residential program using an addiction or disease approach is the Vanguard Compulsive Gambling Treatment Program, in Granite Falls, Minnesota (as described in Rhodes et al., 1997). Assessment includes the

DSM-IV criteria, the SOGS, the GA Twenty Questions, and an assessment of the client's need for gambling "action." The basis of treatment is the GA twelve steps, and clients are expected to work through the first five steps in the month of residential treatment. Although specialized groups address family-of-origin, grief, women's, and men's issues, the program focuses primarily on addiction rather than on underlying issues so as to avoid giving clients the impression that if they "fix" underlying issues, they can gamble again.

The efficacy of the addiction or disease approach is difficult to determine because of a lack of outcome studies (Shaffer, 1999). Evaluations of treatment programs using variations of this model have been plagued by selection bias (outcome questionnaires more likely to be returned by clients who successfully complete the program), fuzzily defined interventions, the unreliability of self-report, and small samples. However, taking all this into consideration, there are several outcome studies that report favorable results for the clients contacted. Six-month and twelve-month outcome data report an abstinence rate of approximately 50 percent of those contacted, and improvement in interpersonal and intrapersonal functioning (National Research Council, 1999; Stinchfield & Winters, 1996). A large study of six treatment programs in Minnesota (all with varying interventions) revealed an abstinence rate of 40 percent at six months among those who reported gambling activity at intake to be once a week or more; 26 percent reported gambling less than monthly (Rhodes et al., 1997).

Cognitive-Behavioral Treatment

Behavioral treatment may involve aversion therapy, imaginal desensitization with relaxation training, and contingency contracting and reinforcement. Cognitive treatments focus on strategies that will reduce irrational thinking and erroneous core beliefs around gambling and will increase problem-solving skills. Combined cognitive and behavioral approaches have demonstrated some success in one of the few controlled investigations (using persons on the waiting list as the control group) in this field (Sylvain, Ladouceur, & Boisvert, 1997). According to the National Research Council (1999), most of the studies of treatment success with cognitive or behavioral strategies or their combinations have had small sample sizes and no control groups, and are not consistent enough to reach any firm conclusions; however, other investigators claim this approach has the best documented efficacy of all the approaches (Blanco et al., 2000). Blanco et al. (2000) suggest behavioral interventions very similar to GA suggestions that may be helpful:

1. Carry the minimum amount of money needed for that day.
2. Turn personal checks and credit cards over to the care of someone else.

3. Require an additional signature to withdraw money from the bank.
4. Voluntarily request a "ban" from frequented casinos or card rooms.
5. Avoid the company of other gamblers.
6. Avoid going to places where gambling is allowed.

Cognitive strategies zero in on the irrational thinking that is typical of compulsive gamblers. The most common errors include a false belief concerning the phenomenon of randomness and the extent to which outcomes can be predicted ("I've put so much money into this machine, it's bound to hit!"), and the personification of the gambling machines or dice (giving them human qualities, as in "Come on baby . . ."). Gender comparisons in one small study ($n = 20$) revealed that women were more likely than men to personify the slot machines (Delfabbro & Winefield, 2000). Other common distortions include (1) the illusion of control—for example, believing that certain conditions, such as a choice of dealer or certain table, choosing a favorite slot machine, walking into a casino through a certain entrance, and so on, will enhance success; (2) flexible attributions, such as transforming losses into "near wins" or predicting a loss after it has happened by identifying "fluke" events that contributed to the loss; (3) availability bias, whereby a person judges the probability of an event based on the sounds of winning around her or on memories of highly publicized winners; and (4) fixation on absolute frequency, whereby the gambler measures the absolute frequency of wins (she wins a lot because she gambles a lot) instead of the relative frequency of wins (she loses more than she wins) (Griffiths, 1994).

The role of the therapist in cognitive therapy is to help the woman identify the irrational thoughts that influence her to continue to gamble, bring them to conscious awareness, monitor them, and replace them with rational and more adaptive thoughts. The assumption is that if the client modifies these erroneous thoughts, the gambling behavior will be reduced or eliminated. There is some research support (Blaszczynski & Silove, 1995) for a cognitive-behavioral approach that uses self-monitoring, addresses cognitive distortions, enhances problem-solving skills by identifying alternative reinforcers, and teaches relapse prevention.

Pharmacological Treatment

Pharmacotherapy is a new approach to treatment based on neurobiological studies that suggest there is neurotransmitter malfunctioning in pathological gamblers. Neurotransmitters that are commonly affected include serotonin, associated with impulsivity and compulsivity; norepinephrine, associated with arousal and novelty seeking; and dopamine, associated with reward and motivation. Although fluvoxamine is the only selective serotonin reuptake inhibitor (SSRI) that has been systematically studied to date (with modest, positive results), experimental placebo-controlled studies of other SSRIs are under way (Blanco et al., 2000). Another promising area is the use of naltrexone, an opioid antagonist that has been used to block the excitement of addictive drugs such as alcohol, cocaine, and heroin. Naltrexone may help mitigate the frequent and intense cravings experienced by compulsive gamblers; new controlled trials of this drug are proceeding (National Research Council, 1999). Drugs such as lithium, used to treat concurrent bipolar disorder, have also been found to decrease compulsive gambling, although it is unclear how much of the success was due to successful treatment of the bipolar disorder.

Other Treatment Models

Alternative treatment approaches may be more a state of mind than a structured treatment protocol. As mentioned earlier, certain beliefs about the nature of problem gambling and the contributing factors run counter to mainstream addiction models and imply a different strategy, such as larger system changes. For example, the Queen of Hearts project in Australia (Brown & Coventry, 1997) elicited suggestions from women for larger system interventions that would be helpful. These included (1) timely access to other supporting services, such as mental health counseling and, especially, financial counseling; (2) access to female counselors because of the need to disclose such problems as physical, sexual, and emotional abuse; (3) easily accessible services in downtown areas as well as in rural environments, where services should be colocated with other supportive services to lessen stigmatization and promote referrals; (4) involvement of all the groups associated with gambling (including financial institutions, gaming operators, and government) in working on solutions, instead of leaving it up to the "victims" to cope; (5) establishing alternative recreations for women in their neighborhoods; and (6) decreasing accessibility of gaming venues—for example, by removing them from shopping centers, strip malls, clubs, and hotels.

Another alternative to the mainstream addiction or disease approach is solution-focused therapy, which treats problem gambling using the same assumptions and techniques that are practiced with any other addiction or problem that a client may bring to the therapeutic environment. Like the feminists, proponents of solution-focused therapy do not see problem gambling as a "unitary disease" that affects everyone in the same way, but instead assist the woman to define her own conception of the problem and goals for change. Specific techniques to find out what is important to the client can involve the following: asking for exceptions to the problem ("When is the last period of time you were not gambling? What was different about that?"); asking scaling questions ("On a scale of one to ten, with ten being the most motivated, where would you rate your motivation to change your gambling patterns?"); and asking questions about coping ("How did you manage to get up and go to work yesterday, after all you've told me about your troubles?"). Such techniques highlight the woman's strengths and past successes in dealing with problems of living, instead of focusing on her deficits or "pathology." She is seen more as a valuable resource for forming goals and finding solutions than as an impaired person with poor judgment. The client's immediate goal is accepted, whether or not it involves gambling (Berg & Miller, 1992).

Recovery Process

"Many compulsive gamblers struggle in the early days of their recovery, through looking back to their past life, burdening themselves with guilt, remorse, money they have lost, opportunities they have missed, or lack of progress at work. Our experience has shown that if we are to recover, these things must be left in the past and we must move on" (GA, 1999b, p. 8).

There is no documentation in the literature on the process of long-term recovery from compulsive gambling for women, but one can speculate that the initial stages mirror the misery and high rate of psychological distress found in the first three months of alcoholism recovery (DeSoto, O'Donnell, & DeSoto, 1989). DeSoto et al. commented, "with a life situation in disarray, suffering a protracted withdrawal syndrome, and experiencing cognitive deficits, it is a challenge indeed for an alcoholic to abstain from the drug that promises at least temporary relief (p. 697)." The financial, social, emotional, health, and spiritual costs from compulsive gambling discussed earlier all come into play, with no escape.

When asked in an on-line survey what has been the hardest part of the recovery process for them, women in recovery from compulsive gambling responded with a variety of issues (Davis, 2000): (1) coping problems ("dealing with my anger, dealing with feelings and life as it comes," "overcoming the guilt," "dealing with the shame about stealing, lying, and cheating," "depression over what I did"); (2) addiction problems ("fighting the compulsiveness," "I liked gambling—it was an escape—sometimes coping is so hard"); (3) practical problems ("not being able to find professional help in my town—no treatment facilities," "going back into making money," "keeping my membership in GA a secret").

When a woman stops gambling, her tried-and-true coping mechanism is gone, with nothing to replace it. This loss occurs just when she starts to be aware of the "wreckage of the past." It may be that one of the most important contributions the clinician can offer at this point is to keep alive the hope that things will get better. Women who do hang on through the difficult early months report satisfaction in several areas (Davis, 2000): (1) self-worth ("holding my head up," "I like me," "the return to being honest," "regaining my self-respect," "getting to know who I am and accepting myself for who I am"); (2) hope ("the best is yet to come"); (3) positive feelings ("loving life again," "peace," "spiritual awareness"); (4) helping others ("involving myself in the GA fellowship," "the ability to be involved in a program that allows me the privilege of helping compulsive gamblers"); (5) resolving past problems ("have own apartment, no debt, emotional freedom").

Clinicians can support these strengths by focusing on what the woman is doing "right" and expanding these qualities to other areas. Because pathological gambling appears to be a chronic condition, ongoing attention to preventing relapse and maintaining recovery is critical.

Conclusion

As noted by Blanco et al. (2000, p. 406), "after more than 10,000 years of the existence of the disorder, the field of pathological gambling research and treatment is still in its infancy." Even in the field's infancy, competing ideologies have sprung up and taken positions. Clinicians have adopted a "more is better" stance and called it multimodal. What little is known is mainly about male, not female problem gamblers. Nevertheless, women problem gamblers are becoming more visible to the general public, research studies have begun to focus on women and to report gender differences, and helping professionals are looking for ways to attend to these problems.

In the future, genetic and brain-imaging studies will help delineate the biological basis of this problem and resolve some of the contested areas around diagnosis and treatment. We can hope that prospective studies will emerge that will tell us more about the course of getting caught in this problem and about the recovery process. Gender differences will be attended to, as will the characteristics of other subgroups that are presently ignored. Social policies will emerge to assist in preventing the problem. In the meantime, clinicians will need to rely on a little bit of knowledge, their compassion, the counseling skills they already possess, and their innate curiosity to find out what this problem is all about for this particular woman.

References

American Psychiatric Association. (1994). *Diagnostic and statistical manual of mental disorders* (4th ed.). Washington, DC: Author.

Arizona Council on Compulsive Gambling. (2000). www.azccg.org.

Berg, I., & Miller, S. (1992). *Working with the problem drinker: A solution-focused approach.* New York: Norton.

Berg, I., Sodersten, E., & Nordin, C. (1997). Altered dopamine function in pathological gambling. *Psychological Medicine, 27,* 473–475.

Blackman, S., Simone, R., & Thoms, D. (1989). The Gamblers Treatment Clinic of St. Vincent's North Richmond Community Mental Health Center: Characteristics of the clients and outcome of treatment. *International Journal of Addictions 24,* 29–37.

Blanco, C., Ibanez, A., Saiz-Ruiz, J., Blanco-Jerez, C., & Nunes, E. (2000). Epidemiology, pathophysiology and treatment of pathological gambling. *CNS Drugs, 13*(6), 397–407.

Blaszczynski, A. (1995, May). Workshop on the assessment and treatment of pathological gambling, presented at the conference of the Australian and New Zealand Association of Psychiatry, Psychology and the Law, Melbourne, as reported in Coman, G., Evans, B., & Burrows, G. (1996). Problem gambling: Treatment strategies and rationale for the use of hypnosis as a treatment adjunct. *Australian Journal of Clinical and Experimental Hypnosis, 24,* 73–91.

Blaszczynski, A. (2000, March). Pathways to pathological gambling: Identifying typologies. *eGambling: The Electronic Journal of Gambling Issues.* Centre for Addiction and Mental Health. Available: www.camh.net/egambling/issue1/feature.

Blaszczynski, A., Huynh, S., Dumlao, V., & Farrell, E. (1998). Problem gambling within a Chinese speaking community. *Journal of Gambling Studies, 14*(4), 359–380.

Blaszczynski, A., & Silove, D. (1995). Cognitive and behavioral therapies for pathological gambling. *Journal of Gambling Studies, 11*(2), 195–220.

Brown, S., & Coventry, L. (1997). *Queen of hearts.* Victoria, Australia: Financial and Consumer Rights Council. Available: home.vicnet.net.au/~fcrc/research/queen/part1.htm.

Comings, D. (1998). The molecular genetics of pathological gambling. *CNS Spectrums, 3,* 20–37.

Cozzetto, D. (1995). The economic and social implications of Indian gaming: The case of Minnesota. *American Indian Culture and Research Journal 19*(1), 119–131.

Cozzetto, D., & Larocque, B. (1996). Compulsive gambling in the Indian community: A North Dakota case study. *American Indian Culture and Research Journal, 20*(1), 73–86.

Crisp, B., Thomas, S., Jackson, A., Thomason, N., Smith, S., Borrell, J., Ho, W., & Holt, T. (2000). Sex differences in the treatment needs and outcomes of problem gamblers. *Research on Social Work Practice, 10*(2), 229–242.

Davis, D. (1996). Women healing from alcoholism: A qualitative study. *Contemporary Drug Problems: An Interdisciplinary Quarterly, 24*(1), 147–179.

Davis, D. (2000). *Women who are taking their lives back from compulsive gambling* [On-line survey]. Available: sswhs.ewu.edu/gambling.

Davis, D., & Jansen, G. (1998). Making meaning of Alcoholics Anonymous for social workers: Myths, metaphors, and realities. *Social Work, 43,* 169–181.

DeCaria, C., Begaz, T., & Hollander, E. (1998). Serotonergic and noradrenergic function in pathological gambling. *CNS Spectrums, 3,* 38–47.

Delfabbro, P., & Winefield, A. (2000). Predictors of irrational thinking in regular slot machine gamblers. *Journal of Psychology, 134*(2), 117–128.

DeSoto, C., O'Donnell, W., & DeSoto, J. (1989). Long-term recovery in alcoholics. *Alcoholism: Clinical and Experimental Research, 13,* 693–697.

Gamblers Anonymous. (1999a). *Sharing recovery through Gamblers Anonymous.* Los Angeles: Author.

Gamblers Anonymous. (1999b). *Gamblers Anonymous: Welcome toward ninety days.* Los Angeles: Author.

Gamblers Anonymous. (2000). *Gamblers Anonymous: A new beginning* (4th ed.). Los Angeles: Author.

Griffiths, M. (1994). The role of cognitive bias and skill in fruit machine gambling. *British Journal of Psychology, 85,* 351–369.

Hraba, J., & Lee, G. (1996). Gender, gambling and problem gambling. *Journal of Gambling Studies, 12*(1), 83–101.

Hulen, D., & Burns, P. (2001). Differences in problem gamblers in Arizona. Arizona Council on Compulsive Gambling. Available: www.azccg.org/about_gambling/action_escp.html.

Johnson, E., Hamer, R., Nora, R., Tan, B., Eisenstein, N., & Engelhart, C. (1997). The lie/bet questionnaire for screening pathological gamblers. *Psychological Reports, 80,* 83–88.

Leshner, A. (1997). Addiction is a brain disease and it matters. *Science, 278,* 45–47.

Lesieur, H. R. (1987). The female pathological gambler. In W. R. Eadington (Ed.), *Gambling research: Proceedings of the Seventh International Conference on Gambling and Risk Taking* (pp. 230–258). Reno: Bureau of Business and Economic Research, University of Nevada.

Lesieur, H. R. (1998a). Costs and treatment of pathological gambling. *Annals of the American Academy of Political and Social Science, 556,* 153–172.

Lesieur, H. R. (1998b, September-October). Social costs of pathological gambling. *Counselor,* pp. 33–34.

Lesieur, H. R., & Blume, S. (1991a). Evaluation of patients treated for pathological gambling in a combined alcohol, substance abuse and pathological gambling treatment unit using the Addiction Severity Index. *British Journal of Addiction, 86,* 1017–1028.

Lesieur, H. R., & Blume, S. (1991b). When Lady Luck loses: Women and compulsive gambling. In N. Van Den Bergh (Ed.), *Feminist perspectives on addictions* (pp. 181–197). New York: Springer.

Lesieur, H. R., & Rosenthal, R. (1991). Pathological gambling: A review of the literature. *Journal of Gambling Studies, 7,* 5–39.

Mark, M. E., & Lesieur, H. R. (1992). A feminist critique of problem gambling research. *British Journal of Addiction, 87,* 549–565.

Miller, W., & Rollnick, S. (1991). *Motivational interviewing: Preparing people to change addictive behavior.* New York: Guilford Press.

Minnesota Institute of Public Health. (1998, December). Gambling problems and women. *Beyond the Odds: A Quarterly Newsletter About Problem Gambling.* Available: www.miph.org/bto/btodec98/1.html.

Minnesota Institute of Public Health. (2000, June). Screening for pathological gambling. *Beyond the Odds: A Quarterly Newsletter About Problem Gambling.* Available: http://www.miph.org/bto/jun00/screen.html

National Gambling Impact Study Commission. (1999, June 18). *Report of the commission.* Washington, DC: U.S. Government Printing Office. Available: www.ngisc.gov/reports/fullrpt.html.

National Research Council. (1999, April 1). *Pathological gambling: A critical review.* Available: www.nap.edu/books/0309065712/html/index.html.

Pavalko, R. M. (1999). Problem gambling. *National Forum, 79*(4), 28–34.

Rhodes, W., Norman, J., Langenbahn, S., Harmon, P., & Deal, D. (1997). *Evaluation of the Minnesota state-funded compulsive gambling treatment programs: Final report, July 21, 1997.* Cambridge, MA: Abt Associates.

Screening for pathological gambling. (1997, July 15). *The Wager: The Weekly Addiction Gambling Education Report 2*(28). Harvard Medical School Division on Addictions. Available: www.thewager.org.

Shaffer, H. J. (1999). Strange bedfellows: A critical view of pathological gambling and addiction. *Addiction, 94,* 1445–1448.

Sheperd, R. (1996). Clinical obstacles in administering the South Oaks Gambling Screen in a methadone and alcohol clinic. *Journal of Gambling Studies, 12,* 21–32.

Steel, Z., & Blaszczynski, A. (1998). Impulsivity, personality disorders and pathological gambling severity. *Addiction, 93,* 895–905.

Stewart, R., & Brown, R. (1988). An outcome study of Gamblers Anonymous. *British Journal of Psychiatry, 152,* 284–288.

Stinchfield, R., & Winters, K. (1996). Gambling treatment outcome study: Treatment effectiveness of six state-supported compulsive gambling treatment programs in Minnesota. Available: www.cbc.med.umn.edu/~randy/gambling/gamtx.htm

Sylvain, C., Ladouceur, R., & Boisvert, J. (1997). Cognitive and behavioral treatment of pathological gambling: A controlled study. *Journal of Consulting and Clinical Psychology, 65,* 727–732.

Taber, J., McCormick, R., Russo, A., Adkins, B., & Ramirez, L. (1987). Follow-up of pathological gamblers after treatment. *American Journal of Psychiatry, 144,* 757–761.

Texas Council on Problem and Compulsive Gambling. (2000, July 7). Women and problem gambling. *e-Update on Problem Gambling News, 1*(23), 1–3.

Turner, N. (2000, August). Randomness, does it matter? *eGambling: The Electronic Journal of Gambling Issues.* Centre for Addiction and Mental Health. Available: www.camh.net/egambling/issue2/research

Volberg, R. (1997, January). *Gambling and problem gambling in Mississippi: A report to the Mississippi Council on Compulsive Gambling* (Social Research Report Series 97-1). Starkville: Mississippi State University, Social Science Research Center.

CHAPTER SIX

WOMEN AND EATING DISORDERS

Susan D. Raeburn

Eating disorders were virtually unknown in undergraduate college classrooms of abnormal psychology in the early 1970s, with the exception of an occasional obscure reference to that mysterious starvation syndrome, anorexia. A frightening photograph of an emaciated girl was offered in the textbook with no seeming recognition that the disorder had any relationship to the crazy eating habits promulgated by weight-loss fads and fashion magazines of the time and already being practiced by countless college women and teenage girls. Fortunately, substantial progress has been made in the understanding and treatment of eating disorders since that time.

This chapter provides a broad overview of the history, prevalence, diagnostic features, etiology, and treatment of the major eating disorders: anorexia nervosa, bulimia, and binge eating disorder. Although there is a rich literature on group and family therapy approaches to eating disorders, this chapter is generally limited to describing individual therapy strategies. It presents a case study of bulimia nervosa that describes an integrative treatment approach, using elements of empirically supported treatments and self psychology principles. The chapter also briefly addresses prevention strategies.

Definition and Scope of the Problem

Although the full-blown clinical manifestations of anorexia nervosa (AN) and bulimia nervosa (BN) remain relatively rare, with estimated prevalence rates of 0.28 to 1.0 percent per hundred thousand for AN and 1.0 to 3.0 percent for BN (American Psychiatric Association [APA], 1994; Hoek, 1995), eating disorder symptoms and syndromes have become increasingly prevalent in industrialized societies in the last three decades (APA, 1994). These disorders also appear to increase in prevalence in non-Western societies as these societies assimilate Western values pertaining to the thin beauty ideal for women. The same process applies with respect to ethnicity and social class, in that signs and symptoms of eating disorders appear to be related to non-Caucasian individuals' degree of assimilation into the Caucasian culture (Wilfley & Rodin, 1995). It is clear that girls and women carry a significantly greater risk of developing these symptoms and disorders than do boys and men. Indeed, an estimated 90 percent of individuals with bulimia and anorexia nervosa are female (APA, 1994).

Descriptions of self-imposed starvation as a form of asceticism have been traced historically to the early religious literature, and the first medical account of anorexia nervosa, by Richard Morton, appeared as early as 1689 (Silverman, 1997). Although early reports of bulimic behaviors (bingeing and purging) may also be found from antiquity to the nineteenth century, bulimia nervosa as it is known today, characterized by a pervasive "fear of fat," was largely unknown until the second half of the twentieth century (Russell, 1997). Indeed, bulimia nervosa first appeared as a disorder in *DSM-III* (1980), but it was not until *DSM III-R* (1987) that the modern "fear of fat" criterion was emphasized. In addition to the academic attention, the public and media consciousness of eating disorders was simultaneously growing, accentuated by the self-disclosure of bulimia histories by such celebrities as actress Jane Fonda, and by the anorexic death of singer Karen Carpenter in 1983.

Binge eating disorder (BED), binge eating without the use of compensatory behaviors, was recently added to the *DSM-IV* appendix for consideration as another distinct eating disorder syndrome (APA, 1994). The estimated prevalence of BED in samples drawn from weight-loss programs averages about 30 percent; females are about 1.5 times more likely to display this pattern than males (APA, 1994; Marcus, 1995). Preliminary studies indicate that African American women are as likely as Caucasian women to binge eat (Wilfley & Rodin, 1995). A prevalence rate of 0.7 to 4.0 percent has been reported in nonpatient community samples (APA, 1994).

Although there is no prevalence rate listed in *DSM-IV* for what are referred to as *eating disorders not otherwise specified* (EDNOS), or what have been called "atypical eating disorders," Fairburn and Walsh (1995) suggest that approximately one-third of those presenting for treatment of an "eating disorder" are subthreshold and would not meet the full criterion for AN or BN.

Although a discussion of the related topic of obesity is well beyond the scope of this chapter, a number of points are worth noting. To begin, simple obesity in and of itself is not considered a psychiatric disorder and thus does not appear in *DSM-IV.* The history of obesity (Brownell, 1995) clearly illustrates that there have been enormous fluctuations in societal judgments of excess weight. The current preoccupation in Western cultures with the "pursuit of thinness" is thus widely understood as time and culture bound. Traditionally there has been a marked separation of emphases between the eating disorder field, influenced primarily by psychology and psychiatry, and the obesity field, influenced predominantly by medicine. The issue of dieting represents the clearest point of contention. Whereas the eating disorder field understands dieting to be a predictable predisposing behavior to the development of an eating disorder in vulnerable women, the obesity field has advocated dieting as a behavioral solution to a significant and growing public health problem (Brownell & Fairburn, 1995).

Despite widespread pressures to diet, U.S. population weights have increased, and there is a growing disparity between actual weights and "ideal" weights, especially for women (Garner, 1997). Indeed, it is estimated that about one-third to one-half of the American people are now obese, up from 25 percent as recently as fifteen to twenty years ago. Women generally have a more variable distribution of body weight over time than men do (Williamson, 1995; "Obesity: Portions out of Control," 2000).

The need for improved integration between the obesity and eating disorder fields is highlighted by the growing recognition of the problem of BED, which affects approximately 5 to 8 percent of the obese in the general population and an estimated 20 to 30 percent of individuals seeking treatment for obesity in university settings (Marcus, 1995).

Diagnoses and Clinical Features

The most recent evolution of the diagnostic criteria for the major eating disorders (AN, BN, and EDNOS, which includes BED) are fully outlined in *DSM-IV* (APA, 1994). What follows are brief summaries of core features of these disorders and some descriptive personality findings.

Anorexia Nervosa

Anorexia nervosa is characterized by refusal to maintain a "minimally normal" body weight for age and height (usually 85 percent of expected weight), fear of fat, a disturbed body image that then unduly influences self-evaluation, and amenorrhea. Once an AN diagnosis has been established, a further classification is made as to whether the behavior is of the restricting or the binge/purge subtype (APA, 1994). The mean age of onset is seventeen years, and the course and outcome may be quite variable. Some anorexics exhibit a full recovery after a single episode; others experience a fluctuating pattern of weight gain followed by relapses; and, sadly, others go through "a chronically deteriorating course of the illness over many years" (APA, 1994, p. 547). The mortality rate for AN is considered one of the highest for psychiatric disorders: it is estimated to be in the range of 6 to 20 percent, usually due to starvation or suicide (Mitchell, Pomeroy, & Adson, 1997).

Various authors (Garner, Vitousek, & Pike, 1997; Strober, 1997; Wonderlich, 1995) have described predictable personality features in anorexics. Strober suggests the following: "high emotional reserve and cognitive inhibition; preference for routine and predictable environments; poor adaptability to change; heightened conformity and deference to others; risk avoidance and dysphoric overarousal by affectively stressful events; excessive rumination and perfectionism" (1997, p. 233). Although Wonderlich (1995) points out that features such as obsessionality, dependency, and introversion may be exacerbated by starvation states, he joins Garner at al. (1997) in citing studies of recovered anorexics in which traits such as conformity to authority, emotional restraint, and risk avoidance remain after many years of weight restoration.

Bulimia Nervosa

Bulimia nervosa is characterized by binge eating and the use of inappropriate compensatory methods to prevent weight gain on the average of at least twice a week for three months. These methods include self-induced vomiting in about 80 to 90 percent of cases, fasting, excessive exercise, misuse of laxatives (in about 30 percent of cases), and misuse of diuretics. A binge is defined as "eating in a discrete period of time an amount of food that is definitely larger than most individuals would eat under similar circumstances" (APA, 1994, p. 545), taking into consideration the context (typical meal versus holiday meal). The definition of what constitutes a "large" quantity has been clinically challenged, as some bulimics perceive any consumption of certain "forbidden foods" as a binge (Walsh & Garner, 1997). The period of time characterizing a binge is generally considered less than two hours. Bingeing usually occurs in secret and is accompanied by a sense of lack of control. Similar to criteria for AN, body shape and weight must "unduly influence" the person's self-evaluation. BN is also subdivided into either purging or nonpurging types. Walsh and Garner (1997, p. 29) caution further that it is sometimes "unclear where the boundary lies between AN in partial recovery and BN" and that the distinctions are often arbitrary.

Most bulimics fall within a normal weight range, although some may be slightly over- or underweight. They are more likely than their peers to have been overweight prior to the onset of the disorder. Some within the normal weight range may actually be underweight relative to their biological "set point" (Garner, 1997). BN typically starts in adolescence or early adulthood with binge eating following a period of dieting. The course of the disorder may be intermittent; times of remission alternate with periods of binge and purge recurrence, or bingeing and purging may become chronic. Although there may be significant variability in functioning, personality features commonly associated with BN include poor impulse control, interpersonal sensitivity, low self-esteem, and low tolerance of frustration (Wonderlich, 1995).

Eating Disorders Not Otherwise Specified

The eating disorder not otherwise specified or "atypical eating disorder" category is used for eating disorders that are subthreshold for AN or BN. Although currently considered an EDNOS in *DSM-IV*, binge eating disorder has commanded increasing attention from researchers as an eating disorder in its own right. The core features of BED are as follows: there are recurrent episodes of binge eating that occur at least two days a week for at least six months; the episodes are characterized by at least three features of marked distress over the bingeing (for example, rapid rate of eating, or feeling uncomfortably full, guilty, and disgusted); there is no regular use of purging behaviors, fasting, or excessive exercise; and symptoms do not occur during episodes of AN or BN (Walsh & Garner, 1997). Studies suggest that people with BED seen in clinical settings have varying levels of obesity but that these individuals report higher rates of depression, anxiety, and other symptoms than do non-BED individuals of equal weight. In weight-loss clinics, these clients are generally more obese and have a history of greater weight fluctuations than non-BED clients (APA, 1994). For a thorough discussion of the important diagnostic issues, see Walsh and Garner (1997), Beaumont (1995), and *DSM-IV* (APA, 1994).

Eating Disorders and Chemical Dependency

Many clients with eating disorders also suffer from other psychiatric problems that complicate the course, prognosis, and treatment of the eating disorder symptoms. Chemically dependent eating-disordered clients often represent a particularly challenging dual-diagnosis subgroup. In addition, controversies continue among clinicians as to how to treat this subgroup effectively.

Comorbidity Between Eating Disorders and Substance Use Disorders

The specificity of the comorbidity between eating disorders and substance use disorders remains unclear because the prevalence of both types of symptoms tends to be elevated in psychiatric patients in general, and the estimates are generally based on patient populations rather than on community samples (Wilson, 1995; Zweben, 1996). Various studies suggest that disturbed eating habits are unexpectedly common among women in treatment for alcohol problems (Wilson, 1995; Peveler & Fairburn, 1990; Goldblum, Naranjo, Bremner, & Hicks, 1992), and alcohol and drug abuse and dependence problems are prevalent among eating-disordered clients (Zweben, 1996; Peveler & Fairburn, 1990; Bulik, 1987; Krahn, Kurth, Demitrack, & Drewnowski, 1992). Krahn et al. report that in a sample of 1,796 college-age women, "Increasing dieting severity was positively associated with increasing prevalence of alcohol, cigarette, and marijuana use and with increasing frequency and intensity of alcohol use" (1992, p. 341). These researchers conclude that the relationship between substance abuse and eating disorders "extends in a continuous graded manner to subthreshold levels of dieting and substance use behaviors" (p. 341).

Reviews generally indicate that the associations between substance abuse and bulimic behaviors are stronger than are those with restricting anorexics, and that dieting-related attitudes and eating disorders may significantly influence the course of substance abuse and dependence disorders (Goldblum et al., 1992; Holderness, Brooks-Gunn, & Warren, 1994; Krahn et al., 1992; Mitchell, Specker, & Edmondson, 1997; Wilson, 1995; Zweben, 1996). As Zweben observes: "eating disorders can precede, coexist with or follow substance use patterns and the variety of possible relationships should be elucidated in the individual case" (1996, p. 364). Therefore, the clinical assessment of women presenting with eating disorders or substance abuse needs to systematically include evaluation for comorbid symptoms.

Eating Disorder as Addiction

Whereas lay people and the recovering alcohol and drug community sometimes equate eating disorders with "food addiction"—because of the obvious similar experiences of "cravings," loss of control, the perceived self-regulatory functions and negative social and personal consequences of the behaviors—eating disorder researchers often dispute the usefulness of that characterization. For example, Wilson

(1995) concludes that these similarities are essentially superficial and that the differences must be accounted for in the treatment of eating disorders. He explains:

> The addiction model prescribes unremitting dietary restraint, featuring absolute avoidance of particular foods (i.e., sugar), highly structured eating patterns, a sense of powerlessness, and reinforcement of a dichotomous thinking pattern. These prescriptions conflict with much of what is now known about the development, maintenance, and modification of binge eating in the case of bulimia nervosa. Those who have attempted to make the 12-Step approach more compatible with the empirical evidence on eating disorders have sought to redefine such core principles as abstinence from particular foods, recasting it as abstention from activities such as binge eating and over exercising; and affirmation of powerlessness, newly interpreting it as the acceptance of body weight and shape. More generic features of 12-Step groups, such as social support, are undoubtedly valuable but not unique to this approach [p. 167].

In contrast, Yeary and Heck (1989) view eating disorders as a type of psychoactive substance abuse, emphasizing the psychophysiological properties of food that affect brain chemistry and alter mood. These clinicians advocate abstinence from certain binge foods for individuals who are unable to moderate their use. Indeed, Overeaters Anonymous (OA), a twelve-step program based on the principles of Alcoholics Anonymous, often advocates complete abstinence from certain foods (such as sugar). Therefore, eating disorder therapists who have been trained using cognitive-behavioral methods that challenge "all-or-nothing" ways of thinking sometimes hesitate to refer eating-disordered clients to OA even though the clients need the social support available at these twelve-step meetings.

Joan Zweben (1996) agrees that it may be counterproductive to apply an adapted twelve-step model as the singular treatment for eating disorders and that integrated treatments remain preferable. Mitchell et al. (1997), for example, describe an intensive, integrative day treatment program for dually diagnosed patients at the University of Minnesota that uses elements of both cognitive-behavioral and twelve-step approaches. As most of the accepted eating disorder treatments were not specifically developed for dually diagnosed clients (indeed, such clients are usually excluded from controlled studies), important research questions remain: (1) Is complete abstinence from certain foods ultimately helpful or hurtful in recovery from eating disorders for this population? and (2) How can empirically supported treatments for eating disorders best be enhanced for practicing (or recovering) alcoholics and addicts? Even within twelve-step approaches, clarification as to what aspects of peer support and program structure are most effective would be useful. For example, informal reports from a small sample of clients attending Food Addicts in Recovery (FA), a relatively recent subgroup of Overeaters Anonymous, suggest that its highly structured approach may be more helpful in normalizing eating patterns and losing weight for some dually diagnosed individuals than traditional OA approaches.

Other Dual Diagnoses

Although a complete discussion of other dual diagnoses is beyond the scope of this chapter, eating-disordered clients often present with comorbid symptoms of depression and anxiety. P. J. Cooper (1995) reports that roughly half the people with eating disorders who are seen in clinics have a lifetime history of major depressive episodes; bulimics (or the bulimic subtype of AN) show a higher rate than restricting anorexics. He suggests that the depressive and anxious (that is, compulsive and obsessional) symptoms in eating-disordered patients are best considered secondary to the primary disturbances of the eating behaviors and related cognitive processes. It has been well established, for example, that psychological and behavioral symptoms of depression and anxiety may be a by-product of the starvation state and remit eventually when normal feeding and weight conditions are resumed (Wonderlich, 1995).

Borderline personality disorder (BPD, in Cluster B) has been shown to be the most predominant of the Axis II diagnoses with respect to bulimia nervosa and the binge/purge subtype of AN; prevalence estimates range between 1.9 to 75 percent and average 34 percent. That is, approximately one-third of the clients with BN or the binge/purge subtype of AN may be expected to present with comorbid BPD. Among restricting anorexics, researchers have found a higher percentage of avoidant, obsessive-compulsive, or dependent personality disorders (in Cluster C) compared to other Axis II disorders (Dennis & Sansone, 1997). As with dually diagnosed chemically dependent clients, the treatment of eating-disordered clients with personality disorders requires specific attention to both problems.

Etiology of Eating Disorders

Despite a diverse and at times conflictual spectrum of theoretical approaches to treatment, there is widespread agreement among researchers and clinicians as to the multifactorial, multidetermined etiology of eating disorders. Within this multidimensional framework, the different models naturally vary in their emphasis and their weighting of factors. Feminist models, for example, see cultural factors and a woman's degree of exposure to them as playing a primary rather than mediating role in the development and maintenance of the disorders (Striegel-Moore,

1995). Cognitive-behavioral models emphasize the interactions between distorted thoughts and beliefs about body shape and weight and extreme dieting behaviors that predispose the individual to binge eating and eventually to purging, thus establishing a self-perpetuating and self-defeating cycle of behaviors (Agras & Apple, 1997; Agras et al., 1992). Psychodynamic, developmental, and self psychology models emphasize self-regulatory deficits and the restorative function of eating-disordered symptoms (Goodsitt, 1997; Kohut, 1984; Sands, 1989). Interpersonal models highlight the role of deficits in interpersonal functioning that predispose the individual to disturbed eating behaviors (Apple, 1999; Fairburn, 1997). Dialectical behavior therapy (DBT), originally developed by Linehan (1993) for borderline personality disorder, has recently been applied to eating disorders as an affect regulation model (Telch, 1997a, 1997b; Wiser & Telch, 1999).

David Garner (1997) explains how these various factors interact to establish eating disorder symptoms. He states: "The symptom patterns represent final common pathways resulting from the interplay of three broad classes of predisposing factors; cultural, individual (psychological and biological), and familial causal factors are presumed to combine with one another in different ways that lead to the development of eating disorders. The precipitants are less clearly understood, except that dieting is invariably an early element" (p. 146). Using this interactive, multidetermined framework, the following sections offer a brief review of cultural, individual, and familial influences implicated in the development of eating disorders.

Cultural Influences

Various aspects of contemporary Western culture's philosophical assumptions, attitudes, and expectations regarding women and their bodies have been implicated in understanding the increase in disordered eating patterns in the past thirty years. Perhaps the most frequently cited aspect is the society's rigid overvaluation of a thin body type as the exclusive standard for female beauty, sexual attractiveness, competence, and success. Striegel-Moore (1995) understands the cultural meaning of thinness as a reflection of the deeply rooted Western philosophy that the body is inferior to the mind, that the body is "passive, untamed, in need of restraint, and feminine; the mind is seen as active, noble, cultured, and masculine" (p. 225). She points out, further, that this philosophy views the human body as "infinitely malleable," whereby weight becomes "a matter of personal choice" (p. 225). Wilfley and Rodin (1995) similarly challenge this philosophy; they say, "The contemporary beauty ideal of 'thinness equals attractiveness' prescribes a body weight that for most women is unrealistically low because of biological and genetic factors. In fact, the body cannot be shaped at will. Genetic factors play a substantial role in limiting one's ability to change body weight and shape. Although the current societal ideal is unrealistic and unattainable for most women, those who do not meet the ideal are often judged to be self-indulgent and lacking in will power" (p. 80). Garner (1997) points out, too, that the actual weights for women of the same age and height as fashion models have steadily increased as the models have become thinner. He cautions that the prevailing body weight and shape standards depicted in the culture "do not even closely resemble the actual body type of the average woman consumer" (p. 149). The cultural prescription for a slender body type results in dieting for many females and, for many who are especially vulnerable, becomes a serious risk factor for eating disorders. This pressure for thinness is particularly pronounced for those in body- and appearance-focused occupations such as dancers, gymnasts, and fashion models (Wilfley & Rodin, 1995).

Other Western cultural factors that have been described as contributory to the development of eating disorders include a female gender socialization that overvalues physical appearance and the role of caretaking, and a power inequity between men and women that further increases women's vulnerability to others' approval, especially during adolescence. Some scholars suggest that shifts in the established beauty ideal toward extreme and unattainable thinness have occurred historically during periods in which women have made political progress and obtained increased personal and economic freedom, thus serving as a way to control and contain women's social goals and sense of empowerment (Striegel-Moore, 1995).

Individual Influences

Individual risk factors for eating disorders may be physical, psychological, or both. Premorbid obesity leading to a subsequent predisposition to dieting has been documented in both anorexia and bulimia. Preexisting affective, anxiety, or personality disorders may increase risk, as does a family history of eating, mood, and substance dependence disorders (APA, 1994). Strober (1997) describes heritable personality traits for both anorexics and bulimics that interact with developmental pressures, sociocultural influences, and life events and that may predispose an individual to eating-disordered behaviors. The previously cited anorexic tendencies toward emotional reserve, compliancy, avoidance of novelty, anxious worry, rumination, and rigidity, for example, are seen as clashing with the normative pressures of adolescent development, which pull for increased emotionality, change, independence, and sociability. Such dispositional traits in bulimics as impulsivity and thrill seeking may similarly interact with developmental and sociocultural pressures, predisposing the individual to dieting or binge eating.

Adverse life events, such as childhood sexual abuse, the death of a loved relative, illness, negative adult sexual experiences, or personal criticism about appearance, may be predisposing factors for either AN or BN (Wonderlich, 1995). Of note is that sexual abuse rates for women with eating disorders are higher than for women in nonpatient community samples but about equal to that for women with other psychiatric diagnoses (Palmer, 1995). Palmer concludes that childhood sexual abuse experiences are "neither necessary nor sufficient causes of clinical eating disorders. They are best viewed as one factor among many that may increase the risk of later disorder, probably via their effects on personality development and self-esteem" (1995, p. 232). Other events that are part of normal development, such as the onset of puberty, leaving home, or starting new relationships, may become precipitating factors as well.

Many authors have examined psychological risk factors for eating disorders from the standpoint of developmental deficits (Goodsitt, 1997; Sands, 1989; Kohut, 1984; Johnson & Connors, 1987). Johnson and Connors suggest that an individual's capacity to self-regulate important functions of the self may be impaired by either under- or overinvolvement by the caregiver, usually the mother. These authors conclude that the anorexic's self-starvation may be an adaptive attempt to defend herself against maternal overinvolvement and that the bulimic's bingeing and purging is a compensation for the pervasive sense of emptiness resulting from maternal underinvolvement.

Susan Sands (1989) describes how problems in the gender self-development of females predispose them to eating disorders. Specifically, she cites the following as areas of concern: distortions in the mirroring of the body self, a lack of idealizable female figures, and the daughter's use as a narcissistic extension of the mother. Building on the ideas of Heinz Kohut (1984) about the restorative function of compulsive eating, Sands says: "The person with an eating disorder has 'given up' on receiving empathic attunement from the caregiving surround and has turned instead to a non-human (and thus more reliable) substitute to find the comfort and inspiration she seeks. Food, of course, is a particularly compelling substitute since it is the first bridge between self and selfobject—the first medium for the transmission of soothing and comfort" (1989, p. 85). In a related vein, Goodsitt (1997) summarizes the psychodynamic view when he writes, "Eating disorders are symptomatic expressions that can occur in a relatively intact or structured psyche and reflect an internal conflict, or can occur in an undeveloped or incomplete mental structure and reflect a disorder of the self. The symptoms of an eating disorder can be either symbolic expressions of psychic aims and defenses (drive-conflict model); symbolic expressions of distorted self and object representations (object relations model); or nonsymbolic, restitutional emergency measures used to stem the tide of disrupted self-states threatened with the loss of cohesion of the self (self psychological model)" (p. 207). Needless to say, a variety of interpersonal problems may result from the developmental deficits described here, and they may become an important focus in treatment.

Familial Influences

Characteristics of eating-disordered families have been described by various authors. Vandereycken (1995) described anorexic families as "consensus-sensitive"—that is, compared to control families, their family organizations were rigid and conflict avoidant, and had interpersonal boundaries that were less clear. The bulimic families were described as "distance-sensitive"; they showed stronger interpersonal boundaries and were less conflict avoidant but also more critical, more chaotic, and less stable. Other descriptions of eating-disordered families have noted that there are often odd eating habits as well as a strong emphasis on appearances and weight (Cooper, Z., 1995). Strober (1995) notes that in contrast to the interactions in restricting anorexic families, which have been characterized as avoidant of intense or novel experiences and conflict, the families of patients who binge eat tend to be characterized by emotional lability, social extraversion, and stimulus seeking in combination with angry and hostile family transactions showing little affection. Strober and Humphrey (1987) further describe the family environments of eating-disordered patients as hindering the development of autonomy, a stable identity, and self-efficacy through disturbed interactions characterized by "enmeshment, poor conflict resolution, emotional overinvolvement or detachment, and a lack of affection and empathy" (p. 657).

◆ ◆ ◆

Although genetically influenced temperament and personality traits may predispose individuals to the development of these disorders, their final expression probably requires the presence of unhealthy family patterns, as described above, in conjunction with sociocultural pressures.

To summarize the interactive processes at work among the cultural, individual, and familial factors identified, Zafra Cooper (1995) states the following: "Whether or not disorder results and whether or not it persists are dependent on the occurrence of circumstances that activate the individual's vulnerability to particular risk factors and on the operation of protective factors. These complex interacting processes unfold over time, and it is a combination of these influences that determines whether an individual follows a path from exposure to a risk factor to the onset of disorder, and whether this disorder then becomes established or even chronic" (p. 199). She emphasizes that understanding these interactive processes is crucial to the development of both primary and secondary prevention efforts as well as improved treatments for eating disorders.

Treatment Strategies

Many controlled clinical trials over the past twenty years have demonstrated that psychological interventions are generally efficacious in reducing eating disorder symptoms (Peterson & Mitchell, 1999; Stein et al., 2001; Wilfley & Cohen, 1997). The majority of these have been outpatient treatment studies and have focused on BN, largely due to difficulties recruiting and retaining anorexics in these treatments: AN is less prevalent than BN; symptoms are often ego syntonic, thereby reducing the anorexic's internal motivation for treatment; and medical complications may become exclusion factors. Inpatient treatments for AN have been more widely studied than outpatient ones, and findings suggest that inpatient behavioral strategies for initial weight restoration are effective (Peterson & Mitchell, 1999). As BED has become better defined, researchers have increasingly developed outpatient treatment applications for BED akin to those for BN (Stein et al., 2001; Telch, 1997a, 1997b; Wilfley & Cohen, 1997; Wilfley et al., 1993; Wiser & Telch, 1999).

Cognitive-behavioral therapy (CBT) has been the most frequently studied and remains the "gold standard" of the empirically based psychological treatments for eating disorders (Agras & Apple, 1997; Agras et al., 1992; Peterson & Mitchell, 1999; Stein et al., 2001; Wilfley & Cohen, 1997; Garner & Needleman, 1997), although interpersonal therapy (IPT) as developed by Klerman and Weissman (1993) and adapted for BN has shown equivalent benefits at one-year follow-up (Apple, 1999; Fairburn, 1997). CBT demonstrates reductions in the frequency of binge eating and purging in BN, averaging about 75 percent; it demonstrates a more modest abstinence rate (the percentage of clients completely free of bingeing and vomiting) of about 40 percent (Peterson & Mitchell, 1999). CBT has also shown significant improvements in related symptoms such as body dissatisfaction, dietary restraint, mood problems, and problems of social functioning (Agras et al., 1992; Peterson & Mitchell, 1999; Stein et al., 2001; Wilfley & Cohen, 1997). Both individual and group therapy formats have been used. CBT has similarly proven helpful in the treatment of BED and, although the conclusion is based on fewer data, AN (Peterson & Mitchell, 1999; Wilfley et al., 1993). Particularly, CBT has been shown to be useful in preventing relapse in weight-restored anorexics (Peterson & Mitchell, 1999).

IPT offers a viable alternative for individuals with BN or BED who do not respond well to direct behavioral directions or whose problematic interpersonal relationships predominate in the development and maintenance of their eating disorders. Few data are available on IPT for AN. Neither CBT nor IPT for BED appear to facilitate weight loss without the addition of behavioral weight-loss interventions (Peterson & Mitchell, 1999). Dialectical behavior therapy (DBT) has only recently been adapted for use with eating disorders, but appears promising with BED (Wiser & Telch, 1999; Telch, 1997a, 1997b).

With regard to pharmacotherapy, generally consistent results from numerous studies indicate the following: (1) CBT is superior to antidepressant medication alone in reducing bulimic symptoms; (2) there is modest evidence that the combination of CBT and fluoxetine (Prozac) may be more effective than CBT alone, but may produce higher dropout rates; (3) fluoxetine in higher doses (60 mg versus 20 mg) has shown significant improvement in eating disorder symptoms, at least in the short run (and longer-term studies are needed); and (4) pharmacotherapy results have been generally poor for AN, in contrast to BN and BED, except for some evidence that psychotherapy and fluoxetine may be useful in preventing relapse after weight restoration; nonetheless, for anorexics, antidepressant medication for comorbid depression and anxiety disorders, such as obsessive compulsive disorder, may be prudent (Peterson & Mitchell, 1999; Bacaltchuk, Trefiglio, deOliveira, Lima, & Mari, 1999; Lennkh, DeZwaan, & Kasper, 1997; Crow & Mitchell, 1994).

While referral to a physician for a medication evaluation is not always necessary, it is always prudent to refer eating-disordered clients for regular physical exams as medical complications can result from their behavioral practices. This is particularly so for anorexics or low-weight bulimics who engage frequently in vomiting or laxative abuse. (See Mitchell et al., 1997, for a discussion of medical problems in eating disorders.)

Despite the incontestable benefit to the pool of knowledge provided by these controlled studies, the generalizability of results to the more diverse population of eating-disordered clients seen in nonresearch settings remains unclear. It is likely that some of the clients seen in clinical practice would have been initially excluded from clinical trials due to comorbid conditions such as substance abuse, or would have been study "dropouts" or treatment nonresponders to brief therapy approaches. This situation has led some researchers and private practitioners to develop integrative approaches that are longer term and not easily formulated into standardized treatment manuals (Garner & Needleman, 1997). As comprehensive technical descriptions of CBT, IPT, and DBT are readily available elsewhere (Agras & Apple, 1997; Apple, 1999; Peterson & Mitchell, 1999; Wilfley & Cohen, 1997; Telch, 1997a, 1997b; Linehan, 1993) and are beyond the scope of this chapter, the current chapter will limit itself to briefly highlighting basic principles of these treatments in the service of describing an integrative strategy for clinical practice that uses elements of these approaches within the context of a psychoanalytic, self psychology therapy (Shane, Shane, & Gales, 1997; Kohut, 1984; Sands, 1991).

Descriptions of Empirically Supported Therapies

Cognitive-behavioral therapy emphasizes an active, highly structured, collaborative approach in a twenty-session outpatient treatment that is generally divided into three stages. The goal of the first stage is to disrupt the self-perpetuating starve-binge-purge cycle and normalize eating patterns using self-monitoring and other behavioral strategies, such as stimulus control. Psychoeducation is routinely offered on matters such as weight regulation, the effects of starvation, and problem solving (Garner, 1997). Stage two emphasizes cognitive restructuring of maladaptive self-talk, attitudes, and beliefs that perpetuate the eating disorder. The last stage teaches relapse prevention strategies to consolidate and maintain the new behaviors (Garner et al., 1997; Agras & Apple, 1997; Agras et al., 1992).

Interpersonal therapy offers a nondirective, noninterpretive approach in a fifteen- to twenty-session outpatient therapy that emphasizes underlying interpersonal problems rather than the eating disorder symptoms per se. The first of three stages identifies the primary interpersonal problem areas that have contributed to the development and maintenance of the eating disorder (for example, grief, interpersonal role disputes, role transitions, or interpersonal deficits). The goal of the middle phase is to support the client in focusing on the interpersonal problems identified, to consider alternatives, and to experiment with ways of changing interpersonal functioning. The final stage reviews progress made in altering interpersonal patterns and explores how the client can continue the work on her own and prevent relapse after termination of the therapy. Discussion of eating behaviors and mood remain tied to the interpersonal context throughout (Apple, 1999; Fairburn, 1997).

Dialectical behavior therapy assumes that dysfunctional behaviors often represent maladaptive attempts at emotion regulation. As recently applied to research in the treatment of BED, a modified form of DBT was offered in a twenty-session group therapy format. Clients were taught new ways to manage their feelings and tension states by learning mindfulness, distress tolerance, and emotion regulation skills (Telch, 1997a, 1997b; Wiser & Telch, 1999; Linehan, 1993). The interpersonal effectiveness component was not included so as not to confound this treatment with IPT. However, this latter component usually teaches skills such as assertiveness and relationship building. Mindfulness teaches clients nonjudgmental, "here-and-now" awareness of their thoughts and feelings, which increases their capacity to observe their internal experience without escalating the feelings. Distress-tolerance skills emphasize open acceptance both of one's affect and of circumstances outside one's control as well as crisis survival techniques such as relaxation, distraction, self-soothing, and evaluating one's options for response. Emotion regulation skills emphasize such elements as self-validation, identification and labeling of affect, clarifying the function of the emotion, and increasing positive affective experiences. See Linehan (1993) and Telch (1997a, 1997b) for a complete description of these components. Preliminary results of the application of DBT to BED are described as encouraging (Wiser & Telch, 1999).

An Integrative Approach for Clinical Practice

Peterson and Mitchell (1999) state, "Although reductions of symptoms in treatment outcome studies are often significant, a large number of people with bulimia nervosa, anorexia nervosa, and binge-eating disorder are not free of symptoms at the end of treatment. In addition, many who improve initially are found to relapse during follow-up. Although research has identified certain therapeutic strategies, such as CBT, that are helpful for a number of individuals, there is clearly a need for alternative, adjunctive, and integrative treatments as well as strategies to identify the most appropriate treatments for specific individuals" (p. 695). Indeed, Garner and Needleman (1997) describe various approaches to the sequencing and integration of treatments for eating disorders.

The goal of an integrated approach is to tailor the treatment to the specific needs of the client over time in a flexible yet thoughtful manner, using proven treatment elements when possible. The current approach draws from psychoanalytic, self psychology principles (Goodsitt, 1997; Kohut, 1984; Shane et al., 1997; Sands, 1991), cognitive-behavioral symptom management techniques (Garner et al., 1997; Agras & Apple, 1997; Agras et al., 1992; Johnson, Connors, & Tobin, 1987), interpersonal therapy (Apple, 1999; Fairburn, 1997), and emotion regulation strategies (Telch, 1997a, 1997b; Linehan, 1993). Adjunctive therapies such as medication, nutrition consultation, group therapy, family therapy, and self-help resources are used as appropriate. For anorexics eighteen years old or younger and living at home, for example, family therapy remains the preferred initial treatment (Garner & Needleman, 1997). Along those lines, Dare and Eisler (1997) recommend the Maudsley model, an interactional systems intervention. Roughly, the integrative therapy approach is divided into early recovery and ongoing recovery stages, although these boundaries may be somewhat fluid at times in any given case. This approach is generally compatible with Stephanie Brown's developmental concept of flexibly tracking the patient's changing relationship with alcohol as he or she recovers (that is, focusing on the "alcohol axis" over time) (Brown, 1985). In eating disorder treatment, the therapist similarly tracks the patient's changing relationship to food and weight. For example, as clients establish abstinence from bingeing and vomiting, the weight/food axis may recede as the central focus of treatment, and other concerns become more prominent. Should relapse occur, the weight/food axis again becomes central.

Early recovery goals include establishing the therapeutic alliance; completing a clinical assessment (see Johnson, 1984, for his Diagnostic Survey for Eating Disorders); enhancing motivation, if necessary (Miller & Rollnick, 1991); increasing new, adaptive eating and interpersonal behaviors while decreasing active symptoms and preoccupation with food and weight; challenging and restructuring distorted cognitions; and improving emotion regulation skills. The focus tends to be on the "here and now." Ongoing recovery represents a consolidation of new behaviors and ways of thinking and a broadening awareness of self-care, interpersonal concerns, and other life issues. The goals are maintenance and generalization of these new behaviors and skills, and relapse prevention. Discussion of the early origins of the maladaptive behaviors, cognitions, core beliefs, and schemas increases in ongoing recovery, as does the analysis of transference, when appropriate. Depending on the client's level of personal deficits, symptom severity and duration, motivation, and comorbid diagnoses, treatment may range from brief strategies akin to the empirically supported treatments previously cited to long-term approaches spanning many years in duration. For a subset of individuals with BN, self-help and psychoeducational interventions may suffice with minimal therapist contact (Peterson & Mitchell, 1999).

Regarding the development of a working therapeutic alliance, I concur with Johnson, Connors, and Tobin (1987) that therapists must "artfully integrate the analysis of transference [that is, understanding how the patient is experiencing the interaction with the therapist] with behavioral symptom management" (p. 669). Another goal, from the perspective of self psychology, is to understand and respond to the eating-disordered symptoms as a "behavioral component of a split-off bulimic self," which requires that the therapist actively empathize with the self-affirming needs of that dissociated self, to reach the archaic needs hidden there (Sands, 1991). This approach is compatible with Linehan's therapeutic focus on balancing change with acceptance (1993).

The following case study from clinical practice illustrates the course of an integrated therapy approach for BN.

The Case of Molly B.

This case spanned sixty individual psychotherapy sessions over a two-year period. Sessions were conducted weekly for the first year, followed by a three-month lapse due to the client's change of location for a school break, and became roughly biweekly thereafter. Details have been changed to protect the anonymity of the client while preserving the therapeutic nature of the case.

Molly B., an attractive, twenty-one-year-old, single, Caucasian woman, sought treatment for BN after her symptoms caused her to drop out of college for a semester during her junior year. She had been in insight-oriented psychotherapy for six months earlier in the year, and although she liked her previous therapist, she felt the therapy did not address her eating disorder. Her binge eating and vomiting behaviors had increased during her previous therapy to four times a week, which occasionally alternated with weeks of semistarvation and short-lived bursts of excessive exercise. There was no history of laxative abuse. At the initial consult, she was 135 pounds and five feet, six inches tall. Historically, her weight had ranged between been 125 and 145 pounds. She told her parents about the bulimia two months before seeking treatment with me and soon thereafter had been evaluated and referred for inpatient care at a well-respected treatment center in Los Angeles, but declined. She had been cleared medically. She seemed sincere in saying that she came to therapy "for herself," even though her parents were very anxious and had encouraged her to return to treatment. In addition to meeting *DSM-IV* criteria for BN, purging subtype, she also reported regularly abusing alcohol at college parties. Not surprisingly, she described periods of depression.

History

Molly was the oldest of two girls. Her father, a successful architect, was highly perfectionistic and had a family and personal history of depression. He was warm, but he overvalued intelligence relative to other characteristics. Prior to the onset of puberty, Molly's relationship with her father was described as "best friends." Once she became a teenager and started separating from the family activities, her father became rigidly obsessed with her achievements in academics and sports. Apparently, his father had chronically devalued him, and nothing he did was ever "good enough."

Molly's mother, a homemaker, was described as kind, noncontingently accepting, passive, and conflict avoidant. She was considerably overweight, unconcerned about her own needs and appearance and dismissive of Molly's appearance concerns as "vain." She had been the caretaker of five younger brothers and sisters as a young teen because her own mother, described as "uneducated but beautiful and fashionable," was not emotionally available.

It became apparent that neither parent adequately mirrored Molly's whole self, leaving her ambivalently relating to herself in fragmented and disconnected pieces. She exhibited problems in affect regulation and self-care and tended to feel overly responsible in interpersonal relationships.

A series of losses further set the stage for the onset of Molly's symptoms as a teenager. She had already become self-conscious about being "chubby" (that is, five to ten pounds over her ideal weight) by twelve years old and had started dieting. A glamorous young aunt who doted on her came to live with the family for the year; Molly identified strongly with her and loved the attention from someone she admired.

When Molly was thirteen, this aunt moved out-of-state to get married and cut down the contact considerably, which Molly experienced as a great loss. The following year, her other maternal aunt was diagnosed with leukemia. Her mother became depressed, threw herself into being her sister's caregiver, and was further unavailable to Molly. Molly's father buried himself in work.

Lonely, depressed, and still struggling to keep her weight down by dieting at fourteen years old, Molly began to binge eat and vomit weekly. She felt extremely self-conscious and embarrassed about being fully sexually developed by fifteen years old. She had a boyfriend until she was eighteen, and gradually became sexually active during this time. However, Molly felt that her boyfriend loved her more than she loved him; she felt compelled to stay with him because she didn't want to hurt him. Later, during her therapy, she became angry when she realized that she had abandoned her authentic feelings in the service of taking care of him rather than herself for those years.

Early Recovery Phase

The initial phase of early recovery emphasized establishing an empathic milieu in which Molly's whole self was welcome; clarifying and intervening in the alcohol abuse; evaluating and slowly modifying her eating-disordered patterns using cognitive-behavioral strategies and psychoeducation; identifying and addressing areas of interpersonal conflict and skill deficit; and addressing deficits in emotion regulation using emotion regulation strategies such as mindful, nonjudgmental observation. Molly self-monitored her eating and drinking, bulimic behaviors, and thoughts and feelings for the first five months of therapy. At the beginning of therapy, she was not eating meals on most days, was snacking at breakfast, "grazing" on candy throughout the day, and bingeing on both "good" and "bad" food in the early evening. We discovered one of her rules to be that if she ate enough to feel satisfied, she had to "get rid of it." I reframed this rule as a "deprivation setup." Because candy did not make her feel full, she mistakenly assumed that the calories were minimal. The relationship between her not keeping down a dinner and her alcohol abuse in the evening also became obvious; she predictably drank more when she was dieting or starving herself.

One initial treatment strategy was the gradual shaping of her eating habits to include eating regular meals, starting with improving her breakfast choices and quantities, decreasing her consumption of candy, and challenging her irrational beliefs about weight regulation and food choices. Additional goals were adopted as she progressed. With many fits and starts, progress and setbacks, she became consistently abstinent from dieting, binge eating, and vomiting by the seventh month of therapy.

Molly's perfectionistic standards and all-or-nothing thinking softened over time as she came to trust that I was not judging her harshly because of her setbacks. She had cautiously returned to her natural weight of 140 pounds, and usually tolerated it well without self-denigration. On those occasions when she resumed her old self-denigrating thinking about her weight, we sought to understand the internal or external triggers and motivation. Her overall body image became more realistic, although she still felt self-conscious about the shape of her thighs. (See Kearney-Cooke and Striegel-Moore [1997] on body image disturbance.) In addition, in a psychology class she was taking at the time, she was starting to learn critical thinking about cultural messages regarding the beauty ideal, which reinforced the work in therapy. Her alcohol abuse stopped after three months, as she was able to turn her attention away from a young alcoholic man whom she tried to take care of and keep up with socially. At the beginning of treatment, we had discussed the progressive nature of addiction and the need for abstinence (and additional support) if she could not modify her drinking. She increased her contact with her other group of friends who were not "partyers." Even with the gradual improvements in her behaviors, her mood tended to fluctuate widely around her menstrual cycles. After much discussion, she had a medication consultation with her family physician and started taking the antidepressant Prozac.

During this period, she thanked me for "seeing through" some of her usual interpersonal patterns. For example, there were a couple of early incidents in which she hugged me at the end of the session. The second time this occurred, I suggested (in a nonrejecting tone) that she say in words what she was feeling instead of acting on it. When she returned the next week I was surprised by the strength of her response. She said that she felt relieved by my attention to her and realized now that she had successfully co-opted her previous therapist by becoming "a friend." I realized that she was reenacting her "taking care of" mode that she felt she needed to do with her mother, among others.

Molly acknowledged feeling frightened about giving up the bulimia and the "romance" of being "thin" (that is, her lowest weight of 125 pounds), and she worried she'd become a "sexless, powerless" person like her mother. She came to see that her symptoms served various purposes: when she was starving, she could tolerate her need to be taken care of by others; her symptoms "de-skilled" her, and she could allow herself to reduce her rigid expectations to achieve; when she had negative emotions, the weight focus and bulimic identity provided an acceptable explanation as well as a distraction from underlying issues.

In addition to the work of changing her eating-related behaviors and thinking, this early recovery phase identified important interpersonal issues: grief, interpersonal role disputes, and interpersonal deficits. Grief was related to the loss of attention from her young aunt, the death of her second aunt from leukemia, her mother's subsequent depression and withdrawal, and, to a lesser extent, the loss of closeness and admiration from her father. Molly carried an inflated sense of responsibility in relationships and believed that she should have been able to protect her aunt from dying as well as prevent her mother's subsequent depression, helplessness, and withdrawal from her. The early adoption of this role accentuated her depression and self-denigration as she was chronically minimizing her own feelings, needs, and wants. In recovery, she began to identify her needs in various relationships, including those with her family, and began to practice self-assertion. New behaviors would typically be followed by a brief slip backwards, at first with eating and later with guilt and self-denigrating thoughts. She gradually developed a greater sense of empathy and tolerance toward herself and her feeling states. She started to understand that her "selfless" need to take care of others defended her against feelings of powerlessness, inadequacy, and at times anger.

Ongoing Recovery Phase

As Molly's new eating and thinking patterns stabilized, the focus of the therapy shifted to issues not related to weight and eating. She was able to discontinue the Prozac. We continued to problem-solve the circumstances surrounding any setbacks in her self-esteem and mood, self-care, eating, and weight. Primarily, the focus intensified on her interpersonal relationships, both with me in the sessions as well as with her friends and family. She became curious about her interpersonal presentation, and we became aware of her use of what we began to call "The Big Emotion." Molly became increasingly aware of how she used exaggeration as a protective shield and felt dissatisfied because she ended up feeling "like a bimbo." Her conscious awareness increased as to how she sometimes resorted to "talking like a little girl" to avoid competition and how this downplayed her considerable intelligence and competence, leaving her feeling inadequate. Overall, she was working hard to integrate her sense of identity to include both her mind and her body as an adult.

Other significant themes in the therapy during the last year included her improving her self-regulation skills in the context of studying and doing work, developing a meaningful love relationship with a fellow student, anticipating the role transition of graduating from college, becoming more psychologically visible to her family, and preventing relapse. (Relapse prevention is a technique developed by Marlatt & Gordon, 1985.) For example, Molly became increasingly able to set limits with her mother when she felt her mother "triangulating" her into the old caretaking role with her younger sister. She could empathize with how difficult it was for her mother to deal directly with her own anxiety, but no longer felt compelled to rescue her. Similarly, she was able to establish a clearer relationship with her own ambition and authentic life goals separate from her father's expectations and to express her desire for closeness to him directly. She learned to really trust her boyfriend's admiration and love for her whole self—including her body at 140 pounds, although she often tested him on this at first. We repeatedly discussed the importance of maintaining her sense of wholeness—her intelligence, personality, and physical attractiveness—in the absence or presence of clear admiration from another person toward any of these aspects of herself.

The termination of Molly B.'s therapy coincided with her successful graduation from college and plan to relocate to start a new job. She planned to live close to her boyfriend to see what would develop there, but no longer worried that she would be taken over by his needs. She felt confident in her ability to continue to assert herself when necessary. At the end of her therapy, she was free of symptoms but concerned about gaining more weight. We discussed healthy methods for weight control, including regular, moderate exercise. We reviewed relapse triggers and prevention strategies, such as returning to the structure of self-monitoring and reaching out for help if she needed it. She was able to take in positive feedback from me about her considerable progress without undermining herself or requiring inflated admiration. Molly told me that for the last session she had planned to write me a letter reiterating her thanks for my help and her feelings about me, but decided that she didn't really have to because she had already told me. I understood that to mean that she felt confident that our connection was solid without her having to take care of me. She did bring me a small gift and gave me a big hug as we said our good-byes, but it was clear that, this time, no interpretations were necessary.

Prevention

In addition to benefiting the individual, recovery for women with eating disorders helps break the intergenerational cycle of dysfunction and suffering and reduces the wasteful "brain drain" of female resources to the society. Instead of engaging in a sterile preoccupation with weight and food, women may redirect their energies and talents toward a greater good. Toward this larger goal, efforts to reverse the tide of eating disorders have most often taken the form of primary and secondary prevention strategies.

Primary prevention is aimed at the prevention of new cases; the goal of secondary prevention is to reduce the duration of the disorder once established. Research suggests that the applications of prevention strategies must be carefully evaluated so as to ensure that benefits outweigh risks (Fairburn, 1995; Shisslak, Crago, Neal, & Swain, 1987; Mann et al., 1997). Mann et al. evaluated an eating disorder prevention program in a sample of female college freshmen and reported that at follow-up, few high-risk participants sought help, and the intervention participants had slightly more eating disorder symptoms than did controls. The program studied was representative of twenty other randomly selected college prevention programs surveyed in that it combined primary and secondary strategies and focused on providing information rather than on teaching skills. The authors state, "Even if both types of prevention programs were effective separately, attempting to accomplish both goals at once may be futile, as ideal strategies for each type of prevention program seem to oppose each other. Programs that are designed to reduce the stigma of eating disorders so that affected women will seek help may make disordered eating habits seem like common behaviors, thereby encouraging other women to try them" (1997, p. 217). Secondary prevention seems to have been emphasized to the detriment of primary prevention.

More specifically targeted interventions, separating primary and secondary prevention goals, appear to be necessary, as do interventions that provide more than just information (Shisslak et al., 1987; Mann et al., 1997; Berger, 2000). Shisslak at al. suggest, for example, that prevention efforts also include training needed to "master the tasks of maturation" (p. 663), such as enhancing a junior high girl's awareness of her body and her social and emotional needs. A recent article in the *New York Times* describes the work of several programs actively emphasizing education and skill enhancement for girls and women to prevent eating disorders. These programs emphasize "function over form" (that is, valuing the function and skill of the body rather than appearance) and range from museum tours exploring body image as expressed through art, to teaching leadership and self-empowerment skills, to teaching media literacy and activism so that girls can critically evaluate the impact of commercial messages and protest offensive messages (Berger, 2000).

More research is needed to discern the effective components of intervention efforts and, indeed, as cited previously, some such activity is obviously under way. Nonetheless, various authors have bemoaned the relative lack of support for prevention efforts in the federal budget as well as the staggering economic power of the prevailing diet, beauty, and fashion industries that serve to promote and maintain the status quo (Fairburn, 1995; Shisslak et al., 1987).

Conclusion

From the closer vantage point of our own communities, it is important that those who are most likely to come into contact with girls and women with eating disorders become well informed about eating disorder symptoms and resources for help. These would include doctors and nurses, social workers, teachers, sports coaches, dance teachers, health and fitness instructors, and parents, for a start. Practitioners need to look beyond the earlier profiles of eating disorder cases as these symptoms become more common among women of color, in various social classes, and even among men (Wilfley & Rodin, 1995; Stein et al., 2001). Clinicians must regularly assess for eating disorders among their depressed, anxious, chemically dependent, and personality-disordered clients, given the high incidence of dual diagnoses in this population. Individually, we benefit from resisting the relentless push of the consumer culture to evaluate ourselves as commodities or in fragments—whether such objectification pertains to weight and shape, age, social class, or any other perceived difference, visible or otherwise—insisting instead on experiencing ourselves as whole people.

References

Agras, W. S., & Apple, R. F. (1997). *Overcoming eating disorders: Therapist guide.* San Antonio, TX: Psychological Corporation, Graywind Publications.

Agras, W. S., Rossiter, E. M., Arnow, B., Schneider, J. A., Telch, C. F., Raeburn, S. D., Bruce, B., Perl, M., & Koran, L. M. (1992). Pharmacologic and cognitive-behavioral treatment for bulimia nervosa: A controlled comparison. *American Journal of Psychiatry, 149,* 82–87.

American Psychiatric Association. (1994). *Diagnostic and statistical manual of mental disorders* (4th ed.). Washington, DC: Author.

Apple, R. F. (1999). Interpersonal therapy for bulimia nervosa. *Journal of Clinical Psychology/ In Session: Psychotherapy in Practice, 55*(6), 715–725.

Bacaltchuk, J., Trefiglio, R. P., deOliveira, I. R., Lima, M. S., & Mari, J. J. (1999). Antidepressants versus psychotherapy for bulimia nervosa: A systematic review. *Journal of Clinical Pharmacy and Therapeutics, 24,* 23–31.

Beaumont, P.J.V. (1995). The clinical presentation of anorexia and bulimia nervosa. In K. D. Brownell & C. G. Fairburn (Eds.), *Eating disorders and obesity: A comprehensive handbook* (pp. 151–158). New York: Guilford Press.

Berger, L. (2000, July 18). A new body politic: Learning to like the way we look. *New York Times,* p. D7.

Brown, S. (1985). *Treating the alcoholic: A developmental model of recovery.* New York: Wiley.

Brownell, K. D. (1995). History of obesity. In K. D. Brownell & C. G. Fairburn (Eds.), *Eating disorders and obesity: A comprehensive handbook* (pp. 381–385). New York: Guilford Press.

Brownell, K. D., & Fairburn, C. G. (1995). Preface. In K. D. Brownell & C. G. Fairburn (Eds.), *Eating disorders and obesity: A comprehensive handbook* (pp. iv–xii). New York: Guilford Press.

Bulik, C. M. (1987). Drug and alcohol abuse by bulimic women and their families. *American Journal of Psychiatry, 144,* 1604–1606.

Cooper, P. J. (1995). Eating disorders and their relationship to mood and anxiety disorders. *Eating disorders and obesity: A comprehensive handbook* (pp. 159–164). New York: Guilford Press.

Cooper, Z. (1995). The development and maintenance of eating disorders. In K. D. Brownell & C. G. Fairburn (Eds.), *Eating disorders and obesity: A comprehensive handbook* (pp. 199–206). New York: Guilford Press.

Crow, S. J., & Mitchell, J. E. (1994). Rational therapy of eating disorders. *Drugs, 48*(3), 372–379.

Dare, C., & Eisler, I. (1997). Family therapy for anorexia nervosa. In D. M. Garner & P. E. Garfinkel (Eds.), *Handbook of treatment of eating disorders* (2nd ed., pp. 307–324). New York: Guilford Press.

Dennis, A. B., & Sansone, R. A. (1997). Treatment of patients with personality disorders. In D. M. Garner & P. E. Garfinkel (Eds.), *Handbook of treatment of eating disorders* (2nd ed., pp. 437–449). New York: Guilford Press.

Fairburn, C. G. (1995). The prevention of eating disorders. In K. D. Brownell & C. G. Fairburn (Eds.), *Eating disorders and obesity: A comprehensive handbook* (pp. 289–293). New York: Guilford Press.

Fairburn, C. G. (1997). Interpersonal psychotherapy for bulimia nervosa. In D. M. Garner & P. E. Garfinkel (Eds.), *Handbook of treatment of eating disorders* (2nd ed., pp. 278–294). New York: Guilford Press.

Fairburn, C. G., & Walsh, B. T. (1995). Atypical eating disorders. In K. D. Brownell & C. G. Fairburn (Eds.), *Eating disorders and obesity: A comprehensive handbook* (pp. 135–140). New York: Guilford Press.

Garner, D. M. (1997). Psychoeducational principles in treatment. In D. M. Garner & P. E. Garfinkel (Eds.), *Handbook of treatment of eating disorders* (2nd ed., pp. 145–177). New York: Guilford Press.

Garner, D. M., & Needleman, L. D. (1997). Sequencing and integration of treatments. In D. M. Garner & P. E. Garfinkel (Eds.), *Handbook of treatment of eating disorders* (2nd ed., pp. 50–63). New York: Guilford Press.

Garner, D. M., Vitousek, K., & Pike, K. (1997). Cognitive-behavioral therapy for anorexia nervosa. In D. M. Garner & P. E. Garfinkel (Eds.), *Handbook of treatment of eating disorders* (2nd ed., pp. 94–144). New York: Guilford Press.

Goldblum, D. S., Naranjo, C. A., Bremner, K. E., & Hicks, L. K. (1992). Eating disorders and alcohol abuse in women. *British Journal of Addiction, 87*, 913–920.

Goodsitt, A. (1997). Eating disorders: A self-psychological perspective. In D. M. Garner & P. E. Garfinkel (Eds.), *Handbook of treatment of eating disorders* (2nd ed., pp. 205–228). New York: Guilford Press.

Hoek, H. W. (1995). The distribution of eating disorders. In K. D. Brownell & C. G. Fairburn (Eds.), *Eating disorders and obesity: A comprehensive handbook* (pp. 207–211). New York: Guilford Press.

Holderness, C. C., Brooks-Gunn, J., & Warren, M. P. (1994). Comorbidity of eating disorders and substance abuse: Review of the literature. *International Journal of Eating Disorders, 16*(1), 1–34.

Johnson, C. L. (1984). Initial consultation for patients with bulimia and anorexia nervosa. In D. M. Garner & P. E. Garfinkel (Eds.), *Handbook of psychotherapy for anorexia nervosa and bulimia* (pp. 19–51). New York: Guilford Press.

Johnson, C. L., & Connors, M. E. (1987). Developmental considerations. In *The etiology and treatment of bulimia nervosa: A biopsychosocial perspective* (pp. 88–125). New York: Basic Books.

Johnson, C. L., Connors, M. E., & Tobin, D. L. (1987). Symptom management of bulimia. *Journal of Consulting and Clinical Psychology, 55*(5), 668–676.

Kearney-Cooke, A., & Striegel-Moore, R. (1997). The etiology and treatment of body image disturbance. In D. M. Garner & P. E. Garfinkel (Eds.), *Handbook of treatment of eating disorders* (2nd ed., pp. 295–306). New York: Guilford Press.

Klerman, G. L., & Weissman, M. M. (1993). *New applications of interpersonal psychotherapy.* Washington, DC: American Psychiatric Press.

Kohut, H. (1984). *How does analysis cure?* Chicago: University of Chicago Press.

Krahn, E., Kurth, C., Demitrack, M., & Drewnowski, A. (1992). The relationship of dieting severity and bulimic behaviors to alcohol and other drug use in young women. *Journal of Substance Abuse, 4*, 341–353.

Lennkh, C., DeZwaan, M., & Kasper, S. (1997). New aspects of diagnosis and pharmacotherapy of eating disorders. *International Journal of Psychiatry in Clinical Practice, 1*, 21–35.

Linehan, M. M. (1993). *Cognitive-behavioral treatment of borderline personality disorder.* New York: Guilford Press.

Mann, T., Nolen-Hoeksema, S., Huang, K., Burgard, D., Wright, A., & Hanson, K. (1997). Are two interventions worse than none? Joint primary and secondary prevention of eating disorders in college females. *Health Psychology, 16*(3), 215–225.

Marcus, M. D. (1995). Binge eating and obesity. In K. D. Brownell & C. G. Fairburn (Eds.), *Eating disorders and obesity: A comprehensive handbook* (pp. 441–444). New York: Guilford Press.

Marlatt, G. A., & Gordon, J. R. (1985). *Relapse prevention: Maintenance strategies in the treatment of addictive behaviors.* New York: Guilford Press.

Miller, W. R., & Rollnick, S. (1991). *Motivational interviewing: Preparing people to change addictive behavior.* New York: Guilford Press.

Mitchell, J. E., Pomeroy, C., & Adson, D. E. (1997). Managing medical complications. In D. M. Garner & P. E. Garfinkel (Eds.), *Handbook of treatment of eating disorders* (2nd ed., pp. 383–393). New York: Guilford Press.

Mitchell, J. E., Specker, S., & Edmonson, K. (1997). Management of substance abuse and dependence. In D. M. Garner & P. E. Garfinkel (Eds.), *Handbook of treatment of eating disorders* (2nd ed., pp. 415–423). New York: Guilford Press.

Obesity: Portions out of control. (2000, August). *Harvard Women's Health Watch, 7*(12), 1.

Palmer, R. L. (1995). Sexual abuse and eating disorders. In K. D. Brownell & C. G. Fairburn (Eds.), *Eating disorders and obesity: A comprehensive handbook* (pp. 230–233). New York: Guilford Press.

Peterson, C. B., & Mitchell, J. E. (1999). Psychosocial and pharmacological treatment of eating disorders: A review of research findings. *Journal of Clinical Psychology/In Session: Psychology in Practice, 55*(6), 685–697.

Peveler, R. C., & Fairburn, C. G. (1990). Eating disorders in women who abuse alcohol. *British Journal of Addiction, 85,* 1633–1638.

Russell, G.F.M. (1997). The history of bulimia nervosa. In D. M. Garner & P. E. Garfinkel (Eds.), *Handbook of treatment of eating disorders* (2nd ed., pp. 11–24). New York: Guilford Press.

Sands, S. (1989). Eating disorders and female development: A self-psychological perspective. In A. Goldberg (Ed.), *Dimensions of self experience: Progress in self psychology* (pp. 75–103). New York: Guilford Press.

Sands, S. (1991). Bulimia, dissociation, and empathy: A self psychological view. In C. L. Johnson (Ed.), *Psychodynamic treatment of anorexia nervosa and bulimia* (pp. 34–50). New York: Guilford Press.

Shane, M., Shane, E., & Gales, M. (1997). *Intimate attachments: Toward a new self psychology.* New York: Guilford Press.

Shisslak, C. M., Crago, M., Neal, M. E., & Swain, B. (1987). Primary prevention of eating disorders. *Journal of Consulting and Clinical Psychology, 55*(5), 660–667.

Silverman, J. A. (1997). Anorexia nervosa: Historical perspective on treatment. In D. M. Garner & P. E. Garfinkel (Eds.), *Handbook of treatment of eating disorders* (2nd ed., pp. 3–10). New York: Guilford Press.

Stein, R. I., Saelens, B. E., Dounchis, J. Z., Lewczyk, C. M., Swenson, A. K., & Wilfley, D. E. (2001). Treatment of eating disorders in women. *The Counseling Psychologist, 29*(5), 695–732.

Striegel-Moore, R. H. (1995). A feminist perspective on the etiology of eating disorders. In K. D. Brownell & C. G. Fairburn (Eds.), *Eating disorders and obesity: A comprehensive handbook* (pp. 224–229). New York: Guilford Press.

Strober, M. (1995). Family-genetic perspectives in anorexia nervosa and bulimia nervosa. In K. D. Brownell & C. G. Fairburn (Eds.), *Eating disorders and obesity: A comprehensive handbook* (pp. 212–218). New York: Guilford Press.

Strober, M. (1997). Consultation and therapeutic engagement in severe anorexia nervosa. In

D. M. Garner & P. E. Garfinkel (Eds.), *Handbook of treatment of eating disorders* (2nd ed., pp. 229–247). New York: Guilford Press.

Strober, M., & Humphrey, L. (1987). Familial contributions to the etiology and course of anorexia nervosa and bulimia. *Journal of Consulting and Clinical Psychology, 55*(5), 654–659.

Telch, C. F. (1997a). *Emotion regulation skills training treatment for binge eating disorder: Therapist manual.* Stanford, CA: Department of Psychiatry and Behavioral Sciences, Stanford University.

Telch, C. F. (1997b). Skills training treatment for adaptive affect regulation in a woman with binge-eating disorder. *International Journal of Eating Disorders, 22,* 77–81.

Vandereycken, W. (1995). The families of patients with eating disorders. In K. D. Brownell & C. G. Fairburn (Eds.), *Eating disorders and obesity: A comprehensive handbook* (pp. 219–223). New York: Guilford Press.

Walsh, B. T., & Garner, D. M. (1997). Diagnostic issues. In D. M. Garner & P. E. Garfinkel (Eds.), *Handbook of treatment of eating disorders* (2nd ed., pp. 25–33). New York: Guilford Press.

Wilfley, D. E., Agras, W. S., Telch, C. F., Rossiter, E. M., Schneider, J. A., Cole, A. G., Sifford, L., & Raeburn, S. D. (1993). Group cognitive-behavioral therapy and group interpersonal psychotherapy for the non-purging bulimic individual: A controlled comparison. *Journal of Consulting and Clinical Psychology, 61,* 296–305.

Wilfley, D. E., & Cohen, L. R. (1997). Psychological treatment of bulimia nervosa and binge eating disorder. *Psychopharmacology Bulletin, 33*(3), 437–454.

Wilfley, D. E., & Rodin, J. (1995). Cultural influences on eating disorders. In K. D. Brownell & C. G. Fairburn (Eds.), *Eating disorders and obesity: A comprehensive handbook* (pp. 78–82). New York: Guilford Press.

Williamson, D. F. (1995). Prevalence and demographics of obesity. In K. D. Brownell & C. G. Fairburn (Eds.), *Eating disorders and obesity: A comprehensive handbook* (pp. 391–395). New York: Guilford Press.

Wilson, T. G. (1995). Eating disorders and addictive disorder. In K. D. Brownell & C. G. Fairburn (Eds.), *Eating disorders and obesity: A comprehensive handbook* (pp. 165–170). New York: Guilford Press.

Wiser, S., & Telch, C. F. (1999). Dialectical behavior therapy for binge eating disorder. *Journal of Clinical Psychology/In Session: Psychotherapy in Practice, 55*(6), 755–768.

Wonderlich, S. A. (1995). Personality and eating disorders. In K. D. Brownell & C. G. Fairburn (Eds.), *Eating disorders and obesity: A comprehensive handbook* (pp. 171–176). New York: Guilford Press.

Yeary, J. R., & Heck, C. L. (1989). Dual diagnosis: Eating disorders and psychoactive substance dependence. *Journal of Psychoactive Drugs, 21,* 239–249.

Zweben, J. E. (1996). Psychiatric problems among alcohol and other drug dependent women. *Journal of Psychoactive Drugs, 28,* 345–366.

CHAPTER SEVEN

SEXUALLY ADDICTIVE BEHAVIOR IN WOMEN

Judith E. Rubin

Sexual addiction in women is a complex disorder that warrants a complex and integrated understanding as well as multimodal treatment strategies. Social conventions, cultural ambivalence about women's sexuality, and gender stereotyping have mitigated against significant clinical research and understanding of the subject. Despite the sexual revolution of the 1960s and the growing acceptance of women's sexuality as a vital component of their holistic well-being, the "Madonna-whore split" continues to exist both in the cultural view of women's sexuality and in the private realm of women's individual psyches. In this view, a woman is seen as either all "good," the nonsexual Madonna to be idealized and worshipped, or all "bad," the whore who is both sexual and willingly available for sex. As a consequence of this split, there has been scant attention given by health professionals to the issue of women's sexuality in general and to the issue of sexual addiction among women in particular.

The concept of sexual addiction, although controversial, has particular importance for addiction professionals. Attempts to achieve abstinence from drug or alcohol abuse may be thwarted by compulsive sexual behavior and the interrelated shame (Goodman, 1998). In addition, because impaired control and impulse disorders are often part of the diagnostic picture of sexual offenders, the sexual exploitation of women is a related concern (Goodman, 1998) and makes women vulnerable to HIV-AIDS and other sexually transmitted disease. The recent growth of cybersex increases the need to understand the issues and dynamics related to sexual addiction in women. In order to enable clinicians to understand sexual addiction better and how it may manifest in women, this chapter includes a review of various theories of etiology and discusses useful treatment strategies for working with sexually addicted women.

Sexual Addiction Defined

How can a clinician determine whether a woman has crossed the line into self-destructive sexual behavior, or sexual addiction? Attempts to craft a succinct and all-encompassing definition of sexual addiction may be harmfully reductionistic. A constructive and gender-neutral definition of sexual addiction needs to include elements from a variety of sources. A practical start, albeit incomplete, are the sexual paraphilias described in *DSM-IV* (American Psychiatric Association, 1994): exhibitionism, fetishism, frotteurism, pedophilia, sexual masochism, sexual sadism, voyeurism, and transvestism. Most clinicians are aware of, if not familiar with, these disorders. Unfortunately, these sexually addictive or compulsive behaviors seem far more common in men.

Sexual addiction in a woman can be described as her loss of control over varying aspects of her sexual thinking and behavior. Carnes (1983) describes sexual addiction as "a pathological relationship with a mood altering experience. . . . The sex addict relies on sex for comfort from pain, nurturing, or relief from stress, etc., the way an alcoholic relies on alcohol or a drug addict relies on drugs" (pp. 4–5). He further states that the sex addict is a person who "transforms sex into the primary relationship or need for which all else may be sacrificed, including family, friends, values, health, safety and work" (p. 5). Braun-Harvey (1997), referring to men, uses the term sexual addiction to describe behaviors that involve "problems of sexual control, excessive and intrusive preoccupation leading to psychological distress" (p. 367), and Schwartz and Brasted (1985) view sexual addiction as "a destructive means of coping with stress, guilt, and passive rage" (p. 104).

A clinically useful definition of sexual addiction in women includes sexual compulsivity, preoccupation, and repeated sexual acting out despite negative consequences to health, self-esteem, interpersonal relationships, psychiatric sequelae, or a combination of these.

As is true in all addictions, the concept of sexual addiction implies that there is a potential for recovery. This recovery is possible if a woman receives the help, education, and support she needs.

Prevalence of Sexual Addiction in Women

Data on the prevalence of sexual addiction in the general population are scarce, and what information exists applies mostly to men. Shame and the fear of potential legal repercussions make it difficult to collect such information and may result in significant underreporting (Goodman, 1998). Using survey data, Carnes (1983) estimated that 3 to 6 percent of Americans suffer from sexual addiction. Coleman (1992) reports that approximately 5 percent of the population meets the diagnostic criteria for "sexual compulsivity" (p. 322). Research findings also indicate that a person with a diagnosis of alcohol addiction, drug addiction, bulimia, pathological gambling, or sexual addiction is at significantly higher risk than the general population of developing one or more of the other addictive processes than is the general population (Goodman, 1998). Thus, individuals with sexual addictions are also likely to have other addictions.

Epidemiological data on women and sexual addiction are absent in the literature. Studies on women, such as they are, tend to be of an ethnographic nature; they focus on quantifiable sequelae of compulsive sexual behavior, such as HIV and other sexually transmitted diseases (Centers for Disease Control and Prevention, 1995) or on women's sexuality in the context of chemical dependence recovery (Carnes, 1991).

Etiological Theories of Sexual Addiction

This section presents a brief review of the more important etiological theories of sexual addiction, each with clinical implications. These theories can be grouped into five general categories: neurological-biological, sociocultural, cognitive-behavioral, psychodynamic, and integrative (Goodman, 1998).

Neurological-Biological Theories

Endocrinological, pharmacological, and anatomical research is currently providing new insights into both normal and pathological sexual functioning in women, and research exploring the relationship between sexual arousal, brain chemistry, and addiction is ongoing. Kafka (1991) has focused on the role of a variety of neurotransmitters in mediating sexual desire. This biological research has resulted in the clinical usage of the new generation of antidepressants referred to as the selective serotonin reuptake inhibitors (SSRIs), such as Prozac, Serzon, and a host of others, to cope with coexisting depressive episodes, and hormones to augment the treatment of sexually addicted women. A five-year project at Vanderbilt University currently under way seeks to identify the neurobiological basis of sexual addiction and its overlap with cocaine and alcohol dependence. It also aims to identify pharmacological agents that may improve treatment outcomes (American Federation of Addiction Research, 2000).

Angier (1999) explores current views of women's anatomy and physiology to draw some interesting conclusions. Her "liberation biology" challenges culturally accepted "Darwinian-based" gender stereotypes (p. xvii) that emphasize monogamous female nature and sexuality, and proposes instead that female anatomy predisposes women to multiple sexual partnering and multiple orgasms, thereby accounting for the flourishing of the species. Although this perspective does not have a direct impact on the understanding of sexually addictive women, it has some important theoretical implications: if cultural norms reflected this viewpoint rather than its opposite, a more realistic understanding of highly sexual women would work to eliminate the current dualistic madonna-whore stance toward women.

Research studies corroborate an increase in sexual desire in women during their menstrual midcycle (Angier, 1999). Although tangentially related, more information regarding the varying contexts in which a change in estrogen secretion might occur (for example, during puberty or menopause) may assist future research efforts in their exploration of the destructive sexual behavior in which some women engage. Although there are no specific findings directly connecting sexual addiction and biological determinants, this is an important area for further exploration.

Sociocultural Theories

Sociocultural considerations provide an important context for clinicians when evaluating women clients for symptoms of sex addiction. The current sociocultural backdrop has several effects on the identification and treatment of sexual addiction in women. First, what is accepted as normal and what is considered pathological sexual behavior need to be defined by women individually, without the interference of culturally imposed stereotypical images and norms resulting from advertisements. Prevailing cultural scripts are influenced by media images and affect what clinicians accept as normative or, by extension, as pathological sexual behavior in women. The acceptance of the concept of sexual addiction as pathological requires that we also explicate what healthy sexuality looks like for the individual woman.

Second, an indirect yet equally important sociocultural influence concerns the role and impact of childhood sexual abuse on the addictive sexual behavior of adult women. Research indicates a strong connection between childhood sexual abuse and sexually self-destructive behavior in women (van der Kolk et al., 1996). More-over, the underreporting and underprosecution of sexual abuse of children by fam-ily members affect both the identification and treatment of this misunderstood and undiagnosed addiction in sexual predators and may contribute to later self-injurious sexual behavior by the victims of this abuse.

A third facet of the sociocultural lens on sexual addiction is the technological orientation of our society. This orientation idolizes the ability to control objects and promotes a reliance on things that can be controlled as a means of solving one's inner emotional and spiritual problems. This orientation fosters an objec-tification of women as sexual objects. Moreover, the ubiquity of images of air-brushed female bodies used for marketing and entertainment purposes can be seen as a covert form of sociocultural aggression.

Sexual norms differ for heterosexual and lesbian behavior; internalized het-erosexism by those working with women with same-sex gender preferences is com-mon and an added complication. Clinicians raised in our homophobic culture must be open to a thorough self-assessment regarding their attitude toward same-sex preferences. Countertransference issues such as unexplored biases and homopho-bic attitudes will most likely contaminate the therapeutic process. In addition, an awareness of the damaging emotional process of internalized homophobia that lesbian clients may bring to the treatment experience is vital (Senreich & Vairo, in press). For some women, compulsive sexual behavior may be a reaction to iden-tifying or accepting themselves as gay (Davis, Cole, & Rothblum, 1996).

Cognitive-Behavioral Theories

Cognitive-behavioral theories emphasize the ways in which cognitive distortions undermine healthy sexuality (Goodman, 1998). From this perspective, the cycle of sexual addiction in women is initiated and perpetuated by a series of mistaken beliefs about self, sexuality, and intimate relationships with others. The system of irrational beliefs resembles those described in the cognitive theories of depression (Beck, 1967; Beck, Rush, Shaw, & Emery, 1979) and is characterized by such thoughts as

1. I'm a bad, unworthy person.
2. No one would love me as I am.
3. My needs will not be met if I depend on others.
4. Sex is my most important need.

Whereas all addicts may hold the first three beliefs, the fourth core belief specif-ically distinguishes sex addicts from other addicts. A faulty belief system develops around these core beliefs, which then promotes impaired thinking that is characterized by denial, rationalization, self-righteousness, and blame of others (Carnes, 1983). This belief system is further complicated by the intense shame that can overwhelm and shape thinking. Low self-esteem, a central problem for the sexually addicted, is inextricably bound with the affect of shame. Consequently, treatment must include an understanding of shame-based cognitions and beliefs (Kaufman, 1989).

Psychodynamic Perspectives

Psychodynamic theories tend to view sexual addiction as fundamentally a disorder of self-regulation (Khantzian, Halliday, & McAuliffe, 1990). These theories focus on impairments in affect regulation, self-soothing, a sense of self, self-esteem, and self-care functions. Such concepts as regression tendencies, aggression, and sadomasochism are "prominent as both etiologic and dynamic factors in psychodynamic theories" (Goodman, 1998). Schwartz (1992) notes that the illusion of intimacy and connectedness provided by sex often replaces emotional voids in the lives of the sexually addicted person, further removing them from genuine closeness with others. Benjamin (1988) revisits the mother-daughter Oedipal struggle with a perspective on how its unsuccessful resolution affects later erotic development in the female. According to this perspective, it is these unresolved conflicts that are often acted out by women sex addicts.

Driven Behavior Spectrum Disorder

Goodman (1998) conceptualizes sexual addiction as *driven behavior spectrum disorder;* according to this perspective, "the psychological formulation of the addictive process and the neurobiological formulation of the addictive process are consistent with each other. . . . [They] are not antagonistic or mutually exclusive, but complementary and mutually enhancing" (p. 219). This integrated perspective also includes an understanding of heredity and the self-perpetuating nature of the addictive process. Goodman further states that it is important not to attempt to choose among different theoretical perspectives, but rather to delineate the conditions under which any particular theoretical perspective is effective.

Such a nondualistic approach would seem to be most useful to clinicians working with female sex addicts. Driven behavior spectrum disorder is a conceptual frame valuable for understanding a variety of addictive processes, which have some overlap or commonality. From this perspective, a sex addict is someone who is coping with an urge for some form of reinforcement (positive, negative, or both) in the short term, which overrides consideration of longer-term consequences (Goodman, 1998).

Assessment

Sexually addicted women need a comprehensive and sensitive assessment. Such assessment should include a complete clinical and psychosocial history, a thorough sexual history, and a sexual behavior inventory. A physical examination, preferably by a urologist or gynecologist, is recommended, as the sexual practices of sexually addicted women can lead to internal or external damage to the genitalia. When using a formal instrument or questioning women about childhood sexual abuse and incest, it is important to be aware of the potential for retraumatization through the act of retelling (van der Kolk et al., 1996).

A sound clinical sexual history should include such issues as gender identity conflict, gender role, sexual preference, and family-of-origin beliefs about sexuality. A complete chronology of the woman's childhood and adolescent sexual behavior, including normal and deviant sexual activities, is vital. Masturbation patterns can also offer clues to sexually compulsive behavior. To avoid vague answers, the clinician needs to ask specific questions and to do so with assumed knowledge. For example, asking "How often do you masturbate?" will prove more effective than "Have you ever masturbated?" (Earle & Earle, 1995).

In addition to taking the formal history, the clinician needs to actively seek information about the client's current sexual behavior and its impact. The following are some of the problematic behaviors to look for:

- A cycle of sexual compulsions, or unsuccessful attempts to control a sexual behavior
- Changing relationships to control sexual fantasy, sexual activities, or both
- Swearing off relationships, only to give in to the next "right" lover
- Breaking promises to self or others to stop abusive fantasy or sexual behaviors
- Switching to caretaking of others, workaholism, overeating, or excessive reading of romantic-erotic material to take the place of a sexual relationship
- Continued sexual behaviors despite negative consequences, such as unplanned pregnancies, abortions, sexually transmitted diseases, or violence
- Terror or shame resulting from sexual activities
- Decreased productivity at work because of time spent preoccupied with sex or sexual partners
- Relationship problems resulting from extramarital affairs or from excessive time spent on sex-related activities or preoccupation with sex or sexual partners

A particularly useful assessment tool is the women's version of the men's Sexual Addiction Screening Test, titled the Women's Sexual Addiction Screening Test, or W-SAST (Carnes, 1991). The W-SAST is designed to assist in the assessment of sexually compulsive or addictive behavior and provides a profile of responses that help the clinician discriminate between addictive and nonaddictive sexual behavior. The W-SAST comprises the following twenty-five questions. Thirteen or more yes answers indicates a likelihood of sexual addiction; ten to thirteen yes answers means there is "early stage addiction." (Permission provided May 2001 by Dr. Patrick Carnes. Copyright 1999 SexHelp.com. All rights reserved. Reproduction in whole or in part without permission is prohibited.)

1. Were you sexually abused as a child or adolescent?
2. Do you regularly purchase romance novels or sexually explicit magazines?
3. Have you stayed in romantic relationships after they become emotionally or physically abusive?
4. Do you often find yourself preoccupied with sexual thoughts or romantic day dreams?
5. Do you feel that your sexual behavior is normal?
6. Does your spouse (or significant other[s]) ever worry or complain about your sexual behavior?
7. Do you have trouble stopping your sexual behavior when you know it is inappropriate?
8. Do you ever feel bad about your sexual behavior?
9. Has your sexual behavior ever created problems for you and your family?
10. Have you ever sought help for sexual behavior you did not like?
11. Have you ever worried about people finding out about your sexual activities?
12. Has anyone been hurt emotionally because of your sexual behavior?
13. Have you ever participated in sexual activity in exchange for money or gifts?
14. Do you have times when you act out sexually followed by periods of celibacy (no sex at all)?
15. Have you made efforts to quit a type of sexual activity and failed?
16. Do you hide some of your sexual behavior from others?
17. Do you find yourself having multiple romantic relationships at the same time?
18. Have you ever felt degraded by your sexual behavior?
19. Has sex or romantic fantasies been a way for you to escape your problems?
20. When you have sex, do you feel depressed afterwards?
21. Do you regularly engage in sadomasochistic behavior?
22. Has your sexual activity interfered with your family life?
23. Have you been sexual with minors?
24. Do you feel controlled by your sexual desire or fantasies of romance?
25. Do you ever think your sexual desire is stronger than you are?

A comprehensive personality inventory, such as the Minnesota Multiphasic Personality Inventory-2 (MMPI-2) may also be helpful, because anxiety and depression, as well as narcissistic, borderline, and antisocial personality disorders, are often comorbid with sex addiction.

Another useful tool is Simpson's Model of the Sex Addiction Cycle (Earle & Earle, 1995). This tool provides a visual instrument to identify the cyclical phases and the accompanying thoughts and behaviors of sexual addicts. Such a tool can be useful to both clinicians and clients in much the same ways that various adaptations of the famous Jellinek chart have been to many substance abusers.

Treatment

Limitations imposed by managed care and inadequate insurance coverage notwithstanding, treatment of women sex addicts should reflect the individualized, comprehensive, biopsychosocial model indicated in the assessment section. Such an approach may include any or all of the modalities discussed in the next sections.

Inpatient Treatment

Inpatient treatment may constitute a useful step in helping stabilize the sexually addicted woman and protecting her from such psychosocial stressors as parenting responsibilities, unsupportive family members, and dangerous self-destructive sexual behavior (Carnes, 1983). During this phase of treatment, the client is encouraged to understand her addiction and increase her motivation to change. Inpatient programs typically include four to six weeks of a combination of individual treatment, group therapy, and psychoeducation for both the client and family members, who are encouraged to participate in adjunctive outpatient meetings.

Outpatient Psychotherapy

Outpatient individual therapy with sexually addicted women will be most effective if it contains elements of psychodynamic work, cognitive therapy, psychoeducation, and bibliotherapy. Individual psychotherapy is most helpful to the sexually addicted woman if it serves to offer unconditional acceptance, build trust, reduce shame, explore resistances, and identify any concurrent addictions or coexisting disorders.

The origins of sexual compulsivity frequently warrant an exploration of childhood sexual abuse or incest (or both) and other trauma, such as physical and psychological abuse and neglect (van der Kolk et al., 1996). Gender identity concerns and sexual preferences can also be a part of the ongoing process of psychodynamic therapy. The negative self-concepts with which the sexually addicted woman struggles can be effectively addressed through cognitive therapy. Cognitive distortions need to be identified and replaced with more positive cognitions. The clinician needs to help identify thoughts that may stimulate urges and cravings and the reflexive affect of shame so frequently bound up with these thoughts, thereby enhancing the client's self-esteem and possibly intervening in the rate and frequency of client relapse. Ongoing education and reading about sex addiction and its dynamics are important in socializing the client to the lifestyle of recovery, an ongoing day-at-a-time process.

Use of Medications

Psychotropic medication can be a useful adjunct to psychotherapy and twelve-step programs, but it should not be thought of as a treatment in and of itself. Medications can be useful in enhancing affect regulation, stabilizing psychobiological functioning, and modulating anxiety and obsessive thoughts. Medications can be effective in controlling emotional flooding and in enhancing the client's coping abilities, thereby improving the effectiveness of psychotherapy. Antidepressant medications, in particular the SSRIs, have been found to reduce the frequency of addictive sexual behavior as well as the intensity of urges (Rubenstein & Engel, 1996).

Twelve-Step and Other Self-Help Programs

Twelve-step and other self-help groups for sexual addiction provide education, acceptance, and support for clients. They include Sex and Love Addicts Anonymous (SLAA), Sexual Compulsives Anonymous (SCA), and Sex Addicts Anonymous (SAA). Based on client feedback and my own observations, SLAA tends to be populated more by women, whereas SCA tends to attract more men.

The primary difference between Alcoholics Anonymous (AA) and the Sex Anonymous groups has to do with the first step: the admission of powerlessness relates to one's sexually addictive behavior, not alcohol. Another difference is in the concept of abstinence. Alcoholics learn how to live a comfortable life while abstaining from all forms of alcohol. Although the concept of "sobriety" varies among different sex addiction groups, compulsive and destructive sexual behaviors are universally considered a relapse. The sexually addicted are encouraged to identify their "bottom-line behaviors" that are uncontrollable and self-destructive. Monogamous sexual connection within a committed relationship is considered part of the recovery from this addiction.

Self-help groups for family members include Co-SLAA (Co-Addicted Sex and Love Addicted Family Members) and Sex-Anon, both based on the Al-Anon model for family members of alcoholics.

Relapse Prevention

Relapse, a cardinal feature of addiction, in fact takes place in the thinking and feeling processes long before the occurrence of any actual self-destructive behavior. The more effective relapse prevention strategies for women are education, one or more unconditionally supportive relationships, and self-awareness. All of these work together to enable a woman to identify destructive arousal triggers and take appropriate action. Sexual recovery involves an ongoing assessment of a client's ability and motivation to establish meaningful intimacy. Encouragement about the ongoing striving toward a healthy erotic life, not merely the elimination of sexually self-destructive behavior, needs to be the focus.

Summary of Treatment Issues

Because clinical work with sexually addicted women shares some similarities with treatment of other addictive disorders, a review of some fundamental concepts of addiction treatment may be of use. First, recovery is about sustaining supportive relationships and becoming interdependent with other people. Frequently, the lifestyles of clients who struggle with addictions exclude relationships except those that center on their addictive substance or behavior. Isolation is common. A client may be unable to make and sustain meaningful relationships with others and, because these relationships are central to the change process, she may be less likely to maintain an ongoing consistent recovery.

Next, countertransference issues can be intense and difficult to process without sufficient peer support and ongoing clinical supervision. Examining and remaining aware of his or her particular biases regarding women's sexuality are important ongoing concerns for any mental health professional. Being responsive to his or her discomfort or judgments allows the clinician to keep the client's best interest in mind and to make appropriate and prompt referrals.

Third, the clinician need not challenge a client's resistances to labeling herself as a "sexual addict," but rather should meet such resistance by nonjudgmentally identifying the discrepancies and incongruities between the client's goals and her actions. The clinician can help increase a client's motivation by fostering a nonadversarial atmosphere that promotes the client's willingness to try unfamiliar ideas and behaviors, which can widen her options, diminish fear and hopelessness, and simultaneously increase her self-esteem. Attending meetings, reaching out to others for support, and being open about her fears and insecurities are essential new behaviors for the client. Fourth, the clinician's therapeutic timing must be particularly sensitive to the qualities of trust and depth of connection between clinician and client. Relapse, a common part of addictive disorders, can stem from many factors. It is important to see that relapse may be the result of lack of education, coping skills, or understanding on the client's part, rather than due to "denial" of the severity of the consequences of the disorder.

Fifth, the clinician's familiarity with local twelve-step resources and self-help groups specific to women and sexual addiction is an integral part of psychotherapy with sexually addicted clients. Without the ongoing contact and support gained through meeting attendance, clients find it difficult to tolerate the shame and self-doubt that are inevitable, particularly in the early phase of abstinence. According to Wolfe (1996), who studied recovering sex addicts using an SLAA sample, only one out of twelve identified their psychotherapist as instrumental in addressing sexual addiction issues and suggesting a support group.

The following case example provides a more nuanced understanding of this disorder.

The Case of Robin

Robin, a thirty-one-year-old White married female, requested treatment for compulsive extramarital affairs. She expressed concern that her days were spent fantasizing about men and strategizing about her next seduction. As a result, she perceived her husband and three children as intruders into her world of fantasy. These fantasies were filled with sadomasochistic scenarios that had in common some form of humiliation, which would bring her to climax. She described her sexual relationship with her husband as "boring." She saw herself as a victim to her often-anonymous partners.

History of the Problem

Robin described a series of relationships with various men over a period of eleven years and complained about their "emotional unavailability." She described her childhood home as lonely and frightening. Her father was an alcoholic, tyrannical and at times physically abusive with her mother, sister, and brother. When he died the previous year, Robin described herself as "feeling nothing." She described her relationship with her mother as a "joke." Robin saw her mother as a passive victim who allowed her father to control the family and offered no resistance to his alcoholic bouts. As a child, Robin had adopted a "Daddy's little girl" strategy, which she described as a protection from his physical outbursts. The family was strict Pentecostal, and any talk of sexual matters was forbidden. She was not permitted to date, and she was still a virgin when she married her husband at the age of eighteen.

Current Sexual Functioning

Robin described her feelings of isolation from her husband, George. She had difficulty relaxing with him and, whenever possible, found various means to avoid sexual contact with him. She described her sexual relationship with her husband as unsatisfying. She had not been orgasmic with him for three years. She knew he felt frustrated with their sexual life and had gained sixty pounds in the past few years; she felt this weight gain made him even less appealing. She described her general contempt for men, whom she believed were "governed by their genitals," unable to function without dominating and abusing women. She was drawn into sado-masochistic fantasies and sought out partners for anonymous sex. She described feeling powerless to stop her seductions despite the increasing shame and humiliation these episodes brought her. She described herself as active in various sexually oriented chat rooms on the Internet, where she adopted sexualized names and spent "way too much time." When her fifteen-year-old son was arrested for shoplifting, she went to a bar the same evening and "picked up this loser" with whom she had unprotected sex.

Initial Phase of Treatment

An integrated, multimodal treatment approach began with outpatient individual psychotherapy by a social worker. A psychiatric referral for assessment resulted in Robin's being diagnosed with borderline personality disorder with depressive features. She was prescribed Serzone, an antidepressant medication. This enabled her to tolerate the feelings that accompanied the recounting of her painful childhood. She was helped to understand how her habitual self-critical thinking reflected her cognitive distortions, how this thinking was connected to her family of origin, and how it led to her acting out sexually with strangers.

Robin was initially resistant to identifying herself as a sex addict, refusing to go to any meeting with "those freaks," and was consequently referred to an Adult Children of Alcoholics self-help group. When she revealed a pattern of compulsively masturbating after attending meetings, the therapist recommended inpatient treatment to provide her with the relief from familial responsibilities and to intervene in what had become a ritualized pattern of compulsive sexual behaviors. The facility provided addiction rehabilitation with a specialty in sexual addiction. Her husband had insurance from his employer to cover the expense of most of the hospitalization, and he agreed to pay out of pocket for the balance.

Inpatient Treatment

While in treatment, Robin identified various attempts at intercourse by her father while she was in grade school, and she began working on the feelings of shame and self-loathing that these memories evoked. She attended a group specifically for women with sexual addiction and learned more about herself and how to intervene during her ritualized behavior, which often preceded her compulsive sexual "acting out." She expressed relief at being in the treatment center especially during times when her feelings of desperation, terror, and rage at her father and mother came to the surface.

Robin identified with a Catholic woman in her group who described a childhood of severe sexual repression. Robin was able to form a relationship with this woman outside the group and continued to stay in contact with her after leaving the facility. She described this relationship as "my first real friendship with a woman."

Bibliotherapy

During Robin's inpatient treatment, her therapist recommended various books in the patient library that addressed topics related to addiction in families and to women's sexuality. In particular, Robin began understanding the lack of boundaries in her family, which was a result of her father's alcoholism and her role as primary caretaker for her mother. She learned how to separate her parents' problems from her own and to address the guilt that this process of individuation stimulated.

Resumption of Outpatient Treatment

When Robin returned to her referring therapist for individual outpatient treatment, she felt motivated to attend self-help groups for sexual addiction, choosing SLAA "because there are more women there, so I feel safe." In addition, she began reading self-help books about women and addiction, which she described as instrumental in her ability to identify and accept herself as a sexually addicted woman. During her therapy sessions, she began more openly divulging the secrets that had been a part of her childhood and current family home. Robin began learning cognitive-behavioral strategies and identified her bottom-line behavior as having sex outside her marriage. She practiced role-playing assertiveness techniques with her therapist and did workbook exercises on these techniques at home. She began creating boundaries with her mother without resorting to aggressive verbal behaviors.

Family Therapy

The boredom that Robin described with her husband was identified in treatment as an inner emptiness and disconnection from herself and her needs. While she was in the residential facility, her husband began learning about his disordered eating patterns and, after some resistance, joined Overeaters Anonymous.

Robin and her husband were referred to another therapist for couples counseling to work on their lack of intimacy. Her son was referred to adolescent group therapy, and he reported that it was "not bad." While Robin began accruing time abstinent from anonymous sex and compulsive masturbation, she was faced with the fact that her daughter had begun a pattern of ritualized cutting and self-mutilation. Robin was able to have her daughter placed in an adolescent facility, despite her husband's misgivings; following her discharge, the daughter joined her siblings in family therapy sessions.

Preventing Relapse

During her treatment, Robin had learned about the potential for relapse, an aspect of recovery from sexual addiction. She had maintained an adamant commitment to abstinence and was devastated when she compulsively masturbated after going back on-line to a self-identified "off-limits" chat room. Robin was able to trace the trigger for her relapse to her feelings of rage and hopelessness that were connected to her mother's deteriorated health and subsequent diagnosis of Alzheimer's disease. After her siblings and her husband criticized her for placing her mother in a nursing home, Robin began isolating herself from her friends in SLAA, and her therapy attendance became inconsistent. In the aftermath of a week-long bout of pornography and compulsive masturbation, she learned that maintaining sobriety was more complicated than she had imagined. She and her therapist did "an autopsy" on the relapse, and she came to see the relapse as an important milestone in her recovery process. She and her SLAA sponsor decided that doing an inventory (corresponding to the fourth of the twelve steps) might help her move forward in her process of growth and self-acceptance.

Conclusion

Sexual addiction in women is a subject of controversy, and, to date, it is a poorly researched area. Clinicians need to take the lead in providing support and education to their clients by understanding and recognizing the basic concepts, signs, and symptoms of this illness. The goals of this chapter have been to deepen clinicians' awareness in recognizing and assessing the severity of sex addiction and in making knowledgeable referrals to treatment and support groups.

Clinical work shows that women can and do recover from sexual addiction. What is badly needed are qualitative studies exploring the therapeutic methods and approaches involved in successful recovery efforts. All clinicians working with women must be open to learning about the ongoing advances in biomedical aspects of addictions and the psychosocial approaches to clinical work with women struggling with sex addiction.

References

American Federation of Addiction Research. (2000). Available: www.addictionresearch.com/priorities.

American Psychiatric Association. (1994). *Diagnostic and statistical manual of mental disorders* (4th ed.). Washington, DC: Author.

Angier, N. (1999). *Woman: An intimate geography.* New York: Anchor Books.

Beck, A. T. (1967). *Depression: Clinical, experimental, and theoretical aspects.* New York: HarperCollins.

Beck, A. T., Rush, A. J., Shaw, B. F., & Emery, G. (1979). *Cognitive therapy of depression.* New York: Guilford Press.

Benjamin, J. (1988). *The bonds of love.* New York: Pantheon Books.

Braun-Harvey, D. K. (1997). Sexual dependence among recovering substance-abusing men. In S.L.A. Straussner & E. Zelvin (Eds.), *Gender and addictions: Men and women in treatment* (pp. 359–384). Northvale, NJ: Aronson.

Carnes, P. (1983). *Out of the shadows: Understanding sexual addiction.* Minneapolis: Comp-Care.

Carnes, P. (1991). *Don't call it love: Recovery from sexual addiction.* New York: Bantam Books.

Centers for Disease Control and Prevention (CDC). (1995, January 27). *The Morbidity and Mortality Weekly Report, 44*(3), p. 50.

Coleman, E. (1992). Is your patient suffering from compulsive sexual behavior? *Psychiatric Annals, 22,* 320–325.

Davis, N. D., Cole, E., & Rothblum, E. D. (1996). *Lesbian therapists and their therapy: From both sides of the couch.* Binghamton, NY: Haworth Press.

Earle, R. H., & Earle, M. R. (1995). *Sex addiction: Case studies and management.* New York: Brunner/Mazel.

Goodman, A. G. (1998). *Sexual addiction: An integrated approach.* Madison, WI: International Universities Press.

Kafka, M. P. (1991). Successful antidepressant treatment of nonparaphilic and paraphilias in men. *Journal of Clinical Psychiatry, 52,* 60–65.

Kaufman, G. (1989). *The psychology of shame: Theory and treatment of shame-based syndromes.* New York: Springer.

Khantzian, E., Halliday, K., & McAuliffe, W. (1990). *Addiction and the vulnerable self.* New York: Guilford Press.

Rubenstein, E. B., & Engel, N. L. (1996). Successful treatment of transvestic fetishism with sertraline and lithium. *Journal of Clinical Psychiatry, 57*(2), p. 92.

Schwartz, M. (1992). Sexual compulsivity as post-traumatic stress disorder: Treatment perspectives. *Psychiatric Annals, 22,* 333.

Schwartz, M., & Brasted, W. (1985). Sexual addiction: Self-hatred, guilt, and passive rage contribute to this deviant behavior. *Medical Aspects of Human Sexuality, 19*(10), 103–107.

Senreich, E., & Vairo, E. (in press). The treatment of the gay, lesbian, and bisexual substance abuser. In S.L.A. Straussner (Ed.), *Clinical work with substance abusing clients* (2nd ed.). New York: Guilford Press.

van der Kolk, B., Pelcovitz, D., Roth, S., Mandel, F., McFarlane, A., & Herman, J. (1996). Dissociation, somatization, and affect dysregulation: The complexity of adaptation to trauma. *American Journal of Psychiatry, 153,* 83–93.

Wolfe, D. B. (1996). *The turning point in committing to a 12 step recovery program for sexual addiction: Is there a spiritual awakening? A phenomenological study.* Ann Arbor, MI: UMI Dissertation Services.

CHAPTER EIGHT

WOMEN AND
RELATIONSHIP ADDICTION

Carol Tosone

"**M**any of us are addicts, only we don't know it. We turn to each other out of the same needs that drive some people to drink and others to heroin" (Peele, 1976, p. 1). With these simple words, Stanton Peele begins his groundbreaking volume on the most common, yet least recognized, form of addiction. Love or relationship addiction to an abusive or unavailable partner can be as injurious as substance abuse and equally as compelling. In such love relationships, the addictive element is not a substance but rather a compulsive need to connect with and remain attached to a particular person.

Akin to other types of addictions discussed in this volume, the person in an addictive relationship often feels empty, incomplete, and in desperate need to connect to something outside herself. There is an internal void, a constant need for stimulation, and an inability to feel sated. According to Peele (1976, 1988), an addiction exists when the individual's attachment to another person lessens her ability to attend to other personal needs. He characterizes addictive relationships as having an exclusively inward focus, one that reduces the person's involvement and capacity to deal with people and activities outside the love relationship. The person's preoccupation with seeking and maintaining a sense of security in the addictive relationship can lead to the dissolution of outside relationships often perceived as threatening to the primary bond. Despite the ensuing isolation and decreasing pleasure, the addictive relationship endures and is often mistaken for love.

Relationship and sexual addictions have been categorized broadly as either attraction or attachment types. Diamond (1988, 1991) observes that women tend to be prone to attachment-type addictions, whereas men are inclined toward addictions of the attraction type. That is, a man may be more focused on romance and attraction and have difficulty committing to one relationship. A woman may commit readily to one person but have difficulty leaving the relationship should it deteriorate. Her attachment may be to an emotionally or physically abusive partner or to one who is essentially unavailable, such as in the single woman–married man syndrome.

For years the popular press has capitalized on this largely women's phenomenon, beginning with the publication of *Women Who Love Too Much* (Norwood, 1985). Subsequently, numerous self-help titles were published on the topic, most notably *Men Who Hate Women and the Women Who Love Them* (Forward & Torres, 1986), *Is It Love or Is It Addiction?* (Schaeffer, 1987), and *Women, Sex and Addiction* (Kasl, 1990). As a trendy social idea, relationship addiction has received substantial attention, but as a clinical construct it has been conspicuously absent in the professional literature. In particular, the psychoanalytic scholarship devoted to the topic of women in addictive relationships is sparse, and, when the subject is discussed, it often comes under the rubric of masochism (Benjamin, 1988; Tuch, 2000). The term *relationship addiction* has been employed largely in the popular press; Peele's work (1976, 1988) is a notable exception. Although there is not a controversy regarding the term, it appears that clinical writers vary their terminology depending on whether they are writing for the lay public or a professional audience. Therefore, this chapter will attempt to bridge these two bodies of literature by applying psychoanalytic theories to the understanding of relationship addiction. Psychoanalytic theory provides a comprehensive explanatory model for understanding the woman's thought process and behavior in such relationships. Accordingly, this chapter uses case material to illustrate the theoretical concepts and to assist clinicians in identifying the syndrome and establishing treatment goals and a course of treatment.

Mature Object Love Versus Relationship Addiction

Women in the throes of an addictive relationship often justify their emotional pain and self-sacrificing behavior as being in the service of love. "I can't leave him because I love him" is a phrase commonly uttered to well-intentioned family and friends and in the privacy of the clinician's office. If a woman is involved in an emotionally or physically abusive relationship, she might add, "He can't help himself. He loves me. He doesn't mean to hurt me." If she is involved with an unavailable or married man, she might instead add, "If he could be with me now, he would. He can't, but I know he really loves me."

Emotions identified as love become the raison d'être for the relationship. Yet the same words that depict this type of love, such as *dependent, destructive, excessive,* and *obsessive,* can also be employed to describe addiction. To better understand the nature of relationship addiction, it would be useful to contrast its qualities with those of mature object love—the goal of treatment.

Mature object love is exemplified by women who are secure in their attachments to others and not preoccupied with abandonment. Such women are capable of and comfortable with mutual dependency. According to Sternberg (1986, 1988), they are capable of maintaining the three ingredients essential to mature love relationships: intimacy, passion, and commitment. Like women in addictive relationships, these women tend to idealize their partners, but their idealization takes place in the context of a mature relationship, with the concomitant capacity for experiencing tenderness, guilt, and forgiveness. Their idealization is distinct from that of women in addictive relationships, who idealize the love object at their own expense. Women capable of mature object love demonstrate a capacity for idealization that exalts the body, as well as the total person and value system, of the love object. Their capacity for passion and mature idealization, coupled with their ability to integrate love and aggression—with love as the dominant feature—constitutes an advanced developmental level of functioning (Kernberg, 1974, 1995).

In contrast, women in addictive relationships are considered developmentally arrested on the way to object constancy (Mahler, Pine, & Bergman, 1975). Many were raised in chronically unpredictable home environments where their mothers were inconsistent in their displays of affection; the children were alternately rewarded and punished for the same behavior. As a result, these children were not highly exploratory and became preoccupied with issues of abandonment. These trends continued throughout childhood, adolescence, and into adulthood.

As I have written elsewhere (Tosone, 1998, 1999), these women tend to present in treatment with masochistic character organization and are often drawn to challenging, unavailable, or abusive people. Out of their tenacious longing for an idealized partner, such women often project these qualities onto potential partners who are not desirable. They readily fall in love out of a need for attachment. The masochistic woman is attracted sexually to an idealized partner who initially provides a whirlwind romance, then may reject or abuse her. In essence, she reexperiences the narcissistic injury created in childhood by the parents. Through submission and caretaking, she attempts to win the love of an admired yet critical partner–parent substitute.

Her experience of love can be described as immature, and it differs significantly from that of a mature love relationship. Indeed, relationship addiction can be considered a type of immature love. Applying Peele's model of love (1988) to a discussion of the qualities of relationship addiction, one can discern sizable differences in their respective descriptions: (1) love as an expansive experience that awakens the individual to opportunities, versus love as an absorption in one person; (2) love as a helping relationship in which there is mutual trust, versus love as an idealization and blind acceptance of another; (3) love as a secure base that allows for enhanced capacity for growth in the outside world, versus love as a private world in which one is concerned solely with how the other person meets his or her needs; (4) love as rooted in a passion for life, versus love as rooted in a painful sense of the world; in mature love, the person benefits from the partner's enjoyment of living; (5) love as a beneficial experience, one that enhances each participant as a person, versus love as an incapacitating experience in which the partners hurt and depreciate one another and foster insecurity in the relationship; (6) love as grounded in one's sense of security and in the belief of the goodness of others, versus love as an accidental occurrence with no stability or longevity; (7) love as an experience consonant with friendship and affection, versus love as an all-or-nothing experience; when an addicted relationship ends, there is rarely the opportunity for an ongoing friendship; and (8) love as an awakened moral state of being, with the concomitant responsibility for nurturing a love relationship, versus love as an unconscious motivation and uncontrollable urge that determines the person's actions in the relationship.

Although many external factors, such as financial and familial obligations, play an important role in sustaining relationship addiction, unconscious factors perhaps best explain the tenacity with which a woman clings to such a relationship. It is important for clinicians to grasp the motivational factors operating in each specific case. In such relationships, the woman often consciously believes that her emotional and physical survival is dependent on the love object, without whom her existence would be meaningless. Her subjective experience of the relationship is echoed in literature, music, and movies that depict the painful nature of dependent, romantic love. Such words and images from popular culture suggest the regressive symbiotic longings of a helpless infant for its powerful mother, as well as a young child's need to elicit affection from a rejecting parent as symbolized by the absent or cruel lover.

Theoretical Perspectives on Relationship Addiction

Theories that illuminate the childhood antecedents of relationship addiction can guide clinicians as they help their clients develop the capacity for mature love. For our present purpose, we will apply multiple theoretical perspectives to aid clinicians in understanding the woman's early childhood relationship patterns and how such patterns contribute to the development of relationship addiction in later life. Accordingly, we will examine relationship addiction in women from the viewpoints of classical, attachment, relational, and feminist theories.

Classical Theory

The classical perspective on addiction incorporates contemporary Freudian and ego psychology views and is best exemplified by the works of Khantzian (1985, 1997), Dodes (1996), and Wurmser (1984), all of whom view addiction as a response to affect intolerance. Khantzian in particular first articulated the self-medication hypothesis, which states that individuals gravitate toward a substance that will fill their psychological void. According to Khantzian (1995), the inability to regulate affective states originates in childhood and reflects the child's lack of internalization of parental care. As a result, in later life, the addicted person has difficulty regulating self-esteem and relationships, and may neglect her own care. This ego deficit is pronounced in women who use their connection to an abusive or unavailable partner to manage their own affective states. When apart from their lovers, many of these women report overwhelming feelings of depression, emptiness, and helplessness.

Dodes (1996) suggests that intolerable helplessness is a core vulnerability in addiction and that addiction serves as a futile attempt to assure oneself that one has the capacity to control one's internal affective state. Loss of control and ego autonomy is a frequent source of shame for addicted individuals and may fuel their denial of the severity of the problem. Women in addictive relationships often feel tremendous shame about the compulsive and self-destructive nature of their behavior, and they often avoid discussing the relationship with others.

Dodes also emphasizes that addictions are a subset of compulsions, and as such are amenable to psychoanalytic inquiry and treatment. Dodes (1996), along with Wurmser (1984), acknowledges the role of intrapsychic conflict in addictions. Both note that addicts tend to have harsh, punitive superegos. As a result, they often feel guilty for their addictive behavior and have difficulties in the areas of self-esteem and establishing healthy relationships with others.

When the addictive "substance" is an abusive or unavailable partner, the classical perspective offers keen insights into the woman's development and her masochistic character structure. Lax (1977) posits that as early as the oral and anal phases, the infant girl experiences her mother as unloving and depriving. Regardless of what the child does, she does not feel accepted as good enough by her mother. Because she needs to believe in the goodness of her mother on whom she depends so heavily, she internalizes the sense of badness and blames herself for the poor treatment she receives.

In addition, the mother's attitude toward her own femininity can contribute significantly to her daughter's developmental process. If the mother has a negative attitude toward her body, genitals, and self, Bernstein (1983) notes that her responses can lead the daughter to view her own body and femininity in a hostile and pain-producing way. In this regard, the daughter is identifying with her mother, as well as adopting aspects of the mother's behavior in an effort to please her. This early mother-daughter dynamic has relevance in the discussion of why women in physically abusive relationships seem to possess a greater tolerance for physical pain. The woman acquiesces to and identifies with a cruel, sadistic love object who reminds her (on an unconscious level) of the original love object, the mother. Through repetition compulsion, these women attempt to resolve elements in their early maternal relationship, the goal being a more satisfying outcome than occurred originally.

Attachment Theory

The nature and quality of the mother-child bond is the core focus of attachment theory as articulated by John Bowlby (1969, 1973, 1979, 1980, 1988). Bowlby held that confidence in the availability of attachment figures, or lack of it, builds up slowly in childhood and adolescence and tends to persist relatively unchanged throughout life. Essentially, people develop mental models of themselves and their partners that largely determine the nature of their feelings and relationship patterns for life. For example, women in emotionally or physically abusive relationships may have learned in early childhood to endure pain in order to maintain a needed attachment. This pattern becomes their working model of the environment and a template for adult relationships.

For Bowlby, all important love relationships, whether between a mother and infant or between adult lovers, constitute attachments. Within either dyad, the anticipation of loss arouses strong emotions, such as crying, anger, and anxiety. Ainsworth, Blehar, Waters, and Wall (1978) applied Bowlby's ideas to their observations of mother-infant pairs and concurred with his point that the mother's attentiveness to her infant's needs is the essential ingredient for secure attachment. Based on their findings, Ainsworth and colleagues delineated three types of attachments, which they referred to as secure, anxious/ambivalent, and avoidant. Unlike the secure infant who is confident in the mother's responsiveness, or the avoidant one who mirrors the rejecting behavior of the mother, the anxious/ambivalent infant is the most prone to crying and anxiety upon separation from the mother. The infant is anxious because he or she is uncertain that the mother will return, and crying serves as an attempt to reengage the mother, thereby assuring her return.

The three-category scheme developed by Ainsworth et al. (1978) has been applied to the study of adult romantic love by Hazan and Shaver (1987), who refer to corresponding qualities of adult attachment using the same terms. Secure lovers are capable of mature object love and have generally attained a mature level of development. In contrast to avoidant lovers who are fearful of intimacy, secure lovers relish it and do not fear abandonment. Women in addictive relationships can be categorized as anxious/ambivalent lovers, given their tremendous fear of abandonment and craving for intimacy. Although their relationships are of a highly dependent nature, they are repeatedly drawn to unavailable or inconsistent partners who frustrate their need and desire for security. Qualitatively different from the avoidant lover who has difficulty trusting others, the woman in an addictive relationship too readily entrusts her care to an intermittently responsive and abusive partner.

Paradoxically, powerful emotional attachment is strengthened by intermittent good and bad treatment and a significant power imbalance in the relationship. This idea represents the basic tenet of traumatic bonding theory first formulated by Dutton and Painter (1993) and extrapolated from Bowlby's attachment theory. Traumatic bonding theory posits that in abusive relationships, the abuser's interpersonal anger arises from frustrated attachment needs and functions as a form of protest behavior. The abuser's goal is to regain contact with the attachment figure or partner. Similarly, for the woman in an abusive relationship, Dutton and Painter observe that threatening conditions, such as physical or emotional abuse, are likely to activate the attachment system. In essence, the abuse serves to enhance the strength of the bond as the abused woman seeks greater proximity to her lover. *The Story of O* and *Return to the Chateau* are poignant literary examples of this phenomenon.

Earlier, Walker (1977) coined the phrase *battered woman syndrome*, which describes a cyclical pattern of domestic violence characterized by three phases. In phase one, tension gradually builds, followed by an explosive battering incident (phase two); in phase three, a calm, loving respite occurs. As the abusive partner attempts to compensate for the violence by providing his partner with exceptionally positive treatment, his improved behavior serves to reduce aversive arousal while also providing reinforcement for the woman to remain in the relationship. She then focuses on the desirable elements in the relationship, often altering her beliefs about the viability of the relationship. Essentially, the woman becomes "hooked" on the relationship. Her partner's intermittent abuse produces a deeper emotional connection that interferes with her leaving and remaining out of the relationship.

Both Walker (1977) and Dutton and Painter (1993) cite animal research (Fischer, 1955; Seay, Alexander, & Harlow, 1964) that supports the hypothesis that inconsistent reinforcement for the same behavior induces greater dependency. That is, when physical punishment was administered intermittently and interspersed with friendly contact, the phenomenon of traumatic bonding seemed most recognizable. The findings of these ethological studies are consistent with those of developmental research, which indicate that abused children are still attached to an abusive caregiver, albeit insecurely (Dutton & Painter, 1993).

Relational Theory

The findings from attachment research are congruent with the relational schools of thought, particularly the works of Fairbairn (1954) and Benjamin (1988, 1995). Defining the relational perspective broadly, it comprises many of the major postclassical schools of analytic thought, including British object relations, self psychology, intersubjectivity, interpersonal psychoanalysis, and multiplicity of self-state theory. For the present purpose, we will consider only relational viewpoints that offer understanding of the salient features of addictive relationships, beginning with Fairbairn.

In his elaboration of an object relations theory of the personality, Fairbairn maintained that infants are object-seeking from birth and originally free of aggression. According to Fairbairn, aggression arises only in response to frustration and deprivation. He suggests that the earliest form of anxiety, separation anxiety, is activated when the infant is temporarily separated from the mother. Such frustration leads to a defensive, unconscious internalization of the object with its exciting and frustrating aspects.

According to Fairbairn, the "masochistic defense" is a result of the unconscious efforts to protect the relationship with the frustrating yet needed object. The masochist internalizes the burden of badness that resides in the object. In becoming bad oneself, one purges the object of its badness.

Fairbairn's concept of internalization as defense can be applied to the understanding of women's addictions to unavailable or abusive partners. Women in both situations experience an obsessive longing, punctuated by short bursts of intense gratification and followed by longer periods of yearning, frustration, or abuse. The exciting object transforms into a rejecting one, but it is difficult for the woman to accept that the previously caring person is now critical and rejecting. The partner is perceived to have all the necessary narcissistic supplies, and the woman desperately tries to get the partner to respond favorably. Her tenacious belief that the partner can provide what she needs is reinforced by the intermittent positive attention, which leaves her feeling that her partner's love is potentially available.

Glickauf-Hughes and Wells (1995), applying Fairbairn's ideas about masochistic defense to work with couples, emphasize the reciprocal nature of the masochistic-narcissistic dyad. They note the partners' interlocking dynamics: narcissists have a propensity for projecting unwanted parts of themselves onto others, whereas masochists tend to internalize aspects of others that are not part of themselves. Women in addictive relationships are vulnerable to the unrealistic promises that narcissists make early in the relationship, thereby enacting their fantasies about ideal love and the ideal partner. That is, by attributing the partner's negative characteristics to herself, the woman is free to view the partner as ideal, much as a child needs to view a parent. Masochistic women generally seek relationships in which they are nurtured and gratified as a child would be by a parent, yet they tend to become caretakers in the relationship by treating others as they wish to be treated themselves. Caretaking assures them a sense of interpersonal control and security.

Benjamin (1988, 1995), adopting an intersubjective point of view, offers a useful model for understanding the masochistic-narcissistic dyad. The intersubjective position holds that a relationship involves a subject in interaction with another subject, both of whom are in need of mutual recognition and connection. Benjamin (1988) proposes that the masochistic woman submits to and adores the man in an effort to gain access to his power. The narcissistic male, controlling the woman by her own submission, loses the sense of recognition and connection he seeks. Rather than a subject in interaction with another subject, she becomes objectified in his eyes, and recognition is no longer possible. It is significant that when women in addictive relationships threaten to leave, they regain their subjectivity, and mutual recognition again becomes possible.

Benjamin notes that when a woman accepts her own object status and denial of self, she is reenacting an early identification with her mother, a replication of the maternal attitude of self-alienation. That is, the daughter adopts her mother's stance of deferring to others' needs and desires at her own expense. The mother, in fact, lacks the recognition of what are her own specific needs. In addition to the mother's contribution, Benjamin also addresses the father's role in the development of a girl's masochism. Benjamin describes "ideal love" as a form of masochism that is rooted in the female child's relationship to her father. He serves as a representative of and link to the outside world, and by his example, he provides a model for freedom and self-realization. Should the girl's identificatory love for her father be thwarted in childhood, it can lead to a solidification of her identification with her mother. This can result in self-debasement and a belief that her abilities are limited.

Feminist Theory

The feminist perspective also considers the subjugation and object status of women, but emphasis is on the imbalance of power between the genders in a patriarchal society. In regard to women in addictive relationships, feminist ideology has explanatory power primarily on the sociopolitical and interpersonal levels. On the macro level, the feminist perspective concludes that economic factors, such as wage differentials, employability, and the need to care for dependents, as well as how men and women are acculturated into their respective gender-stereotyped roles of power and passivity, can account for some women's tendencies to remain in addictive relationships.

In particular, Van Den Bergh (1991) asserts that patriarchal social, political, and economic forces create conditions conducive to the development of addictive behavior in women. The dynamics of control and domination, central to a patriarchal capitalist society, also affect interpersonal relationships between the sexes. Van Den Bergh believes that addiction can develop as a way to numb and deny a sense of powerlessness. Through their efforts to control their partner's behavior, for instance, relationship addicts and codependents acquire a needed sense of power.

Much has been written in the feminist literature specific to the topic of domestic violence (Bartley, 1990; Caplan, 1993; Walker, 1977; Westlund, 1999). Caplan (1993), in particular, argues that survivors of domestic violence exhibit behavior that reflects their efforts to avoid—not seek—punishment, rejection, or guilt. She believes that labels such as masochism do a disservice to women who might blame themselves for their difficulties. Rather, she maintains that behavior labeled as masochistic actually demonstrates a woman's ability to delay gratification and to put the needs of another ahead of her own.

Unfortunately, Caplan adopts a simplistic definition of masochism as the "need to derive pleasure from pain" (1993, p. 1). Her succinct definition does not address the core issue that a woman's attachment to an abusive partner serves as a means of maintaining a relationship to a painfully perceived internal object, one that provides meaning and purpose. Women in addictive relationships do not enjoy pain per se; rather, they see pain as a necessary evil to maintain ties to the desired symbolic love object. Caplan herself acknowledges that the emotional and physical pain the woman endures is more tolerable than facing the loss of a cherished relationship. The woman's bond is not to the abuse but rather to the partner's warmer, affectionate side; this reflects the woman's healthy need to be loved.

Caplan (1993) and other feminist authors, such as Miller (1976), Chodorow (1978), and Gilligan (1982) underscore women's relational developmental needs. In articulating a feminist theory of development, these authors share the view that a woman's sense of herself develops in connection to others. Chodorow, for instance, contends that a woman's core gender identity is formed on a more personal basis than that of a man. That is, because the mother more readily identifies and merges with her daughter due to their shared gender, she may not encourage the same degree of separation for her daughter as she does for her son. For women, development does not involve differentiation as separateness. Rather, it involves changing the nature of their connection to others throughout her life cycle. That is, whereas the boy must separate and individuate from his mother in order to establish a masculine identity, the girl solidifies her identity through attachment to her mother. The nature of her attachment to her mother and others may vary throughout the life cycle, but it is her need to connect that remains constant.

In a similar vein, Gilligan's research (1982) on superego development in men and women supported the proposition that women value responsiveness and caring for others in their social network, whereas men tend to be more focused on abstract concepts, such as equality and justice. Along with Miller (1976), Gilligan (1982) considers the establishment and maintenance of close relationships as the guiding principle in women's lives. Their ideas have direct relevance for understanding women in addictive relationships, who are generally more attuned to their partner's needs than to their own. Pain, whether emotional or physical, becomes the obligatory cost to preserve the bond.

◆ ◆ ◆

Classical, attachment, relational, and feminist paradigms are valuable clinical tools in understanding the etiology of relationship addiction and informing the course of treatment. The following case example will illustrate clinical features of relationship addiction and factors to consider in the general treatment approach.

Case Illustration and Course of Treatment

Janine arrived for her first appointment disheveled and hastily clad in her neighbor's large clothes, which hid her petite frame. As would become her custom in treatment, she began the session with an apology. On this day she apologized for her appearance, drawing attention to her right arm resting in a sling. She spent much of the previous evening in the emergency room awaiting treatment for her sprained arm, an injury sustained when her husband pushed her during an argument. Following the hospital visit, she sought refuge in her neighbor's home, where she planned to remain until her husband, Tom, came to his senses.

Janine spent the initial session and many subsequent ones analyzing and apologizing for his irrational and sometimes explosive behavior. She knew the intimate details of his unmet childhood needs, but none of her own. She focused her discussion on their courtship, when he was loving, generous, and nurturing of her career as a real estate agent. Janine convinced herself that without Tom, life was meaningless. Only he fully knew her and could satisfy her hungry longing for love. His outbursts, she concluded, were primarily her fault. Janine initially sought treatment to understand him better and to make herself a more responsive partner.

Janine and Tom had a well-established pattern, one consistent with the clinical observations of Walker (1977) and Dutton and Painter (1993). Janine and her husband would get into a heated argument, generally over his excessive drinking or her inadequate housekeeping, followed by his berating and sometimes hitting her. She would leave briefly but find the separation intolerable. Each time, she would return convinced that she could not live without him, and more determined to make the relationship work. To do so, she had to neglect other meaningful relationships and her career, two areas that were increasingly being compromised.

During the assessment and early treatment phase, Janine exhibited the classic features of relationship addiction: obsessive longing for and idealization of the symbolic love object, impairment in other areas of functioning due to the preoccupation with the relationship, and lack of control over her affective state. Much of our discussion centered on her feelings of panic and dread at the prospect of living without her husband. When apart from him, she was consumed by unbearable feelings of emptiness and loneliness, especially on those occasions when he left home. Her subjective state was suggestive of an infant unable to self-soothe in her mother's absence, as if there were no certainty of the mother's return. Her preoccupation with abandonment was pronounced: she had difficulty eating, sleeping, and functioning in her daily life. This experience is evocative of an early psychosomatic memory of object loss or an objectless state. When reunited with her husband, however, she enjoyed a blissful symbiotic union in which words were superfluous in communicating mutual love and understanding.

As treatment continued, we spoke at length about her fear of being able to survive alone, not only emotionally but financially. At age thirty-five, she was already an established and successful real estate agent, but she maintained the self-image of a helpless child and "people pleaser." She described herself as a self-proclaimed "codependent," a term she learned in Al-Anon when she was previously married to an abusive alcoholic. She left her first husband to marry Tom, as he was nicer and drank less often. Although Tom did not drink as heavily, he was easily hurt and prone to narcissistic rages that sometimes escalated to physical force.

As we addressed her desire to attune herself to his unmet needs, I observed the disparity between her keen awareness of his desires and her lack of awareness of her own. Although she had an intellectual understanding of how she was repeating the past in the present, she spoke about her childhood without emotion. That is, Janine knew she was negatively affected by her depressed, dependent mother and her critical, alcoholic father, but her emotional energy was centered on her relationship with Tom. According to Janine, her parents were elderly and frail and were not the cause of her current problems. The goals of alleviating her depression and having a healthier marriage provided the only impetus for Janine to explore her harrowing past.

Early memories that she first described as "no big deal," in the later phase of treatment became laden with poignant emotion. Janine's earliest memory at age five, for instance, involved her father smashing a hamburger in her face because she would not eat. Janine had just returned elated from her first dance class, and when she would not heed her father's angry insistence that she eat, he held her head back and forced the hamburger in her mouth. She recalled tearfully her feelings of anger and humiliation at his abusive behavior. Janine also wondered out loud as to her mother's whereabouts on that day. It was rare when she could recall her mother's consistent availability and protection, especially at those times when her father would have angry outbursts. Although he was rarely physically abusive, he was prone to angry outbursts, especially while drunk.

Janine's early memories about her mother proved equally illuminating. She recalls at age seven pacing between her mother and aunt trying to stifle her urge to say a curse word. At the time, Janine rebuked herself for being "a very bad girl." In recalling this memory, Janine mentioned that her mother nearly died when giving birth to her (due to a severe hemorrhage). Her mother was cautioned by the physician not to have other children as doing so might be life threatening. From childhood on, Janine was constantly aware of her mother's frailty and felt guilty whenever she was angry with her.

Janine's frequent violent dreams, however, were filled with gruesome murders of her mother, father, and Tom. There were many murderers in her dreams, but she was never the agent. Treatment addressed her bitter disappointments with these important love objects and her fear that her anger would devastate them. As she gradually came to appreciate the depth of her anger and pain, she began to better understand her fear of being alone. She came to realize that she invested more in the care of others than in her own self-development. The prospect of being alone reminded her of her helpless state as a child.

Janine has taken important steps in the recovery process. She has a better grasp of both the unconscious elements involved in her addictive relationship and the larger familial and societal issues regarding women's traditional role as nurturer. Correspondingly, she understands that her marital relationship represents an addiction, not mature love. She has gained this knowledge through individual therapy, marital counseling, and periodic involvement in Al-Anon. Janine has become more self-protective in the marital relationship and remains committed to the relationship as her husband has sought professional help for himself. Although an arduous process, the journey to recovery has begun and continues to the present day.

Relationship Addiction and Substance Abuse

Janine's narrative is illustrative of the common features of relationship addiction previously described. It is not unusual that these women become involved with substance-abusing partners, nor that they come from families in which substance abuse is an intergenerational pattern. Often such women have been involved with self-help programs such as Al-Anon or Adult Children of Alcoholics. In Janine's case, she was well acquainted with Al-Anon from the days of her previous marriage. During the course of treatment, she came to realize that Tom also had a drinking problem. She attended several Al-Anon meetings to help her gain perspective on the extent of the problem. Additionally, she encouraged her husband to consider attending Alcoholics Anonymous, a step he has not yet taken.

Women in Janine's situation frequently diagnose themselves as codependent. O'Gorman (1991) refers to codependence as a form of intergenerational learned helplessness in which problematic family traditions and rituals pertaining to intimacy and bonding are passed down from mother to daughter. Within this context, O'Gorman considers codependency as a type of relationship addiction in which there is a compulsive dependence on another. In contrast, interdependency, the goal of therapy, involves the mature ability to be together as a couple, as well as alone. Codependency is a rigid stance, whereas interdependence is a fluid process.

In describing the features and etiology of codependency, O'Gorman (1991) observes family patterns similar to those described in traumatic bonding theory. Inconsistent and contradictory messages from the parents to their female child cause her to be dependent and to maintain an external locus of control. The girl learns that her needs and those of other family members are secondary to those of the alcoholic parent. Her attempts to nurture or to change the alcoholic parent are mostly futile. Powerlessness and helplessness become her predominant experience in childhood, and are often repeated in her adult attachments. Sharing her experiences with other women in Al-Anon helps empower her, because it provides personal validation. She comes to realize that other women have had comparable experiences and that change is possible. Insight is gained not only through attendance at Al-Anon meetings but also through individual, family, and group psychotherapy.

Conclusion

Although codependency is a type of relationship addiction, it is important to keep in mind that relationship addiction exists in different variations and that women are more prone to the attachment type. The term relationship addiction has gained a general acceptance in the popular press, whereas the professional literature has largely employed the term masochism to describe the same phenomenon. This chapter has sought to bridge these two bodies of literature by applying multiple theories to better understand the etiology of relationship addiction. Each theory, in its respective lexicon, describes the early mother-daughter dynamic in which the infant does not feel securely attached to her mother. Separation anxiety often develops, as does her tendency to blame herself for her mother's inconsistent attentiveness. In essence, she develops the template for later relationship addiction in that she internalizes the burden of badness that resides in the love object. In relationship addiction, the woman is drawn to an intermittently responsive partner whom she needs to idealize, and so she attributes the partner's negative attributes to herself. In addition to the classical, attachment, and relational theories that elaborate the intrapsychic features of relationship addiction, feminist theory explicates the societal and interpersonal aspects of the syndrome. Case material illustrated the features of relationship addiction and described how theoretical perspectives can inform the course of treatment. It behooves clinicians to understand the many facets of relationship addiction, as it is a common lament of their female clients.

References

Ainsworth, M., Blehar, M., Waters, E., & Wall, S. (1978). *Patterns of attachment: A psychological study of the strange situation.* New York: Wiley.

Bartley, S. (1990). *Femininity and domination: Studies in the phenomenology of oppression.* New York: Routledge.

Benjamin, J. (1988). *The bonds of love.* New York: Pantheon Books.

Benjamin, J. (1995). *Like subjects, love objects: Essays on recognition and sexual difference.* New Haven, CT: Yale University Press.

Bernstein, D. (1983). *Female identity conflict in clinical practice.* Northvale, NJ: Aronson.

Bowlby, J. (1969). *Attachment and loss: Vol. 1. Attachment.* New York: Basic Books.

Bowlby, J. (1973). *Attachment and loss: Vol. 2. Separation.* New York: Basic Books.

Bowlby, J. (1979). *The making and breaking of affectional bonds.* London: Tavistock.

Bowlby, J. (1980). *Attachment and loss: Vol. 3. Loss.* New York: Basic Books.

Bowlby, J. (1988). *A secure base.* New York: Basic Books.

Caplan, P. (1993). *The myth of women's masochism.* Toronto: University of Toronto Press.

Chodorow, N. (1978). *The reproduction of mothering: Psychoanalysis and the sociology of gender.* Berkeley: University of California Press.

Diamond, J. (1988). *Looking for love in all the wrong places: Overcoming romantic and sexual addictions.* New York: Putnam.

Diamond, J. (1991). Looking for love in all the wrong places. In N. Van Den Bergh (Ed.), *Feminist perspectives on addictions* (pp. 167–180). New York: Springer.

Dodes, L. (1996). Compulsion and addiction. *Journal of the American Psychoanalytic Association, 44,* 815–835.

Dutton, D., & Painter, S. (1993). Emotional attachments in abusive relationships: A test of traumatic bonding theory. *Violence and Victims, 8*(2), 105–120.

Fairbairn, W. R. (1954). *An object relations theory of the personality.* New York: Basic Books.

Fischer, A. (1955). *The effects of differential early treatment on the social and exploratory behavior of puppies*. Unpublished doctoral dissertation, Pennsylvania State University.

Forward, S., & Torres, J. (1986). *Men who hate women and the women who love them*. New York: Bantam Books.

Gilligan, C. (1982). *In a different voice*. Cambridge, MA: Harvard University Press.

Glickauf-Hughs, C., & Wells, M. (1995). *Treatment of the masochistic personality: An interactional object relations approach to psychotherapy*. Northvale, NJ: Aronson.

Hazan, C., & Shaver, P. (1987). Romantic love conceptualized as an attachment process. *Journal of Personality and Social Psychology, 52*, 511–524.

Kasl, C. D. (1990). *Women, sex and addiction*. New York: HarperCollins.

Kernberg, O. (1974). Mature love: Prerequisites and characteristics. *Journal of the American Psychoanalytic Association, 22*, 743–768.

Kernberg, O. (1995). *Love relations: Normality and pathology*. New Haven, CT: Yale University Press.

Khantzian, E. (1985). The self-medication hypothesis of addictive disorders. *American Journal of Psychiatry, 142*, 1259–1264.

Khantzian, E. (1995). Self-regulation vulnerabilities in substance abusers: Treatment implications. In S. Dowling (Ed.), *The psychology and treatment of addictive behavior* (pp. 17–42). Madison, CT: International Universities Press.

Khantzian, E. (1997). The self-medication hypothesis of substance use disorders: A reconsideration and recent applications. *Harvard Review of Psychiatry, 4*, 231–244.

Lax, R. (1977). The role of internalization in the development of certain aspects of female masochism: Ego psychological considerations. *International Journal of Psychoanalysis, 58*, 289–300.

Mahler, M., Pine, F., & Bergman, A. (1975). *The psychological birth of the human infant*. New York: Basic Books.

Miller, J. (1976). *Toward a new psychology of women*. Boston: Beacon Press.

Norwood, R. (1985). *Women who love too much*. New York: Pocket Books.

O'Gorman, P. (1991). Codependency and women: Unraveling the power behind learned helplessness. In N. Van Den Bergh (Ed.), *Feminist perspectives on addictions* (pp. 153–166). New York: Springer.

Peele, S. (1976). *Love and addiction*. New York: New American Library.

Peele, S. (1988). Fools for love: The romantic ideal, psychological theory, and addictive love. In R. Sternberg & M. Barnes (Eds.), *The psychology of love* (pp. 159–188). New Haven, CT: Yale University Press.

Schaeffer, B. (1987). *Is it love or is it addiction?* New York: MJF Books.

Seay, B., Alexander, B., & Harlow, H. (1964). Maternal behavior of socially deprived rhesus monkeys. *Journal of Abnormal and Social Psychology, 69*, 345–354.

Sternberg, R. (1986). A triangular theory of love. *Psychological Review, 97*, 119–135.

Sternberg, R. (1988). Triangulating love. In R. Sternberg & M. Barnes (Eds.), *The psychology of love* (pp. 119–138). New Haven, CT: Yale University Press.

Tosone, C. (1998). Revisiting the "myth" of feminine masochism. *Clinical Social Work Journal, 26*, 413–426.

Tosone, C. (1999). Illusion, disillusion, and reality in romantic love. In C. Tosone & T. Aiello (Eds.), *Love and attachment: Contemporary issues and treatment considerations* (pp. 3–24). Northvale, NJ: Aronson.

Tuch, R. (2000). *The single woman–married man syndrome.* Northvale, NJ: Aronson.

Van Den Bergh, N. (1991). Having bitten the apple: A feminist perspective on addictions. In N. Van Den Bergh (Ed.), *Feminist perspectives on addictions* (pp. 3–30). New York: Springer.

Walker, L. (1977). *The battered woman.* New York: HarperCollins.

Westlund, A. (1999). Pre-modern and modern power: Foucault and the case of domestic violence. *Journal of Women in Culture and Society, 24*(4), 1045–1066.

Wurmser, L. (1984). The role of superego conflicts in substance abuse and their treatment. *International Journal of Psychoanalytic Psychotherapy, 10,* 227–258.

CHAPTER NINE

WOMEN AND SPENDING ADDICTIONS

Linda Barbanel

When spending becomes an obsession that consumes a person's thinking and results in repetitive spending behavior, it is considered compulsive spending. As in other addictions, compulsive acts cover up uncomfortable inner feelings, so that spending offers temporary relief. However, sooner or later the person's life becomes out of control because of growing debt. The spender experiences a variety of conflicts and negative feelings, including low self-esteem, boredom, deprivation, inadequacy, loss, and anger. Because the spender does not address these issues but instead just covers them up with additional spending, the cycle continues. Women are especially prone to these symptoms because addressing the problems that prompt spending involves facing their fears of expressing anger, of putting their needs before others, and of saying what they need emotionally. For many women, it is so dangerous to speak up that the acting-out spending behavior continues.

This chapter explores the issues of compulsive spending as they relate to women and seeks to encourage clinicians to help patients learn to identify their needs, wishes, and feelings and put them into words in order to break the compulsive behavioral cycle. Once a woman begins to understand how her behavior is related to her unmet needs, wishes, and feelings—both conscious and unconscious—she can begin to learn more constructive ways of satisfying her emotional needs. Often it is helpful for patients to attend twelve-step groups such as Debtors Anonymous as a way to get support and to hear how others cope with their compulsions.

How Prevalent Is Compulsive Spending?

Compulsive spending can be seen in every part of our society. One could say that it is "American" to spend, considering that our economy depends on the continuous upgrading and replacement of material goods.

It is difficult to know just how prevalent problem spending is, but we do know that millions of people are in debt ("Credit Cards," 2000). About 80 million households have credit card accounts with unpaid balances averaging between $6,000 and $7,000, and bankruptcies are rising. It is not uncommon for individuals to commit suicide as a result of growing credit card debt.

The amount of consumer credit owed to domestic finance companies in 1994 was $244.4 billion, and that sum grew to $323.3 billion by August 1997 (*Federal Reserve Bulletin*, 1997).

Women are still the largest group of spenders. According to a *Ladies' Home Journal* article, "QVC, Inc. network reaches more than 61 million cable subscribers across the country. At any given time 5 to 6 million viewers, some 90 percent of whom are women, are watching QVC, and they buy upwards of $50,000 in merchandise every hour, sometimes as much as $1 million" (Stesin, 1997, p. 166).

With the recent popularity of online investing, indebtedness has increased. Margin loans make up 16 percent of total consumer borrowings, up from 7 percent in 1995 (Morgenson, 2000). Market debt on the New York Stock Exchange has gone up 75 percent to more that $265 billion in the last year. It is not known how many online investors are women, or how many are compulsive spenders, but a growing number of investment firms are targeting women, and every year women receive hundreds of millions of solicitations for credit cards by mail. These offers are difficult to resist, particularly for those women who are addicted to spending.

A Comparison of Compulsive Spending and Other Addictions

Some women who want to feel better about their difficulties in life turn to the use and abuse of substances. Others spend money. Many compulsive spenders and debtors also have a history of drinking, eating, drugging, or "loving too much." Some women who can control their drinking, drugging, eating, and loving turn to spending without realizing that they are continuing their compulsive behavior with a new substance—albeit one that is less immediately destructive.

The common defense mechanisms of denial and rationalization that are seen in women with other addictions are also seen in compulsive spenders. These women not only deny their real feelings but also may deny that their closets are full of unnecessary items and that they need to pay bills. The phrase "I deserve this" is a frequently used overt proclamation of entitlement, which covers up the common underlying feeling of being undeserving.

Similar to women with eating disorders, women with spending compulsions cannot live without their "substance." We all have to eat and to spend money. The need to set limits and to control oneself in both instances is crucial, yet this is impossible to achieve without learning new ways of coping. It is common for a woman with a spending addiction to tell herself, "This is the last time I'll do this," "This was a special opportunity," "It was so cheap, it doesn't count," or "I'll start again tomorrow." Spenders buy things they don't need, just as women with eating problems eat when they are not hungry. Arenson (1991) notes that both debtors and anorexics are self-denying, because they get along with less—whether it is money in the pocket, or food. Compulsive eaters feel controlled by their appetites; compulsive shoppers feel controlled by others. Bulimics vomit food; "shopaholics" return merchandise to regain control.

Shopping is similar to the abuse of alcohol and other drugs in that shopping provides a powerful high. This intense feeling comes on so quickly and becomes so powerful that many shoppers are unaware of their surroundings and other people. All uncomfortable feelings disappear. Often it is only on the day after a shopping binge that the compulsive spender will experience feelings of guilt, shame, and self-hatred. Similar to women with other addictions, compulsive spenders respond to a conscious or unconscious trigger that sets off their compulsion. The impulsive spending is followed by a letdown, or hangover, and a return to the original state of discomfort that led to the initial spending. Relapses are common unless the addicted spender learns new behaviors, such as finding new ways of shopping, taking different routes home to avoid passing stores that act as triggers, and using cash instead of credit cards. For women compulsive spenders, recovery also means learning to cope with difficult feelings and growing in self-awareness and self-acceptance.

Dynamics and Patterns of Compulsive Spending

Research on compulsive spenders is almost nonexistent. Consequently, what we do know is based mainly on clinical experience and reporting in the popular press (Benson, 2000). Spending money is often a great distraction from dealing with other important issues and feelings, both positive and negative. Spending has different meanings and patterns for different women. At times, it can take the form of a temper tantrum. For example, Ellen went shopping as a way of acting out her feelings of rage toward her husband, who, in her view, was not emotionally available to her. By running up large department store bills, she was getting back at him financially, as well as taking care of herself because he was not available.

Some women are binge shoppers who can control their spending for a while and then go out of control as a faulty way to seek relief from life's pressures. Catalogue shoppers sometimes get absorbed in a pile of catalogues as an escape. This focus allows for a "time-out" from life's responsibilities or from internal conflict, which may include feelings of anxiety, depression, and deep need. Shopping, like other addictions, can give women a feeling of taking action, or asserting "control," which can relieve anxiety as much as it causes it. Acting on impulse often can be an assertion of control that then itself becomes out of control.

For lonely, isolated women, TV shopping can provide a pseudo-family. The hosts are friendly sorts of people who try to relate to viewers' need to feel connected. It's possible to shop at odd times and to feel seduced into lengthy hours of watching goods for sale. The act of being absorbed in shopping, whether it is a sudden binge or an extended stay in front of the TV, can produce a numbing, dissociative state that serves to quiet, if not resolve, painful feelings and issues.

Accumulation of material goods is extremely important for women who equate money with security. Women who focus on the money they save by buying something on sale may be reveling in their savvy as shoppers, as well as reducing guilt about their needs, feelings, and wishes. A sense of insecurity and inner emptiness is often behind the need to shop for goods on sale. Most women who are compulsive about sales shopping do not lack for goods, as their drawers and closets are brimming full with everything from soap powder to food. They'll buy things they never use if the price is right. Many go out of their way to buy things on sale even if it costs them more to drive to the store than they save on the sales. The shopping bags, drawers, and closets may be filled, but the "fix" these purchases provide for the inner void is short lived.

Most people appreciate a bargain. Indeed, the idea of a bargain can hold the seductive power of a "win," a great success, or it can be a symbol of the shopper's intelligence and thrift, which are all important American values. But when intense focus is on saving money through sales and coupon redemptions, healthy thrift can become a true compulsion. Some women have been prosecuted for raiding neighbors' mailboxes for coupons, sending in for rebates from someone else's proof-of-purchase labels, and getting refunds under assumed names (Coleman & Hull-Mast, 1992).

Store personnel are accustomed to women who buy, use, then return items. Some women derive satisfaction from using things and returning them for a refund. They may rationalize that the store owes them a service because they shop there often, so they don't see that they are doing anything wrong. Returning merchandise may also be a way of feeling special.

Clinical experience suggests that low self-esteem or lack of recognition or appreciation are central issues for compulsive spenders. Many of these people buy gifts for others because they want the positive response that passes as a form of love. Big tippers may feel appreciated, so they continue to be generous even if they can't afford to be. Unhealthy gift giving occurs when the buyer neglects her own actual needs or when her giving too much creates relationships that are one sided and highly dependent. These dynamics are the same as the unequal roles of caregiving and receiving that often characterize relationship addiction.

The holidays, especially Christmas, create an inordinate need to spend. Some people moonlight for months to purchase the things that will make everybody happy and that in return will make the shopper feel loved and appreciated. Unfortunately, the warm feelings they hope to get usually do not materialize or are short in duration. Instead of feeling good about themselves, they are generally let down and left with months of bills to pay.

The "high" of the planning and shopping gives way to feelings of loss, disappointment, depression, hurt, anxiety, or anger. The wished-for inner relief, comfort, or satisfaction is gone, and the cycle starts again. Like the effects of drinking, gambling, or eating, the effort to fill an inner void or to ward off painful feelings through spending is a temporary solution, and not one that brings resolution.

Some gift buyers express their own deep ambivalence and conflicts by attempting to evoke guilt in the recipients. They may stew about how much money they spent, and convey to the recipients that they are not really worth the gift or that they are not responsive enough. The holder of the gift may feel manipulated rather than pleased. Ironically, the giver does not get the needed emotional response because she induces resentment in others, which makes them back away.

Impact of Early Life

Our earliest influences play an important role in shaping spending patterns in adulthood. The way women spend money can reflect the impact of such early life experiences as the receiving of immediate or insufficient gratification, feeding patterns, and toilet training (Barbanel, 1994, 1996).

The impulsivity inherent in compulsive spending may stem from early parent-child patterns of gratification or withholding in response to the child's needs. For example, parents who are uncomfortable with their child's anxiety may at the first sign of distress turn to pacifiers or food in order to soothe the child. When a parent quickly and repeatedly takes over the satisfaction of needs for the child, the child may have difficulty learning to cope with her feelings or to master the current developmental task herself. Such a quick response by the parent can lead to an expectation of instant gratification later in life, according to Sanger (1981). When parents offer a stress-free environment by putting too many toys within reach or feeding too quickly, the child doesn't learn to tolerate frustration, nor does she learn to know her own feelings. When the child doesn't get the chance to participate actively so as to achieve a sense of satisfaction from a job well done, she will not be able to obtain a sense of mastery or gain self-esteem. Instead, these situations plant the seeds of self-doubt and the need to please others to get attention.

Parents may also withhold help and gratification when a child is not yet able to take care of a need or task herself. This pattern may lead to tremendous frustration, a lack of trust in others on whom the child must depend, and a lifelong hunger that cannot be satisfied. It is interesting that many English words related to money have a direct relationship to eating, such as *money hungry, lettuce, bread,* and *dough.* Compulsive spenders may be seen as having a voracious "appetite" for consumer goods and for the act of spending as a way of satisfying hunger.

Just as growing children can be messy with their food, and even play with it, some adults throw their money around and handle it in sloppy ways. Without being taught better manners or, in the case of money, without learning to manage it well, such dynamics may persist throughout life.

Toilet training involves experiences that are symbolized later in the ways people handle money. The child who "fights" with her mother and won't "give" may not want to pay taxes and bills later. The ambivalence about "giving" can also be seen in last-minute holiday shopping and procrastination in paying bills. The demands of toilet training may be so overwhelming that the child grows into an adult who can't manage daily tasks well and feels that such things as record keeping are "too much." The sense of shame and humiliation one feels as a child when there is an "accident" in training may be felt by compulsive spenders who feel out of control of their money. Emotional scars may develop when toilet training is characterized by guilt or by fear of not being loved. The child can grow up to feel undeserving and unlovable. To combat the worry that "something is wrong with me," compulsive spenders may learn that they are loved and appreciated when they buy things for others and give such things as big tips. Compulsive shoppers also may rationalize that they "deserve" whatever they bought for themselves, as a way to master the underlying feelings of being undeserving that they actually have. Sometimes when parents give excessive encouragement during toilet training, children can learn that giving away their "valuables" gets them loving attention. When they don't learn that they are also lovable for themselves, they may grow up feeling that they need to be generous as a way to get love.

Childhood experiences are powerful in shaping an individual's behavior with money. Children watch, overhear, adopt, and imitate attitudes and habits from their parents that shape their own attitudes and behavior in relation to money. If a parent cannot save or manage money, the child may identify with the parent and behave similarly.

Social Influences

Compulsive spending is the most socially acceptable of all the addictions. Spending is encouraged everywhere. Stores, billboards, Internet shopping, TV shopping, advertisements, cold calls, and direct mail abound. Holidays and special occasions encourage buying, as does the changing of the seasons.

Mother-daughter shopping sprees are hallowed rituals that hold important memories and, often, important conflicts and mixed emotions for many women. For the adult woman, shopping may serve to evoke these memories and feelings, both positive and negative. Acting out both the gratification of happy times and the pain of conflict is easy to do in a material culture.

The ever-present malls are places for entertainment and refreshment as well as "halls of plenty." There are no windows in the stores, so there is an atmosphere of unreality, much like Las Vegas casinos. One loses touch with time when there is stimulation at every turn and exit signs are hard to see. The stores tempt people to touch their goods, with the knowledge that buyers are more apt to purchase if they can feel what they are sizing up. There are no doors in malls, so buyers can wander at will. Sales, special purchases, and no-tax days bring in shoppers who wait for prices to drop. Teenage girls hang out in shopping centers because there are few other places for them to gather. Their needs to conform and to express their individuality depend on what line of clothing or store is "in" and what they can do to rebel against the usual fashions. Many people go to the malls to relax, to exercise, to escape, and to feel cheered up. In a store, everything is new compared to home, where one new item can show up the rest as being old-fashioned, if not plain old.

Assessment

Some compulsive spenders act out their feelings instead of talking them over, so it is no surprise that women who are compulsive spenders do not usually come to therapy with spending or shopping as their presenting problem. Their denial and rationalizations work well to keep their spending hidden from others as well as themselves. The clinician may not know for a long time that shopping is even an issue, much less a central problem. However, just as a therapist assesses a patient's depression and anxiety and asks about her drinking and other problems, it is a good idea to ask about debt and spending habits.

To assess for compulsive shopping, it is helpful to ask such questions as "When and how long do you shop?" "What items do you especially like to buy?" and "How do you feel after shopping?" Ask if she is in debt and how she manages credit. A standardized questionnaire can be helpful, such as Janet Damon's twelve questions (1988) (From *Shopaholics* by Janet E. Damon, copyright ©1988 by Janet Damon. Used by permission of Price Stern & Sloan, Inc., a division of Penquin Putnam, Inc.):

1. Do you "take off for the stores" when you've experienced a setback or a disappointment, or when you feel angry or scared?
2. Are your spending habits emotionally disturbing to you and have they created chaos in your life?
3. Do your shopping habits create conflicts between you and someone close to you (spouse, lover, parents, children)?
4. Do you buy items with your credit cards that you wouldn't buy if you had to pay cash?
5. When you shop, do you feel a rush of euphoria mixed with feelings of anxiety?
6. Do you feel you're performing a dangerous, reckless or forbidden act when you shop?
7. When you return home after shopping, do you feel guilty, ashamed, embarrassed or confused?
8. Are many of your purchases seldom or never worn or used?
9. Do you lie to your family or friends about what you buy and how much you spend?
10. Would you feel "lost" without your credit cards?
11. Do you think about money excessively—how much you have, how much you owe, how much you wish you had—and then go out and shop again?
12. Do you spend a lot of time juggling accounts and bills to accommodate your shopping debts?

Answering yes to more than four of these questions may be an indication of out-of-control compulsive shopping.

Treatment

Spending is a necessary part of life for most people, so treatment must focus on practical help that will foster and support new, healthy spending behaviors. Definitions of abstinence and recovery will still include spending, just as definitions of abstinence and recovery from eating problems must still include eating. In addition to the practical focus on new behaviors, treatment must also illuminate compulsive, out-of-control spending behaviors, attitudes, beliefs, family influences, and other factors that maintain and reinforce the addictive cycle. In therapy, the compulsive spender gains insight into her emotional needs and conflicts in order to identify triggers that lead to a spending binge; she also learns new abstinent behaviors that she can substitute for the impulse to act out via spending. When the behavioral and cognitive structures of "spending recovery" are in place, she can more safely explore deeper issues without relapsing to out-of-control spending to defend against feelings or insights.

There can be no successful treatment outcome until the patient acknowledges her addiction. As is true for other addictions, there has to be recognition that she has a problem that is out of her control. As in every other life situation where change is necessary, the person's attitude is the key.

Initially the therapist may need to focus on the realities of out-of-control spending and the patient's denial of it. When the individual has accepted her loss of control or acknowledged that she has a problem with spending, the clinician can focus on two questions to guide the exploration with the client: What is upsetting the client, whether or not she is conscious of it? and What needs, conscious or unconscious, are unmet?

The therapist then works within behavioral, cognitive, and dynamic frames to help focus on behavioral and cognitive change and on the client's underlying feelings, wishes, and needs that serve as triggers for spending. The therapist must address the concrete out-of-control behavior, the beliefs that reinforce the repetitive behavioral cycle, and the function and symbolic meanings of the spending. The following case illustrates some of these issues, which became evident early in treatment even though the client's presenting problem was depression and low self-esteem.

The Case of Stacey

Stacey, a thirty-three-year-old woman from a White, middle-class family, describes how money was handled in her family. The patient was asked about verbal and nonverbal messages she got regarding saving, spending, debt, investments, lending to relatives, giving to charity, and so on. In the course of exploring her past, Stacey noted that she learned about money from observing her parents' spending. Throughout her childhood there were fights over money that caused her to feel insecure. She saw how her father used money to control her mother. She heard her mother defer to her father at times to keep the peace, a behavior that Stacey didn't respect. It felt as though her mother lost herself when she deferred. Because Stacey did not have an allowance, she did not get a chance to try to manage her own money until she started working after college. As a child and adolescent, Stacey did not feel comfortable with money and worried about how she would take care of herself as an adult. She was overly concerned about success and saw materialism as a fast and easy way to make a statement about her own achievements and position.

Shopping was extraordinarily important to Stacey because her mother overemphasized Stacey's appearance. Stacey also valued her father's attention, which he gave through compliments, which boosted her self-esteem. Compulsive shoppers often rely on outside feedback to feel better, as Stacey illustrates. She did not look in the mirror and feel better about herself. Instead, she presented herself to others and looked for their judgment as to whether she was acceptable or not.

Stacey showed how much she cared for others by how much money she spent or how many gifts she gave, so she continued to purchase gifts that were beyond her budget. She confused love with money. Thus, birthdays and holidays were triggers for overspending. Stacey wanted the look of appreciation in the recipient's eyes, a look that substituted for, or passed for, the love she craved.

In therapy, Stacey explored how feelings, especially anger, were handled as she was growing up. She was told not to feel angry, that feeling angry was bad. So she hid her feelings from herself and others, suppressing her anger, which then built inside her through the years. For her, a spending binge was like a temper tantrum. During her treatment, Stacey became able to connect her spending behavior to her angry feelings. In many cases, her angry feelings were normal reactions to frustrating situations. Through therapy, she learned to acknowledge and take responsibility for the feelings and deal with them constructively. Role playing was helpful, as was envisioning what she would do the next time under similar circumstances.

In the course of treatment, Stacey worked on better ways to express and modulate her angry feelings by using assertiveness techniques. The use of "I" statements was particularly helpful. The therapist helped her identify and experience all of her uncomfortable feelings, empathizing with her and validating her right to feel as she did. When Stacey was emotionally flat or inappropriately smiling, the therapist supplied her own affect: "How come I'm angrier about this than you are, and I just heard about it, while you've been living with it?" In the course of recognizing and experiencing her feelings, Stacey also came to see the ways in which she participated in maintaining her behavior, and some of the "whys."

When Stacey was ready to make behavior changes, she started by taking a different route home from work to avoid the stores that were on her regular route to the subway. Stacey identified these stores as a trigger for her impulse to spend. As she passed them each day, she felt drawn to enter, telling herself that she had to check each one out to keep up on the latest fashion. As part of this ritual, she frequently purchased one of these new items or something on sale that was a "steal." Stacey continued to shop in this manner even though she owed $20,000 in credit card debt. Ultimately, in addition to taking a different route home, she also cut up her credit cards and only used cash, an action that gave her a feeling of more control and thus better feelings about herself.

Instead of bending over backwards to be liked, Stacey learned how to assert herself and her own needs. She had always believed that if she did nice things for others, they would reciprocate. This was a myth. She eventually learned to do what she wanted to do without seeing her behavior as some kind of guarantee of how others would respond. In essence, she let go of the need to control others through her spending.

In working with addictions, the therapist is often helping a patient recognize opposing, even warring, parts within herself. It can be useful to label these parts of the self and to work to make them conscious. The woman in recovery then works to strengthen the healthiest part of herself, her observing ego, which now works to alert her to her impulses and triggers and to substitute new behaviors. This strengthening of the ego in support of "spending recovery" is also what she will experience in Debtors Anonymous.

A cognitive-behavioral interpretation of the classical schema of ego, superego, and id is a useful frame for therapists working with such patients. The ego is the "mature" or "adult" part of the self that can grow the most and benefit the patient. With a healthy ego, a woman will feel confidence and trust in herself. The healthy ego is the core of the self; it gets abused all too often by an untempered, overly harsh superego, which dictates the "shoulds" and "should nots" and is the source of guilt and shame. The id is the troublemaker that I call "the enemy." In an active addiction, the id is the childlike, self-destructive part of the patient that urges her on to repeat her compulsive behavior and forget about making changes in her life. This enemy has to be disciplined if the patient is to recover. Labeling this troublesome voice as an enemy and giving solid evidence of its destructive power to keep the patient captive and to prompt further debt are important ways of dealing with the resulting feelings of guilt and shame.

It is helpful to reassure the patient that this enemy is now outvoted and frightened of losing its power, since the patient's adult voice (the ego) and the therapist's are now working together to gradually diminish the hold that the enemy has held on her. She may feel empowered because the therapist is "lending" her own ego to the patient. She may also feel validated by the therapist's support of her seeking help. She will need continual reminders that it is her enemy's voice that provokes the acting out that will surely occur during the course of treatment; she will also need reminders that her adult voice is perfectly fine, mature, and ready to be there for her if only she can put the enemy in its place. She will have many chances to listen to the adult voice, which will grow as she consciously stops the enemy in its tracks.

To stop the enemy voice, or at least to lower its volume, the woman must first be aware of it, and then be willing to turn it off. At times, talking out loud to herself is helpful, for example, by saying such things as "I'm no longer the overwhelmed child who cannot cope with so many things. I will sort and prioritize what needs to be done. I will put everything on my list and will take care of all things in due time." For some, a simple reminder such as "I am ___ years old, a mother, wife, professional, and tax-paying and voting citizen; I'm able to cope better with uncomfortable feelings!" can also help. These reminders, like the slogans in twelve-step programs, can move the woman from feeling overwhelmed and out of control to feeling calm and rational. The cognitive reminders help mute the "enemy" impulses. When a woman cannot stop or mute the voice or the behaviors, it is an important signal that conflict, conscious or unconscious, is in the way and needs to be addressed.

Sometimes it helps to be very concrete. From a strictly behavioral standpoint, a client might wear a rubber band around her wrist and snap it so it hurts enough to put a stop to the intruding obsessive thoughts that can set the compulsion into high gear. Simply saying "Stop!" or "I'm not going to think that way" can also bring enough consciousness to drive the enemy voice away. Similarly, patting herself on the back at the end of the day can be a great tension reliever as well as a reward. Saying out loud what minimal or very important things she did for herself during the day to further her goals will often raise self-esteem and lower tension. When this strategy does not help, but instead produces guilt, it may be useful to explore underlying conflict. For example, success and good feelings about herself might stimulate feelings of disloyalty to, or betrayal of, a parent. Anxiety about being in control of herself can be as difficult as anxiety about being out of control.

At other times, a symbolic ritual works to calm a woman and decrease her impulses. Patients sometimes ask for a strategy, a silver bullet, that will see them through a difficult time. I'll take a deep breath and sit with my thumbs up in the air and talk while holding this pose. I'll dramatically convey that I do have something so simple yet so profound that it could have an extreme impact on their life. One hand represents my first "rule of thumb," which I call Size Up Your Reality. I will say outright that because they are not psychotic, they are perfectly capable of taking a look at whatever difficult or uncomfortable situation they are in or will be faced with. If they can take only a few minutes to see the pros, cons, and alternatives of the issues facing them, it will help enormously in making constructive decisions.

My second rule of thumb is Don't Hurt Yourself. Because patients know that their addictive behavior and such behaviors as pleasing others instead of themselves, keeping quiet, and being self-critical are destructive, they are forewarned to avoid these activities, behaviors, and thoughts. I tell them that I want them to remember me sitting in front of them in this ridiculous manner with my thumbs up in the air as a way to cope with whatever life deals out. A little laughter in the process will help too.

Once a therapist has introduced this idea, she has an important shorthand to fall back on during the process of therapy. If the patient talks of slipping or relapse, the therapist can raise her Don't Hurt Yourself thumb, and then the client can talk about the frightened enemy that has risen up to hurt her. When there is an anecdote to analyze, the therapist raises her Size Up Your Reality thumb and works with the patient to size up the situation being described. The therapist reassures her client that little by little, she'll be able to do this herself. By using these few strategies, the client strengthens her ego and will be better able to decline and silence the destructive voices that persist.

As treatment progresses, it is helpful to maintain a practical focus while the patient works on emotional issues. For example, the therapist can ask for the patient's thoughts on how she can take responsibility for her behavior. The therapist asks what actions the patient is ready to take and capable of taking in the near and not-too-distant future. Such actions as using cash, cutting up credit cards, and planning ahead to know what she has to shop for can help.

What triggers and opportunities to shop can the client reduce or eliminate? What can she do on days when she feels blue? Can she avoid certain stores by changing her route home, or by just "window shopping"? Exercise is very helpful in fighting the shopping urge. Shopping lists are helpful, as is using only cash or checks. The client should destroy all her credit cards except one for emergencies, and she should avoid discount warehouses, catalogues, and TV shopping channels.

Recognizing the conflicts the patient has in verbalizing can help cement the all-important alliance between the professional and the patient. The therapist offers empathy about how difficult it is to take the time to put feelings into words. The therapist must also be patient as she encourages the woman to feel the uncomfortable feelings instead of act on them. Therapy means change, and the therapist can point up the courage it took to come for help.

Although resistance to change is par for the course and needs to be explored, rewards can eventually win out. What different rewards can the client think of besides buying things? What experiences and new feelings would be gratifying to her? It is hoped that her sense of being more in control will feel welcome and will boost her self-esteem.

Dealing with Relapse

When the patient "slips" into relapse, it is helpful to convey the attitude, "Don't make it a slide." Some women will be so distraught by their behavior that they cannot stop their self-recriminations. It is common for patients to revert to old behavior and feelings, such as guilt and remorse. At this point, it is important to reinstate new behaviors, focus on understanding the reasons for the spending, and consider alternative ways to handle the uncomfortable feelings in the future.

Although our discussion here has focused mainly on cognitive-behavioral interventions, a therapist may need to actively help a woman explore unconscious, dynamic factors that contribute to resistance and slow progress. The "enemy" voice and "enemy" impulses may continue to assert themselves, drowning out the slogans of recovery and clear, mature thinking.

Debtors Anonymous is always a helpful resource for patients that allows them to hear how others deal with relapse and to gain ongoing support. In addition, the therapist continues to help with practical suggestions. As noted earlier, making shopping lists, carrying cash only, and avoiding television shopping shows can help. Considering what she can do differently next time and anticipating and planning how to cope with any tempting situation are also important actions to re-stabilize recovery.

Countertransference

Countertransference is a significant and often difficult issue for therapists who have their own complicated relationships with money and spending, regardless of whether compulsive spending is a problem. Therapists must be aware of their own beliefs, values, and feelings about money and how their own relationship to money will affect their work with clients. For example, a therapist who expects to be paid on time may feel jealous or angry on hearing a patient talk about how much money she spent on a vacation when she cannot afford to pay her therapy bill on time.

It is probably a good idea for therapists to assume that they will automatically be vulnerable to countertransference, a view that can serve as a signal that alerts them to the danger of interference, collusion, or acting out on their part. Therapists may have the same level of discomfort discussing money that their patients have, which will be an obstacle for both. A therapist who can discuss money with ease and comfort and can maintain the same therapeutic boundaries with money that she maintains with everything else will facilitate the patient's exploration.

Conclusion

Compulsive spending is here to stay. Because spending money is necessary, a woman will need a cognitive-behavioral approach to help her make and maintain changes in her relationship with money. She will have a great need for support from a therapist who is comfortable offering concrete, practical help and who is skilled in helping the patient understand her deepest feelings, wishes, and needs. Everyone spends money, and each person can attach significant real and symbolic meaning to it.

References

Arenson, G. (1991). *Born to spend: How to overcome compulsive spending.* Blue Ridge Summit, PA: Tab Books.

Barbanel, L. (1994). *Piggy bank to credit card: Teach your child the financial facts of life.* New York: Crown.

Barbanel, L. (1996). *Sex, money and power: Smart ways to resolve money conflicts and keep them from sabotaging your closest relationships.* New York: Macmillan.

Benson, A. (Ed.). (2000). *I shop, therefore I am: Compulsive buying and the search for self.* Northvale, NJ: Aronson.

Coleman, S., & Hull-Mast, N. (1992). *Can't buy me love: Freedom from compulsive spending and money obsession.* Minneapolis, MN: CompCare.

"Credit cards at fifty: The problems of ubiquity." (2000, March 12). *New York Times,* p. BU11.

Damon, J. (1988). *Shopaholics.* Los Angeles: Price Stern & Sloan. Available: fsap.harvard.edu/moneyaddictions.html.

Federal Reserve Bulletin (1997, December). *83*(12), A33.

Morgenson, G. (2000, March 24). Buying on margin becomes a habit: Investors turn to credit in a bull market. *New York Times,* p. C1.

Sanger, S. (1981, May). Prevention: Key to youth gambling addiction—Part I. *National Council on Compulsive Gambling Newsletter,* pp. 1–3.

Stesin, N. (1997, October). Hooked on home shopping. *Ladies Home Journal, 114,* 166.

CHAPTER TEN

WOMEN AND SMOKING

Jeannine Crouse

The history of cigarette smoking and American women has all the elements of a never-ending and tragic love story: seduction, blind love, control, and deceit. Only seventy years prior to the "You've Come a Long Way, Baby" tobacco campaign of the 1960s aimed at women, smoking was considered strictly a male bonding activity. Women were barred not only from smoking but also from smoking havens, including restaurants, saloons, clubs, and tobacco shops (Christen & Christen, 1998). "Coming a long way" for women thus implied the gaining of permission both to smoke and to travel freely within society.

Once women were permitted to smoke in public, these formerly prohibited behaviors appealed to women, especially to the young, rebellious "flapper" of the 1920s. Between 1925 and 1935, smoking initiation rates among adolescent females tripled. Contributing factors included the use of photography and movies to portray slim, sexy smoking females; cigarette companies' pitching smoking as an effective means of weight control; and teenage rebellion against the antismoking appeals (Christen & Christen, 1998).

Apparently history is repeating itself. As antismoking appeals are heightened, the prevalence of adolescent smoking is again on the rise. In fact, Christen and Christen's reference (1998) to the "new" female smoker image brought to the public in the late 1920s by the tobacco companies—"slender, chic and mildly seductive"—can be applied to the female smoker images brought to us today. Carrie Bradshaw, the intelligent, glamorous, sexy, slim, rebellious, chain-smoking sex columnist character played by actress Sarah Jessica Parker in the popular HBO television series *Sex and the City* is just the latest example of these age-old advertising associations. Past declines in smoking among U.S. adolescents have reversed during the 1990s (Anda et al., 1999), and cigarette smoking among women and adolescent girls is a serious and growing national health threat (American Cancer Society [ACS], 2000; Anda et al., 1999; Brody, 1998; Office of Women's Health, 1996; Christen & Christen, 1998; Fried, 2000; "Tobacco Smoke and Women," 2000).

This chapter discusses the use of tobacco and the current treatment approaches when working with women who are addicted to cigarette smoking.

Why Women Smoke

All addictive substances offer users similar immediate solutions to perceived conflicts. Smoking is no different.

Societal Influences

If one were to view substances on a continuum of social acceptability, nicotine, unlike illegal substances, such as cocaine or heroin, is the more socially acceptable choice. Although both nicotine and alcohol are legal substances, nicotine carries less stigma as an addiction, because the smoker can maintain a higher level of functioning than the alcoholic and is not a potential immediate danger to society. Moreover, smoking may even be considered more socially acceptable than overeating in appearance-oriented cultures, which value and admire the slimness of the female smoker over the chubbiness of the female overeater.

Addictive Properties of Nicotine

Nicotine, like alcohol, is a drug that has both stimulant and tranquilizing effects, depending on the dosage (ACS, 1999; Christen & Christen, 1998). Biochemical experiments have shown that nicotine enhances long-term memory and performance of simple tasks because the neurotransmitters dopamine and serotonin are released in the brain following the inhalation of tobacco smoke (Christen & Christen, 1998). Henningfield, Cohen, and Pickworth (1993) state that the dependence potential of nicotine is influenced by performance enhancement, mood enhancement (anxiolytic and euphoriant effects), high availability, low cost, and high social acceptability. They quote research conducted by the U.S. Department of Health and Human Services in 1988, which concluded that the use of tobacco is more likely to escalate to dependent patterns of use than the use of any other dependence-producing drugs.

Gender Issues

Male and female smokers have become more similar as time goes on. Christen and Christen (1998) quote two studies that report that for women, the three most commonly cited reasons for smoking are weight control, stress reduction, and increased alertness. Of these three, weight control is a major factor for initiating and continuing cigarette use. Although there is evidence to support that smokers tend to weigh less than nonsmokers and that smoking does influence alertness via the norepinephrine pathway, no evidence supports smoking as an effective form of stress reduction.

Persons with negative affect are more likely to start smoking and less likely to be able to quit (Jorenby et al., 1999). People who smoke to decrease negative affect rely more heavily on cigarettes than people who smoke as a response to social or external factors (Christen & Christen, 1998), and these smokers are more often women than men (Fried, 2000). As Christen and Christen point out, although smoking fails to address the roots of problems, it may temporarily assuage negative emotions, which in turn inhibits effective problem solving (for example, changing thoughts, feelings, or behaviors). Paradoxically, the final result is increased stress (ineffective problem solving) in many important life areas, which in turn provides more reasons to smoke.

Research suggests that the social environment is the most influential predictor of teenage and adult smoking, especially during the time of initial use (Christen & Christen, 1998; Fried, 2000). With teenage girls in particular, much depends on whether or not their family, peers, role models, and, especially, their best friends smoke. Anda et al. (1999) found that sexual abuse that occurred by fourteen years of age was associated with a fourfold increase in smoking initiation. Their data showed an inverse relationship between the mean age of smoking initiation and the number of adverse childhood experiences. Their findings support the idea that smoking initiation is a trauma response, an attempt to self-soothe negative affect, or both.

Social Profiles of Female Smokers

The female adolescent smoker is often outgoing (extroverted) and rebellious, but has lower self-esteem and is less confident than her nonsmoking peers in her ability to influence her future (Christen & Christen, 1998). She uses cigarettes as a bonding tool with her peers. She is also more likely to be very concerned with her body weight and outward appearance. Nicotine may provide her with a sense of empowerment, as it bolsters self-confidence through mood alteration (Christen & Christen, 1998). It also serves, at least temporarily, as an effective weight-control tool.

For the adult female smoker, smoking serves as a tool for weight management, social bonding, and a sense of empowerment and control over her changing emotional and physical states. Studies show that most female smokers smoke more heavily just before and during menstruation, suggesting that estrogen plays a role in usage (Christen & Christen, 1998; Fried, 2000).

For the single woman over thirty-five years of age, smoking may become more of a substitute partner or lover. For example, a single woman in her early forties who quit one-and-a-half years ago after smoking for twenty-five years reported to me, "I loved everything to do with smoking. From holding a fresh, hard pack in my hand, to the click of the lighter and its inviting flame; from taking a long, soulful drag, to buying a new ashtray; it was all very sensual to me." Another single woman, age thirty-eight, pointed to her lit cigarette and said, "This is my boyfriend."

Cigarettes may serve as a source of comfort for menopausal and post-menopausal women, who are still greatly concerned with physical attractiveness (including body weight) and may be losing former feelings of attractiveness as they experience the physical aging of their bodies (Christen & Christen, 1998). Ironically, smoking has been identified as an accelerator of the aging process, as it is linked with premature menopause, premature facial wrinkling, and oral and systemic osteoporosis (Christen & Christen, 1998; Fried, 2000).

Problem Definition

About 22 million adult women and at least 1.5 million adolescent girls currently smoke cigarettes. According to Christen and Christen (1998), smoking prevalence among American Indian and Alaskan Native women and female adolescents (40.9 and 44 percent, respectively) remains the highest of all female subgroups. Lesbians have a disproportionately high rate of smoking compared to heterosexual women, though estimates are lower than those for American Indian and Alaskan Native women. Battered women, who have been largely ignored in the literature, are also more likely to smoke than women who have not been abused (Christen & Christen, 1998).

Today, female teens are smoking earlier and heavier than in the past. Women younger than twenty-three years old are the "fastest growing newcomers" (Christen & Christen, 1998, p. 169). Tobacco use usually begins prior to age sixteen, and it is not uncommon for girls to begin smoking regularly at the age of eleven or twelve (Fried, 2000). Education is a major predictor of smoking status (Christen & Christen, 1998). The decline in smoking prevalence has occurred five times faster among the more highly educated than among less educated women and men. Smoking prevalence is also higher among persons living below the poverty level (33.3 percent) than among those above it (24.6 percent) (Centers for Disease Control, 1999).

Health Risks

Tobacco use is responsible for nearly one in five deaths in the United States. Smoking is the most preventable cause of death in our society, and it is estimated that tobacco use costs the U.S. economy more than $100 billion in health care costs and lost productivity (ACS, 2000).

Smoking is responsible for 87 percent of lung cancers and is associated with cancers of the mouth, pharynx, larynx, esophagus, pancreas, uterus, cervix, kidney, and bladder. It is responsible for nearly one-third of all cancer deaths (Office of Women's Health, 1996; ACS, 2000). Smoking increases the risk of coronary heart disease, the leading cause of death among American women (Fried, 2000). In addition, tobacco use in women increases the risk of emphysema, bronchitis, pneumonia (Office of Women's Health, 1996), sinusitis, peptic ulcers (Christen & Christen, 1998; Gilbert, 1988), excessive daytime sleepiness, sleep irregularities, and asthma (Christen & Christen, 1998).

The lung cancer death rate for women has increased by more than 400 percent over the last thirty years and is continuing to increase (Office of Women's Health, 1996). In an article in the *New York Times*, writer Jane Brody (1998, p. F7) states, "An epidemic is raging in this country and no one seems to be paying much attention to it. It is an epidemic of lung cancer in women." Brody reports that in 1996, the federal government invested money toward breast cancer and lung cancer research in a 6:1 ratio. She asks, "Where are the advocacy groups fighting for greater awareness of lung cancer risks to women and pleading for more money for research into this major killer? Are women with lung cancer too embarrassed, knowing that as many as 90 percent of them got sick because they smoked cigarettes? Are they so wedded to tobacco that they are willing to pay for it with their health and lives?" Christen and Christen (1998) point to the acceptance of tobacco industry money by women's organizations as a cause for women's silence.

Several studies suggest that women are more chemically and behaviorally sensitive to nicotine than men, and metabolize it more slowly (Christen & Christen, 1998; Fried, 2000). Results of recent research at Harvard University ("Tobacco

Smoke and Women," 2000) found that women smokers with lung cancer were three times more likely than male smokers to carry a gene mutation known as K-ras, described as a marker for particularly aggressive lung cancer.

The Office of Women's Health (1996) estimates that 18 to 20 percent of pregnant women smoke throughout their pregnancies. The pregnant smoker is more likely to be White than Black and to have a low educational level. Christen and Christen (1998, p. 75) state, "A woman in her reproductive years who smokes is at risk for a wide range of biological alterations, including complications in oral contraceptive use, changes in menstrual cycle, difficulty in becoming pregnant, harmful effects on the placental cord and fetus, changes in gestational duration, retardation of intrauterine fetal growth, varying unfavorable pregnancy outcomes (including significant ill-effects on her newborn infant), early menopause and an increased likelihood of developing cervical cancer."

Secondhand Smoke

Secondhand smoke, or environmental tobacco smoke, is reported to have no safe level of exposure and is responsible for three thousand deaths annually from lung cancer and thirty-five to forty-five thousand deaths from heart disease. It causes lower respiratory infections and asthma in infants and children, and coughing and reduced lung function in nonsmokers; it also increases women's risk for cervical and breast cancers (ACS, 2000; Office of Women's Health, 1996; Christen & Christen, 1998; "Tobacco Smoke and Women," 2000). A nonsmoker who is married to a smoker has a 30 percent greater risk of developing lung cancer than a nonsmoker living with a nonsmoker (ACS, 1999).

Public Health Versus Mental Health Issues

Unlike the treatment of other chemical dependencies, the assessment—and sometimes the entire treatment—of nicotine dependency often occurs in a medical rather than mental health setting. Smokers are permitted more freedom of choice in their treatment than other addicts, because in spite of increasing antismoking sentiments in the United States, nicotine dependency still carries the least social stigma. As the treatment guideline of the American Psychiatric Association points out (Hughes et al., 1996), although nicotine dependence causes significant health problems, it is not usually seen as producing significant negative consequences in other life areas (such as the interpersonal, financial, legal, or psychological), nor does it pose an immediate danger to society, as other chemical dependencies do.

Due to this lower level of social stigma, health care providers have been encouraged to cross boundaries into patients' private lives with regard to cigarette smoking (McGinnis & Foege, 1993).

Moreover, by 1990, tobacco was identified as the most prominent contributor to mortality in the United States, directly related to 400,000 deaths, whereas alcohol was estimated as directly contributing to 100,000 deaths and illicit drug use as directly contributing to 20,000 deaths (McGinnis & Foege, 1993). Once nicotine was identified as the most prominent contributor to mortality in the United States, the medical community and public could no longer afford to ignore it. Consequently, public health and medical community campaigns encouraged medical settings to provide smokers with increased accessibility to at least minimal smoking cessation treatment as part of routine medical and dental care. This procedure also has economic advantages to smokers, as smoking cessation treatment is still not covered by most health insurance plans in the United States. Because smokers make an average of 4.3 physician visits yearly, these visits provide more than four "teachable moments" for medical professionals to provide both motivated and unmotivated smokers with smoking cessation interventions (Orleans, 1993). Inpatient medical hospitalizations were also identified as a prime time to initiate smoking cessation treatment, as they require smokers to quit at least temporarily, due to antismoking laws (Stevens, Glasgow, Hollis, Lichtenstein, & Vogt, 1993).

In addition to these factors that move smoking cessation treatment away from the mental health arena, Christen and Christen (1998) cite several findings which indicate that most smokers who want to quit do so on their own, and with impressive success rates. In 1989, the U.S. surgeon general's report estimated that of all adults who smoked regularly, 50 percent quit (Fisher, Lichtenstein, & Haire-Joshu, 1993).

Assessment of Nicotine Dependence

The American Psychiatric Association (APA) guideline for treating nicotine dependence identifies nicotine dependency as a chronic relapsing disorder (Hughes et al., 1996). Whether the smoker is in a medical or mental health setting, the association recommends that initial and routine assessments of the smoker's status be completed to determine interventions and treatment planning. According to the fourth edition of the *Diagnostic and Statistical Manual of Mental Disorders* (*DSM-IV;* American Psychiatric Association [APA], 1994), the main criterion used for the diagnosis of nicotine dependence is the identification of a group of cognitive, behavioral, and physiological symptoms that exist due to continued use of the substance and in spite of undesirable consequences. This progressive pattern usually results in tolerance, withdrawal, and compulsive nicotine-using behaviors.

In summary, a diagnosis of nicotine dependence is met when a smoker meets a minimum of three of seven criteria in the *DSM-IV.* These criteria describe patterns of negative biopsychosocial consequences caused by continued nicotine use. In addition, the *DSM-IV* reviews features that appear to predict a greater difficulty in cessation. These include the following: smoking soon after awakening, heavy smoking in the mornings versus evenings, smoking when ill, and having difficulty refraining from smoking; the quantity of cigarette smoking; the level of nicotine in the chosen brand of cigarettes; the number of "pack years" smoked; frequent cravings; and reports that the first cigarette of the day is the hardest to give up.

As with other addictive substances, symptoms of nicotine withdrawal can mimic symptoms of mood disorders, which creates diagnostic complications in the early recovery phase. Treatment providers should monitor symptoms closely. Withdrawal symptoms can begin within a few hours of cessation, typically peak in one to four days, and may last three to four weeks (*DSM-IV*). Mild symptoms can also occur when a smoker stops nicotine replacement therapy or switches to a cigarette brand with lower tar. Regarding gender differences, when men and women are equally stressed, women tend to experience a sharper decline in their blood nicotine levels, which thus could produce more intense withdrawal discomfort (Christen & Christen, 1998).

In summary, the following withdrawal symptoms are included in the *DSM-IV*: dysphoric or depressed mood, insomnia, irritability, anger, anxiety, concentration difficulties, and restlessness.

Dual Disorders and Cross Addictions

Most individuals with mental disorders smoke cigarettes, with some estimates as high as 90 percent (*DSM-IV*). For women, depressive disorders occur at least twice as frequently as compared to men, and all patients with depression are more likely to smoke (*DSM-IV;* Christen & Christen, 1998). According to a study by Kozlowski (cited in Christen & Christen, 1998), female smokers were rated as more anxious, restless, nervous, and pessimistic than female nonsmokers.

Tobacco has been identified as a gateway substance, which means it is viewed as opening the door to use of alcohol, marijuana, and other drugs (Christen & Christen, 1998). Adolescent and adult smokers far exceed their nonsmoking peers in alcohol and illegal drug use, and cross addictions among female smokers are common. Tobacco and alcohol are described as multipurpose substance, meaning that both may act as either stimulants or depressants, depending on circumstances surround their intake (Christen & Christen, 1998).

More drinkers and smokers also exhibit bulimic behaviors than nondrinkers and nonsmokers (Christen & Christen, 1998). Perkins (1994, cited in Christen & Christen, 1998) showed an inverse relationship between smoking and eating: food deprivation may magnify the pleasurable effects of nicotine, and nicotine may remove the unpleasant aspects of hunger.

Smokers also drink more coffee than nonsmokers do. Weight management may also be a factor here. The combined effect of nicotine and hunger arousal is intensified with the addition of caffeine. Swanson et al. (1994, cited in Christen & Christen, 1998) showed that nicotine combined with caffeine decreases hunger arousal.

Stepped Care: Linking Public and Mental Health Approaches

The stepped-care approach is a public health model that begins by offering the least intensive, least costly approaches to the largest number of smokers, reserving more costly and intensive treatments for those who do not succeed with minimal treatments (Orleans, 1993). The initial goal of the stepped-care approach is simply to identify smokers, with the intent of getting the treatment provider to the patient before the patient gets to the treatment provider. As outlined by Orleans, this model has the following advantages: (1) it applies to all smokers, whether motivated or not; (2) it outlines five stages, according to Prochaska and DiClemente's model (1983), to identify changes in a smoker's motivation, from "precontemplation" to maintaining abstinence or "recycling"; (3) it incorporates a full assessment and triage to match the smoker with the appropriate intensity of care; (4) it is cyclical, offering the smoker more specialized help as she progresses or does not progress through the stages of recovery; and (5) it can be offered in a wide variety of medical and nonmedical settings. The stepped-care approach has been supported by several medical and mental health researchers in various settings (Curry, 1993; Fiore, Smith, Jorenby, & Baker, 1994; Hughes et al., 1996; Hughes, Goldstein, Hurt, & Shiffman, 1999; Orleans, 1993; Stevens et al., 1993).

If the smoker is considered a precontemplator (unmotivated to quit), it is recommended that the clinician provide advice on the benefits of quitting and to contract with the smoker to revisit this issue at a later date in treatment (Hughes et al., 1996; Orleans, 1993). This method is also recommended when integrating smoking cessation treatment with outpatient psychiatric treatment (Hughes et al., 1996), as will be discussed in a later section.

Smokers for whom intensive or formal treatment is considered more appropriate are those who have experienced prior treatment failures or who are highly dependent on nicotine (which can be easily assessed by asking the smoker how soon after awakening she has her first cigarette of the day). This level of treatment is also recommended for those who have dual disorders or other addictions (or both); issues of self-esteem; or a more chaotic social, environmental, and psychosocial status (Hughes et al., 1996). These traits frequently appear in the female smoker's profile.

Quitting

Once a person reaches later stages of smoking, she is drug addicted. Nicotine is a drug found naturally in tobacco and is as physically and psychologically addictive as heroin and cocaine (ACS, 1999; Henningfield et al., 1993). Therefore, nicotine dependency can be viewed as a progressive medical disease influenced by bio-psychosocial factors, similar to any other chemical dependency.

Studies indicate that women are more likely to make an attempt to quit smoking during pregnancy or when caring for one or more children. All smokers are more likely to attempt quitting when experiencing a smoking-related health crisis or a smoking-related illness or death of a significant other (Christen & Christen, 1998).

Christen and Christen (1998) cite a study by Gritz that profiles the characteristics of women most likely to succeed at smoking cessation: higher educational and income level; strong commitment to change; willingness to use both behavioral and pharmaceutical smoking cessation agents; and ability to establish reliable social support systems. Young women show higher cessation rates than young men, whereas middle-age men show higher cessation rates than middle-age women (Christen & Christen, 1998). Adolescents have the toughest time quitting (APA, 1994). However, for a woman at any age, smoking cessation has immediate and long-term health benefits, whether or not the woman presently has a smoking-related illness (Christen & Christen, 1998).

Quitting Among Women with Coexisting Disorders

Most alcoholics smoke; they tend to be highly nicotine dependent and are more likely to be unmotivated to quit than nonalcoholics (Hughes et al., 1996). The APA guideline states that most smokers who have current alcohol or drug problems are unlikely to quit smoking permanently without treating their coexisting addiction(s) either prior to or at the same time as the nicotine dependency (Hughes et al., 1996).

Similar recommendations are made by the APA regarding treating smoking patients with psychiatric disorders, including depression and mental illness. It is recommended that smokers be psychiatrically stable prior to making an attempt to quit and that they should consider restarting psychiatric medications or psychotherapy (or both), especially if a previous quit attempt preceded a depressive or psychiatric relapse. Smokers with dual disorders (including multiple addictions) tend to be less motivated to quit than others and may benefit from motivational counseling (Hughes et al., 1996). No data are currently available on how smokers with dual disorders, or women smokers in general, should be matched to specific treatment (Hughes et al., 1996).

Smoking cessation is not likely to be successful when a patient is in crisis (Hughes et al., 1996). All smokers have a certain (usually high) degree of attachment to cigarettes. If they are grieving a significant loss (which also may trigger feelings related to previous losses), then grieving the additional loss of cigarettes in their life may be too threatening. However, grieving the smoking-related death or illness of a loved one may be a "teachable moment" that brings a smoker to treatment. Therefore, discussing these timing factors empathically with a grieving smoker on a case-by-case basis is important.

Henningfield et al. (1993) address the psychoactive properties of nicotine in sustaining concentration and logical reasoning, and the importance of this effect for writers. This has been an important issue for me in treating college students—especially graduate students—who must possess the ability to write scholarly papers in a timely fashion and who often smoke most heavily when they write. Do the potential benefits of making a cessation attempt while in a doctorate program outweigh the possibility of altering the student's concentration abilities? Should bupropion, which mimics nicotine's psychoactive properties, be considered earlier on in treatment attempts as a preventive measure with these smokers? Due to lack of research, these decisions are usually left up to the smoker.

Treating Nicotine Withdrawal Symptoms

Nicotine replacement therapies (NRTs) are nicotine substitutes that provide the medicinal benefits of nicotine without the other harmful components of tobacco. One might say that NRTs are to smoking cessation what methadone is to quitting heroin. NRTs include the transdermal patch, nicotine chewing gum, nasal spray, and nasal inhaler. They are beneficial in reducing withdrawal symptoms and cravings, delivering lower doses of nicotine than cigarettes, and providing the quitter with a cleaner form of nicotine by avoiding the tar and thousands of poisons found in burning tobacco (ACS, 1999). All have possible negative side effects, which are generally thought to outweigh the negative consequences of smoking cigarettes.

Research studies support the use of NRT (or combinations of NRTs) as beneficial adjunctive treatment when accompanied by some form of counseling (Fiore et al., 1994; Hughes et al., 1999; Jorenby et al., 1999; Orleans, 1993). However, Fiore et al. and other researchers point out that much of current research has used volunteer subjects who are motivated to quit (Curry, 1993).

NRT research on gender differences indicates that for women, the 4 mg dosage of gum is preferred; however, women have shown more severe withdrawal symptoms than men regardless of dose (Fried, 2000). Also, the gum appears to be more effective than the patch in delaying postcessation weight gain (Fried, 2000). No gender differences in withdrawal symptoms with the patch have been reported (Fried, 2000).

A more recent pharmacotherapy for smoking cessation is the nonaddictive antidepressant bupropion, which in a slow-release form used for smoking cessation is sold under the trade name Zyban. Bupropion helps stabilize the rapid surges and depletions of the neurotransmitters dopamine and norepinephrine, an effect caused by nicotine dependence and withdrawal (Noble, 1999). Bupropion may help a smoker cope with dysphoria, among other withdrawal symptoms, which is often experienced in early recovery. However, smokers with reported symptoms of anxiety and insomnia prior to cessation may find these symptoms exacerbated by bupropion, as will be discussed in the case study later in this chapter. Bupropion may also attract women quitters, as it may be effective in controlling postcessation weight gain (Fried, 2000). More recently, the pharmacotherapies clonidine and nortriptyline have been identified as "second-line" treatment choices, if bupropion and NRTs are not effective (U.S. Department of Health and Human Services [USDHHS], 2000). Like bupropion, these medications have been primarily used for the treatment of depression and anxiety.

Psychotherapeutic Approaches to Smoking Cessation

The APA recommends the use of multimodal behavioral therapy, with the major goals of changing antecedents to smoking (including cognitive components), reinforcing nonsmoking, and teaching skills to avoid smoking in high-risk situations. Multimodal behavioral therapies include skills training, relapse prevention and its variants, cognitive coping, self-help materials, assertiveness training, social support, and relaxation training. The APA recommends establishing a therapeutic alliance with smoking patients and advising them in a nonjudgmental, supportive, and empathic manner. The therapist serves the functions of motivator, educator, coach, and provider of social support (Hughes et al., 1996).

According to Curry (1993), self-help strategies are an important bridge between the clinical approach to smoking cessation (more intensive and offered to motivated patients) and the public health approach (lower-intensity interventions offered to all smokers). Self-help methods can range from completely unaided attempts to quit smoking, to elaborate and intensive clinical programs offered in self-administered formats (Curry, 1993). They include the use of educational materials based on facts and figures, which serve to alter distorted beliefs and to challenge denial, such as through the repeated use of the word *poison* as a nicotine descriptor (ACS, 1999; Gilbert, 1988). Self-help materials play an important role in behavioral interventions (as homework assignments), in intensive treatment programs, and as minimal interventions (in the form of clearly stated medical facts) to help motivate and educate the precontemplator. Self-help support groups, such as Nicotine Anonymous, may also be especially helpful to the female quitter.

Clinical research supports some form of individual or group counseling, including such diverse models as the following: sessions lasting as little as three minutes (U.S. Department of Health and Human Services [USDHHS]], 1996), more than twenty minutes (Hughes et al., 1999), or up to thirty minutes (ACS, 1999); telephone sessions, which can be as successful as face-to-face sessions (Hughes et al., 1999); and treatment lasting from four to seven sessions, over a minimum of two weeks. The more intense the program is in session length, number of sessions, and number of weeks, the greater the likelihood of long-term abstinence from tobacco (ACS, 1999; USDHHS, 1996, 2000).

One cannot overestimate the importance of treating the cognitive components of psychological addiction in the treatment of all chemical dependencies, especially nicotine dependence. As stated previously, women more commonly than men have been found to use smoking as a means of coping with negative mood states. Smoking produces immediate gratification in response to discomfort, and through repeated exposure (sometimes all day for many years) it becomes a learned response. Memory helps form and maintain an association between psychic pain and the pleasurable aspects of nicotine (Grady, 1998), thus creating psychological cravings. Moreover, cravings are usually accompanied by a cognitive rationalization, whether conscious or not, defined as "a mistaken belief that seems to make sense at the time but is not based on facts" (ACS, 1999). An example would be the belief, "I cannot cope with stress without smoking." For such a smoker, the perceived stress (or intensified negative affect) related to attempting to quit smoking can actually cause increased smoking. This early treatment response, called *stress mobilization response* by Gritz (cited in Christen & Christen, 1998, p. 155), has been observed in those who smoke particularly to cope with negative affect. If this phenomenon is not noticed and explained to a smoker, she may feel more shameful and hopeless.

Other powerful and essential alternative behavioral techniques used in smoking cessation treatment are diaphragmatic or deep breathing training, and exercise (ACS, 1999; Fried, 2000; Gilbert, 1988). I have found diaphragmatic breathing training particularly helpful for smokers with comorbid anxiety and panic disorders. Exercise can relieve the temporary depressive symptoms that smokers experience in early recovery (ACS, 1999) and also counteracts the decrease in metabolic rate that follows quitting.

Hypnosis has also been identified as a promising treatment intervention (Hughes et al., 1996). Self-hypnosis training is also available for smokers quitting on their own (Gilbert, 1988). However, not everyone is a good candidate for hypnotic suggestion, and those who are not may interpret this as a personal failure.

The Use of Psychodynamic Principles in Smoking Cessation Treatment

Hughes et al. (1996) acknowledge that although psychodynamic therapies have been used with other drug dependencies and might be applicable to smoking cessation, research is almost nonexistent in this area. This is not surprising given the large amount of medically oriented research and increased availability of pharmacotherapies, coupled with lack of third-party reimbursement for talking therapies. Clinicians may also play a role in minimizing, ignoring, or denying that smoking is a potential treatment issue. Clinicians who smoke may feel unauthorized to help other smokers or shameful about their own smoking. As pointed out by Resnick (1993), prior to antismoking laws, many clinicians may have even smoked with or in the presence of smoking patients; others may, for conscious or unconscious reasons, play enabling roles with their smoking client.

It is helpful to review the history of a smoker's attachment to nicotine in order to understand the intensity of this bond and its meaning to the smoker. When exploring the meanings and associations that cigarettes hold for the smoker, frequently a tale of attachment will follow in which cigarettes are personified as a consistent, reliable friend or even lover substitute.

Societal customs play a role in the attachment process. Smoking is viewed as a rite of passage into adulthood (Fisher et al., 1993), as a sort of teenage transitional object (as originated by Winnicott and discussed by Levin, 1991) from one's family of origin into the adult world. Through social, physiological, and psychological reinforcement, the bonding (attachment) strengthens over time. In later stages, some smokers may associate smoking with every waking moment.

Bowlby's attachment theory (1980), which minimizes pathology and explains disturbed patterns of attachment and loss (grieving) at any age, can be a valuable therapeutic and assessment tool, in combination with previously discussed cognitive-behavioral interventions. Detachment or separation from a valued object or person causes a grieving state to begin. Disturbances in attachment or separation stages (for example, young adulthood) can set the stage for a mood or substance abuse disorder. When an addict eventually decides to detach from the substance originally used to soothe separation discomfort, a secondary grieving of the substance itself occurs.

In certain circumstances (perhaps related to previous losses, parental unavailability, neglect, abuse, and others), an anxious attachment, or a clinging to the attachment figure, can occur (Bowlby, 1980), resulting in even more intense dependency and difficulty detaching. Such clinging behavior, due to separation anxiety, provides an alternate and deeper explanation of the stress mobilization response seen in smokers.

Bowlby (1980) also makes important points that may cause acting-out behaviors in treatment. He explains that threat of loss arouses anxiety, and actual loss gives rise to sorrow; both will likely arouse anger. This may translate into unconscious or conscious resistance (for example, missed sessions or anger projected onto the therapist). Approaching and normalizing grief reactions with a patient can often bring her relief and allow for increased trust, a necessary ingredient for verbalizing negative affect. As a sort of preventive measure for certain smokers, I often choose to introduce these possible treatment reactions during early treatment, before they happen.

Bowlby further explains that just as attachment behavior is activated under certain conditions (such as when one is fearful or fatigued or when attachment figures are unavailable), it is also terminated under certain other conditions, such as when there is a familiar environment and a readily available and responsive attachment figure. Alternative attachment figures, whether a support group or individual therapist, should be available and responsive. Research has shown that even a brief telephone call to a smoker in early recovery can be very helpful.

The process of grieving and the need to normalize grief reactions in recovery have been discussed in relation to treating other chemical dependencies (Levin, 1991). However, given the high prevalence of mood disorders found in smokers and the degree of attachment, grieving may play a more significant role in treating nicotine dependence as compared to other chemical dependencies.

Ego psychology (Goldstein, 1984) also offers helpful assessment techniques and treatment-friendly approaches to integrating more precise and individualized smoking cessation treatment with ongoing short- or long-term psychotherapy. Ego psychology provides clinicians with guidelines for assessing the extent of pathology;

delineating what ego functions are most impaired and, therefore, where smoking is most intensely used as a coping tool. Ego psychology allows flexibility of the therapist's roles (as educator, motivator, and social supporter, for example) in providing treatment using problem-solving techniques and deciding when to use interpretations of unconscious resistance. In addition, ego psychology acknowledges the roles of social factors and environmental influences in creating and maintaining presenting problems. For example, a smoking patient assessed as having a severe and pervasive deficit in the ego function of regulation and control of drives, affects, and impulses may be classified as a negative affect smoker. Such a smoker might benefit from a more intense treatment early on, with a focus on affect education and management, until her changing feeling states become less threatening. In contrast, a patient whose smoking behaviors are assessed as being related to a deficit in the stimulus barrier function (for example, an identified low or high tolerance for stimulation) may benefit from treatment focused on environmental or behavioral changes. A smoker with primitive defensive functioning or deficits in object relations (or both) may require a focus on establishing a trusting and corrective experience with the clinician.

Relapse Management

Many smokers attempt quitting, and most make several (often more than five) attempts before quitting permanently (Hughes et al., 1999). Two-thirds of quitters relapse within the first week (Hughes et al., 1996). After six months in recovery, 50 percent of individuals reported having had the desire to smoke within the past twenty-four hours (APA, 1994). Given the high likelihood of relapse, it is crucial to both the patient and the clinician to accept relapses and learn from them. When assessing the chronic relapser, Hughes et al. (1999) advise physicians to search for poor medical compliance, comorbid psychiatric problems (especially alcohol abuse or depression), and apparent reasons for the last treatment failure, and to determine whether or not a new treatment approach might be appropriate. One reason why relapses may be more common in smoking cessation treatment than in treatment of other chemical dependencies is the probability that life will not change dramatically if a smoker relapses. Often smokers will treat a relapse as if they were going off a diet, describing it as "cheating a little." Therefore, a smoker usually requires more time and needs to make more quit attempts before admitting her powerlessness over nicotine.

Another reason why relapses may be more common with nicotine dependency is that there is usually a delay before the smoker receives physical gratification from quitting. Many smokers in early recovery experience an exacerbation of smoking-related illnesses, such as breathing difficulties, coughing, or sore throat. This can have an aversive effect on the smoker who initiated quitting because of these symptoms in the first place.

Although NRT boosts the rates of smoking cessation, 70 to 80 percent of smokers who use these therapies still start to smoke again (Jorenby et al., 1999). Women tend to have a more difficult time quitting, reporting more relapses and more severe withdrawal symptoms than males (Christen & Christen, 1998). Studies report that over two-thirds of pregnant quitters relapsed within six months postpartum (Christen & Christen, 1998; Fried, 2000). Postpartum women are more likely to relapse if they live with a smoker or are not breastfeeding (Fried, 2000). This suggests a need for educating new mothers regarding the effects of environmental tobacco smoke on infants—including the impact of there being two smokers in the household as opposed to one—and not just education regarding the effects of smoking on breastfeeding.

Females gain relatively more weight than males following cessation, and a small subset of women are "super gainers"—that is, they gain up to 28.6 pounds (ACS, 1999; Christen & Christen, 1998). However, research shows that women who quit smoking tend to gain no more than five pounds, and often this gain is temporary (Office of Women's Health, 1996). It is important to investigate whether food or alcohol, which also has calories, is being used as a reward for not smoking or as a repeated means of affect management.

Many addicts tend in think in an "all or nothing" manner, which often shows up in other areas of health. This is particularly dangerous because a perceived failure in one area can cause failures in many areas. Sometimes a smoker contemplating quitting may find that instead of attempting to change all these areas simultaneously, she can focus on achieving goals to improve other behavioral areas prior to quitting smoking; these successes are then helpful motivation in preparing a quitting plan. For example, one older adolescent female patient, who initially rated her motivation to quit smoking as a five on a scale of ten, wanted to begin swimming regularly and improve her eating habits prior to quitting. She found these new behaviors to be pleasurable and self-esteem building, and her desire to increase her lung capacity for swimming increased her motivation to quit smoking, which she did after a few weeks of treatment.

A long-term female smoker in her middle sixties recently asked me, "What makes us continue when we know how bad it is for us? It is an ugly addiction, and one I wish I did not have. How can I be so in tune with so many things and oblivious to this? Is it weakness or self-destructive behavior for some reason? I have tried the patch, hypnotism, and just cutting back, and nothing worked. I guess I did not try hard enough, or I have not been scared enough so far—that is, no cough, etc." Like many addicts, this woman acknowledges that an addiction is taking place but still questions whether her addiction and relapses are "weaknesses" rather than parts of the disease process. This contributes to a pervasive sense of self-defeat. She exemplifies the reports stating that compared to men, women are less confident in their ability to quit and view relapses as defeats rather than learning opportunities (Christen & Christen, 1998).

Nicotine and alcohol are commonly consumed together by female smokers, and alcohol increases cigarette cravings (ACS, 1999; USDHHS, 1996; Christen & Christen, 1998). However, quitting smoking has not been identified as a relapse factor for alcoholics in recovery (Hughes et al., 1996). It is important to remind the recreational drinker that avoidance of alcohol will increase her chances of success and may need to be only temporary, until she becomes more accustomed to a nonsmoking existence.

Major depressive disorder, relatively more common in women, has been firmly linked to smoking (Christen & Christen, 1998). Cessation of smoking can actually provoke the onset of a major depressive episode or panic disorder, which are important factors to monitor and treat, especially in early recovery. This issue highlights the importance of a smoking cessation counselor's mental health knowledge.

Clinicians working with older female smokers have observed that, because most of her friends have probably quit, the older female smoker may view herself as "one of the few who cannot," which adds to her shame and sense of hopelessness. She may also have more difficulty with weight gain as she attempts quitting, because it is harder to lose weight as one ages.

◆ ◆ ◆

The following case of Susan illustrates both the use of multiple treatment interventions and successful collaborative efforts between public and mental health providers.

Case Study

Susan, a thirty-six-year-old, separated, White heterosexual female author, was referred to a mental health clinic for smoking cessation treatment by her primary physician, who had recently treated Susan for chronic upper respiratory ailments attributed to smoking. The doctor advised Susan to quit smoking and to seek help through this program because her own past repeated efforts at quitting did not have permanent results.

Susan began smoking at the age of fifteen and had been smoking one pack a day for four years. She had been trying to quit smoking cigarettes on her own for years, "cold turkey" only. She had heard of bupropion and verbalized particular interest in it. After the counselor explained the benefits of both medication and counseling, Susan agreed to both treatment interventions.

Susan's longest time abstinent had been two months, achieved earlier that year. At that time, she quit along with her boyfriend, who had also relapsed. She denied any other addictions and described herself as an occasional drinker (two glasses of wine per use). Her identified smoking triggers included alcohol and socializing with other smokers. Writing was also an identified performance anxiety trigger, as she had experienced writing "blocks" in the past, especially when nearing deadlines. Weight control was not a major issue, but a concern; she was noted as thin, though her appetite was good. She had begun exercising two weeks previously.

Susan denied current anxiety and depressive symptoms, but described periods of anxiety and depression in the past. She had sought medical treatment for anxiety during a crisis six years previously and was successfully treated with the antidepressant Zoloft, which she took for three months then stopped due to feeling more adjusted to the transition. She had never sought counseling in the past. Her mother had a history of depression and had been treated with antidepressant medication briefly in the past. Susan's mother also smoked cigarettes throughout Susan's life. No other addictions in the family were reported.

Assessment

According to Susan's reports, six of the seven criteria for a diagnosis of nicotine dependence were met. An atypical depressive disorder was also suspected (with mixed depressive and anxiety symptoms); however, her bout of performance anxiety in the past might have been related to a life transition. Because Susan had experienced positive results with an antidepressant in the past, it was expected that it would be helpful again. Although Susan had not sought counseling in the past for her anxiety and depression, she agreed to smoking cessation counseling at this time. Susan attended a total of twelve sessions for smoking cessation over the course of two-and-a-half months (six sessions each with a counselor and a psychiatrist).

Counseling Sessions One and Two

These initial sessions focused on providing educational, cognitive, and behavioral interventions for smoking cessation. A psychiatric assessment was scheduled. Susan identified a target quit date two weeks from session two.

Psychiatric Sessions One Through Three

Susan's first psychiatric session occurred two weeks prior to her first projected quit date. The psychiatrist noted that although Susan's stated chief complaint was that she wanted to quit smoking, upon questioning, Susan described escalating depressive and anxiety symptoms for one week, including dysphoric mood, difficulty sleeping, poor concentration, low energy, increased appetite, and increased anxiety. The identified precipitants were ongoing conflicts related to a divorce settlement from her husband.

This also threatened her current financial situation. She also described past depressive cycles in more detail, suggesting a pattern of recurrent major depression, especially in winter. She described having at least low-level anxiety on most days. Given her anxiety symptoms and a past positive response to Zoloft, Susan agreed to the doctor's recommendation to begin a low dose of Zoloft and to return in one week for monitoring. Susan forgot the second appointment and did not show up, but rescheduled when called at home that day. In the next session, after taking Zoloft for two weeks, she complained of extreme fatigue, increased sleeping, nausea, and poor concentration due to fatigue, though she also reported improved mood and decreased anxiety. Susan was informed that initial negative side effects are common with SSRIs and that suspected sedation would likely subside. However, by her third psychiatric session, they had not, and Susan asked to discontinue Zoloft and to try bupropion, as her smoking had increased while she was depressed, and she hoped to improve her concentration and energy levels. After speaking with Susan about the possibility that bupropion would exacerbate her anxiety symptoms, the doctor agreed to a trial of bupropion.

Counseling Session Three

Susan decided to delay her target quit date for one week due to her recent reported depressive and anxiety symptoms, which were also interfering in her interpersonal relationships and contributing to social isolation. Susan also feared that her inability to concentrate and excessive fatigue would again interfere with her writing performance. The session focused on maintaining motivation (coaching) and developing adaptive coping skills that were pleasurable and social in nature.

Psychiatric Session Four

Susan reported taking bupropion for one week; she described a vast improvement in concentration and had not smoked for a few days, nor had she felt the desire to smoke. She noted feeling slightly more nervous and complained of insomnia. She also noted the loss of social ease that she experienced while taking Zoloft. The doctor explained that insomnia and nervousness may be temporary side effects. She was given a time-limited prescription for insomnia, and the doctor explained that there might be temporary negative side effects.

Counseling Sessions Four Through Six

Susan was congratulated for her ability to quit smoking, having achieved an initial period of abstinence of two weeks while taking bupropion. Over the next month, she reported smoking one to three cigarettes per week, usually in the morning while drinking coffee with her smoking boyfriend, and smoking in response to feeling anger related to her long-awaited divorce.

Sessions focused on assertiveness training in her interpersonal relationships, accepting relapses, and learning coping alternatives to smoking. She was encouraged to exercise more regularly. Susan's two missed counseling sessions during this time period were briefly addressed. She stated that morning appointments were now inconvenient; therefore, the next session was moved to the afternoon. The counselor chose to remain in an ego-supportive stance while Susan was experiencing multiple losses and stressors, and did not choose to confront or explore her resistance more deeply at that point.

Psychiatric Sessions Five and Six

Susan reported continued nervousness while taking bupropion, although the sleep medication had improved her insomnia. She still complained of social anxiety but did not want to take an SSRI again, due to past sedative side effects. When she discontinued the brief trial of sleeping medication because of concern about its habit-forming properties, her insomnia returned; the doctor prescribed an alternate nonaddictive sleeping medication, which caused grogginess in the mornings. Susan was encouraged to do aerobic exercise to treat insomnia; between psychiatric sessions five and six, Susan reported running three times, but her insomnia did not improve. The psychiatrist also decreased her dosage of bupropion in an effort to minimize negative side effects.

Susan missed the next appointments scheduled with the counselor and psychiatrist. Outreach attempts were made by letter, which Susan responded to by mail one month later, stating that she had been traveling. Susan reported that she had not smoked for the past six weeks and that her insomnia had improved on a self-determined lower dosage of bupropion. She also described her counseling sessions as having been helpful, and identified her self-doubt as her main obstacle in achieving the things most important to her.

Susan's medical doctor took advantage of a teachable moment (while treating Susan's upper respiratory ailment) during a time when Susan would likely be motivated to quit (while experiencing a smoking-related illness) and encouraged Susan to seek intensive treatment (due to her history of relapses). Susan's mental health practitioners monitored comorbid vulnerabilities (history of and current depression and anxiety in Susan and her family) and applied appropriate clinical and psychopharmacological interventions. More specific counseling challenges pertaining to this case are discussed in the next section.

Transference, Countertransference, and Counseling Issues

Public health literature encourages counselors to be very directive with smoking patients, an approach that might raise ethical dilemmas for a trained mental health professional, who tends to be less directive and more respectful of starting where the patient is. One guideline (USDHHS, 1996) goes so far as to encourage the instilling of guilt as a tool for increasing patient motivation, such as saying to the patient, "You know your children need you." This is a high-risk intervention when the clinician is forming a therapeutic alliance with a patient, especially considering the potential profile of an older, long-term female smoker possessing longer-term shame. However, such an intervention given by staff in a medical setting during a brief checkup may have a different impact than when used by a smoking cessation clinician, with whom an ongoing positive alliance is crucial.

The newer governmental guidelines delineate treatment styles for three different types of patients: the "willing" patient, the "not yet willing" patient, and the patient who has recently quit (USDHHS, 2000). Transference and countertransference issues vary depending on the stage that a patient is in when entering treatment. A clinician must tread carefully (if at all) in areas of the unconscious. For instance, in the case of Susan, her missed appointments were met by the counselor with an ego-supportive, rather than ego-modifying, approach (Goldstein, 1984), which acknowledged the absences but did not confront the unconscious resistance. It was evident to the counselor during the assessment phase that Susan's past treatment of her anxiety and depression (that is, her seeking medication versus talking therapy), her social anxiety, and her constricted or controlled affect all indicated that Susan would likely trust medication far more quickly and easily than she would a person or the counseling process. Supporting this initial hypothesis were her more frequent missed appointments with her counselor (as compared to her psychiatrist) and the noticeably increased disclosure of her current and past history of depressive and anxiety symptomatology with her psychiatrist rather than her counselor. Susan appeared to view her counselor as more of a peer at that point, and her psychiatrist as an authority. The counselor felt that while too many internal and external stressors were present, Susan might feel easily criticized by exploration of unconscious resistance. However, Susan did verbalize a high degree of motivation to quit smoking and to read and learn about this area of the counselor's expertise. The counselor built on these strengths and focused primarily on helping Susan quit smoking. As a teacher and coach, she provided Susan with information, and Susan in turn completed her homework readings. Only in later sessions did Susan voluntarily begin to increase her disclosure concerning the interpersonal conflicts that contributed to her comorbid features.

Because patients often rely more on pharmacotherapy than on counseling (Hughes et al., 1999), smoking cessation counselors must be narcissistically capable of playing a secondary role in the overall treatment. The counselor must also be flexible, because a patient may use an entire forty-five-minute session, as she would in psychotherapy, or she may feel more comfortable with shorter sessions or sessions conducted by telephone.

In private practice, I have worked toward integrating smoking cessation treatment with ongoing general psychotherapy by taking advantage of teachable moments (for instance, when a patient brings up a health crisis or arrives at the session short winded from asthma) and by offering motivational information and concern. When a therapeutic alliance is already in place, I often feel that it is appropriate to confront resistance.

All clinicians must examine their own reactions to nicotine addiction, as we are not exempt from the tendency to stigmatize smokers. Smokers are not "just stupid," which has become a popular idea. Destigmatization of all addicts will allow for more precise problem solving, uncontaminated by emotional reactivity. Although it is quite challenging to do so, the clinician can achieve a balance between motivating and also conveying realistic information about the possibility of relapse, without seeming pessimistic to the patient; this allows a quitter to accept slips or the possibility of slips. The clinician must be able to model acceptance of her own failures in order to help others find this in themselves. Humor can also be a very valuable tool.

Conclusion

When we examine women's smoking behaviors from a historical perspective, we are reminded of the truth in the statement, "Be careful of what you ask for lest you may get it." The very symbol of women having found their voice in the 1920s silenced them with laryngitis and throat cancer in later years. Perhaps the recent record $144.8 billion awarded by a Florida jury against the tobacco industry may finally change some of its practices, especially its targeting of young people in cigarette advertising.

In the treatment arena, now that we are reaching more smokers through the stepped-care approach, are we serving them well? Or are we asking too much of health care providers and allowing smokers who do not respond to minimal interventions (and therefore probably belong in mental health settings) to fall through the cracks? One danger of the stepped-care model is its similarities to managed health care, as both offer lowest-cost, minimal interventions first—but then what? Many mental health care providers are familiar with treating depressed patients whose managed-care provider refused to pay for treatment when the patient was not willing (or ready) to take antidepressant medication. Smokers (and practitioners) can take on the dangerous view that "what works for one should work for all."

For poorly trained medical practitioners, teachable moments can quickly become moments of perceived failure. Moreover, identifying smokers is a first step, but can medical practitioners identify smokers with special needs? The greatest need for prevention, treatment, and low-cost or reimbursable services lies in the less-educated, lower socioeconomic populations. These women may be more likely to smoke but less likely to show up in either medical and mental health settings.

References

American Cancer Society. (1999, July). *Quitting smoking.* Available: www.cancer.org/tobacco/quitting.html.

American Cancer Society. (2000). *Cancer facts and figures 2000: Tobacco use.* Available: www.cancer.org/statistics/cff2000/tobacco.html.

American Psychiatric Association. (1994). *Diagnostic and statistical manual of mental disorders* (4th ed.). Washington, DC: Author.

Anda, R. F., Croft, J. B., Felitti, V. J., Nordenburg, D., Giles, W. H., Williamson, D. F., & Giovino, G. A. (1999). Adverse childhood experiences and smoking during adolescence and adulthood. *Journal of the American Medical Association, 282,* 1652–1658.

Bowlby, J. (1980). *Attachment and loss: Vol. 3. Loss.* New York: Basic Books.

Brody, J. E. (1998, May 12). A fatal shift in cancer's gender gap. *New York Times,* p. F7.

Centers for Disease Control and Prevention. (1999). Cigarette smoking among adults— United States, 1997. *Morbidity and Mortality Weekly Report, 48,* 993–996.

Christen, J. R., & Christen, A. G. (1998). *The female smoker: From addiction to recovery.* Indianapolis: Creative Services, Medical Educational Resources Program, Indiana University School of Medicine.

Curry, S. (1993). Self-help interventions for smoking cessation. *Journal of Consulting and Clinical Psychology, 61,* 790–803.

Fiore, M. C., Smith, S. S., Jorenby, D. E., & Baker, T. B. (1994). The effectiveness of the nicotine patch for smoking cessation: A meta-analysis. *Journal of the American Medical Association, 271,* 1940–1947.

Fisher, E. B, Jr., Lichtenstein, E., & Haire-Joshu, D. (1993). Multiple determinants of tobacco use and cessation. In C. T. Orleans & J. Slade (Eds.), *Nicotine addiction: Principles and management* (pp. 59–88). New York: Oxford University Press.

Fried, J. L. (2000). Women and tobacco: Oral health issues. *Journal of Dental Hygiene, 74*(1), 49–55.

Gilbert, I. (1988). *Stop smoking through self-hypnosis.* Rocklin, CA: Prima Publishing & Communications.

Goldstein, E. G. (1984). *Ego psychology and social work practice.* New York: Free Press.

Grady, D. (1998, October 27). Hardest habit to break: Memories of the high. *New York Times,* p. F1.

Henningfield, J. E., Cohen, C., & Pickworth, W. B. Psychopharmacology of nicotine. (1993). In C. T. Orleans & J. Slade (Eds.), *Nicotine addiction: Principles and management* (pp. 64–65). New York: Oxford University Press.

Hughes, J. R., Fiester, S., Goldstein, M. G., Resnick, M. P., Rock, N., & Ziedonis, D. (1996). American Psychiatric Association practice guideline for the treatment of patients with nicotine dependence. *American Journal of Psychiatry, 153*(Suppl.), pp. S1–S31. Available: www.psych.org/clin_res/pg_nicotine.html.

Hughes, J. R., Goldstein, M. G., Hurt, R. D., & Shiffman, S. (1999). Recent advances in the pharmacotherapy of smoking. *Journal of the American Medical Association, 281,* 72–76.

Jorenby, D. E., Leischow, S. J., Nides, M. A. Rennard, S. I., Johnson, J. A., Hughes, A. R., Smith, S. S., Muramoto, M. L., Daughton, D. M., Doan, K., Fiore, M. C., & Baker, T. B. (1999). A controlled trial of sustained-release bupropion, a nicotine patch, or both for smoking cessation. *New England Journal of Medicine, 340,* 685–691.

Levin, J. D. (1991). *Treatment of alcoholism and other addictions: A self-psychology approach.* Northvale, NJ: Aronson.

McGinnis, J. M., & Foege, W. H. (1993). Actual causes of death in the U.S. *Journal of the American Medical Association, 270,* 2207–2212.

Noble, H. B. (1999, March 2). New from the smoking wars: Success. *New York Times,* pp. F1–F3.

Office of Women's Health. (1996, March). *Tobacco use.* Available: www.cdc.gov/od/owh/whtob.htm.

Orleans, C. T. (1993). Treating nicotine dependence in medical settings: A stepped-care model. In C. T. Orleans & J. Slade (Eds.), *Nicotine addiction: Principles and management* (pp. 145–161). New York: Oxford University Press.

Prochaska, J. O., & DiClemente, C. C. (1983). Stages and processes of self-change of smoking: Toward an integrative model of change. *Journal of Consulting and Clinical Psychology, 51,* 390–395.

Resnick, M. (1993). Treating nicotine addiction in patients with psychiatric co-morbidity. In C. T. Orleans & J. Slade (Eds.), *Nicotine addiction: Principles and management* (pp. 327–366). New York: Oxford University Press.

Stevens, V. J., Glasgow, R. E., Hollis, J. F., Lichtenstein, E., & Vogt, T. M. (1993). A smoking-cessation intervention for hospital patients. *Medical Care, 31*(1), 65–72.

Tobacco smoke and women: A special vulnerability? (2000, May). *Harvard Women's Health Watch, 17,* 9.

U.S. Department of Health and Human Services. (1996, April). *Smoking cessation clinical practice guideline no. 18.* Rockville, MD: U.S. Department of Health and Human Services.

U.S. Department of Health and Human Services. (2000, June). *Treating tobacco use and dependence* (Summary). U.S. Public Health Service. Available: www.surgeongeneral.gov/tobacco/smokesum.htm.

PART THREE

LIFE CYCLE ISSUES FOR ADDICTED WOMEN

CHAPTER ELEVEN

ADOLESCENT GIRLS AND ADDICTION

Rose Fajardo Latino

There are a lot of things that I pretty much have to figure out on my own now. I can't talk to my mom about stuff; she tries to push in on me too much. I like drugs because for a while I can just be solo; I can forget about whatever's got me down. I just don't care anymore. Drugs always work. I can't trust other people, but I know that my weed will always be there.

HEATHER, AGE SIXTEEN, WHITE EUROPEAN DESCENT

Chemical dependency at any age can devastate a woman's ability to function, but adolescence leaves girls particularly vulnerable to the consequences of substance abuse. In previous generations, women's addiction began later in life (Center for Substance Abuse Prevention, 1996). This has changed as increasing numbers of girls begin to use drugs in early adolescence, perhaps in response to changing social roles. Although teenage boys have traditionally had higher rates of substance abuse, girls are now equally likely to use alcohol or illicit drugs (National Center on Addiction and Substance Abuse at Columbia University, 1996). Unfortunately, a linear relationship has been found between serious drug usage in youth and negative effects on future work conditions, education, social integration, emotional health, criminal involvement, and family stability (Newcomb, 1995).

To work effectively with adolescent girls, it is essential to understand both the unique developmental aspects of this life stage and the diverse issues that girls today must negotiate (Hersch, 1998). More than ever before, adolescent girls are bombarded with unreal female images ranging from underweight models in magazines to hypersexualized female dancers on MTV. Many teenage girls face daily pressures ranging from confronting drug dealers at school to becoming sexually active, issues that are typically difficult for most girls to discuss with their parents. Although some parents may have faced similar experiences in adolescence, many others cannot conceive of the world their daughters live in daily. In her book

Reviving Ophelia, Mary Pipher (1994) suggests that the stressors girls face create a "girl poisoning culture." Sociocultural, psychological, and physiological factors function as risk factors or as protective elements in relation to substance use. Girls of color and girls from poor families must also meet the extra challenges of racism and poverty. At each stage of adolescence, girls may experience distinctive negative consequences and effects of substance abuse. Adolescents should not be treated as young adults (Lamb, 1978). Because teenagers differ developmentally from adult women, it is essential to provide informed interventions that meet their special needs. This chapter will review the basic developmental achievements for the adolescent girl, the unique features of adolescent chemical dependency, and the factors clinicians must consider for adept assessment, treatment, and continuing care.

Adolescent Development

Adolescents are a heterogeneous group, and girls at different stages within this age group will have widely different issues with which to contend. Throughout the period, girls negotiate the tasks of establishing an adult personality, developing relationships outside the family, and negotiating closeness and separateness within the family structure. These tasks may be complicated by several factors. For example, for girls whose culture places high value on family cohesiveness, the pursuit of outside goals and relationships may be perceived as abandoning the family (Canino & Spurlock, 1994; Aguilar, 1999).

Whereas the lines between childhood and adulthood are clearly defined, the differences between adolescents and adults are blurred. Increasingly, adolescents are treated legally and socially as adults despite their immature mental and emotional development. Adolescents' notorious poor judgment and impulsivity, which relate to many of their behavioral troubles, have been shown to be a result of the immature state of the brain's frontal lobe, which continues its development into the mid-twenties (Sowell, Thompson, Holmes, Jernigan, & Toga, 1999). Compared to those of teenage boys, girls' brains mature earlier; thus, in general, they may demonstrate better self-control, organizing, and emotional regulation. Nonetheless, research by Nancy Gilligan (1982) suggests that, rather than becoming more confident during adolescence, many girls develop self-doubt. Gilligan found that as adolescent girls encounter the sociocultural disempowerment experienced by women, they experience a disconnection between what they know and what they feel is acceptable to voice.

The teenage years can be framed as early, middle, and late adolescence, each with its own particular challenges and achievements. We will give special attention to early adolescence, as these years are particularly difficult due to the radical changes occurring at this time.

Early Adolescence: Ages Twelve to Fourteen

The years between twelve and thirteen are often the most vulnerable for teenagers (Golombeck, Martin, Stein, & Korenblum, 1986; Schave & Schave, 1989). Having lost the security of childhood, many girls turn to substance use to achieve a pseudo-maturity and to alleviate the painful emotions of the early teens. This period may be the time of greatest variability among teen girls due to major developmental differences in physical and emotional maturity. Whereas some girls are still interested in latency-age play, others may be fully sexually active.

In contemporary Western societies, girls reach menarche at about age twelve and a half, with a two-year range in either direction. In general, girls reach puberty two years earlier than boys. Girls who develop prematurely report more dissatisfaction with body appearance and increased self-consciousness (O'Dea & Abraham, 1999), and earlier maturity has been linked to earlier sexual behavior as well as increased likelihood for eating disorders. Because the self-assessment of girls in early adolescence may be particularly harsh, dissatisfaction with their changing bodies contributes to depression, eating disorders, and negative self-evaluation (O'Dea & Abraham, 1999; Rierdan & Koff, 1997). A girl's sense of loss of control of her body is unnerving at a time when other parts of life are also in flux.

During early adolescence, teenagers begin a critical scrutiny of parents and other significant adults. This de-idealization process is considered one of the primary forces that move girls from childhood to adolescence. Yet it leaves adolescent girls at a heightened risk for substance use. Where once they turned to parents for definition and feedback, now they rely on peers, popular culture, and themselves. The lack of certainty in self-definition may create a vacuum that drug use can fill. Substances may provide a soothing reassurance during this uncomfortable period, allowing the girl to avoid anxious feelings (Pipher, 1994).

Alcohol and drug use also may be the result of ordinary adolescent curiosity about trying new life experiences. In 1998, 42 percent of eighth-grade girls reported using alcohol in the past year, and 17 percent of them reported having been drunk during the year (Johnston, O'Malley, & Bachman, 1999). Of girls this age, 15 percent reported using marijuana in the past year, and 9 percent reported marijuana use during the thirty days prior to the national survey. The use of alcohol and other drugs can have profound harmful implications if it continues unchecked. Entering the junior high school environment, adolescents must decipher new rules, expectations, and norms. The experience is stressful, but the process of learning to negotiate these experiences is important to successful psychological and emotional development. Without learning to negotiate this aspect of social acculturation, the girl may flounder in performing important tasks related to identity formation.

More than in later years, early adolescents experience feelings of shame (Schave & Schave, 1989). These feelings relate both to the multitude of new developmental issues they face at that time, such as physical changes and new school environments, and to their increased tendency to be self-critical. Drug use temporarily alleviates these stressors while providing a social point of connection with peers. Simultaneously, drug use creates the illusion of being older, independent, and daring—three commonly held adolescent values.

Another characteristic of early adolescence is girls' absorption with sameness and difference among peers. A constant scrutiny of themselves and their friends is a part of classic socialization that contributes to identity formation. This narcissistic absorption, although bringing uncomfortable self-consciousness, aids in creating a new self-definition. Peer relationships also function as agents in negotiating a second separation-individuation process (Blos, 1962) and encourage the development of sensibilities that are often starkly different from those of their parents. For many girls, this separation process may entail experimenting with radical changes in dress styles, music tastes, and use of nouveau slang as they explore the new adult roles. In 1998, the annual survey of teenagers conducted by the National Institute on Drug Abuse (NIDA, 1999) found that eighth-grade girls surpassed boys in annual prevalence of use of cocaine (3.1 percent versus 2.9 percent), amphetamines (4 percent versus 2.4 percent), and inhalants (11.6 percent versus 10.6 percent). The causes for this gender difference are not fully understood; multiple risk factors and such protective factors as an involved family and community, effective coping skills, and spirituality are thought to contribute to the strengths or vulnerability of all adolescents (Winters, 1999a). Several studies have found that girls in this age group report experiencing affect more intensely than in later teen years (Greene, 1990). The NIDA report also finds that Latino youth at this age have the highest rates of cocaine use, marijuana use, and binge drinking. This may partially account for the higher than average school dropout rates of Latino students. For girls of color, culture-specific stressors such as language barriers, higher poverty rates, and the cumulative effects of racism contribute to the overall life challenges.

Familial and community dynamics have been recognized as playing an especially strong role in substance use at this age. For example, the high mobility of modern families, a family history of alcoholism, high levels of family conflict, and lack of bonding to the school increase the likelihood of substance abuse (Hawkins, 1999). Girls living in the inner city may have a greater exposure to drugs in their neighborhoods, a stressor that may normalize substance abuse (Canino & Spurlock, 1994). Jessor and Jessor (1975) found that teenagers who were poorer students academically and who perceived a lower level of parental support and a higher level of parental and peer approval of drinking were more likely to drink at younger ages. Family conflict, which interferes with secure bonding between parents and their children, has been identified as contributing to youthful drug use (Jessor & Jessor, 1975; Needle, Lavee, Su, Brown, & Doherty, 1988).

Successful interventions at this age may prevent or delay development of an addiction process. Indeed, postponement of the age of onset for alcohol use effectively delays the risk for use of marijuana, a drug commonly associated with the initiation of other drug use (Yamaguchi, 1990). As is true of all adolescent substance abuse counseling, involvement of parents or guardians is recommended (Liddle & Dakof, 1995).

Middle Adolescence: Ages Fifteen to Sixteen

During middle adolescence, girls are generally more psychologically integrated, having had more experiences to help them adjust to their changing physical, social, and psychological selves. One observes the maturation of ego strengths in their improved ability to manage life demands and unexpected challenges. Cognitively they are more capable of entertaining the gray shades of uncertainty; they also have the capacity to move beyond the ongoing self-scrutiny so ubiquitous in early adolescence. This is reflected by Annie, age fifteen, the daughter of a White mother and a Chinese father:

> It was like I was a different person every few months. For a while, I was a "prep" dressing all perfect in my pink button-down shirts and khaki pants. Then I was a skater girl wearing just super-baggy clothes and hanging out with the skater guys. We got high after school together and smoked [cigarettes] before school. After that I went "goth," wearing all black; I dyed my hair blue-black, wore heavy, dark makeup and tons of silver jewelry. That was when I tried other stuff—acid and even cocaine. My mom was like, what is wrong with you? It was like I was trying to find myself . . . be someone, you know. Now I'm just me. I figured out that I want to be a fashion designer, so drugs will get in the way. I still smoke sometimes, but I wear whatever I want to.

Gilligan's early research (1982) demonstrated the importance of healthy relationships with others, without which girls' sense of identity may be precarious. This gender difference is reflected in adolescent girls' substance use, as girls more often adjust their drinking to match that of their close friends but not that of their larger peer group (Downs, 1985). In contrast, boys' substance use matched the larger group. Commonly, girls at this stage will have heightened de-idealization of their parents and will give more value to the ideas and opinions of peers. Adolescent girls with stronger coping skills will verbally process feelings with friends and trusted adults to successfully manage their intense feelings (Booth, 1997), but girls with fewer coping abilities may turn to drugs as a method of establishing connections with others. Further, teen girls reporting low family support have been found to be more vulnerable to problems with alcohol (Windle, 1992).

Although a general reprieve from the stress experienced in early adolescence occurs as girls move into the middle years of adolescence, this is also the age at which girls report their highest use of most substances (Johnston et al., 1999). At present there is no explanation given for this in the literature. Gilligan (1982) theorized that girls are left feeling disillusioned as they begin to piece together some of the inherent conflicts between what is expected of them as females in a Western society and their personal wishes and goals. For example, most teen girls recognize the double standard regarding sexual mores, which condemn sexually active girls more strongly than they do adolescent boys.

According to the 1998 Monitoring the Future Survey (Johnston et al., 1999), tenth-grade females, as compared to their male cohorts, report slightly higher annual rates of using tranquilizers (5.4 percent versus 4.7 percent) and amphetamines (12.3 versus 9 percent), and virtually the same rate of alcohol use (63.9 percent versus 63.5 percent). Their reported rates of use of marijuana, LSD, hallucinogens, MDMA, and tranquilizers are double the rates for girls in the eighth grade. The high rate of amphetamine use might be attributed to the sociocultural value placed on maintaining a thin prepubescent body type.

The possible effects of substance use in this period include the negative consequences of the earlier period plus impairment in the ability to plan ahead, further stunting of emotional growth, reduced self-esteem, increased depression, and higher truancy and school dropout rates.

Late Adolescence: Ages Seventeen to Eighteen

At this age, teenage girls once again stand at the gates of major life changes. Many face leaving home and living away from their parents for the first time. This can be a time of both exhilaration and anxiety, and the accumulation of past success and failure contributes to their sense of expectancy about the future. Those who have learned that their efforts effect change will feel more confident with the gradual move into adulthood. In contrast, girls with fewer life successes will need extra support and encouragement to tackle future goals. Developmentally, the primary issues for girls in this stage are to achieve autonomy while balancing their needs for closeness and separateness. Maintaining meaningful intimate relationships with both genders is prized.

According to the 1998 Monitoring the Future report (Johnston et al. 1999), 45 percent of twelfth-grade girls reported having used marijuana; 19 percent of them reported use during the thirty days prior to the survey. Alcohol, the most commonly used substance, was used by 81 percent of senior high school girls, and 26 percent of them reported having been intoxicated in the previous thirty days. Although it is not possible to accurately ascertain from these figures the number of chemically dependent girls, it is clear that substance use among adolescent girls is a common occurrence.

Girls who have developed chemical dependency face an impairment in their ability to achieve independence. Their resulting pseudo-independence leaves them lacking the self-confidence or skills necessary for exploring future life plans. Paradoxically, they often believe they are staunchly independent, denying all dependency needs. These girls may reason in a more concrete and magical manner more common to younger adolescents. This tendency may not be immediately evident because they appear physically older and may be quite articulate and intellectually advanced. Nevertheless, they may have difficulty in interpersonal relationships as a result of their substance use and may be highly self-critical, a dynamic more common to early adolescence.

Maria, a seventeen-year-old Mexican American girl, portrayed some of these issues after her arrest for public intoxication at a high school basketball game.

Maria: It's really no big thing being suspended, because I was planning to quit and get my GED anyway.

Clinician: It'd be pretty rough to quit in the twelfth grade. You've worked a lot of years in school to get to this point.

Maria: I worked my you-know-what off! But a GED is just as good, and faster.

Clinician: Sounds like the arrest has really got you down and discouraged.

Maria: I'd do it all over again, because basically I have always liked to drink.

Clinician: That's saying a lot; I mean, you'd give up twelve years of school for it. What do you like about it?

Maria: I like the freedom it gives you. I remember the first time I got drunk like it was yesterday. Right away I knew I was going to always like to drink. I thought, how come no one ever told me about this? It's great! My family disapproves of drinking, I think because of my uncles.

Clinician: They have trouble with alcohol?

Maria: Yeah, and so my mom thinks it's a sin or something, but to me, it's legal and fun.

Clinician: Even though it's not really legal for you yet. You're still underage, right?

Maria: Well . . . I'm at the age now when I make my own decisions.

Clinician: Some decisions get you into trouble, but you feel able to take care of yourself.

Maria: Yeah, I always have. For alcohol though, it's my boyfriend who can usually get it with his fake ID. A lot of times we just stay at his place and have a few drinks. Then we usually end up having sex, which I only like after I've had something to drink. Otherwise, I'm self-conscious, you know? And if anything goes wrong or whatever, I know that really I'm not totally responsible because I'm drunk. It wouldn't be my fault.

Clinician: So alcohol gives you freedom to do things that you think you couldn't do otherwise. Is that right?

Maria: *(smiles)* Excuse me, but do you always have to put a negative on whatever I say?

Clinician: Sorry, Maria. Just trying to get you to think about this a bit. I think it's a pretty important thing going on in your life right now.

Maria: Yeah, I know. I just don't feel ready to start just being a "good girl" right now. Too boring for me.

Etiology of Substance Abuse by Girls

The etiology of substance abuse varies by gender and ethnicity, and there is a growing recognition that the meaning of substance use by adolescents may also vary. For example, teenage girls, more often than boys, readily talk out their feelings and experiences with others. This tendency is a strength that allows for the possibility of helpful feedback or support from others. This same quality, however, has recently been related to reasons for initiating substance use among some girls (Donovan, 1996). For example, whereas boys tend to use alcohol for recreation and the known effect of the drug, girls have been found to use alcohol as a means of connecting to others. Thus when faced with a drug-using group, some girls may use substances in order not to make the others feel uncomfortable by their lack of participation. Motivationally, this differs from the traditional notion of peer pressure, as girls appear more concerned with fitting in to make group members feel at ease.

Adolescent girls of color have the lowest reported drug use of any subgroup of teens (Johnston et al., 1999). Paradoxically, these girls must negotiate life in a culture that frequently devalues females and people of color. For example, whereas African American girls have a greater likelihood of exposure to such risk factors as being raised in single-parent homes, living in high-crime neighborhoods with fewer available amenities, residing in substandard housing, and coming from poorer families (Biafora & Zimmerman, 1998), their drug use remains lower compared to their White counterparts. Because ethnic families traditionally maintain closer family units (Gibbs, 1985; Canino & Spurlock, 1994), parents' antidrug messages may resonate more strongly because of the tighter connection between parent and child.

Depression, sexual abuse, and eating disorders have been identified as factors strongly associated with substance abuse by adolescent girls. If drug use is understood as a mechanism to cope with emotional pain and trauma, then it is not difficult to comprehend this connection.

Depression

Compared to teenage boys, girls are more likely to suffer from depression. By the ages of fourteen and fifteen, the rate of depression is twice that of boys; girls are also less likely to report feeling securely self-confident (Pipher, 1994). This dynamic has been identified for several decades now; although explanations for it vary, all point to sociocultural expectations for girls as a leading contributor. Adolescent girls may consciously or unconsciously begin to deny aspects of themselves that do not fit the culturally determined values for femininity. Although many successfully negotiate these social challenges, those who lack secure family or social support systems may feel disillusioned and devalued. Too many girls respond by quelling their true voices, thus disrupting their natural desire to express themselves openly and authentically, and leaving them more vulnerable to depression (Pipher, 1994).

Compared to adults seeking drug treatment, adolescents are more likely to have attempted suicide. In one study of teens surveyed at eleven drug rehabilitation centers, 10 percent of boys and 30 percent of girls were found to have attempted suicide in the year prior to admission. More so than adolescent boys, adolescent girls with combined substance abuse, depression, and conduct disorder are at higher risk for suicide (Wannan & Fombonne, 1998). Adolescent girls attempt suicide at twice the rate of boys (National Institute of Mental Health, 1999); however, because teenage girls tend to use less lethal methods, boys more often die from suicide. Certain populations of teens appear more at risk for suicide. For example, the rate of suicide attempts and suicide among gay and lesbian teenagers is three times that for heterosexual teens (Remafedi, 1987). White adolescent girls maintain the highest suicide rate among teen girls, twice that of African American girls (U.S. Bureau of the Census, 1995). Nonetheless, the rate of suicide among African American girls has doubled between 1960 and 1995 (U.S. Bureau of the Census, 1995).

Approximately 40 percent of all adolescents seen in drug rehabilitation centers are dually diagnosed with alcohol dependence and depression (Lysaught & Wodarski, 1996). Their increased difficulty with family conflicts, interpersonal relationships, and other psychosocial difficulties may be caused or complicated by the use of substances. And even though many adults consider marijuana to be a "safer" drug, recent research has found that weekly marijuana users report higher rates of depression and feelings of isolation compared to nonusers (Greenblatt, 1999).

Sexual Abuse

There is a clear relationship between substance abuse and childhood physical, sexual, and emotional abuse and neglect (Winters, 1999b), and this issue should be included in every chemical dependency assessment for adolescent girls. An estimated 75 percent of female alcoholics report having been sexually violated by the age of ten (Covington, 1986). They are also more likely to have experienced rape as a result of impaired judgment due to intoxication. These abusive experiences lower self-esteem and foster feelings of distrust, emotional isolation, depression, and self-destructiveness. Although injurious, substance use can be seen as a coping mechanism for adolescents with a history of sexual abuse. Such substance use may provide a temporary disassociation and a reprieve from painful memories. Many girls who have been sexually abused will have difficulty discussing their history; they should be allowed to establish a secure rapport with the clinician and be reasonably stable in their recovery before delving into memories of past abuse. Because girls' early experiences may be a template for later sexual experiences, providing adolescent girls with information regarding safe dating and sexuality may help them make wiser decisions in their relationships (Pipher, 1994).

Disordered Eating

An estimated 10 percent of American adolescent girls have an eating disorder (American Academy of Child and Adolescent Psychiatry, 1997), and countless others have subclinical disordered eating, accounting for restricted food intake and excessive dietary restrictions. The interplay of the culturally valued thin body type and teenage girls' vulnerability to dissatisfaction with their bodies contributes to the heightened risk for disordered eating. Particularly during early adolescence, more physically developed girls are at higher risk for eating disorders (Cauffman & Steinberg, 1996; Swarr & Richards, 1996). Their body's natural gain of weight and curves during this time is often perceived as becoming "fat." Girls dissatisfied with their weight are also more at risk of using drugs for appetite control. Research has shown an association between bulimia and increased substance use for adolescent girls (Krahn, Kurth, Demitrack, & Drewnowski, 1992; Wiederman & Pryor, 1997).

The psychological problems associated with coexisting eating disorders and substance abuse can be quite complex. From early life, the individual's sense of self is located in the body (Applegate & Bonovitz, 1995). Eating disorders can be understood as stemming from the very core of a person, leaving her unprotected yet also very defended against intervention. The teenage girl who, in response to societal pressures or other stressors, fights to retain a prepubescent figure will deeply alter her experience at the most primary levels. For example, her relationship with food and substances outweighs the value of any person, place, or thing in her life. Her sense of self is permeated by a skewed assessment of her physical appearance, limiting other formative experiences. This concern is not limited to girls with eating disorders, as most teenage girls feel concerned with their weight and attractiveness (Pipher, 1994). For many girls, there is a constant scrutiny of weight and a striving for an elusive sense of beauty. Vicki, a sixteen-year-old of White European descent, said the following during her initial screening session:

> I like uppers because they do just that: make you feel up. I need them for studying—I can get more done, all my homework, and then work on projects for debate team. I want to get into a college, so I need to make good grades. They're also good for my eating habits—I mean they take away your appetite, so I'm not eating all the time like I used to do. I had been getting huge before this. Sometimes I have to vomit when I do eat. My mom makes me eat sometimes, so afterwards, I sneak to my room and vomit out the window! It's gross, but it's the only thing I can do to not get any fatter than I already am. I try to eat only fruit and drink Diet Cokes every day, but sometimes I slip and then I just eat everything! My boyfriend likes skinny girls, and I'm not one of those people who is naturally thin so . . . it helps.

It is no surprise that girls who assess themselves as unattractive have been found to be more likely to use substances (Page, 1993). This finding may play a part in explaining the puzzle of the steady increase in girls' substance abuse throughout most of the 1990s.

Assessment

Adolescents who abuse substances are prone to many other emotional and behavioral problems (Newcomb, 1995; Winters 1999a). The major challenge facing therapists is differentiating problems related to substance use from issues that are not drug related. For example, such classic substance abuse symptoms as depression, serious familial conflict, and chronic school truancy are also common mental health issues for adolescent girls. Recent research finds that girls with conduct problems are at greater risk for substance abuse (National Institute on Drug Abuse, 1997). Despite the challenges, early detection is key in intervention assessments, and it is better to be overly inclusive in identifying addiction in adolescents than to underdiagnose the problem (Winters, 1999a). In assessing adolescent girls, clinicians must take care not to be unduly influenced by manners of dress, hairstyle, makeup, or body art. Many teenagers express their need for separation from parents in this way but have no interest in drug use. Initially, even affect and cooperation with the interviewer may not be clinically indicative of substance abuse. Because the referral circumstances are most often related to negative behavior, most girls enter the room with a certain degree of defensiveness. The depressed or anxious girl may be as guarded as the chemically dependent girl when it comes to discussing her most troubling issues with an unknown adult. Maintaining a calm and supportive tone throughout the interview will increase rapport, and reasonable self-disclosure on the part of the clinician may decrease negative transference. These girls often enter the assessment with a template of conflictual relationships with adults; to speak openly, they must first perceive that the clinician is nonjudgmental, interested in their circumstances, and capable of understanding their point of view.

Adolescent substance abuse is best viewed on a continuum of drug use progression (Newcomb, 1995). Differentiating drug experimentation from substance abuse is a critical issue in conducting an assessment with adolescents. For many seasoned counselors, any drug use by a teenager is classified as dangerous. But many adolescent girls use drugs experimentally and eventually quit of their own volition at the first negative consequence. It is a characteristic of the vitality of adolescent girls to be curious and interested in trying new experiences, and some experimentation is normal for teenagers (Newcomb, 1995; Winters, 1999a). Unfortunately, whereas some girls may briefly experiment, others will go on to harmful abuse and dependence. Like their adult counterparts, teens who develop addiction continue to use despite negative repercussions in their family, school, and personal life. For many girls, a decline in school academics and behavior is one of the earliest signals of substance use noticed by their parents.

The initial interview for an assessment ideally will include the adolescent girl and her parents or guardians. To increase the accuracy of information and the effectiveness of the meeting, the clinician should give special emphasis to developing a therapeutic alliance with both the girl and her parents or guardians (Winters, 1999a). When obtaining the history of substance use, it is important to note the types of drugs used, age at first use, frequency and pattern of use, mode of ingestion, and previous drug treatments. The clinician should be aware that minimizing drug use is very common among drug-using teens. When treating teenage girls, the clinician should assess for abuse of pills, including Ritalin, over-the-counter diet aids, and herbal energy supplements, which may be used for weight control. Medical history should include age at first menses, disability status, sexual activity, and whether the girl makes use of safer sex practices. Sensitive issues such as sexual promiscuity, pregnancy, or concern about body image may be uncovered in this discussion.

Assessment of dual diagnosis should rule out depression, anxiety, attention deficit disorder, oppositional disorder, and conduct disorder (Chatlos, 1994). Feelings of depression, anxiety, and peer rejection have been found to be general predictors of drug disorders among females (Reinherz, Giaconia, Hauf, Wasserman, & Paradis, 2000). Special attention should be given to suicidality. This is especially important when assessing marijuana users, as their rate of suicidal ideation is three times as high as that of nonusers (Greenblatt, 1999). Girls who identify as lesbian will require extra support due to the strong presence of homophobia among teens and in society in general (Appleby & Anastas, 1998).

It is particularly important to assess the girl's home life, including family discord; physical, emotional, or sexual abuse; a history of running away from home; and the quality of her relationships with others in the household. Devoting equal focus to the strengths of the girl and her family, such as family closeness and concern, religious involvement, or community supports, will decrease defensiveness and increase openness in the interview process.

More than addicted adolescent boys, chemically dependent girls are more likely to have experienced severe familial conflict (Gross & McCaul, 1991). Because of this, girls and their parents or guardian will each need some portion of the assessment period for a separate confidential interview. Many parents will have feelings of anger, guilt, hurt, and inadequacy in response to their daughter's behaviors. Allowing the adult caregivers time to express their concerns helps reduce the anxiety that they may feel regarding the assessment process. Finally, because parental addiction is associated with children's drug use, the substance abuse history of parents and other household members should be assessed. Any history of serious physical and mental illnesses also needs to be explored.

A validated and reliable chemical dependency instrument, such as the Substance Abuse Subtle Screening Inventory–Adolescent Version (Winters & Stinchfield, 1995) or the Personal Experience Inventory, should be used as part of the assessment process (Winters, 1999a). These tests may be invaluable in the assessment because adolescents are notorious for minimizing or denying substance use. A thorough assessment combines the use of a dependable test with a semistructured interview. A skillful interviewer may learn not only about substance abuse but also about interpersonal problems.

Intervention and Treatment Protocols

A wide range of interventions for chemically dependent girls exists. The clinician must give careful consideration to the individual girl's personal, familial, and social strengths and needs in order to successfully match the level of intervention to the level of need. Attention to healing familial strain has been found to be particularly important in adolescent treatment (Liddle & Dakof, 1995). Unfortunately, even though treatment for adolescents has been found to be effective, it is in "extremely short supply" (Center for Substance Abuse Treatment, 2000). Although there are approximately ten levels of treatment and service options for adolescents, this review will discuss only those that are most commonly available.

Prevention and Intervention Counseling

At early stages of substance abuse, counseling that focuses on interrupting substance use and addressing problematic family dynamics may be an effective measure to prevent the development of chemical dependency.

Weekly counseling should focus on building an alliance that allows the clinician input into the adolescent's decision-making process. The clinician thus functions as an external ego for the girl, while working to strengthen such ego functions as judgment and perception. Family therapy is key to success in this process because the family dynamics can support or inhibit drug use (Liddle, Rowe, Dakof, & Lyke, 1998). Group therapy is also an effective approach, as girls value their peers' opinions, and the dynamics of a strong group can enhance recovery. As counseling progresses, the basic goals should always include development of social, communication, and problem-solving skills.

The following interchange took place between Lucinda, a thirteen-year-old of African American and Puerto Rican descent, and her clinician during Lucinda's third month of outpatient individual and family counseling. The dialogue illustrates the development of improved judgment and decision making through the use of the therapist as an external ego.

Lucinda: Mostly it was kid stuff we did—we were bored, and there was always Glade [air freshener] around. We huffed at my house mostly because my mother always bought it. She thought I just used it a lot because I liked the smell! *(laughs)* It was fun at the time—a cheap high.

Clinician: You didn't know it was so dangerous to your brain?

Lucinda: No! I didn't know that till my support group. No one ever said it could like, burn your brains out.

Clinician: So if you had known, you wouldn't have done it?

Lucinda: I'm not *that* crazy! Hey, I've got a little common sense!

Clinician: I see! *(laughs)* OK, so how will you use that common sense with this big beer party coming up this weekend?

Lucinda: I knew you were going to bust me on that! *(laughs)*

Clinician: How'd you know that I would bring that up?

Lucinda: Because you always end up getting into that stuff with me—the bad stuff.

Clinician: And how do I know about that "bad stuff"?

Lucinda: 'Cause I tell you! *(laughs)* I think I secretly want you to stop me or something!

Clinician: Maybe it's so I can help you stop yourself.

Lucinda: You and my mom too. She's gotten psychic lately!

Clinician: Seems like you tell her stuff so she can help you make decisions, too.

Outpatient Treatment

Teenage girls who report problems caused by low to moderate rates of drug use without withdrawal are best served in an outpatient setting (Winters, 1999b). Girls needing this level of care have impaired coping skills and difficulty with such emotions as depression or anger, and they exhibit low self-esteem. At this early stage of addiction, the girls have social environments that are not solely populated with drug-using friends; they still have friends and acquaintances who are substance free and available for drug-free socialization. The family's functioning level needs to be stable enough for consistency in office appointments and for transportation to Alcoholics Anonymous (AA) or Narcotics Anonymous (NA) meetings. Parents should be agreeable to attend family sessions, Al-Anon, or Families Anonymous meetings.

Teenaged girls beginning outpatient treatment are generally quite resistant. To develop an effective working alliance, the clinician must first allow the girl to tell her story, thus assuring her that the clinician is capable of hearing and understanding her experiences (Diamond & Liddle, 1996). Ideally, the treatment plan comprises a mix of individual, family, and peer group therapy, such that there is contact with the girl two to three times weekly. Flexibility in treatment planning is important, because such issues as sexual abuse or depression will influence the treatment needs of the individual girl and her family. The goal of treatment at this point is to foster a stable relationship in the family and a secure connection to an AA or NA group, including the girl's having a sponsor. The clinician provides family members with information about the process of addiction and the normal developmental issues for teenaged girls. Clinicians must be able to make therapeutic use of themselves, making parts of their own personalities available to the adolescent to foster growth (Khantzian, 1999; Lamb, 1978).

In the following interchange, Chessie, a fifteen-year-old girl of Irish-English descent, and her mother illustrate resistance and denial in their second week of outpatient family therapy.

Chessie: I don't think I need to go to those AA meetings. Everyone is so old!

Mom: Yes, I noticed the same thing. I've been wondering, would it be all right if we just came and saw you each week, instead of my dragging her to those meetings? There really don't seem to be many kids there. And the people at the Al-Anon meetings seemed to have a lot more trouble than Chessie and I have ever had.

Chessie: Yeah, the kids I saw are the hard-core druggies. I've never been that bad. Besides, I think I've learned all I need from the two meetings I went to this week.

Clinician: What did you learn?

Chessie: That you can get in a lot of trouble drinking too much!

Mom: So true.

Clinician: When we started off in our very first assessment interview together, both of you described a lot of trouble that Chessie was having: truancy court, caught smoking weed at the football game, getting drunk with your boyfriend every weekend. Seems like you were having a lot of trouble too.

Mom: Yes, but do you really think it is as bad as those people at AA? I mean, she's only fifteen years old . . .

Clinician: Right, Chessie is only fifteen, but she's already having some fairly significant problems. Do we want to see her get worse so she can fit in better at an AA meeting?

Chessie: I think I learned my lesson, though; I don't want to get into any more trouble, so I'm just going to quit on my own.

Mom: I think she could do it too, especially with my support. We've talked about it this week and came up with a plan where she'll carry her pager with her at all times and promises to call me whenever I page her. Plus, she'll keep a reasonable curfew and keep her room clean and her chores done.

Clinician: Hmmm . . . this sounds a lot like the plan you'd made two times last school year when this trouble with drugs and alcohol first started. Remember how after Chessie was suspended for intoxication at school, you made that behavioral contract with the school social worker about Chessie stopping drinking? As I recall, you did that twice, and both times you were very, very serious about it.

> *Mom:* We have tried it on our own before, Chessie, I forgot about that.
>
> *Clinician:* This is a really good example of the denial that we've been talking about lately. Denial tells us that maybe Chessie isn't so bad and that she could stop on her own.
>
> *Chessie:* Well, but the AA meeting was so boring, I almost fell asleep. I don't think it will help me.
>
> *Clinician:* Geez—it sounds like you were really bored, Chessie! Did you speak to any of the kids at the meeting? I'm asking because a lot of teenagers find AA boring when they first start, and a lot of that is because in the beginning, it's hard to know what's really going on.
>
> *Chessie:* Two girls came up and spoke to me after the meeting. They said they'd been clean for almost one year.
>
> *Clinician:* That's a long time. That's part of what you can get from going to AA meetings—clean time. Let's do this: let's take it one week at a time. I want you to attend three AA meetings this week, and this time, make a point to sit near those other teenagers and talk to them after the meeting.
>
> *Chessie:* They'll think I'm some kind of weirdo.
>
> *Clinician:* Just tell them your social worker is making you do it. Will you do that?
>
> *Chessie:* (nods) But this is the last week that I have to go?
>
> *Clinician:* We'll see. For now, let's just focus on attending this week.
>
> *Mom:* I heard some people in Al-Anon say going out after the meetings was a good thing to do. Maybe we could try that this Friday, Chessie?
>
> *Chessie:* Whatever.
>
> *Clinician:* I'm glad you're willing to give it a try. Shows what a lot of guts you've got.
>
> *Chessie:* Yeah, right, they're overflowing my pants since I stopped smoking cigarettes!
>
> *Clinician:* We'll talk about that next week.

Intensive Outpatient Treatment

Adolescent girls referred for intensive treatment fit similar treatment criteria as those needing outpatient care, with some important exceptions. This level of care is intended for girls who report moderate to heavy drug use, require a moderately structured setting, and can be safely detoxified with social supports (Winters, 1999b). Sessions are scheduled three to four times weekly and consist of individual, family, and group counseling. Family therapy is particularly important for girls, as they have high rates of family conflict. Group therapy, which may consist of peer group counseling, a multifamily group setting, or both, is helpful in providing a safe holding environment for members. Successful working groups also provide emotional refueling and empathic mirroring that is so often missing for girls and their families. Random drug testing is used to ensure that the outpatient intervention provides adequate support for this less restrictive method of treatment.

Intensive Inpatient Treatment and Residential Care

Girls referred into inpatient treatment or residential care have a higher level of difficulty with drug use. These girls report moderate to heavy drug use that has significantly impaired their overall ability to function at home, school, or work or with friends. The inpatient setting provides a retreat from the people, places, and things that fostered the addictive lifestyle. Such treatment is particularly important for those who are actively suicidal or at risk for subacute drug withdrawal. This extra support allows the girl and her family to prepare for more intensive therapy.

Longer-term stays allow for deeper therapeutic work on character issues and strengthen the girl's overall ability to use the tools of recovery. These tools include a positive connection with an AA or NA sponsor and peers in recovery, improved ability to self-reflect, and more time to recognize the consequences of the addiction on her life. Because the inpatient program provides a safe environment, issues that may be too overwhelming to discuss in an outpatient setting can be more fully processed. For many girls, the longer-term setting provides the time and place to safely discuss such issues as severe sexual or physical abuse, rape, unresolved grief and loss, or long-term family dysfunction.

LaTherese, an eighteen-year-old African American girl who has been in residential treatment for three months, exemplifies the importance of feeling secure and safe in the longer-term setting:

LaTherese: I remember I used to wake up every morning and wish I was dead. It was like, after I was raped, I just didn't care anymore. My boyfriend broke up with me the next day. He said it was my own fault for being drunk at the time.

Clinician: It was a terrible time in life for you, the time you hit bottom.

LaTherese: And I wouldn't be here now if I didn't overdose. I'd still be out there losing my life slowly.

Clinician: You were so alone with all that pain. How has it been for you to talk about this in the group?

LaTherese: You know, it's been tough, but the other girls have been good to me. Someone else had the same thing happen, and she told me all about it. I could see if it wasn't her fault, it wasn't my fault either.

Clinician: That's so hard to learn, isn't it? That it is not your fault.

LaTherese: That's right. It's crazy too, you know? I never did anything to deserve that. No one has—doesn't matter how drunk you are.

Clinician: You've really gained self-respect and compassion for yourself here, LaTherese.

LaTherese: Yeah, I never could have learned that before I got clean and sober. A girl in group said I was too busy trying to drug away my feelings, and she's right. I'm tired of doing that. I'm ready to live my life now.

Continuing Care and Relapse Prevention

In most instances, teenage girls and their families perceive the completion of a treatment program as the completion of treatment. Counselors should emphasize, ideally while the girl and her family are still in the program, that this is only the beginning of the recovery process, and should refer the family to aftercare services. Uninterrupted sobriety after treatment is rare among adolescent addicts, and early intervention after a relapse is key to regaining sobriety for the teen. For some, success is measured by the brevity of the relapse, as opposed to complete abstinence. Winters (1999b) found that girls who completed a treatment program had a 53 percent rate of sobriety, compared to only 15 percent for those who did not complete treatment. This difficulty in maintaining full abstinence is a reflection not only of the challenges that girls face in recovery but also of the challenges of adolescence. Khantzian (1999) suggests that relapse may also reflect a deficit in the ego's function of self-care, whereby an addicted person lacks the ability to think through decisions that may be harmful. This may be the case for girls who did not receive a secure and nurturing support system during their earlier years.

The primary goals of continuing care are to assist the girl in connecting to a stable twelve-step support group and sponsor, continue with any needed family work, and address special individual therapy needs. It is also vital that the girl learn to identify relapse signals and make plans for coping with drug-using peers. Prior to treatment, the addicted girl lacks positive mirroring because substances have replaced any significant relationships. Finding mirroring through positive peer friendships satisfies a girl's natural need for knowing others like herself (Berzoff, 1989). Clinicians need to help girls develop sober relationships based on closeness and communication. Such relationships enhance the girl's sobriety and her capacity to benefit more fully from recovery.

Conclusion

Working with chemically dependent adolescent girls can be a creative and rewarding clinical practice. Assisting girls in finding their true voices as they evolve through recovery touches the lives of many, including the treating clinician. To combine compassion, a sense of humor, knowledge of the developmental period, and flexibility is the best formula for working successfully with this population. Knowing that an intervention, even an imperfect one, can positively change the course of a girl's life makes the extra challenges well worth the effort.

References

Aguilar, M. A. (1999). Promoting the educational achievement of Mexican-American young women. In P. L. Ewalt, E. M. Freeman, A. E. Fortune, D. L. Poole, & S. L. Witkin (Eds.), *Multicultural issues in social work: Practice and research* (pp. 175–188). Washington, DC: NASW Press.

American Academy of Child and Adolescent Psychiatry. (1997). *Teenagers with eating disorders.* Available: www.aacap.org/factsfam/eating.htm.

Appleby, G. A., & Anastas, J. W. (Eds.). (1998). *Not just a passing phase: Social work with gay, lesbian, and bisexual people.* New York: Columbia University Press.

Applegate, J. S., & Bonovitz, J. M. (Eds.). (1995). *The facilitating partnership: A Winnicottian approach for social workers and other helping professionals.* Northvale, NJ: Aronson.

Berzoff, J. (1989). The role of attachments in female adolescent development. *Child and Adolescent Social Work, 6*(2), 115–125.

Biafora, F., & Zimmerman, R. (1998). Developmental patterns of African American adolescent drug use. In W. A. Vega, A. G. Gill, & Associates (Eds.), *Drug use and ethnicity in early adolescence* (pp. 149–175). New York: Plenum.

Blos, P. (1962). *On adolescence: A psychoanalytic interpretation.* New York: Free Press.

Booth, C. M. (1997). The development of affect. In J. Noshpitz (Series Ed.) & L. T. Faherty & R. M. Sarles (Vol. Eds.), *Handbook of child and adolescent psychiatry: Vol. 3. Adolescence: Development and syndromes* (pp. 53–59). New York: Wiley.

Canino, I. A., & Spurlock, J. (1994). *Culturally diverse children and adolescents: Assessment, diagnosis, and treatment.* New York: Guilford Press.

Cauffman, E., & Steinberg, L. (1996). Interactive effects of menarcheal status and dating on dieting and disordered eating among adolescent girls. *Developmental Psychology, 32,* 631–635.

Center for Substance Abuse Prevention. (1996). *Closing the gap: CSAP initiates Girl Power.* Available: www.omhrc.gov/ctg/chil-08.htm.

Center for Substance Abuse Treatment. (2000, January). *Successful treatment for adolescents: Multiple needs require diverse and special services.* Available: www.samshsa.gov/csat/inbriefs/jan2000.htm.

Chatlos, J. C. (1994). Dual diagnosis in adolescent populations. In N. S. Miller (Ed.), *Treating coexisting psychiatric and addictive disorders: A practical guide* (pp. 85–110). Center City, MN: Hazelden.

Covington, S. S. (1986). Facing the clinical challenges of women alcoholics' physical, emotional, and sexual abuse. *Focus on Family, 10,* 37–44.

Diamond, G. M., & Liddle, H. A. (1996). Resolving a therapeutic impasse between parents and adolescents in multidimensional family therapy. *Journal of Consulting and Clinical Psychology, 64,* 481–488.

Donovan, J. E. (1996). Gender differences in alcohol involvement in children and adolescents: A review of the literature. In J. M. Howard, S. E. Martin, P. D. Mail, M. E. Hilton, & E. D. Taylor (Eds.), *Women and alcohol: Issues for prevention research* (NIH Publication No. 32, pp. 133–162). Bethesda, MD: U.S. Government Printing Office.

Downs, W. R. (1985). Using panel data to examine sex differences in causal relationships among adolescent alcohol use, norms, and peer alcohol use. *Journal of Youth and Adolescence, 14,* 469–486.

Gibbs, J. T. (1985). City girls: A psychosocial adjustment of urban Black adolescent females. *SAGE: A Scholarly Journal on Black Women, 2,* 28–36.

Gilligan, C. (1982). *In a different voice: Psychological theory and women's development.* Cambridge: Harvard University Press.

Golombeck, H., Martin, P., Stein, B., & Korenblum, M. (1986). A study of disturbed and non-disturbed adolescents: The Toronto adolescent longitudinal study. *Canadian Journal of Psychiatry, 50,* 340–356.

Greenblatt, J. C. (1999). *Adolescent self-reported behaviors and their association with marijuana use.* Rockville, MD: Substance Abuse and Mental Health Services Administration, Office of Applied Studies.

Greene, A. L. (1990). Patterns of affectivity in the transition to adolescence. *Journal of Experimental Child Psychology, 50,* 340–356.

Gross, J., & McCaul, M. E. (1991). A comparison of drug use and adjustment in urban adolescent children of substance abusers. *International Journal of Addictions, 25,* 495–511.

Hawkins, J. D. (1999). *Activating communities to reduce risks for health and behavior problems.* Available: www.tyc.state.tx.us/prevention/activate.htm.

Hersch, P. (1998). *A tribe apart: A journey into the heart of American adolescence.* New York: Ballantine.

Jessor, R., & Jessor, S. L. (1975). Adolescent development and the onset of drinking: A longitudinal study. *Journal of Studies on Alcohol, 36,* 27–51.

Johnston L. D., O'Malley, P. M., & Bachman, J. G. (1999). *National survey results on drug use from the Monitoring the Future study, 1975–1998* (NIH Publication No. 99-4660). Washington, DC: U.S. Government Printing Office.

Khantzian, E. J. (1999). *Treating addiction as a human process.* Northvale, NJ: Aronson.

Krahn, D. D., Kurth, C., Demitrack, M. A., & Drewnowski, A. (1992). The relationship of dieting severity and bulimic behaviors to alcohol and drug use in young women. *Journal of Substance Abuse, 4,* 341–353.

Lamb, D. (1978). *Psychotherapy with adolescent girls.* San Francisco: Jossey-Bass.

Liddle, H. A., & Dakof, G. A. (1995). Family based treatment for adolescent drug use: State of the science. In E. Rahdert & D. Czechowicz (Eds.), *Adolescent drug abuse: Clinical assessment and therapeutic interventions* (NIH Publication No. 95-3908, pp. 218–254). Rockville, MD: U.S. Government Printing Office.

Liddle, H. A., Rowe, C., Dakof, G. A., & Lyke, J. (1998). Translating parenting research into clinical interventions for families of adolescents. *Clinical Child Psychology and Psychiatry, 3,* 419–443.

Lysaught, E., & Wodarski, J. S. (1996). Model: A dual focused intervention for depression and addiction. *Journal of Child and Adolescent Substance Abuse, 5*(1), 55–72.

National Center on Addiction and Substance Abuse at Columbia University. (1996). *Substance abuse and the American woman.* Available: www.casacolumbia.org/publications1456/publications.html.

National Institute on Drug Abuse. (1997). *Child psychopathology risk factors for drug abuse: Features and mechanisms.* Available: http://165.112.78.61/MeetSum/Meeting-SUM1.html.

National Institute on Drug Abuse. (1999). *NIDA research priorities and highlights.* Available: http://165.112.78.61/STRC/Role6.html.

National Institute of Mental Health. (1999). *Suicide facts.* Available: www.nimh.nih.gov/research/suifact.htm.

Needle, R., Lavee, Y., Su, S., Brown, P., & Doherty, W. (1988). Familial, interpersonal, and intrapersonal correlates of drug use: A longitudinal comparison of adolescents in treatment, drug-using adolescents not in treatment, and non-drug-using adolescents. *International Journal of Addictions, 23,* 1211–1240.

Newcomb, M. D. (1995). Identifying high-risk youth: Prevalence and patterns of adolescent drug abuse. In E. Rahdert & D. Czechowicz (Eds.), *Adolescent drug abuse: Clinical assessment and therapeutic interventions* (NIH Publication No. 156, pp. 7–38). Rockville, MD: U.S. Government Printing Office.

O'Dea, J. A., & Abraham, S. (1999). Onset of disordered eating attitudes and behaviors in early adolescence: Interplay of pubertal status, gender, weight, and age. *Adolescence, 34,* 671–679.

Page, R. M. (1993). Perceived physical attractiveness and frequency of substance use among male and female adolescents. *Journal of Alcohol and Drug Education, 38*(2), 81–91.

Pipher, M. (1994). *Reviving Ophelia: Saving the selves of adolescent girls.* New York: Ballantine.

Reinherz, H. Z., Giaconia, R. M., Hauf, A.M.C., Wasserman, M. S., & Paradis, A. D. (2000). General and specific childhood risk factors for depression and drug disorders by early adulthood. *Journal of the American Academy of Child and Adolescent Psychiatry, 39,* 223–231.

Remafedi, G. (1987). Homosexual youth: A challenge to contemporary society. *Journal of the American Medical Association, 258,* 222–228.

Rierdan, J., & Koff, E. (1997). Weight, weight-related aspects of body image, and depression in early adolescent girls. *Adolescence, 32,* 615–624.

Schave, D., & Schave, B. (1989). *Early adolescence and the search for self.* New York: Praeger.

Sowell, E. R., Thompson, P. M., Holmes, C. J., Jernigan, T. L., & Toga, A. W. (1999). In vivo evidence for post-adolescent brain maturation in frontal and striatal regions. *Nature Neuroscience, 2,* 859–861.

Swarr, A., & Richards, M. (1996). Longitudinal effects of adolescent girls' pubertal development, perceptions of pubertal timing and parental relations on eating problems. *Developmental Psychology, 32,* 636–646.

U.S. Bureau of the Census. (1995). *Statistical abstract of the United States.* Washington, DC: U.S. Commerce Department.

Wannan, G., & Fombonne, E. (1998). Gender differences in rates and correlates of suicidal behavior amongst child psychiatric patients. *Journal of Adolescence, 21,* 371–381.

Wiederman, M. W., & Pryor, T. (1997). The relationship between substance use and clinical characteristics among adolescent girls with anorexia nervosa or bulimia nervosa. *Journal of Child and Adolescent Substance Abuse, 6*(2), 39–47.

Windle, M. (1992). A longitudinal study of stress buffering for adolescent problem behaviors. *Developmental Psychology, 28,* 522–530.

Winters, K. C. (1999a). *Screening and assessing adolescents for substance use disorders* (Treatment Improvement Protocol Series No. 31). Rockville, MD: Center for Substance Abuse Treatment.

Winters, K. C. (1999b). *Treatment of adolescents with substance use disorders* (Treatment Improvement Protocol Series No. 32). Rockville, MD: Center for Substance Abuse Treatment.

Winters, K. C., & Stinchfield, R. D. (1995). Current issues and future needs in the assessment of adolescent drug abuse. In E. Rahdert & D. Czechowicz (Eds.), *Adolescent drug abuse: Clinical assessment and therapeutic interventions* (NIH Publication No. 156, pp. 146–171). Rockville, MD: U.S. Government Printing Office.

Yamaguchi, K. (1990). Drug use and its social covariates from the period of adolescence to young adulthood: Some implications from longitudinal studies. In M. Galanter (Ed.), *Recent developments in alcoholism* (Vol. 8, pp. 125–144). New York: Plenum.

CHAPTER TWELVE

ADDICTION AND RECOVERY IN MIDLIFE

Nancy Waite-O'Brien

W omen currently in midlife represent a cohort of individuals whose life experience is much different from that of any other group of women in
American history. They are daughters of women of the 1950s. Daughters of
women who, after a brief period of independence because of being employed
during World War II, returned to homemaking and expectations of conformity.
These daughters, now in their fifties, received mixed messages as they grew up
(Ehrenreich & English, 1978). On one hand, their mothers told them to strive
toward independence and accomplishment; on the other, the message was to conform, to behave, and not to make waves. These women reached their teen years
in a time of great cultural change. For the first time, being young was something to be valued and prolonged instead of a life phase to be hurried through.
The civil rights movement of the 1950s and early 1960s had spilled over into
employment law, creating equal employment standards, which opened opportunities for women as well as other minorities. At the same time, the women's movement was taking root on college campuses and in consciousness-raising groups
throughout the nation. Young women examined their lives, shared their experiences, and, with the support of others, changed and expanded their lives. In concert with this expanding awareness, reliable birth control allowed women new
sexual freedom. Finally, the Vietnam War became a rallying point for people of
all ages to question the status quo (Evans & Avis, 1999).

These seismic changes in culture reverberated through women's lives. They moved into the workplace, often into careers once the exclusive domain of men. They were politically active, at times taking to the streets to let the world know how they felt. They shocked and sometimes disappointed their elders as they questioned long-held taboos and claimed their independence from old social mores. These were women on the vanguard of change. They had few role models to emulate, because the women who preceded them had structured their lives around the demands of mothering and home care. As a result, these cultural pioneers created lives they could never have imagined when they were children. The lessons of childhood—self-sacrifice, conformity, and deference—were tucked away in favor of assertiveness, independence, and self-care. With the encouragement of other women, often in support groups, these women made having a career a priority over marriage and motherhood. As part of this shift, they learned to put their own needs ahead of, or at least equal to, those of others, particularly men.

All this change came at some cost.

This chapter seeks to examine the experience of addiction in women who are currently in midlife. This includes examining the cultural and social environment in which they grew up and currently live, the physiological implications of drug or alcohol use at this time of life, the psychological problems that accompany addiction at this age, and the process of treatment and recovery during this transitional period of life.

Sex, Drugs, and Rock and Roll: Drugs and Alcohol Use in the 1960s and 1970s

One of the taboos that was tossed aside in the 1960s and 1970s was the prohibition against women's using drugs and alcohol. College and young adult experience often included an introduction to drugs that in previous generations had been used only outside of the mainstream. This was the first generation to recreationally use mood-altering chemicals other than alcohol. Marijuana, cocaine, and LSD were extolled as agents of consciousness raising, and it was claimed that these drugs were safe and nonaddictive. Patterns of consumption of alcohol changed as women joined their male counterparts in drinking to intoxication at parties, in bars, and at other social events.

Women claimed the right to use alcohol and other drugs in the same way men did. They also claimed the right to be sexual. They embraced "free love" with the exuberance of liberated youth, having sex with multiple partners without the requirement of marriage. At least on the surface, these changes seemed to be accepted if not applauded by young men. A closer examination of this phenomenon suggests that this was not always the case, as many women found that being drunk was an invitation to unwanted sexual advances and sexual assault. Because there was such an enthusiastic acceptance of both drug use and sexual freedom within the culture, and because recognizing rape as an act of aggression was a relatively new thought, women found themselves ashamed and secretive about these assaults (Brownmiller, 1975). After all, these were women who were likely to have grown up hearing, "There is no such thing as rape because a woman can run faster with her skirt up than a man can with his pants down."

The incidence of sexual assault among intoxicated women provides insight into the underlying cultural bias relative to women and alcohol and other drugs. If one examines the pejorative terms ("slut," "whore," "easy") used to describe intoxicated women, the association between this intoxicated state and women's sexuality is immediately apparent. These terms imply that drunken women are promiscuous, an assumption not born out in reality. A study done by Klassen and Wilsnack (1987) found that only 8 percent of women drinkers had ever become less particular in their choice of sexual partners when they had been drinking. Conversely, 60 percent of the women surveyed said that someone who had been present during a drinking episode had been sexually aggressive toward them. The incidence of aggression did not vary depending on whether the woman was a light, moderate, or heavy drinker.

Assaults on intoxicated women are not solely sexual. In a study of social victimization of drinkers, researchers found that women who drink in bars are more likely to be victimized than their male counterparts, whether or not they were heavy drinkers (Fillmore, 1985). Another study (Miller & Downs., 1986) found that women suffering from alcoholism were significantly more likely than nonalcoholics to have been victims of violent crime, including rape.

The shaming messages about sexual availability and loss of control are internalized into the belief system of every addicted woman—young, old, or in midlife. A woman who has lost control of her drinking or drug use is as critical of herself as are those around her, because she too is a part of the culture that carries those attitudes. It makes no difference when the assault occurred; the scars remain. A woman in midlife who was victimized early in her drinking or drug use history and who has received no treatment carries that memory with her as if it had just happened.

Every culture in the world, past and present, views an intoxicated woman with opprobrium (Wilsnack & Beckman, 1984). Women are punished for being intoxicated. This punishment may be as mild as a lifted eyebrow or as harsh as being beaten or killed for the sin of drunkenness. The result of this punishment is to make women's drinking and drug use patterns secret and isolative. This fact strongly differentiates women drinkers and drug users from their male counterparts. Men's drinking, at least at the beginning, is usually a group activity. They are often admired for their capacity to consume large quantities of alcohol. This is never the case for women. Every addicted woman, no matter her age, feels shame about her inability to control her drinking or drug use (Waite-O'Brien, 1991). This shame is associated with the first experience of intoxication and continues throughout the course of the disease until the drinking or drug use ends or the woman dies. The shame exists not only because the world looks askance at her intoxication but also because she is a part of the culture that carries this prohibition. She has absorbed the critical messages such that she needs no one else to remind her of her failure. Judgment comes from within as well as from those around her.

Alcoholic and addicted women in midlife—those who had claimed independence in so many parts of their lives—find themselves keeping their use of alcohol or other drugs secret or using them defiantly in an effort to ward off the pervasive sense of shame that is attached to loss of control.

Demands and Pressures at Midlife

Life is complicated at any age, but the demands on women during midlife can be consuming. More women ages fifty-five to sixty-four are working now than in the past. In 1955, 26 percent of women in this age group were employed; in 1999, 50 percent held a job (Bureau of Labor Statistics, 2001). A woman's career path is often much different than a man's. It is likely that she has made a number of job changes or has taken time away from work to attend to children or to accommodate the demands of her partner's career. She may also have had to adjust her work life to take care of children following a divorce. Clearly, a woman's career path is seldom linear. More often it is complex and circuitous (Bateson, 1989). For women in the working world, midlife is often the time her efforts are beginning to be rewarded. The addition of addiction to the pressure of work creates a new tension in the career path. Active addiction exerts powerful demands on attention, causing a woman to be distracted from the work she may love or perhaps forcing her into a work life that provides little in terms of psychic rewards. One fifty-year-old woman's résumé told the story of her addiction as it described the shift from positions of responsibility and authority to jobs that just provided the money to keep her drinking and to pay for shelter. She sought help for her drinking when she could no longer hold the minimum-wage job that kept her off the streets. As she tried to put together the chronological history of her drinking, she found that her résumé described the tale most accurately.

Other phenomena exert pressure on midlife families. First, over one-quarter of adults ages fifty-five to sixty-four are living with an adult child (Speare & Avery, n.d.). These children may have never left home, or they returned home after finding that on their own they couldn't achieve the level of comfort they could by living with their parents. In addition, grandparents are often the primary caretakers of grandchildren. This often occurs because the parents are addicts or alcoholics. Women who thought their years of child care had ended when their children left home have found they need to continue this responsibility in caring for their grandchildren. At the other end of the life course, the parents of midlife adults are living longer (Speare & Avery, n.d.). They live longer, but not always in the best of health, so care of aging parents exerts demands on the family. The responsibility of providing help with household tasks, shopping, transportation, and companionship usually falls to the female children—women now in midlife (Cobbs & Ralapati, 1998). Again, if the woman is an alcoholic or addict, she feels the additional demand of the disease, which leaves her with few emotional resources to cope with the demands of others.

Another stressor with significant impact on the lives of women at midlife is the physiological change inherent to the aging process. Menopause is often a mark of this change, although this event may be too circumscribed to fully describe the years of changes included in this period of a woman's life. Medically, menopause is the two-year period following a woman's last menses. A more accurate term may be *the climacteric*, the fifteen-year period beginning when a woman is between forty and forty-five, during which her body makes the transition away from reproductive capability (Boston Women's Health Book Collective, 1984). This period is marked by changes in appearance, changes in internal physiology that may include such phenomena as hot flashes or vaginal dryness, and often changes in emotions. Some women describe themselves as more susceptible to tears, more irritable, less patient, or forgetful and disorganized at this time. It's hard to tell if this change in emotion is a result of hormone fluctuations or if it occurs because women in midlife find themselves in a culture that does not value women of this age. These women often describe themselves as "invisible" or "disappearing." A review of current movies, fashion magazines, or the multitude of catalogues that arrive in the mail on a daily basis reinforces this perception. There are virtually no middle-aged women in these publications (Friedan, 1993). It's as if she has disappeared.

Many women say that managing weight becomes much more difficult after menopause and describe themselves as feeling helpless as their body shape changes. It's normal for a woman's waistline to expand at this time, but women who have prided themselves on being thin now are shameful and self-critical about their inability to maintain their youthful figure. For the woman who has centered her self-worth on the admiring glances of men around her, this change in physical appearance is devastating. Along with the changes already mentioned, chronic health problems such as arthritis or heart disease may emerge, which serve as another marker of the aging process (Cobbs & Ralapati, 1998).

In our culture, it is common to seek a chemical release from emotional distress. For a woman who isn't coping well with aging, a visit to her physician gives her a prescription for a tranquilizer or an antidepressant, and a visit to the grocery store provides alcohol or food to cope with the losses she is experiencing.

Women's Psychology and Midlife Developmental Tasks

Hollis (1993) describes the transition to midlife as a shift from a provisional personality to an adult personality. The provisional personality is one patched together in childhood based on youthful interpretations of traumatic experience. Hollis describes trauma experience as falling into one of two categories: the experience of being overwhelmed or the experience of being abandoned or neglected. The experience of being overwhelmed may fall anywhere on a continuum ranging from the disappointment a child experiences at being prevented from having her own way to the emotional injury suffered in physical or sexual abuse. Similarly, the sense of abandonment or neglect exists on a continuum: on one end, the child spends her first fearful night alone in her own room; on the other, she is left to take on the care of younger siblings when she is too young to accept this kind of responsibility, or she is left in the care of strangers. As children we interpret our own experiences as statements about our value as individuals, about life in general, and about our power to affect the direction of our own destiny. These assumptions are unlikely to be accurate, but they do shape how we see the world.

Our provisional personality is an attempt to create a sense of safety in an unsafe world. In essence, we cobble together a personality based on our best efforts to defend against trauma and disappointment. We do this any number of ways. We gather friends and family to prevent feeling lonely, we accumulate wealth to defend against feelings of worthlessness, we study and learn to protect against feeling inadequate because we don't know enough, and we develop any number of psychological defenses to bolster our sense of self-worth. We may drink or use other mood-altering chemicals. Alcohol and other mood-altering chemicals provide instant and predictable relief from the sense of unease and fear associated with trying to fend off an underlying feeling of inadequacy.

Initially these defenses work well to fend off the fears we project onto life experience. Hollis (1993) states that somewhere in midlife, these defenses seem to become less effective. There is a seismic shift occurring in the psyche. This shift is often marked at first by a sense of ennui, much like Peggy Lee's song "Is That All There Is?" We begin to question the assumptions of early life, and the invitation to change begins to assert itself. This questioning process is painful. Old ways of behaving and defending ourselves are familiar even though they have become less effective at protecting the self. It's here that some of us become stuck. Even though the old defenses aren't as effective as they have been, the temptation is to use them anyway, but with greater frequency or intensity. We accumulate more, we hurry to keep from being alone, we study more, and some of us drink or seek other chemical release with more frequency.

The failure to achieve this developmental shift is marked by increasing anxiety and depression. For the woman who drinks or uses to defend against this psychic shift, the drinking or using takes on a life of its own. She is drinking or using not only to defend against the ominous sense that the world is no longer the same but also because the addiction now exerts its own demands on her using patterns. She will continue this use until recovery begins or until illness or death ends the progression. Hitting bottom, or the collapse of the defense system, occurs when the soul or psyche can no longer tolerate what the body is doing. It is the moment when the person recognizes that her behavior no longer satisfies the need for wholeness in the self. It is at this point that recovery can begin. Hollis (1993) describes this change as a process of replacing the person who was with the person who will be.

A look at midlife developmental tasks also requires a review of women's psychology. Relational psychology as developed by Jean Baker-Miller, Judith Jordan, and others describes significant differences between traditional intrapsychic psychology and psychological theory incorporating women's relational needs (Miller, 1986; Jordan, Kaplan, Miller, Stiver, & Surrey, 1991; Jordan, 1997; Baker-Miller & Stiver, 1997). These theorists describe the need for relationship as fundamental to women's psychological health. (Actually, the need for relationship is undoubtedly not gender specific, but the intent of this chapter is to focus on women.) Contrary to traditional psychology, these theorists describe the need for relationship as fundamental to women's psychological health and development. A woman's care and concern for others is not a sign of weakness or dependency but a reflection of her attempts to maintain psychological health by maintaining healthy relationships with those around her. Healthy, growth-fostering relationships are mutual, creative, and energy producing for all participants (Miller, 1986). They provide an environment for the expression of feelings and thoughts. In a healthy relationship, each participant has the capacity to be affected by the thoughts and feelings of the others, and each person feels a sense of empathy toward the others (Baker-Miller & Stiver, 1997).

It has been suggested that addictive substances assist women in coping with relationships that fail to provide the ingredients necessary to nurture emotional health. The drug may function to create the illusion of relationship, allow the woman to tolerate the lack of relationship, lower her resistance to pressure to accommodate someone else's expectations, or provide a way to connect with a drinking or using partner (Surrey, 1991). The connection with the using partner is limited because it is based on the parallel need for the drug. For women in midlife, all these dynamics may have been part of the underpinnings of her addiction.

When drug use shifts from elective to addictive use, the chemical asserts its own demands. These demands permeate all aspects of the woman's life in ways both dramatic and subtle. It's easy to see the impact addiction has on a woman's life when it involves legal problems, such as a DUI or a shoplifting charge; occupational problems, such as job loss; or relationship problems, such as divorce or separation. But addiction also affects relationships in sly, insidious ways. The woman is distracted. The call of the drug is persistent, so she attends to each of her relationships as if there were always a voice from another room calling to her. She is never fully present in the relationships in her life. Genuine connection with others ceases. The addiction becomes the "Plexiglas" barrier that cuts the woman off from all genuine relationship. Addiction has been described as a passionate relationship to a drug. It is this passion that shapes all other relationships. The woman alcoholic or addict may not be able to identify this phenomenon, but those around her do. Anyone who grew up in an alcoholic home can immediately identify with the sense of never feeling fully "seen" by the alcoholic parent. Addiction becomes the "chemical disconnection" that separates the woman from those she needs in her life. This disconnection is both psychic and concrete as relationships crumble in the face of this pressure.

Women alcoholics and addicts who are married are often left by their non-addicted spouse (Lane, Burge, & Graham, 1992). The leaving may be through divorce or separation or may occur in the form of a shift of attention to other things, such as work or hobbies. The partner may still have residence in the home, but the emotional connection to the woman drinker or user has been severed. Her partner may have made some attempts to intervene or provide help, but if these have failed, it is likely he will move on.

For women who are in a relationship with another drinker or user, the likelihood is that the relationship will last until one or the other either gets sober or dies. Active addiction accommodates another user because the demands of the disease are parallel, so the use of the drug is normalized.

The dynamics described here predict that the woman drinker or user in midlife is likely to be either alone or in a relationship with another user. If her partner has physically left, her economic circumstances are likely to be limited. If her children have left also, her isolation is more complete. Her only partner is her disease. Addiction distorts thinking such that the drinker who is isolated is separated from the kind of information or interventions from loved ones that could interrupt the progression of the disease.

Incidence of Addiction in Midlife

It is difficult to ascertain the incidence of addiction in midlife women. This is due to a number of methodological circumstances. First, research tends not to measure incidence of addiction in later ages for either men or women. The 1995 *Substance Abuse and Mental Health Sourcebook* (Substance Abuse and Mental Health Services Administration [SAMHSA], 1995) looked at illicit drug use and heavy alcohol use differentiated by age and gender, but grouped all users over the age of thirty-five in one group. More recently, the 1999 National Household Survey of Drug Abuse (SAMHSA, 2000) gave more information about age and addiction, but did not separate the sexes.

Second, looking at women's drug-using patterns at all is a relatively recent phenomenon. There is limited information available about women's addiction in any age group. Information about women and drinking is collected by the National Institute on Alcohol Abuse and Alcoholism (NIAAA). Their data indicate that in 1988, there were 94,000 women ages forty-five to sixty-four who met criteria for the diagnosis of alcoholism, and another 93,000 abusing alcohol. By comparison, in 1992 there were estimated to be 119,000 women in the same age group who were thought to be alcoholic and 127,000 estimated to be using alcohol abusively. This suggests an increase in a four-year period of 41,000 women in this age group who are either alcoholic or alcohol abusers. One wonders if the shift in numbers of alcohol abusers compared to alcoholics during that time period indicates a rate at which abuse is converting to addiction. In 1988, 3,665 women ages forty-five to sixty-four died of cirrhosis; in 1992, 3,061 died; and in 1996, the number was 3,043 (Saadatmand, Stinson, Grant, & Dufour, 1999). It appears that the numbers dying of cirrhosis did not change significantly over this eight-year period. That the number of deaths due to cirrhosis did not increase at the same rate as the incidence of alcoholism raises some questions. It is possible that the number stayed low because physicians were cautious about assigning cirrhosis as the cause of death for women if there were other factors that could contribute to the death. If this is the case, it appears to be a reflection of the cultural blindness regarding the identification of alcoholism in women in midlife.

Data about women's abuse of or dependence on prescription medications are virtually nonexistent. This is significant, considering that women, particularly women in this age group, are the largest consumers of prescription painkillers, antidepressants, and benzodiazepines.

Third, the current criteria to diagnose addiction are not geared to the kind of life problems addiction creates in a woman's life. Women of any age are expert in hiding their addiction. Their drinking and using are likely to be done in isolation because there is so much shame attached to a woman's use of alcohol or other drugs. The fourth edition of the *Diagnostic and Statistical Manual of Mental Disorders* (American Psychiatric Association, 1994) enumerates criteria for the diagnosis of dependency that are gender-neutral, but the criteria are often applied in ways that fail to identify women. Many assessment instruments, such as the CAGE questions (Mayfield, McLeod, & Hall, 1974), the Addiction Severity Index (McClellan, Luborsky, O'Brien, & Woody, 1980), or the Short Michigan Alcohol Screening Test (Selzer, Vinokur, & van Roojien, 1975) focus on the kind of acting-out behaviors and legal problems that characterize men's drug and alcohol use patterns. In contrast, women's symptoms of addiction tend to be more in the form of "withdrawal" from the mainstream of life, and as a consequence are frequently misdiagnosed as depression or anxiety. If this is the case, the woman seeking help is likely to be seen in a mental health setting rather than in an alcohol or drug treatment setting. Also, female addicts, particularly in this age group, are likely to exhibit physical symptoms of their disease as opposed to behavioral disturbances, so they end up in the offices of their family physician or in a hospital rather than in drug or alcohol treatment (Cobbs & Ralapati, 1998). Both of these factors suggest that midlife women alcoholics and addicts are likely to receive medications that mask and prevent diagnosis of the real problem in their lives: active addiction.

Physiological Issues

Alcohol affects women differently than it does men (Brady, Grice, Dunstan, & Randal, 1993; Freeza et al., 1990; Lane et al., 1992; Hill, 1984). At every age, women appear to be vulnerable to more adverse physical consequences of drinking than men. Women achieve higher concentrations of alcohol in the blood and become more impaired than men after drinking equivalent amounts of alcohol (Freeza et al., 1990). This occurs because most women have less body water than men of similar weight, and this results in a higher blood alcohol level. Women also metabolize alcohol from the blood faster than men. This puts a higher demand on liver function, resulting in more liver disease. There is also some indication that women alcoholics have lower levels of alcohol dehydrogenase, an enzyme responsible for breakdown of alcohol in the gastrointestinal tract. If the alcohol isn't broken down there as part of the metabolic process, more alcohol moves into the bloodstream, also increasing the demand on the liver (Galaver & Arria, 1995). Women in midlife who have a long history of drinking are likely to have more extensive liver damage in the form of cirrhosis and alcoholic hepatitis as a cumulative effect of the stress placed on the liver.

Postmenopausal women who drink moderate to heavy amounts of alcohol also have other health problems. They are at higher risk for breast cancer and heart disease even if the amount they drink is less than that of their male counterparts (Urbano-Marquez et al., 1995; Smith-Warner et al., 1998; Zhang et al., 1999). Again, it's likely that these health problems will emerge at this time in the woman's life. Women drinkers may also be more vulnerable to alcohol-induced brain damage. Magnetic resonance imaging (MRI) suggests that the area of the brain responsible for coordinating multiple brain functions appears to be more damaged in women drinkers than in male drinkers (Hommer et al., 1996; Wang et al., 1998). Women who drink are less likely than men to drive drunk, but when they do, they are more likely to be involved in a serious accident. This appears to be a result of gender differences in the effects alcohol has on some visual cues and motor tasks (Waller & Blow, 1995).

The accumulation of symptoms like those just mentioned, as well as hypertension, anemia, malnutrition, and gastrointestinal hemorrhage, is often described as *telescoping*, because the symptoms escalate much more rapidly in women than in men (Lane et al., 1992). The result of this phenomenon is death. Women who chronically abuse alcohol have death rates 50 to 100 percent higher than men who have the same alcohol use patterns (Wilsnack & Beckman, 1984). These deaths are directly related to the cumulative effect of alcohol on the body and don't include those women who die of suicide, alcohol-related accidents, or assault by violent partners.

There is a limited amount of research describing specifically how other addictive drugs react in women. Some studies suggest that the presence of estrogen in women changes the effect cocaine has on the body. It may increase the stimulant or reward effect of the drug, which suggests that women cocaine addicts may have more trouble stopping their use of the drug. Conversely, estrogen appears to protect women from the vasoconstrictive effects of cocaine; therefore there may be some protection against the increased risk of stroke associated with use of this drug. One study indicated that chronic use of the drug MDMA (ecstasy) might cause more neurological dysfunction in women than it does in men. It's likely that this difference too is related to the presence of estrogen in women. It will require further investigation to see what happens to women users whose estrogen levels change as they move into perimenopause and menopause.

Psychological Concomitants of Addiction in Midlife

Differentiating addiction from the psychological problems that often accompany it is difficult because the effect the drug has on thinking and emotion mimics psychiatric disorders. Long-term consumption of a depressant such as alcohol is likely to cause depression, and long-term consumption of a stimulant drug such as cocaine or amphetamines is likely to cause anxiety or in some cases disrupt logical thought processes, resulting in psychosis. The emotional upset the woman is experiencing is likely to include both the pharmacological effect of the drug and the sadness and discouragement that result when problems created by the use of the chemical begin to mount. The level of depression or anxiety she experiences is commensurate with the disarray present in the woman's life. The most conservative approach to differentiating psychiatric syndromes from addiction is to do a very careful assessment and, if it seems reasonable, see what happens when the person experiences several months of sobriety. For many women, the reduction in life problems and the experience of spiritual transformation that often accompanies the beginnings of recovery predict lower levels of depression and anxiety.

A second approach to differentiating comorbid psychiatric conditions from the residual effect the drug has on the nervous system is to note the number of previous treatments the person has had. For women who have had multiple treatments and who have difficulty maintaining long-term sobriety, the likelihood exists that there is a co-occurring psychiatric condition needing treatment. Research indicates that clinical depression is frequently a comorbid condition with addiction. A study of a group of cocaine and alcohol abusers showed that 70 percent of the women sampled had at some time in their lives been diagnosed with an affective or anxiety disorder; 40 percent had been diagnosed as having experienced at least one episode of a major depressive disorder; 46 percent had at some time been diagnosed with posttraumatic stress disorder (PTSD) (Brady, Dansky, Saladin, & Sonne, 1996). If one notes the likelihood that a using or drinking woman's partner is likely to be using and that the woman is likely to have been a victim of violence, the high numbers of women diagnosed with PTSD makes sense. In a study of shame and depression comparing men and women alcoholics with a similar population of nonalcoholics, it was found that the women alcoholics reported significantly higher levels of shame and depression than the male alcoholics and both male and female nonalcoholics (Waite-O'Brien, 1991).

The rate of incidence of depressive disorders with alcoholism ranges from 30 percent to 70 percent, depending on the definition of depression and on the instrument used to assess it (Hesselbrock & Hesselbrock, 1993). What is clear is that no matter how depression is measured, when the measure is applied to women versus men, women—particularly women alcoholics—report more depression. It seems that depression often precedes the diagnosis of addiction in women.

Joan Borysenko (1996) suggests four reasons for the prevalence of depression among women. First is the cultural prohibition against the expression of anger for women. She suggests that some forms of depression are an expression of anger turned inward in a way that protects the woman from this prohibition. This passive stance certainly is characteristic of many women. Second, women, particularly alcoholic and addicted women, are likely to be survivors of childhood physical or sexual abuse. The helplessness these women experienced when they found themselves unable to protect themselves persists into adulthood as both anxiety and depression. This contention is supported by a study by Brady et al. (1996), which found that 46 percent of women alcohol and cocaine abusers had, at some time, been diagnosed with PTSD, compared to 24 percent of men with the same drug use pattern. The same study indicated that 70 percent of women alcohol and cocaine abusers had at some time been diagnosed with an affective or anxiety disorder; 40 percent of the total group had at one time been diagnosed with a major depressive episode. Third, Borysenko suggests that women tend to be more sensitive to and feel more responsible for relationship problems than do their male counterparts. This tendency to assume blame and responsibility is also likely to lead to depression. This dynamic is significant when one considers the numbers of addicted women who have been left by their husbands or who are in dysfunctional relationships. These women are likely to report significant levels of depression along with their addictive symptoms. Finally, Borysenko hypothesizes that women's tendency toward depression begins at puberty when they realize their relative powerlessness in a male-dominated society. This powerlessness is demonstrated later in life in the wage discrepancies between men and women and the other limitations women experience in their professional lives. This hypothesis may be supported by a study of cocaine- and alcohol-abusing men and women that found no significant differences in incidence of major depressive episodes but noted that for women, the depression was significantly more likely to precede the use of the drugs (Brady et al., 1993).

The presence of depression makes treatment of the addictive disorder more difficult. When one is depressed, the feelings of hopelessness and lack of interest in life in general, the sense of isolation from others, and the low energy level predict that it will be harder to engage in the process of recovery. It all seems like too much effort. This suggests the need for addiction treatment to be sensitive to the need for attention to depressive or anxiety disorders. Because anxiety and depression so often exist as parallel diagnoses with addiction, treatment assessments need to be sensitive to these diagnoses, and treatment planning should incorporate cognitive behavioral approaches to management of these conditions.

Beginning the Process of Recovery

For women in midlife, denial may be prolonged by the inability of those around her to identify what the problem is. Family members think the woman is depressed and needs to see her doctor, her doctor thinks she needs an antidepressant and a psychiatrist, and she thinks she needs a drink and to be left alone. She is working harder but accomplishing less in her job. No one knows quite why she isn't doing as well as she used to, often attributing the change to the fact that she is just "getting older." She is skilled at hiding her use both from others and from herself. Eventually, if she is lucky, someone may suggest or infer that the problem truly rests in her addiction, but she's likely to deny this with some energy. For many women, the decision to enter treatment does not feel like their own. A formalized intervention involving concerned family and friends and orchestrated by a therapist skilled in this approach may help leverage her into treatment. Adult children often intervene in an informal but powerful way when they deny a woman alcoholic or addict access to beloved grandchildren. They do this when it appears that it's no longer safe to allow the children to be with their grandmother because her behavior has become too unpredictable. Less frequently, women are confronted on the job or are arrested for drunk driving, and in the interest of avoiding the loss of employment or driving privileges, they elect to go to treatment. Most often it is the physical debilitation accompanying advanced alcoholism that gets the attention of the physician or the family and moves the woman toward treatment.

The decision to come into treatment is often complicated for women because of their multiple responsibilities. Even though the addicted woman in midlife may not have young children to care for, there are still many other responsibilities to attend to. These may include the care of the home, the care of elderly parents, and community and job responsibilities. All must be attended to before the woman can extricate herself to attend to herself. A woman's apparent resistance to putting aside these responsibilities is often thought of as another level of denial, but it is more likely to be a genuine relational demand. Most women would say they have never devoted any significant period of time to themselves, so the decision to attend to their drinking or drug use in a treatment setting is likely to be complicated by feelings of guilt associated with not being present to care for others.

At this point it's important to remember that it is only the minority of using women of any age that get appropriate treatment. Women die of addiction in alarming numbers. This happens because the disease is underdiagnosed and because it is more lethal in women than in men.

Age-Appropriate Treatment

Treatment for midlife women alcoholics and addicts needs to be sensitive to a number of factors: the aging process, the cultural view of women who use alcohol or other drugs, the likelihood of a trauma history, the presence of comorbid psychiatric conditions, and the need to reconnect with others to engender a sense of hope and empowerment. The best of women's treatment occurs with other women. There is no research that indicates the need for women's treatment to be stratified by age, and in fact the mix of ages often allows women to look at their own addiction from a different perspective. One fifty-year-old woman described the understanding she gained of her own drinking history after she heard a twenty-five-year-old woman describe how she had shaped her family life to accommodate her need to drink during the day. The sharing of experience in a treatment setting allows the possibility of connection with others who can reflect a similar experience and model feminine empowerment.

A review of the issues presented by alcoholic or addicted women in midlife suggests that the ideal treatment should begin with gender-sensitive, age-appropriate assessment. Assessment should cover the woman's physical health, including her gynecological and nutritional needs; her family, work, and social networks; her psychological well-being; and her spiritual needs. Attention should be paid to women who live in violent relationships and to those who have experienced trauma in other times of their lives. From this assessment, an individualized treatment plan can evolve that addresses her specific needs.

A recent study of several models of women's treatment (Kearney, 1998) described women's drug use as *self-destructive self-nurturing.* Kearney suggests that the beginning of a woman's drug use is an effort to ease discomfort, both physical and psychological, or take care of herself. This effort at self-nurturing fails because the drug use is harmful to the woman's body, self-concept, relationships, family, and community, and because even though the drugs provide the illusion of relief from unhappiness, they don't address the source of the pain. Kearney then describes treatment for addiction as *truthful self-nurturing:* a process of coming to an honest understanding of the self, and learning to care for that self. It begins with an internalized shift in awareness such that the woman sees substance use as the problem rather than as the solution. Kearney describes the work of recovery as occurring in three distinct phases:

1. Abstinence work: the process of learning ways to avoid using drugs. This is the basic work of recovery and involves learning one's own using patterns, and seeking ways to avoid triggers for relapse. This kind of awareness often comes in a formalized treatment setting or in twelve-step meetings.
2. Self work: an honest self-appraisal of the underpinnings of one's own addiction, and becoming more aware of one's own needs.
3. Connection work: the process of reaching out to family, culture, heritage, and spirituality. This part of recovery is the one that brings the richness and sense of meaning that provide hope and genuine relief from pain. Connection work allows a woman at this life stage to reevaluate her spiritual self in relation to the direction her life has taken.

Twelve-Step Recovery

It has become common to question the appropriateness of a twelve-step approach to recovery for women (Kasl, 1993). The concern focuses on the issue of powerlessness as a foundation of recovery for women. It is true that women lack power in many areas of their lives. Women are physically smaller than most men, earn less, get fewer promotions, have less political clout, and are shamed for having a disease that is killing them. It is hard to begin recovery with a statement of powerlessness when women genuinely lack power. A review of the language of the first step of AA provides another perspective, however: "We admitted we were powerless *over alcohol*—that our lives had become unmanageable" (emphasis added) (Alcoholics Anonymous, 1976, p. 59). Alcohol and drug dependency does cause the sufferer to lose control. The lack of control results in a feeling of powerlessness. It causes a woman to lose whatever possibility of experiencing a sense of empowerment or strength she has in the world. The source of the powerlessness is the drug.

One derivation of the word addict comes from the Latin word *addicere: ad* means "to," *dicere* "to say or pronounce." Together, they describe the giving over of voice, describing the state of the Roman slave, the addict—the one without voice or power (Leonard, 1989). In truth, the woman addict is a person without voice. She has lost the capacity to influence her own life because of the dominant force addiction exerts on her life. In this framework, one can then ascribe the powerlessness to the demands of addiction and see that the admission of powerlessness over the drug paradoxically begins the restoration of the possibility of power in other parts of life. The beginning of recovery is the return of voice. The woman can begin to speak her own truth and influence her life in ways her addiction had never allowed.

The environment of women's twelve-step meetings is inherently feminine. The structure of the meeting is horizontal rather than hierarchical; there are no CEOs, presidents, or chiefs. Instead there is a trusted servant who has no power other than to assist in structuring the meeting (Kurtz, 1988). The format of the meeting is familiar to many women; the sharing of experience instead of advice is a feminine communication style. Telling stories has historically been the role of women. The group setting allows the woman to tell her own story and, from that experience, connect with others who share the same experience.

The selection of a sponsor allows a woman to receive guidance from a feminine mentor, an experience most women have never had, particularly those women who have attached much of their identity to men. Witnessing courageous action on the part of others in the group suggests a new model of change for the group participants. Judith Jordan (1990, p. 2) describes courage as "the capacity to act meaningfully and with integrity in the face of acknowledged vulnerability." She further goes on to say that the actions of courage are different when one has the sense that one is not alone. Fear escalates in isolation and is reduced when one has the sense of connection with others. The connection Jordan refers to can exist either in fantasy or reality. For example, in a women's therapy group, one participant struggled with the prospect of having a painful conversation with her mother. She shared her concern with other group members and received encouragement and support to help her accomplish this task. In the next session, she reported with some pride that she had accomplished her goal. When asked how this had come about, she reported that she had mentally placed in the room images of the other group members smiling and nodding encouragement to her as she spoke. At difficult points in the conversation, she mentally shifted to those images of encouragement. The sense that she was not alone and had the support of others helped her accomplish her goal. In similar ways, a woman in a support group can internalize images of others in the group and carry with her the courage to act in ways that allow her to do what she has always feared.

A feminine model of recovery honors women's need to maintain relationship while supporting courageous action. It helps women use the strength and experience of other women in support of recovery. For a woman who has never liked or trusted other women, the task is not easy, because it demands a willingness to trust those whom she has never trusted. For women alcoholics and addicts in midlife, this experience can be life changing. The movement out of isolation and helplessness is witnessed and applauded by other women, other women model courageous actions, and the sense of empowerment provides the woman a new feeling of intoxication.

Conclusion

Midlife can be a time of transition, when a woman may reevaluate the direction her life has taken and make a significant life change. This chapter has described how active addiction can disrupt this process for women. The identification of this disease in this age group is complicated by cultural attitudes and the woman addict's own ability to cover up her disease. Treatment for women in this age group requires sensitivity to the problems they face, which means paying attention to the impact drugs and alcohol have on her body; being aware of the responsibilities she has in other parts of her life; being sensitive to her history, including her experience of trauma; and having the psychological sophistication to address issues of anxiety and depression likely to accompany the diagnosis of addiction. Most important, treatment needs to support the spiritual self of the recovering woman. Without active addiction in her life, the woman can continue the growth process and move into old age with a sense of having lived a meaningful life. Anthropologist Margaret Mead called this a time of "postmenopausal zest." For the recovering alcoholic or addicted woman, it is an opportunity to experience the paradoxical power of admitting powerlessness.

References

Alcoholics Anonymous. (1976). *Alcoholics Anonymous* (3rd ed.). New York: Alcoholics Anonymous World Services.

American Psychiatric Association. (1994). *Diagnostic and statistical manual of mental disorders* (4th ed.). Washington, DC: Author.

Baker-Miller, J., & Stiver, I. P. (1997). *The healing connection: How women form relationships in therapy and in life.* Boston: Beacon Press.

Bateson, M. C. (1989). *Composing a life.* New York: Penguin Books.

Borysenko, J. (1996). *A woman's book of life: The biology, psychology, and spirituality of the feminine life cycle.* New York: Riverhead Books.

Boston Women's Health Book Collective. (1984). *The new our bodies, ourselves: A book by and for women.* New York: Simon & Schuster.

Brady, K. T., Dansky, B., Saladin, M., & Sonne, A. (1996). *PTSD and cocaine dependence: The effect of order of onset.* Presentation at the annual meeting of the College on Problems of Drug Dependency, San Juan, Puerto Rico.

Brady, K. T., Grice, D. E., Dunstan, L., & Randal, C. (1993). Gender differences in substance use disorders. *American Journal of Psychiatry, 150,* 1707–1711.

Brownmiller, S. (1975). *Against our wills: Men, women, and rape.* New York: Fawcett Columbine.

Bureau of Labor Statistics. *Labor force statistics from the current population survey.* Available: http://stats.bls.gov.hlpselec.htm.

Cobbs, E. L., & Ralapati, A. N. (1998). Health of older women. *Medical Clinics of North America, 82*(1), 127–145.

Covington, S. S. (1994). *A woman's way through the twelve steps.* Center City, MN: Hazelden.

Ehrenreich, B., & English, D. (1978). *For her own good: 150 years of experts' advice to women.* New York: Doubleday.

Evans, S. B., & Avis, J. P. (1999). *The women who broke all the rules.* Naperville, IL: Sourcebooks.

Fillmore, K. M. (1985). The social victims of drinking. *British Journal of Addictions, 80,* 307–314.

Freeza, M., et al. (1990). High blood alcohol levels in women: The role of decreased gastric alcohol dehydrogenase activity and first pass metabolism. *New England Journal of Medicine, 322,* 95–99.

Friedan, B. (1993). *The fountain of age.* New York: Simon & Schuster.

Galaver, J. S., & Arria, A. M. (1995). Increased susceptibility of women to alcoholic liver disease: Artifactual or real? In P. Hall (Ed.), *Alcoholic liver disease: Pathology and pathogenesis* (2nd ed., pp. 123–133). London: Edward Arnold.

Hesselbrock, M. N., & Hesselbrock, V. M. (1993). Depression and antisocial personality disorder in alcoholism: Gender comparison. In E.S.L. Gomberg & T. D. Nirenberg (Ed.), *Women and substance abuse* (pp. 142–161). Norwood, NJ: Ablex.

Hill, S. Y. (1984). Vulnerability to the biomedical consequences of alcoholism and alcohol related problems. In S. C. Wilsnack & L. J. Beckman (Eds.), *Alcohol problems in women: Antecedents, consequences and intervention.* New York: Guilford Press.

Hollis, J. (1993). *The middle passage: From misery to meaning in midlife.* Toronto: Inner City Books.

Hommer, D., et al. (1996). Decreased corpus callosum size among alcoholic women. *Archives of Neurology, 53,* 359–363.

Jordan, J. V. (1990). *Courage in connection: Conflict, compassion, creativity.* Wellesley, MA: Stone Center.

Jordan, J. V. (Ed.). (1997). *Women's growth in diversity: More writings from the Stone Center.* New York: Guilford Press.

Jordan, J. V., Kaplan, A. G., Miller, J. B., Stiver, I. P., & Surrey, J. L. (Eds.). (1991). *Women's growth in connection: Writings from the Stone Center.* New York: Guilford Press.

Kasl, C. D. (1993). *Many roads, one journey: Moving beyond the 12 steps.* New York: HarperCollins.

Kearney, M. H. (1998). Truthful self-nurturing: A grounded formal theory of women's addiction recovery. *Qualitative Health Research, 8,* 495–512.

Kilbourne, J., & Surrey, J. L. (Speakers). (1991). *Women, addiction and codependency* [Cassette recording]. Wellesley, MA: Stone Center.

Klassen A. D., & Wilsnack S. C. (1987). Sexual experience and drinking among women in a U.S. national survey. *Archives of Sexual Behaviors, 15,* 363–392.

Kurtz, E. (1988). *AA: The story.* New York: HarperCollins.

Kwo, P. Y., et al. (1998). Gender differences in alcohol metabolism: Relationship to liver volume and effect of adjusting for body mass. *Gastroenterology, 114,* 1552–1557.

Lane, P. A., Burge, S., & Graham, A. (1992). Management of addictive disorders in women. In M. F. Fleming & K. L. Barry (Eds.), *Addictive disorders* (pp. 260–269). St. Louis, MO: Mosby-Year Book.

Leonard, L. S. (1989). *Witness to the fire: Creativity and the veil of addiction.* Boston: Shambhala.

Mayfield, D., McLeod, G., & Hall, P. (1974). The CAGE questionnaire: Validation of a new alcoholism screening instrument. *American Journal of Psychiatry, 131,* 1121–1123.

McClellan, A. T., Luborsky, L., O'Brien, C., & Woody, G. E. (1980). An improved instrument for substance abuse patients: The Addiction Severity Index. *Journal of Nervous and Mental Disease, 168,* 26–33.

Miller, B. A., & Downs, W. R. (1986). *Conflict and violence among alcoholic women as compared to a random household sample.* Paper presented at the 38th Annual Meeting of the American Society of Criminology, Atlanta, GA.

Miller, J. B. (1986). *Toward a new psychology of women* (2nd ed.). Boston: Beacon Press.

Saadatmand, F., Stinson, F. S., Grant, B. F., & Dufour, M. C. (1999). *Liver cirrhosis mortality in the United States, 1970–1996* (Surveillance Report No. 52). Rockville, MD: National Institute on Alcohol Abuse and Alcoholism, Division of Biometry and Epidemiology.

Selzer, M., Vinokur, A., & van Roojien, L. (1975). A self administered short Michigan Alcoholism Screening Test. *Journal of Studies on Alcohol, 36,* 117–126.

Smith-Warner, S. A., et al. (1998). Alcohol and breast cancer in women: A pooled analysis of cohort studies. *Journal of the American Medical Association, 279,* 535–540.

Speare, A., Jr., & Avery, R. (n.d.). *Who helps whom in older parent-child families* (Survey of Income and Program Participation, No. 163). Washington, DC: U.S. Department of Commerce, Bureau of the Census.

Substance Abuse and Mental Health Services Administration. (1995). *Substance abuse and mental health sourcebook.* Washington, DC: Author.

Substance Abuse and Mental Health Services Administration. (2000). *1999 National Household Survey on Drug Abuse.*

Surrey, J. (1991). The self in relation: A theory of women's development. In J. Jordan, A. Kaplan, J. Miller, M. Stiver, & J. Surrey (Eds.), *Women's growth in connection: Writings from the Stone Center.* New York: Guilford Press.

Urbano-Marquez, A., et al. (1995). The greater risk of cardiomathopathy and myopathy in women compared with men. *Journal of the American Medical Association, 274,* 149–154.

Waite-O'Brien, N. (1991). *Shame and depression differences in male and female alcoholic and non-alcoholic populations.* Unpublished doctoral dissertation, United States International University, San Diego.

Waller, P. F., & Blow, F. C. (1995). Women, alcohol and driving. In M. Gallanter (Ed.), *Recent developments in alcoholism* (Vol. 12, pp. 103–123). New York: Plenum.

Wang, G. J., et al. (1998). Regional cerebral metabolism in female alcoholics of moderate severity does not differ from that of controls. *Alcoholism: Clinical and Experimental Research, 22,* 1850–1854.

Wilsnack, S. C., & Beckman, L. J. (Eds.). (1984). *Alcohol problems in women: Antecedents, consequences and intervention.* New York: Guilford Press.

Zhang, Y., et al. (1999). Alcohol consumption and risk of breast cancer: The Framingham Study revisited. *American Journal of Epidemiology, 149*(2), 93–101.

CHAPTER THIRTEEN

OLDER WOMEN AND ADDICTIONS

Renee S. Katz

Substance abuse among older women in the United States has been deemed an "invisible epidemic." Indeed, until recently, the subjects of alcohol and prescription drug abuse and addiction among older women were glaringly absent from both the gerontology and substance abuse literature. And to a degree, they still are. Yet there are more than 25.6 million older women (age sixty and over) in the United States today. Of these, close to five million are at risk for abuse of prescription drugs or alcohol. Furthermore, the baby boom generation is fast approaching old age. These "boomers" will include 40.1 million women in the year 2020 and are predicted to have even greater substance abuse issues, given the relative acceptance of drinking and drug use in this cohort (National Center on Addiction and Substance Abuse at Columbia University [CASA], 1999).

Scope of the Problem

Alcoholism and prescription drug abuse are the top two chemical dependency issues for older women today (CASA, 1999; Gurnack, 1997; Substance Abuse and Mental Health Services Administration [SAMHSA], 1998). Prevalence rates for alcohol problems in older adults range from 3 to 25 percent. The discrepancy in the literature is due to differences in (1) the population studied (for example, hospitalized patients, community dwellers, visitors to physicians' offices), (2) the definition of "old" used in the study (ranging from forty-five years to sixty-five years and older), and (3) assessment criteria used to define alcoholism (for example, *DSM* criteria, CAGE Questionnaire or other screening instrument, use of supplemental questions). Aside from these differences, prevalence rates for chemical dependency in older women are likely to be significantly underestimated (CASA, 1999; SAMHSA, 1998). This is because prevalence rates are often based on surveys that underrepresent older adults in general and older women in particular. In addition, older women, if they *are* surveyed, frequently underreport their alcohol consumption (DeHart & Hoffmann, 1997).

Although few published data exist, clinical evidence reported in the literature suggests that prescription drugs, especially benzodiazepines, sedatives, and hypnotics, are frequently prescribed for and abused by older women. In fact, older women are prescribed benzodiazepines more than any other age group (Finlayson, 1997; Gomberg, 1992; SAMHSA, 1998). Psychosocial problems are inherent to the addiction process, but for older women, the dangers of these prescription drugs are even more alarming. Age-related changes in drug metabolism, as well as interactions with other prescriptions, over-the-counter drugs, and alcohol, all contribute to greater risks for cognitive impairment, dementia, falls, and institutionalization (Roy & Griffin, 1990; SAMHSA, 1998).

How is it that substance abuse in older women—one of the fastest-growing health problems facing this country—has been so invisible? Is it because older women are more likely to "hide" their substance abuse? Is it because older women are less likely to seek treatment? Perhaps. But if we are perfectly honest about this invisible epidemic, we must first start with our societal view of older people in general and of older women in particular. We must first start with ageism and with sexism.

Impact of Ageism

We live in a society fueled by the media's worship of youth and beauty. Obsessed with a fast-paced lifestyle, we emphasize efficiency, autonomy, and productivity. We promulgate youthful appearance, activity, and independence as standards of personal worth. In the United States, young is beautiful, self-sufficient, and powerful; old is worthless, sexless, senile, and lonely. Instead of regarding old age as a valuable culmination of the life cycle, we are victims of negative, stereotypical views of aging as less than normal (Genevay & Katz, 1990). Like sexism and racism, ageism promotes stereotyping and discrimination against individuals—in this case, simply because those individuals have lived a certain number of years.

Further, ageism serves to protect our youth-oriented society against its fears related to helplessness, vulnerability, and inferiority. By projecting negative attributes onto older people and by avoiding discussion of or contact with the aging process, we use ageism to protect our own self-esteem and perceived status in life when we are younger. Ageism ultimately protects our youth-oriented society from its anxieties about death, illness, and loss of meaning in life (Genevay & Katz, 1990; Levin & Levin, 1980).

We are, in fact, so preoccupied with defending ourselves against the reality of death that we ignore the fact that human beings are alive until they actually die. "At best, the living old are treated as if they were already half dead" (Butler, 1975, p. 2), when in reality most older people are reasonably healthy.

Ageism contributes to the lack of identification, diagnosis, and treatment of substance abuse in older women. Physicians, social workers, chemical dependency workers, and family members often explain away problems as a function of being old. For instance, an older woman may be classified as "senile" without being examined for underlying etiologies. In reality, she may suffer from a treatable condition such as depression, multi-infarct dementia, alcoholism, or prescription drug abuse.

In addition, our society unconsciously assigns different quality-of-life standards to older adults. Mom's dependency on her evening cocktails may be dismissed as "her only joy in life." Grandmother's prescription drug habit may likewise be overlooked because "What difference does it make? She's going to die soon anyway."

There is an unspoken but pervasive assumption that it's not worth treating older adults for substance use disorders. Behavior considered a problem in younger adults does not inspire the same urgency for care among older adults. Along with the (false) impression that alcohol or substance abuse problems cannot be successfully treated in older adults, there is the assumption that treatment for this population is a waste of health care resources (SAMHSA, 1998).

Impact of Sexism

For older women, ageism combined with sexism puts their lives in double jeopardy. This generation of older women grew up before the impact of the women's movement. Women's stature in life was based on beauty, "femininity," and eligibility to be a wife and mother—none of which are compatible with our society's notions of aging and growing older. As early as 1972, Susan Sontag described the double standard of aging in our society—a standard that denounces older women with particular severity. She noted that added to the pressures felt by every person in our society to look young for as long as possible "are the values of 'femininity,' which specifically identify sexual attractiveness in women with youth" (Sontag, 1972, p. 33).

For a woman, a much greater part of her sense of self-esteem and pleasure in life is threatened when she faces aging. Aging, a perfectly natural process, is regarded as a humiliating defeat in a woman (Sontag, 1972). Witness the host of antiaging creams marketed to women, hair dyes to hide the gray, face lifts, tummy tucks, liposuction, and breast lifts—frantic yet fruitless efforts to appear young, to delay the inevitable. Note the relative lack of such gimmicks aimed at men. Note also our society's generally positive reframing of the natural process of aging for men: wrinkles in an older man are signs of "character"; gray hair makes a man look "distinguished"; added weight is simply "huskiness." Men are even considered sexually eligible well into old age. For an older man, to date or marry a woman twenty years younger is acceptable. For a woman, it is scandalous. "The double standard about aging sets women up as property, as objects whose value depreciates rapidly with the march of the calendar" (Sontag, 1972, p. 38).

Collette Browne comments that even though "women should refuse to let society define their social lives and worth on such superficial criteria, it is difficult not to become demoralized when one is bombarded by such negative images and messages" (Browne, 1998, p. 43).

Is it any wonder, then, that in combination with the myriad of biopsychosocial stressors faced by older women, self-esteem is often negligible and depression rampant? On one level, seeking comfort and emotional numbness from alcohol and prescription drugs is understandable, yet these substances also contribute to loneliness; lower life satisfaction (Hendricks, Johnson, Sheahan, & Coons, 1991); increased depression; and a host of declines in other emotional, social, cognitive, and physiological spheres (Gambert & Katsoyannis, 1995; Tarter, 1995; SAMHSA, 1998).

◆ ◆ ◆

In sum, when older women internalize ageism and sexism, they are less likely to seek help for mental health or substance abuse problems (Patterson & Dupree, 1994). In addition, when helping professionals are themselves influenced by ageism and sexism, they are less likely to identify and treat substance abuse in older women.

Barriers to Identifying and Treating Chemical Dependency in Older Women

While ageism and sexism can more subtly influence our attitudes toward older women and addictions, there are additional covert and overt factors that significantly affect proper diagnosis and treatment for older women with chemical dependency problems.

Stigma and Shame

Many of today's older women grew up and formed their attitudes about alcohol before the 1950s, when advertising and greater accessibility helped change society's view of alcohol use from a moral failing to a symbol of postwar prosperity (SAMHSA, 1998). Rather, these older women grew up at a time when social mores attached great stigma to women drinking at all. "Nice girls don't drink" was the motto. And actually to *be* drunk meant destroying a good reputation and placing it on a par with promiscuity. Furthermore, many of today's older women were influenced by the era of prohibition.

Thus, more than any group, this cohort of older women is most likely to believe that addiction is a moral flaw—a sign of weakness and irresponsibility—rather than a disease. Ashamed and embarrassed, older women of today hide their drinking and drug problems under a cloak of denial, isolation, and despair (CASA, 1999; SAMHSA, 1998).

Lack of Awareness and Training on the Part of Health Care Professionals

Many older women present for treatment with complaints of depression, memory loss, falls, fatigue, and chronic pain. Health care professionals frequently mistake these common symptoms of alcohol and prescription drug abuse and dependence for what they believe are the "inevitable" consequences of aging. In actuality, the symptoms of psychoactive substance abuse may disguise themselves as those very complaints that initially triggered the prescription medication, such as anxiety, loss of energy, depression, or insomnia. Rather than attempt to determine the potential *cause(s)* of these problems, health care providers often jump right into treating the *presenting symptom*. The truth is, most health care workers do not diagnose substance abuse and chemical dependency in older women because they simply are not looking for it.

In addition, there is a lack of understanding about the increased sensitivity to and decreased tolerance of alcohol and drugs in older women. Because lean body mass and water decline with age, and because alcohol and drugs are metabolized differently in older women, what was safe, moderate drinking in their younger years places women at high risk for abuse and addiction in their older years. Older women experience problems related to alcohol and prescription drugs sooner and get addicted faster, consuming smaller amounts, than any other group—a phenomenon known as *telescoping* (CASA, 1999). Most health care professionals—including those working in the chemical dependency field—are totally unaware that current standards from the National Institute on Alcohol Abuse and Alcoholism recommend no more than one drink per day for older women, and even one drink is considered risky (National Institute on Alcohol Abuse and Alcoholism, 1997; SAMHSA, 1998).

Finally, despite studies indicating that older adults are more likely to complete treatment and have outcomes as good as or better than younger adults (CASA, 1999; SAMHSA, 1998), health care providers continue to believe that older women cannot change and, therefore, cannot benefit from treatment. Further, many health care providers simply do not wish to address drinking and drug use in older women because the topic is uncomfortable, or they believe that these dependencies are one of the last few pleasures left for older women. It is here that ageism and ignorance contribute to denial, pessimism, and "therapeutic nihilism" vis-à-vis older women and chemical dependency.

Psychosocial Issues

The following psychosocial issues also become barriers to treatment for older women.

Decreases in Social Network. Many older women are widowed or living alone. Their social networks shrink due to death and disability of friends and family members, and their access to social networks may be severely limited due to transportation and accessibility problems. Homebound older women are especially vulnerable to social isolation. Thus, because of these women's limited social contacts, the actual number of opportunities for others to witness chemical dependency problems in older women is significantly reduced and may thereby allow serious abuse to go undetected. Even if chemical dependency is detected, treatment becomes more difficult if there are few friends and family members to participate in and support treatment.

Financial Difficulties. Many managed care organizations or insurance companies are reported to refuse to cover the costs of chemical dependency treatment for older women. Medicare itself covers inpatient treatment for substance abuse only if it is provided in a hospital setting—which in many instances solely covers detoxification (CASA, 1999). Even in a psychiatric setting, Medicare covers only 50 percent of most types of outpatient treatment. Because older women are frequently unemployed or retired, their income is significantly more limited than at any other time in their lives.

Lack of Expertise in Treatment Programs. Few drug and alcohol treatment programs have gerontology specialists or treat many older adults in general. Older women may be screened out of standard treatment programs because of poor cognitive tests or because they cannot drive to a program or to AA meetings that operate in the evening hours. Many treatment programs are frequently ill prepared and ill designed to accommodate even the functional disabilities of older women—such as hearing loss, vision changes, or ambulation problems—let alone the specific treatment needs of older women.

Early- and Late-Onset Alcoholism and Prescription Drug Dependence

One of the most striking discoveries in contemporary gerontological research is the finding that alcohol- and drug-related problems in older women begin both in young adulthood and in later life. It is estimated that up to 50 percent of older women develop late-onset alcoholism and that upwards of 35 percent develop late-onset prescription drug dependence (CASA, 1999).

Early-onset alcoholics and prescription drug abusers are more likely than late-onset alcoholics to experience chronic medical problems and organic brain damage, as well as comorbid affective disorders such as depression, anxiety, and bipolar disorder. "They are more likely to have exacerbated their adverse circumstances through their history of [substance abuse]" (SAMHSA, 1998, p. 20). They are also more likely to have alienated family and friends, and thus may be more socially isolated.

In comparison, older women with late-onset chemical dependency issues present psychologically and physically healthier. They experience fewer and less severe psychosocial problems as well as less severe and more reversible cognitive losses. Gerontologists believe that late-onset chemical dependency occurs not only because of the aging body's greater sensitivity to drugs and alcohol but also because older women turn to these substances to cope with age-related stresses and losses (CASA, 1999, p. 16; Gurnack, 1997).

Unlike their younger peers, who cite impulsiveness, sensation seeking, socializing, and desires to be unconventional as motives for their drinking and drug use, older women report using alcohol to alleviate and soothe feelings of depression, hopelessness, and isolation (CASA, 1999; Gomberg, 1990; SAMHSA, 1998). Older women incur significantly more losses due to death, disability, divorce, retirement, and loss of status in life. They experience with particular severity financial stresses, chronic pain, and loneliness. A late-onset chemically dependent woman may drink and self-medicate to escape the stresses of long-term caregiving for a spouse or parent, or she may take up drinking as a new vocation when she discovers the "happy hour" in her new retirement community. Whatever the trigger or reason, late-onset chemical dependency problems are even more likely to be overlooked by health care providers because these older women "appear too healthy, too 'normal' to raise suspicions about problem drinking [and drug use]" (SAMHSA, 1998, p. 20).

There is virtually no research comparing treatment approaches or outcomes for early- versus late-onset chemically dependent older women. However, it is generally believed that late-onset alcohol- and drug-dependent women may respond better to brief interventions—in part because their problems tend to be milder and are thought to be more sensitive to informal social pressure (SAMHSA, 1998). Further, because these women have successfully used other coping mechanisms prior to turning to chemicals, it is believed that they are more amenable to recouping those coping mechanisms.

Diagnostic Criteria for Drug and Alcohol Problems in Older Women

Because of the biopsychosocial changes intrinsic to aging, standard criteria for diagnosing chemical dependency problems in older women are often inadequate. If, for example, *DSM-IV* criteria (American Psychiatric Association, 1994) were used to diagnose alcohol or drug abuse or dependence in older women, a huge percentage of women with these problems would go unidentified because many of the criteria for alcohol abuse in younger women are simply not relevant to older women.

An older woman abusing alcohol or prescription drugs, for example, may still be unlikely to report social or legal problems if she is homebound, living alone, or socially isolated. She is unlikely to fail in "role obligations" if she is no longer parenting or employed. She is unlikely to report "persistent, recurrent problems" due to chemical use, because she is frequently unaware of them, or she may, like her health care providers, attribute these problems to the aging process (CASA 1999; SAMHSA, 1998). And because older women's physiological changes cause them to be sensitive to even small amounts of drugs and alcohol, "tolerance" may not be a relevant diagnostic criterion either.

In addition, because late-onset chemically dependent women typically have a shorter history of alcohol or prescription drug dependence, they frequently have fewer health and family relationship problems. They lack a history of prior work or social problems, they may not develop physiological dependence, and they may not exhibit classic signs of withdrawal—all of which contradict the familiar clinical picture of chemical dependency (CASA, 1999; SAMHSA, 1998).

To be useful in assessing older women, the *DSM-IV* criteria must be interpreted in an age-appropriate manner. "For many adults, the phenomenon of aging, with its accompanying physical vulnerabilities and distinctive psychosocial demands, may be the key risk factor for alcohol [and prescription drug] problems" (SAMHSA, 1998, p. 19).

In fact, the American Medical Association (AMA) has taken steps to refine the definition of alcoholism for older adults. The AMA begins with the American Society of Addiction Medicine's definition of alcoholism as "characterized by impaired control over drinking, preoccupation with the drug alcohol, use of alcohol despite adverse consequences and distortions in thinking, most notably denial." To this definition, the AMA recommends adding the following: "The onset or continuation of drinking behavior that becomes problematic because of physiological and psychosocial changes that occur with aging, including increased sensitivity to alcohol effects" (American Medical Association, 1995, n.p.). We can extrapolate this definition to the effects of prescription drugs as well.

Assessing Drug and Alcohol Problems in Older Women

Because older women are acutely sensitive to the stigma associated with drug and alcohol abuse, it is recommended that alcohol and drug use questions be embedded in a general medical questionnaire and history taking. Prefacing these questions with a link to a medical condition can make them more palatable (CASA, 1999; SAMHSA, 1998).

Thus, when approaching an older woman, the clinician should spell out clearly that these questions are being asked to diagnose health status accurately. Patients are likely to respond most accurately if the interviewer appears friendly and concerned, nonjudgmental and matter-of-fact—for example: "Now I am going to ask you some questions about your use of alcoholic beverages during the past year. Because alcohol use can affect many areas of health and may interfere with certain medications, it is important for us to know how much you usually drink and whether you have experienced any problems with your drinking" (Babor, de la Fuente, Saunders, & Grant, 1992). Or, "I'm wondering if alcohol may be the reason that your diabetes isn't responding as it should," or "Sometimes one prescription drug can affect how well another medication is working. Let's go over the drugs you're taking and see if we can figure this problem" (SAMHSA, 1998, p. xviii). At times, the interviewer will need to ask for specifics: "You say you drink just every so often. Is that just on weekends? Or do you drink more or less every day?" Then the interviewer will need to probe further to determine exactly how much is actually consumed.

Cognitive deficits in older women may make it difficult to obtain complete, accurate answers to interview questions. In such cases, it may be necessary to obtain collateral information from family members, neighbors, home health aids, clergy, or other individuals in the woman's support system. If possible, this should be done with the older woman's permission and should be done in private. Because families are vulnerable to their own ageism and denial, approaching them gently and in a nonconfrontational manner is ideal—for instance: "I'm concerned about your mother's medical condition. I wonder if perhaps her use of alcohol could be complicating the picture and causing her decline. Have you or any one else had any concerns about her drinking?" (SAMHSA, 1998).

Age-Specific Assessment Instruments

A useful screening instrument, which was developed to consider the special vulnerabilities and presentation of alcohol problems in older adults, is the Michigan Alcoholism Screening Test–Geriatric Version (MAST-G), which appears in Exhibit 13.1. It has a high sensitivity and specificity for use in the older population. The well-known Alcoholics Anonymous list of twenty questions about alcoholism has been adapted as a self-test for older drinkers, and it may be used to assess for alcoholism or drug dependency in older women. It is reproduced in Exhibit 13.2.

These screening instruments are most useful when accompanied by (1) education regarding drinking and drug use in late life—its social, emotional, cognitive, and physical effects—as well as current medical recommendations; (2) explorations of history, pattern of use, and reasons for drinking; (3) inquiry into the consequences of drinking—familial-social, cognitive, physical, and emotional; and (4) education about issues specific to older women (for example, shame, hiding, social isolation, multiple losses of aging, grief, and stresses of caregiving).

When to Assess

Because alcohol and prescription drug abuse can trigger or exacerbate serious physical and mental health problems in older women, every older woman should be screened for alcohol and substance abuse as part of any mental health intake interview and as part of a regular physical exam. Such symptoms as depression, irritability, stomach upset, malnutrition, weight loss, memory loss, self-neglect, insomnia, anxiety, and frequent accidents should be considered red flags.

Exhibit 13.1. MICHIGAN ALCOHOLISM SCREENING TEST– GERIATRIC VERSION (MAST-G).

1. After drinking have you ever noticed an increase in your heart rate or beating in your chest?   Yes   No
2. When talking with others, do you ever underestimate how much you actually drink?   Yes   No
3. Does alcohol make you sleepy so that you often fall asleep in your chair?   Yes   No
4. After a few drinks, have you sometimes not eaten or been able to skip a meal because you didn't feel hungry?   Yes   No
5. Does having a few drinks help decrease your shakiness or tremors?   Yes   No
6. Does alcohol sometimes make it hard for you to remember parts of the day or night?   Yes   No
7. Do you have rules for yourself that you won't drink before a certain time of the day?   Yes   No
8. Have you lost interest in hobbies or activities you used to enjoy?   Yes   No
9. When you wake up in the morning, do you ever have trouble remembering part of the night before?   Yes   No
10. Does having a drink help you sleep?   Yes   No
11. Do you hide your alcohol bottles from family members?   Yes   No
12. After a social gathering, have you ever felt embarrassed because you drank too much?   Yes   No
13. Have you ever been concerned that drinking might be harmful to your health?   Yes   No
14. Do you like to end an evening with a nightcap?   Yes   No
15. Did you find your drinking increased after someone close to you died?   Yes   No
16. In general, would you prefer to have a few drinks at home rather than go out to social events?   Yes   No
17. Are you drinking more now than in the past?   Yes   No
18. Do you usually take a drink to relax or calm your nerves?   Yes   No
19. Do you drink to take your mind off your problems?   Yes   No
20. Have you ever increased your drinking after experiencing a loss in your life?   Yes   No
21. Do you sometimes drive when you have had too much to drink?   Yes   No
22. Has a doctor or nurse ever said they were worried or concerned about your drinking?   Yes   No
23. Have you ever made rules to manage your drinking?   Yes   No
24. When you feel lonely, does having a drink help?   Yes   No

Note: Five or more yes responses are indicative of an alcohol problem. For further information, contact Frederic C. Blow, Ph.D., University of Michigan Alcohol Research Center, 400 E. Eisenhower Parkway, Suite A, Ann Arbor, MI 48108; (734) 998-7952.

Source: From "The Michigan Alcoholism Screening Test–Geriatric Version (MAST-G): A new elderly-specific screening instrument," by F. C. Blow, K. J. Brower, J. E. Schulenberg, L. M. Demo-Dananberg, J. P. Young, & T. P. Beresford, 1992, *Alcoholism: Clinical and Experimental Research, 16,* p. 372. Copyright 1991 by the Regents of the University of Michigan. Reprinted with permission.

Exhibit 13.2. AA'S TWENTY QUESTIONS ADAPTED FOR OLDER CHEMICALLY DEPENDENT INDIVIDUALS.

1. Do you dislike or condemn yourself after you have drunk to intoxication?	Yes	No
2. Do you drink with the attitude, "It doesn't really matter" or "What's the use?"	Yes	No
3. Do you frequently miss prescheduled activities like social events, doctor's appointments, or dates with hair dressers?	Yes	No
4. Do you often use the money needed to pay the rent or bills to buy alcohol?	Yes	No
5. Are there occasions when drinking is more important than your relations with your family, friends, or neighbors?	Yes	No
6. Have you ever suffered an injury from falls, burns, or cuts when you were drinking?	Yes	No
7. Is drinking the answer for coping with boredom when you have time on your hands and little to do?	Yes	No
8. Have you ever experienced a black out because of drinking, causing you to have a complete loss of memory for days, even weeks at a time?	Yes	No
9. Has your doctor ever expressed concern about your use of alcohol?	Yes	No
10. When your confidence is low, do you turn to alcohol to rebuild your self-worth?	Yes	No
11. Do you wake up during the night and get up to pour yourself a drink?	Yes	No
12. Do you have to consume a drink to get to sleep?	Yes	No
13. Does alcohol enable you to participate in special events and holidays?	Yes	No
14. Are your relationships with family, friends, or neighbors deteriorating because of your drinking?	Yes	No
15. After you drink do you find it advisable to avoid contact with friends who are not drinking buddies?	Yes	No
16. Does consumption of alcohol result in your inability to make personal decisions promptly?	Yes	No
17. Do you prefer to drink alone, and do you deny to others that you drink excessively?	Yes	No
18. Is alcohol your answer to covering up fears, worry, or sadness?	Yes	No
19. Do you ever refuse to answer the telephone or doorbell when you are intoxicated because you don't want contact?	Yes	No
20. Have you ever been hospitalized for medical problems that have resulted from your drinking?	Yes	No

Note: The Twenty Questions may be adapted to other addictive drugs as well. A yes answer to three or more of these questions indicates a problem with alcohol or drugs.

Source: From *Alcohol, Medications, and Older Adults,* by C. Vandeputte, 1991, Minneapolis: Johnson Institute. Reprinted with permission.

To assess for alcohol and drug problems just once is insufficient. When illnesses and medical symptomatology present or if any of the physical symptoms listed in Exhibit 13.3 are present, the practitioner should be alert to the possibility of drug or alcohol problems. Further, when other psychosocial warning signs are evident (see Exhibit 13.4) or if the older woman is experiencing major life transitions or psychosocial stressors, the practitioner should again initiate questions regarding her alcohol and medication use.

Interventive Approaches with Older Women

Treatment techniques and treatment programs are most effective for older women when they are modified to meet the specific needs, styles, and developmental challenges of this population.

Exhibit 13.3. PHYSICAL SYMPTOMS THAT MAY INDICATE CHEMICAL DEPENDENCY PROBLEMS IN OLDER WOMEN.

- Sleep complaints, erratic sleep patterns, fatigue, daytime drowsiness
- Cognitive impairment, changes in memory or concentration, inability to "track," confusion, disorientation
- Malnutrition, weight loss, muscle wasting
- Seizures, tremors, unsteady gait, changes in motor coordination
- Depression, irritability, anxiety, altered mood
- Frequent, unusual, or neglected injuries
- Bruises—especially on arms and legs and at furniture height
- Burns, fractures, or other trauma—especially if there is no memory of when or how they happened
- Blurred vision, blackouts
- Unexplained chronic pain or other somatic complaints
- Edema, leg cramps
- Urinary incontinence, urinary retention, difficulties urinating
- Poor hygiene, self-neglect
- Unusual restlessness, agitation
- Slurred speech
- Frequent falls
- Chronic gastrointestinal problems (for example, heartburn, indigestion, ulcers, diarrhea)
- Hypertension of recent onset

Sources: Adapted from Pacific Northwest Extension Publication No. 342, September 1989; *Substance Abuse Among Older Adults,* (SAMHSA) Series 26, by the Substance Abuse and Mental Health Services Administration, 1998, Washington, DC: Author.

Exhibit 13.4. PSYCHOSOCIAL FACTORS THAT MAY INDICATE CHEMICAL DEPENDENCY PROBLEMS IN OLDER WOMEN.

- Loss of interest in usual activities and social relationships
- Empty cupboards
- Neglect of home, bills, pets, mail, or newspaper
- Cigarette burns on clothing, furniture, self
- Financial difficulties
- Minor traffic accidents, erratic driving
- Personality changes
- Defensiveness about prescription drug use
- Seeing more than one doctor or using more than one pharmacy for prescriptions
- Excessively worrying about whether prescription drugs are actually working
- Complaints that a prescribed drug has lost its effectiveness
- Ascribing great significance to a specific drug and its efficacy
- Worrying about having enough pills or the correct time to take them—so much so that other activities revolve around their use
- Continuing to use or request refills for drugs when the original condition for which it was prescribed should have improved
- Resisting cessation or decreases in doses of a prescribed drug or drugs
- Complaining about physicians who refuse to write prescriptions or who don't take symptoms seriously
- Self-medicating by increasing doses of drugs that "aren't helping anymore"
- Rating social events by the amount of alcohol dispensed
- Drinking before a social event to "get started" or "warm up"
- Guarding the supply of alcoholic beverages or insisting on mixing own drinks
- Empty liquor, wine, or beer bottles or cans in the garbage/recycling bin or concealed under the bed, in a closet, or other location

Sources: Adapted from Pacific Northwest Extension Publication No. 342, September 1989; *Substance Abuse Among Older Adults,* (SAMHSA) Series 26, by the Substance Abuse and Mental Health Services Administration, 1998, Washington, DC: Author.

Brief Intervention Strategies

Many older women may not know that their alcohol or prescription drug use is affecting their health. Thus physicians and other health care providers are in a unique position to use medical problems and cognitive changes as opportunities to leverage older women into treatment. In fact, brief interventions by health care providers (of even five to fifteen minutes) have been shown to be effective in significantly reducing problems associated with prescription drug and alcohol abuse—particularly with late-onset chemically dependent individuals (CASA, 1999; SAMHSA, 1998).

A brief intervention by a health care provider looks like this. First, the physician, home health nurse, or other health professional describes the impact that the alcohol or prescription drug use is having on the older woman's health or functional abilities. This is followed up with a statement about how reducing or ceasing the use of the chemical will improve her life and is then followed by a brief recommendation—for example: "This is very treatable. Using other methods to help you sleep [or discontinuing your drinking or reducing your Xanax] will help you maintain your independence [or help your memory or help keep you out of a nursing home]" (SAMHSA, 1998).

Although mental health professionals may not have the same leverage as other health professionals vis-à-vis physical health issues, exploring the effects of the older woman's alcohol or prescription drug abuse and its negative consequences is still the starting point. Because older women frequently feel hopeless about their future and about their abilities to change their relationships to alcohol and prescription drugs, a "motivational counseling" style (Miller & Rollnick, 1991) has been found to be especially useful in this population (SAMHSA, 1998).

A motivational counseling approach begins with the principle that the counselor starts where the client is—listening respectfully to her perspective and honoring it as a starting point. The counselor uses reflective listening techniques and empathy to reflect his or her understanding of the older woman's perspective—thus "joining" with her. Then, using the older woman's perspective as a starting point, the counselor begins to help her identify the negative consequences of her drinking and prescription drug use. When the client is ambivalent or resistant, the counselor "rolls" with the resistance, working gently to help the client more clearly see the impact of her drinking or drug use. The counselor encourages the older woman to generate insights about solutions to her problem, and, perhaps most important, the counselor holds on to hope and overtly expresses his or her belief that change is possible. "When older adults are motivated to take action on their own behalf, the prognosis for positive change is extremely favorable. Key to inspiring motivation is the clinician's caring style, willingness to view the older adult as a full partner in his or her recovery, and capacity to provide hope and encouragement as the older adult progresses through the referral, treatment, and recovery process" (SAMHSA, 1998, p. 67).

For some older women—especially those who present with late-onset chemical dependency, strong social supports, and good mental health—a brief intervention or series of brief interventions combined with empathic support may be all that is necessary for continued recovery (SAMHSA, 1998).

Structured Intervention

Formal, structured intervention also can be effective for older women, but with some modifications. A structured intervention involves family members and close friends of the alcoholic or drug abuser in confronting their loved one with their personal experiences of her drug or alcohol use. A counselor meets with the individuals involved to help them clarify their concerns and identify specific situations in which their loved one's behavior has been affected by her drug and alcohol use. Together, these family members determine what they would like to ask their loved one to do to address her addiction and what each individual's response or consequence will be if the loved one does not comply. For some family members, this may mean that they will no longer supply the alcohol to Mom; for others, this may mean that they cannot continue to have contact with her; for others, it may mean they will no longer maintain their silence when questioned by the family physician.

It is recommended that besides the health care provider, no more that two relatives or close friends be involved in an intervention with an older woman (SAMHSA, 1998). Too many individuals taking part in an intervention may be too emotionally overwhelming or confusing to an older woman. In addition, careful consideration should be given when involving grandchildren in an intervention because many older women feel humiliated when their "dirty laundry" is aired in the presence of much younger family members.

Detoxification

Older women, especially those who have been long-term abusers of drugs or alcohol, may require inpatient detox in order to withdraw from alcohol or drugs safely. This is especially important for women who present with multiple medical problems or cognitive deficits; she may not be able to monitor her own "tapering," for example. Inpatient detox may also be necessary when it is not clear whether the cognitive changes are due to medications, a separate dementia, another medically induced reason, or mixed addictions (whereby drugs or alcohol can potentiate each other). Detox is of course indicated if there is significant potential that dangerous withdrawal symptoms—for example, seizures, delirium, or mental confusion—could occur or if prior attempts at abstinence have caused these symptoms.

It is recommended that such detox be undertaken by a physician and nursing staff specially trained to work with older adults, particularly because the initial dose of drugs used to manage withdrawal symptoms in older women is substantially less than the usual adult dosage and because detox may take longer, as drugs and alcohol are more slowly excreted from the aged body.

Age-Specific Treatment Settings

The life contexts and concerns of older women differ significantly from those of younger adults, and treatment works best when the issues addressed are congruent with the life stage of the client (SAMHSA, 1998). Whether in inpatient or outpatient treatment, older women generally do better in settings geared specifically to older adults (SAMHSA, 1998).

Many older women report that they cannot tolerate the profanity used in some treatment and AA settings; they cannot relate to the addict who uses or sells illicit drugs. The vocational and social consequences experienced by younger people as a result of their chemical use often feel irrelevant to older women; and, conversely, the depression, social isolation, chronic illness, multiple losses, and age-related stressors of older women may not resonate for younger people (CASA, 1999). Rather than dealing with child-care issues, for instance, older women are often coping with elder-care issues involving increasing caregiving responsibilities for older parents and spouses while they are simultaneously adjusting to changed relationships with their children. Rather than coping with the stresses of establishing themselves in jobs and careers, many older women are struggling with establishing and re-creating identities in retirement. Rather than facing the loss of driving privileges due to DUIs, older women may be facing sensory losses or chronic health problems that are forcing them to give up driving completely. Further, "Concern with mitigating the social isolation experienced by women caring for children within the nuclear family structure shifts to concern for the social isolation of nuclear family spouses when one requires long term care or dies. . . . Issues of sexuality move toward exploring varieties of sexual expression available to women who inhabit in old age a largely single-sex social world" (Rosenthal, 1990, p. 2), and who now must cope with changes in physical health and abilities in themselves and in their partners.

Treatment Approaches

Older women tend to do better in treatment when the approach is supportive, respectful, and nonconfrontational. Classic "break down their defenses" styles generally have not proven effective with older women—nor have treatment styles that demand that they use the terms *alcoholic* or *addict* (CASA, 1999; SAMHSA, 1998). Rather, in working with older women, addressing their "problems with alcohol or drugs" in a nonjudgmental, nonthreatening manner respects their long-held denial of the problem and associated guilt. It permits older women to face their shame, despair, and denial with dignity and self-respect.

Many older women have adopted the attitudes of their time: "don't air your dirty laundry in public"; *sex* and *sexuality* are words only to be whispered behind closed doors; people should handle their own problems without imposing on others. These attitudes require special recognition and accommodation in treatment. The chemical dependency counselor must understand and work with the fact that older women will approach self-revelation with caution; identification of feelings may be slower; and discussion of personal foibles and needs will take longer and will require modeling, support, and encouragement on the part of the counselor. Also important in this approach are assurances of confidentiality and overt statements that express confidence in the older woman's ability to participate and succeed in treatment. Educational components must normalize the experiences, attitudes, and feelings of older women; must describe and delineate the way treatment works; and must provide hope for change. "Treatment programs should cultivate a culture of respect for older clients. Nurturing clients' self-esteem and reawakening their sense of themselves as valuable, competent human beings are central. . . . Older adults frequently enter treatment depleted physically, socially, and emotionally, convinced that their situation is hopeless. Adding the stigma of addiction to the stigma of aging can compound their despair" (SAMHSA, 1998, p. 74).

Physiological, Sensory, and Cognitive Accommodations

In addition to the pace and style of treatment, treatment facilities and programs must accommodate sensory changes and deficits as well as information-processing differences in older women. For instance, due to physiological changes related to aging, older women often require larger type on handouts and overheads; the volume of presentations may need to be louder; rooms will need to be controlled for glare and superfluous noise; and a warmer temperature in the actual physical environment may be necessary.

Older women will assimilate information most thoroughly if it is presented more slowly and if it is repeated or reviewed. It is also useful to present material both visually and aurally and to keep sessions brief (no longer than fifty minutes). Because many older women do not drive or cannot drive at night because of age-related changes in vision or because it may actually be unsafe to go out at night, they can best use treatment programs and AA meetings that are held during the day and that accommodate their special transportation needs.

Case Management and Community Resources

Because older women are frequently faced with multiple and complex financial, legal, housing, caregiving, transportation, and medical concerns, these potential obstacles to treatment and recovery must be addressed in order to support older women's sobriety. Case management and linkage to community resources are critical in this population and will require extra effort on the part of the professional helper. In addition, many older women already have several health care providers—physicians, visiting nurses, adult day care staff, clergy, social workers—and it will be important for all members of this network to coordinate treatment information and care on an ongoing basis. Attending to psychosocial factors helps support the older woman's sobriety by alleviating external stressors that might otherwise contribute to potential relapse. Coordinating care with the entire team ensures that symptoms related to alcoholism, drug addiction, or withdrawal are not mistaken for other medical issues; it also becomes crucial when psychotropic or pain-relief medications are being considered for prescription.

◆ ◆ ◆

To summarize, older women do better in treatment when

> They are treated in age-specific treatment programs that are supportive, respectful, and nonconfrontational, and that aim to rebuild an older woman's feelings of self-worth and self-esteem.

> The focus of treatment includes coping with depression, loneliness, loss, and other stage-of-life issues relevant to older women.

> There is a focus on rebuilding social support networks.

> The pace, approach, and content of treatment are appropriate for older women.

> Staff members are trained in gerontology or are interested and experienced in working with older people.

> Linkages to community resources (such as medical services and social work services) as well as case management are used in conjunction with treatment (SAMHSA, 1998; Schonfeld & Dupree, 1997).

Psychotherapy and Recovery Issues for Older Women

As indicated previously, the life stage of older women means that their developmental challenges and the foci of their internal worlds are different from those of their younger peers. Psychotherapeutic work with substance-abusing older women and those in recovery needs to consider their special place in the life cycle and the physical, psychosocial, and cognitive changes they face.

The Drinking-Using Stage

Whether older women come to their addictions early in life or later, this first stage of alcohol or drug dependency is characterized by behavior and thinking that revolves around the increased need for chemicals and the concomitant belief that there is no problem with drinking or drug use. This becomes the central organizing principle in the older woman's life.

Jan's husband of forty years, Al, died after a long battle with Alzheimer's disease. Jan spent five years caring for him at home, playing the roles of nurse, physical therapist, dietician, and coordinator of medical appointments. She answered Al's numerous, repetitive questions; she helped him "remember" to toilet himself; she fed him when he couldn't remember how to use a fork; she struggled with how to handle his sexual advances. Jan found herself depleted of energy, tired, and without time to see friends in her previously large support system. "My doctor gave me a little pill to help steady my nerves. I just take one when I really need it . . . one or two times a day, sometimes more. I thought once Al died I'd just stop taking them; then I thought, well, maybe after the funeral is over. . . . Actually, I find it really helps me if I start with one in the morning to help my `shakes.' You know, my nerves. I used to say, `I don't know what I'd do without my friends.' Now, I don't know what I'd do without my little pills."

The therapist's role in this stage is to challenge denial gently. Using the techniques described in the prior section, the therapist listens with an ear toward uncovering the turn to alcohol or drugs, and works to bring that turn, along with its consequences, into focus (Brown, 1995). In Jan's case, the therapist would work to help Jan see the psychological function that her "little pills" were serving in her life. She would explore Jan's grief, loss, and role stress that she experienced in caring for Al, as well as Jan's subsequent bereavement after his death. In coordination with Jan's physician, the therapist would explore the role of those "little pills," how they might contribute to Jan's "shakes" and how they might help or hinder Jan's anxiety ("nerves"). With this information, the therapist is in a position to examine how Jan's dependency has shifted from her support system to her pills. She will explore Jan's prior coping mechanisms and look to support Jan in reclaiming them. The goals are to illuminate the problem with the drug dependency and to help Jan embrace abstinence.

For some older women, a focus on abstinence and the problems that alcohol or drugs cause them physiologically or cognitively may be as far as they go at this stage, and, with improved health and mental acuity, this suffices. For other women, this is just the starting point on a journey into recovery.

Transition: The Struggle with the Chemical Dependency Identity

The older woman in transition is struggling with her identity as a chemically dependent person. The therapist's role is to challenge denial and help the client uncover evidence that supports the reality of her loss of control and her identity as a chemically dependent person. The process of transition is frightening, painful, and fraught with internal conflict. The older woman struggles with denial of her problem, yet is confronted with the reality of it. When she can no longer hide behind the mask of denial, the tension breaks. She "surrenders" to her identity as an alcoholic or addict, and there is a sense of relief in that alone. It "solves" her struggle for control over alcohol, for control over alcohol is impossible for an alcoholic (Brown, 1995).

With this shift, the role of the therapist becomes more active. She moves between the roles of coach, educator, and counselor, to help the client learn new behaviors to replace drinking behaviors. She enrolls the help of AA, a sponsor, and perhaps a formal treatment program to support abstinence.

At sixty, Sylvia found herself in her son's living room surrounded by her children, grandchildren, two childhood friends, and one unknown face. She was surprised to see everyone at what she thought was going to be an intimate Sunday brunch. Sylvia was even more surprised when the stranger introduced herself as a chemical dependency counselor who was there to help her family and friends talk to her about their concerns about her drinking.

This announcement took Sylvia's breath away. "I couldn't believe what I was hearing! I felt so humiliated! And, to think, in front of the grandchildren! I agreed to go to inpatient treatment, but I hated every minute of it. I couldn't relate to the adolescent behavior of the 'adults' there, and I would never say I was an alcoholic. When they went around the circle, I never said, 'I'm an alcoholic'; I said 'alcohol.' I returned home with no aftercare in place and was drinking within a month.

"I went for regular check-backs with my general practitioner and cardiologist and would always look at the liver function tests. They were within range, so I felt safe. I couldn't admit that I was increasing my drinking—waking up at 3 A.M. and pouring myself a sherry to get back to sleep, then coming back home after exercise class and pouring vodka into my orange juice! And that doesn't even include my two eight-ounce Tom Collinses before dinner!

"Just before my seventy-ninth birthday, my counselor expressed concern about my health. She pointed out what I already knew: my hand tremors had gotten so bad I could barely recognize my signature; my gait was so unsteady I had to hold on to the walls when I walked; and my memory was going. She suggested I go to a neurologist. He took some tests and told me it was alcohol related and that if I quit I stood a good chance of getting my cognitive functioning back. He said I could just taper myself off. Day one I followed his instructions, but by day two I found myself cheating! It was then that I knew this was for real. It scared me into recovery. I'm an alcoholic, and I know I can't ever go back; if I do, I'll be dead."

At her counselor's suggestion, Sylvia enrolled in an outpatient older adult chemical dependency program. She found herself learning about the effects of alcohol on the aging brain, finding support and companionship with other women her age, and choosing all-women AA meetings to support her recovery. In coordination with the team at the chemical dependency program, Sylvia's counselor worked to help Sylvia replace her drinking behaviors with positive abstinent actions to fortify her sobriety.

At this stage of recovery, Sylvia's therapist must also remain "on call" in the psychotherapeutic realm. The long-term trauma of Sylvia's alcoholism may unleash painful guilt, remorse, and depression, which could lead to relapse. Thus the therapist needs to move between gentle encouragement of action through AA attendance and standing ready to raise or examine painful memories and issues that may make action difficult (Brown, 1995). The therapist's moving between active coaching and gentle uncovering of defenses will help Sylvia look at any resistance she may have to long-term involvement in AA or to the lifestyle changes necessary to achieve stability in recovery.

Early Recovery

Early recovery marks the time when an individual has achieved a period of stable abstinence. The seemingly uncontrollable impulses of transition have been quieted, and individuals have a growing trust that they need not be overwhelmed by a desire to drink or use. This is often a result of regular attendance at twelve-step meetings; it is also due in large part to the stability provided by putting cognitive, behavioral, and lifestyle changes into place.

The tasks of early recovery expand the parameters of the transition stage. In addition to maintaining behavioral abstinence, older women grapple with the emergence of their feelings and with strategies for how to regulate them. They select permanent sponsors and come to develop new understandings of their alcoholism, addiction, and recovery. Like transition, this stage is often a time of extremes: excitement and growth go hand in hand with depression and struggle (Katz & Ney, 1995).

The therapist stands by, ready to help her client through the web of deep loss and sorrow that often emerges in response to the loss of the chemical that once provided an illusion of safety and protection. The therapist remains alert to the possibility of difficulty in abstinence, watching for relapse indicators or "holes" in behavior and cognitive change; she offers additional concrete support if feelings threaten to overwhelm the older woman or threaten abstinence. Then, once behavioral and cognitive abstinence is secure, the client can move to uncovering work (Brown, 1995).

At sixty-two, Muriel had been sober for six months, and she had never felt better. She felt mentally sharp and energized at work, her physical stamina was palpable, and she was making new friends through AA. Her only concern was her partner of twenty years,

Diane. Muriel described trying to talk to Diane about her recovery but feeling stuck. "What do you need to stop drinking for?" asked Diane. "You don't have a problem with alcohol!" Muriel described a "tornado" of feelings that this unleashed for her. She was enraged that Diane could not see the reality of her alcoholism; she missed their evening "cocktail hour"—a time when they would often "connect" over a drink, or several; she worried that Diane would reject her and her commitment to AA, and she had already been rejected by her immediate family for her "lesbian lifestyle." Muriel just couldn't face one more loss. Suddenly, the pink cloud of recovery had turned dark. Muriel wondered if it was really worth it.

At this juncture, the therapist will be working to support Muriel's hard-won pro-recovery behaviors while "holding" her painful feelings in relation to her life partner and the felt abandonment of her family of origin. The therapist will work with Muriel on strategies that allow her to recognize and acknowledge her feelings without acting them out. Helping Muriel express and work through the pull she feels between recovery and maintaining the status quo of her relationship is a critical step in securing long-term behavioral abstinence and personal recovery. The therapeutic process here will require careful, titrated work and lots of support as Muriel copes with her painful history and the power of her affects and defenses—without relying on alcohol to quell her discomfort.

Ongoing Recovery

With the security and stability of sobriety in place, the older woman enters ongoing recovery. This is a time when cognitive, behavioral, and lifestyle changes are second nature. The tumult of the transition and early recovery phases is quelled, and affect related to past and present can emerge without stimulating a return to drinking. With this secure base, the older woman often begins an intense, deeper exploration of her self. This is facilitated by a more complex exploration of the twelve steps. Here, the twelve steps are used as an uncovering process, much like the depth work in psychodynamic psychotherapy. The twelve steps are powerful vehicles on the road to the heart of recovery: spiritual development that is encompassed in the belief in a power greater than the self (Brown, 1995).

Dovetailing with this rich work of ongoing recovery is the developmental and internal work that is inherent to this life stage. Late life is a time when older women are working on "meaning-making"—on ascribing meaning to their past and working toward meaningful involvement during the last portion of their lives. Many older women have the maturity and skills, acquired over a lifetime, to review, reappraise, and modify their life structures (Genevay, 2000). Others need the support of twelve-step work and psychotherapy to integrate the complexities of their personalities and personal histories, to let go of disappointments—personal, professional, and familial—to move toward acceptance and recognition of their ageless selves, and ultimately to find meaning in their lives and in their legacies.

It is here that "the art of psychotherapy flourishes" (Brown, 1995, p. 48). Uncovering work, addiction issues in recovery, and the developmental tasks of life review and reconstruction merge to propel the older woman forward on her journey. The uncovering process of psychotherapy often makes this movement possible.

Here, Marsha describes her life review process—a process that has been set in motion by looking back at life in sobriety and by looking ahead toward the end of the life cycle:

"I sought out psychotherapy five years ago. My sobriety was stable. I was working the steps and attending meetings, but I felt stuck. I was still uneasy with my relationships and with my place in life. I knew I needed additional help to deepen my process. I used to love life, but I found I was getting so despondent about growing older. I think it must have been the years of alcohol abuse. I didn't feel good about the last thirty years; what a waste. How could I have let it happen? Why didn't I stop? In therapy I realized that I had to tackle the past so that I could move forward in the future. I wanted and needed to continue to grow and change at seventy-five. I finally realized that I could not enrich my relationships until I'd changed internally. I was totally unaware before. Now I am learning to forgive and let go of and remember the horrible abuse I experienced as a child. I am learning to separate my alcoholic identity from that of my mother's. I must—so that the hurt and rage and resentment don't haunt me and so I don't turn it in on myself.

"I am learning to forgive myself for my mistakes and focus on what I have learned from them. Freeing myself from this burden has allowed me to pursue my relationships with meaning and depth and joy. Joy. What a concept: I no longer feel compelled to drown out my sorrow in alcohol. I have learned to see this all as part of my spiritual journey. Examining the meaning of this pain in my life was excruciating, then exhilarating. What was I waiting for? I am a guest here. So I am making every day count. I am clearer about my priorities and what I want to accomplish. I am taking better care of myself. I am allowing myself to heal old wounds, pursue my personal passions, and deepen my relationships inside and outside of AA. I have only so much energy, so I am trying not to get derailed from this final stage of my life's journey."

Here, we see how Marsha has successfully used psychotherapy in combination with a solid recovery program to work on many levels. We can surmise that with her abstinence secure and with the strong attachments of sobriety in place, her denial and repression softened, which allowed her to begin the painful process of resolving trauma. She was able to return to early childhood memories and to struggles with her alcoholic identity—areas that had previously kept her "stuck." Through the exploration of these conscious and unconscious conflicts and affects,

Marsha was able to move forward along her spiritual path. She ultimately was able to use recovery, psychotherapy, and her place in the life cycle to face aging with dignity, integrity, and hope.

Conclusion

Older women with addictions are in the unique position to embrace recovery with a wealth of wisdom, life experience, and skills honed over a lifetime. Perhaps more than any other population, older women, in freeing themselves from the ravages of alcohol or drug dependencies, may experience the most remarkable turn-arounds in the physical, social, psychological, and spiritual arenas. Each woman's path is as unique as her history, but the benefits are great. Renewal, new energy, a "technicolor" view of the world, the move from alienation to reconciliation, self-acceptance, and self-esteem are all possibilities. Our role is to facilitate this potential while respecting each woman's process, internal structures, and place in the life cycle.

References

American Medical Association. (1995). *Alcoholism in the elderly: Diagnosis, treatment and prevention: Guidelines for primary care physicians.* Chicago: Author.

American Psychiatric Association. (1994). *Diagnostic and statistical manual of mental disorders* (4th ed.). Washington, DC: Author.

Babor, T. F., de la Fuente, J. R., Saunders, J., & Grant, M. (1992). *AUDIT: The Alcohol Use Disorders Identification Test: Guidelines for use in primary health care.* Geneva, Switzerland: World Health Organization.

Brown, S. (1995). A developmental model of alcoholism and recovery. In S. Brown (Ed.), *Treating alcoholism* (pp. 27–53). San Francisco: Jossey-Bass.

Browne, C. V. (1998). *Women, feminism, and aging.* New York: Springer.

Butler, R. (1975). *Why survive? Being old in America.* New York: HarperCollins.

DeHart, S. S., & Hoffmann, N. G. (1997). Screening and diagnosis: Alcohol use disorders in older adults. In A. M. Gurnack (Ed.), *Older adults' misuse of alcohol, medicines, and other drugs* (pp. 25–53). New York: Springer.

Finlayson, R. (1997). Misuse of prescription drugs. In A. M. Gurnack (Ed.), *Older adults' misuse of alcohol, medicines, and other drugs* (pp. 158–184). New York: Springer.

Gambert, S. R., & Katsoyannis, K. K. (1995). Alcohol-related medical disorders of older heavy drinkers. In T. P. Beresford & E. Gomberg (Eds.), *Alcohol and aging* (pp. 70–81). New York: Oxford University Press.

Genevay, B. (2000). There is life after work. In N. Peterson & R. C. Gonzalez (Eds.), *Career counseling models for diverse populations* (pp. 258–269). Pacific Grove, CA: Brooks/Cole.

Genevay, B., & Katz, R. S. (1990). *Countertransference and older clients.* Thousand Oaks, CA: Sage.

Gomberg, E.S.L. (1990). Drugs, alcohol and aging. *Research advances in alcohol and drug problems, 10*, 171–213.

Gomberg, E.S.L. (1992). Medication problems and drug abuse. In F. J. Turner (Ed.), *Mental health and the elderly* (pp. 355–374). New York: Free Press.

Gurnack, A. M. (Ed.). (1997). *Older adults' misuse of alcohol, medicines, and other drugs.* New York: Springer.

Hendricks, J., Johnson, T. P., Sheahan, S. L., & Coons, S. J. (1991). Medication use among older persons in congregate living facilities. *Journal of Geriatric Drug Therapy, 6*(1), 47–61.

Katz, R. S., & Ney, N. H. (1995). Preventing relapse. In S. Brown (Ed.), *Treating alcoholism* (pp. 231–276). San Francisco: Jossey-Bass.

Levin, J., & Levin, W. C. (1980). *Ageism: Prejudice and discrimination against the elderly.* Belmont, CA: Wadsworth.

Miller, W. R., & Rollnick, S. (1991). *Motivational interviewing: Preparing people to change addictive behavior.* New York: Guilford Press.

National Center on Addiction and Substance Abuse at Columbia University. (1999). *Under the rug: Substance abuse and the mature woman.* New York: Author.

National Institute on Alcohol Abuse and Alcoholism. (1997). *Ninth special report to the U.S. Congress on alcohol and health from the Secretary of Health and Human Services.* Rockville, MD: U.S. Department of Health and Human Services, Public Health Service, National Institutes of Health, National Institute on Alcohol Abuse and Alcoholism.

Patterson, R. L., and Dupree, L. (1994). Older adults. In M. Hersen & S. Turner (Eds.), *Diagnostic interviewing* (2nd ed., pp. 373–397). New York: Plenum Press.

Rosenthal, E. R. (1990). Women and varieties of ageism. In E. R. Rosenthal (ed.), *Women, aging and ageism* (pp. 1–6). Binghamton, NY: Haworth Press.

Roy, W., & Griffin, M. (1990). Prescribed medications and the risk of falling. *Topics in Geriatric Rehabilitation, 5*(20), 12–20.

Schonfeld, L., & Dupree, L. W. (1997). Treatment alternatives for older alcohol abusers. In A. M. Gurnack (Ed.), *Older adults' misuse of alcohol, medicines, and other drugs* (pp. 113–131). New York: Springer.

Sontag, S. (1972, September 23). The double standard of aging. *Saturday Review*, pp. 29–38.

Substance Abuse and Mental Health Services Administration. (1998). *Substance abuse among older adults.* (SAMHSA) Series 26. Washington, DC: Author.

Tarter, R. E. (1995). Cognition, aging, and alcohol. In T. P. Beresford & E. Gomberg (Eds.), *Alcohol and aging* (pp. 82–97). New York: Oxford University Press.

PART FOUR

ADDICTIONS ISSUES FOR ETHNICALLY DIVERSE WOMEN

CHAPTER FOURTEEN

BLACK WOMEN AND ADDICTIONS

Muriel Gray and Melissa B. Littlefield

Although they share a history of racism and sexism in the United States, Black women are not a monolithic group. They comprise a diverse range in terms of cultural and ethnic identification, income, education, marital status, occupation, and lifestyle. Effective treatment of addiction in this population requires an understanding of the variation among Black women's life circumstances and experiences, for socioeconomic and cultural variables play a strong role in the patterns of substance use and abuse. Moreover, effective treatment of an individual Black woman must be socially and culturally relevant.

Despite the importance of cultural factors, researchers have not explored ethnic or cultural differences in addiction among Black women. Therefore, this chapter will focus on the addiction issues that are particularly salient among Black women as a group in the United States.

The existing body of literature primarily focuses on substance addiction (Boyd, Hill, Holmes, & Purnell, 1998; Brook, Balka, Brook, Win, & Gursen, 1998;

For the purposes of this chapter, the term *Black* rather than *African American* is used in acknowledgment that there are many persons of African descent in the United States who identify racially as Black but do not identify ethnically or culturally with being African American. These may include but are not limited to persons of West Indian, African, and Latin American or Hispanic heritage, whose families immigrated to the United States and who, in many cases, continue to live in their ethnic communities and retain their native culture.

Carter & Rogers, 1996; Cohen, 1999; Davis, 1997; National Institute on Alcohol Abuse and Alcoholism [NIAAA], 2000; Substance Abuse and Mental Health Services Administration [SAMHSA], 1999; Sanders-Phillips, 1998), with few studies exploring eating disorders (Ross-Durow & Boyd, 2000; Striegel-Moore, 2000; Molloy, 1998; Laws & Golding, 1996; Walcott-McQuigg, 1995; Thompson, 1994; Root, 1990) and one article exploring sexual addiction in African American women (Robinson, 1999). There is no literature addressing gambling addiction among Black women. However, given anecdotal data regarding the prevalence of gambling in society in general and among economically disadvantaged people in particular, this issue deserves clinical exploration.

Demographic Overview of Black Women in the United States

Although Blacks in the United States share a history of oppression and continued discrimination, there is a great deal of variation in their everyday experiences, the strategies they employ for negotiating their social environments, and their resulting treatment needs. Black clients differ in their geographical distribution, their ethnic culture, the degree to which they identify with mainstream White culture, and by such socioeconomic factors as income, education, and employment.

Geographical Distribution

The U.S. Bureau of the Census reports race but not ethnicity. As a result, most Blacks are considered African American, and their ethnicity (for example, Haitian, Jamaican, Guyanese, Nigerian, Ghanaian) is not identified. According to the U.S. Bureau of the Census (1999), the majority of the African American population in the United States (54.6 percent) resides in the South. West Indian and Hispanic Blacks, including Jamaicans, Dominicans, Puerto Ricans, and Haitians, are concentrated in the Northeast, although there is a large population of Haitians and Cubans, many of whom are Black, in the South as well. As the overall Black population statistics suggest, Black females primarily reside in the South (54.4 percent); almost a fifth live in the Northeast (19 percent) and in the Midwest (19.3 percent). A much smaller portion, 7.6 percent, resides in the western states.

The great majority of Blacks live in metropolitan areas (88 percent); over half reside within central cities of metropolitan areas (53.1 percent) (U.S. Bureau of the Census, 1999). The high percentage of Blacks living in the inner city has led many to equate the two; however, it should be noted that slightly more than one-third of Blacks (34.9 percent) live in the suburbs, and 12 percent reside outside metropolitan areas altogether (U.S. Bureau of the Census, 1999).

Due to historical patterns of discrimination, Blacks have historically lived in predominantly Black communities and often in ethnic enclaves within those communities. This includes Black immigrants from the West Indies, Latin America, and Africa. Despite ethnic differences among these groups, they share a Black racial identity arising out of the common experience of oppression (historical and ongoing) of Black people in the United States. However, many Blacks whose families immigrated to the United States identify with their national heritage and may not be acculturated to African American culture.

Due to the demise of legalized segregation in housing and to increased access to economic opportunities over the past three decades, many Blacks have moved into neighborhoods (mostly in the suburbs) that are racially diverse or predominately White. Although some have suppressed their ethnic identity and adapted to the mainstream White culture in exchange for economic and social benefits, many Blacks have maintained strong ties with their ethnic communities through their religious institutions, social organizations, or volunteer work. As a result, many are bicultural in that they are able to operate proficiently in both their ethnic Black culture and mainstream White culture.

As indicated previously, a large percentage of Blacks live in central cities. As metropolitan growth and development moved outward to the suburbs after the 1960s, conditions in central cities declined. Housing and building stock deteriorated, and retail shops and services moved out; crime increased. Those who could not afford to move out or who were prevented from doing so were faced with limited access to transportation to jobs (which were moving to the suburbs) and retail outlets, and higher prices for essentials such as groceries. Thus, even though inner-city Blacks have remained in their ethnic communities, isolation and poor conditions have strained their culture-bearing institutions, including families, churches, and schools. As a result, many of the prominent values and behaviors that are associated with Black inner-city culture bear little or no resemblance to traditional Black ethnic cultures.

Income

The median income for Black women was between $15,000 and $19,000, compared to a national median household income of $30,056 in 1998, but one-third (33.6 percent) had a total income of $20,000 or more, and 13.7 percent had an income of $35,000 or more. Black women are more likely to be poor than the general population (U.S. Bureau of the Census, 1999): 24.4 percent of Black women ages eighteen to sixty-four and 30 percent of those sixty-five years and older live below the poverty level, compared to the national rate of 12.5 percent of persons eighteen to sixty-four and 12.8 percent of those sixty-five and older. Although there is a much higher percentage of poor Black females relative to the population at large, the vast majority—75.6 percent of Black females ages eighteen to sixty-four and 69.8 percent of those ages sixty-five and older—live above the federal poverty level.

As a group, married Black women are better off financially than single Black women. The median household income for married Black women in 1998 was between $35,000 and $49,000, compared to $10,000 to $14,999 for Black women with no spouse present. It bears noting, however, that 12.9 percent of Black women with no spouse present had income in the range of $25,000 to $34,000, 11 percent had income from $35,000 to $49,000, and 9.3 percent had income of $50,000 and over. Thus, being single does not necessarily indicate that a Black woman is low income.

When one considers the high cost of living in metropolitan areas, especially central cities, the likelihood of Black women, especially single Black women, experiencing financial difficulty is great. This factor is likely to affect a woman's ability to meet her basic needs. The stress associated with limited finances and the psychological impact associated with racism and sexism have been found to make Black women vulnerable to problems related to substance abuse (Taylor, Henderson, & Jackson, 1991) and eating disorders (Thompson, 1994; Walcott-McQuigg, 1995).

Substance Use by Black Women

The National Household Survey on Drug Abuse (NHSDA) (SAMHSA, 1999) is relied on to estimate the incidence and prevalence of substance use, abuse, and dependence among people in the United States according to their racial or ethnic identification, gender, and age. However, sampling limitations in measuring actual substance use, race or ethnicity identification, subgroups among racial and ethnic groups, and covariates of race or ethnicity make it difficult to know the actual incidence and prevalence of substance use among Black women, and even more difficult to understand cultural aspects of addiction over their life span.

The NHSDA found that other sociodemographic variables better explain differences in the incidence and prevalence of substance use among women than does race. The survey also offered a social context in which the use of substances by some Black women may be understood. For instance, it found that individuals (1) in households with low family income, (2) living in the West or in large metropolitan areas, (3) who spoke English rather than Spanish in the NHSDA interview, (4) who lacked health insurance, (5) who were unemployed, (6) who had nine to eleven years of education, or (7) who have never been married were more likely to report use of alcohol and illicit substances. The NHSDA also found that adolescents who dropped out of school or who reside in households with fewer than two biological parents were more likely to have used illicit drugs, cigarettes, and alcohol within the past year. The same study found that although the rate of illicit drug use is higher among the unemployed, most drug users are employed either full- or part-time.

Therefore, if we are to understand the complex phenomenon of addiction in Black women, we must take into account not only the personal characteristics of the individual addicted woman but also the sociopolitical factors that make up the context within which she lives and is defined. In that regard, several studies have explored the relationship between environment, personal characteristics, and specific substance use.

Alcohol

According to the *Tenth Special Report to Congress on Alcohol* (NIAAA, 2000), Black women report drinking less than other women until the age of twenty-six, at which age the comparative drinking patterns for Black, White, and Hispanic women change. Thereafter, drinking among Black women increases along the developmental life span. For example, Black women between the ages of 26 and 45 report drinking less than White women but more than Hispanic women; and in all age groups between 46–50 and 61–65, Black women report drinking more than White and Hispanic women. However, it should be noted that the use of alcohol and illicit drugs was found to be consistently low among Caribbean woman in the United States (SAMHSA, 1999). Among youth between the ages of 12 and 17, Black girls were less likely than Black male youth or White male and female youth to report use of alcohol and other drugs (SAMSHA, 1999).

It has been established that there are gender differences in the medical consequences of substance use, patterns of use, and the progression and development of substance dependence (Straussner & Zelvin, 1997). In general, women are reported to experience more medical consequences related to substance use than men and to have a much shorter substance use history before developing a dependence on the substance. Moreover, the incidence of fetal alcohol syndrome (FAS) among Blacks who drink is seven times higher than among Whites, even though more Black women in general abstain from drinking than White women (NIAAA, 1994). It is speculated that greater abstinence may, in part, be related to religious influences, but Black women who do drink, drink more than White women (Straussner & Zelvin, 1997).

Tobacco

In a study comparing Mexican American women, Mexican immigrant groups, and Black women, it was found that Black women were more likely to be smokers (Zambrano, Hernandez, Dunkel-Schetter, & Scrimshaw, 1991). The Centers for Disease Control and Prevention (1997) found that White women and Black women smoke at similar rates. Manfredi, Lacy, and Warnecle (1992) found that among Black women, education is negatively related to age of smoking onset, amount of smoking, and perceived difficulty in quitting. Conversely, Black women with more education were more likely to live in environments with fewer smokers. Taylor et al. (1991) found that tobacco use and alcohol consumption among Black women was associated with stressful life events.

Although this finding is not related specifically to women, Blacks and Whites have been shown to metabolize nicotine differently, resulting in higher levels of metabolized nicotine in Blacks than among Whites or Mexican American smokers (Caraballo, 1998), a factor that may contribute to an increased likelihood of addiction among Blacks.

Illicit Substances

Although surveys of the general population show that Black women are more likely to abstain from alcohol and other drug use (SAMHSA, 1999), surveys of the drinking and drug-using population find that African American women are overrepresented among crack cocaine users (Lundy, Gottheil, Serota, Weinstein, & Sterling, 1995) and heavy drinkers (Battle, 1990). Similarly, the use of intravenous drugs is increasing among women in general, and Black women in particular. Among all women, Black women have been found to be the hardest hit by HIV (Carter & Rogers, 1996; Quinn, 1993). The Center for Substance Abuse Prevention (2000) notes that the incidence of HIV and AIDS has increased dramatically among Black women infected through heterosexual contact and that AIDS is the leading cause of death for Black women.

Socioeconomic Aspects and Substance Abuse

By their nature, incidence and prevalence studies provide little insight into the specific social realities of the Black women surveyed. They are not designed to explore the impact, if any, that gender, ethnic, and cultural identification have on Black women's use of illicit substances. However, other types of studies have explored the impact of gender, ethnicity, cultural identification, and specific life experiences on substance use.

A study of ethnic differences in illicit drug use patterns (Lillie-Blanton, Anthony, & Schuster, 1993) found no ethnic differences in use patterns after controlling for drug availability, mechanisms for coping with life stressors, and distribution of wealth and access to social resources.

Trauma has been identified as an important variable in the lives of addicted Black women (Davis, 1997). Ross-Durow and Boyd (2000) found that 61 percent of Black women who use crack cocaine have a history of sexual abuse in their lifetime. Similarly, a qualitative phenomenological study by Davis (1997) of Black addicted women in the Northeast also found histories of sexual and other physical abuse, as well as childhood neglect and abandonment.

The relationship between poverty and substance abuse is complicated. On the one hand, the unemployment, underemployment, or erratic employment brought about by substance abuse may contribute to keeping families headed by women in poverty. There are many anecdotal observations that poverty and homelessness often result among addicted women who once were financially self-sufficient. On the other hand, a woman living in poverty with limited economic support and education is more vulnerable to using substances. For instance, a study of female recipients of Aid to Families with Dependent Children found that one-third of the women assessed had a substance abuse problem (Sisco & Pearson, 1994).

Most of the literature on socioeconomic aspects focuses on risk factors related to addictive behaviors. However, Brook et al. (1998) conducted a study of protective factors; they found that Black adolescents who strongly identify with their communities and cultures, have strong family bonds and attachment to wholesome role models, and have a religious commitment are less vulnerable to risk factors associated with drug use. A look at the convergence of these factors may be seen in the case of LaKeisha.

LaKeisha

LaKeisha is a twenty-eight-year-old single woman who was born into a middle-class, Christian, African American family. Both parents are employed. LaKeisha's father is a recovering alcoholic who is a deacon in their church. The entire family attends the same church. LaKeisha is the youngest of three children.

At fifteen years of age, LaKeisha started drinking at weekend parties with her friends. She was introduced to crack cocaine just before graduating from high school and continued to use during college. She went to a predominantly Black college out of state, where she knew few people. She continued to attend chapel on campus on Sunday, but started to drink heavily and use cocaine regularly during the week and weekends. Her grades suffered, and she began isolating herself from old friends and hanging out with a new drug-using crowd. Her drug use progressed, but she did not feel that it was a problem because she was still in college and still attending church. Eventually, some of her church friends confronted her and contacted her parents. They got her involved in their ministry for young college students with drug problems.

LaKeisha's story highlights several issues: (1) education and socioeconomic status alone are not protective factors in the development of substance addiction; (2) support of family and friends and the support associated with having a religious affiliation are important—not the affiliation alone; (3) both protective and risk factors must be addressed simultaneously.

Theoretical Perspectives on Black Women and Addiction

Historically, mainstream treatment of substance addiction has not considered the unique needs of women in general, and Black women in particular. Most of the literature addressing addiction among Black women focuses on substance addiction and identifies environmental stressors as a major contributor. An exploration of those stressors suggests that they are psychosocial and economic in nature and are a consequence of historical sexism and racism (Carter & Rogers, 1996). Furthermore, it is speculated that personal trauma, style of coping with life stressors, and lack of social support are the major factors that predispose many Black women to initiate substance use. These factors also impact on their continued use of substances and on their utilization of treatment. Thus, unlike addiction in either Black or White men or White women, addiction in Black women is viewed more from a sociocultural theoretical perspective than from a medical or disease model.

Substance Addiction Treatment and Black Women

Although research data are limited, it appears that Black women are underrepresented in treatment. Moreover, the traditional disease model treatment approach may be less effective with this population (Uziel-Miller, Lyons, Kissiel, & Love, 1998).

Many addicted Black women have child-rearing responsibilities and few supports (Luthar & Walsh, 1995). They also exhibit more signs of depression and lower self-esteem (Dempsey & Wenner, 1996) than men. Moreover, Black women addicts typically have fewer financial resources and are more likely to be involved in the child welfare system. Treatment utilization among poor Black women is therefore lower because of these economic and social realities.

These realities may lead to other life circumstances that can be significant treatment barriers. For instance, in a study of treatment barriers for African American women, Allen (1995) found that the most frequently reported barriers were household responsibilities, inability to pay, and the unavailability of drug treatment program slots. The same study revealed attitudinal barriers: lack of knowledge and fear of treatment, fear of others' reactions, shame associated with drug use, and the belief that they would be unable to remain drug free. Another identified barrier was the fear of losing their children to the child welfare system (Abbott, 1994; Allen, 1995; Corse, McHugh, & Gordon, 1995). Veronica's case illustrates some of these barriers and the emotional struggles that must be addressed in overcoming them.

Veronica

Veronica was a twenty-three-year-old single mother of two. She had a tenth-grade education and an erratic work history in low-paying jobs. She first started using alcohol at age twelve, crack cocaine at fifteen. She was sixteen when her son was born. She moved out of her mother's home to live with her son's father, Deon, and his friends. She and Deon both worked erratically, but primarily supported their addiction by selling drugs. Both of Veronica's children had been diagnosed with medical conditions and manifest behaviors associated with drug exposure. Because Veronica was pregnant with her third child and had made multiple unsuccessful attempts at abstinence, the nurse and social worker at the local health department recommended a public residential treatment program that would put her on their wait list. Deon, who used drugs with her, did not believe her problem was "that bad" and threatened to leave her if she "abandoned" him and the children. Veronica put herself on the wait list but did not enter the program because she feared losing the relationship with Deon and losing her children. She eventually entered an intensive outpatient program because she feared that she would lose her children if her third child was born drug affected. The outpatient program offered child-care services and a welfare-to-work training component.

As Veronica's case shows, the combination of social and economic factors and attitudinal beliefs or misconceptions about treatment result in resistance and low rates of treatment utilization among Black women.

Assessment and Treatment Considerations

Studies of treatment efficacy have identified treatment models, components, and approaches that have been effective in treating selected Black women addicts. Although the components of the few programs designed for Black women are similar, the philosophy or worldview differs. Ethnic and cultural identity is the foundation of one's view of the world. It is the lens by which most people filter their life experiences. Studies have stressed the importance of considering a woman's ethnic and cultural orientation and have emphasized that treatment approaches must be "culturally sensitive and congruent" (Terrell, 1993) with the women's values (Davis, 1997; Longshore, Grills, Annon, & Grady, 1998; Smith, Buxton, Bilal, & Seymour, 1993; Uziel-Miller et al., 1998).

Hence, it is important to assess and determine the ethnic and cultural orientation of each Black woman, keeping in mind that Black women are not a monolithic group. Some may be guided by a worldview that is more Western, Eastern, or African; others may be guided more by identification with a specific ethnic group or geographical region. For instance, a Black woman who identifies herself as American may place more value on being American than on being of African descent. A Black woman who identifies as African American may place the most value on being a person of African descent in America and may interpret her life circumstance as a consequence of U.S. slavery. Another woman may identify more with her African ancestry and draw from her heritage in Africa to define who she is. Still another woman may identify with being Southern, West Indian, or a member of the culture of some other geographical region. Therefore, it is important to learn how a woman identifies herself. Once treatment is used, the inclusion of components that address a woman's African, African American, or American identity have been found to be effective in addressing resistance and promoting recovery (Longshore, Grills, Annon, & Grady, 1998; Smith, Buxton, Bilal, & Seymour, 1993). It is therefore important to assess the woman's ethnic identity. For example, if she identifies more with her African ancestry, incorporating aspects of African culture may be effective. If she identifies more with her gender (and not her ethnicity), a gender-sensitive approach may be more effective. In order to address resistance and promote recovery, ethnic, cultural, and gender differences need to be taken into account (Uziel-Miller et al., 1998). The chart shown in Exhibit 14.1, used by Dr. Cheryl Hyde at the University of Maryland School of Social Work as a tool for understanding social identity, may be adapted to understand ethnicity.

This exercise may be modified and used specifically as a tool in understanding a Black woman's racial and ethnic identity. However, when making treatment placement decisions, the counselor should also make sure that the approaches used in treatment are congruent with her social identity.

Programs with an African American–centered approach (Davis, 1997; Smith et al., 1993; Uziel-Miller et al., 1998) focus on the experiences of being African in America by incorporating interventions designed to address low self-esteem, sense of powerlessness, institutionalized racism and sexism, and internalized racism. It has been observed that African American women and men may not

Exhibit 14.1. INFLUENCES ON SOCIAL IDENTITY.

Directions: In order to understand the various influences on your social identity, as well as your perception of the relative "weight" of each influence, rank order the following social identity categories in terms of level of influence or importance. Use a scale of one to eight, with one being the most important. For example, if religion is the most influential or important aspect of your overall identity, give it a one (1). If gender is the least influential or important aspect of your overall identity (which does not mean it is unimportant), give it an eight (8). No tied rankings, please.

Social Identity Category	Rank (1–8)
Race __	
Ethnicity __	
Gender __	
Sexual orientation __	
Religion __	
Disability __	
Age __	
Class __	

initially embrace some of the recovery concepts, such as twelve-step programs, that are considered the cornerstone of traditional treatment in the United States (Smith et al., 1993). Such resistance is thought to be a reaction to the twelve-step concept of powerlessness, which is also associated with slavery, racism, and sexism. However, because spirituality is the foundation of twelve-step programs, and spirituality has been found to be a protective factor for substance use among Black women, strategies highlighting the spiritual aspects of twelve-step programs and reframing the concept of powerlessness have been developed. One such program is the HAFC/Glide African American Extended Family Program of the Haight-Ashbury Free Clinics and Glide Memorial Methodist Church. This program for African American addicts adapted the twelve steps to address some of the cultural and social points of resistance (Smith et al., 1993). The program addresses women's issues of low self-esteem and powerlessness by placing emphasis on the role of women in the matriarchal African American family and using the archetypal "grandmother" as both a positive role model and as representing a "Higher Power."

Some programs have an African-centered approach (Longshore et al., 1998; Jackson, 1995) that incorporates such traditional African principles as communalism and collective support. These models embrace the African belief that "it takes a village" as the guiding philosophical theme. Such programs may also include African history classes, African attire, and rituals to enhance self-esteem. Thus a sense of group and community is the focus (as opposed to focusing primarily on the self-interest and recovery of an individual woman). Regardless of the specific approach, if a program is to be effective, it must address the appropriate ethnic, cultural, and gender-specific needs of each Black woman.

Effective Treatment Approaches

The most compelling theme in the research literature is the need to address all the various dimensions of Black women's social reality, including racial, ethnic, and cultural identification, in order for treatment to be effective. In addition, studies have shown that effective treatment must also address gender-specific issues (Allen, 1995; Roberts, Jackson, & Carlton-LaNey, 2000; Straussner & Zelvin, 1997).

Because Black women often present with multidimensional issues that include limited educational and employment histories, child care needs, histories of victimization, and psychological distress, treatment must address these issues in addition to the substance addiction (Davis, 1997; Uziel-Miller et al., 1998). Gender-sensitive programs typically have a long-term and residential component for women and their children. They also need to include ancillary services, such as child care, parenting classes, job training and educational opportunities programs, as well as individual, group, and family counseling services available not only to the women but also to their children. A study of treatment effectiveness (Uziel-Miller et al., 1998) for African American women and their children enrolled in a comprehensive gender- and culture-sensitive, long-term (approximately nine-month) residential program found that 88 percent of the women remained substance free throughout treatment and at discharge. Because many Black women who are addicted to substances report physical and sexual trauma, effective programs also need to offer clinical services focusing on trauma recovery. A study of treatment retention (Lewis, Haller, Branch, & Ingersoll, 1996) found that coed therapy groups (especially those addressing sexuality and trauma) were barriers to women's remaining in treatment.

Black Women and Eating Disorders

Some of the psychosocial factors associated with substance addiction have also been associated with other addictions, especially eating disorders. However, most research has studied and defined the eating behaviors as disorders, not addiction.

Eating disorders have been socially constructed as being unique to White women, but according to Striegel-Moore (2000), women of color in general, and Black women in particular, appear to be as likely as White women to engage in binge eating and to use laxatives for weight control. The prevalence of clinical eating disorders appears to be higher for Black women than White women. In her study of a community-based sample of Black and White women between the ages of eighteen and forty in two New England states ($n = 7,369$), Striegel-Moore found that when the severity level of binge eating was considered, Black women were twice as likely as White women to have a clinical eating disorder.

Theoretical Perspectives

A fundamental misconception held by many is that eating disorders stem from misguided vanity; in other words, women who are overly concerned with their appearance can develop eating disorders as a result of a weight-control strategy gone bad. Feminist analysis has challenged this notion, arguing that women's limited access to power within and outside the family is at the root of eating disorders. Thompson's groundbreaking qualitative research (1994) on women with eating disorders expands earlier feminist analysis. Thompson collected and analyzed the life histories of eighteen women between the ages of nineteen and forty-five: five African Americans, five Latinas, and eight Whites; of these women, twelve were lesbians (all of the White women and four of the women of color). The majority of these women had a combination of eating disorders (bulimia, compulsive eating, anorexia, extensive dieting), the most common of which were bingeing and extensive dieting. The specific type of eating problem was not related to race, class, sexual orientation, or nationality. Moreover, the particular type of eating problems they experienced often changed during their lives.

According to Thompson (1994), women—across race, class, and sexual orientation—begin to binge and diet in response to trauma, including sexual abuse, racism, acculturative stress, poverty, homophobia, emotional and physical abuse, witnessing the abuse of siblings and parents, and loss—including physical, psychic, and spiritual losses. Women begin to diet or binge to help them numb difficult emotions. Food works like a drug: bingeing "sedates, lessens anxiety, and induces sleep" (p. 96); dieting serves a similar function by giving women a goal to focus on as a way to avoid painful feelings.

Thompson (1994) asserts that bingeing and dieting may over time become generalized responses to stress, as women eventually come to construe these coping strategies as methods of caring for themselves and dealing with their problems on their own. They may begin to feel as though they have regained a degree of the personal power lost as a result of their traumatic experiences. Other people in women's lives often reinforce this false sense of empowerment. For example, anorexic or bulimic women may be praised for having the will power to be thin.

In Thompson's research (1994), food was the "drug" of choice, even in instances where alcohol and other drugs were used, because it could be easily accessed by traumatized girls long before they had access to the money and transportation that would be required to obtain drugs to cope with their pain. As noted previously, much of the trauma experienced by the respondents began when they were young girls. Beyond childhood, food continued to be a more viable option than drugs for many women because it is available, accessible, and affordable, and does not carry the social stigma of drugs. The women in Thompson's study reported that they viewed food as less expensive than alcohol and its effect less dangerous for them and their children. Specifically, women could binge without getting a hangover and could still perform their daily responsibilities adequately.

The findings of Walcott-McQuigg's research (1995) on stress and weight-control behavior in African American women are consistent with Thompson's assertions (1994). Walcott-McQuigg conducted in-depth interviews with a convenience sample of thirty-six professional Black women between the ages of twenty-five and seventy-five. Over half of the respondents identified themselves as "stress eaters"; in other words, their eating behavior increased when they were under stress. The women who were experiencing higher levels of stress had a lower physical self-concept (measured by the Tennessee Self-Concept Scale). Caregiver stress and stress in the workplace—including on-the-job politics, lack of respect for their authority on the part of Whites, and sexual harassment—were the two primary types of stress they associated with their increased eating. They also reported other stressors, such as the difficulty of being a Black woman, safety issues, lack of career options, and lack of attention to issues specific to Black women.

Betty

Betty is a forty-two-year-old married African American woman with two preteen children; she works as a middle manager in a social service agency. She has a strong cultural identification as a Black woman and is committed to improving the community. She is a member of several organizations that provide services to her home community, including Black women's clubs and a church group.

Betty has been active at her job and in her community work for as long as she can remember, but lately they seemed to be taking more of a toll on her. In the months before she sought professional help, she often felt tired and overworked, but would not cut back on her activities because she felt a real sense of accomplishment and gratification from her success in her professional, community, and family life. Despite her general positive feelings about her life, Betty was aware that her success had been in spite of the racism and sexism she had experienced from Whites and other Blacks. Although these experiences were a source of great pain for her, she felt proud that she had been able to surmount the obstacles she faced. She took great pride in being viewed as a "together Black woman" and drew strength from this image. This self-image, although affirming on one level, prevented Betty from admitting to herself or her family and friends that her seemingly high functioning was actually taking a toll on her mental and physical health. Due to her strong religious beliefs, she did not partake of alcohol or any other substances, including cigarettes, to relax her when she was stressed out. Before her best friend passed away a few years back, Betty used to confide in her, but now there was no one with whom she felt comfortable sharing her struggles, not even her husband; she felt that he had his own struggles and that she needed to be strong for him, too.

Several times a week, when she was working late or at one of her numerous community meetings, Betty snacked on sweets, chips, and other readily available food. Often she consumed a family-size bag of chips or a whole box of cookies. Most times she was not even hungry. She had gained a lot of weight since she had started getting more involved in the community and taking on more responsibilities at work. She was uncomfortable with her weight and often experienced bloating or indigestion after snacking, but eating always comforted her, so she did not stop. She often thought to herself that she really needed to cut back on her snacking and lose some weight. But her husband and friends told her she looked good for a woman her age—and many of her friends were heavyset too. She thought she would get around to addressing her weight issue one day, but she had more pressing matters to deal with. Besides, she thought, at least she was not like some people she knew who chain smoked or went out drinking every other night.

Debilitating anxiety attacks occurring around the due date of a big project at work ultimately scared Betty into seeking professional help. Upon finding no physical basis for her attacks, she entered treatment to learn to deal with her stress. In therapy, Betty was able to admit that she was an overachiever because she continuously struggled with an inferiority complex due to the racism and sexism she had experienced. Eventually, she also revealed her snacking behavior to the therapist. The therapist helped Betty deal with her issues of internalized oppression. She focused in on Betty's strong spirituality and encouraged her to release her problem to God, affirming her worth by assuring her that God doesn't make mistakes. She helped Betty critically analyze the negative messages she received about being African American and being a women; develop more authentic, affirming images of Black womanhood; and balance her work, family, and community roles. She also referred Betty to Overeaters Anonymous for ongoing support with her binge eating.

Assessment and Treatment Considerations

Eating disorders often go undiagnosed in Black women (Striegel-Moore, 2000; Thompson, 1994). When they are detected, they are usually more advanced and therefore tend to be more persistent and severe. Thus, they are more difficult to treat (Kempa & Thomas, 2000; Root, 1990; Thompson, 1994). Root reports that Black women often experience shame or a sense of betrayal as a result of having what is considered to be a White women's disorder. When Black women dare to express their eating difficulties to others, they often encounter disbelief and are discouraged from seeking help. This suggests a need for greater public awareness and for education efforts targeted to Black communities, as well as to helping professionals who work with Black women.

There are several factors that contribute to the failure to diagnose and treat Black women for eating disorders. First, researchers and practitioners have maintained a somewhat unidimensional focus on anorexia nervosa and, increasingly, on bulimia, to the exclusion of other eating disorders, such as binge eating, which are more likely to be experienced by Black women; this has limited our understanding of eating disorders in this population. For example, in a study of sexual assault history and eating disorder symptoms among White, Hispanic, and Black women and men (Laws & Golding, 1996), sexual assault was found to be unrelated to eating disorders among African Americans but significantly related for Whites and Hispanics. However, these authors operationalized eating disorders as symptoms and behaviors from the anorexia nervosa section of the Diagnostic Interview Schedule, and did not explore other types of eating disorders, such as binge eating, that Blacks may experience as a result of sexual trauma.

Second, the tendency of mainstream researchers and practitioners to view Black women through the lens of White culture rather than from a Black female perspective has led to erroneous conclusions about the role of Black culture in the development of eating disorders. Black women are believed to be "protected" from eating disorders because of more flexible definitions of beauty and the preference or higher tolerance for a larger female body size (Molloy, 1998; Root, 1990). The conceptualization of eating disorders as "vanity-related" disorders rather than as maladaptive modes of coping with stress and oppression underlies this belief and gives the false impression that Black women are not concerned with their weight and do not practice weight-control behavior.

Third, many health professionals do not recognize Black women's symptoms, or they lack the cultural awareness that would allow them to assess the psychological dimension of the physical problems with which Black women present (Thompson, 1994). As noted earlier, eating disorders in Black women may have a different course or manifest different symptoms from those of Whites. Binge eating is more common than anorexia and bulimia, and therefore needs to be specifically and routinely screened for when Black women present with trauma and other crisis situations. In addition, the onset of eating disorders may occur later in life for Black women relative to White women, who are likely to develop such disorders in their teen years (Kempa & Thomas, 2000).

Finally, cultural norms and expression can discourage Black women from seeking help. The insistence of Black culture on women's strength and independence may prevent women from revealing eating problems, particularly because such problems can seem minor relative to some of the other difficulties they may be experiencing. Black women may take comfort in being able to handle their personal problems on their own and may be reluctant to identify their disordered eating as a problem until it impairs their functioning in other areas or until some personal crisis pushes them into seeking treatment. If they do seek treatment, Black women may lack the terminology to name the eating problems they are experiencing, as they are not widely discussed within the culture (Thompson, 1994).

Culture is also significant in that food (for example, African American soul food) is an important part of Black cultural identity, expression, and celebration. As the primary preparers of food, Black women are esteemed as culture bearers. Restrictive dietary habits may be viewed as a threat to the maintenance of cultural traditions and may eliminate one of the few areas where African American women are publicly affirmed and validated and can thereby derive self-esteem. Compounding this is the appreciation of a more voluptuous female body type among many Blacks, which may prevent Black women from receiving support or affirmation for their efforts to curtail their bingeing. Thus, culture provides the backdrop against which normative and non-normative eating is defined.

Kempa and Thomas (2000) assert that, in addition to aspects of Black culture(s), acculturation to mainstream White culture and confused ethnic identity are risk factors for eating disorders among Black women. Historical and ongoing oppression has resulted in the devaluation of non-European physical features and of ethnic foods, rituals, and customs. A common response by Black women is to reject their ethnic culture and internalize mainstream White standards of culture and norms of beauty. In so doing, women who are highly acculturated may be at risk for developing such eating disorders as anorexia and bulimia as they strive to attain the idealized Caucasian ultrathin body type. Kempa and Thomas also suggest that the degree of identification a Black woman feels with her own ethnic culture and with mainstream White culture influences the manifestation of her presenting symptoms. For example, those who reject their ethnic culture may develop eating disorders as a result of a search for uniqueness, whereas those who identify strongly with mainstream values may develop a hatred for their own appearance and may engage in excessive dieting out of a desire to be thin.

The following case illustrates the impact of acculturative stress on Black women's disordered eating.

Rita

Rita is a sixteen-year-old girl who moved with her mother from Nigeria to the United States when she was seven years old to join her father, who had finished his degree at a U.S. college. The family settled in a predominantly White suburb close to the engineering firm where her father had gained employment. Rita's family maintained ties with their extended families in Nigeria, who visited for lengthy periods from time to time. Rita's uncle and his family lived two hours away, and the families often visited each other on weekends.

Rita spoke English prior to coming to the United States and was a good-natured, gregarious girl. She appeared to adjust well upon entering school and made friends with relative ease. Rita had always been taller and proportionately larger than the other girls in her class, and at age ten she began to develop breasts and hips, which made her stand out even more among her peers. When her friends would joke with her about it, she would laugh along with them, but inside she would cringe. She had always felt that she looked very different from everyone else and had worked very hard at fitting in.

Rita's parents gave her conflicting messages about her size. She enjoyed attending the frequent family functions that centered around large meals because she was able to connect with her family and express her native culture and heritage. Her parents encouraged her to eat heartily during these events, although they would also mention that she should be careful to watch her weight. They would also stress that she must do well in school and look nice so that they could show the Americans that their family was proud and could do well in a new country.

Rita felt conflicted about the expectations placed on her. She wanted to feel important and do things right, and she wanted to please her family. She knew that her family had sacrificed everything to come to the United States, and she felt that she had to be successful and perfect to pay them back. She began to diet and work out in an attempt to fit the image of the skinny American girl. She began to obsess over what she should eat and how much. When she began to lose weight, her parents became concerned and insisted that she eat more at family meals. She began to purge after meals, using laxatives and diuretic herbal teas.

Initially, Rita felt as though she was managing the conflicting needs of her home and school environment well, but eventually she began to become withdrawn and fatigued from not having anyone with whom to talk about her adjustment issues. A teacher recognized the change in her demeanor and referred her to the school social worker. After much searching, the social worker found a group for immigrant girls in a community-based social services agency. She spoke with Rita's parents, who, after much discussion, agreed to let her attend. The social worker realized that the parents also needed help understanding what their daughter was experiencing, and persuaded them to attend the parents' group at the same center.

Sexual Addiction and Black Women

The clinical recognition of sexual addiction is increasingly common; however, the literature and research have not kept pace with this clinical reality. Much more is known about male sexuality than female sexuality. Perhaps this is because female sexuality is highly value laden in American society and therefore has not been the subject of objective study.

There are even fewer scientific studies about sexuality and Black women specifically. Robinson (1999) speculates that the paucity of scientific study focusing on sexuality among Black women may be the result of the historical relationship between sexual exploitation and slavery, and the contemporary relationship between sexual exploitation, poverty, and racism.

What literature there is on female sexual addiction finds that a high percentage of women who identify themselves as having a sexual addiction report having been sexually assaulted at some point in their lives (Ross, 1996). Because a large number of women with substance addictions report similar histories, one might speculate that there will be some incidence of sexual addiction among Black women who have substance or other types of addictions. However, this is not recorded in the literature. The limited literature that exists primarily focuses on sexual addiction among African Americans in general (not women as a group) as a response to posttraumatic stress (Robinson, 1999) or to sexual assault and rape (Barbee, 1992; Danziger, 1995).

Conclusion

Efforts to identify and understand addiction among Black women and to develop successful programs of intervention should be guided by findings regarding incidence and prevalence, risk and protective factors, personal characteristics, and social factors that affect Black women's lives. Although there have been studies of substance addiction among African American women and some studies exploring the impact of ethnic and cultural identity as risk and protective factors, there have been no studies of addiction among Black women that have attempted to account for differences in ethnicity and culture. For example, there have been no studies exploring differences in addiction between Black North American women and Black Caribbean women, African women living in America, or Black Hispanic women. There have been even fewer studies of eating disorders or food addiction among Black women and no studies of Black women and sexual and gambling addiction.

A major theme in both the substance and food addiction literature on Black women is the importance of understanding and assessing how Black women's ethnic and cultural identity may make them more vulnerable or may help protect them from developing an addiction. The same literature identifies such personal characteristics as low self-esteem, depression, experience of posttraumatic stress, and style of coping with the stresses of day-to-day life (including few financial resources and limited education) as factors that need to be addressed in the treatment of these addictions.

References

Abbott, A. (1994). A feminist approach to substance abuse treatment and service delivery. *Social Work in Health Care, 19,* 67–83.

Allen, K. (1995). Barriers to treatment for addicted African American women. *Journal of the National Medical Association, 87,* 751–756.

Barbee, E. (1992). African American women and depression: A review and critique of the literature. *Archives of Psychiatric Nursing, 6,* 257–265.

Battle, S. (1990). Moving targets: Alcohol, crack and Black women. In E. White (Ed.), *The Black women's health book* (pp. 251–256). Seattle, WA: Seal Press.

Boyd, C., Hill, E., Holmes, C., & Purnell, R. (1998). Putting drug use in context: Life-lines of African American women who smoke crack. *Journal of Substance Abuse Treatment, 15,* 235–249.

Brook, J., Balka, E., Brook, D., Win, P., & Gursen, M. (1998). Drug use among African Americans: Ethnic identity as a protective factor. *Psychological Reports, 83,* 1427–1446.

Caraballo, R. (1998). Racial and ethnic differences in serum cotinine levels of cigarette smokers: Third National Health and Nutrition Examination Survey, 1988–1991. *Journal of the American Medical Association, 280,* 135–139.

Carter, J., & Rogers, C. (1996). Alcoholism and African-American women: A medical sociocultural perspective. *Journal of the National Medical Association, 88,* 81–86.

Center for Substance Abuse Prevention. (2000). Substance abuse prevention and HIV prevention initiative for youth and women of color. In *CSAP—Prevention Works!* Rockville, MD: Author.

Centers for Disease Control and Prevention. (1997). Cigarette smoking among adults— United States, 1995. *Morbidity and Mortality Weekly Report, 46,* 1217–1220.

Cohen, E. (1999). Exploratory attempt to distinguish subgroups among crack-abusing African American women. *Journal of Addictive Diseases, 18*(3), 41–54.

Corse, S., McHugh, M., & Gordon, S. (1995). Enhancing provider effectiveness in treating pregnant women with addictions. *Journal of Substance Abuse Treatment, 12*(1), 3–12.

Danziger, S. (1995). Family life and teenage pregnancy in the inner city: Experiences of African-American youth. *Children and Youth Services, 17,* 183–202.

Davis, R. (1997). Trauma and addiction experiences of African American women. *Western Journal of Nursing Research, 19,* 442–465.

Dempsey, M., & Wenner, A. (1996). Gender specific treatment for chemically dependent women: A rationale for inclusion of vocational services. *Alcoholism Treatment Quarterly, 14*(1), 21–30.

Jackson, M. S. (1995). Afrocentric treatment of African-American women and their children in a residential chemical dependency program. *Journal of Black Studies, 26*(1), 71–29.

Kempa, M. L., & Thomas, A. J. (2000). Culturally sensitive assessment and treatment of eating disorders. *Eating Disorders, 8,* 17–30.

Laws, A., & Golding, J. M. (1996). Sexual assault history and eating disorder symptoms among White, Hispanic, and African-American women and men. *American Journal of Public Health, 86,* 579–582.

Lewis, R. A., Haller, D., Branch, D., & Ingersoll, K. S. (1996). Retention issues involving drug-abusing women in treatment research. *NIDA Monograph, 166,* 110–121.

Lillie-Blanton, M., Anthony, J., & Schuster, C. (1993). Probing the meaning of racial/ethnic comparisons in crack cocaine smoking. *Journal of the American Medical Association, 269,* 993–998.

Longshore, D., Grills, C., Annon, K., & Grady, R. (1998). Promoting recovery from drug abuse: An Africentric intervention. *Journal of Black Studies, 28,* 319–333.

Lundy, A., Gottheil, E., Serota, R., Weinstein, S., & Sterling, R. (1995). Gender differences and similarities in African American crack cocaine abusers. *Journal of Nervous and Mental Disease, 183,* 260–266.

Luthar, S., & Walsh, K. (1995). Treatment needs of drug addicted mothers: Integrating parenting psychotherapy interventions. *Journal of Substance Abuse Treatment, 12*(5), 341–353.

Manfredi, C., Lacey, L., & Warnecle, P. (1992). Smoking-related behavior, beliefs, and social environment of young Black women in subsidized public housing in Chicago. *American Journal of Public Health, 82*(2), 267–272.

Molloy, B. L. (1998, April). Body image and self esteem: A comparison of African American and Caucasian women. *Sex Roles: A Journal of Research.* Available: www.findarticles.com.

National Institute on Alcohol Abuse and Alcoholism. (1994, January). Alcohol and minorities. *Alcohol Alert* (No. 23). Rockville, MD: Author.

National Institute on Alcohol Abuse and Alcoholism. (2000). Alcohol and women: An overview. In *Tenth Special Report to Congress on Alcohol* (pp. 253–257). Rockville, MD: Author.

Quinn, S. (1993). AIDS and the African American woman: The triple burden of race, class, and gender. *Health Education Quarterly, 20,* 305–320.

Roberts, A., Jackson, M. S., & Carlton-LaNey, I. (2000). Revisiting the need for feminism and Afrocentric theory when treating African American female substance abusers. *Journal of Drug Issues, 30,* 901–918.

Robinson, D. (1999). Sexual addiction as an adaptive response to post-traumatic stress disorder in the African American community. *Sexual Addiction and Compulsivity, 6,* 11–22.

Root, M.P.P. (1990). Disordered eating in women of color. *Sex Roles, 22,* 525–530.

Ross, C. (1996). A qualitative study of sexually addicted women. *Sexual Addiction and Compulsivity, 3,* 43–53.

Ross-Durow, P., & Boyd, C. (2000). Sexual abuse, depression and eating disorders in African American women who smoke cocaine. *Journal of Substance Abuse Treatment, 18,* 79–81.

Sanders-Phillips, K. (1998). Factors influencing health behaviors and drug abuse among low-income Black and Latino women. In C. Wetherington & A. Roman (Eds.), *Drug addiction research and the health of women* (pp. 439–465). Rockville, MD: National Institute on Drug Abuse.

Sisco, C., & Pearson, C. (1994). Prevalence of alcoholism and drug abuse among AFDC recipients. *Health and Social Work, 19,* 75–77.

Smith, D., Buxton, M., Bilal, R., & Seymour, R. (1993). Cultural points of resistance to the 12-step recovery process. *Journal of Psychoactive Drugs, 25,* 97–108.

Straussner, S.L.A., & Zelvin, E. (Eds.). (1997). *Gender and addiction: Men and women in treatment.* Northvale, NJ: Aronson.

Striegel-Moore, R. H. (2000). Recurrent binge eating in Black American women. *Archives of Family Medicine, 9*(1), 83–87.

Substance Abuse and Mental Health Services Administration (SAMHSA). (1999). *National Household Survey on Drug Abuse.* Main findings, 1997. (pp. 99–115). Rockville, MD: Author.

Taylor, J., Henderson, D., & Jackson, B. B. (1991). A holistic model for understanding and predicting depressive symptoms in African-American women. *Journal of Community Psychology, 19,* 306–320.

Terrell, M. D. (1993). Ethnocultural factors in substance abuse: Toward culturally sensitive treatment models. *Psychology of Addictive Behaviors, 7*(3), 162–167.

Thompson, B. W. (1994). *A hunger so wide and so deep: A multiracial view of women's eating problems.* Minneapolis: University of Minnesota Press.

U.S. Bureau of the Census. (1999, March). *Current population survey.* Washington, DC: U.S. Department of Commerce.

Uziel-Miller, N., Lyons, J., Kissiel, C., & Love, S. (1998). Treatment needs and initial outcomes of a residential recovery program for African-American women and their children. *American Journal on Addictions, 7*(1), 43–50.

Walcott-McQuigg, J. A. (1995). The relationship between stress and weight-control behavior in African American women. *Journal of the National Medical Association, 87,* 427–432.

Zambrano, R., Hernandez, M., Dunkel-Schetter, C., & Scrimshaw, S. (1991). Ethnic differences in the substance use patterns of low-income pregnant women. *Family Community Health, 13,* 1–11.

CHAPTER FIFTEEN

LATINAS IN CULTURAL TRANSITION: ADDICTION, TREATMENT, AND RECOVERY

Juana Mora

Latinas are members of one of the fastest-growing segments of the U.S. population, representing nearly half of the thirty-three million Latinos living in the United States. According to U.S. Census projections, Latinos are expected to become the largest ethnic group in the United States (U.S. Bureau of the Census, 2000). Like other women in U.S. society, Latinas are largely working women who raise their children and confront daily economic and cultural challenges as they build their lives and the lives of their children. Latinas are not a homogeneous population; rather, they are ethnically diverse, coming from various Latin and Caribbean cultures. As an individual, every Latina represents her own unique personal history and experience of who she is, where she comes from, why she came to the United States, and how she is adapting to a new culture and society.

For Latinas, U.S. cultural adaptation means that they enter new educational, social, and work arenas and opportunities. Like other women, contemporary Latinas experience the "superwoman" syndrome—the desire to be exceptional in their work and careers, to be good mothers and spouses or partners, and to remain committed to the extended family. The pressures and desires to fulfill expected and new roles can take a toll. Very little support is forthcoming, as Latinas are usually expected to provide the support to others. Because Latinas come from different countries that have their own political and cultural histories, the challenge for those who work in substance abuse and addiction treatment is to explore the variety of personal experiences and histories Latinas bring into treatment in order to best help them confront their addictions and rebuild their lives. The purpose of this chapter is to give a sense of the Latina U.S. experience and of how various aspects of this experience may affect both the development of addictions and the recovery process.

Latinas in the United States: Cultural and Other Forms of Diversity

Latinas represent culturally diverse groups of women who have migrated to the United States from South America, Central America, and the Caribbean. Mexican Americans are the largest of the Latino groups in the United States, representing more than half of all Latinos. The majority of Mexican Americans live in the southern and midwestern United States. The next largest group are Puerto Ricans, who live primarily in or near the New York area, followed by Cubans, who live primarily in the city of Miami, Florida. In some regions, there are growing numbers of Central American and Latin American immigrants. In New York City, Dominican and Colombian immigrants are prominent, and in Los Angeles there are large communities of Guatemalan, Salvadoran, and Nicaraguan immigrants. Although Latinas come from such places as Mexico, Puerto Rico, Cuba, Guatemala, El Salvador, Argentina, and Chile, and experience life from their unique cultural and historical perspective, they share many cultural, linguistic, religious, and family traditions and values. For example, all Latinos share a common language, a largely Catholic upbringing, and a strong belief in the importance of extended family and family connections.

As a group, Latinas are ethnically diverse but also diverse in many other important ways that are relevant to the treatment of addictions. For example, whereas some Latinas have recently immigrated to the United States, a large majority of Latinas are U.S. born or are from Puerto Rico. Many U.S. born Latinas live very different lives compared to more recently immigrated women from Mexico or Central America, who are generally less educated, are primarily Spanish speaking, and tend to work in lower-paying jobs. Women in this latter group are more likely to experience grief, loss, and depression associated with immigration, and stress related to language barriers. They are also more limited in their ability to seek treatment and require targeted outreach and assistance in their native language. Later-generation or U.S. born Latinas are more likely to be English speaking or bilingual and to have various levels of education (Buriel, 1987), and thus may not have the same language barriers as women who have recently immigrated. However, other barriers, including the stigma attached to women addicts in Latino cultures, may prevent these women from seeking treatment.

There are also important and growing differences between U.S. born Latinas who are well educated and have professional careers, and the larger number of U.S. born Latinas who have limited education and generally work in low-wage jobs or experience intermittent employment. In addition, the growing number of adolescent Latinas experience life in the United States under circumstances that are quite different from those of their mothers, aunts, and older sisters. Because of their age and exposure to conflicting cultural expectations, young Latinas are perhaps more vulnerable than older Latinas to substance abuse and addictions.

According to U.S. Census population estimates, there are more than 5.5 million Latina girls under the age of eighteen living in the United States, constituting 15.2 percent of the total number of American girls (Council of Economic Advisers, 1998). Although very little is known about the lifestyles, needs, or aspirations of young Latinas, recent public health data show a growing severity of substance abuse and increased rates of suicide attempts, depression, and unprotected sex among these girls.

Gender, Culture, and Changing Roles in the United States: Impact on Substance Abuse

Latinas experience the same pressures and stressors that other U.S. working and family women encounter in their daily lives. Like other women, many Latinas work outside the home, maintain their own homes, have significant social relationships with men and women, and deal with school systems and the needs of their children. Some life stressors, however, are unique to the Latina U.S. experience, such as the stress of adapting to changes in the role of Latinas in the family and community.

In recent years, the traditional role of Latinas has gone through major modifications as a result of the influence of the women's movement and the large number of Latinas in the labor force (Padilla & Salgado de Snyder, 1995). Nearly half of all Latinas work outside the home (U.S. Bureau of the Census, 1994). The majority work in jobs that involve long working hours and are low paying and difficult. Many Latinas hold more than one job and often are employed in jobs that do not include health care coverage (Quinn, 2000).

In addition to economic pressures, there are intrapsychic stresses that produce guilt and anxiety. For example, like other U.S. women, Latinas have experienced drastic changes in traditional gender role expectations, sanctions, and pressures in the last four decades. In Latino cultures, women are given special roles and are highly respected as the central figures in the extended family networks (Falicov, 1998). Although this special cultural place gives women much prestige and cultural power, it is also a role that requires them to sacrifice their needs for the needs of others. Gender socialization in Latino cultures is reinforced by family and by the Catholic Church. "Good women" are defined as those who care for and nurture others and put their own needs aside for the sake of others (Rodriguez, 1999). These cultural expectations influence the lives of Latinas in ways that are still unexplored. One can ask, for example, Does teaching women to care for others above themselves lead to their developing unhealthy attachments to abusive partners? Can the neglect of the self become a risk more than a virtue and lead to depression and other disorders? These pressures may create an environment in which some Latinas resort to the use of substances either to rebel against these cultural-gender prescriptions or to seek relief from the strain. Latinas in treatment need assistance to unravel the cultural messages that have become detrimental in their lives and to salvage those that empower them and their families. To be effective in helping women with these tasks, the clinician must be extremely knowledgeable and competent with regard to cultural norms and their impact on the female addict.

Because cultural expectations change more slowly than economic needs, many Latinas are expected both to work outside the home yet also to maintain the household, care for the children, and behave like a "respectable" woman in public and the workplace. Latinas experience a high degree of family and spousal pressure because they are not able to maintain their family life at the same level as they could when they were not employed, so they feel that they are failing in their family obligations (Zavella, 1987). Although research shows that Latinas employed outside the home experience guilt and stress, these women also report a high level of satisfaction with their jobs because employment brings economic and social freedom that empowers them personally (Williams, 1990; Zavella, 1987). The power and personal freedom that employment outside the home brings also provides new opportunities for alcohol and tobacco use, as well as the use of some illicit drugs. Personal and economic pressures, combined with more access to alcohol and other drugs, may contribute to greater alcohol- and drug-related problems.

Use of Alcohol, Tobacco, and Other Drugs Among Latinas

When reviewing the epidemiological literature on substance abuse, it is important to look deeper than Hispanic, White, and Black differences. Large-scale, national substance abuse surveys often focus only on these broad groups and fail to examine differences within groups and between men and women. Several recent reports, however, include substance abuse data that compare alcohol, tobacco, and other drug use by Latino subgroups (Cuban, Puerto Rican, Mexican, South

American, and other Latino) and by gender (Substance Abuse and Mental Health Services Administration, 1998; Vega et al., 1998). These studies provide some insights into the Latina groups that might be at greater risk for developing addictions and in need of special outreach and treatment efforts.

Until recently, it was believed that Latinas were unique in their abstinence and freedom from problems related to substance abuse. Because cultural sanctions against women's alcohol use and smoking, particularly in public places, are so strong in Latin America, it was assumed that Latinas who immigrated to the United States maintained these traditional norms and behaviors and resisted the social pressures to use certain substances. In the last decade, however, research has shown that substance abuse patterns, particularly alcohol use, among Latinas are more complex than had been supposed. The most important variations in alcohol and other drug use among Latinas are associated primarily with age and degree of acculturation. That is, second- and third-generation Latinas drink more frequently and use other drugs more often as they become more acculturated into U.S. society, and younger Latinas generally drink and use other drugs more often than older Latinas (Gilbert, 1987).

The majority of substance abuse research among Latinas has focused on alcohol use. For example, an early 1984 national survey of drinking patterns among Latinos in the United States found that although the majority of Latina women in the United States have a higher abstention rate than U.S. women (47 percent as opposed to 36 percent), Mexican American women report more "heavy" drinking (14 percent) than Cuban (7 percent) or Puerto Rican women (5 percent) (Caetano, 1985). In an article published by Gilbert in 1987, she compared abstention and drinking rates of immigrant, second-, and third-generation Mexican American women and women in the U.S. general population. In this review, Gilbert found a high abstention rate among Mexican immigrant women (75 percent) and a lower rate among Mexican women who were U.S. born (38 percent for third-generation women). Third-generation Latinas and women in the general U.S. population exhibit a similar rate of what is considered heavy drinking (12 percent and 13 percent, respectively). Thus, as early as the 1980s, U.S. born Mexican American women were emerging as a group that exhibited high rates of heavy alcohol use.

In more recent surveys, other differences among Latina subgroups have been reported. In 1998, for example, the Substance Abuse and Mental Health Services Administration (SAMHSA) published national substance abuse prevalence data for U.S. racial and ethnic subgroups based on data collected by SAMHSA between 1991 and 1993. This report includes a subgroup and gender analysis of the data, which is presented in the tables that follow in the next sections.

Most large-scale surveys collect substance abuse data based on self-reports of the amount of substances used in the past month or year. They also collect data on self-reports of "heavy" use or "dependence" on a particular substance. In the SAMHSA report, each of these categories has slightly different findings among different groups of Latinas. The highest-risk groups and most indicative of treatment need are those that report heavy use and dependence.

Use of Alcohol

Latinas' rates of alcohol use in the past year, of heavy alcohol use, and of alcohol dependency, in the order of highest to lowest rates, are shown in Table 15.1.

It is interesting to note that although Cuban women are among the top four groups reporting alcohol use in the last year, they are not among those who report heavy alcohol use or dependence. This may reflect the higher economic status of the Cuban American population compared to Mexican American, Puerto Rican, or other Latino immigrants. It is possible, for example, that higher incomes allow Cuban American women to seek counseling and other forms of private care and avoid advancing to more progressive stages of alcohol dependence. Qualitative research that can explore lifestyle differences and substance abuse rates related to income levels would help us understand this difference better.

"Other Latina" women (defined in the report as other than Caribbean, Central American, Cuban, Mexican, Puerto Rican, or South American), however, report a high rate of alcohol use in the last year and the highest rate of heavy alcohol use, and they are second among those who report alcohol dependence. The Mexican women who do drink report the highest level of alcohol dependence.

Based on this study, "Other Latina" and Mexican women have the highest rates of heavy alcohol use and dependence, and consequently need to be targeted for research, outreach, and treatment services.

Table 15.1. RATES OF ALCOHOL USE AND DEPENDENCY (PERCENTAGE).

Alcohol Use in Last Year		Heavy Alcohol Use		Alcohol Dependency	
South American	65.2	Other Latina	2.5	Mexican	2.6
Other Latina	59.7	Mexican	1.7	Other Latina	1.9
Cuban	58.7	Caribbean	1.4	South American	1.8
Puerto Rican	54.1	Puerto Rican	1.2	Puerto Rican	1.6
Mexican	52.5	Cuban	0.8	Central American	0.8
Caribbean	50.2	South American	0.7	Cuban	0.5
Central American	40.3	Central American	0.3	Caribbean	0.3

Source: Data are from *Prevalence of Substance Use Among Racial and Ethnic Subgroups in the United States, 1991–1993,* by the Substance Abuse and Mental Health Services Administration, 1998, Rockville, MD: Department of Health and Human Services.

Use of Cigarettes

Rates of cigarette use in the past year and self-report of smoking one pack or more per day also differ among Latinas. Table 15.2 shows the rates reported, in order from the highest to the lowest.

According to these data, Puerto Rican women are at greatest risk for developing smoking addictions and related health problems. Intervention and smoking cessation programs are needed to reduce these rates in this group of Latinas. Other high-risk groups are Caribbean, Cuban, and South American women.

Use of Illicit Drugs

The SAMHSA data on the use of illicit drugs by Latinas compare use of any illicit drug, marijuana, and cocaine in the past year. Table 15.3 displays the rate in order from the highest to the lowest.

Puerto Rican, Mexican, and "Other Latina" women have the highest rates of reported overall illicit drug use, marijuana use, and cocaine use. These are clearly high-risk groups who are most in need of targeted outreach and treatment efforts.

The data reported here are important because they present trends in the use of various substances across distinct segments of the U.S. Latina population, thus giving us a sense that there are some substances that are more prevalent among certain groups (for example, cocaine among Mexican American women, cigarettes among Puerto Rican women). This information that can be used to develop specialized

Table 15.2. RATES OF CIGARETTE USE (PERCENTAGE).

Cigarette Use in Past Year		One Pack or More per Day	
Puerto Rican	29.3	Puerto Rican	8.9
South American	27.1	Caribbean	4.3
Other Latina	25	Cuban	4.1
Mexican	22	South American	4.0
Cuban	22	Other Latina	2.9
Caribbean	21	Mexican	2.8
Central American	11.4	Central American	1.5

Source: Data are from *Prevalence of Substance Use Among Racial and Ethnic Subgroups in the United States, 1991–1993,* by the Substance Abuse and Mental Health Services Administration, 1998, Rockville, MD: Department of Health and Human Services.

Table 15.3. RATES OF ILLICIT DRUG USE (PERCENTAGE).

Use of Illicit Drugs in Past Year		Use of Marijuana in Past Year		Use of Cocaine in Past Year	
Other Latina	10.7	Other Latina	9.2	Mexican	2.6
Mexican	9.2	Puerto Rican	7.0	Other Latina	1.9
Puerto Rican	9.2	Mexican	5.5	Puerto Rican	1.8
Caribbean	7.1	South American	4.2	South American	1.5
South American	5.8	Cuban	3.7	Caribbean	1.5
Cuban	5.5	Caribbean	3.5	Cuban	0.8
Central American	4.2	Central American	1.5	Central American	0.1

Source: Data are from *Prevalence of Substance Use Among Racial and Ethnic Subgroups in the United States, 1991–1993,* by the Substance Abuse and Mental Health Services Administration, 1998, Rockville, MD: Department of Health and Human Services.

outreach and treatment services to these populations. The data are also important because although the relative rates of use, heavy use, and dependency are small, the data indicate a trend of increased use that needs to be monitored in the future.

Substance Abuse Among Latina Adolescents

The 1999 Youth Risk Behavior Surveillance Survey (YRBSS), conducted by the Centers for Disease Control and Prevention (Kann et al., 2000), includes substance abuse data on Latina girls who are in school. Latina girls who are in school have a higher rate of lifetime cigarette use than non-Latina White girls (71.1 percent versus 70.9 percent) and a higher rate of lifetime alcohol use (84.8 percent versus 82.3 percent). Latina girls also begin drinking at a younger age. According to this report, 30.7 percent of Latina girls began drinking before the age of thirteen, compared to 25.2 percent of non-Latina White girls; Latina girls are also more likely to have tried marijuana before the age of thirteen (8.9 percent versus 6.8 percent). A higher percentage of Latina girls are also more likely than non-Latina White girls to have experimented with cocaine (12.3 percent versus 8.7 percent). Moreover, Latina female students are almost twice as likely as non-Latina White girls to report current use of cocaine (5.4 percent versus 2.8 percent). Latina girls also lead in lifetime use of marijuana, inhalants, methamphetamine, illegal steroids, and heroin.

According to one report, Latina girls are also using LSD, PCP, speed, ecstasy, and mushrooms (COSSMHO Press, 1999). This report identifies acculturative stress and gender role conflicts as factors that may contribute to higher levels of substance abuse, depression, low self-esteem, and eating disorders. Further research is needed to understand the etiology of these disorders for young Latinas within a U.S. and

Latino cultural context. For example, it is important to understand the impact of family pressures to maintain traditions and the external pressures to "Americanize," and the degree to which Latina girls use substances to cope with these pressures.

These data clearly indicate that outreach, education, and treatment targeted to Latina girls are important in order to arrest a trend that is quickly becoming problematic and has the potential to affect future generations of Latinos.

Multiple Risks: Relationships, Age, Culture Change, and Acculturation

Most Latinas living in the United States are truly in transition as they move into a new and rapidly changing culture. Young Latinas are especially vulnerable because they struggle with the desire and expectation to retain aspects of their culture of origin and with pressures to adapt to the new one (COSSMHO Press, 1999). These changes, although at times positive and exciting, are also difficult and can result in personal and family stress and conflict, and ultimately in a greater vulnerability to high-risk substance use and behaviors (Vega & Gil, 1999).

Although it is known that rapid social and cultural change may be a factor in substance use and abuse norms among Latinas, it is unclear what aspects of cultural change create and promote these patterns. A new focus on women's health has shed some light into the social, cultural, and biological vulnerabilities that are unique to women (Center for Substance Abuse Treatment [CSAT], 1995). This work has produced various models and approaches for understanding and treating substance abuse among women. Some of these, such as the relational model as described by Miller (1986) and the risk and resiliency model (Hawkins, Catalano, & Miller, 1992), have some applications to Latinas. Although these models and approaches have some relevance to Latinas, acculturation must also be addressed due to the importance of this concept to the Latina and other immigrant experience.

An important and useful framework for examining the etiology of addictions is one that identifies the risks and protective factors associated with the onset or delay of substance abuse (Hawkins et al., 1992). Research that utilizes this framework, however, has focused more on the risks and less on the protective factors. It is important to understand what aspects of Latinas' lives provide the support and safety net to protect them from developing addictions, and why some women remain resilient in the face of many personal and social obstacles. At this point, however, there is more information about specific risks associated with substance abuse and addiction among Latinas. These risk factors are related to relationships, age, and acculturation.

Relationships

An important emerging area of study and application in treatment settings is the role of personal relationships in the development of addictions among women in general, and Latinas in particular. Research on female addicts has found that relationships, particularly with men, play an important role in the initiation into alcohol and drug use. Men often supply women with drugs, and women use drugs to "get a man," to "keep a man," or to self-medicate to deal with the end of a relationship (Amaro & Hardy-Fanta, 1995). In contrast, relationships with supportive men and women, including parents, extended family, friends, or neighbors, are important for encouraging a woman to seek treatment, supporting her through the treatment, and helping her after treatment. Such relationships are particularly important for Latinas. The help and support of such individuals as an aunt, a grandmother, an uncle, a neighbor, a coworker, or a social service worker can be instrumental in a Latina's treatment program and later recovery. They can help by encouraging the woman to stay in treatment, by assisting her with child care so she can seek treatment, and sometimes even by participating in her treatment program.

Age

Another risk factor associated with greater substance abuse among Latinas is age. As reviewed earlier, studies of teenage drinking show that Latina girls in school are experimenting with alcohol and marijuana at around age thirteen and are more likely to be lifetime users of alcohol and marijuana than are non-Latina White girls (Kann et al., 2000). Overall, then, it isn't surprising that it is the younger generation of Latinas who are most likely to be drinkers and users of other drugs. Given the drinking rates and the increases in the adolescent Latina population, we can project higher treatment needs among future generations of young adult Latinas. In addition, the experience of older Latinas in relation to substance abuse and addictions has not been explored. This is perhaps because older Latinas generally are believed to be nonabusers or because the Latina population overall has been neglected in research. As Latinas grow and age in the population, this will become an important area of study.

Acculturation

The issue that has received the most attention in the research literature and has been associated with increases in alcohol and drug abuse among Latinos in general, and Latinas in particular, is the issue of acculturation. Research on alcohol and drug abuse rates among Latinas has found, for example, that immigration to the United States begins a process that leads to some fascinating changes in Latina women's drinking and drug use behaviors—changes that do not become apparent until the second generation, when acculturation into this society is more advanced (Alaniz, Treno, & Saltz, 1999; Caetano & Medina-Mora, 1988; Gilbert, 1991). In general, immigrant Latinas do not show much of a change in their drinking and drug use habits when they come to the United States. In fact, if anything, they have been found to be more abstinent than the women they leave behind in Latin America (Gilbert, 1987; Vega et al., 1998). This may be explained by the fact that older-generation immigrant women tend to be quite isolated from family and friends and as a result do not have culturally sanctioned opportunities to consume alcohol, even moderately, at family gatherings, and generally do not have access to other illicit drugs.

However, for the second generation—the more acculturated daughters who are born and raised in the United States—the situation is very different. It is among this second generation of Latinas that dramatic changes in drinking and drug use behaviors take place. In the third generation (U.S. born daughters of U.S. born parents), there are even fewer nondrinkers and nonusers of drugs (Alaniz et al., 1999; Gilbert, 1987).

What is it about acculturation that increases the risk among Latinas and reduces the usual resiliency found in this population? In thinking about this subject, we must remember that acculturation is a process that involves giving up some of the customs and ways of thinking that were learned in the culture of origin. Part of acculturation involves experiencing the pain, loss, and grief associated with leaving a country and culture that are familiar and comforting. The grief and pain associated with this loss has intergenerational effects far beyond the immigrant generation, and sometimes it is the second and third generations who exhibit the deleterious effects of this trauma (Falicov, 1998). Although learning the ways of a new culture can be very exciting for some people, for many it is an intimidating process that threatens a familiar and safe core sense of self. For many, learning a new culture means unlearning all that is familiar, and at times individuals may feel disconnected from both cultures. It is this sense of loss, confusion, and fear, part of learning a new culture, that perhaps pushes some Latinas to use alcohol and other drugs as a way of coping with rapid change.

In describing their experiences as Latinas living in the United States, several Chicana and Latina writers have referred to themselves as living in the "borderlands" between two worlds, languages, and sets of customs and expectations, not belonging to one or the other. In her book *Borderlands/La Frontera: The New Mestiza,* Gloria Anzaldua (1987, pp. 2–3) writes about the border of the United States and Mexico as a geographical space as well as a metaphor for her body and life as a "mestiza," Latina woman:

1,950 mile-long open wound,

dividing a pueblo, a culture,

running down the length of my body,

staking fence rods in my flesh,

splits me, splits me,

me raja, me raja,

this is my home

this thin edge of barbwire.

From this perspective, the lives of Latinas represent a border, or the area where two cultures meet and where people of different cultures occupy the same space. A person who inhabits this border space may feel that she or he is not connected to or accepted by either culture. Young Latinos, particularly, often speak of this disconnection and lack of acceptance as they travel across the two borders. For example, family in Mexico may be hostile or may tease a younger member of the family who is being raised in the United States and speaks Spanish with an American accent. In the United States, this same individual may not feel connected to or accepted by the larger society and may be rejected for not speaking English "properly." A border crosser is someone who can occupy both spaces, speak both languages, and live two realities. For some Latinas, this maneuver is difficult. One Latina (Montoya, 1994, p. 185) describes the experience this way:

Because I, a mestiza,

continually walk out of one culture

and into another,

because I am in all cultures at the same time,

a soul between two worlds, three, four,

my head buzzes with the contradictory,

I am disoriented by all the voices

that talk to me simultaneously.

For most addicts, male or female of any culture, becoming addicted to a drug or other substance is a process that results in a loss of spirit, energy, and hope. For many Latina addicts, there may also be a loss of a cultural self through the process of acculturation. In this society, Latinos, particularly youth, receive subtle but strong messages that they will be more successful if they drop everything that might identify them as different, including language, accent, form of dress, sense of family, and spirituality. When one abandons the cultural self, there is a sense of emptiness and falseness that is expressed in the following passage (Montoya, 1994, p. 185):

> I put on my masks, my costumes
> and pose for each occasion. I
> conducted myself well, I think,
> but an emptiness grew that no
> thing could fill. I hungered for
> myself.

Many Latinas maneuver two worlds successfully, but others, particularly young women, do not, and they need support and assistance with this difficult process, particularly in treatment settings. Younger Latinas, particularly those born in the United States to immigrant parents or those who immigrated to the United States at a young age, do not have the benefit of knowing much about their country or culture of origin compared to those who immigrate to the United States at an older age. These young women struggle to understand who they are and where they belong. In a poem titled "I Am from . . .," another young Latina (Araujo, 2000) expresses this dual experience:

> I am from my grandfather's rain forests in Chiapas . . .
> I am from America's white suburbs . . .
> I am from my mother's teachings of Spanish . . .
> I am from being too Mexican for the Americans and too
> American for the Mexicans . . .

A Latina addict will need help unraveling how all the various messages she receives from her culture and the larger society affect her abuse. A competent staff person should identify these obstacles to recovery, and help the client understand how they have hurt her and how to overcome them to achieve sobriety.

◆ ◆ ◆

In addition to relationships, age, and acculturation, there are other risk factors that are also part of the addiction process for Latinas and need further research and attention in treatment settings, including early trauma and sexual abuse, violence, sexual orientation, stressful environments, and racism. Often these are not isolated issues. A Latina may experience multiple traumas that the treatment staff must diagnose and adequately treat.

The Role of Substance Abuse and Other Addictions in the Lives of Latinas

Like other disorders, an addiction to alcohol, a prescription drug, an illegal drug, tobacco, or food can develop for a variety of reasons. The etiology of substance abuse has not been studied for Latinas; therefore, the following discussion and examples are based on my own work in community-based treatment settings and federally funded treatment programs for women and their children.

Some Latinas depend on a particular substance to cope with the stress associated with rapid cultural change and adaptation. An example might be a young Latina who privately turns to alcohol to cope with the stress associated with the pressures she feels as the oldest of a large immigrant family. As the eldest child in her family, she carries the weight of the many expectations placed on her; she wants to live up to them, but it is difficult for her to fulfill her role, because in this new culture there are more options open to her. She knows other women who have the freedom and opportunity to pursue their dreams. They may be working to save money so that they can attend college, or they may be in college.

In this context, cultural rules and options are changing rapidly for this young girl, but her parents and elders want to maintain a strong hold on traditions with which they were raised and traditions that they feel are the "right" ones for their family (Falicov, 1998; Rodriguez, 1999). The following case example illustrates some aspects of this dilemma.

Adela

Adela is a high school student who is the oldest of nine children. She works after school to help her family. They live on a farm where her father works. Many times, however, he does not work because he is an alcoholic, and his drinking is now interfering with his work. Adela is referred to a counseling center by her school counselor because she is having problems in school and has also started to drink. Adela's counselor finds a young girl under tremendous pressure to do well in school, to help her family financially, and to remain a virgin until she marries. Adela is angry at her father for his alcoholism and because he is sometimes mean and rough with her mother and siblings. She wants to do well in school and go to college so that she can help her family get out of the situation they are in. She is smart and wants to study psychology. She is finding it harder and harder to abstain from sex so that she can marry in white as her family expects her to do. When she is with her boyfriend, she drinks in order to engage in sexual activities and later tells herself that she could not help herself because she was under the influence of alcohol. She feels that if she engages in sex while sober and uses contraceptives, she is betraying her family and traditions and becoming "Americanized" like the White girls in school who use contraceptives and have sex. She is very confused and is beginning to drink more as she thinks about her options and choices.

This young girl could eventually be expected to drop out of school to work and help the family, to delay marriage, and to deny her own needs. Her drinking will probably get worse because she has an internal life and feelings that are not allowed to be expressed or resolved. And she feels tremendous guilt for having her own needs and desires while her family is suffering from poverty, the father's alcoholism, and other family problems.

A woman also may begin to use a substance in order to keep a relationship with a partner who uses, or to deal with the loss of a relationship. The following case example illustrates the effects of loss:

Dolores

Dolores is a young woman who was raised to aspire to marriage and a family. She marries a man who is financially well off and owns a restaurant. Dolores feels neglected and lonely much of the time because her husband spends lots of time at the restaurant. She begins to drink privately at home while he is at work. Over the years, she has several children, thinking that this will make her feel better, yet her drinking continues. She begins to drink in public and embarrasses her husband. He divorces her and takes custody of the children. Dolores is devastated and drinks even more to cope with the loss and the guilt. Her family and his family blame her because she did not exhibit the "traditional and proper" behaviors expected of a wife and mother. Eventually, she is rejected by everyone and decides to leave the state.

Many Latinas who divorce do so against extreme cultural pressure. They are often pressured by family members to stay married even if the marriage is abusive. When a Latina divorces, she may be temporarily isolated from family and may be criticized if she begins to date other men. Under these circumstances, alcohol use may be one way to deal with the shame, pain, frustration, and isolation that divorce brings to a Latina woman.

Some Latinas may use drugs to cope with the loneliness and stress associated with demanding work and careers, or the pain of childhood trauma and sexual abuse. In the case of Latinas who experience childhood sexual abuse, the shame is so deep and the family denial so strong that these women often have few options for dealing with this pain and often resort to alcohol or drug abuse. The following examples illustrate these issues:

Career and Stress: The Case of Alicia

Alicia is an executive with a major television network. She works long hours, lives alone, and has little time for personal relationships. She had had to move in order to pursue this career, so her family lives outside the state. Her main relationships are with coworkers, with whom she drinks to cope with the stress and loneliness of the job. Alicia has recently become concerned because she is now drinking more and more at home alone and late at night. This is affecting her life; she feels more tired and is less effective at work. She does not know what to do.

Sexual Abuse: The Case of Rita

Rita is a Latina with a B.A. in public administration. She grew up in a large city as one of the middle children of a large, poor, working-class immigrant family. Rita is very smart; she excelled in high school and got into college. When Rita was in college, she ended up in counseling because she was having problems with school, drinking too much, and feeling depressed a lot. In counseling she admitted to herself and her counselor that she was a victim of incest. Her father had molested her for several years during her childhood. She felt very guilty and angry. She was angry at her father for the molestation and at her mother for allowing it to happen.

After several years of counseling, Rita decides to tell the family about the abuse and to press charges against her father. When she does this, her entire extended family gets mad at her: they think she is not being loyal to her father and that she is breaking up the family. Her father finally leaves the country, and her family slowly comes to understand her motives. This is an issue that Rita continues to work on with her family as well as in her own recovery.

Healing Through Treatment and Recovery: Regaining Culture and Spirit

Substance abuse and other addiction treatment programs differ in philosophy, approach, setting, and duration (U.S. Department of Health and Human Services [USDHHS], 1995). Some programs are brief and use a confrontational mode of therapy; others are longer in duration (for example, six months to one year) and use therapeutic community approaches in which the individuals in treatment take leadership roles in the therapeutic setting. Very few treatment approaches or philosophies have been applied and tested in relation to their effectiveness for Latinas. However, over several decades, federally funded treatment programs for women and their children have demonstrated that there are some essential elements necessary for the effective treatment of substance abuse among women. To a large extent, these gender-based strategies for treatment, combined with culturally competent staff and strategies, can form the basis of effective treatment programs for Latina addicts.

Effective substance abuse treatment involves a continuum of care that includes outreach, intake and assessment, diagnosis, treatment planning, detoxification, residential or outpatient care, relapse prevention, life skills development, discharge, and aftercare (USDHHS, 1995). Substance abuse treatment for women also requires the provision of child care, transportation, medical care, testing and screening for HIV and other sexually transmitted diseases, reproductive health care, parent education and training, sexual abuse and domestic violence counseling, and other forms of support to help women and their children recover from addictions (CSAT, 1995).

Some treatment philosophies and approaches are more consistent with Latino cultural norms than others. These, as well as selected essential elements for the effective treatment of Latina addicts, are briefly outlined and discussed in the next sections.

Treatment Philosophy

There are various philosophical frameworks and models available in the substance abuse treatment field, including the social model, the therapeutic community model, feminist and gender-based models, and medical, self-help, and cultural models (CSAT, 1995). Usually a program will adopt a philosophy consistent with that of the executive director or the board of directors. For a Latina, a program philosophy that supports her personal growth and empowerment within a cultural and family context will most likely retain her in the program and thus have a greater possibility of being effective. For example, a program that provides opportunities for Latinas to identify and express their feelings, develop their language and job skills, and learn how to attain sobriety—all provided by other Latinas or women who understand the Latina experience and bring cultural and family issues into treatment—has a better chance of retaining these women in treatment.

Treatment Approach

For Latinas, a recommended approach to the treatment of substance abuse is a combination of *empowerment* and *regaining culture* approaches. An empowerment approach to the treatment of Latinas includes services that encourage and promote internal and external power and strength. This can include basic assertiveness training as well as teaching English and job skills.

An empowerment approach is recommended because Latinas, like other women of color in this society and in their own cultures, are socialized to be unempowered and not to have a voice or sense of self. According to mental health experts and practitioners, women of color who come into treatment for mental health have spent so little time in their lives focusing on their own needs rather than those of others that they are often unaware of what their needs are and cannot easily express them (Comas-Diaz, 1994). Often, as stated earlier, traditional cultural gender expectations, combined with dominant cultural pressures to be assertive in order to succeed, sometimes clash and force these women to confront role expectations. A gifted and trained program staff can work with Latinas on a daily basis to help them find their voices, slowly identify and express their feelings, and ultimately gain more control of their lives and the lives of their children. In addition, support groups are extremely helpful for Latinas' positive development because in these settings they can learn positive coping skills and learn, perhaps for the first time, to trust someone outside the family.

Part of empowering Latinas includes helping them find strength and beauty in their cultural background—a sense that perhaps is lost in the process of acculturation. Again, this approach requires highly skilled staff, because some Latinas, particularly third- or fourth-generation women, may not be in touch with their cultural identity and background and may experience anger at the staff for raising the issue. These women have internalized the messages told to them as they grew up: it is not OK to speak Spanish or to be Mexican, and it is best to deny your culture and become "American" as soon as possible. However, a skilled practitioner can find ways to educate these women about the meaning and roots of such internalized racism to help them regain strength and spirit in their cultural and familial roots. When this is done successfully, clients take cultural values and traditions back into themselves, usually with much joy and curiosity, and through these the women gain a depth of internal power that helps them live a life without drugs.

Outreach

Outreach is an important element of treating substance abuse among Latinas, because many are still highly stigmatized by this problem and are not self-motivated to seek treatment. Thus, targeted outreach efforts by other Latinas are necessary to encourage Latinas to step forward and seek treatment. Latinas need to know that there is a "safe" place where they can seek basic assistance with this problem. A safe place for Latinas is a family-like environment where they will be accepted and not judged, where they and their children will be greeted warmly by other

Latinas and in their own language. It is important that more than the front-office staff speak Spanish—the language must permeate the premises and the environment. This will help with the recruitment and retention of Latina clients. In my experience in treatment settings, when a Latina, even if she is third or fourth generation, enters a facility where her background is reflected in familiar family-like surroundings and where she hears Spanish used freely, she will perceive such an environment as accepting of her and her culture, and she will be more likely to stay in treatment.

In Latino communities, outreach is most effective if it is done person-to-person and less effective if it relies too much on written or other less personal forms of communication. The reason for this is twofold: first, literacy levels may vary in some Latino communities, and thus families may rely more on friends and neighbors for information; second, Latino cultures are oriented toward personal contact and relationships, which are perceived to be more reliable and gratifying than written forms of communication (Falicov, 1998; Rodriguez, 1999). To begin community outreach efforts, it is best to hire a person who can visit Head Start centers, community-based organizations, faith-based groups, and local events, and through word of mouth inform the community about the program and its services.

Effective treatment programs in Latino communities need to link with other community groups and organizations in health, education, housing, and the legal system to build credibility and cross-referral networks. For example, the most "popular" programs in Latino communities are those that are connected to other programs and work together to provide the best support to individuals and families. Important connections can and should be made with local parishes, health clinics, and employment and education institutions.

Child Care and Transportation

Child care and a "children are welcome" attitude at the program facility, whether it is outpatient or residential, are crucial for forming long-lasting bonds with Latina clients and for retention. The provision of transportation, whether via van pickup or cab or bus vouchers, is extremely important because many Latinas do not have access to transportation.

Intake, Assessment, and Diagnosis

Because so few treatment programs have been developed for Latinas, intake, assessment, and diagnosis procedures for this population have not been perfected. Currently, in treatment programs that happen to recruit one or two Latina clients or residents who are primarily Spanish speaking, staff may translate intake and assessment forms designed for the general population. When this occurs, or when intake forms used for the general population are applied to an English-speaking Latina, there may be some areas unique to the Latina experience, such as her extended family networks or immigration history, that will not be properly assessed. These areas may prove to be important for understanding the woman's addiction and for treatment planning.

Some programs that are beginning to serve Latinas with substance abuse problems have reported to me that Latinas will not divulge substance abuse histories at the time of intake. Because Latinas have traditionally not sought help or treatment outside the family, Latinas in treatment may be more reticent to open up or share their histories until after they get to know the program staff.

Through the work that has been done in the last two decades with female addicts, we have learned that women who are addicted often enter treatment presenting with several mental health or psychiatric disorders in addition to the addiction to drugs. This pattern is likely to be the same for Latinas in treatment, as there is evidence from the mental health literature that Latinas suffer from disproportionate levels of depression (Vega et al., 1998). Thus, when treatment programs are developed to serve Latinas, diagnosis and treatment of mental health disorders should be incorporated into the overall treatment plan.

Outpatient Treatment

Outpatient care usually consists of various forms of individual, group, or family counseling at a treatment center or facility. Outpatient care is best suited for women whose addiction is not yet severe enough to require inpatient, residential care but who can benefit from weekly contact with a treatment professional. A Latina is much more likely to utilize outpatient care than residential care because outpatient treatment does not require her to leave her family or home environment. Outpatient programs also need to develop outreach and treatment approaches that are culturally appropriate, hire licensed counselors who are Latina or who are competent in the Latina experience, and provide services that are consistent with the risk factors unique to Latinas (as outlined earlier). In addition, family involvement in treatment and in the recovery process can be very useful for the long-term sobriety of Latina addicts. Sometimes, however, the family is resistant, particularly if there is much denial. Family members may not be willing to accept that a family member, particularly a female member, has a substance abuse problem because it means that they too may have to change their alcohol or drug use. When family members refuse to participate or support a Latina in substance abuse treatment, the counselor must work closely with the client to help her accept their decision. Over time, the counselor can also help the client understand that she must develop other supportive relationships that at times may substitute for a family that is absent in her life.

Detoxification and Residential Care

The most expensive, but perhaps the most effective, treatment, particularly for difficult and severe addictions, is long-term (six- to twelve-month) comprehensive residential care. Residential treatment programs for women often function as small, family-like households and communities of women, their children, and a community of staff. The women and their children live in these settings for months at a time and engage in individual, group, and family counseling and in parenting training and education. Learning how to live sober and to prevent relapse is an important element of these programs.

Many Latinas may be reluctant to seek residential treatment because it will take them away from their spouse, partner, family, or children. Residential treatment for women that includes residential space and educational child care for children is most desirable and can be a draw for women to seek treatment. The more effective residential programs are well linked with other community resources and provide case management for the women and children to help with legal, educational, job training, health, housing, and other support systems. When possible, health care is provided on-site for the women and children, including medical detoxification services when the women first enter the program. Comprehensive residential programs aim to change the women's lives, treat their addictions, and help them through life skills training to go out into the community and maintain a drug-free life. Therefore, life skills training, including assertiveness training, anger management, and specific job training, is usually part of the overall goals of residential care. For Latinas, this may also include English language training.

Publicly funded comprehensive residential treatment programs that provide an array of services are most effective and are desirable for the treatment of addiction among Latinas, who, like other women in treatment, tend to have multiple problems and needs. Most come to these programs not only with a substance abuse problem but also with a need for health care, education, job training, legal assistance, and mental health treatment.

Twelve-Step Groups and Programs

Twelve-step groups and programs are extremely popular and have worked for many individuals in Mexico and other Latin American countries. There are twelve-step groups available in most Latin American countries; in Mexico alone there are nearly thirteen thousand Alcoholics Anonymous groups (Alcoholics

Anonymous, 2001). Twelve-step meetings in English and Spanish can be an important support for Latinas in either outpatient or residential treatment and are an important supplement to the treatment program. For Latinas, the "fellowship" environment and the focus on spirituality in these self-help groups are consistent with cultural views and traditions. They are also useful to Latinas as lifelong sources of support following the completion of formal treatment.

Discharge and Continuing Care

Residential treatment programs are more likely to offer discharge planning and continuing care. Discharge planning begins several months before the woman leaves the program and helps her apply for various jobs, enroll the children in appropriate educational settings, and plan for where she and her children will live if she does not have a home to return to. Continuing care can take various forms, including an "alumni" group of women who return to the facility once a week and who serve as a support network in the community (CSAT, 1995). Social networks—particularly with other women, such as godmothers or "comadres," sisters, aunts, and other elder women—are an important part of Latino culture (Rodriguez, 1999). Thus, the establishment of new networks of sober women who have similar experiences can be very effective for maintaining long-term sobriety and recovery for Latinas.

The Case of Diana: A Latina Addict's Journey

Diana was a twenty-one-year-old undergraduate student, the first in her family to attend college. Diana had dark hair and dark skin. When she arrived at college, she felt different and alone. This college was located in a beach town, and many of the students were blond, carefree, and wealthy. Diana's family was not wealthy. She was one of nine children, and her parents were farmworkers. Her family did not understand her desire to go far away from the family to attend college, and Diana felt isolated from them.

Over time, she felt overwhelmed with the amount of schoolwork, and she was not prepared to compete with students of privileged backgrounds. She felt less prepared academically than them. Diana also began questioning her sexuality. She grew up hearing horrendous stories of domestic violence from her *tias* (aunts) and wanted no part of that. She was lonely and began to hang out with a group of lesbian White women who partied and drank a lot. She found that the White lesbian women also felt like outsiders, and she felt accepted by them. She also found that she could outdrink many of the women she partied with. Her body at first had a high tolerance for alcohol. But after almost four years of heavy partying, she ended up in the hospital. Her doctor told her she had to stop drinking or she would die. Her liver was damaged. The doctor helped Diana enroll in a six-week treatment program, where she learned that her alcoholism had advanced quickly because of her family predisposition to addictions—she had a sibling who was a heroin addict.

As one of two Latinas in the program, she felt uncomfortable, but was open to learning about her illness. In the program, she also learned that she drank to cope with her feelings of loneliness, her sense of not belonging as a dark Latina in a White environment. She began to examine her sexuality. The program was brief, but it gave her a base of knowledge about her alcoholism and addiction and also introduced her to self-help programs, where she continued to pursue her sobriety after she left the program. Diana has now been sober for twenty years.

Conclusion

Substance abuse and other forms of addiction are increasing in the Latina population, particularly among young Latinas. As Latinas grow in numbers and become more prominent in social, political, criminal justice, and educational arenas, it will become imperative that effective outreach and treatment efforts be developed to treat these addictions. These programs should be accessible, and staffed by culturally competent women who understand the diverse life experiences and backgrounds that Latinas will bring to treatment. The programs also need to attend to how acculturation and culture change, conflicting role expectations, sexual abuse, family history, and relationships with men and women contribute to the development of addictions among Latinas. This knowledge can then be used to fashion recovery programs that are long lasting and life changing.

References

Alaniz, M. L., Treno, A. J., & Saltz, R. F. (1999). Gender, acculturation and alcohol among Mexican Americans. *Journal of Substance Use and Abuse, 34,* 1407–1426.

Alcoholics Anonymous. (2001). Available at: www.alcoholicsanonymous.org

Amaro, H., & Hardy-Fanta, C. (1995). Gender relations in addiction and recovery. *Journal of Psychoactive Drugs, 27,* 325–337.

Anzaldua, G. (1987). *Borderlands/la frontera: The new mestiza.* San Francisco: Spinsters/Aunt Lute Press.

Araujo, O. (2000, March). "I am from . . ." Poem presented at the HOPE Education and Leadership Fund Ninth Annual Symposium, Los Angeles.

Buriel, R. (1987). Ethnic labeling and identity among Mexican Americans. In J. S. Phinney & M. J. Rotherman (Eds.), *Children's ethnic socialization: Pluralism and development* (pp. 134–152). Thousand Oaks, CA: Sage.

Caetano, R. (1985). Drinking patterns and alcohol problems in a national sample of U.S.

Hispanics. In D. Spiegler, D. Tate, S. Aiken, & C. Christian (Eds.), *Alcohol use among U.S. ethnic minorities* (Research Monograph No. 18, National Institute on Alcohol Abuse and Alcoholism, DHHS Publication No. ADM 89-1435, pp. 147–162). Washington, DC: U.S. Government Printing Office.

Caetano, R., & Medina-Mora, M. (1988). Acculturation and drinking among people of Mexican descent in Mexico and the United States. *Journal of Studies on Alcohol, 49,* 462–471.

Center for Substance Abuse Treatment (CSAT). (1995). *Practical approaches in the treatment of women who abuse alcohol and other drugs.* Rockville, MD: Department of Health and Human Services.

Comas-Diaz, L. (1994). Introduction. *Women of color: Integrating ethnic and gender identities in psychotherapy.* New York: Guilford Press.

COSSMHO Press. (1999). *The state of Hispanic girls.* Washington, DC: COSSMHO Press. Available at: www.cossmho.org.

Council of Economic Advisors. (1998). *Changing America: Indicators of social and economic well-being by race and Hispanic origin.* Washington, DC: U.S. Government Printing Office.

Falicov, C. J. (1998). *Latino families in therapy: A guide to multicultural practice.* New York: Guilford Press.

Gilbert, M. J. (1987). Alcohol consumption patterns in immigrant and later generation Mexican American women. *Hispanic Journal of the Behavioral Sciences, 9,* 299–313.

Gilbert, M. J. (1991). Acculturation and changes in drinking patterns among Mexican American women: Implications for prevention. *Alcohol Health and Research World, 15,* 234–238.

Hawkins, J. D., Catalano, R. F., & Miller, J. Y. (1992). Risk and protective factors for alcohol and other drug problems in adolescence and early adulthood: Implications for substance abuse prevention. *Psychological Bulletin, 112*(1), 64–105.

Kann, L., Kinchen, S., Williams, B., Goss, J., Grunbaum, J., Kolbe, L., & Lowry, R. (2000). *Youth Risk Behavior Surveillance Survey, United States, 1999.* Atlanta, GA: Centers for Disease Control and Prevention.

Miller, J. B. (1986). *Toward a new psychology of women.* Boston: Beacon Press.

Montoya, M. E. (1994). Mascaras, trenzas, y grenas: Un/masking the self while un/braiding Latina stories and legal discourse. *Harvard Women's Law Journal, 17,* 185–220.

Padilla, A. M., & Salgado de Snyder, N. V. (1995). Hispanics: What the culturally informed evaluator needs to know. In M. A. Orlandi, R. Weston, & L. G. Epstein (Eds.), *Cultural competency for evaluators: A guide for alcohol and other drug abuse prevention practitioners working with ethnic/racial communities* (Center for Substance Abuse Prevention Cultural Competence Series, Vol. 1, pp. 117–146). Rockville, MD: Department of Health & Human Services, Public Health Series.

Quinn, K. (2000). *Working without benefits: The health insurance crisis confronting Hispanic Americans.* New York: Commonwealth Fund.

Rodriguez, G. (1999). *Raising nuestros ninos in a bicultural world.* New York: Fireside Books.

Substance Abuse and Mental Health Services Administration. (1998). *Prevalence of substance use among racial and ethnic subgroups in the United States, 1991–1993.* Rockville, MD: Department of Health and Human Services.

U.S. Bureau of the Census. (1994). *The nation's Hispanic population—1994.* Washington, DC: U.S. Department of Commerce.

U.S. Bureau of the Census. (2000). *Resident population estimates of the United States by sex, race and*

Hispanic origin: April 1, 1990–July 1, 1999. Washington, DC: U.S. Department of Commerce.

U.S. Department of Health and Human Services. (1995). *White paper: Effectiveness of substance abuse treatment.* Washington, DC: Center for Substance Abuse Treatment.

Vega, W. A., & Gil, A. (1999). A model for explaining drug use behavior among Hispanic adolescents. *Drugs and Society, 14*(1/2), 57–74.

Vega, W. A., Kolody, B., Aguilar-Gaxiola, S., Alderete, E., Catalano, R., Caraveo-Anduaga, J. (1998). Lifetime prevalence of DSM-III-R psychiatric disorders among urban and rural Mexican Americans in California. *Archives of General Psychiatry, 55,* 771–778.

Williams, N. (1990). *The Mexican American family: Tradition and change.* Dix Hills, NY: General Hall Press.

Zavella, P. (1987). *Women's work and Chicano families: Cannery workers of the Santa Clara Valley.* Ithaca, NY: Cornell University Press.

CHAPTER SIXTEEN

ASIAN AND PACIFIC ISLANDER WOMEN AND ADDICTION

Kerrily J. Kitano and Liane J. Louie

Asian and Pacific Islander (API) Americans are the most diverse and fastest-growing minority group in the United States. In 1995, the API population reached 9.5 million and is expected to surpass 30 million by the year 2050 (Andersen, 1996). According to the U.S. Census, the API category comprises over forty separate ethnic groups, many with distinct languages and dialects, all with unique cultures and customs.

Analyzing aggregate data regarding APIs obscures the disparities between specific ethnic groups. For example, if one were to look at median income, APIs as a whole appear to have achieved parity with whites. However, closer scrutiny reveals that API families have more wage earners contributing to household income, that there is a high prevalence of poverty among some API subgroups despite the higher median income, and that there the relationship between education and income is not what one would expect (Sue & Sue, 1990). Age, immigration status, and educational levels are also wide ranging among API ethnic groups.

The popular stereotype of Asians as the "model minority," the highly successful immigrant, is pervasive. This myth has created division among other minority groups who have been criticized for not living up to the same standards. It has also served to disguise the existence of a host of social problems that Asians face in the United States. Pacific Islanders, by contrast, do not fit the image of a successful model minority in the continental United States and in fact report disproportionate rates of poverty (Barringer, Gardner, & Levin, 1993). Asians and

Pacific Islanders are invisible in the United States. Grouping them together further obscures any distinction between the unique and complex picture of their problems with addiction.

Asian American women have been cast in several polarized stereotypes over the years. They have been depicted as sneaky and loyal, promiscuous and sexless, evil and obedient, opium-addicted and abstinent, controlling and submissive. They are dragon ladies, China dolls, goody-goodies (Fung, 1991; Tajima, 1989), and "sexless worker bees" (Homma-True, 1990, p. 479). Representations of Pacific Islander women have been limited to those of sensual, naked women who are eager to accommodate mainland men. All these images fail to capture the multi-faceted nature of API women and serve to oversimplify the intricacies of their lives. Further, these stereotypes affect how individuals who are not exposed to API women view them, how API women see themselves, and how they see themselves in relation to others.

Despite the shallow portrayal of API women in the dominant culture and their invisibility in the addiction world, they do indeed exist. In this chapter, we will identify patterns of addiction among Asian American and Pacific Islander women, identify cultural and familial factors that protect women from and contribute to risk of substance abuse, discuss limitations of current assessment tools and treatment modalities, and provide recommendations as to the best treatment approaches for this population. The chapter also creates a historical and cultural context through which to explore the complexity of addiction with regard to API women.

Historical Background

The history of API women in the United States is invariably connected to family. Asian women largely came into this country as mothers, daughters, wives, picture brides, war brides, and refugees. As did Pacific Islander women, they stood alongside their husbands, fathers, and children as their families were excluded, interned, colonized, and conquered. Large numbers of Asian women also came into the United States through the exploitation of men: as prostitutes, domestic servants, and mail-order brides.

China

Few women accompanied the early Chinese male sojourners. Traveling was dangerous for them; the long voyage by sea was rigorous, and there were reports of sexual molestation by sailors. In 1850, there were a reported 7 Chinese women to 4,018 Chinese men in San Francisco, growing to 1,784 women and 33,149 men a decade later (Yung, 1986). The predominantly "bachelor" community was beset by problems common to societies dominated by males, including prostitution, gambling, violence, and drug use (Glenn, 1986).

Economic conditions in China, in conjunction with the devaluation of women in the culture, led desperately poor parents to sell their daughters for as little as $70 to $150. Many other women were kidnapped, lured under false pretenses, and purchased as part of a lucrative prostitution trade. The women, ranging in age from sixteen to twenty-five, were stripped for inspection, sold to the highest bidder, and then forced into prostitution. They were subject to physical, mental, and sexual abuse, and most could not possibly outlive their contracts. They essentially were slaves and usually did not survive longer than six years. Their only hope for escape was at the hands of a wealthy client, a rare occurrence. Typically these women ended their lives diseased, discarded in the street, and left to die. Suicide or madness was the only other way out of their misery (Yung, 1986).

Japan

A loophole in the "Gentleman's Agreement" of 1907–1908 brought the arrival of more than twenty thousand Japanese "picture brides" in the early 1900s. They came to marry Japanese men with whom they had only exchanged pictures through the mail. This first generation of women, the *issei*, lived hard lives; they were at the mercy of their husbands and subject to the mores of their new country, where they were unable to become citizens. Severely affected by intense racism and sexism, they toiled daily, subordinating their own needs and wants for the sake of their children and future generations (Nakano, 1990). Their initial hopes and dreams of living a rich life or even a remotely better life than the one they had left behind were shattered with the internment of 110,000 Japanese Americans during World War II for the "crime" of being of Japanese ancestry. The fatalistic cultural belief *shikata ga nai*, that things cannot be changed, helped them through the drudgery and disillusionment of their lives.

The Philippines

Although the Philippines is a country of skilled and educated laborers and a wealth of natural resources (gold and copper), the economy has not overcome governmental corruption, the failure of land reform, and huge foreign debt. The $30 billion foreign debt has caused oppression, underdevelopment, a brain drain, and the exploitation of women (Glodava & Onizuka, 1994). Filipina women have become "the domestic servants of the world," as maids overseas in many countries, supporting the families they have left behind in their homeland. Countless

Filipinas are hired to work abroad as "entertainers" and find themselves tricked into prostitution, an issue just receiving global attention (Glodava & Onizuka, 1994; Krich, 1986).

Another consequence of the extreme poverty in the Philippines is the exploitation of women as so-called mail-order brides, a multimillion-dollar business playing on the economic desperation of Third World women. The stereotype of Asian women as passive, obedient, erotic creatures plays perfectly into the business scheme. The men who "purchase" brides from such companies as Cherry Blossoms, Lotus Blossoms, Pearls of the Orient, and the like are typically White, older, politically conservative, and socially alienated. Because the man "bought" his wife, he feels that he owns her; because of his advanced age, he is also striving to obtain a "live-in nurse" (Kim, 1984). Over 50 percent of mail-order brides come from the Philippines, but they also come in large numbers from such countries as Thailand, Indonesia, Malaysia, India, and Pakistan (Glodava & Onizuka, 1994).

Korea

Over forty thousand "war brides" arrived in the United States between 1952 and 1982 under the "second wave" of Korean immigration (Min, 1988). As wives of White American servicemen, they were an invisible minority clustered around army bases. They knew that by marrying a non-Asian man they would experience some degree of alienation and ultimate separation from their parents and kin, but they didn't know to what extent or what fully to expect (Glenn, 1986). A study of these women conducted by Bok-Lim Kim (1980) reports that Korean war brides suffered from culture shock, lack of education, isolation, problems with communication, alienation, physical abuse, suicide, attempted suicide, and high divorce rates. Korean wives were marginal both to the dominant culture and to the Korean community (Kitano & Daniels, 1995; Kim, 1980). Japanese and Filipina war brides were also numerous during this time period and endured similar hardships.

Southeast Asia

The first group of Southeast Asian refugees to arrive in the United States was from the relatively "privileged" class, who were fearful that their lifestyles would be targets of the communists. The second group arrived in 1975 following the fall of Saigon. Many of this group suffered from posttraumatic stress, having witnessed wartime atrocities perpetrated against their countrymen and loved ones and having themselves been raped and subjected to other terrors. After enduring numerous traumas, these refugees were then faced with living in a state of limbo in holding camps in countries of "first asylum," marked by tremendous uncertainty for an indeterminate time.

Refugees differ from voluntary migrants in that they leave their homelands against their will with no personal desire to settle anywhere else (Bousquet, 1987). When they are finally accepted into a new country for long-term resettlement, they are received by "hosts" who commonly exude a sense of cultural superiority and to whom the refugees respond with childlike deference (Schein, 1987). This kind of experience served only as a starting point for a long, painful, and difficult adjustment period for thousands of Vietnamese, ethnic Chinese, Hmong, and Cambodian women.

The Pacific Islands

The Pacific Island nations were colonized and occupied by the United States and, in the case of Hawaii, invaded and stolen. Hawaii was a thriving culture with a population of over three hundred thousand in 1778, which was decimated to fifty-seven thousand after its first hundred years of contact with White people. Native peoples lost their independence and identities, as well as their land (Trask, 1990).

◆ ◆ ◆

These historical vignettes depict the varying climates from which API women came and began their new lives in the United States. The women shared many commonalities, however, with hardship as their dominant theme. Although these women hoped for much, they expected and received little. Many were exploited until they perished, but others endured and survived with impressive resilience and strength. Their stories of early arrival mark only the beginning of the difficulty and diversity of API women's experiences in the United States.

Impact of Addiction Problems

There is scant research documenting the prevalence of addiction in API women, but clinical experience reveals that they have substance abuse disorders, eating disorders, gambling problems, and other addictive behaviors like anyone else. The inability to identify addictive behavior in these women, denial of addiction, lack of access to culturally competent resources, and a cultural proclivity to hide their difficulties have ensured the invisibility of these problems and allowed them to go unrecognized and untreated. The imperceptibility of their problems combined with the marginal status of API women are responsible for the lack of attention and focus given to these women. There are no philosophical frameworks or academic theories, treatment modalities, or assessment tools developed with API women in mind. Thus such questions as Why do these women use, whereas other API women do not? and How best can we treat them? remain unexplored areas.

API women differ in their degree of knowledge of addiction and health issues. Most are unaware of problems associated with addictive behaviors. This lack of knowledge of risk factors and preventive behaviors may explain why so few seek attention to screen for or assess addictive behavior and why so few seek treatment. Through ignorance about the existence and dangers of addiction, and the denial of addiction, API women often overlook symptoms and may fail to seek help until problems are so severe that the individual or family is incapacitated, hospitalization is required, or there is a suicide (Ja & Aoki, 1993).

Because many API immigrant women are unable to communicate in English, their vocational and employment opportunities are substantially limited. This creates significant dependence on their partners, husbands, and families, both financially and socially. Even if an addiction problem is identified for treatment, the lack of support from the woman's family creates yet stronger barriers to seeking or receiving treatment. Going to treatment is viewed as a self-indulgent luxury that takes away from familial responsibilities, causing disruption to the whole family unit. In addition, API immigrant women are financially impoverished and have the second-highest uninsured rates (28 percent) among women, behind Latinas (35 percent) (Jang & Penserga, 1999). Taking off time from work for treatment is not something that their economic realities will allow.

Access to treatment is worsened by a complex set of cultural, linguistic, structural, and financial barriers to care (Office of Women's Health, 2000). Existing resources that do not have the capacity to communicate in the women's native language simply cannot provide adequate services. These issues are even further complicated for those living illegally in the United States. These women may fear the use of such public services as clinics, mental health centers, or substance abuse treatment programs, because they believe that they may be deported or that the unwanted attention might create immigration difficulties. Although they may recognize the need for treatment, they will not seek help because of these fears.

Traditional Asian American values include the concept of shame, which serves to reinforce familial expectations; "loss of face" if an individual behaves "improperly"; and a belief in fatalism, that things are as they are and that no one has the ability to control or change events. An individual's behavior is seen as a reflection on the entire family and, to an extent, the community (Ja & Aoki, 1993; Ho, 1983; Ohnuki-Tierney, 1984). Thus, open admission of addiction by an API woman is rare because of the shame she feels, the loss of face that it brings to her and to her family, and the perceived condemnation she feels from the "outside."

Furthermore, families may discourage her from seeking treatment, in part due to the lack of understanding of addiction and to a larger extent due to the embarrassment brought to the entire family. Some addicted API women report feelings of deep guilt or even betrayal for seeking outside help, because they know they are subjecting their families to outside scrutiny. The strong desire to "keep up appearances" may also lead her to seek confidential treatment from herbalists and acupuncturists. In extreme cases, she may withdraw from her family and community, and even attempt suicide.

API women who have partners who are addicts are often perceived to be codependent and enablers in their partner's addictions. However, the consequences of not behaving in their culturally prescribed role leaves them vulnerable to physical, financial, verbal, and psychological abuse. Their limited power keeps them from urging their partner into treatment. Separation or divorce may in the long run be an easier and safer strategy of protection than exposing herself to the consequences of trying to facilitate his entry into treatment (Sun, 1991).

Regardless of the number of generations Asian families have been in the United States, many traditional values are still upheld in the upbringing of an Asian American child, among them deference to authority, emotional restraint, specified roles, carrying on the family line and name through childbearing, and a hierarchical family structure (Sue & Sue, 1990). Women are still expected to play a passive and subservient role. However, American-born, educated API women, who have more choices with regard to employment and marriage, recognize that the family system is more responsive to the needs of men than women (Rimonte, 1989) and may challenge some of the gender-defined roles and cultural expectations, changing the hierarchical organization of the family unit. Acculturation needs to be viewed as a continuum and as an important facet of how API individuals and families view and treat addiction.

Alcohol and Drug Use

Common myths describing API substance abuse include the picture of APIs as the model minority—a homogeneous group with homogeneous drug-using patterns—and the notion that APIs have fewer alcohol and drug problems relative to other ethnic minority groups (Kuramoto, 1995). These myths are so pervasive that API alcohol and drug use behavior is largely ignored by health professionals, researchers, and community members, including those in the API community (Nemoto et al., 1999). Cultural, social, and institutional barriers combined with lack of knowledge about prevalence of drug abuse add to this problem (Ja & Aoki, 1993).

The limited data on API alcohol use support the stereotype of a more moderate drinking group (Chi, Lubben, & Kitano, 1988; Higuchi, Parrish, Dufour, Towle, & Harford, 1994; Johnson & Nagoshi, 1990; Stinson et al., 1998). However, when API ethnic groups are analyzed separately, notable differences emerge. Consistently, Native Hawaiians and Japanese are found to have higher drinking levels than other API groups, followed by Filipinos and Koreans; Chinese report the lowest drinking rates (Ahern, 1985; Cheung, 1993; Chi, Lubben, & Kitano, 1988). Higher rates of alcohol consumption were reported among Asian nationals than among Asian Americans at all ages, suggesting that acculturation tends to inhibit drinking patterns among Japanese men (Higuchi et al., 1994) and among Korean-American men and women (Yamamoto, Yeh, Lee, & Lin, 1988).

Data on API women are even more scarce. Most data that do exist, however, confirm the stereotype of a restrained drinker. According to national data (Stinson et al., 1998), API women of all age groups drink less than their API male counterparts. However, one study among Korean adolescents in Los Angeles reported that the number of males and females in the group of heaviest drinkers was the same (Nakashima & Wong, 1999). National data suggest that Japanese and Filipino women have higher percentages of current drinkers among API groups, and higher percentages of heavy drinkers among those who do drink (Kitano, 2000). In addition, Kitano & Chi (1986) found that heavy drinking of alcohol among Japanese American men and women in Los Angeles was not uncommon. A higher percentage of Japanese American women report being heavy drinkers than Chinese, Korean, and Filipino American females. Contrary to the aforementioned findings for Asian men, it appears that alcohol use among API women tends to increase with acculturation. Data that group all Asians and Pacific Islanders together lose these important and meaningful distinctions.

Some believe that Asians have built-in protection from alcoholism because of their physiological propensity to "flush" when they drink. Many studies have been conducted to examine this phenomenon. Results are ambiguous and do not explain the great variance in drinking patterns among Asian people. Although it is still a topic for debate, the controversy is dying out. There is just not enough evidence, even with numerous studies, to claim a physical, biological factor that somehow makes Asians different from other racial groups in their reactivity to alcohol and other drugs (Nakawatase, Yamamoto, & Toshiaki, 1993; Sue, Kitano, Hatanaka, & Yeung, 1985; Park et al., 1984).

In a study in San Francisco of 104 API drug users not in treatment (36 percent of whom were women), Vietnamese women started using drugs at a much later age than Chinese and Filipina women. All Chinese and Vietnamese immigrants in this sample began taking drugs after immigrating to the United States.

Depression and stress were the reasons cited. Filipino and Japanese subjects were more likely to inject drugs, and Chinese and Vietnamese were more likely to smoke crack. Of the participants, 75 percent reported that they had good relationships with their families, yet half the sample hid their drug use from family members (Nemoto et al., 1999).

In a study of thirty-seven female API methamphetamine users in Hawaii, Joe (1995) reports a background of economic marginality, a family history of alcohol and drugs, and a family history of violence and abuse. These women also confront poverty, homelessness, and domestic violence, all risk factors for substance abuse and addiction.

U.S. national data on the use of marijuana, hashish, THC, cocaine, crack, heroin, methamphetamine, and barbiturates reveal that the rate of API drug use is lower than for all other racial groups. Drug use among API females is consistently lower than among API males and among all other females in the United States (Stinson et al., 1998). Thus it can be inferred that APIs "use less" than other groups, and API females use less than API males.

The low documented rates of alcohol and drug problems for API women should not be misunderstood to mean that API women do not have these problems. On the contrary, the aforementioned studies by Nemoto et al. (1999) and Joe (1996) provide some evidence of the existence of drug use in API women, although little is known about this group of women. The low numbers could also be due to underreporting, underuse of services, and sampling methodologies that overlook API women who use drugs. There are tremendous numbers of API women who marry outside their race and who no longer have API surnames. Data collection methods that use telephone books or other lists of names fail to recruit these API women. In addition, subjects may not fully understand questionnaires and interviews conducted in English only and in a manner that is not culturally sensitive, which would lead to confused responses or missing data.

Tobacco Use

Although API women overall are seen as exhibiting healthful lifestyle behaviors, such as a lower smoking prevalence (10 percent) than among other American women (25 percent), there is clear variation by subgroup population in both healthful behaviors and prevalence of illness. For example, a recent California survey found higher rates of smoking among Japanese (19 percent) and Filipinas (11 percent), and lower rates for Chinese (7 percent). Additional state data report high prevalence of cigarette smoking among Korean and Filipino men as well as among Japanese and Korean women (Office of Women's Health, 2000).

Aggregated 1994 and 1995 national survey data report that 15.3 percent of APIs smoke (Asian Pacific Islander American Health Forum, 2000). Another national survey (National Asian Women's Health Organization, 1998) that interviewed its subjects in Vietnamese and Korean reported higher usage: 34 percent prevalence among Vietnamese males and 31 percent among Korean males. This study demonstrates the higher levels of accuracy resulting from interviews conducted in the native language of the respondent. Estimates for Southeast Asian American men range from 34 percent to 43 percent. Smoking prevalence among Native Hawaiian men is 42 percent and 34 percent for women. Overall, Asian Americans are reported to be a high-risk population for smoking and for tobacco-related diseases. Most begin smoking when they are teenagers. Asian American women have an extremely high rate of environmental tobacco smoke exposure due to daily contact with secondhand smoke, and lung cancer is the leading cause of preventable death among Asian American women over the age of fifty-five (National Asian Women's Health Organization [NAWHO], 1998).

Asian women born in the United States are seen as more likely to smoke than their counterparts born in Asia. Furthermore, Asian American girls are seen to have the highest risk of depressive symptoms among racial groups, and girls with such symptoms have double the prevalence of risky behaviors and are more likely to turn to drinking or smoking for relief. NAWHO (1998) identified a variety of issues complicating tobacco use for Asian American females, including those of body image and self-esteem, substance abuse, and cultural values and pressures.

Gambling

Although there are no formal data documenting Asian Americans or Pacific Islanders with gambling addiction, it is believed that Asians participate in gambling and pathological gambling more than non-Asian ethnic groups. Culturally speaking, gambling is seen as a significant activity among APIs in general. This is another topic that elicits shame. Female gambling addicts tend to suffer deeply from guilt and shame, and are hesitant to speak out about their problem. They often begin gambling later in life as a way to make themselves feel good and for the sense of empowerment and freedom they feel while gambling, which they lack in other areas of their life. Women gambling addicts are often characterized as "closet" gamblers who seldom talk about their winnings (California Council on Problem Gambling, 2000).

We can only assume that the same factors that drive API women away from formal treatment for substance abuse, mental illness, HIV-AIDS, and other "social ills" by which "model minority" women are not supposed to be affected will also hold true for API female gambling addicts. This is another stigmatized issue and therefore subjects its victims to secrecy.

Discussions among API women regarding gambling are met with whispered stories of aunties, sisters, mothers, and grandmothers who gamble excessively on horse races, chicken fights, or slot machines and who experience problems with the Internal Revenue Service—nothing formal, but everyone knows that gambling is a common behavior in the API community. To date, no significant studies have been conducted on this population, although one community-based organization in San Francisco is currently studying this issue in the API community (D. Inaba, personal communication, September 2000).

Eating Disorders

There is an upsurge in the number of Asian Americans seeking treatment for eating disorders at mental health clinics throughout the country, challenging the myth that anorexia and bulimia are "white girls' diseases" (Park, 2000). This trend may be due to a number of factors, including the increasing population of Asian Americans and more exposure to the concept of eating disorders that prompts help for treatment.

According to the sparse literature on this issue that specifically addresses Asian American women, the pressure to conform to lingering stereotypes of the exotic, petite Asian woman may be at the heart of the anorexic or bulimic woman's motivation. Western ideals of a tall, thin body have propelled Asian women in the United States and in Asia toward this goal. Expectations found in traditional households still encourage girls to marry into prominent families. Understanding that physical attractiveness can buoy girls' chances of success, Asian families may inadvertently or blatantly encourage unhealthy dietary practices for their daughters so that the girls will more closely conform to these mainstream standards of beauty.

Lack of knowledge about the existence and dangers of eating disorders means that families and individuals cannot detect a problem when it is presenting. The words *anorexia* and *bulimia* themselves may not have equivalent terms in Asian languages. It is difficult to define a problem when there is no language to describe its existence. If the problem is not visible, it can more easily lead to tragic consequences, because symptoms are then left unidentified and unrecognized.

It is reported that eating disorders appear to be as prevalent in Asian American females as in other ethnic groups. In fact, clinicians who work with young Asian females report that they appear more conscious of and self-conscious about their bodies than other ethnic females. Moreover, some therapists report that because of stereotypes API women hold, their self-esteem and self-worth are more closely tied to these self-perceptions than is true of other women (Park, 2000).

Risk Factors

Whether immigrant families left their home countries to flee political turmoil, persecution, or the ravages of war, or simply in an attempt to create a better life, the daily stresses they experience are vastly different from those of families who have been settled in the United States for generations. Family dynamics and role reversals by gender and age are not uncommon (Abe & Zane, 1990). The delicate balance, harmony, and hierarchical structure that were in place in the home country have been radically and irrevocably changed. Children are better able to navigate and negotiate through the U.S. system than their parents, sometimes even serving as translators in complicated legal and financial dealings on behalf of their families; women are working and even becoming primary breadwinners.

Confusion and insecurity about individual role take their toll on all family members. The surge of power for working women and for acculturated children, combined with the resultant lack of power attributed to the less successful male parent, can create deep tension and frustration that affect the entire family unit. A bicultural existence—comprising both socialization from the home country and exposure to new ideas about gender roles garnered from life in the United States—provides a tremendous challenge to all family members to forge a new understanding of their familial roles.

API immigrants constitute one of the most economically disadvantaged segments of the population. These economic disadvantages, combined with the stresses and related risk factors associated with immigration, put the API newcomer population at high risk for substance abuse and mental health problems. For refugees and wartime survivors from Southeast Asia, these troubles are compounded by separation of family members during the immigration process, strain related to relocation, personal tragedies, traumas of war, and political turmoil.

Other significant risk factors include overcrowding, social isolation, family strife, underemployment in multiple service jobs that do not have the status of jobs held in their home communities, inadequate job opportunities, and intergenerational conflicts between immigrant parents and latch-key children over the adoption of Western values. The pressure on the members of the nuclear family to support themselves both financially and emotionally and to fulfill all social functions—often without the benefit of the close proximity to friends and extended family to which the nuclear family is accustomed—can be burdensome (Lee, n.d.).

Traditional families face conflict between their native world values of family, hierarchical relationships, and social conformity, and American values of individualism, egalitarianism, and independence (Ja & Yuen, 1997). These conflicts become apparent in all interactions with mainstream society, at school and work, but also at home with the children. In times of crisis back at home in the "old world," the family, community, and social structure facilitated harmony. Everyone knew what to expect, what the rules were—how to play by them and how to circumvent them. In this new environment, in contrast, the native country structures are not only unavailable but also perhaps inappropriate. Not everyone plays by the same rules, and expectations are often unknown and unpredictable.

Asian women born in the United States or who have been in the country for at least two or three generations experience a different set of pressures and problems that may put them at risk for addictive behaviors. These include lack of ethnic identity, feelings of isolation because they do not feel a sense of belonging either to their ethnic community or to the mainstream, the experience of racism and sexism, and the high expectations from their families to excel. As they acculturate, the traditional emphasis on moderation and family that served to protect them from vulnerability to "social ills" becomes diluted (Sun, 1991).

The term *model minority* was coined in the 1960s to describe the Japanese American population that was scared into conformity following World War II and that has now settled into this country for four to five generations. The stereotype then extended outward to all Asians, promoting the notion that they do not have social problems. For those API individuals who do have addiction and other social problems, the failure to live up to this gilded reputation brings deep shame and can pressure them further into hiding.

Pacific Islander migrants also face a number of stresses in attempting to live on the U.S. mainland. They are a true minority in terms of numbers and are at a tremendous disadvantage when competing for federal funds under the combined grouping of the Asian/Pacific Islander race category. When Pacific Islanders move to the U.S. mainland, like other immigrants they oftentimes lose their status, rank, and prestige, and commonly find themselves in jobs below their education and skill level. Hierarchical familial roles are threatened through the weakening of the traditional kinship group and village culture. In addition, the skills they have attained in an island culture are vastly different from those valued in a modern technological society (Kitano and Daniels, 1995).

Whether immigrant or fifth-generation American, API female addicts inevitably discover that it is more socially acceptable for API addicts to be male. There is a higher degree of shame and guilt connected with substance abuse for women, perpetuating their invisibility and isolation. These feelings of shame and guilt may explain, in part, the increase in suicide rates for Asian women addicts as compared with Asian men and non-Asian women (D. Inaba, personal communication, June 2000).

Asian and Pacific Islander women, like other women, are often led to substance abuse and addiction by a husband, lover, or older brother. Joe (1996) found that a large number of the API women addicts in her study of methamphetamine users admitted to using alcohol and drugs initially to enhance sex. Many had problematic childhoods fraught with domestic violence, incest, homelessness, and poverty. During chaotic episodes, the women became vulnerable to drinking and drug use.

◆ ◆ ◆

API women face a number of environmental, social, cultural, and familial risk factors. These risk factors are complicated by culture, gender, and levels of acculturation, all of which have a direct impact on the development and maintenance of their addictions.

Experience of Addiction for API Women and Their Families

Although cultural factors differ among API ethnic groups, particularly when generational, social class, and educational differences are considered, most API families react universally to the news that their children and other family members have problems related to stigmatized issues such as substance abuse, mental illness, or HIV-AIDS. All these areas are taboo when they occur within the immediate family. In fact, if any of these problems do not significantly impair the functioning of the individual, if the individual fulfills the obligations to the family, and if the problem is neither overtly visible nor talked about, then there is no problem. Addictive behaviors are viewed in the same way: if the addiction does not impede familial obligations or expectations set by the family, then the family may not even consider the addiction detrimental (Ja & Aoki, 1993).

The family becomes concerned when psychiatric symptoms, illegal behavior, or drug use become publicly visible. These behaviors are then perceived as a defect or weakness in character. Shame and loss of face are heightened, and the woman's behavior is seen as a negative reflection on her parents, family, and community. An initial response from family members of an API addict is to ignore or deny the existence of these problems in hopes that they will disappear. They may also isolate or insulate the individual from the community to save face for her and the family (Ja & Aoki, 1993). If these options do not work, and if the family is forced to directly confront these problems, the embarrassment and loss of face

may force specific cultural responses, such as the act of shaming or scolding to resolve the issue. In extreme situations, the family rejects the individual by disown-
ing her or sending her to another family member or even "back home" to the
family's original homeland. Interventions are initially kept within the extended
family network. When all else fails and the individual's problems or behaviors are
perceived as too severe or unbearable, the family may seek help beyond their family network and go to "outsiders." It is at this pivotal point that social and human
service practitioners may be called on for assistance (Ja & Aoki, 1993).

At this point, the API family may be looking for a quick fix for their problems,
believing that once the individual goes to a doctor, she will be taken care of. This
reflects their hope and their high expectations of the treatment provider as the expert. The family likely has little understanding of their role in the problems of
addiction.

API families operate with a cultural perspective of family interdependence,
in contrast to the more Western view of independence of the individual (Ja & Aoki,
1993). API substance abusers take advantage of the existing levels of family interdependence. It is not unusual to find exasperated parents who are frustrated
and angry with their adult child who uses drugs and exhibits bizarre behavior, yet
the individual continues to live at home and receive money from the family.

API women appear to be relatively functional throughout most of their addiction experience. They are able and expected to hold many roles in their lives
and in their families; thus their addictions can progress for quite some time without detection. Some report experiencing increased feelings of shame and intrapsychic distress over their dependencies, reinforced by cultural values placed on
them by their families and communities. The intense pressure perpetuates self-
destructive behavior. Feelings of powerlessness and self-hatred increase as their
drug use or compulsive behaviors, such as bingeing, purging, or gambling, increase.
They become anxious about being able to maintain their addictions and fearful
that others will discover "the secret." As their ability to function decreases, they
lose control over other responsibilities. Meanwhile, the pleasures of addiction wane
as the hardship of continuing it increases. Their compulsive behavior requires
more and more drugs, alcohol, control over their food intake, or money for gambling bets to relieve the increasing feelings of anxiety and tension. These women
report losing touch with their sense of self, not liking the person they are becoming, and finally being unable to stop the addictive behavior. Suicide becomes a
strong option.

Issues of identity development may be at the forefront for American-born API
addicted women. These women report liking who they become when they use
drugs or alcohol, or the exuberance they feel when gambling, the control they feel
when they don't eat, or the relief they feel after they purge. The problems begin

when the addiction takes over, and they realize they cannot stop the behaviors that once brought pleasure and now bring anxiety.

API cultures encourage self-discipline and self-control. Addictions such as eating disorders are suspected to be symbolic representations of psychological control over oneself or others, yet ironically these obsessions and compulsions eventually create a loss of self-control. The API woman's relationship to addiction may reflect her underlying feelings of inadequacy or anger, or may serve as a replacement for personal intimacy. It is imperative that she understand the underlying issues behind her addiction if she is to effectively address the resultant behaviors.

Assessment

The issues that an addicted API woman faces are complex and therefore require unique perspectives from which to assess the woman's cultural, social, and biological background. As we stated earlier, these women remain invisible in the addiction world, as in the larger society. Although they are just as vulnerable to addiction as other women—perhaps more vulnerable, considering their marginalized status by race and gender—they are still perceived as a group that does not have problems. Enabled by their own families and overwhelmed by shame and guilt in admitting their addiction, these women keep their plight hidden, further promulgating this myth.

A comprehensive assessment is needed to thoroughly appraise the biological and psychosocial interactions of the API woman and her addiction. The Multidisciplinary Assessment Profile (MAP), developed by Denning (2000), is a good tool for this purpose. MAP includes motivational interviewing (Miller & Rollnick, 1991) and stages of change (Prochaska, DiClemente, & Norcross, 1992). MAP guides the interviewing process by addressing twelve components: stage of change, decisional balance, types of drug(s) used, level of abuse or dependence, prescribed medications, past treatment history, support system, self-efficacy, psychiatric diagnoses, client's stated goals, therapist's stated goals, and the developmental grid. This assessment tool is seen as one that incorporates a culturally competent and flexible approach to assessing API women and their relationship to addiction.

Motivational interviewing (Miller & Rollnick, 1991) is both an interviewing technique and a treatment approach. The therapist assesses and encourages the client's motivation for change, while building a strong and trusting relationship between himself or herself and the client.

Stages of change theory (Prochaska, DiClemente, & Norcross, 1992) guides the clinician in assessing a client depending on "where she is" in her addiction and accepting her wherever she is. The stages of change are precontemplation, contemplation, preparation, action, and maintenance. Relapse can occur at any stage in the process. This perspective supports where the client is in her own view of addiction and helps support her move through the cycle of treatment.

In the case of immigrant API women, clinical assessments may need to be performed by bilingual and bicultural therapists to obtain a thorough and accurate picture of the API client's situation and to deal with her shame. The counselor must explicitly ensure confidentiality, as most API individuals are concerned about who will find out about their addiction and the fact that they are in treatment.

Asian clients may register psychosomatic complaints to express underlying psychological or somatic problems that they are unable to identify or are too embarrassed to report. Somatic complaints can be viewed as culturally driven verbal expressions of psychological distress or as a safe way of expressing psychological problems, given the stigma and negative consequences of reporting emotional complaints. Moreover, some API clients may actually experience physical pain and discomfort in their bodies when they are undergoing emotional stress (Sue & Morishima, 1982). Counselors need to be cognizant of this type of cultural expression and provide services aimed at the reduction of symptoms while at the same time exploring the underlying problems.

After she has been identified as having an addiction, an API woman must be assessed in the context of her culture, immigration status, and level of acculturation. Treatment recommendations also must reflect her cultural background and history. Counselors also need to consider other issues, such as domestic violence, sexual abuse, cultural roles, lack of a support system, and family histories of addiction.

A recent study (Sullivan, Chen, & Lu, 2000) suggests that APIs remain severely underrepresented in mental health services; APIs were also found to present with more severe mental symptoms and to remain longer in services once they sought them, as compared to other racial-ethnic groups. This study also found that API clients were more likely than other racial groups to use outpatient and day treatment programs. Furthermore, the API clients who received treatment tended to be older, less educated, unemployed, and female.

This study underscores the importance of early diagnosis and the need for early entry into treatment. However, no assessment tools have been "normed" on API people, let alone API women, nor are there any specific psychological or assessment measures that can facilitate early detection of addiction behaviors. Although this population is relatively small, language- and culture-specific, culturally sensitive measures are needed to ensure that the number of API women with addiction problems does not increase.

Treatment Strategies and Approaches

As we have stated elsewhere, few API people seek treatment for addiction. If an API woman does seek treatment, she has likely been mandated by the court system or pushed into it by desperate family members. Her receptivity to treatment is affected by a host of factors, of which her level of acculturation plays a principal part. The concept of addiction treatment is alien to API newcomers. Western-trained therapists place great emphasis on talk therapy, working through issues, individual growth and change, long-range treatment goals, pathology, and use of corrective emotional experiences to resolve psychological deficits and shortcomings. Immigrant API women are unfamiliar with these notions and are unlikely to be willing to participate in treatment based on these ideas and modalities. They are also likely to be intimidated by the high use of verbal expression and will have a difficult time seeing the value in telling problems to strangers.

Unless specifically trained, practitioners can easily overlook addictive behavior in API women. The unknowing eye may also be confused by what appears to be denial of use and enabling of others to use, when in fact these women are merely behaving in a culturally determined manner. Treatment strategies may need to involve the API woman's immediate family, as the addict is especially concerned about being able to remain responsive to the family's needs. If the family is educated about the addiction and is an integral part of recovery, the client is less likely to relapse when she formally ends treatment.

The hierarchical nature of API families needs to be remembered in the education and treatment process. Communication within the family is generally indirect and based on roles. It is vital for the counselor to respect the implicit power of both parents and extended family members and to be aware of the group's nonverbal communication. Language barriers are naturally a big problem. The use of a translator or interpreter might also be problematic, not only because it makes for difficult and slow communication but also because API families who are in treatment do not want someone else in their community to know of their family problems. The use of a variety of oral and visual activities to encourage verbal and nonverbal communication, such as storytelling or sharing pictures, is essential.

API women who have recently immigrated from war-torn countries have significant histories of rape, trauma, and other experiences that affect their current functioning, addictive behaviors, and treatment. Experiences of torture, starvation, rape, forced labor, and witness to murder and other atrocities, combined with the stress related to dislocation and resettlement, have resulted in unique medical conditions. One example is the psychosomatic or nonorganic blindness reported among Cambodian women forty years of age or older (Office of Women's Health, 2000). Mental health and addiction problems are not uncommon among these women. Clinicians report depression, anxiety, posttraumatic stress disorder (PTSD), and psychosomatic illness in addition to impaired physical health (Gibbs & Huang, 1989; O'Hare & Tran, 1998). Therapists who work with these women must be aware of the environmental and psychological triggers that might re-traumatize them in their treatment, and need to understand how these experiences affect their addiction. General therapy guidelines might include a focus on multiple losses, related somatic concerns, and daily problems of adaptation as they are connected to addictive behavior. Therapists who work with these clients should utilize the sizable literature on PTSD.

For acculturated API women, seeking addiction treatment may not be as threatening, despite the stigma and shame attached. They are more familiar with Western therapeutic processes that include "talk therapy" or psychodynamic therapy. Many clinicians have recommended directive approaches such as cognitive-behavioral therapy (CBT) in working with acculturated API clients. In particular, CBT is seen as both practical and familiar and is less threatening in conveying information to clients. It encourages the teaching modality inherent in psycho-educational and skill-based approaches. This method can address the client's perceptions of a problem without being unnecessarily intrusive or emotionally threatening, while encouraging stress management techniques based on Asian philosophies that clients find familiar. Furthermore, API women may find this approach less intrusive because it initially addresses the behavioral problems and attitudes around the problems rather than the underlying issues.

Incorporating and integrating indigenous treatment modalities such as healing ceremonies (Mien culture); *hooponopono* (Hawaiian culture), which means "setting it right" in a spiritual, physical, and emotional sense (DeCambra, Marshall, & Ono, 1999); and other Eastern treatment modalities are effective in engaging API clients in treatment. Acupuncture, meditation, massage, tai-chi, and herbal medicines all contribute to a more comprehensive treatment approach for addictions. Martin and Zweben (1993) found that for substance-abusing clients in the Mien (Laotian) population, massage, acupuncture, and liniment patches are more culturally acceptable treatment modalities for withdrawal or relapse than are pills or oral liquid.

Another holistic treatment model seen as effective in working with API women, whether immigrant or acculturated, is a harm reduction approach. The damage resulting from drug or alcohol use is the focus of attention rather than the actual drug or alcohol use itself. Abstinence is not necessarily the absolute goal; instead, the goal is reduction in harm, with an emphasis on the biological, psychological, and social relationships that placed the individual at higher risk for abuse. Slips, relapses, and reduction of use are integrated into treatment in a realistic manner. Harm reduction principles support the client's ability to make choices that incorporate cultural mores into individualized recovery. This approach is flexible, pragmatic, and client-centered.

Although API addicts may be isolated or have a difficult relationship with their families, many still rely on their family members for assistance and may also be relied on by the family in some ways (Joe, 1996). Old, familiar expectations dictated by the family can play an important part in the API woman's perceptions of healing. On the other end of the spectrum, there are API female addicts who have had to disconnect from their families in order to begin the recovery process. Healing could begin only after they moved away from the intense shame, judgment, and pressure they experienced in their families.

Twelve-step programs, although one of the more popular and successful models of self-help treatment in this country and around the world, are philosophically incongruent with some Asian cultures, because of these programs' heavy emphasis on self-examination and public confession. Some Asian ethnic groups are not comfortable with the concept of admitting "powerlessness" or with public disclosure, integral parts of twelve-step programs. These concepts are in direct conflict with the API cultural penchant to avoid "airing dirty laundry." An approach that focuses on personal strengths rather than deficits—a "challenge model"—may be seen as more effective for API clients.

Treatment Recommendations

The problems of addiction in API women are complex. Their help-seeking patterns and perceptions of their dependencies differ from those of their male counterparts and other women. Cultural expectations and gender roles dictate that the API woman addict be silent and invisible, even while problems are becoming blatant and difficult to hide. Her shame makes it hard initially to admit her addiction to herself and then to others, but her denial should not be seen as limiting her desire for help. Treatment strategies must be considerate of her cultural need to address her problems in a private way, while at the same time offering her the benefit of support from others with whom she develops genuine trust.

A crucial component in working with an API woman in recovery is to reduce the stigma of her addiction. When addiction-related services are presented in a context of promoting overall health rather than treatment focused on substance abuse, the addict and her family are able to view her dependence as an interconnected problem rather than as an isolated, individual character flaw. An outpatient treatment center based in San Francisco that specifically caters to API clients views substance abuse problems on a continuum of life issues and places the healing of addiction in the context of body, mind, and spirit; both of these are philosophical modalities that are successful in maintaining their API clients.

The education of individuals, families, and communities about the topic of addiction reduces the stigma of these issues; clients and their families talk about addiction, learn of its existence in the API community, and learn about structural, genetic, and situational factors that put individuals at risk for abuse. Education about symptoms, resources, and treatment options, provided by bilingual and bicultural staff, also helps normalize the problem. A one-stop health service center provides a less stigmatized point of entry for those accessing addiction services.

Another critical strategy for successfully treating API female addicts is to use a nurturing approach that is careful not to exacerbate the woman's cultural and gendered tendencies toward self-blame. Psychological attribution theory suggests that women tend to internalize or attribute internal reasons for positive and negative events, blaming themselves for negative events (Fiske & Taylor, 1991; Weiner, 1986). In contrast, male addicts tend to externalize negative events, attributing blame for their difficulties or negative circumstances to those outside themselves (Straussner, 1997). This theory supports the confrontational treatment approach in traditional substance abuse treatment programs designed for male addicts. This same treatment approach is less likely to be effective for women, especially API women, because it increases their levels of shame, guilt, and self-blame, disengaging them from seeking help (D. Inaba, personal communication, September 2000).

API female addicts require a more supportive, compassionate approach to engage them in addiction treatment. Strategies to obtain and retain clients therefore must encourage the development of trust and a positive therapeutic alliance while decreasing internalized feelings of guilt and shame. Developing a strong relationship with the API woman in recovery and her family is an important factor in her treatment. Doing so may take some time, even months or years, and cannot be hurried (Minkoff, 2000). Those who harbor a historical distrust of authority generally take longer to forge a working bond. However, Asian groups tend to place great value on relationships, even on contrived ones like the therapeutic relationship. In some cases, sharing information about the therapist's credentials, family background, and marital status will assist in developing a rapport between the therapist and the immigrant API client and family. It is not uncommon for clients to ask about personal matters, such as how many children the therapist has or if he or she is married. While maintaining personal boundaries, the therapist needs to feel comfortable in answering some questions in order to deepen the level of trust.

Some of the approaches we have already discussed—harm reduction strategies, the Multidisciplinary Assessment Profile, motivational interviewing techniques, and stages of change theory—enable the practitioner to develop a positive therapeutic relationship with the API woman. These approaches support developing a positive clinical relationship in a flexible, culturally competent manner.

Another way to promote trust as well as to gain important diagnostic information is for the therapist to make home visits into the individual's or family's environment. API women are likely to appreciate the therapist's willingness to do this. In this way, the therapist makes services more accessible to the client and, more important, demonstrates respect. The gesture of attempting to accommodate the API woman's schedule and life would go a long way, as many women would have to find child care and deal with public transportation to come and see the counselor.

Acculturated API women are generally able to gain from insight-oriented therapy with an emphasis on ethnic identity issues and expectations based on gender role, and on how these interplay with her addictive behavior. Individual supportive counseling is seen as a successful treatment modality in that the client is emotionally supported and confidentiality is ensured. In addition to individual counseling, women's groups and family counseling are other important modes of available treatment. Counselors who have led coed API groups acknowledge that API women are not as successful in these groups because they find it difficult to admit intimate details and issues in the presence of males. Furthermore, the women are less likely to impose their feelings of suffering, as well as their successes, on others. Groups tend to be difficult initially because API women are less likely to openly share their problems and more likely to accommodate the men (D. Inaba, personal communication, September 2000).

Successful treatment modalities depend on the individual addict. Her ethnic, cultural, and historical background, immigration status, social and familial role and relationships, and socioeconomic condition are all integral components that affect her relationship to her addiction. Her addictive behaviors need to be understood in these contexts, and her psychological and emotional processes can be seen, in part, as survival and coping strategies.

Getting API female addicts into treatment and retaining them are difficult. Problems with access are monumental due to cultural inhibitions, language, lack of support, finances, and such logistical considerations as transportation, child care, time off from work, and time off from familial duties. Overcoming these obstacles is half the battle. It is likely that the woman does not have enough sense of self-worth to feel that she is worth the time and hassle involved, which is a symptom of her addiction in the first place. Once she has connected to services, the

API woman is likely to utilize treatment well (D. Inaba, personal communication, June 2000; Sullivan et al., 2000).

Conclusion

Three themes have echoed throughout this chapter, which described the lives, histories, culture, and addiction of API women: invisibility, complexity, and hardship. API women are invisible and unknown in the addiction and treatment world. Their addictions are a complex issue because of the diversity and lack of knowledge surrounding their experiences and needs. The breadth and depth of the hardships that API women have been taught to bear silently is a part of their historical and cultural legacy, affecting how their addictions are defined, acknowledged, and treated.

The emergence of addiction in an individual is a symptom that something is not right and hasn't been right for quite some time. The presence of addiction in an API woman is particularly compelling because it denotes problems in someone who isn't supposed to have them. If she denies the addiction, as her culture expects, and if her family and community denies it, then she remains invisible. The consequences of her invisibility are tragic. If she does recognize her addiction and wants help, she must traverse into a world where few others look like her, speak her language, or know who she is. Moreover, others may have preconceived ideas about her that don't match her own perception.

API women are under a lot of pressure to excel, to uphold the API community, to meet the dominant culture's expectations of a member of a model group without problems, and to overcome an extremely severe historical past. Any attempt to examine their departure from their exalted stereotypes must be made in the context of seeing these women as individuals, as family members, and as community members, and of seeing them in relationship to the mainstream, in the multiple roles in their lives. Their relationship to addiction is only a small piece of the puzzle that makes up the intricacies of their lives.

References

Abe, J., & Zane, N. (1990). Psychological maladjustment among Asian and white college students. *Journal of Counseling Psychology, 37*, 437–444.

Ahern, F. M. (1985, September 11–14). *Alcohol use and abuse among four ethnic groups in Hawaii: Native Hawaiians, Japanese, Filipinos, and Caucasians.* Paper presented at the Epidemiology of Alcohol Use and Abuse Among U.S. Minorities conference, sponsored by the National Institute on Alcoholism and Alcohol Abuse, Bethesda, MD.

Andersen, P. (1996, January 19–25). Growing into the 21st century: Asians and Pacific Islanders one-tenth of the U.S. population by 2050. *Asian Week*, 16–17.

Asian Pacific Islander American Health Forum. (2000). *Tobacco fact sheet.* San Francisco: National Asian Women's Health Organization.

Barringer, H., Gardner, R., & Levin, M. (1993). *Asians and Pacific Islanders in the United States.* New York: Russell Sage Foundation.

Bousquet, G. (1987). Living in a state of limbo: A case study of Vietnamese refugees in Hong Kong camps. In S. Morgan & E. Colsen (Eds.), *People in upheaval* (pp. 34–53). New York: Center for Migration Studies.

California Council on Problem Gambling. (2000). Available: www.calproblemgambling.org.

Cheung, Y. W. (1993). Beyond liver and culture: A review of theories and research in drinking among Chinese in North America. *International Review of the Addictions, 28,* 1497–1513.

Chi, I., Lubben, J. E., & Kitano, H. H. (1988). Differences in drinking behavior among three Asian-American groups. *Journal of Studies on Alcohol, 50,* 15–23.

DeCambra, H., Marshall, W. E., & Ono, M. (1999). Ho'omau ke ola: "To perpetuate life as it was meant to be." In N. Mokuau (Ed.), *Responding to Pacific Islanders: Culturally competent perspectives for substance abuse prevention* (pp. 73–96). Washington, DC: U.S. Department of Health and Human Services.

Denning, P. (2000). *Practicing harm reduction psychotherapy: An alternative approach to addictions.* New York: Guilford Press.

Fiske, S. T., & Taylor, S. E. (1991). *Social cognition.* Reading, MA: Addison-Wesley.

Fung, R. (1991). Center the margins. In R. Leong (Ed.), *Moving the image: Independent Asian Pacific American media arts* (pp. 62–67). Los Angeles: University of California-Los Angeles Asian American Studies Center.

Gibbs, J. T., & Huang, L. (1989). *Children of color: Psychological interventions with minority youths.* San Francisco: Jossey-Bass.

Glenn, E. N. (1986). *Issei, nisei, war bride.* Philadelphia: Temple University Press.

Glodava, M., & Onizuka, R. (1994). *Mail-order brides: Women for sale.* Fort Collins, CO: Alaken.

Higuchi, S., Parrish, K. M., Dufour, M. C., Towle, L. H., & Harford, T. C. (1994). Relationship between age and drinking patterns and drinking problems among Japanese, Japanese-Americans, and Caucasians. *Alcoholism: Clinical and Experimental Research, 18,* 305–310.

Ho, M. K. (1983). *Family therapy with ethnic minorities.* Thousand Oaks, CA: Sage.

Homma-True, R. (1990). Psychotherapeutic issues with Asian American women. *Sex Roles, 22,* 477–486.

Ja, D., & Aoki, B (1993). Substance abuse treatment: Culture and barriers in the Asian American community. *Journal of Psychoactive Drugs, 25,* 61–71.

Ja, D., & Yuen, F. (1997). Substance abuse treatment among Asian Americans. In E. Lee (Ed.), *Working with Asian Americans: A guide for clinicians* (pp. 295–308). New York: Guilford Press.

Jang, D., & Penserga, L. J. (1999, August). Beyond the safety net: Health services for low-income Asian and Pacific Islander women and children in California. In *Asian and Pacific Islander American Health Forum policy report.* San Francisco: Asian Pacific Islander American Health Forum.

Joe, K. A., (1995). Ice is strong enough for a man but made for a woman. *Crime, Law and Social Change, 23,* 269–289.

Joe, K. A. (1996). The lives and times of Asian Pacific American women drug users: An ethnographic study of their methamphetamine use. *Journal of Drug Issues, 26,* 199–218.

Johnson, R. C., & Nagoshi, C. T. (1990). Asians, Asian-Americans and alcohol. *Journal of Psychoactive Drugs, 22,* 45–52.

Kim, B.-L. (1980). *The Korean American child at school and at home.* Washington, DC: U.S. Department of Health, Education, and Welfare.

Kim, E. (1984). Sex tourism in Asia: A reflection of political and economic inequality. *Critical Perspectives of Third World America, 2*(1), 214–232.

Kitano, H. L., & Chi, I. (1986, Winter). Asian Americans and alcohol use: Exploring cultural differences in Los Angeles. *Alcohol, Health and Research World,* pp. 42–47.

Kitano, H. L., & Daniels, R. (1995). *Asian Americans: Emerging minorities* (2nd ed.). Englewood Cliffs, NJ: Prentice Hall.

Kitano, K. J. (2000). *National longitudinal alcohol epidemiologic survey: A secondary analysis looking at Asians and Pacific Islanders.* Unpublished article.

Krich, J. (1986, February/March). Here comes the bride. *Mother Jones,* pp. 34–37, 43–46.

Kuramoto, F. (1995). Asian and Pacific Island community alcohol prevention research. In P. A. Langton (Ed.), *The challenge of participatory research: Preventing alcohol-related problems in ethnic communities* (pp. 411–428). Special collaborative National Institute on Alcoholism and Alcohol Abuse/Center for Substance Abuse Prevention monograph based on an NIAAA conference, May 18–19, 1992.

Lee, E. (n.d.). *Family therapy with Chinese American families: A practical guide for clinicians.* Unpublished paper.

Martin, M., & Zweben, J. (1993). Addressing treatment needs of southeast Asian Mien opium users in California. *Journal of Psychoactive Drugs, 25,* 73–76.

Miller, W. R., & Rollnick, S. (1991). *Motivational interviewing: Preparing people to change addictive behavior.* New York: Guilford Press.

Min, P. G. (1988). The Korean American family. In C. Mindel (Ed.), *Ethnic families in America* (pp. 223–253). New York: Elsevier.

Minkoff, K. (2000, May). *Dual diagnosis.* [Clinical training]. Contra Costa County Mental Health Services, Concord, CA.

Mokuau, N. (Ed.). (1991). *Handbook of social services for Asian and Pacific Islanders.* Westport, CT: Greenwood Press.

Mokuau, N. (1996). *Reality and vision: Health and well-being for Pacific Islanders: Status, barriers and resolutions.* Washington, DC: U.S. Department of Health and Human Services.

Nakano, M. (1990). *Japanese American women: Three generations 1890–1990.* Berkeley, CA: Mina.

Nakashima, J., & Wong, M. (1999). *Characteristics of alcohol consumption and correlates of alcohol misuse among Korean American adolescents.* Unpublished manuscript.

Nakawatase, T. V., Yamamoto, J., & Toshiaki, S. (1993). The association between fast flushing response and alcohol use among Japanese-Americans. *Journal of Studies on Alcohol, 54,* 48–53.

National Asian Women's Health Organization. (1998). *Smoking among Asian Americans: A national tobacco survey.* San Francisco: Author.

Nemoto, T., Aoki, B., Huang, K., Morris, A., Nguyen, H., & Wong, W. (1999). Drug use behaviors among Asian drug users in San Francisco. *Addictive Behaviors, 24,* 823–838.

Office of Women's Health. (2000, May 18). Factors affecting the health of women of color: Asian Americans. In *Women of Color Health Data Book.* Washington, DC: U.S. Department of Health and Human Services.

O'Hare, T., & Tran, T. V. (1998). Substance abuse among Southeast Asians in the U.S.: Implications for practice and research. *Social Work in Health Care, 26*(3), 69–80.

Ohnuki-Tierney, E. (1984). *Illness and culture in contemporary Japan.* Cambridge: Cambridge University Press.

Park, E. (2000, June 15–21). Starving in silence: Eating and body image disorders plague young Asian and Asian American women. *Asian Week,* pp. 17–19.

Park, J. Y., Huang, Y. H., Nagoshi, C. T., Yen, S., Johnson, R., Ching, C., & Bowman, K. (1984). The flushing response to alcohol use among Koreans and Taiwanese. *Journal of Studies on Alcohol, 45,* 481–485.

Prochaska, J. O., DiClemente, C. C., & Norcross, J. C. (1992). In search of how people change: Applications to addictive behaviors. *American Psychologist, 47,* 1102–1114.

Rimonte, N. (1989). Domestic violence among Pacific Asians. In *Making waves: An anthology of writings by and about Asian-American women* (pp. 327–337). Boston: Beacon Press.

Schein, L. (1987). Control of contrast: Lao-Hmong refugees in American contexts. In S. Morgan & E. Colsen (Eds.), *People in upheaval* (pp. 88–107). New York: Center for Migration Studies.

Stinson, F., Yi, H-Y., Grant, B., Chou, P., Dawson, D. A., Pickering, R., & Dufour, M. C. (1998). *Drinking in the United States: Main findings from the 1992 National Longitudinal Alcohol Epidemiologic Survey.* Bethesda, MD: U.S. Department of Health and Human Services, National Institute on Alcoholism and Alcohol Abuse.

Straussner, S.L.A. (1997). Gender and substance abuse. In S.L.A. Straussner & E. Zelvin (Eds.), *Gender and addictions: Men and women in treatment* (pp. 3–27). Northvale, NJ: Aronson.

Sue, D. W., & Sue, D. (1990). Counseling Asian Americans. In D. W. Sue & D. Sue (Eds.), *Counseling the culturally different: Theory and practice.* New York: Wiley.

Sue, S., Kitano, H., Hatanaka, H., & Yeung, W. T. (1985). Alcohol consumption among Chinese in the United States. In L. Bennett & G. Ames (Eds.), *The American experience with alcohol* (pp. 359–375). New York: Plenum.

Sue, S., & Morishima, J. K. (1982). *The mental health of Asian Americans: Contemporary issues in identifying and treating mental problems.* San Francisco: Jossey-Bass.

Sullivan, N. Y., Chen, S., & Lu, Y. E. (2000, March 31-April 1). *Asian Americans and mental health services: A historical, theoretical and empirical examination.* Paper presented at the Conference on Effective Clinical Practice with Asians and Asian Americans, New York.

Sun, A. P. (1991). Issues for Asian American women. In P. Roth (Ed.), *Alcohol and drugs are women's issues: Vol. 1. A review of the issues* (pp. 125–129). Metuchen, NJ: Scarecrow.

Tajima, R. (1989). Lotus blossoms don't bleed: Images of Asian women. *Making waves: An anthology of writings by and about Asian-American women* (pp. 308–317). Boston: Beacon Press.

Trask, H.-K. (1990). Politics in the Pacific Islands: Imperialism and native self-determination. *Amerasia Journal, 16,* 1–19.

Weiner, B. (1986). *An attributional theory of motivation and emotion.* New York: Springer-Verlag.

Yamamoto, J., Yeh, E. K., Lee, C. K., & Lin, K. M. (1988). Alcohol abuse among Koreans and Taiwanese. *National Institutes of Alcoholism and Alcohol Abuse Research Monograph Series, 19,* 135–175.

Yung, J. (1986). *Chinese Women of America: A pictorial history.* Seattle: University of Washington.

PART FIVE

SPECIAL POPULATIONS AND SETTINGS

CHAPTER SEVENTEEN

ADDICTION AND WOMEN
IN THE WORKPLACE

Jane M. Nakken

Addicted women work. Most of us know that; we recognize addiction in our employed clients and sometimes among our professional colleagues whose erratic behavior, irritability, or dangerous mistakes tip us off to their problem with alcohol or drugs. Perhaps we know this firsthand, because we ourselves have been employed while in the throes of our own addictions. In fact, two out of three adults in the United States know someone who has gone to work under the influence of drugs or alcohol (Hazelden Foundation, 1996), and alcohol and drug use costs American business more than $170 billion every year. About a third of the nation's eighteen million alcoholics and drug addicts are women (Substance Abuse and Mental Health Services Administration, 1998).

Yet as a society we pay little attention to addiction as a problem of women in the workplace. Further, we as professionals, influenced by societal stereotypes, sometimes fail to recognize addiction as a source of the problems of the employed and often highly successful women we treat. Underdiagnosis of addiction in women is exacerbated by the fact that they are less likely than men to seek help in the form of addiction treatment services; instead, they prefer to consult physicians and mental health professionals in settings in which their chemical problems are less likely to be diagnosed (Beckman, 1994).

Health care professionals can make a difference and reduce the odds against women's receiving the treatment they need for addiction problems. Remaining alert to the signs and symptoms of addiction that prompt a thorough evaluation is one step. Becoming aware of the treatment options and how to refer women is a second step. Third, helping professionals can guide women in establishing recovery lifestyles that address their experience in the workplace. A review of the literature, however, turns up less information than we might expect on the topic of addiction and treatment issues of women who work.

This chapter will present what we know about women and addiction in the workplace. Most of this information concerns addiction to alcohol and drugs. Unfortunately, we are left to wonder about the applicability of this discussion to women with other addictions. This chapter shares some of what recovering women themselves have to say about their own addiction and recovery experiences as those relate to their careers and workplaces, and discusses some of the implications of their stories for other women in recovery and for us, the professionals who assist them.

Women, Work, and Addiction: Exploring the Relationships

Does the added stress of the workplace make women more vulnerable to addiction? Women's entrance into the modern workforce during the 1960s and 1970s led to predictions of dire consequences for women's mental health and emotional balance (Wilsnack, 1996). It was assumed that paid employment would have adverse effects on women's mental health and drinking behavior, particularly when employment was combined with marriage and family roles. Researchers suspected that excessive responsibility from multiple roles (role overload) or competition among these roles (role conflict) created stress that might lead to more and heavier drinking (Wilsnack, 1996).

In fact, research studies found that women with jobs are no more, and no less, likely to be addicted than women outside the workforce. Most studies found that although women employed outside the home are more likely to drink and to drink more often than homemakers, they are no more likely to drink heavily or to experience adverse consequences (Wilsnack, 1996). Even women in high-level professional and executive positions, who presumably have very stressful jobs, do not have higher rates of alcoholism (Wilsnack, 1996). Whereas a study of men in high-stress job situations found that they were 3.4 times more likely to develop an alcohol problem than men in less stressful jobs, women in high-stress jobs were found not to be at higher risk for alcohol addiction or abuse than other women (Crum, 1995). Thus, neither the stereotype of the destitute, unemployed addicted mother nor that of the hard-driving, hard-drinking female executive presents a meaningful profile of women who are addicted to alcohol or drugs; most alcoholic and drug-dependent women fall between these extremes. Research and clinical data show that any woman—teacher, nurse, engineer, attorney, waitress, banker, artist, psychologist, adventurer, office worker—can become an addict.

There are, however, specific situations in women's work lives that do influence the likelihood that a woman will have an alcohol or drug problem (Wilsnack, 1996):

- Women who work in occupations in which their peers are predominantly male have higher rates of heavy drinking. These jobs cut across blue-collar and professional workplaces, and the effect is the same on men's alcohol use: heavy drinking is more prevalent among both women and men in male-dominated workplaces.
- A woman is more likely to be a heavy drinker if she is unhappy with her work role or the status of her work life.
- Women with incomes below $9,000 or above $75,000 do have slightly higher rates of drug use.

Karen's Story: Portrait of a High-Achieving Addict

Karen, a successful author and retired publisher, believes that many high-achieving women are alcoholic and drug dependent. Her story, she said, is similar in many ways to the lives of many other addicted women she has met in her recovery program.

Karen has always struggled with a sense of inadequacy, and worked hard to compensate for her shame. Ever since high school, she's been a high achiever looking for accolades. When she was a retail sales clerk after high school, her boss wanted her to go into merchandising; even then, Karen remembers thinking, "Oh, he doesn't know I'm just pretending to be good."

In her quest to feel more adequate, she went to college and became a teacher. Married to an alcoholic, she grew in anxiety and feared that it affected her work, although the world saw her as a dependable and talented teacher. She began looking forward to her first martini every evening at the end of the school day. Drinking made her feel like a real grown-up, and she liked it because it gave her relief from her anxiety and tension-induced stomachaches. She became a daily drinker.

After her marriage ended, Karen went to graduate school. Her good feelings came from being a very good student and teaching assistant. She was still plagued by feelings of anxiety, this time concerning her teaching performance. She was afraid now that her alcohol and drug use were affecting her ability to teach; she had added use of amphetamines to her chemical repertoire. Karen tells her story:

"So many times I had mini-blackouts while I was teaching and sort of 'woke up' wondering if I was in the middle of a sentence and the class was waiting for me to finish it, or if perhaps someone had asked me a question and everyone was waiting for me to answer. By this time I was in my mid-thirties, and I was consuming great volumes of booze daily, getting little sleep because I was up half the night drinking. I told myself, 'This is my life and it's OK. I'm having fun. Self-doubt is normal—it's part of being human. Isn't it nice I can get out of myself, have some fun, and dance on the bar?' I was proving I could do it, and that was the whole reason I was going to school anyway—to prove I could get a master's degree.

"I was dating people who were trouble, and I was doing tons of drugs. I didn't hide my lifestyle from my colleagues, but I don't think they knew how bad it was. I earned almost half my credits in independent study courses, which made my life as a drinker easier and helped me keep a lower profile with the faculty—luckily, I don't remember any of the faculty ever catching me in my after-hours bar scene. They would have seen me as out of control. My behavior was wild, crazy. I ran into students all the time. I went to bed with a couple of my students! It was not a pretty sight. My room-mate moved out because she was afraid of the people I brought home with me. But I never saw danger, just risk and excitement. I even instigated an affair with one of my professors. I thought I was cute and exciting.

"Alcohol and drugs gave me a great deal of courage to go for it in a big way. Even though I didn't believe I had the smarts, the discipline, or the courage to do it, I de-cided to go on for a Ph.D. As crazy as it sounds, I'm grateful I was an active drinker at that time. It fueled me. It muffled the overwhelming fear that I couldn't do it. I doubt I would ever have gotten my doctoral degree if I had gotten sober first.

"I hit the wall with my dissertation. I just couldn't do it. I went to a counselor at the university, who talked with me about my drinking. I stopped drinking and using and went into a counseling group and Alcoholics Anonymous. I loved AA right from the start. I spent the first year of my recovery being an AA party girl, still intent on find-ing the next relationship with a man. I was exhilarated. I still couldn't face my disser-tation for the first year in recovery; it just seemed like it would never happen. But then I finally did it, and I got a great job at a recovery-oriented publishing house.

"I believe my alcoholism is how I became a successful person! I think my insecurity led to my alcoholism, which gave me the courage to aim high and get a terrific edu-cation, which allowed me to get great work and begin a really significant career. Re-covery came for me at the end of my education, and now I no longer have anxiety. Now I know that nothing I think or say or do is important enough to get worried about. I'm not so ego-involved; I let my Higher Power take care of outcomes. My re-covery has defined the kind of person I want to be on and off the job and what I want to model to others. The fellowship gave me a structure for the kind of leadership I've grown comfortable with. It's like I got the courage from drinking to get my Ph.D., and recovery has taught me what to do with it. I truly feel happy and successful now."

The fact that Karen attributes her educational ambition and professional suc-cess to her addiction is an eye-opener; it speaks to the many dimensions of suc-cess and the complicated uses and meanings of drinking. Karen's aggressive, addiction-fueled confidence served as a defense against recognizing her feelings of inadequacy and her impaired performance, and in this sense, drinking served her in the short term. But, as she continued, this defense began to backfire. She was fortunate that she recognized her addiction and entered recovery before her career was destroyed.

Addicts like Karen are difficult to help; they often are unable to see their addiction—especially when they see drinking and drug use as helpful to them. The clinician can help a woman like Karen by helping her identify the negative consequences of her use, using any leverage provided by her supervisor's feedback, and pointing out sobriety as a better path to accomplishing her goals.

Identifying the Addicted Woman in the Workplace

According to figures supplied by the National Institute on Drug Abuse (Backer, 1987), employees who have problems with alcohol and other drug use arrive late to work three times as often as the average employee, use three times the normal level of sick benefits, are five times more likely to file a worker's compensation claim, and are involved in accidents three times more often. In fact, substance-abusing employees are responsible for more than 40 percent of all industrial fatalities and nearly half of all injuries (Bernstein & Mahoney, 1989). Other symptoms include decreased and erratic productivity, increasing neglect of details and lower quality of work, and greater relationship problems with coworkers. Any of these kinds of behavior or consequences occurring at work should tip off the helping professional to assess the individual for addiction.

For women, however, many of the effects of addiction are less easily observable. Addiction in women is often accompanied by anxiety, depression, and other emotional and physical ailments, and compounded by relationship problems and domestic violence (Kinney, 1991). Considering that addicted women who seek the help of professionals often cite other problems as primary, it helps to be aware that the workplace behavior that often accompanies addiction may be harder to identify in women; rather, key symptoms for women are shame, low self-esteem, depression, and feelings of powerlessness and unmanageability in general living.

By the time problems show up in a woman's behavior or work performance, addiction is often well established. For example, although Janet was never confronted by anyone at work about her addiction-related performance problems, she was well aware of them:

My compulsive overeating interfered with my work as a counselor. I worked with adolescents in a lot of pain, struggling with addictions to alcohol and drugs. And there I was trying to help them, hiding my own pain and shame about my active addiction to food. Just before I started going to Overeaters Anonymous (OA), I was truly over-powered by the addiction. I remember sneaking out of work during the afternoon, driving two miles down the road to get a sugar fix. I didn't want anyone to see me. I pretended that I was invisible when I was in my car. I certainly wasn't in my office, where I was supposed to be, recording my patients' progress in their charts or making phone calls to concerned parents, social workers, and teachers.

Janet doesn't know whether her behavior went undetected; she does know that there seemed to be little concern among her colleagues about her overeating as a problem. That an addicted woman has experienced no repercussions at work may indicate that her workplace has a culture that accepts the manifestations of her particular addiction. According to another woman, Sherry, her alcoholic drinking was actually a social asset in two of her early careers, as a singer and as a waitress. As a waitress, she joined her coworkers in drinking after the evening's shift was over.

Assessing Women in the Workplace

Women present for counseling or therapy in a number of ways: through self-referral, referral by a work supervisor or human resources professional, or through intervention resulting from an incident outside of work, such as domestic abuse or an arrest for impaired driving.

Working women are less likely than men to be identified with alcohol and other drug-related problems, and they require different types of outreach (Pape, in press). For many women, workplace employee assistance programs (EAPs) provide the doorway to help. In companies with EAPs, women learn about services available through word of mouth, brochures or posters in the workplace, mailings sent to employees' homes, or referral through a supervisor or the human resources department. It is important, especially for women, that EAPs address a wide range of problems and issues, because women may avoid services that are identified as addiction focused, due to shame and stigma surrounding addiction, which are especially high for women.

Whether in an EAP or another clinical setting, addicted women often present with a host of issues. Depression, anxiety, relationship issues, and job problems are a few of their common presenting problems. Financial problems and violence may be factors in their personal lives. Addicted women almost always experience low self-esteem and shame. For these reasons, Pape (in press) suggests that traditional approaches to intervention, which focus on breaking down denial, are contraindicated with women. Confrontation with women is best approached constructively and accompanied by education about addiction as a disease. The goal of intervention with women is to motivate them to recognize and acknowledge addiction as a primary problem for them and to accept treatment (Spiegel & Friedman, 1997).

If addiction-related performance issues have put the woman's job in jeopardy, the clinician has a powerful lever to support a recommendation for treatment. Yet the workplace problems associated with addictions that alert colleagues and supervisors to intervene with the individual are, for women, only part of the story. Although addiction typically affects every part of a woman's life, she is likely to be very invested in hiding it. Surveys of over five hundred recovering women (conducted by Hazelden, the Betty Ford Center, and the Caron Foundation) found that women list shame about telling family members as the biggest barrier to entering treatment, followed by shame about telling their employers. Other significant barriers include child care and the cost of treatment (Gordon, 2001).

Treatment Needs of Working Women

Effective treatment for addiction can take place in a variety of settings, including counseling with referral to a mutual-help group, structured outpatient day or evening treatment programs, and inpatient or residential treatment. Recommending the appropriate level of treatment depends on the severity of the individual's addiction, her need for treatment of other physical or mental illness, and the risks to recovery and the level of support for recovery in her personal and work life.

Severity of Addiction

The bottom-line question regarding addiction severity is this: How much support and structure will the addicted woman need in order to initiate and maintain a sober lifestyle? A woman whose use pattern permeates her working days will likely need inpatient treatment; the combination of her cravings with the triggers in her daily environment will make abstinence difficult and perhaps even unlikely with any less intensive approach. On the other end of the spectrum, a woman with a binge drinking pattern who recognizes that she has a problem but gets through most days without using may be a candidate for individual or group counseling and a mutual-help recovery program. Physical or mental illness or the anticipation of withdrawal symptoms should also enter into the determination of the appropriate level of care.

Risk and Support in the Woman's Personal Life

Many addicted women have little support or modeling for sobriety. Family issues, such as codependent relationships with using partners, domestic abuse, child care demands, and financial stresses, may increase the need for structure in the early days and weeks of treatment. The optimal situation—one in which a healthy, loving family not only supports the woman's treatment but also becomes involved with their own recoveries in Al-Anon or another family recovery program—is rare. It is extremely important to carefully assess the barriers that families may introduce with their own expectations of the woman, and to determine her readiness to make her recovery her first priority in the face of the daily demands of her life. The woman without a strong personal network faces other risks; she needs to develop a supportive network as part of her recovery program. Women with high risk and low support need inpatient treatment. Women with low risk and high support can often recover with outpatient treatment or counseling and participation in mutual-help recovery programs. The most well known and widely respected of these are Alcoholics Anonymous (AA), Narcotics Anonymous, or other twelve-step programs.

Risk and Support in the Woman's Work Life

It is important in assessment and treatment planning to examine the relationship of the woman's addiction to her work life. Work is where many women come face-to-face with issues of self-esteem and self-confidence, relationships and power, ambition and glass ceilings. Work is likely to be an important issue for attention well into a woman's recovery from addiction. In planning her treatment, the key question is this: Can she quit using while she is going to work as usual? If not, what modifications to her work life are advisable? If the workplace, work colleagues, or work-related stress are triggers for a woman's use of alcohol or other substances, then she may well need to take a leave from work while she is in treatment, or even seek other employment. Here are some key questions to consider:

- Does she use before, during, or after work, or even throughout the workday?
- If so, does she use alone or with others?
- Is using part of the workplace culture and relationships, either on a regular basis or on special occasions?
- Does she have particular relationships at work that involve using or that create stress that she relieves by using?
- Can she navigate the issues and stresses that are likely to arise for her in her workplace, while staying sober?

- Does she use after her workday to relieve work-related stress?
- Do her colleagues know about her addiction?
- If so, what is the level of gossip or stigma she is likely to face from colleagues as she enters recovery?
- Does she know people at work who are in recovery or who can understand and support her?
- Is there help available at the worksite from an EAP counselor?

Careful probing of these three issues—severity of the woman's addiction and other health issues, her personal life, and her work life—will assist both the clinician and the addicted individual in developing an understanding of the appropriate level of treatment. In today's health care environment, however, clinically appropriate treatment is not always easily accessible. Sometimes it is the practical demands of child or elder care that necessitate an alternative plan of treatment. Whatever the level of treatment that becomes advisable as a result of the assessment, both the clinician and the woman entering treatment should be aware that other options can work and that other levels of care are available and can be pursued if they are needed.

Considerations in Referrals to Treatment

Having a clear picture of the individual's condition, situation, and treatment needs, as we have discussed in this chapter, makes it easier to design or select an appropriate treatment. Perhaps the first consideration is the availability of financial support for treatment. Working women are often covered by employer-provided health plans, many of which manage care according to their own guidelines. Managed care health plans often have standards of care that provide only detoxification and medical stabilization, or require failure of a less intensive treatment approach before authorizing increasingly intensive treatment. In some cases, failure of less intensive treatment results in the health plan's denying further care and labeling the addicted woman as "not amenable to treatment." In this or similar cases, it is appropriate to advocate for the patient, pointing out to health plans and to employers directly that a policy of providing employees with needed treatment, even expensive residential treatment, saves money through reduced overall health care costs, increased productivity, and improved workplace safety (Fearing, 2000).

Familiarity with local and national treatment resources is essential for the referring professional. When the clinician is making a treatment referral for an employed woman, a key decision is whether to refer to outpatient or inpatient treatment. Outpatient treatment allows the individual to continue with some aspects of home and work life, which poses both benefits and additional stresses. Although outpatient treatment is less expensive when it proves sufficient, inpatient treatment is successful for the most patients (Walsh et al., 1991).

When possible, women should enter gender-specific treatment. Women have a higher rate of recovery when they receive treatment in women-only groups (Straussner & Zelvin, 1997). There are gender-specific inpatient and outpatient treatment programs, some of which include children.

Work as a Treatment and Recovery Issue

Work, like every other aspect of an addicted woman's life, is related to her addiction and her recovery in a holistic way. Aspects of her work life are likely to be both part of the solution and part of the problem in establishing a new sober lifestyle. Job stress for women often relates to social, competency, and political issues. For some women, drinking or using drugs with colleagues has been a way to connect and find inclusion in the work culture. Other women use chemicals to cope with uncomfortable or abusive workplaces. Staying sober in these situations requires a woman to develop clarity about the culture in which she works and to plan strategies and develop skills for handling relationships and feelings in new and sober ways.

A key role for the clinician is to give support and direction in helping the addicted woman assess the role of her work life in attaining and maintaining her recovery. Each woman faces societal and individual challenges and has her own coping mechanisms, goals, and skills. The challenge is to find a fit that is comfortable enough for her to maintain her sobriety.

The Early Days of Sobriety at Work

Whether she takes an absence from work to concentrate on treatment or begins her recovery while staying on the job, the newly recovering woman faces a host of challenges. Her addiction may have provided her the courage or energy to face her work, and abstinence may bring a flood of self-doubt ("Can I do this job sober?") as well as require demanding new social skills. Without a plan and some attention to developing coping strategies, a woman may find that stresses in the workplace threaten her recovery.

The clinician's role includes coaching the newly sober woman as she thinks ahead, assesses the threats and triggers she can reasonably anticipate encountering in her workplace, and rehearses ways to avoid or handle slippery situations. Asking the client to read such self-help books as *Working Clean and Sober: A Guide for All Recovering People* (Skibbins, 2000) can be an important supplement to treatment, encouraging planning and providing practical coaching on returning to work and dealing with foreseeable problems.

Clinicians can use the following list in helping newly sober women formulate a plan for continuing their recovery at work:

1. *Using the EAP.* Many companies have EAPs that actively support women in recovery by staying in touch with them, providing free counseling, and sometimes even testing for alcohol and drugs. This last practice is most likely to be found in industries with high needs for safety or for security of intellectual property. Drug testing is often required of nurses and physicians, too. EAPs with strong follow-up services for employees who have received treatment for addiction are effective in raising recovery rates for their employees.

2. *Deciding whether to be open with colleagues and bosses.* Deciding whether to tell colleagues or bosses the truth about one's addiction is an important decision that may make life easier or present more obstacles in the future; such decisions should be made very carefully. What kind of reactions can the woman anticipate, and how will she handle them? Whether sympathetic or not, most people in the workplace simply do not understand addiction or the amount of energy that it takes to work a recovery program. They may not understand why it is such a big deal, why the newly recovering person isn't simply "fixed"—normal—and why she can't drink, use drugs, or eat sweets in moderation like everyone else. All these issues need to be considered before they come up.

3. *Dealing with stigma.* Addiction is still widely misconstrued as a moral issue. Whether a woman chooses to openly disclose her addiction and recovery or not, she will be subjected to others' views, and there are times when these views may cause pain. At the same time, a newly recovering woman may be too sensitive to how other people see her, or she may project her own negative self-image and think that people are gossiping about her when they are not.

4. *Regaining the trust of coworkers and employers.* By the time they get into recovery, many addicted women have left a trail of poor performance and unmet commitments at work. If this is the case, employers and coworkers will need to see not only improvement but also consistency over time before the scrutiny subsides. Dealing with such distrust is stressful, and clients should be prepared to deal with this stress. Reaching out to a recovery support system can be a very helpful step.

5. *Identifying people, places, or things on the job that might trigger the urge to use.* One of the first things a woman needs to realize is the importance of paying attention to monitoring the people, places, and things that are triggers for her addictive

thinking, cravings, and behavior. Work life is teeming with people, places, and things that may be helpful, dangerous, or both. It is important for the woman to identify any triggering habits or routines that come up before, during, or after work, to make plans to avoid them, and to learn how best to handle triggers when she must face them.

6. *Being left out or feeling left out.* Returning to work after a leave for treatment may lead to feelings of having been left out of the information loop as well as the social network at work. Moreover, even an environment that is supportive of recovery from one kind of addiction may be less supportive of an addict with a different problem. Janet's experience is an example:

I was lucky to be working in a chemical dependency treatment center when I got into recovery for my food addiction. It helped, because so much of my daily work centered on the spiritual principles that were part of my own recovery program. But I found myself reluctant to tell people what I was doing. What if I shared that I had an addiction of my own, and then failed to recover? Wouldn't it be better to keep my recovery program secret, so that if I cheated a bit or plunged full force into bingeing they would never know? I didn't want people watching whether I was joining in the coffee-and-caramel-roll ritual that followed our morning staff meeting. I didn't want to join the ritual and be tempted by the sweets. But I didn't want to be left out, either. I felt lonely. It was hurtful to me that when I did share with some of my coworkers, who understood alcoholism and drug addiction so well, they simply did not understand or accept my addiction as real or serious.

7. *Developing a supportive network at work.* A central theme among recovering women is the need for support from at least one other person. Making a list of telephone numbers of sponsors or other recovery support people and keeping it handy all day are very important. Attending a lunchtime twelve-step meeting near the workplace may help the woman identify nearby people in recovery who may serve as supports when needed.

8. *Developing positive rituals.* Positive triggers and rituals can support a woman's new sobriety. These need not be things that are obvious to others, as long as they are meaningful to the woman herself. They may include having a coffee mug that is imbued with a special meaning, placing a photo of a sponsor or other supportive person on the desk, hanging a favorite poem or affirmation on the bulletin board, taking a nature walk at lunchtime, or making two calls each day to a sponsor or other support person.

9. *Planning a new routine for after work.* If a woman in recovery is accustomed to going out for a drink with colleagues, going home and smoking marijuana, taking a pill, or stopping at a particular convenience store to buy junk food or lottery tickets, she will need to change her routine. She may need to schedule a self-help

or therapy meeting after work instead of going out, or take a different route home to avoid a tempting store. She will also need to make her home a "recovery-friendly" place. The more specific the alternative plans the better.

10. *Dealing with the challenges of business entertaining and traveling.* It is important for the woman to think through how to handle business entertaining and to develop a plan that will minimize access to her addictive substance. Many women recovering from alcohol dependence will use the excuse that they are on a special diet as a way of not having to join in a business drink. Business traveling, if done in early recovery, can be made safer by staying at a hotel without a stocked refrigerator in the room or by calling ahead to ask that it be emptied.

11. *Finding confidence.* A woman who has functioned for months or years under the influence of a chemical may indeed face a situation in which the work, learned while in an altered state, seems strange once sobriety sets in. "In early sobriety, I was still feeling sick and tired, as well as scared, and nothing seemed the same," said Kathy of her job working in a railroad yard. "I pretty much used regularly on the job after the first few months. It came natural to do my job under the influence. Sober, it felt like I had to learn the job all over again."

Slippery Workplaces

Workplaces have their own cultures: their particular attitudes toward alcohol and drug use on and off the job, pressures to overperform, and tolerance for low performance; they may encourage employees to become workaholics or to enjoy a balanced approach to life. Some workplaces are supportive of recovery, but many are not. Depending on the industry, the particular organization, and the specific people who work closely together, work can be helpful in early recovery or can make staying sober even more difficult.

Some workplace cultures condone drinking or using drugs—sometimes even on the job—and these environments are very difficult places to work for chemically dependent women. The food service industry, as one example, is one of the tougher businesses for a newly recovering woman. With higher than average rates of heavy drinking (18.6 percent of employees) and use of illegal drugs (15 percent), the food service industry is an example of an enabling culture that demonstrates a high tolerance for "partying" (Anthony, 1992; Backer, 1987). Trying to stay sober while working in such an atmosphere is difficult; it's the kind of work environment recovering people label as *slippery.*

Sherry's experience waiting tables spanned both her using life and recovery: "When I was using and working as a waitress, no one cared what kind of shape I was in when I came in to work my shift—as long as I came in. Everyone who worked in that nightclub partied pretty hard, and it was kind of taken for granted. I tried working in that business after I got sober, and it was really uncomfortable. It was really obvious that I didn't fit in. I was miserable, so I left. I'm glad I did; it wasn't a good place for me."

That's not to say all restaurants are "slippery" places to work. On the extreme other end from Sherry's experience at the nightclub is work at the Day by Day Café in St. Paul, Minnesota, where the staff and many of the clientele are in recovery. "Fitting in" in this work environment means abstaining from alcohol and drugs on and off the job, and living a recovery lifestyle as well.

White-collar professions can have drinking and drug-using cultures, too, as Patty's situation illustrates:

Patty worked in advertising. Forgoing a drink with the team after work put some crimps in relationships for her. And the culture was so accepting of alcohol that it entered right into the workday. Patty says, "Returning to work was just awful. Alcohol and drug use was really normal at the ad agency where I worked. One month into recovery, we landed a huge account, and I was pouring the champagne at the office party we threw to celebrate. This was not a good situation! I was very lucky because someone else at work let me know that they were in recovery, too. After that, we supported each other. That made it somewhat better. And the next year, my boss went into treatment!"

Working situations in which one's peer group is predominantly male is slippery. There is more drinking and drug use in industries with a higher percentage of male employees. As pointed out earlier, women who work in male-dominated industries and workplaces drink more than women who work in female-dominated workplaces. That does not mean that recovering women can't return to work or pursue a career in male-dominated fields; it does mean, however, that it may be harder. Kathy's case is an example:

For Kathy, a railroad engineer, being happily sober in her male-dominated job meant calling on the relationship skills she learned in her rough-and-tumble family. Rather than "being nice," she ratcheted up her "gotchya" sense of humor, in-your-face honesty, and determination to do her fair share of the work. Her strong personality works for her in this setting, and she likes the work itself. Kathy says, "Although I'm more of a feminist now, and I draw boundaries about sexist and racist humor, in a lot of ways I'm sort of one of the guys. I can pretty much give as good as I get, and I get along fine with most of the men I work with. We've all been there a long time, and they know me, and pretty much respect my boundaries now. They may act differently when I'm not around, but they're OK around me. It's worth it to me because I really like working the railroad—I like the excitement and risk of working the yard, and the powerful engines and the fresh air. And I like the fact I can make good money."

Kathy had to get through really difficult times to reach her current comfort level in what many women would consider a hostile environment. Her determination and heavy reliance on AA saw her through many tests. She describes her first night back on the job:

"It was really hard that first night back at work after getting out of treatment. I told everyone where I had been and that I was going to stay sober. My old boyfriend was giving the assignments that night, and he sent me off to the other end of the yard. When I pulled the engine down to his end later, I saw the pot smoke wafting out the window of one of the cars, and I knew he was with the only other woman on the shift, doing what we used to do together. That really hurt. I went in one of the shacks and had a good cry, and wouldn't you know they walked in on me? I sucked it up and got out of there, and I knew work would never be the same if I was going to get well."

Many women would not choose to develop the tough coping skills Kathy needed in her job environment. It would seem to be a perfect setup for relapse, yet Kathy has maintained her sobriety in that work environment for over ten years. Kathy's case demonstrates the importance of making examined and conscious decisions about how to survive each day in recovery.

Many women, Kathy included, find valuable help with relationship and personal boundary issues in Al-Anon. Al-Anon helps women focus on personal awareness and development while finding healthy balance in relationships with others applies naturally to workplace relationships. Al-Anon sponsors can be a valuable complement to sobriety sponsors, helping create a strong support system for the working woman in recovery.

After the Crisis: Helping Clients Stay Motivated for Sobriety

Planning to stay sober is a pretty simple thing to do. However, for many women early in recovery it is hard to keep caring about staying sober. As Marjie says:

I got sober through Narcotics Anonymous and Alcoholics Anonymous meetings. Those first months were awful. Since I started using at age eleven and was basically stoned for sixteen years, my whole personality was based on using. I was a flirt, a party girl, and my whole world expected me to be that person. I didn't fit in with the people in my life any more, because you only fit as long as you do what they're doing.

When I got sober, I was an empty shell—at least, I felt that way. I didn't know who I was or even what I liked to do. There was no real reward in sobriety yet—I didn't yet have what I've gotten since, one day at a time, to fall back on.

Marjie says that there were two things that helped her stay sober in those early days. The first was going to lots of twelve-step meetings. The second was that her boss and one friend at her catering job were in recovery too. "It only takes reaching out to one other person to avoid being alone. That's the worst thing: feeling like you're alone."

Growing Pains: The Ongoing Challenges of Recovery

Being content with one's role and with one's workplace is healthy as well as helpful to women. It is important for women to carefully consider the choices open to them. Although the need for economic survival may dictate the necessity to earn a paycheck, and personal ambition may lead women to particular career paths, most women have at least some choice regarding what kind of work they do and the work environment in which they will spend their time and energy. This choice is very important for all women, and especially for women in recovery. It is an important element of creating a life that fits comfortably. For some women, that means changing jobs. Marjie, for example, changed careers early in recovery in order to stay sober. Her work environment as a caterer was too dangerous a place to be; coworkers were drinking and snorting lines of cocaine on the job. Seven years later, she is still convinced she made the right choice.

Finding a fit in one's work life is not always a matter of changing jobs, although it is uncomfortable to stay in a stressful work situation. Women in this situation must identify stress factors and develop strategies for coping with their work situations. Early in recovery, Karen had the experience of struggling with an authoritarian boss who abused her emotionally yet also promoted her. In spite of the high stress of dealing with her boss, she was excited by her work and absolutely convinced that she needed to stay in her job for the time being. After seeking therapy to help her deal with her work problems, she ultimately was promoted into her dream job.

Creating Balance

Most employed women lead busy lives, and finding time for recovery in addition to work, family, community involvement, and taking care of their personal needs is a physical and spiritual challenge. Nevertheless, having multiple roles is helpful for women in maintaining sobriety. Busy lives pull women forward, and momentum helps maintain balance. Many women find that the very structure of twelve-step recovery programs—their regular meetings, social and service opportunities, prescriptions for reading and writing, and role assignments both as mentor and student through the tool of sponsorship—introduces variety and balance into their lives.

Betsy, in recovery for over twenty years, says that her recovery program has taught her helpful ways of defining and handling work stress:

Every week I go to these meetings where everyone is talking about all of the tragedies that just occurred in the last week in their life, and we can sit around laughing about it because we can see how we exaggerate these little things in our life and turn them into major tragedies. I think that it is really important for an organization and the people in it to be able to admit that they made mistakes and to not get beat up for it, to be able to laugh at themselves. Besides encouraging honesty and sincerity, the twelve steps also encourage us not to take ourselves too seriously and to have a clearer perspective of what is important in our life. The job is incredibly important, and we all need to do as much as we possibly can to get the job done; however, you are not your job, and you have a life outside of your job, and that needs attention, too. The program fosters balance.

Finding Meaning

Women in recovery from addiction are engaged in a way of life that forces them to question all aspects of the way they live. Because women change and grow, these life issues are revisited many times over the years. Recovering women may enter therapy many years after attaining sobriety, engaged in and unsettled by new areas of growth and spiritual development.

Work is often high on the list of critical issues for the woman looking for meaning; the recovery process leads women to question their perspectives on work. Often, goals of making money or achieving promotions begin to recede in importance, as they are challenged by new goals of finding satisfying work, being happy at work, or doing something one believes is making an important contribution.

The observant therapist can encourage this process by pointing out that the client's current unrest may be related to her growth in recovery, and by framing her presenting need for more self-discovery as positive and exciting. Marjie is an example of someone who reached this stage years after she entered recovery; she was surprised to find that advancement in her work became a concern for her as she approached her twelfth sobriety anniversary. As she described her recovery process, the first years were devoted to staying sober, the next years were focused on learning to live successfully, and only in the last few years has she really begun to appreciate that she has something special and worthwhile to contribute.

Accepting Success and Leadership

Recovery leads women to success. It teaches women the skills of living in the paradox of accepting responsibility and recognizing powerlessness and walking the fine line between taking control of making something happen and letting go. It teaches women to value community and teamwork.

Many women in recovery eventually find themselves in leadership positions and situations because others appreciate the character the women develop through practicing the twelve-step recovery program. Other people recognize their wisdom, love, and attitude of service. Colleagues trust them. Recovering women find, and others recognize in them, that one of the promises of the twelve-step program has come true: "We will intuitively know how to handle situations that used to baffle us." Such intuition develops as recovering women apply the lessons of recovery to the rest of their lives, including their work.

AA's *Twelve Steps and Twelve Traditions* says that when it is bestowed, leadership is to be worn humbly, as a simple exercise of the Higher Power's will for the alcoholic (Alcoholics Anonymous, 1953). The program also asks recovering alcoholics to practice twelve-step principles in all their affairs. For leaders, a natural and pressing question is, How do I apply the twelve steps to the tasks of running my organization? Karen, the publisher, talked about the relationship of her recovery to her role as a leader of an organization:

The twelve steps became so ingrained in my life; they became my philosophy so that I didn't know how to manage any other way. When I go to an AA meeting, I know we aren't sitting here to judge each other, but to help each other figure out how to live our lives better. At work, I knew that when I called a management meeting, we were there without anyone trying to "outshine" another. There was no sense that we were going to "sabotage" one another. There was an absolute sense that we were together to solve a common problem. In AA, the common problem was alcoholism. As a team at work, the common problem was how do we get our message out to the community. What marketing strategies do we need to use? What books do we need to be publishing? It became clear to me that it was a spiritual set of tools; I don't mean religiously spiritual, but the spirit of what we were trying to reach together meant all the difference in the world. What we were doing every day is purposeful, like a fun challenge. We were trying to solve problems to help people.

Recovery Teaches a Feminine Model of Leadership

The groundbreaking theory on a new model of women's psychology being developed at the Stone Center at Wellesley College states that women develop and mature in relationship with others. These researchers reject the notion of autonomy as the goal of personal growth. They believe that women are aware at a core level that they are part of a constellation of relationships and that all growth and maturation takes place in connection with others (Jordan, Kaplan, Miller, Stiver, & Surrey, 1991). If we apply the thinking of Jordan et al. to women's style of power and leadership, the dynamics of the work group take on a key role. Competition becomes irrelevant. Authority is less important than information and creativity, and power arises as energy from the group. Karen's description of her recovery-based leadership style fits the description of feminine leadership:

One of the incredible things about us as a team was that we really didn't have the answers as individuals. We would gather together around the table in my office not having the answer, and believing that if we sat there and talked it out together, the right answer would emerge. It wasn't a whole lot different than a one-on-one counseling session that a person might have or a whole lot different than something that would occur at an AA meeting. People are just saying how it feels or seems to them, and the wisdom that would arise was the result of people just kind of being willing to say that they don't know what looks right or what feels right. It seems to me that part of the reason the business was so successful was that we were so willing to intuit, to let our intuition guide us. I think that that is one of the things that in some kind of management programs needs to be honored more. I learned that the collective inner-wisdom of a group of people sitting around a table is so much greater than the individual inner-wisdom, because you never know when ego is trying to lead you astray.

This model is less threatening than the traditional authoritarian style of leadership, in part because it is less lonely. Still, in many work situations, leadership positions bring not only new opportunities and new professional challenges but also new personal stresses: stronger pressure to function like the men in a male-oriented power framework, "glass ceiling" barriers to advancement, increased demands on time usually spent on personal or family needs, and other ongoing stresses. For women in leadership roles, the support of a recovery group or a continuing therapeutic relationship is very helpful, because, as Marjie said about stress in the workplace, "That's the worst thing: feeling like you're alone." No woman needs to be alone in dealing with the challenges her life and her work deliver.

A Leadership Model for Tomorrow's Workplace

The value of the twelve-step model is being recognized by leading scholars in organization leadership and change theory (Hammond, 2001; Mitroff & Denton, 2000; Mitroff, Mason, & Pearson, 1994; Robbins, 1987, 1992). As our society and workplaces are diversifying in a rapidly changing world, the importance of creating strong relationships among people in our workforces is gaining recognition. Women are naturally interested in facilitating relationships. Recovering women are practiced at the skills of self-aware and responsible relationship building. They make good leaders—the kind of leaders that will increasingly be in demand in the more diverse workforce of the future.

Conclusion

Working women with addictions are not always offered the help they need to enter recovery. Internalized societal stereotypes of addicted women often keep clinicians from recognizing addiction as a primary problem among employed women seeking help. Consequently, the symptoms of addiction among employed women often show up in the workplace long after addiction has become well established.

Helping professionals play a key role in aiding addicted women recognize their addiction as a problem that needs treatment and in supporting them to let go of their shame. The clinician's careful assessment and strong advocacy for appropriate treatment are extremely important; by taking the disease and treatment seriously, the clinician helps the addicted woman value her self and her right to treatment and recovery.

A woman's ability to maintain sobriety at work is one factor that must be considered in designing an appropriate treatment plan to arrest her addiction. Women who are busy with multiple roles in their lives do better in recovery than women with fewer roles. Being busy with several roles appears to create momentum and healthy balance for women. The quality of the relationships within those roles is important for women's health; statistics tell us that working women do better in recovery if they work with predominantly female colleagues rather than in settings dominated by men. Introducing recovery practices and rituals into women's workdays is recommended, as well as incorporating the support of sponsors and other recovery support persons.

Working a recovery program strengthens a woman's capabilities and talents in leading others. Practicing recovery principles in the workplace results in a more comfortable, feminine approach to management and leadership well suited to meeting the needs of today's workforce. For the recovering woman called to leadership, continuing support from a therapist and her recovery support group can provide the balance and perspective to help her keep her recovery lifestyle as her highest priority. For recovery must take priority over work. It's a simple matter of "first things first."

References

Alcoholics Anonymous. (1953). *Twelve steps and twelve traditions.* New York: Alcoholics Anonymous World Services.

Anthony, J. C. (1992). Psychoactive drug dependence and abuse: More common in some occupations than in others? *Journal of Employee Assistance Research, 1*(1), 148–186.

Backer, T. E. (1987). *Strategic planning for workplace drug abuse programs.* Rockville, MD: National Institute on Drug Abuse.

Beckman, L. (1994). Barriers to alcoholism treatment for women. *Alcohol Health and Research World, 18,* 208.

Bernstein, M., & Mahoney, J. J. (1989). Management perspectives on alcoholism: The employer's stake in alcoholism treatment. *Occupational Medicine, 4,* 223–232.

Crum, R. M. (1995). Occupational stress and the risk of alcohol abuse and dependence. *Alcoholism: Clinical and Experimental Research, 19,* 647–655.

Fearing, J. (2000). *Workplace intervention: The bottom line on helping addicted employees become productive again.* Center City, MN: Hazelden.

Gordon, S. (2001). *Barriers to treatment for chemically dependent women: A survey of participants in Women Healing Conferences.* Wernersville, PA: Caron Foundation.

Hammond, W. C. (2001). *Twelve step wisdom at work: Transforming your life and your organization.* London: Kogan Page.

Hazelden Foundation. (1996). *National survey shows alcohol and drug use has strong impact on workplace.* Unpublished article. Results available from Hazelden Corporate Communications, P.O. Box 11, Center City, MN.

Jordan, J. V., Kaplan, A. G., Miller, J. B., Stiver, I. P., & Surrey, J. L. (1991). *Women's growth in connection.* New York: Guilford Press.

Kinney, J. (1991). *Clinical manual of substance abuse.* St. Louis, MO: Mosby.

Mitroff, I. I., & Denton, E. (2000). *A spiritual audit of corporate America: Multiple designs for fostering spirituality in the workplace.* San Francisco: Jossey-Bass.

Mitroff, I. I., Mason, R. O., & Pearson, C. M. (1994). *Framebreak: The radical redesign of American business.* San Francisco: Jossey-Bass.

National Council on Alcoholism and Drug Dependence. (2000, March 7). *Use of alcohol and other drugs among women.* Available: www.ncadd.org/women.html.

Pape, P. A. (in press). Assessment and intervention with alcohol- and drug-abusing women. In S.L.A. Straussner (Ed.), *Clinical work with substance-abusing clients* (2nd ed.). New York: Guilford Press.

Robbins, L. P. (1987). *Learning in organizations: The effects of interactive planning and twelve step methodologies.* Unpublished doctoral dissertation, University of Pennsylvania, Philadelphia.

Robbins, L. P. (1992). Designing more functional organizations: The 12 step model. *Journal of Organizational Change Management, 5*(4), 41–58.

Skibbins, D. (2000). *Working clean and sober: A guide for all recovering people.* Center City, MN: Hazelden.

Spiegel, B. R., & Friedman, D. D. (1997). High-achieving women: Issues in addiction and recovery. In S.L.A. Straussner & E. Zelvin (Eds.), *Gender and addictions: Men and women in treatment* (pp. 151–166). Northvale, NJ: Aronson.

Straussner, S.L.A., & Zelvin, E. (Eds.). (1997). *Gender and addictions: Men and women in treatment.* Northvale, NJ: Aronson.

Substance Abuse and Mental Health Services Administration. (1998). *1997 National Household Survey on Drug Abuse.* Rockville, MD: Author.

Walsh, D. C., Hingson, R. W., Merrigan, D. M., Levenson, S. M., Cupples, L. A., Heeren, T., Coffman, G. A., Becker, C. A., Barker, T. A., Hamilton, S. K., McGuire, T. G., & Kelly, C. A. (1991). A randomized trial of treatment options for alcohol-abusing workers. *New England Journal of Medicine, 325,* 775–782.

Wilsnack, S. C. (1996). Patterns and trends in women's drinking: Recent findings and some implications for prevention. In J. M. Howard, S. E. Martin, P. D. Mail, M. E. Hilton, & E. D. Taylor (Eds.), *Women and alcohol: Issues for prevention research* (NIAAA Research Monograph 32, NIH Publication No. 96-3817, pp. 19–63). Bethesda, MD: U.S. Department of Health and Human Services, Public Health Services, National Institutes of Health.

CHAPTER EIGHTEEN

EFFECTIVE INTERVENTION AND TREATMENT FOR LESBIANS

Laurie Drabble and Brenda L. Underhill

Providing clinical services for lesbians who are abusing or are addicted to chemicals or other behaviors necessitates working within a complex, multilevel, multitheoretical perspective. The experiences of addiction and of recovery among lesbians are shaped by individual dynamics and continuing interaction with the larger contexts of community, culture, and societal structures and values. Because helping professionals are not exempt from overt and covert societal messages that underpin homophobia and heterosexism, effectively working with lesbians entails becoming adept at self-assessment and recognizing our own countertransference. Determining the line between normative and problematic or pathological behavior has long been a challenge in the addiction field. The dilemma of distinguishing what is personally or culturally normative from what is problematic is particularly pertinent in working with lesbians, a diverse population whose very existence has been marginalized, pathologized, and stigmatized.

Despite gains by the women's and gay rights movements, individual and systemic homophobia (fear of same sex sexuality) and heterosexism (presumption of heterosexuality and belief that heterosexual relationships are superior to homosexual relationships) pervade the larger culture and create barriers to effective treatment for lesbians with addictions (Underhill & Ostermann, 1991). Additional barriers are created by the common failure to consider the specific needs of lesbians from different racial, ethnic, age, regional, or other subcultural groups.

Historically, scant research and few prevention and treatment efforts have focused on lesbians with substance abuse problems, eating problems, pathological or problem gambling, or compulsive sexual behavior; even less work has been done on lesbians of color and young lesbians. However, a growing body of literature and clinical experience offers direction for the clinician in providing lesbian-sensitive services. This chapter examines the prevalence and etiology of substance abuse and several other behavioral problems among lesbians; it offers clinical frameworks that are useful in facilitating recovery, and specific strategies for assessment, intervention, and treatment.

Epidemiology and Etiology

Studies suggest that lesbians have lower rates of abstention from alcohol use, higher rates of reported alcohol-related problems, less decrease of alcohol use with aging, and higher rates of tobacco and illicit drug use (Bradford, Ryan, & Rothblum, 1994; McKirnan & Peterson, 1989; Roberts & Sorensen, 1999; Skinner, 1994). Most studies about alcohol and drug use among lesbians have been conducted with limited, nonrandom samples, such as selecting respondents from lesbian and gay bars. The strongest study to date, an analysis of national population-based data, found higher rates of alcohol and drug dependency among lesbians and bisexuals in comparison to heterosexual women (Cochran & Mays, 2000). In contrast, two other studies conducted in different urban areas found no significant differences in levels of drinking between lesbians and heterosexual women, but found that lesbian abstainers were more likely to report being recovering alcoholics (Bradford et al., 1994; Hughes, Hass, Razzano, Cassidy, & Matthews, 2000). These findings may suggest that some lesbians are at higher risk for alcohol- and drug-related problems, or they may reflect a continuing trend, which began in the 1980s, toward increased awareness of alcohol problems and greater abstinence in some lesbian communities (Bradford et al., 1994; Hughes et al., 2000).

Several theories suggest factors that may be unique or particularly significant to the etiology of alcohol and drug problems among lesbians and gay men. These factors include internalized and external homophobia, stress related to the coming-out process, isolation, and reliance on alcohol and other drugs to counter stigma and shame associated with same-sex sexual activity (Bradford et al., 1994; Kus, 1990; Paul, Stall, & Bloomfield, 1991). Hughes and Wilsnack (1997) suggest that lesbians may be disproportionately affected by risk factors that are known to correlate with alcohol consumption among women, including underemployment, job discrimination, and stressors related to multiple roles and family conflict. Hypotheses explaining differences in substance use have yet to be verified through research studies (Bux, 1996).

Some studies of eating problems among lesbians suggest that the rates of bulimia, frequent dieting, and binge eating are generally similar to those of heterosexual women (French, Story, Remafedi, Resnick, & Blum, 1996; Striegel-Moore, Tucker, & Hsu, 1990), whereas others suggest that lesbians may be more likely to binge eat than heterosexual women (Heffernan, 1996). Compulsive sexual behavior, defined by Coleman (1995) as sexual behavior that is based on a drive to reduce anxiety rather than sexual desire, appears to be more common among men than women (Rosen & Leiblum, 1995), as is pathological and problem gambling (Mark & Lesieur, 1992). However, compulsive sexual behavior, other sexual issues, and pathological gambling in women, particularly subpopulations of women (including lesbians), remain relatively unexplored (Hughes & Norris, 1995; Mark & Lesieur, 1992).

Clinical Frameworks

Several compatible models for the process of change serve as a useful foundation for working with lesbians. The developmental model of recovery by Stephanie Brown (1985) is a useful framework for understanding the dynamic process of recovery. Brown's model recognizes the relationship between stages of recovery (for example, drinking, transition, early recovery, and ongoing recovery) and key components of recovery (focus on the problem, the interaction between the individual and the environment, and interpretation of self and others). The transtheoretical model is an empirically based comprehensive framework of change for treating addiction (DiClemente & Prochaska, 1998). Using this model, the clinician helps the client move through stages of change (precontemplation, contemplation, preparation, and action and maintenance) and address the tasks of each stage. Motivational interviewing, a strategy that emphasizes the importance of empathy and uses a client-centered focus to enhance the client's motivation for change, is a useful approach, particularly when working with individuals in the early stages of the change process (that is, precontemplation and contemplation) (Miller & Rollnick, 1991).

Feminist theory also provides a framework for addressing addictions among lesbians. Feminist frameworks stress (1) recognizing power imbalances and the importance of client empowerment; (2) defining and naming "problems" based on the client's perceptions of harm and healing rather than on dominant social norms; (3) maintaining flexibility and a commitment to honor individual and cultural preferences in the process of recovery; (4) understanding that recovery is a process; and (5) accounting for the sociocultural and political context of recovery (for example, addressing the impact of societal prescriptions about what women should look like in relation to a client's body image issues or eating problems) (Van Den Bergh, 1991). Some feminists challenge the constructs and language that are often used to frame "addictive" problems. For example, some feminists prefer the term *eating problems* rather than *eating disorders* because these problems "often begin as orderly and sane responses to insane circumstances" (Thompson, 1996, p. 106). Saulnier (1996) suggests that the concept of sex addiction should be viewed critically by helping professionals because it is often poorly defined and has been loosely used to explain diverse and complex phenomena, from violent sexual acts to sexual behavior that falls outside traditional norms. This criticism is particularly pertinent to lesbians and bisexuals, whose same-sex sexuality has often been stigmatized and pathologized.

Other theoretical frameworks, compatible with the models described previously, are salient to working with lesbian clients. Trauma theory provides a framework for clinicians and clients to understand the impact of trauma (including the harmful impact of homophobia) on client affect, consciousness (for example, dissociation), self-perception, and relationship to physical self (Finnegan & McNally, 1996). Relational theory provides a perspective for understanding the importance of relationships in women's development and the dynamics of intimacy in lesbian relationships (which have often been framed as "fusion") (Mencher, 1997). Systems-cultural approaches acknowledge the importance of the mutual interaction between individuals and systems, such as families and cultural groups (Fassinger, 2000). The strengths model "empowers and validates lesbian and gay clients in a social climate characterized by homophobia and hostility, on the one hand, and by the triumph of gay identity and community on the other" (van Wormer, Wells, & Boes, 2000, p. xvii).

Assessment

For all clients, treatment goals are developed from information gathered during a biopsychosocial assessment. Given the complexity of issues linked to addiction recovery for lesbians, the clinician must actively listen and assess the client's concerns about her addiction problems and related issues, such as her family-of-origin concerns, life stressors (for example, financial, emotional, and relationship issues), and interpersonal conflicts. In order to target issues that are key for individual lesbian clients, it is beneficial to focus assessment and the development of therapeutic goals on problems that are most important to the client and that are the most acute and disruptive to the client's daily life. Lesbians, like other clients, need to be assessed for their motivation to change and their current stage of change in relation to the issues for which they are seeking help. In addition, clinicians need to explore the multilevel concerns that are integral to addiction recovery among lesbians, including clients' cultural identity and sense of connection to community, and the impact of internalized and external oppressions, such as homophobia, racism, and sexism.

It is critical for clinicians to develop respectful, empathetic, and collaborative relationships with lesbians seeking help for addiction or other behavioral problems. Effective client assessment will include questions about sexual orientation and sexual behavior. It is important to use gender-neutral language on all assessment forms and during interviews. Assessment tools can be easily designed or adapted to use the term *partner*, instead of the more traditionally used terms for male significant others. Operating on the principle of "do ask, do tell" means explicitly asking about relationships with partners who may be male, female, or both, in a manner that communicates acceptance and normalizes different sexual orientations and sexual behaviors.

It is also important to be aware of issues that may disproportionately affect lesbians when using standardized assessment tools. Because assessment forms the basis for treatment planning, clinicians need to be alert to a lesbian's individual strengths and community assets that may support the recovery process. Even when using well-established instruments, clinicians need to be aware of how sexual orientation may affect some of the domains of assessment. For example, the Addiction Severity Index Instrument, Expanded Female Version (ASI–F), in addition to assessing alcohol and drug use, provides information about other domains: medical status, employment status, legal status, family and social relationships, and psychiatric status (Center for Substance Abuse Treatment, 1998). Assessment of lesbians could be skewed toward greater individual severity and could miss important individual and social assets, unless this test and others like it are administered with awareness of the interaction between social context and a lesbian client's experiences in each of these domains. For example, lesbians, particularly lesbians of color, are for financial reasons more likely than heterosexual women to be uninsured, to experience a lack continuity of medical care, and to be unable to obtain medical or mental health care (Bradford et al., 1994; Stevens, 1993, 1998). Lesbians are also less likely to receive preventive health services (for example, Pap smears and clinical breast exams) and more likely to avoid medical care because of fear of homophobia and heterosexism among health providers (Cassidy & Hughes, 1997). Lesbians may face discrimination in employment because of their sexual orientation or face barriers to some sectors in the job market if their appearance and style of dress, which may be integral to their personal and community identity, do not conform to traditional sex-role expectations (for example, appears masculine or "butch"). Lesbians may also rely on different social support networks than heterosexual women. For example, a lesbian may be more likely to turn to friends ("family of choice") than to her family of origin for support (Bradford et al., 1994).

According to research studies, lesbians are not likely to have greater mental health problems than heterosexual women, but are more likely to experience a wide array of stressors related to experiences of homophobia and discrimination (Institute of Medicine [IOM], 1999). A national lesbian health study found that over half the sample had been verbally attacked for being lesbian, and 13 percent had lost employment because of discrimination (Bradford et al., 1994). Racism, sexism, and homophobia create particularly high levels of stress for lesbians of color. A national survey of homosexually active African American women and men found that lesbian and bisexual women displayed higher levels of depressive distress than gay men (except for men that were HIV positive) (Cochran & Mays, 1994). Examination of potential mental health issues in addiction assessment will ideally use a bifocal lens: one that recognizes the traumatic impact of social oppression and at the same time evaluates individual symptoms and strengths.

Past and potential suicidality and violence are important assessment areas. Lesbians are more likely than heterosexual women to have thought about suicide and to have attempted suicide, particularly during adolescence and young adulthood (Bradford et al., 1994; Hughes et al., 2000). Lesbians, like all women seeking help with addictive problems, need to be assessed for past experiences of child abuse, other sexual abuse, and (contrary to popular mythology that battering does not occur between women) domestic violence (Hughes & Norris, 1995).

Case Example: Jo

Jo is a thirty-two-year-old Latina lesbian who describes her background as crazy but loving. Her mother lives nearby, and her father died at an early age from alcoholism. An older male cousin who lived with the family sexually abused Jo as a child. Jo did not disclose the abuse to her family, stating that she is certain that no one would have believed her.

Jo is just over five feet tall, is considered heavy for her height (185 pounds), has short hair, and dresses in men's clothing. She began drinking at the age of twelve, when she was given alcohol by the cousin who subsequently sexually molested her. Jo says that she became seriously involved with alcohol and drugs at age fifteen after she ran away from home as a result of being "caught" with another girl. She describes her parents as religious and says they "went crazy"; as a result, Jo fled to stay with a distant relative who was just over twenty-one and provided no supervision. Jo is back in touch with her family, is "out" to some of her siblings and cousins, but says that, in general, her sexuality is just "not talked about." She states that she can't control her alcohol and drug use and has had problems with work, relationships, and "feeling crazy" because of her use. She sought help at another women's treatment agency two years ago, but left when her counselor encouraged her to "keep her lifestyle to herself to protect her from possible misunderstanding from other participants in group" and suggested that she try adopting more feminine attire so that she "might better fit in."

Jo is not in a permanent partnership and describes having "acted out" sexually in the past with women and, occasionally when drunk, with men. Jo did have a primary relationship with another woman for four years, which ended last year. She describes that relationship as "full of drama," though she states that she still misses her ex-lover and looks forward to becoming friends with her in the future. She mentions, with some embarrassment, that she and her partner argued toward the end of their relationship and that Jo threatened to hit her girlfriend a couple of times in anger. She is currently dating and having sexual relationships with two different women. In the last year, Jo has become involved in a local Latina lesbian social and political organization. She describes this as "the best thing to happen to her in years" but is worried about continuing to participate in social events where alcohol is available.

There are a number of opportunities for inaccurate assessment and misdiagnosis in Jo's case. Domestic violence literature and interventions generally focus on male-female partners, although violence in same-gender relationships is also a problem (Hughes et al., 2000) and is often correlated with substance use (Schilit, Lie, & Montagne, 1990). The verbal threats Jo described may be problematic but isolated events, or they may be indicative of a pattern of intimidation and intent to control a partner commonly found in battering relationships. Jo's verbal threats should be explored, but the clinician should avoid prematurely labeling Jo as a batterer and not assume that the violence is always perpetrated by the partner who may be perceived as more "masculine." When domestic violence is an issue in a lesbian relationship, it is essential to assess and address issues related to immediate safety, recognizing that traditional services for domestic violence are almost always oriented to the needs of heterosexual women.

Most lesbians, like heterosexual women, tend to place a high value on intimacy, monogamy, and physical contact (Herbert, 1996). It is important that clinicians exercise caution in pathologizing or labeling lesbian sexual behaviors as "addictive," even when they may be perceived as outside the boundaries of traditionally accepted sexual behavior. Clinicians need to be cognizant of their own attitudes about sexuality and work carefully with clients to distinguish between normative sexual behavior, problematic sexual behavior, and behavior that is reflective of underlying psychological distress (Coleman, 1995). Lesbians have historically been pathologized for their sexuality, and sexual norms for women are often more restrictive than those for men. Social context informs which sexual behaviors are defined as deviant; for example, current norms may define recreational sex among women as "out of control" (Saulnier, 1996). The focus of clinical work with Jo must include her own perceptions of her past sexual behavior, the relationship between her substance abuse and sexuality, the degree to which her current choices are positive or harmful, and her goals for her personal and sexual relationships. Jo's choices should be considered in the context of the significant diversity found among lesbian communities in terms of values about sexuality and sexual behavior. For example, Faderman (1991), an historian and analyst of lesbian culture, discusses differences between lesbian cultural feminists, who eschew objectification of women and value egalitarian relationships, in contrast to a younger subculture of "lesbian sex radicals" who embrace "conquering a historically male bastion of privilege—the right to free-wheeling sexuality" (p. 252).

Although all women need to be asked about eating habits and weight gain or loss as part of a standard assessment, clinicians working with lesbian clients should not presume that larger physical size is necessarily evidence of an eating disorder. A greater proportion of lesbians appear to have a high lifetime body mass index (a measure of overweight) than heterosexual women (IOM, 1999). Although cultural prescriptions for size and appearance for women have changed over time, the current preoccupation with thinness in Western culture has contributed to a propensity to pathologize large women, whether or not an eating disorder is present (Fallon, Katzman, & Wooley, 1994). Consequently, lesbians like Jo are more likely to be presumed to have eating problems. Although lesbians are affected by the same cultural messages about physical appearance as heterosexual women, there is some indication that lesbians place less stress on traditional physical attractiveness and have fewer problems related to body dissatisfaction and weight preoccupation (Heffernan, 1996; Siever, 1994).

Assessment of lesbians, as for all other women, is ideally centered on defining the problem from the client's perspective and takes personal, cultural, and environmental factors into account. At the same time, assessment should determine whether a client is in a precontemplative or "denial" stage about her addiction and identify the possible health and social consequences of her harmful behavior. The clinician needs to be mindful of the community and cultural contexts in which the client lives, while exploring any discrepancies between the client's goals and her current behavior, disparities between the client's and others' perceptions of what constitutes problem behavior, and the significance of the events that brought her to treatment.

Principles for Intervention and Treatment

Lesbians are often rendered invisible, inundated with homophobic messages, and beleaguered by discrimination and the harmful impact of social stereotypes. Effective clinicians will be cognizant of these contextual issues and accordingly will adopt principles in their practice that guard against unintended clinical bias and promote client empowerment.

Addressing Countertransference and Clinician Bias

Even though the American Psychiatric Association removed homosexuality from the list of mental disorders and embraced a nonpathologizing construct of homosexuality in 1975, clinicians' overt and covert homophobia and heterosexual bias continue to create barriers for lesbians seeking addiction recovery and other mental health services. Homophobic practices in the form of "conversion" or "reparative" therapies are still occurring. These practices are ineffective and unethical, and they affirm the need for practice that is based on evidence and consistent with professional principles (Alexander, 1999; Haldeman, 1994). The codes of ethics and conduct of both the National Association of Social Workers and the American Psychological Association clearly affirm that helping professionals should not discriminate based on sexual orientation and should obtain the consultation and training required in order to provide competent services.

Bias and ignorance on the part of professionals with regard to lesbians are not uncommon (Berkman & Zinberg, 1997; Underhill & Ostermann, 1991). Clinicians' countertransference and bias can interfere substantially in their conducting an accurate assessment and developing an appropriate treatment plan with lesbian clients. Consequently, it is critical for clinicians to monitor, question, and obtain consultation about their own assumptions and biases throughout the assessment, intervention, and treatment processes. Clinician bias helped drive Jo away from her first treatment attempt. The clinician relinquished responsibility for creating a safe, therapeutic environment that would permit Jo—and other clients—to be open about their sexuality and sexual issues, and reinforced the stigma attached to Jo's identity and style of dress as a lesbian. The clinician also encouraged Jo to remain silent about her life and her sense of identity—a counterproductive suggestion for anyone entering recovery, and a particularly harmful one for a survivor of sexual abuse.

Guiding principles for clinicians working with lesbians in addiction treatment include (1) obtaining consultation for countertransference issues; (2) examining one's practice for more subtle forms of bias and ignorance; (3) actively seeking research data and other sources of information to continuously learn about issues related to the treatment of lesbian clients; and (4) developing knowledge about lesbian community resources and lesbian-friendly services for client support and aftercare services.

Using a Client-Centered Developmental Approach

As is true for all clients, the foundation for providing effective intervention and treatment services to lesbians with addictions entails establishing a relationship based on respect, empathy, trust, and nonjudgmental care. These are ingredients essential to creating an environment in which clients can examine their lives and take the risks involved in initiating and maintaining change. Interventions that are built on this foundation should be informed by the lesbian client's stage in the developmental process of change, sense of personal identity, and connectedness to community. Working with lesbians also requires a commitment to ensuring that clients' interactions with clinicians and helping organizations are lesbian affirming—that practice and policies are rooted in knowledge of and respect for the needs and strengths of this population (Underhill, 1993). The following are several questions (adapted from Kowszun & Malley, 1996) that may assist the clinician in providing lesbian-affirming support, using Jo as an example:

- What are Jo's presenting problems, and who is defining the addictive problems (the client, her sexual partner(s), her family, friends)?
- What problems, or elements of Jo's problems, may be socially constructed or based on internalized misinformation? Which are the result of addictions and thus appropriate for intervention?
- Where is Jo in relation to considering, acting on, or maintaining change in her drinking and drug using and other areas of concern?
- What are the perceived costs and benefits of Jo's current drinking and using behavior, and what are the advantages and disadvantages of change?
- How does Jo perceive the level of harm associated with her drinking, using, and any other addictive problems, and what are the consequences of not addressing the issues?
- Where is Jo in her development and maintenance of a lesbian identity? In what ways do sexual identity, cultural identity, community, and experiences of discrimination interact with Jo's addiction issues, and what are the implications for supporting Jo's positive change?
- What process will be used to assist Jo in prioritizing issues related to her addiction and identifying "next steps" for change?

- What support is available and acceptable to assist Jo in the change process?
- What information, support, or resources might be needed by the clinician to work effectively with Jo?

Clinical Issues in the Treatment of Lesbians

Clinicians in treatment agencies or private practice must be prepared to address addictive behavior among lesbians and bixesual women for several reasons. First, there are few resources specifically directed to lesbian, gay, bisexual, and trans-gendered clients. Second, some lesbians and bisexual women may elect to seek treatment in settings outside this community or prefer to seek service that may match other needs, related to race, culture, or religion. Finally, it is incorrect and harmful to assume that all clients are heterosexual. Instead, clinicians and program managers ideally will be prepared to address the clinical issues of women with addictive problems who have diverse sexual orientations or sexual behavior or issues related to sexuality.

Creation of Safety

Once a lesbian has sought or been referred for help with an addiction, she must determine whether she will disclose her sexual identity and share important facets of her social world. It is the responsibility of the clinician to create an atmosphere of safety that fosters trust. Failure to explicitly create opportunities for disclosure may encourage silence, impede the development of a productive helping relationship with the clinician or other clients in a program, and ultimately undermine a lesbian's opportunity to succeed in addiction treatment. The absence of expressions of homophobia does not automatically create a neutral or safe environment. It is the clinician's task to take every opportunity to make lesbians, bisexuals, and a lesbian lifestyle visible and clearly acceptable. Specific statements in individual or group settings that acknowledge and affirm differences in sexual orientation and sexual behavior should be customary. Antilesbian statements by other clients need to be clearly addressed as inappropriate and unacceptable. In addition, clinicians should avoid stating or implying that there is "no difference" between lesbian and nonlesbians; such assertions reflect ignorance, deny the reality of a lesbian's life experiences, and may alienate the lesbian client from treatment. Stereotypes about lesbians (for example, lesbianism is solely a sexual issue, all lesbians are masculine or want to be men, lesbians hate men) undermine safety and the sense of acceptance necessary in the recovery process.

Provision of Information and Options

The clinician should give support and information to the client regarding what she can expect as she navigates through different developmental phases of addiction recovery and stages of change. Similarly, the clinician needs to support lesbian clients in the parallel process of exploring and affirming sexual, cultural, and community identities. Jo, for example, has long identified as lesbian, but her involvement in a culturally specific lesbian support group is relatively new. Another woman in early recovery may be more confused or ambivalent about her sexual orientation or sexual experiences. It is essential for the clinician to communicate a clear sense of permission for the client to be who she is and to feel free to explore the issues that are of concern to her. It may also be appropriate to provide information about what is normative in relation to human sexuality. Use of bibliotherapy or referral to other sources of information about lesbian sexuality, culture, or history is also an effective way to present information in a nonthreatening manner.

Coming-Out and Identity Issues

Several facets of the coming-out process—the process of acknowledging sexual orientation to self and to others—are important to consider in relation to clinical work with lesbians. Acceptance of sexual orientation may be important to recovery for some individuals. For example, a study of lesbians in recovery found that drinking was an important strategy for coping with feelings about sexuality and stigma, although some women used alcohol to avoid same-sex feelings, and others drank to "be" lesbian (McNally & Finnegan, 1992). The authors found that the process of recovery entailed acceptance and integration of two distinct identities: lesbian identity and identity as a recovering alcoholic. Using a developmental framework, a clinician working with Jo should address the interaction between Jo's identification with her recovery and her identities as a lesbian and Latina.

The coming-out process is often described in terms of stages, or as a developmental process through which lesbian or bisexual identity is formed and integrated (Coleman, 1982; Lewis, 1984), although these stages are not necessarily linear or applicable to all individuals. For example, Coleman (1982) describes developmental stages that include pre–coming out, coming out, exploration, first relationships, and integration. In the case of Jo, developmental models may be helpful for understanding her relationship to and integration of multiple identities (for example, lesbian, racial and ethnic, and recovery and change identities). Other theorists and practitioners emphasize that it is important, particularly when working with culturally diverse lesbians, to use a contextual approach that considers the individual lesbian or bisexual woman as part of a larger family system and cultural context (Smith, 1997). A clinician would do well to use a contextual approach in supporting Jo's recovery from addiction while considering the complexities related to Jo's life as a lesbian of color in relation to family, community, cultural norms, and societal oppressions. Clinicians must be aware of how their own cultural background informs their perceptions and responses to a Latina lesbian client like Jo (Espin, 1987).

Coming out is not always linear and is not a singular event. Lesbians and bisexual women continuously face issues related to disclosure to family, friends, coworkers, and community members. For some lesbians in recovery, coming out may be a pressing issue and even a relapse trigger; for others, it is a matter of course. Clinicians should support the client's choice to be "in" or "out" in different settings or to different degrees in relation to the client's preference and cultural context and to the very real possibilities of discrimination. However, if a client is struggling with internalized homophobia or is uncomfortable with her choice of being in the closet, a therapist needs to work on these issues carefully, particularly as they are likely to affect the client's establishing and maintaining recovery from addictions.

Smith (1997) points out that some of the common assumptions about the coming-out process may be more salient for White Americans than for other ethnic groups. One such assumption is the belief that the degree of "outness" is related to self-concept and that failure to come out is a form of denial. According to the National Lesbian Health Care Survey (Bradford et al., 1994), 88 percent of the respondents were openly lesbian to other gay and lesbian people, 27 percent were out to all of their family members, 28 percent were out to heterosexual friends, and 17 percent were out to coworkers. However, White lesbians in this sample were more likely to be out to various people than African American or Latina lesbians. A study of African American lesbians and gay men (Mays, Chatters, Cochran, & Mackness, 1998) points out that in this population, disclosure to family members poses specific risks, such as scorn and rejection, and that the respondents often preferred disclosing sexual identity to women (both sister and mother). The authors suggest that confiding in sympathetic family members may mediate reactions of disclosure throughout the family network.

Sexual identity in the dominant culture is generally perceived as dichotomous, and sexual behavior is presumed to be uniformly congruent with identity. In order to work appropriately with women in recovery, clinicians need to be aware of normative variations in self-definition and sexual behavior among women. Many women who have sex with women may not identify with the terms *lesbian, gay,* or *bisexual.* For example, a study of different dimensions of same-sex identity found that nearly all women who self-identified as lesbian reported same-sex desire and behavior, yet many women who reported same-sex behavior or desire (or both) did not identify as lesbian (Laumann, Gagnon, Michael, & Michaels, 1994). Contrary to popular assumption, many adults who identify as lesbian and gay have had sex with opposite-sex partners (Diamant, Schuster, McGuigan, & Lever, 1999). For example, Jo's sexual interactions with men have been incidental and associated with her alcohol and drug use.

Clients' sexual history and current behaviors, and the significance of sexual interactions with either gender, may vary considerably among women and may have important implications for understanding their addictions, recovery, and relapse prevention needs. Lesbian identity may also vary across generations (Parks, 1999b), among racial and ethnic groups (Greene, 1997), and in different regions and communities (for example, urban or rural). Jo feels able to be open about her identification as an adult Latina lesbian in an urban area where she feels part of a community, but she might not have felt the same in a different context. The many dimensions of coming out and self-identity have important implications for recovery.

Access to Group Support

One of the most stressful aspects of lesbian and bisexual life is social isolation, and many lesbians are well into their adult lives before they meet other lesbians. Moreover, substance abuse literature indicates that women are more likely than their male counterparts to use alcohol and other drugs in isolation (Braiker, 1984). Thus, isolation can be compounded for addicted lesbians, and connection to supportive individuals and community is an important aspect of recovery for lesbians.

Jo experienced many of the problems, such as flight from home because of her family's negative reaction to her sexual orientation, that are endemic among lesbian, gay, and bisexual youth and that may need to be addressed in group treatment during her early recovery. Lesbian, bisexual, and gay youth are at greater risk than heterosexual youth for a number of health, social, and emotional problems, including sexual risk taking, poorer health maintenance, suicide attempts, substance abuse, depression, dropping out of school, running away from home, or being rejected by their families (Lock & Steiner, 1999; Rosario, Meyer-Bahlburg, Heino, Hunter, & Gwadz, 1999; Savin-Williams, 1994). These experiences have important implications for the health, mental health, educational, and social support needs of some lesbians in recovery.

Recovery groups can provide lesbians with a supportive environment for exploring and addressing complex problems, including individual concerns and the impact of marginalization (Saulnier, 1997). Group interaction can support recovery and positive interaction with peers; it can also break down the stigma and normalize common adolescent and adulthood experiences of lesbians, and help the client sort out which problems are individual and which are the result of societal discrimination. Facilities that are not specifically for lesbians need to conduct or link with lesbian-specific recovery groups and other support groups in the community. For example, some women's addiction treatment programs conduct lesbian-specific support groups as part of their array of services. If it is not possible for a group to be lesbian-specific, its composition must at least include other lesbians. It is also helpful for the group leader or coleader to be an "out" lesbian clinician.

Family Counseling

Lesbians in recovery from an addiction may need counseling with significant others, be they family, friends, or lovers. For example, Jo will need to examine potential supports or impediments to change in the context of her significant others. These significant others may include her family of origin or her family of choice, which may comprise a partner, other close friends, and ex-lovers. The significance of relationships with members of lesbians' family of origin may vary considerably depending on the degree of acceptance, appreciation, denial, or rejection clients have experienced. Consequently, some lesbians may benefit from support in forging stronger relationships with members of their family of origin, whereas others, whose reunification with rejecting family members is not possible, may need help finding resolution through grief work.

Cultural traditions will have a significant impact on family counseling. For example, Latino cultural values of *familismo* (valuing familial loyalty and closeness) and *marianismo* (valuing traditional sex-role expectations for women) can be sources of both support and conflict for some Latina lesbians in relation to their family of origin (Marsiglia, 1998; Reyes, 1998). The clinical task is to help Jo explore issues related to her family of origin, family of choice, and cultural traditions with the goal of obtaining and maintaining support for her recovery. Family-focused treatment should include significant others as determined by the client, recognize the unique stressors that lesbians experience in relation to their family of origin, and respect the importance of the family of choice.

Many lesbians are involved in long-term relationships. Although lesbian couples face many of the same basic issues in recovery as those faced by other couples, it is important to consider internal and external factors that may differ for lesbians and that may call for different interventions in addressing addictive behaviors. For example, the process of working with a lesbian couple addressing compulsive sexual behavior will likely involve sorting through individual and relational issues in the context of a dominant culture that pathologizes lesbian sexuality. Other issues, such as those related to the unique structure and nuances of relationships in which both partners have been socialized as women, are also important. A study of social distancing and conflict resolution in lesbian relationships in a nonclinical sample found moderate fusion among lesbian partners; it also found that partners' sharing a large amount of time with each other was not problematic (Causby, Lockhart, White, & Greene, 1995). However, the study did find that sharing concrete items, such as money, clothing, or professional services (for example, a therapist) made the maintenance of healthy boundaries more difficult. Mark and Lesieur (1992) point out that the suggestion of Gamblers Anonymous that financial assets be relinquished to a partner may not be appropriate for women in traditional marriages where they may already be financially dependent. Although relinquishment of financial assets in a lesbian relationship may not reinforce gender-based power differences, it may nevertheless be equally ill advised in terms of maintaining healthy boundaries. Addressing financial issues when one partner has a gambling or spending problem will also necessitate understanding the role and perceived meaning of money and financial sharing or separation for a lesbian couple. For example, what meaning might financial separation have for a lesbian couple whose merging of finances is symbolic of commitment in a society where legal sanctioning of relationships is not available?

Many lesbians are parents and, contrary to popular mythology, the parenting skills of lesbian mothers and the psychosocial development of their children are comparable to that of heterosexual women (Parks, 1998). However, lesbian mothers in addiction recovery often have special concerns, including absence of social validation from the heterosexual and nonparenting lesbian social worlds, variable support from immediate or extended family (depending on homophobia), and threats to child custody on the part of former spouses or other family members.

Unfortunately, addiction treatment services for mothers tend to presume heterosexuality and often fail to integrate lesbian-specific program elements into their treatment services. For example, some clinicians and treatment programs are unwilling or ill prepared to include the lesbian partner in treatment when an ex-husband or biological father is still involved with any children of the primary client. Although there is no single "right" approach to this situation, the client will need the clinician to help address the potentially complex emotional and legal issues of her lesbian blended family. Services for recovering lesbian mothers should include lesbian-specific groups, written materials that reflect respect and affirmation of diverse family structures, inclusion of members of the family of choice in program activities, linkages to community resources for lesbian mothers, and protocols that address the special legal and social concerns of lesbians.

Use and Expansion of Social Support

Social supports within lesbian communities are important aspects of the recovery process. A national survey of lesbians found that they were more likely to turn to friends than family for support and that most of the sample frequently attended lesbian-specific events (Bradford et al., 1994). Unfortunately, lesbian-identified domains (bars, sports events, social events) that frequently serve as entry points into lesbian subcultures and provide opportunities for development of a lesbian identity and immersion into lesbian community are also places where alcohol is often served (Parks, 1999a). Moreover, researchers who have studied African American, Asian American, and Latina lesbians have all found that respondents perceive their race and ethnicity and their sexual orientation as integrated identities but that they often experience homophobia in their cultural communities and racism in lesbian communities (Chan, 1989; Espin, 1987; Mays, Cochran, & Rhue, 1993). All these issues may be salient to Jo, for example, in her efforts to maintain and build social support for her recovery, and Jo expresses appropriate concern about alcohol availability in the context of a Latina lesbian social network that is important to her.

It is not uncommon for clinicians to caution clients to avoid "people, places, and things" associated with drinking or drug use. This approach erroneously assumes that the client has easy access to sober social support. Intervention strategies and relapse prevention planning are crucial to continued recovery and need to be developed in the context of the client's community and culture. For example, Jo may be able to identify other clean and sober individuals as potential sources of support in her Latina lesbian social network. She may be able to ally with friends to organize alcohol-free social events, facilitate alcohol-safe practices (for example, having plenty of alcohol-free beverages at social events), or attend social events with a supportive group. At the same time, she might expand her social support network by developing relationships with other lesbian-friendly people in recovery. Clinicians working with lesbians with addictions need to familiarize themselves with the wide range of social, political, and support organizations that are available to lesbians and bisexual women and their families. These organizations can be important sources of information and referral during treatment and are particularly important in aftercare planning for lesbian and bisexual clients.

Issues Related to Sexual Abuse

Childhood sexual abuse is correlated with substance abuse and other addictive problems among lesbians, as it is among heterosexual women. Hall (1996), who conducted in-depth interviews with lesbians in recovery from alcohol problems, found that sexual abuse survivors were polydrug users and "were also likely to report multiple addictions involving food, sex, money, and relationships" (p. 233). However, the stigma attached to same-sex sexuality requires that the clinician be both adept at addressing these issues and alert to the impact of homophobia on the client and on the therapeutic relationship. For example, clinicians do not generally question (or have clients question) whether sexual abuse may be an etiological factor for heterosexual orientation. By contrast, a study of lesbian survivors of sexual abuse found that although no respondent believed her sexual orientation was a result of childhood abuse, "the societal presumption of sexual abuse as an etiological factor in determining lesbian sexual orientation, nevertheless, was pivotal for these survivors because they had to constantly protect themselves from others' judgements about whether they were 'real lesbians'" (Hall, 1998, p. 8). Jo, for example, will need to address her childhood sexual abuse at some point in her recovery. It will be imperative that her therapists see this issue as important in Jo's relationships to self and others (Jo may have used substances to medicate feelings related to childhood abuse, for example) but not causal to her sexual orientation.

Issues Related to Sexuality

Clinicians must also be knowledgeable about lesbian sexuality and avoid superimposing heterosexual norms on their perception of, and approach to, lesbian sexual relationships. Jo is described as masculine in her style of dress and may (or may not) identify as butch. Some lesbians embrace identification as butch or femme; others may reject these constructs. Even if Jo does identify as butch, the clinician should not assume that this identification aligns with traditional male sex roles in Jo's sexual, interpersonal, and social behaviors. If Jo chooses to go to a treatment program, her outward appearance as butch may be a source of problems for her from other clients and even from staff. It will be important that the clinicians and treatment agencies take a proactive role in creating an environment that affirms rather than stigmatizes differences.

Saulnier (1996) suggests several steps for providing appropriate assessment and intervention in relation to sexual behavior that are particularly pertinent for lesbians. The clinician's first task is to help the client separate her real problems from nonconformist behaviors, which are labeled deviant based on current social norms and therefore are not appropriate for intervention. The clinician's second task is to work with the client to "disentangle the cluster of genuine problems and then identify responses that fit each of these issues" (Saulnier, 1996, p. 166). This includes examining and reframing the harmful messages that the client may have internalized and that contribute to the client's inflexibility or excessive shame about her sexual expression. Finally, individuals who perceive their sexual behavior as harmfully excessive or who engage in dangerous risk-taking behaviors should be helped to examine these behaviors and set goals "for meeting their needs in a way that suits them better and keeps them out of danger" (Saulnier, 1996, p. 166).

Self-Help and Lesbians

Jo may benefit from involvement in self-help groups. However, any clinician working with Jo needs to be flexible about promoting participation in self-help groups and open to addressing both the assets and drawbacks to such participation. Self-help programs for substance abuse problems are easily accessible and can provide substantive support for lesbians in recovery. In some areas, it appears as though Alcoholics Anonymous (AA) has replaced the bar as a social center for many lesbians (Hall, 1994). Although the basic tenets and supports of AA can be useful, the emphasis on "nonuniqueness," the presence of religious undercurrents, and a sense of orthodoxy regarding how recovery should be accomplished may be alienating to some lesbians (Bittle, 1982). Lesbians in recovery appear to have mixed perceptions of AA as potentially liberating but also potentially oppressive (Hall, 1993). A majority (74 percent) of recovering lesbians in one study (Hall, 1994) relied on other sources of support in addition to AA. Participants in this study described experiencing ambivalence about the ideological underpinnings of AA and feeling tension between assimilating into the program and having a strong sense of autonomy.

Twelve-step programs are not always homogenous in their content and dynamics and seem to take on different meanings and dynamics when adapted by distinct cultural groups (Hall, 1993). Although culturally specific self-help groups are available to lesbians recovering from substance abuse problems, other self-help groups such as Gamblers Anonymous tend to be Caucasian and male dominated (Mark & Lesieur, 1992). It is helpful for clinicians to be flexible about promoting twelve-step participation, able to recognize that resistance to twelve-step programs may be grounded in substantive cultural and political conflict rather than solely "denial," and knowledgeable about alternative self-help and support options. Such alternatives (although less readily available and largely focused on substance abuse recovery) include Women for Sobriety, Secular Organization for Sobriety, and Rational Recovery.

Design of an Effective Treatment Program

Because addiction treatment services are often provided in the context of an agency setting, appropriate institutional policies, staffing patterns, program design, and training plans are also essential to the provision of lesbian-sensitive recovery services.

Addiction treatment agencies should adopt administrative policies that explicitly affirm the organization's commitment to serving lesbians and prohibit discrimination based on sexual orientation, gender, and cultural background. Open lesbians should be on the board of directors, and clients should have access to out lesbian clinicians. A recent study comparing lesbian and heterosexual women's mental health found that a vast majority of lesbians preferred having a counselor of the same sex (94 percent) and the same sexual orientation (79 percent) (Hughes et al., 2000). Initial development of appropriate addiction treatment programming could involve convening focus groups of lesbians to help design services, developing lesbian-specific "tracks" or workshops, and providing education and guidelines for heterosexual participants about appropriate language and behaviors for interacting and supporting lesbian peers in recovery. Ongoing staff training needs to address current research on lesbian issues, provide opportunities for staff to explore their fears and prejudices in a safe environment, and orient staff to community resources. This training should include a combination of didactic information relevant to addiction treatment, and process work through which clinicians can integrate new insights and skills into their practice with diverse lesbian clients.

Conclusion

In working with lesbian and bisexual clients in addictions treatment, it is best to use a client-centered model that recognizes the developmental process of recovery in the context of lesbian identity and community; builds on individual strengths and community assets; recognizes the context of homophobia, sexism, and racism as integral rather than diversionary to the process of change related to addictive behaviors; and avoids pathologizing nonharmful behavior merely on the basis that it goes against prevailing social norms and gender expectations.

Lesbians are often rendered invisible, inundated with homophobic messages, and beleaguered by discrimination and the harmful impact of social stereotypes. Lesbian partnerships are not legally sanctioned, and access to domestic partnership benefits is rare. Lesbians have frequently experienced discrimination and harm from legal, religious, health, mental health, and substance abuse treatment institutions. Clinicians treating women who are addicted must be cognizant of these contextual issues and need to guard against both overt and unintended biases against lesbian clients. Facilitating positive change that supports recovery occurs not only in the individual realm but also in social and political spheres. Clinicians have an important role as advocates for lesbians and bisexual women in recovery to promote legal equity and the creation of healthier familial, professional, organizational, and social environments free of discrimination and bias.

References

Alexander, C. J. (1999). Reparative therapy for gays and lesbians. *Journal of Gay and Lesbian Social Services, 9*(4), 115–118.

Berkman, C. S., & Zinberg, G. (1997). Homophobia and heterosexism in social workers. *Social Work, 42,* 319–332.

Bittle, W. E. (1982). Alcoholics Anonymous and the gay alcoholic. *Journal of Homosexuality, 7*(4), 81–88.

Bradford, J., Ryan, C., & Rothblum, E. D. (1994). National lesbian health care survey: Implications for mental health care. *Journal of Consulting and Clinical Psychology, 62,* 228–242.

Braiker, H. B. (1984). Therapeutic issues in the treatment of alcoholic women. In S. C. Wilsnack & L. J. Beckman (Eds.), *Alcohol problems in women* (pp. 97–116). New York: Guilford Press.

Brown, S. (1985). *Treating the alcoholic: A developmental model of recovery.* New York: Wiley.

Bux, D. (1996). The epidemiology of problem drinking in gay men and lesbians: A critical review. *Clinical Psychology Review, 16,* 227–298.

Cassidy, R., & Hughes, T. L. (1997). Lesbian health: Barriers to care. In B. J. McElmurry & R. S. Parker (Eds.), *Annual review of women's health* (Vol. 3, pp. 67–87). New York: National League for Nursing Press.

Causby, V., Lockhart, L., White, B., & Greene, K. (1995). Fusion and conflict resolution in lesbian relationships. *Journal of Gay and Lesbian Social Services, 3*(1), 67–82.

Center for Substance Abuse Treatment. (1998). *Supplementary administration manual for the expanded female version of the Addiction Severity Index (ASI) Instrument, the ASI-F* (DHHS Publication No. SMA 98-3180). Rockville, MD: Substance Abuse and Mental Health Services Administration.

Chan, C. S. (1989). Issues of identity development among Asian-American lesbians and gay men. *Journal of Counseling Development, 68*(1), 16–20.

Cochran, S. D., & Mays, V. M. (1994). Depressive distress among homosexually active African American men and women. *Journal of Psychiatry, 151,* 524–529.

Cochran, S. D., & Mays, V. M. (2000). Relation between psychiatric syndromes and behaviorally defined sexual orientation in a sample of the US population. *American Journal of Epidemiology, 151,* 516–523.

Coleman, E. (1982). Developmental stages of the coming out process. *Journal of Homosexuality, 7*(2/3), 31–43.

Coleman, E. (1995). Treatment of compulsive sexual behavior. In R. C. Rosman & S. R. Leiblum (Eds.), *Case studies in sex therapy* (pp. 333–349). New York: Guilford Press.

Diamant, A. L., Schuster, M. A., McGuigan, K., & Lever, J. (1999). Lesbians' sexual history with men: Implications for taking a sexual history. *Archives of Internal Medicine, 159,* 2730–2736.

DiClemente, C., & Prochaska, J. O. (1998). Toward a comprehensive, transtheoretical model of change: Stages of change and addictive behaviors. In W. R. Miller & N. Heather (Eds.), *Treating addictive behaviors* (2nd ed., pp. 3–24). New York: Plenum.

Espin, O. M. (1987). Issues of identity in the psychology of Latina lesbians. In Boston Lesbians Psychologies Collective (Ed.), *Lesbian psychologies* (pp. 35–55). Urbana: University of Illinois Press.

Faderman, L. (1991). *Odd girls out and twilight lovers: A history of lesbian life in the twentieth century.* New York: Columbia University Press.

Fallon, P., Katzman, M. A., & Wooley, S. C. (1994). *Feminist perspectives on eating disorders.* New York: Guilford Press.

Fassinger, R. E. (2000). Applying counseling theories to lesbian, gay, and bisexual clients: Pitfalls and possibilities. In R. M. Perez, K. A. DeBord, & K. J. Bieschke (Eds.), *Handbook of counseling and psychotherapy with lesbian, gay, and bisexual clients* (pp. 107–131). Washington, DC: American Psychological Association.

Finnegan, D. G., & McNally, E. (1996). Chemically dependent lesbians and bisexual women: Recovery from many traumas. In B. L. Underhill & D. G. Finnegan (Eds.), *Chemical dependency: Women at risk* (pp. 87–107). Binghamton, NY: Haworth Press.

French, S. A., Story, M., Remafedi, G., Resnick, M. D., & Blum, R. W. (1996). Sexual orientation and prevalence of body dissatisfaction and eating disordered behaviors: A population-based study of adolescents. *International Journal of Eating Disorders, 19*(2), 119–126.

Greene, B. (1997). *Ethnic and cultural diversity among lesbians and gay men.* Thousand Oaks, CA: Sage.

Haldeman, D. C. (1994). The practice and ethics of sexual orientation conversion therapy. *Journal of Consulting and Clinical Psychology, 62,* 221–227.

Hall, J. M. (1993). Lesbians and alcohol: Patterns and paradoxes in medical notions and lesbians' beliefs. *Journal of Psychoactive Drugs, 25,* 109–117.

Hall, J. M. (1994). The experiences of lesbians in Alcoholics Anonymous. *Western Journal of Nursing Research, 16*(5), 556–576.

Hall, J. M. (1996). Pervasive effects of childhood sexual abuse in lesbians' recovery from alcohol problems. *Substance Use and Misuse, 31,* 225–239.

Hall, J. M. (1998). Lesbians surviving childhood sexual abuse: Pivotal experiences related to sexual orientation, gender, and race. *Journal of Lesbian Studies, 2*(1), 7–28.

Heffernan, K. (1996). Eating disorders and weight concern among lesbians. *International Journal of Eating Disorders, 19*(2), 127–138.

Herbert, S. E. (1996). Lesbian sexuality. In R. P. Cabaj & T. S. Stein (Eds.), *Textbook of homosexuality and mental health* (pp. 723–742). Washington, DC: American Psychiatric Press.

Hughes, T. L., Hass, A. P., Razzano, L., Cassidy, R., & Matthews, A. (2000). Comparing lesbians' and heterosexual women's mental health: A multi-site survey. *Journal of Gay and Lesbian Social Services, 11*(1), 57–76.

Hughes, T. L., & Norris, J. (1995). Sexuality, sexual orientation, and violence: Pieces in the puzzle of women's use and abuse of alcohol. In B. J. McElmurry & R. S. Parker (Eds.), *Annual review of women's health* (Vol. 2, pp. 285–317). New York: National League for Nursing Press.

Hughes, T. L., & Wilsnack, S. C. (1997). Use of alcohol among lesbians: Research and clinical implications. *American Journal of Orthopsychiatry, 67,* 20–36.

Institute of Medicine. (1999). *Lesbian health: Current assessment and directions for the future.* Washington, DC: National Academy Press.

Kowszun, G., & Malley, M. (1996). Alcohol and substance misuse. In D. Davies & C. Neal (Eds.), *Pink therapy: A guide for counsellors and therapists working with lesbian, gay and bisexual clients* (pp. 170–187). Philadelphia: Open University Press.

Kus, R. J. (1990). Alcoholism in the gay and lesbian communities. In R. J. Kus (Ed.), *Keys to caring: Assisting your gay and lesbian clients* (pp. 66–81). Boston: Alyson.

Laumann, E. O., Gagnon, J. H., Michael, R. T., & Michaels, S. (1994). *The social organization of sexuality: Sexual practices in the United States.* Chicago: University of Chicago Press.

Lewis, L. A. (1984). The coming out process for lesbians: Integrating a stable identity. *Social Work, 29,* 464–469.

Lock, J., & Steiner, H. (1999). Gay, lesbian, and bisexual youth risks for emotional, physical, and social problems: Results from a community based survey. *Journal of the American Academy of Child and Adolescent Psychiatry, 38,* 297–304.

Mark, M. E., & Lesieur, H. R. (1992). A feminist critique of problem gambling research. *British Journal of Addictions, 87,* 549–565.

Marsiglia, F. F. (1998). Homosexuality and Latino/as: Towards an integration of identities. *Journal of Gay and Lesbian Social Services, 8*(3), 113–121.

Mays, V. M., Chatters, L. M., Cochran, S. D., & Mackness, J. (1998). African American families in diversity: Gay men and lesbians as participants in family networks. *Journal of Comparative Family Studies, 29*(1), 73–87.

Mays, V. M., Cochran, S. D., & Rhue, S. (1993). The impact of perceived discrimination on the intimate relationships of black lesbians. *Journal of Homosexuality, 25*(4), 1–14.

McKirnan, D. J., & Peterson, P. L. (1989). Alcohol and drug use among homosexual men and women: Epidemiology and population characteristics. *Addiction Behaviors, 14,* 545–553.

McNally, E., & Finnegan, D. G. (1992). Lesbian recovering alcoholics: A qualitative study of identity transformation—a report on research and application to treatment. *Journal of Chemical Dependency Treatment, 5*(1), 93–103.

Mencher, J. (1997). Intimacy in lesbian relationships: A critical reexamination of fusion. In J. V. Jordan (Ed.), *Women's growth in diversity: More writings from the Stone Center* (pp. 311–330). New York: Guilford Press.

Miller, W. R., & Rollnick, S. (1991). *Motivational interviewing: Preparing people to change addictive behavior.* New York: Guilford Press.

Parks, C. (1998). Lesbian parenthood: A review of the literature. *American Journal of Orthopsychiatry, 68,* 376–389.

Parks, C. (1999a). Bicultural competence: A mediating factor affecting alcohol use practices and problems among lesbian social drinkers. *Journal of Drug Issues, 29,* 135–154.

Parks, C. (1999b). Lesbian identity development: An examination across generations. *American Journal of Orthopsychiatry, 69,* 347–361.

Paul, J. P., Stall, R., & Bloomfield, K. A. (1991). Gay and alcoholic: Epidemiological and clinical issues. *Alcohol Health and Research World, 15,* 151–160.

Reyes, M. (1998). Latina lesbians and alcohol and other drugs: Social work implications. *Alcoholism Treatment Quarterly, 16*(1/2), 179–192.

Roberts, S. J., & Sorensen, L. (1999). Health related behaviors and cancer screening of lesbians: Results from the Boston Lesbian Health Project. *Women and Health, 28*(4), 1–12.

Rosario, M., Meyer-Bahlburg, H.F.L., Heino, F. L., Hunter, J., & Gwadz, M. (1999). Sexual risk behaviors of gay, lesbian, and bisexual youths in New York City: Prevalence and correlates. *AIDS Education and Prevention, 11,* 476–496.

Rosen, R. C., & Leiblum, S. R. (1995). Sexual addiction and compulsion. In R. C. Rosen & S. R. Leiblum (Eds.), *Case studies in sex therapy* (pp. 331–334). New York: Guilford Press.

Saulnier, C. F. (1996). Sex addiction: A problematic concept. *Journal of Applied Social Services Research, 20*(2), 159–168.

Saulnier, C. F. (1997). Alcohol problems and marginalization: Social group work with lesbians. *Social Work with Groups, 20*(3), 37–59.

Savin-Williams, R. C. (1994). Verbal and physical abuse as stressors in the lives of lesbian, gay male, and bisexual youths: Associations with school problems, running away, substance abuse, prostitution, and suicide. *Journal of Consulting and Clinical Psychology, 62,* 261–269.

Schilit, R., Lie, G., & Montagne, M. (1990). Substance use as a correlate of violence in intimate lesbian relationships. *Journal of Homosexuality, 19*(3), 51–65.

Siever, M. D. (1994). Sexual orientation and gender as factors in socioculturally acquired vulnerability to body dissatisfaction and eating disorders. *Journal of Consulting and Clinical Psychology, 62,* 252–260.

Skinner, W. F. (1994). The prevalence and demographic predictors of illicit and licit drug use among lesbians and gay men. *American Journal of Public Health, 84,* 1307–1310.

Smith, A. (1997). Cultural diversity and the coming-out process: Implications for clinical practice. In B. Greene (Ed.), *Ethnic and cultural diversity among lesbians and gay men* (pp. 279–300). Thousand Oaks, CA: Sage.

Stevens, P. E. (1993). Lesbian health care research: A review of the literature from 1970 to 1990. In P. N. Stern (Ed.), *Lesbian health: What are the issues?* (pp. 1–30). Washington, DC: Taylor & Francis.

Stevens, P. E. (1998). The experiences of lesbians of color in health care encounters: Narrative insights for improving access and quality. *Journal of Lesbian Studies, 2*(1), 77–94.

Striegel-Moore, R. H., Tucker, N., & Hsu, J. (1990). Body image dissatisfaction and disordered eating in lesbian college students. *International Journal of Eating Disorders, 9,* 493–500.

Thompson, B. (1996). Multiracial feminist theorizing about eating problems: Refusing to rank oppressions. *Eating Disorders, 4*(2), 104–114.

Underhill, B. L. (1993). *Creating visibility: Providing lesbian-sensitive and lesbian-specific alcoholism recovery services.* Los Angeles: Alcoholism Center for Women.

Underhill, B. L., & Ostermann, S. (1991). The pain of invisibility: Issues for lesbians. In P. Roth (Ed.), *Alcohol and drugs are women's issues: A review of the issues* (Vol. 1, pp. 71–77). New York: Women's Action Alliance and Scarecrow Press.

Van Den Bergh, N. (1991). Having bitten the apple: A feminist perspective on addictions. In N. Van Den Bergh (Ed.), *Feminist perspectives on addictions* (pp. 3–30). New York: Springer.

van Wormer, K., Wells, J., & Boes, M. (2000). *Social work with lesbians, gays, and bisexuals: A strengths perspective.* Needham Heights, MA: Allyn & Bacon.

CHAPTER NINETEEN

ADDICTIONS AND WOMEN WITH MAJOR PSYCHIATRIC DISORDERS

Diana M. DiNitto and Catherine Crisp

Women with addictive disorders—substance abuse or dependence—frequently have a coexisting psychiatric disorder (Reed & Mowbray, 1999). Consequences of these coexisting conditions are severe and include increased likelihood of poor psychosocial functioning, health problems, medication noncompliance, relapses, hospitalizations, homelessness, and suicidal and violent behavior (see Drake, Mueser, & McHugo, 1996; RachBeisel, Scot, & Dixon, 1999; Reed & Mowbray, 1999 for reviews). Although people with alcohol or drug disorders and a psychiatric disorder are more likely to receive treatment than those with a single disorder (Kessler, Nelson, et al., 1996), coexisting problems can complicate the course of treatment.

This chapter focuses on women with dual diagnoses. As used in this chapter, the terms *dual diagnosis* and *comorbidity* refer to a person's having one or more diagnoses of substance abuse or dependence in combination with one or more major psychiatric disorders. The term *major psychiatric disorder* may refer to specific diagnoses (for example, major depression, bipolar disorder, schizoaffective disorder, schizophrenia) or to any mental disorder that significantly impairs a woman's ability to function, especially with regard to self-care (see, for example, Zweben, 1996).

The purpose of this chapter is to better equip practitioners to assist women with dual diagnoses. It covers the prevalence of dual diagnoses among women;

theories of dual diagnoses; dynamics of dual diagnoses; screening, diagnosis, and assessment; and suggestions for treatment.

The Prevalence of Comorbidity Among Women

Few major studies report the prevalence of comorbidity among women, but Kessler, Crum, et al. (1997) found that 72 percent of women with a diagnosis of alcohol abuse and 86 percent of women with a diagnosis of alcohol dependence met lifetime criteria for another psychiatric disorder (including drug dependence). The major psychiatric disorders of concern in this chapter are mood, anxiety, and psychotic disorders. These disorders are discussed in the following sections with regard to gender.

Mood Disorders

Among the severe mood or affective disorders are major depression, dysthymia, bipolar disorder, and cyclothymia (American Psychiatric Association, 2000). Depending on the disorder, symptoms include mania (for example, grandiosity, racing thoughts, psychomotor agitation) or depression (for example, insomnia or hypersomnia, feelings of worthlessness, suicidality). According to the National Comorbidity Study, affective disorders occur in 24 percent of women in the general population over the course of their lifetimes, compared with 15 percent of men (Kessler, McGonagle, et al., 1994), in 34 percent of women with alcohol abuse, and in 54 percent of women with alcohol dependence (Kessler et al., 1997). The Epidemiological Catchment Area (ECA) study found that women with alcohol abuse or dependence had higher rates of major depression and mania than did men with alcohol abuse or dependence; they also had higher rates of these disorders than did both men and women in the general population (Helzer & Pryzbeck, 1988).

Anxiety Disorders

Anxiety disorders are the most common psychiatric disorder among women (Kessler et al., 1994) and are characterized by nervousness, tension, apprehension, and fear (see Zweben, 1996). They include panic disorder, phobias, obsessive-compulsive disorder, acute stress disorder, posttraumatic stress disorder (PTSD), and generalized anxiety disorder (American Psychiatric Association, 2000). Anxiety disorders are estimated to occur in 30 percent of women during their lifetimes, compared with 19 percent of men (Kessler et al., 1994), in 49 percent of women with alcohol abuse, and in 61 percent of women with alcohol dependence (Kessler et al., 1997). The ECA study indicates that women with alcohol abuse or dependence had higher rates of panic disorder and phobic disorders than did men with alcohol abuse or dependence, and they had higher rates of these disorders than did men and women in the general population (Helzer & Pryzbeck, 1988).

Psychotic Disorders

Psychotic disorders involve some combination of delusions, hallucinations, disorganized speech or thoughts, and disorganized or catatonic behavior. These disorders include schizophrenia, schizoaffective disorder, and delusional disorder. There is little difference in the prevalence of psychotic disorders experienced by men and women: 0.8 percent of women have a psychotic disorder during their lifetimes compared with 0.6 percent of men (Kessler et al., 1994). Although these disorders occur infrequently, they are often severely debilitating. The ECA study found that 47 percent of individuals with a lifetime diagnosis of schizophrenia or schizophreniform disorder had a substance abuse or dependence diagnosis (Regier et al., 1990); however, few studies have reported gender differences among people with schizophrenia and substance use disorders (Brunette & Drake, 1997). In a study of 172 men and women with schizophrenia or schizoaffective disorder, Brunette and Drake (1997) found little support for gender differences in the severity of drug abuse and no significant differences in age of onset of drug use.

◆ ◆ ◆

The high incidence of psychiatric problems among people of both genders who have substance use disorders means that addiction practitioners need to be versed in psychiatric disorders and, conversely, that mental health practitioners must be versed in substance use disorders. Practitioners who are trained in both fields are better equipped to address the unique needs of people with dual diagnoses.

Theories of Dual Diagnoses

No one knows exactly why some people develop both psychiatric and substance use disorders, but a consideration of theories purporting to explain comorbidity should be of interest to practitioners as they assist women with dual diagnoses. Mueser, Drake, and Wallach (1998) group the many theories into four models.

The first model suggests that the same factors, such as genetics or antisocial personality disorder (ASPD), contribute to major psychiatric disorders and substance use disorders. Mueser et al. (1998) believe that more evidence supports the ASPD explanation than shared genetic vulnerability. Although there is a high probability of ASPD in alcoholic women, this explanation may be less satisfying in explaining women's dual diagnoses, because women in the general population and women with substance use disorders are less likely than men to have ASPD (Kessler et al., 1994, 1997).

The second model suggests that major psychiatric disorders increase the risk of developing substance use disorders. This model includes the widely debated self-medication hypothesis, which is that people with psychiatric disorders select drugs to alleviate symptoms specific to their diagnosis (Khantzian, 1985). For example, people with bipolar disorder may use alcohol (a central nervous system depressant) to control a manic episode or to slow rapid thoughts (Stasiewicz, Carey, Bradizza, & Maisto, 1996), thus increasing their risk for developing alcohol abuse or dependence. Zweben (1996) notes no single temporal relationship between eating disorders and substance use disorders but suggests that women with eating disorders may use stimulants to suppress appetite, heroin to induce vomiting, and alcohol to calm the panic accompanying bingeing and purging. Mueser and colleagues (1998) found less support for the self-medication theory than for a general alleviation of dysphoria theory, whereby people with major psychiatric disorders begin using alcohol and other drugs for the same reasons that other people with substance use disorders do—to feel better. Mueser et al. suggest that increased dysphoria among people with major psychiatric disorders may explain their high rates of co-occurring substance use disorders, although in the long run, substance use produces negative rather than positive outcomes. This model also includes a theory of multiple risk factors or "supersensitivity." In these cases, genetic factors may interact with early life events and other environmental stressors, making people with major psychiatric disorders vulnerable to the effects of even small amounts of alcohol or other drugs, as sometimes seen in clinical settings.

Mueser et al. (1998) give little credence to a third model: that substance use disorders cause major psychiatric disorders; for example, alcohol use disorders are common among people with psychiatric disorders, yet they are not considered a cause of major psychiatric disorders such as schizophrenia or bipolar disorder.

The fourth model suggests that psychiatric and substance use disorders exacerbate each other. Though Mueser and colleagues (1998) call this model largely untested, it is widely referred to by practitioners in the dual-diagnosis field. Practitioners generally caution clients that alcohol and nonprescribed drug use can precipitate an episode of mental illness and that failure to control mental illness by taking prescribed medications or attending treatment sessions can precipitate substance use.

Practitioners who espouse postmodernism or social constructionism may appreciate Naegle's perspective (1997) on the four functions or meanings of drug use in women's lives. First is to modulate emotional experiences or achieve an equilibrium they do not otherwise have. Mosley (1996), for example, describes the importance of "identifying and labeling feelings, expressing feelings, assessing the intensity of feelings, managing feelings, delaying gratification, controlling impulses, reducing stress and knowing the relationship and difference between feeling and actions" in treating women with dual diagnoses (p. 386).

The second function of drug use Naegle (1997) describes is to escape or avoid painful memories, perhaps troubling family relationships or losses. In these cases, drugs may provide "an illusion of safety and coping" (p. 570). The third function is to facilitate behaviors that women are not comfortable engaging in while drug free. For example, alcohol and drug use may enhance feelings of self-efficacy in social situations. Fourth is to provide a lifestyle or identity, which Naegle indicates may be common among women with dual diagnoses who have experienced traumatic life events.

Dynamics of Dual Diagnoses Among Women

Women with dual diagnoses experience problems related to their addiction, their psychiatric disorder, and the interaction of the two illnesses. These problems include a history of victimization, health problems, psychotropic medication issues, chaotic relationships, insufficient income, and barriers to treatment.

History of Victimization

Many dually diagnosed women have experienced emotional, physical, and sexual trauma (Alexander, 1996; Gearon & Bellack, 1999; Zweben, 1996) that may result in PTSD. For example, women with schizophrenia and addictive disorders may have increased vulnerability to sexual and physical abuse due to the deficits in their cognitive and social skills (Gearon & Bellack, 1999). Victimization of women with dual diagnoses may begin in childhood or adolescence and continue into adulthood (Palacios, Urmann, Newel, & Hamilton, 1999). Boyd and Hauenstein (1997, p. 79) suggest that "women who report feelings of paranoia or strange ESP phenomena that sound psychotic may be suffering from the sequelae of victimization" and that "as detoxification progresses, memories of traumatic experiences may resurface causing significant anxiety and depression" that should be addressed in treatment.

Health Problems

Reed and Mowbray's review of the literature (1999) indicates that the health of women with dual diagnoses is worse than that of other women and of dually diagnosed men. These women have more medical hospitalizations and more alcohol- and drug-related health problems, such as hepatitis, cirrhosis, fractures, anemia, kidney and bladder ailments, and breast cancer than women in the general population. Sexual dysfunction and gynecological and reproductive problems are also common in alcoholic women, though it is unclear whether these conditions are more a cause or a consequence of substance use disorders (Wilsnack, 1982). In addition to increased risk for sexual and physical violence, women with substance use disorders are at greater risk for sexually transmitted diseases like HIV and AIDS; women with major psychiatric disorders may also be at increased risk for these health problems (RachBeisel et al., 1999).

Women with dual diagnoses may not seek medical treatment because alcohol and drug use may obscure pain or other symptoms and because substance and mental disorders often interfere with self-care (depression, for example, makes it difficult to initiate action); women also may avoid treatment providers who they believe will stigmatize them or report their illegal drug use to authorities (see Reed & Mowbray, 1999). The neglect of women's health care, particularly gynecological care, in chemical dependency and mental health treatment programs is alarming, and the health problems of women with psychiatric and substance use disorders are sometimes ignored because health practitioners assume they will not comply with treatment or because these practitioners prefer to avoid this clientele (see Reed & Mowbray, 1999). Women are also more likely to be uninsured and to lack funds to pay for health care (Greenberger, 1998).

Psychotropic Medication Issues

Women receive psychotropic medications more often than men, and although these medications are often necessary in treating psychiatric disorders, they can cause side effects, including constant dry mouth, menstrual irregularities, constipation, pseudopregnancy, excessive weight gain, skin problems, and sexual difficulties (see Reed & Mowbray, 1999). The picture becomes more complicated when women use street drugs to avoid unpleasant effects of psychotropic medications.

Clients' resistance to taking psychotropic medications due to the stigma of mental illness is an important issue in treating many women with major psychiatric disorders. Maureen Veech, a nurse and president of the Washington, DC, chapter of the Alliance for the Mentally Ill, who finally sought help for depression, expressed it well (as reported by Greenberger, 1998, p. 407): "I was afraid and ashamed to try medication for quite a long time. I didn't even want to consider it, mainly because of how I saw others treated—and by others, I mean other fellow healthcare professionals, including a very capable nurse who was laughed at and whispered about behind her back because she was on medication." Even when Veech began taking medication for her depression, she experienced side effects, such as severe headaches and weight gain. "But," she said, "I tolerated all of that because I was able to function again."

Chaotic Relationships

Many dually diagnosed women have chaotic relationships. Alcohol and other drug use among women frequently begins following involvement with an addicted partner (see Davis & DiNitto, 1998, for a review), as illustrated by a woman with bipolar disorder who began using methamphetamine when she became involved with a man who "cooked" the drug at home. Because she could not bear to inject the drug herself, she relied on him to "shoot her up." As Gearon and Bellack (1999, p. 410) note, "Years of experiencing stigma and social isolation may make this group of women eager to please individuals who give them attention and the promise of love and affection—regardless of how they are treated or what they are asked to do."

Among chemically dependent mothers, the desire to retain custody of their children is said to be a strong motivation to seek treatment. At the same time, women may be reluctant or unable to enter treatment if they cannot make arrangements for the care of their children or if they fear losing custody while in treatment. Dually diagnosed women may have children, but those with severe symptoms may not have custody. In a study of dually diagnosed patients whose mental illness was schizophrenia, women were more likely than men to have children, but they had very little contact with their children, suggesting substantial problems in their ability to function (Brunette & Drake, 1997).

Insufficient Income

Although the causal relationship is unclear, the correlation between poverty and psychiatric disorders has been well documented (Belle, 1990). Kessler et al. (1994) found that people in the lowest income group ($19,000 a year or less) were more likely to have a diagnosable psychiatric disorder than those in other income groups. The combination of mental and addictive disorders puts dually diagnosed women at greater risk for homelessness. Many are too severely impaired to hold jobs and may receive Supplemental Security Income (SSI), a form of public assistance, or Social Security Disability Insurance (SSDI) if they have a work history. They may also rely on food stamps and Medicaid or Medicare for health care. Some are not connected to these services and may fail to qualify due to stringent eligibility requirements, especially where alcohol and drug disabilities are concerned.

Barriers to Treatment

Compared to men, women who are addicted to alcohol and drugs lack social supports, including support to get treatment (Davis & DiNitto, 1998). Addicted partners may discourage women from seeking treatment. Women may also have concerns about disclosing the nature of their dual diagnoses to treatment providers and peers. For example, at an Alcoholics Anonymous (AA) meeting, a woman may be comfortable discussing her alcoholism but uncomfortable discussing her anxiety disorder; conversely, she may be comfortable discussing her anxiety disorder in a support group for people with mental illness but uncomfortable discussing her alcoholism. Women may also have concerns about the ability of treatment providers to effectively address their dual diagnoses, particularly when they have had prior negative experiences with treatment for both disorders. Thus, women with dual diagnoses may reject treatment altogether or feel as if the barriers to treatment are too great to overcome.

The case of Jane illustrates several dynamics of dual diagnoses discussed in this section.

Case Study of a Dually Diagnosed Woman

Jane was diagnosed with bipolar disorder and alcohol dependence in her senior year of college, following a period in which she had been feeling depressed for several days and drinking heavily. Persuaded by friends to attend a party, she woke up the next morning in the bed of a man she did not know and with no memory of the events of the past several days. She returned to her room feeling ashamed and depressed and attempted to commit suicide by taking a bottle of Tylenol. Friends discovered her a few hours later and took her to the emergency room (ER). After being evaluated in the ER, she was admitted to the psychiatric unit, where she stayed for two weeks. She was given a prescription for lithium, advised to attend AA meetings and abstain from alcohol and other drugs, and given an appointment to see the psychiatrist at the student health center four weeks after her discharge.

Jane initially took the medication, but soon stopped because it made her feel "flat" and "as if [she] had no feelings." She also doubted she was an alcoholic, believing that she used alcohol only to control her mood swings. She cancelled her appointment at the counseling center and subsequently entered a cycle of mania-depression that lasted for several months. She continued to drink and minimized the extent of both her mood swings and her alcohol dependence. Despite this cycle, she remained out of the hospital and graduated from college, albeit with much lower grades than she preferred.

Following college, Jane returned to her parents' home and began a series of jobs that she had difficulty keeping. Although she had no trouble getting and maintaining a job when she was manic, she could not perform the required tasks when she became depressed, and often fell behind. She also called in sick frequently. When she lost a job, it was most often due to excessive absences. Despite being confronted on several occasions by her parents, she increased her consumption of alcohol as well as the number of her sexual partners and denial of the severity of both her bipolar disorder and her alcoholism. After her parents discovered she had contracted a sexually transmitted disease (STD), they gave her an ultimatum: get treatment for her mental illness and alcoholism or find alternative living arrangements. Having no job and few friends on whom she could rely, she reluctantly agreed to seek treatment.

With no insurance, Jane sought help at the community mental health center. After an extensive intake process in which she was asked to provide information regarding her mood swings, alcohol and drug use, sexual behavior, and health problems, Jane was given an appointment for the following week to meet with a psychiatrist and social worker who were trained in the treatment of dual diagnoses.

Jane began attending twice-weekly therapy sessions with the social worker and monthly medication management sessions with the psychiatrist. During the first two years of treatment, these sessions focused on (1) education about her diagnoses and the actions she needed to engage in to effectively cope with her illnesses, (2) treatment of her STD, and (3) cautions about engaging in high-risk behaviors that might lead to self-harm or harm by others. She was also encouraged to attend AA and a peer counseling group for people with dual diagnoses. During this time, Jane struggled to accept her diagnoses and was minimally compliant with treatment. She often failed to attend sessions, refused to take her medication, and continued to drink alcohol. She also continued to have a variety of sexual partners, particularly when she became manic after going off her medication for more than a week. Neither the social worker nor the psychiatrist expected immediate compliance with treatment, but helped Jane learn from the consequences that resulted when she did not comply.

Over the next several years, Jane increasingly accepted the nature of her illness and the required treatment. Although she continued to float in and out of treatment, she was able to build longer periods of compliance with her medication, treatment sessions, and abstinence from alcohol. Consequently, the focus of her sessions shifted to a relationship she was building with a man she had met at an AA meeting and had been seeing for several months. She expressed an interest in marrying and having a family but also remained fearful that she could not be an equal partner in the relationship and a good mother, given her illnesses. As her relationship progressed, she asked her boyfriend to attend counseling sessions with her. Although she felt he understood her addiction, she wanted him to have more understanding of her bipolar disorder.

Jane married the man she met in AA. She wanted children and discussed this desire with her psychiatrist and social worker. She had been stable on lithium for over two years but had concerns about taking it while she was pregnant. At the same time, she did not want to stop her medication because she knew all too well the consequences of not taking it. She was afraid her bipolar disorder would flare up and that she would start drinking again to help her cope with her mental illness. After several consultations with her social worker, psychiatrist, and medical doctor, Jane agreed to be slowly tapered off the medication before trying to become pregnant. She agreed to increase her sessions with her psychiatrist and social worker so that her bipolar disorder could be more closely monitored, and to increase her attendance at AA to support her efforts at sobriety while off medication. In addition, she agreed to enter the hospital if her bipolar disorder or alcoholism worsened to the point where she or the child she hoped to conceive were at risk of harm.

Jane did not drink during her pregnancy, though she was hospitalized once when she experienced a brief manic episode. Following her hospitalization, she was advised to resume a low dose of lithium or consider other medications, but she chose to remain off all medications until after she gave birth. Shortly after her daughter was born, Jane resumed her lithium treatment and continued to do well in managing both of her illnesses.

Screening

Practitioners in alcohol and drug treatment programs often screen clients for mental disorders, and mental health practitioners often screen clients for alcohol and drug problems. Women more often than men present at medical (Reed & Mowbray, 1999) and mental health settings (Zweben, 1996) for symptom relief. In general medical settings as well as in social service programs, practitioners often need to screen for both mental and substance disorders. Women (and men) may seek help in these settings because they are less stigmatizing than mental health or chemical dependency treatment programs.

In screening clients with major psychiatric disorders for alcohol and drug problems, clinicians are looking for the same symptoms or behaviors as they are in screening others for these problems, such as the client's spending increased time acquiring and using drugs and continuing drinking or "drugging" despite life problems associated with drug use (see Chapter Three for more information on screening for alcohol and other drug problems). Some additional screening factors should be kept in mind when dual diagnoses are suspected. Even minor use of alcohol or nonprescribed drugs may result in exacerbation of psychiatric disorders, whereas these small amounts may be clinically insignificant with other populations. For example, DiNitto and Webb (1998) describe a woman whose caseworker saw no indication of an alcohol or drug problem; however, when the client met with her treatment team to explore the causes of her hospitalizations, she mentioned that when she drank even one beer, she ended up in the psychiatric hospital. Toxicology testing (for example, urine screens or blood tests) is commonly used for screening (see Orlin & Davis, 1993), especially in acute situations, such as a psychotic episode. Though detection of alcohol and drugs through laboratory testing is not synonymous with a substance use disorder, these tests can help to detect such problems. Practitioners may want to consider using these tests in screening clients as well as in monitoring progress. Although such tests may seem intrusive or punitive, some clients see them as a useful tool in their recovery.

Screening for alcohol and drug problems in cases of dual diagnoses also involves inquiries about whether a woman with a psychiatric disorder is taking psychotropic medications as prescribed. Some women use nonprescribed drugs to modulate the unwanted side effects of prescribed psychotropic medications. Others abandon their psychotropic medications and rely on alcohol or street drugs to counteract symptoms of mental illness, despite the propensity of these substances to increase psychiatric dysphoria.

It is difficult to recommend standardized tools for alcohol and drug screening for women who have major psychiatric disorders, because the most widely used brief screening instruments were developed primarily with male populations, and they were not devised for people who have major psychiatric disorders. Depending on the setting and the severity of a client's psychiatric diagnosis, practitioners may wish to consider the following instruments:

- In settings where screening time is severely limited, one of the briefest screening instruments for alcohol problems, the four-item CAGE (see Ewing, 1984), may be used with patients who have psychiatric disorders (see Sciacca, 1991). The newly tested CAGE Adapted to Include Drugs (CAGE-AID) may also be used with instructions to the patient or client that "when thinking about drug use, include illegal drug use and the use of prescription drugs other than as prescribed" (Brown, Leonard, Saunders, & Papasouliotis, 1998, p. 102). These instructions are useful in screening women with psychiatric disorders who have often been prescribed psychotropic medications and who may be taking them inappropriately.
- The Michigan Alcoholism Screening Test (MAST) (Selzer, 1971) is another well-known screening tool. A recent meta-analysis found that the MAST had sufficient validity in psychiatric settings and that validity increased when study samples contained higher proportions of women (Teitelbaum & Mullen, 2000).
- The Drug Abuse Screening Test (DAST) (Skinner, 1982) is often used to screen for drug problems other than alcohol. Rosenberg, Drake, Wolford, and Meuser (1998) found that it did not classify hospitalized patients with severe mental illness as well as some other instruments, but Cocco and Carey (1998) found

both good reliability and validity with outpatients who had major psychiatric disorders.

• The TWEAK and the T-ACE questionaires were designed to be more sensitive to women's drinking problems (see Russell, 1994). Both were devised to screen for risk drinking during pregnancy. Validation with women who have psychiatric disorders is needed.

• The Substance Abuse Subtle Screening Inventory (SASSI) (Miller, Miller, Roberts, Brooks, & Lazowski, 1997), contains many items that do not inquire directly about alcohol and other drug problems. It may be useful when there are concerns that the client may not respond candidly to many obvious questions about substance use and related problems. The SASSI has a separate scoring profile for women, and subscales provide some information about psychological distress, such as whether the client has a depressed affect. Some questions may be too abstract for people with severe thought disorders, and its sixty-seven subtle items make it longer than other instruments noted here.

• The eighteen-item Dartmouth Assessment of Lifestyle Instrument (DALI) was recently developed to address the frequent underdetection of alcohol and other drug disorders among psychiatric patients (Rosenberg et al., 1998). It is apparently the only instrument of its kind reported in the literature. The DALI focuses on the substance use disorders most common among psychiatric patients—alcohol, cannabis, and cocaine. Initial evidence suggests that gender is not related to the DALI's accuracy and that it may perform better than other tools frequently used to detect substance use disorders (Rosenberg et al., 1998).

In screening psychiatric patients for alcohol and other drug problems, interviews are preferable to self-administered paper-and-pencil tests (Carey & Correia, 1998; RachBeisel et al., 1999). Clear and simplified wording and response options also make it easier for patients to comply (Carey & Correia, 1998). In addition to the usual conditions for adequate screening, such as the test administrator's building rapport with the client, the client should be free of intoxicating substances and psychiatrically stable (see Skinner, 1984). Responses are also generally more accurate when the client does not fear negative repercussions, such as psychiatric hospitalization. Underreporting is common, but overreporting may occur as a way to gain access to services or other resources (Carey & Correia, 1998). In addition to toxicology testing and records and information from family, friends, and service providers who are knowledgeable about the client are especially important when the client is unable or unwilling to provide accurate information.

More validation of the commonly used alcohol and drug screening instruments is needed for people with major psychiatric disorders, particularly women, and new tools are needed to improve screening. Many tools are available to help chemical dependency professionals screen adult clients for psychiatric problems, such as the Brief Psychiatric Rating Scale (BPRS) (see Miller & Faustman, 1996) and the Beck Depression Inventory (BDI) (see Steer & Beck, 1996).

Diagnosis and Assessment

Confirmation of psychiatric and substance use disorders usually relies on criteria found in the *Diagnostic and Statistical Manual of Mental Disorders,* fourth edition, text revised *(DSM-IV-TR)* (American Psychiatric Association, 2000). The Structured Clinical Interview for DSM-IV (SCID) can be useful in making these diagnoses (First, Spitzer, Gibbon, & Williams, 1995). The Psychiatric Research Interview for Substance and Mental Disorders (PRISM) (Hasin et al., 1996), also based on *DSM* criteria, may also help clinicians detect psychiatric problems among patients with substance use disorders. There are probe questions to improve women's responses to PRISM items and for people of various ethnic groups. The brief Alcohol Use Scale (AUS) and Drug Use Scale (DUS) also rely on *DSM* criteria and use practitioners' ratings to assess (and monitor) the alcohol and drug use of clients with major psychiatric disorders (Drake et al., 1996).

In addition to establishing a diagnosis, women with major psychiatric disorders and substance use disorders need comprehensive, ongoing, biopsychosocial assessment. The five axes of *DSM-IV-TR* provide an approach for conducting these assessments. Axis I contains the substance-related disorders and most of the mental disorders. Dually diagnosed women may present with more than one psychiatric disorder. A critical issue, especially in acute situations, is differentiating alcohol and drug disorders and psychiatric illnesses. Zweben (1996) reports a situation in which "a staff member in a social model community recovery center prepared to eject a participant who was talking loudly to herself, on the grounds that she was intoxicated. The director, observing the interchange, asked the participant if she was hearing voices" (p. 348), and indeed she was. Drug effects and symptoms of psychiatric disorders often mimic each other. Stimulant use can produce an episode that appears to be paranoid schizophrenia, but if it is indeed drug induced, the episode usually remits quickly (Zweben, 1996). Alcoholics and others dependent on sedative-hypnotic drugs may exhibit depressive symptoms during detoxification, but such symptoms usually ease within a few weeks (Zweben, 1996). When they do not, a diagnosis of a depressive disorder may be supported.

Diagnostic errors may result in inappropriate treatment; in particular, mistaking a substance-induced psychosis for a primary psychotic disorder could cause a client to receive antipsychotic medications for needlessly long periods (Carey & Correia, 1998). A firm diagnosis often cannot be established until the woman is alcohol and drug free, but when patients are known to have psychiatric disorders requiring psychotropic medication, such medication is usually administered. A woman's diagnoses may need to be modified over time as additional information becomes available.

A careful history may reveal whether an alcohol or drug problem predated a woman's psychiatric disorder or whether a psychiatric disorder predated her substance use disorder. One condition may appear to have contributed to the other, or they may appear to be independent of each other. These temporal distinctions can be important in treatment planning, but in cases where the drug use began early in life, they can be difficult to make (also see Zweben, 1996). Many women have primary diagnoses of mental and substance use disorders, meaning that the substance use disorder will not disappear once the mental disorder is treated and that the mental disorder will not go away once the substance use disorder is treated. Early detection and appropriate intervention are important in stemming the psychosocial dysfunction that accompanies dual disorders (see Rao, Daley, & Hammen, 2000).

Axis II contains the personality disorders (for example, borderline, antisocial, narcissistic) that may be difficult to identify because their diagnostic criteria are often confused with symptoms of substance use disorders (Zweben, 1996). Personality disorders complicate treatment for chemical dependency and dual diagnoses because they result in impulsiveness, unstable affect, and identity confusion (Naegle, 1997). As Naegle describes, "a narcissistic woman who is perceived as constantly complaining and never satisfied is avoided by health professionals, and her unmet health needs reinforce her drug using patterns and negative behaviors" (p. 573). These diagnoses often elicit negative reactions among staff, including the presumption of a poor prognosis, but clients with personality disorders can benefit from the structured environment of many rehabilitation programs (Zweben, 1996).

Axis III is used to report medical problems that affect the course and treatment of a woman's psychiatric disorder (American Psychiatric Association, 2000). Conditions such as liver and kidney damage (whether or not they are related to alcohol or drug use) can complicate the treatment of psychiatric disorders, because some psychotropic medications are contraindicated when these conditions are present. Providers of mental health services and chemical dependency treatment should see that appropriate evaluation is done to identify any health problems that need attention or that may interfere with treatment.

Axis IV covers psychosocial and environmental problems that affect the course and treatment of Axes I and II diagnoses. They include problems related to social supports, the environment (for example, discrimination), education (for example, illiteracy), occupation (for example, unemployment), housing, finances (for example, poverty), access to health and social services, and legal concerns. Problems on Axis IV may also result from positive changes, such as a job promotion that the client has difficulty handling due to low self-esteem or difficulty with stress and anxiety, as is often the case with women who have major psychiatric and substance use disorders.

Axis V is synonymous with the Global Assessment of Functioning (GAF) Scale used by clinicians to describe clients' overall functioning (American Psychiatric Association, 2000). It is especially useful in detecting urgent situations. Scores range from 1 to 100. Scores of 91 to 100 indicate "superior functioning," whereas at the low end of the scale, 1 to 10, there is "persistent danger of severely hurting self or others (e.g., recurrent violence) OR persistent inability to maintain minimal personal hygiene OR serious suicidal act with clear expectation of death" (American Psychiatric Association, 2000, p. 34).

Many chemical dependency professionals use the Addiction Severity Index (ASI) (McLellan et al., 1985), a structured interview, for assessment and treatment planning (see RachBeisel et al., 1999; Carey & Correia, 1998). The ASI addresses medical, employment, alcohol, drug, legal, family-social, and psychiatric problems. Few other tools address all these domains, but some items may not be relevant to the life experiences and substance use of people with major psychiatric disorders (Corse, Hirschinger, & Zanis, 1995). The Substance Abuse Treatment Scale (SATS) (Drake et al., 1996) was developed specifically for dually diagnosed clients. This brief eight-point scale helps clinicians identify the client's stage of treatment for substance use disorders (ranging from no contact with treatment providers through remission) in order to match her with appropriate services. It is also used to monitor a client's progress.

Clinicians may find it useful to help clients identify behavioral chains—relationships between increases and decreases in substance use and symptoms of mental illness, including the antecedents and consequences of both types of behaviors (Stasiewicz et al., 1996). A behavior chain includes the following: Trigger → Thought → Feeling → Behavior → Consequence (Stasiewicz et al., 1996, p. 97). A woman who works with her therapist to identify this sequence can make plans to break the chain and avoid negative consequences, but clients often need considerable coaching to engage in this process. Miller and Rollnick's motivational interviewing approach (1991) may reduce women's denial and defensiveness and increase their willingness and ability to identify this chain of events. In motivational interviewing, the treatment provider "begins where the client is." Reflection, education, objective feedback, and other techniques are used to help clients gain a greater understanding of the problem. Removing barriers, increasing choices, negotiating goals, and other strategies are used to help clients identify and initiate new behaviors to address the problem.

Guidelines for Treating Women with Dual Diagnoses

Because of the number and magnitude of their problems, women with dual diagnoses require comprehensive biopsychosocial services. Yet these women may have difficulty following treatment plans, and crises and relapses typically occur. Relapse may also occur because psychotropic medications fail to produce the intended results even when taken as prescribed and because much is still unknown about how to treat both single and dual disorders.

Many strategies for assisting women with addictive disorders presented throughout this book have been used to help women with major psychiatric disorders and women with dual diagnoses, such as feminist approaches (for example, consciousness raising and empowerment) and women-only groups (see Avery, 1998; RachBeisel et al., 1999; Zweben, 1996). The field of dual diagnoses practice is still in its infancy, and treatment models have generally not distinguished between male and female clients. We do, however, offer some guidelines for treating women with dual diagnoses. Many of these guidelines are discussed in Drake, Bartels, Teague, Noordsy, and Clark, 1993.

Ensure That Women with Dual Diagnoses Receive Coordinated Services

The mental health and chemical dependency treatment systems developed independently of each other, and their philosophies and approaches differ. Mental health systems rely on professional service providers, individual treatment, and the use of psychotropic medications. Help for alcoholics and addicts emerged through peer-led self-help groups that may have eschewed the use of medications (pharmacotherapy) following detoxification. Mental health programs have traditionally excluded clients who used alcohol and street drugs on grounds that they were disruptive or might encourage other clients to use. Conversely, chemical dependency programs have traditionally rejected clients who used psychotropic medications because they were not considered "clean and sober," thus leaving dually diagnosed clients without a good source of care (see DiNitto & Webb, 1998).

Most treatment for clients with dual disorders has been sequential or serial: one disorder (either the mental illness or the substance use disorder) was treated before the other. When clients did not get help in negotiating the two systems, they often ended up with "ping-pong ball" treatment—referrals back and forth between the two systems—until a crisis arose. Today, treatment providers generally seek either parallel or integrated treatment for clients with dual diagnoses.

In parallel treatment, the client's substance use disorder and psychiatric disorder are treated simultaneously—one individual or team treats the substance use disorder and another treats the mental illness. Optimally, the two agree on treatment plans and consult periodically so as to avoid sabotaging each other's efforts and to avoid triangulation by clients. To optimize service delivery, however, mental health and chemical dependency professionals should be prepared to take the lead in coordinating services when using the parallel model.

Integrated models combine elements of treatment for substance use and psychiatric disorders into one program for people with dual diagnoses. Services are provided by a single treatment team comprising clinicians and case managers who are knowledgeable about substance use disorders, psychiatric disorders, and dual diagnoses. Among the best-known models of integrated treatment is the New Hampshire dual-diagnosis program (Drake, Teague, & Warren, 1990). Integrated treatment seems reasonable, considering the similarities between mental and substance use disorders. Both are chronic conditions in which clients are prone to relapse, both may stem from neurobiological causes, and both require vigilance in order to prevent relapse (Bricker, 1995; Orlin & Davis, 1993). Integrated treatment is often unavailable, however, because funding streams for mental health and chemical dependency services remain separate, and many service providers are still not conversant or comfortable treating both disorders.

Although integrated treatment services for people with dual diagnoses have been embraced as the optimal approach, only a handful of controlled studies have evaluated them. Few have identified superior dual-diagnoses models or shown such services to be clearly more effective than standard mental health services (see DiNitto, Webb, & Rubin, in press, for a review). These studies have paid little attention to gender differences, though Jerrell and Ridgely (1995) did a post hoc comparison of outcomes by gender ($N = 31$ women and 101 men) in their study of three treatments (intensive case management, behavioral skills training, and a twelve-step recovery model) for people with dual diagnoses. The small number of women makes it difficult to generalize, but men and women did equally well on the outcomes measured. Women fared somewhat better in the twelve-step model than in the other interventions. Although the authors did not discuss the reasons for this finding, it may be that the twelve-step model provided services more consistent with the participants' needs. For example, participants spent all their time addressing substance abuse issues, and the component was staffed by women who provided supportive rather than confrontational treatment.

Ensure the Client's Safety and Address Other Needs

It is difficult for women to remain mentally stable and free from alcohol and improper drug use when living on the streets or with others who are not working toward these goals. The literature stresses dually diagnosed women's fears of victimization and their need for safety (see, for example, Alexander, 1996; Rach-Beisel et al., 1999; Watkins, Shaner, & Sullivan, 1999), but service providers may still spend a great deal of time coaxing women with major psychiatric illnesses to accept shelter or housing services. Many supported or assisted housing programs have been developed to improve outcomes for clients with psychiatric disorders; some include teaching them skills necessary to maintain a household and live more independently. Some now focus on women with dual diagnoses (see Mosley, 1996).

Until chronic medical and dental problems are treated, women may have difficulty concentrating on mental health and chemical dependency services. The need for child care must also be addressed. As a client progresses in treatment, assistance with social skills and vocational services may also be needed.

Many women who have severe mental illness and substance use disorders are served through public or nonprofit agencies. They do not have resources to access private, for-profit services, and private providers may not offer the wide range of services these clients need, such as housing. Sometimes private practitioners offer pro bono or reduced-fee services and may see some women with severe disabilities who could not otherwise afford these services. These private practitioners must maintain a broad knowledge of community services to assist these clients adequately. These practitioners also benefit from knowledge of Medicaid and Medicare and the coverage they provide for mental health and chemical dependency services. Some women with dual diagnoses are high functioning and maintain employment or have access to other resources that cover private mental health and chemical dependency treatment. These women may not need the community housing services, socialization groups, assistance in negotiating public assistance, or other services that many other women with severe mental illness require.

Provide Dual-Diagnosis Services Oriented to Women

Traditional mental health and chemical dependency treatment approaches must be altered to better serve those with dual diagnoses (Drake et al., 1993). Because chemical dependency services in particular have been designed to meet the needs of men, they must be further altered to address the needs of dually diagnosed women. For example, Zweben (1996) notes that women with PTSD are doomed to fail if they follow admonitions to put their trauma issues on hold until they achieve stable abstinence. Confrontation—seen as necessary to break the denial that stands in the way of the client's recognition of the problem—has been a hallmark of chemical dependency treatment, but such punitive approaches may revictimize women (Zweben, 1996). Motivational interviewing, used by many chemical dependency treatment providers, is an alternative to confrontation that may increase acceptance of help (Miller & Rollnick, 1991). Cognitively impaired women may require additional program modifications, such as repetition and reinforcement, because they can easily forget or misunderstand information (Mosley, 1996).

Women-focused services must also consider life cycle or developmental stages, including relationship issues at each stage. The young adult with dual diagnoses may need services geared to addressing issues of sexuality and protection from sexually transmitted diseases, including negotiating intimate relationships with partners of the same or opposite gender. Drug-using peers are often influential in the lives of these young women, and treatment providers often assist young clients in developing relationships through support groups that focus on remaining clean and sober. Women of childbearing age may struggle with issues of pregnancy and the contraindications of using certain psychotropic medications during this life stage, as illustrated earlier in Jane's case. They may have former or current partners to contend with, including abusive partners and those using alcohol and other drugs. Older women may be faced with the accumulation of health problems that arise from long-term alcohol and drug use and lack of attention to health care. They may be alienated from family and have few, if any, friends on whom to rely. In some cases a family member may be the woman's caretaker or guardian. These relationships can be fraught with struggles, especially if the caretaker or guardian controls an SSI or SSDI check that the woman receives.

Adopt an Incremental Approach

Osher and Kofoed (1989) conceptualized treatment for dual diagnoses as occurring in four stages: engagement, in which providers develop a relationship with the client; persuasion, in which providers help the client identify the negative consequences of substance use and encourage the client to consider accepting services; active treatment that results in the client's stability; and relapse prevention to maintain recovery. Drake and colleagues (1996) have expanded the model to include eight stages. The importance of the first stage is underlined by mental health workers known as "engagement specialists," who reach out to dually diagnosed clients, help them obtain the concrete services they want, and patiently assist them until they are willing to accept mental health and chemical dependency services.

The transtheoretical model (TTM) or stages of change model (Prochaska, DiClemente, & Norcross, 1992), which has gained popularity in the chemical dependency field, has also been applied to treatment of dual diagnoses (see Velasquez, Carbonari, & DiClemente, 1999). The TTM stages are precontemplation, in which the individual lacks awareness of the problem or is not considering change; contemplation, in which the individual considers changing; preparation, in which the individual makes plans and a commitment to change; action, in which the individual takes action and achieves change; and maintenance, in which the individual sustains the change and makes it a part of her life. Clients do not necessarily progress in a linear fashion through any of these stages. In fact, the TTM is conceptualized as a spiral, a depiction well suited to mental illness and chemical dependency, in which relapses are common. Whichever of these models a clinician might prefer, their importance lies in matching services to the client's stage or phase of change.

In most alcohol and drug treatment programs and in twelve-step programs, one is either clean and sober, or not. In working with women with dual diagnoses, a harm reduction approach, which rewards decreased use and supports incremental gains in recovery from chemical dependency and mental illness, may be more appropriate. Insistence on sobriety may cause a woman in the precontemplation or contemplation phase to reject the treatment provider, thus losing an opportunity for engagement. Insistence on a particular level of service intensity may also cause client flight. As Watkins et al. (1999) describe, "one woman's paranoia led her to leave a treatment program for alcohol. She said 'I got too mentally sick, because contact everyday is too much for me. It's just overwhelming for me'" (pp. 120–121).

Conceptualize Services as Lifelong

In chemical dependency treatment programs, providers often expect clients to "graduate" from the program and move on. Though clients may return to treatment should a relapse occur, most aftercare is done through Alcoholics Anonymous and other twelve-step groups. Those with major mental illnesses generally do not graduate from the treatment system; instead they are encouraged to participate in services on a consistent basis. Treatment gains often come slowly, and providers should be flexible with regard to a woman's length of stay in any phase or stage of a treatment program.

Maintain Regular Contact with Clients and Advocate for Them

Assertive Community Treatment and continuous treatment teams are the standard of care in assisting clients with major psychiatric disorders, particularly those who are homeless (see Drake et al., 1993; Stein & Santos, 1998). These teams see that clients get comprehensive services for the multiple problems they face, and as the words *assertive* and *continuous* imply, they are not shy about reaching out to clients. In fact, when a woman does not maintain contact, the team regards this as an indication that it should reach out to her. Naegle (1997) notes that for women with dual diagnoses, "low self-esteem, compromised social skills, and lack of assertiveness make advocacy key to clients' access and use of the comprehensive services they need" (p. 573). Regular contact can result in early identification of problems, thus perhaps preventing crises and other serious consequences, such as hospitalizations or incarceration. Various case management models used in mental health and chemical dependency treatment also promote regular contact with clients (see Sands, 2001).

Pay Attention to the Client's Reactions to Medication and Medication Compliance

Despite their negative side effects, psychotropic medications may be essential to controlling mental illness, and growing attention is being paid to pharmacotherapy in the long-term management of substance dependence. Newer medications can present concerns because their long-term safety profile may be unknown, and medical personnel often fear repercussions when prescribing for women of childbearing age. There are also serious concerns about the use of some well-known medications in treating clients with chemical dependency and dual diagnoses. For example, benzodiazepines should be considered judiciously when treating conditions such as anxiety disorders, because of their cross-addiction and overdose potential with alcohol and other abused sedative drugs. Newer medications for treating anxiety and depression, such as the selective serotonin reuptake inhibitors (SSRIs), are effective, are not habit forming, and may produce fewer side effects than previous generations of antidepressants, thus making them more acceptable to patients (Greenberger, 1998).

It often takes time and a good relationship with a psychiatrist for a woman to find the right type and dosage of medication. This point was driven home by a woman who attended psychoeducational dual-diagnosis treatment groups where she learned about her diagnoses and the medications used in treating her psychiatric illness. She had not been educated on these subjects during her previous treatments and reacted to her newfound knowledge by saying, "Boy, is my psychiatrist going to be ticked when he finds out that you are teaching this stuff!" This woman has become a much more equal partner in her treatment planning and works closely with her psychiatrist to modify her medications as needed.

It is also important to help clients and even other professionals interpret medication effects. As Mosley notes, "a depressed client prescribed medication may be criticized by her peers for appearing 'lazy' or unwilling to participate in the daily routine" (1996, p. 386).

Emphasize the Positive, and Reward Treatment Gains Liberally

Dual diagnoses, like other chronic illnesses, are demoralizing for clients and their families (Drake et al., 1993). For dually diagnosed women, this demoralization may be compounded not only by multiple illnesses but by multiple role losses if children have been removed from their care (Alexander, 1996), if they have lost a spouse or other partner or are estranged from family, and if they are unable to maintain employment. Treatment providers should help clients maintain hope (Drake et al., 1993; Webb, 1997). They should encourage clients at every step of the way and reward them liberally for even small gains in utilizing services, maintaining sobriety, and the like. Women with dual diagnoses need help in recognizing their self-worth. The threat of suicide looms large in this population. Professional education should help providers learn not only how to prevent suicides but also how to cope themselves when suicides occur.

A Model Program for Dually Diagnosed Women

The PROTOTYPES program (Mosley, 1996) offers comprehensive residential and outpatient drug treatment to dually diagnosed pregnant and parenting women, consistent with the treatment guidelines discussed in the preceding section. It is a model for treating dually diagnosed women in general. The program's philosophy is women-sensitive, focusing on empowerment, on women's multiple roles, and on providing a safe and nurturing environment. Staff use practical strategies to help clients resolve complex life issues. They give clients provisional diagnoses at entry, make diagnoses carefully so as not to confuse psychiatric and substance use disorders, and review the diagnoses periodically. Staff see recovery as a lifelong process, and in this process they consider a woman's experiences and her place in the life cycle. Staff serve as role models for clients and work with mental health therapists to achieve service integration. They provide services at different levels and intensities, ranging from "highly structured and intensive to minimally structured and more self-directed," and they match services to clients' needs (p. 383).

Stages of treatment include intake and orientation, stabilization, reparenting and support, and community reentry. Residential services generally last six to eighteen months, and participants decide if they would like to extend a stage, allowing them to pace treatment according to their psychosocial needs and progress. The program also provides aftercare services.

An important program component is crisis management, which may be needed to address negative reactions to medications, relived trauma, suicidal thoughts, emotional outbursts, and desires to leave prematurely. Should clients be administratively discharged or leave against professional advice, case managers help them obtain other community services that will promote recovery. Relapse does not necessarily result in discharge. Instead, staff help the woman resume recovery and measure her progress "by longer periods of abstinence, fewer relapses, improved quality of life and well-being and improved medication management rather than by total and absolute compliance" (Mosley, 1996, p. 385). Children also receive services.

Use of Self-Help and Other Support Groups

Although there is agreement that clients with dual diagnoses should be coached on how to participate in Alcoholics Anonymous, Narcotics Anonymous, and other twelve-step groups and be accompanied to initial meetings (see DiNitto & Webb, 1998; Mosley, 1996; Noordsy, Schwab, Fox, & Drake, 1996), the extent to which clients use and benefit from these groups continues to be discussed. AA supports the use of medications when judiciously prescribed and cautions members not to play doctor (Alcoholics Anonymous, 1984), but there is always the concern that well-meaning but misinformed members might encourage individuals with a major psychiatric disorder to abandon their prescribed psychotropic medications. Through role plays or other means, professionals can assist women in developing the self-efficacy necessary to handle these situations. Zweben (1996) encourages professionals working with women who have psychiatric disorders to recognize and discuss the demoralization that may occur when they see other members of twelve-step groups progress faster than they do. She also notes that self-image and concerns about appearance may hamper the participation of women who have diagnoses of depression, HIV, and eating disorders.

DiNitto, Webb, Rubin, Morrison-Orton, and Wambach (2001) found substantial attendance in self-help groups among dually diagnosed clients (most of whom had mood rather than thought disorders) in the ninety days following inpatient chemical dependency treatment, with no relationship to diagnosis or gender. Clients with more education attended more meetings, suggesting that cognitive functioning may affect ability to participate in twelve-step programs that are not specifically adapted for people with psychiatric disorders.

In contrast, Noordsy and colleagues' research (1996) indicates that few dually diagnosed clients used self-help groups consistently, though most attended at some point. Those with affective disorders attended more than those with schizophrenia, and better social skills were positively related to attendance. Those who pursued attendance commented on the support and accessibility of the groups; they could speak at meetings but did not have to do so. The religious tone appealed to some, as did the groups' routines and structure. However, other clients noted that program philosophy and jargon minimized their life problems. Other hindrances to initial attendance may be fear of crowds, clients' concern that others will be watching them, and their feeling different from others. At meetings, some clients had difficulty sitting still or felt that others' stories made them want to use substances. Some had difficulty relating to stories about losses (spouse, job, or car) because they had never had these things. The delusional connotations of such phrases as "Let go and let God" may also be a concern for some. Noordsy et al. note that dually diagnosed clients generally achieve remission without self-help group attendance and that insisting on attendance can be counterproductive. Because these groups are voluntary, the researchers suggest backing off if the client is not interested and trying again at a later stage when the client might be more receptive.

To better assist people with dual diagnoses of mental and addictive disorders, self-help groups such as Double Trouble in Recovery (DTR) and Dual Recovery Anonymous (DRA) have emerged. Both are based on the twelve steps of AA. Information about DRA can be obtained at www.draonline.org or by calling (888) 869-9230.

Some groups, such as Good Chemistry Groups (Webb, 1997), use a professional facilitator along with a facilitator in dual recovery. Zweben (1996) recommends several approaches to treating dually diagnosed women that are incorporated in Good Chemistry Groups: psychoeducation to address denial and counteract erroneous information and myths, sufficient time to discuss and process information, the reducing of shame and denial and the building of self-esteem and hope, a coleader who is in dual recovery, and tokens (similar to chips in AA) to reinforce accomplishments. Each session of Good Chemistry begins with the program's "Dos and Don'ts" and mottoes to reinforce principles. Good Chemistry empowers attendees by encouraging them to be active participants in their own treatment and recovery. A similar program is Support Together for Emotional and Mental Serenity and Sobriety (STEMSS) (Bricker, 1995). Though Good Chemistry and STEMSS groups are coed, they could be conducted for women only.

Conclusion

Integrated treatments for clients with dual diagnoses are relatively new, especially with regard to a focus on women. Greenberger (1998) calls for greater attention to ways in which "gender-based biology can be used to determine how mental illness and addiction operate differently in women than in men" (p. 410). Perhaps this knowledge will lead to desperately needed improvements in treatment, such as more effective ways of combining medications with psychosocial treatments for women. Zweben (1996) notes that clinicians often focus on improving their treatment skills rather than on working to restructure the systems that serve clients. This chapter has focused primarily on clinical issues, but a broad policy response that views dually diagnosed women in a holistic fashion could do much to improve the quality of their lives.

References

Alcoholics Anonymous. (1984). *The AA member—medications and other drugs.* New York: Alcoholics Anonymous World Services.

Alexander, M. J. (1996). Women with co-occurring addictive and mental disorders: An emerging profile of vulnerability. *American Journal of Orthopsychiatry, 66*(1), 61–70.

American Psychiatric Association. (2000). *Diagnostic and statistical manual of mental disorders* (4th ed., Text revised). Washington, DC: Author.

Avery, L. (1998). A feminist perspective on group work with severely mentally ill women. *Women and Therapy, 21*(4), 1–14.

Belle, D. (1990). Poverty and women's mental health. *American Psychologist, 45,* 385–389.

Boyd, M., & Hauenstein, E. (1997). Psychiatric assessment and confirmation of dual disorders in rural substance abusing women. *Archives of Psychiatric Nursing, 11*(2), 74–81.

Bricker, M. G. (1995). The STEMSS supported self-help model for dual diagnosis recovery: Applications for rural settings. In *Treating alcohol and other drug abusers in rural and frontier areas* (Technical Assistance Publication Series 17, DHHS Publication No. [SMA] 95-3054). Rockville, MD: Center for Substance Abuse Treatment, Substance Abuse and Mental Health Services Administration. Available: www.treatment.org/TAPS/TAP17/tap17stemss.html.

Brown, R. L., Leonard, T., Saunders, L. A., & Papasouliotis, O. (1998). The prevalence and detection of substance use disorders among inpatients ages 18 to 49: An opportunity for prevention. *Preventive Medicine, 27,* 101–110.

Brunette, M. F., & Drake, R. E. (1997). Gender differences in patients with schizophrenia and substance abuse. *Comprehensive Psychiatry, 38*(2), 109–116.

Carey, K. B., & Correia, C J. (1998). Severe mental illness and addictions: Assessment considerations. *Addictive Behaviors, 23,* 735–748.

Cocco, K. M., & Carey, K. B. (1998). Psychometric properties of the Drug Abuse Screening Test in psychiatric outpatients. *Psychological Assessment, 10,* 408–414.

Corse, S. J., Hirschinger, N. B., & Zanis, D. (1995). The use of the Addiction Severity Index with people with severe mental illness. *Psychiatric Rehabilitation Journal, 19,* 9–18.

Davis, D. R., & DiNitto, D. M. (1998). Gender and drugs: Fact, fiction, and unanswered questions. In C. A. McNeece & D. M. DiNitto (Eds.), *Chemical dependency: A systems approach* (2nd ed. pp. 406–442). Needham Heights, MA: Allyn & Bacon.

DiNitto, D. M., & Webb, D. K. (1998). Compounding the problem: Substance abuse and other disabilities. In C. A. McNeece & D. M. DiNitto (Eds.), *Chemical dependency: A systems approach* (2nd ed., pp. 347–390). Needham Heights, MA: Allyn & Bacon.

DiNitto, D. M., Webb, D. K., & Rubin, A. (in press). The effectiveness of an integrated treatment approach for clients with dual diagnoses. *Research on Social Work Practice.*

DiNitto, D. M., Webb, D. K., Rubin, A., Morrison-Orton, D., & Wambach, K. G. (2001). *Self-help group attendance among clients with dual diagnoses.* Manuscript accepted for publication.

Drake, R. E., Bartels, S. J., Teague, G. B., Noordsy, D. L., & Clark, R. E. (1993). Treatment of substance abuse in severely mentally ill patients. *Journal of Nervous and Mental Disease, 181,* 606–611.

Drake, R. E., Mueser, K. T., & McHugo, G. J. (1996). Clinician rating scales: Alcohol Use Scale (AUS), Drug Use Scale (DUS), and Substance Abuse Treatment Scale (SATS). In L. I. Sederer & B. Dickey (Eds.), *Outcomes assessment in clinical practice* (pp. 113–116). Baltimore: Williams & Wilkins.

Drake, R. E., Teague, G. B., & Warren, R. A. (1990). New Hampshire's dual diagnosis program for people with severe mental illness and substance use disorder. *Addiction Recovery, 10,* 35–39.

Ewing, J. A. (1984). Detecting alcoholism: The CAGE questionnaire. *Journal of the American Medical Association, 252,* 1905–1907.

First, M. B., Spitzer, R. L., Gibbon, M., & Williams, J.B.W. (1995). *Structured clinical interview for* DSM-IV *Axis I disorders—Patient edition.* New York: Biometrics Research Department, New York State Psychiatric Institute.

Gearon, J. S., & Bellack, A. S. (1999). Women with schizophrenia and co-occurring substance use disorders: An increased risk for violent victimization and HIV. *Community Mental Health Journal, 35,* 401–419.

Greenberger, P. (1998). News from the Society for the Advancement of Women's Health Research: Targeting mental illness and substance abuse among women. *Journal of Women's Health, 7,* 407–410.

Hasin, D. S., Trautman, K. D., Miele, G. M., Samet, S., Smith, M., & Endicott, J. (1996). Psychiatric Research Interview for Substance and Mental Disorders (PRISM): Reliability for substance abusers. *American Journal of Psychiatry, 153,* 1195–1201.

Helzer, J. E., & Pryzbeck, T. R. (1988). The co-occurrence of alcoholism with other psychiatric disorders in the general population and its impact on treatment. *Journal of Studies on Alcohol, 49,* 219–224.

Jerrell, J. M., & Ridgely, M. S. (1995). Gender differences in the assessment of specialized treatments for substance abuse among people with severe mental illness. *Journal of Psychoactive Drugs, 27,* 347–355.

Kessler, R. C., Crum, R. M., Warner, L. A., Nelson, C. B., Schulenberg, J., & Anthony, J. C. (1997). Lifetime co-occurrence of *DSM-III-R* alcohol abuse and dependence with other psychiatric disorders in the National Comorbidity Survey. *Archives of General Psychiatry, 54,* 313–321.

Kessler, R. C., McGonagle, K. A., Zhao, S., Nelson, C. B., Hughes, M., Eshelman, S., Wittchen, H., & Kendler, K. S. (1994). Lifetime and 12-month prevalence of *DSM-III-R* psychiatric disorders in the United States. *Archives of General Psychiatry, 51,* 8–19.

Kessler, R. C., Nelson, C. B., McGonagle, K. A., Edlund, M. J., Frank, R. G., & Leaf, P. J. (1996). The epidemiology of co-occurring addictive and mental disorders: Implications for prevention and service utilization. *American Journal of Orthopsychiatry, 66,* 17–31.

Khantzian, E. J. (1985). The self-medication hypothesis of addictive disorders: Focus on heroin and cocaine dependence. *American Journal of Psychiatry, 142,* 1259–1264.

McLellan, A. T., Luborsky, L., Cacciola, M. A., Griffith, J., Evans, R., Barr, H. L., &

O'Brien, C. P. (1985). New data from the Addiction Severity Index: Reliability and validity in three centers. *Journal of Nervous and Mental Disease, 173*, 412–423.

Miller, G. A., Miller, F. G., Roberts, J., Brooks, M. K., & Lazowski, L. G. (1997). *The SASSI-3.* Bloomington, IN: Baugh Enterprises.

Miller, L. S., & Faustman, W. O. (1996). Brief Psychiatric Rating Scale. In L. I. Sederer & B. Dickey (Eds.), *Outcomes assessment in clinical practice* (pp. 105–109). Baltimore: Williams & Wilkins.

Miller, W. R., & Rollnick, S. (1991). *Motivational interviewing: Preparing people to change addictive behavior.* New York: Guilford Press.

Mosley, T. M. (1996). PROTOTYPES: An urban model program of treatment and recovery services for dually diagnosed perinatal program participants. *Journal of Psychoactive Drugs, 28*, 381–388.

Mueser, K. T., Drake, R. E., & Wallach, M. A. (1998). Dual diagnosis: A review of etiological theories. *Addictive Behaviors, 23*, 717–734.

Naegle, M. A. (1997). Understanding women with dual diagnoses. *Journal of Obstetric, Gynecologic, and Neonatal Nursing, 26*, 567–575.

Noordsy, D. L., Schwab, B., Fox, L., & Drake, R. E. (1996). The role of self-help programs in the rehabilitation of persons with severe mental illness and substance use disorders. *Community Mental Health Journal, 32*, 71–81.

Orlin, L., & Davis, J. (1993). Assessment and intervention with drug and alcohol abusers in psychiatric settings. In S.L.A. Straussner (Ed.), *Clinical work with substance-abusing clients* (pp. 50–68). New York: Guilford Press.

Osher, F. C., & Kofoed, L. L. (1989). Treatment of patients with psychiatric and psychoactive substance abuse disorders. *Hospital and Community Psychiatry, 40*, 1025–1030.

Palacios, W. R., Urmann, C. F., Newel, R., & Hamilton, N. (1999). Developing a sociological framework for dually diagnosed women. *Journal of Substance Abuse Treatment, 17*, 91–102.

Prochaska, J. O., DiClemente, C. C., & Norcross, J. C. (1992). In search of how people change: Applications to addictive behaviors. *American Psychologist, 47*, 1102–1114.

RachBeisel, J., Scot, J., & Dixon, L. (1999). Co-occurring severe mental illness and substance use disorders: A review of recent research. *Psychiatric Services, 50*, 1427–1434.

Rao, U., Daley, S. E., & Hammen, C. (2000). Relationship between depression and substance use disorders in adolescent women during the transition to adulthood. *Journal of the American Academy of Child and Adolescent Psychiatry, 39*, 215–222.

Reed, B. G., & Mowbray, C. T. (1999). Mental illness and substance abuse: Implications for women's health and health care access. *Journal of the American Medical Women's Association, 54*, 71–78.

Regier, D. A., Farmer, M. E., Rae, D. S., Locke, B. Z., Keith, S. J., Judd, L. L., & Goodwin, F. K. (1990, November 21). Comorbidity of mental disorders with alcohol and other drug abuse: Results from the Epidemiologic Catchment Area (ECA) study. *Journal of the American Medical Association, 264*, 2511–2518.

Rosenberg, S. D., Drake, R. E., Wolford, G. L., & Meuser, K. T. (1998). Dartmouth Assessment of Lifestyle Instrument (DALI): A substance use disorder screen for people with severe mental illness. *American Journal of Psychiatry, 155*, 232–238.

Russell, M. (1994). New assessment tools for risk drinking during pregnancy: T-ACE, TWEAK, and others. *Alcohol Health and Research World, 18*(1), 55–61.

Sands, R. G. (2001). *Clinical social work practice in community mental health.* Needham Heights, MA: Allyn & Bacon.

Sciacca, K. (1991). An integrated treatment approach for severely mentally ill individuals with substance disorders. In K. Minkoff & R. E. Drake (Eds.), *Dual diagnosis of major mental illness and substance disorder.* Social and Behavioral Sciences Series, no. 50 (pp. 69–84). San Francisco: Jossey-Bass.

Selzer, M. L. (1971). The Michigan Alcoholism Screening Test: The quest for a new diagnostic instrument. *American Journal of Psychiatry, 127,* 1653–1658.

Skinner, H. A. (1982). The Drug Abuse Screening Test. *Addictive Behaviors, 7,* 363–371.

Skinner, H. A. (1984). Assessing alcohol use by patients in treatment. In R. G. Smart, H. D. Cappell, F. B. Glaser, Y. Israel, H. Kalant, W. Schmidt, & E. Sellers (Eds.), *Research advances in alcohol and drug problems* (Vol. 8, pp. 183–207). New York: Plenum.

Stasiewicz, P. R., Carey, K. B., Bradizza, C. M., & Maisto, S. A. (1996). Behavioral assessment of substance abuse with co-occurring psychiatric disorder. *Cognitive and Behavioral Practice, 3,* 91–105.

Steer, R. A., & Beck, A. T. (1996). Deck Depression Inventory (BDITM). In L. I. Sederer & B. Dickey (Eds.), *Outcomes assessment in clinical practice* (pp. 100–104). Baltimore: Williams & Wilkins.

Stein, L. I., & Santos, A. B. (1998). *Assertive community treatment of persons with severe mental illness.* New York: Norton.

Teitelbaum, L., & Mullen, B. (2000). The validity of the MAST in psychiatric settings: A meta-analytic integration. *Journal of Studies on Alcohol, 61,* 254–261.

Velasquez, M. M., Carbonari, J. P., & DiClemente, C. C. (1999). Psychiatric severity and behavior change in alcoholism: The relation of the transtheoretical model variables to psychiatric distress in dually diagnosed patients. *Addictive Behaviors, 24,* 481–496.

Watkins, K. E., Shaner, A., & Sullivan, G. (1999). The role of gender in engaging the dually diagnosed in treatment. *Community Mental Health Journal, 35,* 115–126.

Webb, D. K. (1997). *Good Chemistry co-leader's manual.* Austin, TX: Deborah K. Webb.

Wilsnack, S. (1982). Alcohol abuse and alcoholism in women. In E. M. Pattison & E. Kaufman (Eds.), *Encyclopedic handbook of alcoholism* (pp. 718–735). New York: Gardner Press.

Zweben, J. E. (1996). Psychiatric problems among alcohol and other drug dependent women. *Journal of Psychoactive Drugs, 28,* 345–366.

CHAPTER TWENTY

HOMELESS ADDICTED WOMEN

A. Meredith Deming, Karen McGoff-Yost, and Anne L. Strozier

Homelessness is a problem of national proportion in the United States. The rise of female-headed homeless families has been a growing concern for government officials and service providers alike. What makes these women distinct is that often the most pressing issue they face is one of sheer survival. Homeless addicted women compose possibly the most marginalized and economically impoverished demographic group in the country.

Tonya is a twenty-six-year-old, single, African American woman with six children. She bore her first child, a daughter, at the age of fourteen, and four different men fathered her children. None of the men has been found, in spite of efforts to collect court-ordered child support; therefore, Tonya receives none. Each of the children has, at one time or another, been removed by the state. Tonya has managed to reunite her family, but once more she finds herself in jeopardy. She struggles with a virulent crack cocaine addiction, as well as with increasingly crippling bouts of depression. She has arrived at a social service agency clutching a three-day eviction notice, asking for help with move-in costs for yet another apartment. When questioned by the social worker, she admits that she has no real plan in place to ensure that she will be able to maintain this apartment either. Tearful and despondent, Tonya wonders aloud how long it will be before her children are back in foster care. She tells the social worker, "I am not a homeless woman—I am just a woman without a place to live!" The social worker asks what Tonya perceives to be the difference between these conditions. Tonya explains, "People call me a homeless woman, and their voices are full of judging me. It's like that's all I am, and all I'll ever be, in their eyes. Why can't they see me, and not think they know me?"

Estimates of the number of homeless individuals in general are difficult to gauge due to the number and variety of definitions of the issue itself. For the purposes of this chapter, the definition of homeless individuals used is one put forward by Baxter and Hopper (1981), which states that the homeless are "those whose primary nighttime residence is either in publicly or privately operated shelters, or in streets, doorways . . . or other hidden sites known only to their users" (p. 129).

Although there are particular skills and techniques that will assist the clinician in developing a therapeutic alliance with clients who are homeless, the practitioner must also have a basic grasp of the systemic issues relevant to this population. It is crucial to this effort for the clinician to possess the skills and the willingness to forge a genuine relationship with the client and to keep in mind that homelessness is "more than just the loss of a home: it almost inevitably disrupts the sense of identity and feeling of self-worth and self-efficacy. The ability to retain a measure of human dignity is constantly challenged by the humiliation and terror of daily life without a home" (Buckner, Bassuk, & Zima, 1993, p. 385). This chapter reviews the wide range of issues affecting homeless women and discusses assessment and treatment approaches with this population.

Scope of the Problem

According to the National Coalition for the Homeless (1999a), an estimated twelve million adult U.S. residents have experienced homelessness at some point; this estimate does not include, nor begin to address, the vast numbers of children affected by homelessness. A recent estimate puts the number of people experiencing homelessness on a given night at over seven hundred thousand, and suggests a yearly total of up to 2 million.

For the past several years, the National Coalition for the Homeless (NCH) has reported that an increasing proportion of this nation's homeless population are women. Single mothers with dependent children are the fastest-growing subpopulation of those without housing in the United States (National Coalition for the Homeless, 1999b). In 1998, families consisting mainly of women and children accounted for 36.5 percent of the homeless in this country (Bassuk, Buckner,

Perloff, & Bassuk, 1998). Race and family size appear to have an impact on homelessness for women. One study reported that with each additional child, the chances of obtaining permanent housing decreased, and that African American mothers had vastly increased problems in finding such housing (Rocha, Johnson, McChesney, & Butterfield, 1996).

A public awareness poster produced by NCH shows the changing face of homelessness over the decades: the 1960s and 1970s are personified by a middle-aged male, the 1980s by a Black female, and the 1990s by an African American family with dependent children. Although these trends are due to a number of systemic and interpersonal factors, addiction is certainly one of the major contributing themes.

In 1999, NCH reported that "people who are poor and addicted are clearly at increased risk [of becoming homeless] . . . in the 1970s and 1980s, competition for increasingly scarce low-income housing grew so intense that those with disabilities, such as addictive or mental disorders, were more likely to lose out and find themselves on the street."

Homeless women present as a largely vulnerable population engaging in high-risk behaviors that result in negative consequences for themselves and their children. They run an increased risk of adverse pregnancy outcomes, including miscarriage, low birth weight, and infant mortality due to poor nutrition, lack of prenatal health care, and limited access to health and treatment services (Danzig, 1997; Tessler & Dennis, 1989).

The presence of dependent children can be both a blessing and a curse to women at risk of homelessness. Although children can provide emotional support and a sense of purpose to their mothers, they can also be the source of great emotional and financial demands.

Tonya speaks to the social worker about this: "I love my kids, and I have fought to keep them with me . . . still, it sure would be an easier road if there weren't so many of them. How am I supposed to find a house for all of us, with the little bit of money I got? When I go to work, to get the money to pay the bills, my kids get taken away 'cause I 'abandoned' them. God, what am I gonna do?"

The presence of children may allow for access to some services available only to families with children; at the same time, they may create a barrier to accessing affordable housing. In addition, children who are homeless do poorly in school, often develop a wide range of medical problems, present emotional and behavioral problems, and experience cognitive and developmental delays (Weinreb & Rossi, 1991).

Stages of Homelessness

Three distinct, progressive stages of homelessness have been identified (Belcher, Scholler-Jaquish, & Dremmond, 1991). The first is a state of "marginal" homelessness, during which the woman experiences subsistence at a level of poverty that keeps her living situation tenuous, at best. During this period, service providers would do well to address the immediate problems; food stamps, job training, budget counseling—each could strengthen the foundation that would allow this woman to keep out of the downward spiral she has begun.

In the next phase, one of sudden or unexpected homelessness, the woman often believes that she will quickly regain what has been lost; there is a heavy reliance on neighbors, family, and friends, who may provide temporary shelter, albeit in overcrowded conditions. During this phase, shame, guilt, and depression may appear, as well as an exacerbation of any existing substance abuse. Should thorough assessments for drug usage and depression take place at this time, the cycle might well be interrupted before the client loses everything, including the positive feelings of her family and friends.

In the last stage, a woman enters chronic homelessness, as she has most likely exhausted any resources she may still have retained in stage two. At this point, she may be resigned to life on the streets, and could become suspicious and distrustful of others. Reduced economic status, a loss of social support, and a perception that she is powerless to alter her circumstances can all contribute to a sense of hopelessness. This is compounded when alcohol or other substances are used as coping mechanisms. At this stage, substance use may deepen into dependence, and any preexisting mental health symptoms may grow into severe depression, anxiety, or psychosis. This is a crisis point in the life of this client, one at which she may remain, unless a caring practitioner can break through the suspiciousness of the client and offer the help she needs. The clinician will have to show acceptance and patience, as recovery from this stage can be painstakingly slow, if it occurs at all. One real problem does remain, however: often, even when the client is willing to enter a treatment program, none may exist for which she qualifies. Clinicians must be ever vigilant in discovering the available resources in their communities.

Systemic Issues Affecting Homeless Women

Pervasive systemic issues that create multiple barriers to accessing treatment and other services make work with homeless women distinct from work with other addicted women. Practitioners find that homeless women may be one of the most vulnerable and disenfranchised groups that exist in this country. Due to the widespread judgments that exist when society is confronted with the issues of substance abuse, and the additional stigma of homelessness, many women in this situation are faced with obstacles that are difficult to overcome. Attitudes toward "junkies," including the assumption that drug addiction is a choice, and societal beliefs concerning homelessness, including a conviction that homeless people are eager to take advantage of the system, compound the loss of self-worth and self-esteem on the part of many homeless women. Accepting the belief system thrust upon her, such a woman becomes convinced that she is in fact worthless. Counseling a homeless woman through her feelings of despair and hopelessness as she faces the seemingly uncaring world can be challenging.

Tonya agrees with this and expresses her frustration with the system that is supposed to be helping her. "I can't get a job when they find out I got no address—I get looked at like I am nothin'. I want to get out of this hole I'm in, for me and my kids, but I don't see how I ever will. I try to get work, and I can't—I try to get a place for my family, but I got no money. What do y'all expect from me? Sometimes I just get so down, I don't even want to keep tryin'. . . . It seems like I don't got a chance, anyhow."

Issues Affecting Homeless Addicted Women

Homeless women often deal with issues of substance abuse, though questions of cause and effect, or correlation, remain unanswered. Does addiction perpetuate homelessness, or does being homeless lead one deeper into drug abuse? Regardless of which problem occurred initially, women who apply for services at agencies for the homeless often struggle with the added burden of an addiction. Not all addiction disorders involve the use of chemicals; other addictions include eating disorders, sexual addiction, and gambling. They can have equally destructive consequences for the affected woman.

Based on the authors' clinical observations, the most common eating disorder exhibited among homeless women appears to be compulsive overeating. As in other forms of addiction, using the desired substance begins as a method of self-comfort. Snack foods, easily acquired at the corner store, are affordable and legal; breads, cookies, and candy, as well as many soft drinks, can provide a sugar "rush" that can mirror a drug-induced state, however short lived.

Clinical observation also indicates that sexual addiction plays a part in the lives of many homeless women. For these women, sex-trade activities are initially enacted in order to obtain money, drugs, or even shelter. This can lead to a sexual compulsion; the woman does not feel wholly alive without the frequent act of sex. Acting out in this manner makes the woman vulnerable to STDs, HIV, pregnancy, and violent treatment from her sex partners. It can, in addition, put her children at increased risk, given the woman's casual yet intimate contact with strangers.

Addiction to gambling is another real threat. The woman may be prone to purchasing various types of lottery tickets, lured by the promise of something for nothing. In a vain attempt to alter her financial state, she can spend large sums of her already insufficient cash. There is a definite aspect of this addiction that resembles the rush of drug use: a quick high while she has fantasies of the big score, followed by the crash when she realizes she has lost yet again. Despite the woman's numerous losses, the behavior can continue, as she is always looking for the easy way out.

Nicotine addiction is (relatively) socially acceptable and inexpensive, at least when compared to the high cost of many other drugs; however, there is nothing benign about this insidious form of self-medication. Clients have reported that cigarette smoking eases the pangs of hunger, and a moment to "light up" is often a welcome break from the stress of the day. The consequences of this habit, however, can be devastating and lethal. At the very least, money is spent on cigarettes that would be better used to purchase food, school supplies, or other necessities. Serious health risks can result from the use of tobacco products (many women use chewing tobacco in the false belief that it does not cause cancer), and families often face the consequences of this "harmless" pastime. One immediate problem that stems from a mother's using tobacco is the effect it has on her children. They must deal with the adverse effects from secondhand smoke, and they often become smokers themselves.

In addition to the problems that result from addiction, homeless women confront many other issues, such as the threat of violence and victimization, the risk of pregnancy, loss of the custody of their children, involvement in prostitution, and social stigma (Grella, 1996). A large proportion of this population faces disabilities and other health problems. Medical problems that are direct consequences of being homeless include untreated injuries or traumas, assaults, dehydration and malnutrition, infectious diseases, and hypothermia (exposure). Many homeless women have STDs and are at high risk for HIV infection.

One condition, too often overlooked in the assessment of this population, is poor dental hygiene. Oral infection can result in, among other problems, a constant low-grade fever, making it difficult to perform the simplest of tasks.

Tonya arrives at the agency with a mouth that is both missing teeth and full of bad teeth, infections, and abscesses. She expresses deep shame about the condition of her mouth and rarely smiles. Dental care is simply not affordable. Tonya sees the same things happening in the mouths of her children, causing her to feel even worse about her performance as a mother. "I can't even take my babies to the dentist—I'll never get the money to take them all for their checkups; and what if they need fillings?" she wails. The social worker tries, without success, to get pro bono care for this family.

Domestic violence (DV) has been observed to be one of the prime causes of homelessness for women and children, and those who use substances appear to be at a particularly high risk. It has been reported that as many as 80 percent of homeless mothers have had experiences with physical abuse and that violence has been a major factor in their becoming homeless (Grella, 1996). Among homeless women who are substance abusers, up to 97 percent are estimated to be victims of domestic violence. Violence often is an experience that begins in childhood, resulting in a diminished degree of self-worth and a lack of appropriate coping skills (Goodman, Dutton, & Harris, 1995). Substance abuse can exacerbate these problems. It has been found that addicted women suffer more frequent and pervasive sexual and emotional abuse, including incest and rape, than is experienced by women without substance abuse problems. These events are often the acts of multiple perpetrators (Covington & Surrey, 1997). In treating addicted homeless women, clinicians must understand that they are likely to be treating victims of multiple traumas.

Barriers to Treatment Delivery

The Center for Mental Health Services, part of the federal Substance Abuse and Mental Health Services Administration, released findings from 1998 focus groups of formerly homeless women with mental health or substance abuse issues (or both). These women rated the services they received, the services they felt were the most helpful to them, and the barriers they encountered during their homelessness. Among the identified barriers to treatment and services were (1) high staff turnover in homeless programs, due to low funding; (2) lack of proper and timely information and referral to available services, such as child care, food pantries, and job training; (3) lack of transportation, or placement in shelters that were not in proximity to other needed services; (4) shelter environments that lacked privacy or were unclean or unsafe; (5) the use of drugs and alcohol by other shelter residents, creating a threatening environment; and (6) lack of space in existing shelters, resulting in women in need being turned away. Other problems included the inflexible regulations of many shelters, such as strict hours by which one had to vacate the bed, and unavailable child care, often leading to the expulsion of many women, who had no alternative but to return to the streets. Formerly homeless women also reported the grave need for drug counseling available twenty-four hours a day in the shelter (Center for Mental Health Services, 1998).

A population that remains vastly underreported is that of the "hidden homeless": women who are doubled up, or even tripled up, in the homes of family members or friends. As they have no permanent domicile of their own, they are homeless; yet, because they are not sleeping in a vehicle or on the street, they are not eligible for many of the services that might enable them to achieve stability.

Assessment

Addicted homeless women present with a variety of deficits and needs, requiring careful and thorough assessments from social workers and other service providers. As discussed earlier, this population has often experienced multiple traumas, and an insensitive worker runs a risk of causing more harm than good.

As reported by Tonya, all too often women arrive at service agencies prepared to be subjected to yet another in a seemingly never-ending series of indignities. Tonya explains that "I go from one place to another, answering the same questions at each one, and it takes all day sometimes . . . and I still got no help at the end of the day. Everyone got reasons why I don't get the help—but I don't care about the reasons. I get a bunch of 'referrals,' but they're just paper—I need food."

Service providers would do well to assess for a multitude of needs and to offer solutions for the complex problems reported by the women they serve.

Family Needs

Does this woman have custody of children? Is she striving for reunification with any of her children not currently in her custody? How effective are her parenting skills? Does she need child care, involvement of protective services, family reunification services, or some combination of these? Does she have adequate knowledge of child development? Does she have an active relationship with any family members at this time? Has she bonded with her own children? Does the woman have family members who can provide emotional support during recovery? Have family relationships been damaged by the client's history of substance abuse? Have the family members "given up" on the client? Is the client the family's scapegoat? Does she want family members to know her whereabouts? What are her thoughts about family therapy?

Financial Needs

Is there a source of income? How has the client been supporting herself thus far? Has she received consistent child support? Is she eligible for Social Security, food stamps, or other entitlements? Is she in debt (including having items in pawn that she has been attempting to retrieve)? Does she have a poor credit rating or previous evictions?

Health Needs

When was the last time she received medical care or a comprehensive examination? Where has she been receiving her primary health care? When did she last see a dentist? How has she been practicing birth control (if she has been)? Is she aware of safe sex practices and risk behaviors? What signs or symptoms are present that may require immediate referral to a medical provider?

Mental Health Needs

Is there any history of involvement with the mental health system? Does the woman have a dual diagnosis? Has she been taking her medication? Has she been able to access community mental health services? Does she show any symptoms of depression or anxiety?

Domestic Violence

Is there a history of DV? How recently? Is the woman currently fleeing a potentially dangerous situation? Does she have a safety plan? How has DV affected her physical and mental health? Are the children involved as witnesses or victims? Is the woman agreeable to legal and police involvement?

Vocational Needs

Could the woman benefit from career counseling, vocational assessment, job training, mentoring, job placement assistance, training in job-seeking skills, and referrals to vocational rehabilitation? Is she employed? Has she ever been employed? What is her highest educational level? Does she have any job skills that are marketable? What about job coaching? What have been barriers to employment in the past (for example, transportation, lack of child care)? To what extent has substance abuse been a factor in employment difficulties? Are there any other potential difficulties with employability?

Housing History

How long has the woman been homeless? How many times has she been home-less previously? Are there any events that, as a pattern, have triggered homeless-ness (for example, relapse, job loss, disability, child-care problems, family illness)? Is there a history of eviction? Does she have a history of living in shelters? Is she aware of emergency housing resources? Which ones has she already used, and has she exhausted her stay? Is she aware of or using any resources such as HUD or Section 8?

Social Supports

Whom does the client identify as part of her support network? Does her family provide her with positive support? Does she have friends? Does her entire social network consist of others who also abuse substances? Does the client feel that she has anyone to confide in? Does she feel that she has "burned all of her bridges"? Has she ever used the church or other religious institutions for support?

Life Skills

Can she read and write in English or in any other language? What is her demon-strated ability to create and follow a budget? What is her assessed level of problem-solving skills? What is her knowledge of resources and pattern of resource utilization? What is the self-reported level of household and daily living skills and time management skills? Does she have any leisure activities that she enjoys? Is she able to use basic services, such as public transportation—that is, can she read maps, schedules, and so on?

Tonya responds to the social worker conducting the assessment, "I'm glad to get a chance to talk about other stuff besides needing a place to stay—we got so many other things goin' on along with that. I wouldn't be in this mess if someone could just get my kids' fathers to pay what they owe . . . but no one can find 'em. And I know they'll take away my kids again if I can't get a place soon. I got no way to get a decent job, one that would pay enough to really help, and no place to leave the kids if I had a job. We been lucky—my kids hardly ever get sick, but what if I do? What'll happen to them? I got no insurance, and all our teeth are goin' bad. God knows, I got no money for a dentist. Tell me somethin', though—once you're done asking me all these ques-tions, are you going to help me? Or am I just wastin' my time talkin' about this stuff, when there's nothin' to help at all."

It is clear to the social worker that Tonya's needs go much deeper than a simple lack of affordable housing. A history of spousal abuse (which led to her initial descent into homelessness), the presence of depression, and a lack of job and social skills create a challenge for the clinician; every aspect of Tonya's case affects the other, and none can be ignored. A thorough and comprehensive assessment is an essential first step in a long treatment process.

Treatment Issues

When seeking to design a treatment approach for women who are homeless, the practitioner must remember to look at the women first and then the situation. During a meeting of the steering committee of the Homeless Families Program, a joint project of the Center for Mental Health Services and Center for Substance Abuse Treatment (1999), current and former consumers spoke of the issues they hoped would be addressed in the course of the five-year study that the centers were undertaking. These included social, psychological, and physical consequences of addiction; racism within service agencies and communities; gender discrimination; issues of the disabled; the need for mentoring to assist in navigating the system; domestic violence; custody issues; grief and loss; trauma issues (such as rape and incest); the constant demand for affordable housing; and the need for treatment services far exceeding the available supply. The women who attended this meeting were extremely vocal in their insistence not to be "lumped together" and identified as a group. They wished to be seen as individuals, with problems and circumstances unique to each; none was willing to accept any label referring to their circumstances—"junkie" being particularly abhorred. It was agreed that addiction, as well as poverty, counted as the largest risk factors leading to homelessness.

Few service providers, shelters, or case management agencies will have the funding necessary to provide therapy for homeless clients. The lack of available resources makes it imperative that the basic necessities of life, such as food and shelter, get met prior to addressing the therapeutic needs of this population. Nonetheless, many, if not most, homeless women have need of therapeutic services from a clinically trained staff.

Relationships are a key factor to consider when addressing women who are homeless. For example, women frequently begin using substances and alcohol when their partners are engaging in this behavior. Amaro and Hardy-Fanta (1995) identified numerous ways in which relationships with male partners contributed to substance abuse in women, hindering their recovery. Male friends or partners often introduce women to drugs or heavy drinking. Whether or not he caused her to use, the male often becomes the supplier of the substances. Men often disappoint their female partner, failing to care adequately for the woman or her children. Violence in the relationship may cause the woman to seek relief in the use of drugs or alcohol. And the male partner may not support the homeless woman's motivation to seek treatment. Moreover, should both partners be agreeable to the pursuit of drug treatment, there are few, if any, facilities that offer the possibility of staying together during the course of treatment, particularly if the couple is unmarried. A woman may be hesitant to live apart from her partner, fearing abandonment or isolation. As these women often deal with grief issues brought about by multiple losses—loss of security, loss of self-worth—the concept of losing her partner at the same time that she is expected to give up her drugs can heighten her sense of grief.

Approaches to Working with Addicted Homeless Women

Working with addicted homeless women can present particular challenges for practitioners. These challenges can frequently be met effectively through the use of specific treatment approaches when addressing he unique concerns of this population.

Use of Feminist Treatment Approaches

Feminist theory, by its very focus, can provide a powerful springboard from which a clinician can approach treatment issues. This perspective brings a deep belief in the client's ability to heal, the conviction that women are not subservient to men, and the clinician's projection of her own wellness as a model for the client. The feminist perspective, with its emphasis on strengths, can assist the client in revealing her perceived needs and deficits without creating a sense of pathology. In addition to furthering the trusting relationship between the individual and the clinician, helping to strengthen the client's sense of empowerment and self-awareness, "feminist social work practice is committed to promoting change in any oppressive system" (Valentich, 1996, p. 291).

This methodology has a positive effect on Tonya, who responds to the focus on her being a strong woman learning to reclaim her locus of control. She tells her social worker that she has never before had the sense that women had any real power. She speaks frankly about her experiences and reveals a long-held belief that she somehow deserved what had been happening in her life. "I didn't ever know my daddy, 'cause he left when I was a kid. Now my kids are going through the same thing, and I feel bad. I know I'm strong when it comes to getting through everything we been facing, but I always thought that women were weak. . . . After all, don't men really run the world?"

After the clinician has engaged in numerous interactions with Tonya that remain focused on a feminist viewpoint, Tonya begins to raise her head and look the clinician in the eye. Even though her living conditions are still difficult, she has started to accept the possibility that she is not totally responsible for her circumstances. The clinician has taken care to disclose to Tonya some of the issues other women, including the practitioner, have had to face and have overcome. This allows the clinician to delve deeper into issues that the client formerly was reluctant to approach.

Use of Empowerment

Empowerment theory is a second approach that can be helpful with this population. Empowerment practice is "based on a simultaneous concern for people and environments, to assist people who experience poverty and oppression in their efforts to empower themselves to enhance their adaptive potentials and to work toward changing environmental and structural arrangements that are oppressive" (Lee, 1996, p. 230). In working with the homeless population, the clinician can develop the role of partner in the quest for the client's stability, as opposed to taking an authoritative stance. It is necessary to promote such a partnership, as many homeless women often perceive themselves as having to accept whatever happens to them, without any real voice in their own futures. By using this approach to therapy, the practitioner can effectively reframe a client's self-perception and help her see that she has a role in society. This practice entails specific exercises and "deals with a particular kind of block to problem solving: that imposed by the external society by virtue of a stigmatized collective identity" (Salomon, Bassuk, & Brooks, 1996, p. 521). Once the basic needs of the client have been met, she is able to look at some of the barriers she has put in place that keep her from self-actualization, as well as at those that are truly beyond her individual control. In using clinical approaches such as feminist and empowerment theories, the clinician, in concert with the client, can begin to address issues the client may never have considered before.

Use of Group Treatment

Group treatment has proven to be particularly effective with this population, as it involves women in helping each other learn to trust and to share their fears. Groups allow women, sometimes for the first time in their lives, to hear other voices echoing their own experiences and thoughts. When facilitated carefully and attentively, group process can draw a client into an emotional wellspring from which healing can take place in a safe arena.

One group exercise, which requires the client to speak for thirty seconds to a partner who must remain silent and listen, is an example of empowerment during group work with women. This may be the first occasion in either woman's recent memory in which she has felt heard or important. When this technique is used with a homeless woman, the clinician can often see a palpable change in the woman's affect, just from the unfamiliar experience of having a voice (Eisenstadt, 2000).

In another exercise (Eisenstadt, 2000), an example of working within transpersonal theory, each woman writes her name in the middle of a page of paper. In one corner, she writes a time or place that she was the happiest in her life. In another corner, she writes the name of a well-known woman she admires or wants to emulate. In the third corner she writes two qualities that she believes to be important, such as humor or honesty. In the fourth corner, the woman writes five things she likes to do, such as riding a bike or reading. When the page is complete, each woman uses tape to attach the page to her shirt. Then, without speaking, each woman walks around and reads all the other pages. This can provoke a discussion about similarities and differences, likes and dislikes, and aspirations. Homeless women often are asked only about such issues as shelter, food, and child care, while their dreams and talents may be all but ignored.

In an exercise called Fantasy Introduction, participants begin by pairing off. Each woman introduces her partner to the group as if they had been friends for ten or more years. The "friend" tells the group at least three things that she likes about the other, using her imagination to do so. For example, "This is my friend Jane. I've known her for twelve years. The three things I like the best about her are that she always dreamed of being a ballet dancer, she writes poetry, and she's a really attentive mother." This exercise often brings out the inner longings of the speaker, as she tries to invent the introduction of someone whom she truly likes.

Clinicians can use these and many other exercises to encourage a group of often guarded women to open up and engage with one another. Homeless women, who often have deep-rooted difficulties with trust, may find that participating in such group activities releases long-held secrets and beliefs (Eisenstadt, 2000).

Nontraditional Therapies

For clinicians, the traditional, office-based private practice model will not work with this population. Clinicians need to be extremely creative and find ways to meet the client where she is—literally. The social worker may have to visit the client in the shelter or at a food pantry, or even find the vehicle in which the family is living, in order to build trust and a rapport. Unlike traditional clinical work in which the client seeks services and in which services are provided in an agreed-on office and time frame, the clinician may need to conduct outreach repetitively at irregular hours and locations prior to establishing any credibility with the client.

Women who have been relying on substance use and other forms of addictive behavior to provide self-comfort in difficult circumstances will need some direction in their efforts to reestablish a productive life. The clinician's being familiar with community resources, such as twelve-step groups, is vital to successful work with this population. When clients are encouraged to view attendance at twelve-step meetings as an integral part of the services they are receiving, this can prove to be a motivating factor in continuing to attend such groups. Regular attendance at twelve-step groups remains, arguably, the most powerful tool to ensure long-term recovery.

Tonya works hard to rise above her sense of victimization and to focus on those aspects of her life that she can affect in a positive manner. A life spent in poverty and abuse has left her with a lingering feeling of defeat that she struggles to alter, with the help of the clinician. Some days she appears to make great strides in this direction; other days seem more difficult. The practitioner keeps the focus on "one day at a time" and assures Tonya that she has the capacity to change.

During Tonya's regular office visits, the clinician pays close attention to her client's continuing cocaine use. Tonya's progress is slow, but her struggle to persevere is evident to the clinician, who greets even small efforts with enthusiastic support and encouragement. Tonya reports sporadic attendance at her twelve-step meetings, due, she claims, to her lack of transportation and child care. The clinician reminds Tonya that many meetings offer lists of attendees willing to give rides, and some have on-site babysitters. Tonya acknowledges, "I gotta try somethin' different, 'cause my way sure ain't working."

Use of Spirituality

Addiction is often described as a physical, emotional, and spiritual disease. Physical needs can be addressed by food baskets and stable housing, and emotional distress alleviated by a referral to a counselor, but spirituality is often ignored by mental health assessments. Addiction can rob a woman of this aspect of life and leave her feeling empty and without connection. Using the modality of transpersonal theory, the clinician can employ a holistic approach, incorporating body, mind, and spirit. This takes the form of "a biopsychosocial spiritual journey that takes the individual across a continuum from an egocentric position that believes 'I am the universe,' toward a position beyond ego where the person can potentially realize a sense of unitive consciousness and an experience of oneness with all that is" (Cowley, 1996, p. 672). Homeless addicted women, conditioned to deal with numerous losses and having developed coping mechanisms that do not involve maintaining hope for the future, often appear to have lost their spiritual selves. When using this framework with a client whose recent experience is solely focused on physical survival, the clinician can help that client begin to see other possibilities for her life. One caveat, however: this approach is futile until the client ceases to use mind-altering substances, including alcohol. Such substances keep the woman in a wholly self-absorbed state, wherein it is all but impossible for her to allow spirituality into her frame of mind.

Once drugs have been removed from the client's system, the practitioner can explore the client's beliefs, and offer the possibility that the client can invite a connection with the spiritual. It does the client a disservice to assume that because the presenting problems relate to the need for shelter, food, and the like, there is no place for this kind of therapeutic intervention. Clinical observation has led us to the awareness that homeless women differ not at all from the rest of society in their search for meaning in their lives. Aspects of the client's experience can often be seen most clearly in the context of a spiritual wound. The deficits in the lives of these women can lead to a profound sense of grief; transpersonal work, with its pursuit of higher consciousness, can bring relief and hope into what seems to be intractable pain.

Not to be confused with a religious focus, transpersonal theory refers to a focus on the human need for connection with something larger than ourselves and a willingness to explore this need with the client. It is imperative, however, to keep one's own biases out of the therapeutic forum, in order to allow the client to find her own truth. Although this is not, in any sense, the therapeutic intervention a clinician would initially employ, it can have a definite value in the healing process once trust has been established.

While working with Tonya, the clinician attempts to explore issues of spirituality with her. "I believe in God," Tonya says. "I just am not sure he believes in me." After long discussions on how Tonya believes she has disappointed God, the clinician presents an exercise. "Make a list with three columns. In the first column, list all the things you would want God to be, all the qualities God has—kindness, love—anything you want to see as God. In the second column, put down all the things you think God expects from you—obedience, trust, compliance—anything. In the third column, list all the things you expect from God—relief, a sense of protection—anything you want from your relationship with the God you believe exists." This exercise takes Tonya two weeks to complete, as she does not like to write. She states that she has not done drugs "much" over the course of the two weeks and that she really tried to think about the list. "I haven't thought about God for a long time, unless I was prayin' that He 'get me out of this one, and I'll be good.' This got me thinking about God again."

Other Considerations

Many other therapeutic methodologies can also be effectively employed when working with homeless women. The ideal scenario for treatment is for the woman successfully recovering from homelessness and addiction to move directly from residential treatment to transitional housing to permanent housing. Although programs tend to have strict timelines, there is tremendous variability in the amount of time it takes these women to achieve their goals. One of the most important things for the clinician to bear in mind is the heterogeneity of this population and the importance of avoiding stereotypes and further labeling.

Because women who are addicted face issues unique to them as women, gender-specific treatment often results in better outcomes than generic treatment models. In particular, successful treatment takes a holistic view of the female client and does not limit its focus to one facet alone. The National Women's Resource Center (Finkelstein, Kennedy, Thomas, & Kearns, 1997) reported that elements of a female-focused treatment model would include a perspective focusing on strengths, conducted in a nonconfrontational manner. Child-care issues would be addressed, and women would have female modeling from both staff and each other.

When attempting to provide services to homeless women with substance dependence or other addictions, clinicians must realize that the women who most need the assistance may be reluctant to seek it or use it. This can be due, in part, to the threat of losing custody of dependent children should it be discovered that a woman is addicted and lacks stable housing. A homeless family often must struggle to access the services of numerous agencies to meet its needs; few agencies exist that use a comprehensive approach to address issues of addiction, medical and health needs, job training, child care, housing assistance, and psychiatric services. This splintering may inadvertently add to the reluctance of these women to seek services.

Need for Advocacy

Clinicians working with homeless women should be strong advocates for systemic changes. For example, one of the key macro problems encountered by these women is the lack of affordable housing. Depending on the geographical location and specific policies of local housing authorities, women are likely to face several problems: extremely long waiting lists for the limited public housing available; multiple barriers to entering subsidized housing; policies that make it nearly impossible for them to access services; and major gaps in the available housing continuum, such as lacks in transitional housing, affordable permanent housing once having completed a transitional program, Section 8 vouchers, and so on.

Clinicians in this field should consider the possibility of forming a coalition with other community agencies. The saying "There is power in numbers" certainly applies in this case. One agency alone, with limited financial resources, may not be able to engender significant change in public policy, but a group of community agencies, each committed to working with the homeless, could be a force for positive change.

Conclusion

It is far too simplistic to look at homeless women with substance abuse issues and conclude that all they need is housing and drug treatment. This population warrants and demands a complex, intensive systems approach that addresses the multiple challenges with which these women live on a daily basis. Such issues include safety, employment and job skills, violence and trauma, co-occurring diagnoses, child care and custody, medical and dental care, legal issues, and relationship skills. Treatment models that dismiss or ignore any of these pressing issues run the risk of failing to meet the client's true needs.

Clinicians are faced with difficult and challenging tasks: to offer hope in situations that often appear bleak and hopeless, to assist women in finding their voice when society and despair may have driven them into silence, to become a partner in the process of discovering worth in a human being who may perceive herself as having none, and to attend to a segment of our populace that is all too frequently ignored. Perhaps the greatest gift any clinician can offer is a genuine interest in the woman she treats.

Homeless women, especially those who are addicted, face almost unimaginable obstacles in their daily lives. Treatment providers must look at these women in a holistic and nonjudgmental manner. Clinicians must examine their own biases and stereotypes and recognize the dangers of presenting a condescending or judgmental face to homeless and addicted women.

References

Amaro, H., & Hardy-Fanta, C. (1995). Gender relations in addiction and recovery. *Journal of Psychoactive Drugs, 27,* 325–337.

Bassuk, E. L., Buckner, J. C., Perloff, J. N., & Bassuk, S. S. (1998). Prevalence of mental health and substance abuse disorders among homeless and low income housed mothers. *American Journal of Psychiatry, 155*(11), 1561–1564.

Baxter, E., & Hopper, K. (1981). *Private lives/public spaces: Homeless adults on the streets of New York City.* New York: Institute for Social Welfare Research.

Belcher, J. R., Scholler-Jaquish, A., & Dremmond, M. (1991). Three stages of homelessness: A conceptual model for social workers in health care. *Health and Social Work, 16*(2), 87–93.

Buckner, J. C., Bassuk, E. L., & Zima, B. T. (1993). Mental health issues affecting homeless women: Implications for intervention. *American Journal of Orthopsychiatry 63*(3), 385–399.

Center for Mental Health Services. (1998). *Focus group summary and report on formerly homeless women.* Washington, DC: Author.

Center for Mental Health Services/Center for Substance Abuse Treatment. (1999, December 15–17). Homeless Families Program steering committee meeting, Washington, DC.

Covington, S., & Surrey, J. (1997). The relational model of women's psychological development: Implications for substance abuse. In S. Wilsnack and R. Wilsnack (Eds.), *Gender and alcohol: Individual and social perspectives* (pp. 335–351). New Brunswick, NJ: Rutgers Center of Alcohol Studies.

Cowley, A. (1996). Transpersonal social work. In F. J. Turner (Ed.), *Social work treatment* (4th ed., pp. 663–698). New York: Free Press.

Danzig, R. A. (1997). Children in homeless families. In N. K. Phillips & S.L.A. Straussner (Eds.), *Children in the urban environment* (pp. 191–208). Springfield, IL: Thomas.

Eisenstadt, B. (2000, August). *Actions speak louder: Women's issues. Innovative approaches to make treatment work.* Workshop at the Florida School of Addictions Studies, Jacksonville, FL.

Finkelstein, N., Kennedy, C., Thomas, K., & Kearns, M. (1997). *Gender-specific substance abuse treatment.* National Women's Resource Center for the Prevention and Treatment of Alcohol, Tobacco, and Other Drug Abuse and Mental Illness, Center for Substance Abuse Prevention.

Goodman, L. A., Dutton, M. A., & Harris, M. (1995). Episodically homeless women with serious mental illness: Prevalence of physical and sexual assault. *American Journal of Orthopsychiatry, 65*(4), 468–478.

Grella, C. E. (1996). Background and overview on mental health and substance abuse treatment systems: Meeting the needs of women who are pregnant or parenting. *Journal of Psychoactive Drugs, 26,* 319–339.

Lee, J.A.B. (1996). The empowerment approach to social work practice. In F. L. Turner (Ed.), *Social work treatment* (4th ed., pp. 218–249). New York: Free Press.

National Coalition for the Homeless. (1999a, February). *How many people experience homelessness?* (NCH Fact Sheet No. 2.) Available: www.nationalhomeless.org/numbers.html.

National Coalition for the Homeless. (1999b, April). *Addiction disorders and homelessness.* (NCH Fact Sheet No. 6.) Available: www.nationalhomeless.org/addict.html.

Rocha, C. R., Johnson, C. K., McChesney, K. Y., & Butterfield, W. H. (1996). Predictors of permanent housing for sheltered homeless families. *Journal of Contemporary Human Services, 77*(1), 50–56.

Salomon, A., Bassuk, S. S., & Brooks, M. G. (1996). Patterns of welfare use among poor and homeless women. *American Journal of Orthopsychiatry, 66*(4), 510–525.

Tessler, R. C., & Dennis, D. L. (1989). *A synthesis of NIMH funded research concerning persons who are homeless and mentally ill.* Rockville, MD: National Institute of Mental Health.

Valentich, M. (1996). Feminist theory and social work practice. In F. J. Turner (Ed.), *Social work treatment* (4th ed., pp. 282–318). New York: Free Press.

Weinreb, L., & Rossi, P. (1991). *Programs and evaluation. Homeless families with children: Research perspectives* (pp. 53–57). Rockville, MD: National Institute on Alcohol Abuse and Alcoholism.

CHAPTER TWENTY-ONE

ADDICTIONS AND WOMEN
IN THE CRIMINAL JUSTICE SYSTEM

Katherine van Wormer

Women become involved with the criminal justice system most often be-cause of problems related to alcohol and other drugs. Many of these women are referred by their lawyers or the courts to substance abuse treatment, which means that many substance abuse practitioners are likely to be working with female offenders as a part of their normal caseload. Knowledge of the facts pertaining to women's involvement in the criminal justice system is therefore a crucial component of a book on clinical and theoretical aspects of substance-abusing women. Exploring the link between female crime and women's in-volvement with substance abuse is the first and major task of this chapter. This link will be examined through a look at relevant statistics and a description of the typical pathways to crime for individual women. That the War on Drugs (and on drug users) has drastic repercussions for poor women of color is one of the basic assumptions of this chapter. The effects of this war are seen in the increased rate of arrest and imprisonment of minority women. This chapter will examine the treatment needs of this offender population, a population more apt to be punished than counseled, more apt to be stigmatized than understood. It will compare a strengths-based model of offender treatment to the traditional "crim-inal personality," male-focused model. In a manner consistent with the strengths perspective, the chapter will also identify and describe various exemplary woman-centered community-based programs.

Scope of the Problem

Women compose only 6.5 percent of the total number of prison inmates (up from 4 percent in 1980), and approximately 10 percent of those in jail. (Jails, unlike prisons, hold persons awaiting trial and convicts serving short sentences.) Women's rate of incarceration tripled between 1983 and 1993, and doubled from 1990 to 1999 (Bureau of Justice Statistics [BJS], 2000). Largely because of the War on Drugs, the rate of increase in the female prison population over the past two decades has exceeded the male rate. During 1996, for example, the number of female inmates grew 9.1 percent, nearly double the male rate of increase ("U.S. Prison Population Rises," 1997). Meanwhile, the crime rate has shown a steady decline for both men and women.

According to a recent study by the General Accounting Office (1999), the number of female prisoners increased over the past two decades by more than 500 percent, and the number of female inmates serving time for drug offenses has nearly doubled since 1990. This increase reflects the crackdown on drug use and the tendency today to arrest wives and girlfriends of male drug dealers along with the dealers. Due to the substantial number of female inmates and other offenders with drug problems entering the criminal justice system, both state and federal agencies have established substance abuse treatment programs throughout the correctional system (Office of the National Drug Control Policy, 2001).

Characteristics of Female Offenders

Many female offenders come from impoverished, abusive backgrounds, are addicted to drugs and alcohol, and have severe emotional and mental health problems. Their experience with the criminal justice system can be favorable or unfavorable depending on the helpfulness or harshness of the sanctions provided. Sadly, our society has often overlooked the special needs of female offenders and the extent to which addiction, unhealthy relationships, or both have figured in the crimes for which they are punished. Incarceration of female substance abusers is disempowering in many respects: it weakens ties to family and community; punishes innocent children, which further increases the mother's sense of guilt; and deepens women's sense of shame and dependence. At the same time, community programs, such as probation and parole, often lack the resources and womanpower to provide the intense but nurturing monitoring required for sober living. As is often said in this field, the rich get treatment and the poor get prison.

Under federal law, sentences for most drug cases are determined by a single factor: the quantity of the drugs confiscated. There is little or no regard for the defendant's background, actions or motives, level of involvement, or history of victimization. Women who have become addicted to illegal substances (and their children who are parted from them) have been especially hard hit by the harsh sentences that are being handed out. The unequal impact of these mandatory sentencing requirements on nonviolent female offenders, unfortunately, has not been matched by a commensurate investment in substance abuse programming to meet their special needs. Moreover, female drug dealers often wind up with longer sentences than the drug-dealing males with whom they're involved because they lack the information about the drug trafficking operations the prosecutors want in exchange for more lenient sentences, or because they are unwilling to go undercover or inform on drug-dealing family members (Stodghill, 1999).

The drug-dependent women incarcerated in U.S. jails and prisons suffer from the multiple risk factors that complicate substance abuse in women: poverty, psychological problems, and histories of trauma and abuse. In her review of the current research on women inmates serving time in jails and prisons, Kassebaum (1999) concluded that incarcerated women often had serious mental and emotional problems.

At least 80 percent of women behind bars were involved in various ways with alcohol or other drugs at the time of their crime (Acoca, 1998). Many of these women who committed a crime while in a drug-induced state stole property or engaged in prostitution to buy drugs, or got involved in the sale of drugs, often through an addicted partner (van Wormer, 2001). Analysis of state prison data reveals that 45 percent of female prisoners require treatment for chronic substance abuse, a figure that is double the male rate (BJS, 1999a). A profile of the typical female prisoner compiled by the New Jersey Department of Corrections (Gonzalez, 1996) reveals that a high proportion of women arrested for drug-related activities were severely addicted to their drugs of choice. The typical woman offender spent approximately $1,000 per week to support her habit, had been addicted an average of nine years, and used alcohol in conjunction with the other drugs.

Unlike those of male offenders, most of women's drug convictions relate to the use of drugs and not to drug trafficking (Phillips & Harm, 1997). Consumption of illegal substances, however, is highly associated with the commission of other crimes. In a comprehensive survey conducted by the Substance Abuse and Mental Health Administration (1997), 38 percent of drug-using women in the general population reported the commission of crimes such as burglary, theft, and prostitution over the past year; only 5.5 percent of women not using drugs made this admission. Most female offenders are sentenced for nonviolent offenses; when women do commit murder, the victims are most likely to be their partners or other family members, often persons who abused the offender, but sometimes infants and small children.

Three out of four female offenders in the correctional system are on probation. In a special report on DWI (driving while intoxicated) offenders, the Bureau of Justice Statistics (1999b) reported that among probationers, females accounted for 17 percent of DWI offenses. Each year there are approximately eighty thousand women under supervision for DWI offenses, most of whom will require some sort of educational or treatment services.

Substance abuse is not only directly linked to criminality due to the drug laws themselves; substance abuse (especially alcohol, cocaine, and methamphetamine) is also *indirectly* related to crimes of violence such as robbery and assault. Drugs lower inhibitions in people and also adversely affect the judgment area of the brain (Butterfield, 1997; Fishbein & Pease, 1996). In addition, such "process addictions" (Straussner & Zelvin, 1997) as gambling and spending addictions can lead, because of the addict's financial desperation, to the commission of serious economic crimes such as theft and embezzlement. One of the most effective ways to prevent crime, therefore, is to make addiction treatment readily available as soon as problems first begin to manifest themselves. According to Kassebaum (1999), effective treatment results in savings to society that outweigh the costs of treatment by a factor of 4:1.

Race, Class, and Gender

The interplay of race, class, and gender is highly visible in the criminal justice system. In a number of ways, problems related to childhood poverty set the stage for offenders' entry into homelessness, unemployment, drug use, survival sex, and, ultimately, more serious criminality (Chesney-Lind, 1997). Harsh penalties against users of the drug associated with residents of the inner city—crack cocaine— weigh heavily on women of color. Because of disproportionately harsh sentencing for users of crack cocaine compared to more expensive varieties of cocaine, African American women are more than twice as likely as Hispanics and eight times more likely than Whites to go to prison (BJS, 1999c).

The prosecution of drug-addicted mothers also has disproportionately affected the poor. Under the rationale of protecting the fetus, poor, Black, drug-addicted pregnant women are being hauled into court. This is part of an alarming trend toward greater state intervention into the lives of pregnant women, as Roberts (1994) suggests. Fortunately, however, in response to a case involving the testing done on pregnant women at South Carolina's public hospitals, the U.S.

Supreme Court recently ruled that hospitals may no longer turn over medical information pertaining to drug use to the police without the patient's consent (Greenhouse, 2001).

Personal Pathways to Crime

For women, victimization and criminalization typically are intertwined. In women's lives, the connection between addiction and crime is manifest both directly through drug-induced lawbreaking and indirectly through involvement in destructive relationships with people involved in the criminal underworld. Poverty compounds a woman's dependency on drug-abusing, often battering, men. The racial dimension is reflected in the fact that African American women are more likely than White or Latina women to be recruited to deviant street networks through domestic ties, whereas White and Latina women are more likely to be recruited into these networks through running away, drug use, or both, behaviors often associated with physical and sexual abuse in their families of origin (Farr, 2000; Miller, 1986). The typical pattern is for the girl who runs away from a violent or sexually abusive family to join other runaways on the streets. Once there, she learns how to survive through various illegal means (see Weiner & Pollack, 1997).

Compared to male offenders, female offenders have a disproportionately high rate of multiple victimization. Chesney-Lind (1997) maps out the pathway that would lead a girl, desperate to escape the sexual and physical abuse at home, to run away; seek solace in drugs and the company of drug users, gang members, and the like; and survive on the streets through prostitution. This pattern is highlighted in inner-city females for whom prostitution may serve as a means of survival in circumstances of extreme economic hardship. Rolison (1993) also stresses the role of poverty and sexual and physical abuse in women who assist the men in the commission of crime.

Surveys of women in trouble with the law indicate that early childhood victimization—for example, sexual molestation—is highly correlated with later involvement in prostitution (BJS, 1999a). Victimization during childhood is associated with feelings of distress and low self-esteem. To dull the pain, the woman may use drugs, such as alcohol, cocaine, heroin, or methamphetamines. Sometimes the drugs are introduced to the woman by her boyfriend. Many female addicts report that their drug-using male partners initiated them into drug abuse; and once she is hooked up with an alcohol- or drug-dependent man, it is very hard for a recovering woman to maintain sobriety (National Institute on Drug Abuse, 1999).

In her interviews with women at Rikers Island Correctional Facility in New York, Richie (1996) identified six paths through which these women entered the criminal justice system: (1) being tried along with an abusive partner in the death of a child, (2) committing violence toward a nonabusive man, (3) committing violence in self-defense against a partner, (4) committing drug-related crimes to sustain the habit, (5) committing economically motivated offenses, and (6) engaging in illegal drug work.

Treatment Needs and Approaches

Female offenders tend to be addicted or drug abusing, young, poor, African American or Latina, and often with a history of psychological trauma. The crimes for which they are sentenced, more often than not, were committed in the context of a relationship. Their greatest needs are for multifaceted treatment for alcohol and other drug abuse, trauma recovery, and relationship issues (Covington, 1999).

Mandatory minimum sentencing designed to remove judicial discretion ensures that women in trouble with the law are treated according to a male model of justice (or injustice). As Chesney-Lind (1995) argues, women are caught up today in the societal mood of "getting tough on crime," driven in part by society's reaction to violent male criminals "getting away with murder" (p. 105). When women are provided with court-ordered treatment for substance abuse problems, their treatment tends to follow a one-size-fits-all model. Yet a woman's substance abuse, like her criminality, is different from that of a typical man (Kassebaum, 1999).

Because in the United States equality is often falsely equated with sameness, women in the correctional system are classified and treated according to a gender-neutral model of risk, rather than in light of women's unique treatment needs (Farr, 2000). In contrast to the U.S. approach, in Canada, innovative woman-specific (usually called gender-specific) programs are being designed to address female offenders' special needs (Blanchette, 1997). The intake and periodic assessment of female offenders in these Canadian programs are based on empirically validated classification instruments. Psychological and addictions assessments and treatment interventions are tailored to the offender, as well as for risk of behavior problems within the Canadian correctional system (Blanchette, 1997). Such gender-specific programs have identified the following treatment needs of addicted female offenders: learning the skills of assertiveness in relationships, understanding how substance abuse increases vulnerability to all forms of abuse, and finding alternative ways to deal with negative feelings other than through use of chemicals.

Tapping into Women's Strengths

"In the thicket of trauma, pain, and trouble you can see blooms of hope and transformation" (pp. 3–4). With these words, Saleebey (1997) eloquently captures the essence of the strengths approach. A perspective based on strengths offers a dramatic departure from the adversarial, negative labeling characteristics of traditional offender treatment. The strengths approach is versatile, relying heavily on ingenuity and creativity; strengths-based therapy is collaborative rather than authoritative in focus (Saleebey, 1997). The strengths-oriented therapist strives to help his or her client tap into the same resources that helped the client survive on the streets or in the criminal milieu and to redirect her energies along a path more consistent with her needs, such as regaining custody of her children. Instead of dwelling on the client's problems, the strengths therapist works to help mobilize the client to find realistic solutions to her problems.

Stephanie Covington (1999) has introduced a broad-based treatment curriculum, *Helping Women Recover: Special Edition for Use in the Criminal Justice System*, which is both woman-centered and focused on empowerment. This curriculum, which is widely use in correctional settings, is eclectic in design and geared toward women who are recovering from both substance abuse and psychological trauma. Instead of seeing an addicted woman's issues as problems needing to be solved, Covington views them collectively as the "level of burden" a woman carries (p. 31). The level-of-burden concept avoids further stigmatizing a woman who probably already has borne a good deal of scorn from society, family members, and correctional personnel. The four components contained in Covington's program each pertain to a key segment of the client's being: self, relationships, sexuality, and spirituality. A woman's specific treatment needs vary, as Covington further indicates, according to the level of correctional control. The woman on probation or parole, for example, requires special monitoring in the community to help her both meet her child-care needs and deal with relationships, which may well be a source of stress. If she is living with a drug-using boyfriend, for example, her own sobriety may be in constant jeopardy. Moreover, she will be at high risk of losing custody of her children. The option of a halfway house may offer a practical solution to the female offender in need of a sober and clean living arrangement. The following two case vignettes from van Wormer's files exemplify some of these issues.

The Case of Mimi

Although Mimi was placed on probation for shoplifting, it soon became apparent that it was her addiction to methamphetamine (meth) that was at the root of the problems. When Mimi admitted how she had first started taking meth (a highly potent and dangerous stimulant that produces a euphoric state that lasts much longer than cocaine and is much cheaper besides), her probation officer referred her to a local outpatient treatment center.

At the center, a social worker assessed Mimi's strengths as follows: love and concern for her six-year-old daughter, intelligence, a positive work ethic, ambition, and thoughtfulness. The following were areas that needed work: accepting her large body size (she had started using meth to lose weight), finding supportive and caring friends, preparing for a career, and overcoming her tendency to seek out people who mistreated her. Through encouragement, Mimi connected with Narcotics Anonymous, a group she attended once a week. As Mimi's mind and body began to heal from the drug abuse and long periods of sleep deprivation associated with meth, she decided to enroll in courses in human services at the local community college. Participation in family therapy, meanwhile, helped restore her relationship with her mother and sisters. In the end, Mimi came to view her conviction for crime as a blessing in disguise, in that it helped her embark on some major life changes.

The Case of Rosie

Rosie was so drunk when she stabbed her equally intoxicated and violent husband that she was unable to help in her defense. Her lawyer, a public defender, did his best but was too overwhelmed with a case overload to do more than go through the motions. Once in prison, Rosie had virtually no contact with her children, who were eventually placed with their paternal grandmother. In prison, Rosie was on a waiting list for several years before getting the substance abuse treatment she required to prepare herself for a return to the outside.

Rosie related well to other women in the treatment group and gradually was able to turn her life around. In retrospect, she attributed the breakthrough, her recovery, to the church visitors and a helpful chaplain who listened to her and urged her on to get her G.E.D. Attendance at AA meetings once a week was helpful during the early period following incarceration. A progressive welfare program (in Iowa) provided Rosie with financial support to attend a community college. Her children, now young teenagers, returned to her care. They attended Al-Ateen (a self-help program for children of alcoholics) to help them deal with the impact of growing up in a violent, alcoholic household.

Using Motivational Enhancement Therapy

Motivational enhancement therapy (MET) is a promising development making inroads today in substance abuse treatment circles. It is an approach that can be especially empowering for women (van Wormer, 2001). For female offenders, MET is especially relevant because of its ability to build trust in a population that, in light of the victimization commonly found in their backgrounds, has rarely had much reason to trust.

Instead of fighting the client's resistance to being in treatment, the counselor using the motivational approach meets the client where she is. Listening intently and following the logic of the client, the motivational counselor makes such statements as, "Maybe you'd be happier just keeping things the way they are" or "Your problems with drugs don't sound real serious." The goal is to help the client reflect on her denial or minimization of problems and to encourage the client to move from the contemplation level of change toward the action stage (Miller & Rollnick, 1991).

Key clinical skills involved in MET are designed to build and enhance client motivation through actively involving the client in identifying her own concerns and goals for change. This approach stresses empathy rather than confrontation; the counselor deals with resistance by creating a supportive and trusting environment. Strategies for treatment of a given client are based on an assessment of that client's particular problems (for example, with drugs and relationships) but mostly on the assessment of strengths—strengths of the client herself and of those in the client's family and environment. William Miller (1999) spells out his principles in a U.S. Department of Health and Human Services publication, *Enhancing Motivation for Change in Substance Abuse Treatment*. The key elements of this approach, summarized by the acronym FRAMES, are as follows (Miller, 1999):

*F*eedback is based on formal assessment.

*R*esponsibility for change is placed on the individual.

*A*dvice about needed change is suggested rather than told.

*M*enu of self-directed change options is offered to the client.

*E*mpathic counseling is provided.

*S*elf-efficacy leading to change in behavior is encouraged.

In Project Match, a carefully controlled research design, this technique was found to be as effective as both the traditional twelve-step approach and a cognitively based technique in work with substance-abusing clients (Project Match Research Group, 1997). What makes MET highly attractive is its usefulness when dealing with clients who, due to legal, economic, or other factors, may only be seen for a brief period of time. In Project Match, the cognitively based and twelve-step facilitation approaches took twelve sessions each, whereas MET took only four sessions to achieve the same result.

Treatment Services for Women Offenders

Empirical evidence indicates that treatment for drug-abusing women is effective and that its effectiveness is not diminished when women offenders are coerced into treatment by the criminal justice system as a condition of probation or parole (Wellisch, Anglin, & Prendergast, 1993). Within prison walls, women are usually eager for services, and there may be a waiting list to attend. The benefits of group treatment within prison walls are that the members are eager for an outsider to talk to, absences are rare, and the women often have an extended period of sobriety. On the negative side, there is no family or community involvement, nor is there a chance for women to become independently resourceful. Moreover, there is no testing ground for inmates to learn to resist temptation—there is little or no temptation to resist. The outpatient setting is just the opposite in terms of advantages and disadvantages: clients relapse and disappear, and they may resent being forced to attend when they have pressing family and work demands to attend to (Wellisch et al., 1993; Wellisch, Prendergast, & Anglin, 1996). Their support system may still be intact, however, and family members' involvement in the program enhances the addict's chances of recovery. Referral to nearby resources, such as community treatment and self-help groups, can reinforce social skills learned in treatment.

Many prisons (and some jails) subcontract out with substance abuse treatment centers for the provision of counseling services. This approach provides the counseling staff with more professional freedom than would otherwise be the case if their first loyalty were to the correctional authorities. In addition, confidentiality is better maintained by having practitioners answer to their own agencies, not to the correctional system. In any case, inmates—so in need of a friendly professional to talk to, and usually with time on their hands—often are highly motivated for treatment, and they welcome the individual attention to their needs. But, as such research as that surveyed in Kassebaum (1999) shows, for treatment to be effective in the long term, adequate supervision must be provided to ex-inmates who were abusing substances prior to their arrest. Therefore, extensive services are needed to help a woman during the tough transitional period to the community as she begins to seek work, housing, and regaining custody of her children.

Halfway homes providing residential care for mothers and their children are a tremendous aid in enabling ex-convicts to make this difficult transition. While the mother has been away, children develop new attachments; many resent their mother for having left them. Some are ashamed of their mother's criminal behavior and are disrespectful and refuse to listen to her. Living in a therapeutic, transitional environment with their children can help mothers reestablish their family roles.

The need for assertive case management services for parolees is highlighted by Martin and Inciardi (1997) and Kassebaum (1999), and the numerous needs of these women make such services vital in reintegrating them in a supportive and law-abiding community. In her book *Making It in the "Free World,"* Patricia O'Brien (2001) draws on the personal narratives of women in transition from prison to graphically document the difficulties in returning to freedom after an experience of incarceration. Without sufficient financial resources and professional guidance, women ex-inmates are likely to return to the life that led them into criminality in the first place.

Women Offenders with Special Needs

Most female offenders assessed as drug dependent can be categorized as dually diagnosed. In other words, they have a co-occurring substance abuse addiction and mental disorder. Posttraumatic stress disorder (PTSD) is the most common secondary disorder in this population (Covington, 1999). Major depression is also common.

Because jails have become dumping grounds for mentally ill persons with behavioral problems, it is not surprising that several small-scale studies of women in jail (Acoca, 1998) have estimated a two-thirds prevalence of psychotic disorders. In the National Council on Crime and Delinquency Survey coordinated by Acoca, 45 percent of female prisoners reported that they currently needed mental health treatment; 36 percent reported having attempted suicide on at least one occasion. Few female offenders, however, get the psychological attention they need.

AIDS is a major concern in women's institutions. At the end of 1995, 4 percent of all female state prison inmates were HIV positive, compared to just over 2 percent of male inmates (BJS, 1997). At some prisons, such as the York Correctional Institution for Women in Connecticut, as many as 30 percent are HIV positive (Acoca, 1998). This high rate probably reflects the prevalence of intravenous drug use among women of color in the Northeast. As Acoca indicates, the treatment of prisoners living with AIDS is often seriously inadequate, both from a medical and a psychological standpoint. Acoca recounts a harrowing tale of a young woman showing signs of psychosis, who was placed in administrative segregation for behavioral infractions. In fact, she had full-blown AIDS and was probably suffering from AIDS-related dementia.

With as many as two-thirds of female inmates requiring mental health services, attention to this dimension of treatment is essential (Pomeroy, Kiam, &

Abel, 1998). Within prisons, substance abuse and psychiatric services tend to be separate. Consequently, almost no treatment programs are available for substance-abusing women with mental disorders (Kassebaum, 1999). A few short-term substance abuse programs, such as the one at the Baltimore detention center, will admit women with mental disorders if they can be stabilized on psychotropic medications.

If treatment does exist, it may be based on a male model that may not be therapeutic for women. Correctional treatment has been designed to deal with male offenders with antisocial personality disorder, who require harsh confrontation to break down their defensive cognitions so that they can admit their wrongs. Research demonstrates, however, that the confrontational approach is not appropriate or effective with women (van Wormer, 2001).

Depression, anxiety, and other mood disorders are common among substance-abusing women (Covington, 1999). And, as pointed out earlier, so is a history of physical and sexual abuse. All these "dual diagnoses" are often related to trauma. Heney and Kristiansen (1998) urge that female inmates should be viewed as likely adult survivors of childhood sexual abuse and that such labels as *borderline personality disorder* be avoided for a condition that may well be related to the psychological wounds of trauma. Clinicians who work with female inmates also should be cognizant of the retraumatization aspects of body cavity searches and other invasive prison procedures that are routine in custodial settings. As described in van Wormer and Bartollas (2000), these procedures entail strip searches, including vaginal and anal searches for contraband. Lack of privacy for women in the toilet and shower areas are additional problems for women with histories of sexual abuse.

Community Aftercare

A major shortcoming in the correctional system is the lack of integrated community services for offenders. Increasingly, however, linkages between the criminal justice system and substance abuse treatment are occurring through the use of the case management model.

Because the most critical period for female offenders is during their transition to the community, when the freedom to reoffend can be overwhelming, supervised aftercare is essential. The Center for Substance Abuse Treatment has funded a number of residential programs for women ex-convicts to meet their special needs (Kassebaum, 1999). Such programs encourage autonomy, trust, bonding, and maintenance of close family ties. Ideally, community service providers will work with women at the facility to help them arrange for child care, housing, supportive supervision, and a sober lifestyle upon their release. Unfortunately, women offenders who are returning to the community are especially hard hit by restrictive "welfare reform" initiatives. Recent federal legislation deprives women convicted of a drug offense from receiving welfare support unless the state makes an exemption. Similar restrictions on financial aid for college education also apply, not to violent offenders, but only to persons convicted of drug offenses.

Alternatives to Prison

Increasingly, research is highlighting the superiority of substance abuse programs delivered in the community over those conducted in institutional settings (Weekes, 1997). One of the most promising developments in recent years is the drug court, an alternative to prison that was first launched in Florida. According to a news account (Johnson, 1998), these new courts, which divert nonviolent drug offenders from the prison system into treatment, prove that such programs are cost-effective to society and still allow people to obtain treatment and maintain their work and family roles. Today there are close to three hundred drug courts in forty-eight states. The specific impact of these courts on women is still to be determined.

Because many women offenders are mothers (BJS, 1999a), correctional programs delivered in the community are particularly important for women who have young children. Community centers that house mothers together with their children are especially valuable, as they can provide counselors who model appropriate parenting skills as issues arise spontaneously in the common living situation. Knowing that jail time awaits them if they begin abusing drugs again can offer women a strong incentive to change. By the same token, without help and the educational and vocational skills necessary to survive on their own, some women seem to deliberately get themselves in trouble in order to return to the safety of the prison environment.

Exemplary woman-focused community-based programs are designed to meet women's special needs. Such programs transform the male-model, confrontational therapeutic communities into a nurturing, family-like setting (Kassebaum, 1999). Even the traditional twelve-step model is adapted, especially in its group bonding and structural components, to suit the needs of women who already feel powerless over most aspects of their lives. In one program, official ceremonies to honor women clients were developed as affirming events to celebrate completion of the program and follow-up achievements. This activity served as a bonding experience to bring the community together (Kassebaum, 1999).

The Women's Re-entry Resource Network in Cleveland, Ohio, is a voluntary counseling and support network that offers ex-offenders the kind of close monitoring that they need following the shock of release. Over two hundred women have been helped through these reentry services to decrease the stress and stigma they experience in returning to the community (Farkas, 1998). Parent education is a vital part of this program. Intensive outreach services are badly needed, however, to draw more newly released women into treatment.

Follow-up data on the rate of recidivism of women in Oregon three years after treatment showed that the treated group of one hundred clients had a re-arrest rate three times lower than did a matched sample of untreated women. Similar studies in Ohio, Texas, and Minnesota revealed even more striking results (Kassebaum, 1999). A major element in all the successful programs is that they are long-term, preferably nine months to a year, and that they are linked to community services. The long-term period is essential to monitor women through the difficulties that face a returning ex-convict who needs to start a new life. The community links help open doors to a brighter and more secure future.

In an anonymous letter to me (July 13, 1998), an inmate describes the help she obtained from a drug treatment program while incarcerated:

> After arriving at this facility in July of 1996, being transferred for the sole purpose of having access to educational and programming opportunities, I applied for admission to the Bureau of Prison's 500-Hour Comprehensive Drug Treatment Program. I graduated in August of 1997 and remained on the unit as a mentor for addicted women participating in the program. This opportunity was the single most important thing that I have ever done. The courses, which included work on life skills and relationship issues, gave me the answers to *why* I did some of the things I did as well as *why* I kept relapsing when I had every intention of staying clean and reestablishing my life. I still work closely with the program and now lead self-help groups myself. This program had given me the understanding of myself and my addiction that I needed in order to prevent future relapse and problems, and the tools to live more productively. This was an incredible opportunity for me and because of it, if nothing else, I am confident there will be no more problems with addiction and/or relapse. The Drug Treatment Specialists at this facility are outstanding and extremely well versed in addiction and treatment and I basically owe them my life. . . .

From Pembroke Station, Danbury, Connecticut

Conclusion

As we have seen in this chapter, much of the substance abuse treatment that women offenders are receiving for addiction problems is taking place through the criminal justice system. Most of the treatment is offered in highly punitive settings behind prison walls. Even in the disempowering environment of prison, however, effective counseling programs can help women learn healthier ways of coping than using drugs or getting entangled in destructive relationships. To prepare women to make a successful transition into the community and to resume their parenting duties and work roles, halfway houses with professional supervision can be an invaluable aid.

Clearly it costs far less money to treat a woman offender for addiction than to incarcerate her. The cost savings of innovative treatment programs are incalculable; they include prevention of the spread of HIV-AIDS and fetal alcohol syndrome, and reduction of crime rates and of extensive welfare and foster care costs. In short, what is good for substance-abusing and addicted women is good for the children, and what is good for both mothers and children is good for the society as a whole. Most women who are incarcerated will one day be returned to society. How well they are prepared—psychologically, educationally, and emotionally—for life in the community will depend on the level of investment that our society is willing to make in their care.

References

Acoca, L. (1998). Defusing the time bomb: Understanding and meeting the growing health care needs of incarcerated women in America. *Crime and Delinquency, 44*(1), 49–69.

Blanchette, K. (1997, January). Classifying female offenders for correctional interventions. *Forum in Corrections, 9*(1), 1–8.

Bureau of Justice Statistics. (1997). *Lifetime likelihood of going to state or federal prison.* Washington, DC: U.S. Department of Justice.

Bureau of Justice Statistics. (1999a). *Prisoners in 1998.* Washington, DC: U.S. Department of Justice.

Bureau of Justice Statistics. (1999b). *DWI offenders under correctional supervision.* Washington, DC: U.S. Department of Justice.

Bureau of Justice Statistics. (1999c). *Women offenders.* Washington, DC: U.S. Department of Justice.

Bureau of Justice Statistics. (2000). *Prison and jail inmates at midyear 1999.* Washington, DC: U.S. Department of Justice.

Butterfield, F. (1997, October 27). Drop in homicide rate linked to crack's decline. *New York Times,* p. A10.

Chesney-Lind, M. (1995). Girls, delinquency, and juvenile justice: Toward a feminist theory of young women's crime. In B. R. Price & N. J. Sokoloff (Eds.), *The criminal justice system and women: Offenders, victims, and workers* (pp. 71–88). New York: McGraw-Hill.

Chesney-Lind, M. (1997). *The female offender: Girls, women, and crime.* Thousand Oaks, CA: Sage.

Covington, S. (1999). *Helping women recover: A program for treating substance abuse.* San Francisco: Jossey-Bass.

Farkas, K. (1998, February). Women's re-entry resource network: A specialized program for ex-offender women and their children. *Issues of Substance,* pp. 6–7.

Farr, K. A. (2000). Classification for female inmates: Moving forward. *Crime and Delinquency, 46*(1), 3–17.

Fishbein, D., & Pease, S. (1996). *The dynamics of drug abuse.* Needham Heights, MA: Allyn & Bacon.

General Accounting Office. (1999, December 18). *Women in prison: Issues and challenges confronting the U.S. correctional system.* Washington, DC: Author.

Gonzalez, F. (1996, January). *Profile of the female offender: A statistical analysis.* Trenton: New Jersey Department of Corrections, Bureau of Community and Correctional Services.

Greenhouse, L. (2001, March 22). Court curbs drug tests during pregnancy. *New York Times.* Available: www.nytimes.com/2001. . ./politics/22SCOT.html.

Heney, J., & Kristiansen, C. M. (1998). An analysis of the impact of prison on women survivors of childhood sexual abuse. *Women and Therapy, 20*(4), 29–44.

Johnson, K. (1998, May 15). Drug courts help addicts find way back. *USA Today,* p. 12A.

Kassebaum, P. A. (1999). *Substance abuse treatment for women offenders: Guide to promising approaches.* Rockville, MD: U.S. Department of Health and Human Services.

Martin, S. S., & Inciardi, J. A. (1997). Case management outcomes for drug-involved offenders. *Prison Journal, 77*(2), 168–183.

Miller, E. (1986). *Street woman.* Philadelphia: Temple University Press.

Miller, W. R. (1999). *Enhancing motivation for change in substance abuse treatment* (Treatment Improvement Protocol Series No. 35). Rockville, MD: Center for Substance Abuse Treatment.

Miller, W. R., & Rollnick, S. (1991). *Motivational interviewing: Preparing people to change addictive behaviors.* New York: Guilford Press.

National Institute on Drug Abuse. (1999). *Infofax: Treatment methods for women.* Available: www.drugabuse.gov/pp1-4.

O'Brien, P. (2001). *Making it in the "free world": Women in transition from prison.* Albany: State University of New York Press.

Office of National Drug Control Policy. (2001). *National drug control strategy: 2001 annual report.* Washington, DC: U.S. Department of Health and Human Services.

Phillips, S. D., & Harm, N. J. (1997). Women prisoners: A contextual framework. *Women and Therapy, 20*(4), 1–9.

Pomeroy, E. C., Kiam, R., & Abel, E. (1998). *Health and Social Work, 23*(19), 71–75.

Project MATCH Research Group. (1997). Matching alcoholism treatments to client heterogeneity. *Journal of Studies on Alcohol, 58,* 7–27.

Richie, B. E. (1996). *Compelled to crime: The gender entrapment of battered black women.* New York: Routledge.

Roberts, D. (1994). *The color of welfare: How racism undermined the war on poverty.* New York: Oxford University Press.

Rolison, G. (1993). Toward an integrated theory of female criminality and incarceration. In

B. Fletcher, L. D. Shaver, & D. G. Moon (Eds.), *Women prisoners: A forgotten population* (pp. 137–146). Westport, CT: Praeger.

Saleebey, D. (1997). Introduction: Power in the people. In D. Saleebey (Ed.), *The strengths perspective in social work practice* (2nd ed., pp. 3–19). New York: Longman.

Stodghill, R. (1999, February 1). Unequal justice: Why women face abuse. *Time,* pp. 50–51.

Straussner, S. L., & Zelvin, E. (Eds.). (1997). *Gender and addictions: Men and women in treatment.* Northvale, NJ: Aronson.

Substance Abuse and Mental Health Administration. (1997). *Substance use among women in the United States.* Rockville, MD: Department of Health and Human Services.

U.S. prison population rises. (1997, August). *Corrections Today, 59,* 12.

van Wormer, K. (2001). *Counseling female offenders and victims: A strengths-restorative approach.* New York: Springer.

van Wormer, K., & Bartollas, C. (2000). *Women and the criminal justice system.* Needham Heights, MA: Allyn & Bacon.

Weekes, J. R. (1997, July). Substance abuse treatment for offenders. *Corrections Today,* pp. 12–16.

Weiner, A., & Pollack, D. (1997). Urban runaway youth: Sex, drugs and HIV. In N. Phillips & S.L.A. Straussner (Eds.), *Children in the urban environment: Linking social policy and clinical practice* (pp. 209–226). Springfield, IL: Thomas.

Wellisch, J., Anglin, M. D., & Prendergast, M. L. (1993). Treatment strategies for drug-abusing women offenders. In J. A. Inciardi (Ed.), *Drug treatment and criminal justice* (pp. 5–29). Thousand Oaks, CA: Sage.

Wellisch, J., Prendergast, M. L., & Anglin, M. D. (1996). Needs assessment and services for drug-abusing women offenders: Results from a national survey of community-based treatment programs. *Women and Criminal Justice, 8*(1), 27–60.

CHAPTER TWENTY-TWO

WOMEN AFFECTED BY ADDICTIONS

Elizabeth Zelvin

Recent research confirms the belief, long a truism in the popular recovery move-ment, that the adverse consequences of addictions seriously influence four to six significant others around each addicted individual (Abbott, 2000). Yet in both research and treatment, the partners and other loved ones of chemical dependents are still gravely underrepresented, and the significant others of compulsive gam-blers and sexual compulsives are barely considered. Women in particular, such as the wives of alcoholics or the mothers of young women with eating disorders, are more likely to be seen as enablers who contribute to the problem and even sab-otage recovery than as women who are in pain and in need of help.

Although lip service is paid to the necessity of getting family members into treatment, in the majority of treatment programs, the needs of partner, parent, or adult child are addressed in a perfunctory way with advice to attend Al-Anon or another self-help program. In mental health and family-oriented social service agencies, and even in private practice, where a variety of presenting problems can mask distress over a loved one's addiction, assessment may not include an ade-quate appraisal of addiction problems in the family system. And in most women's programs, helping professionals tend to respond more promptly and compre-hensively to the needs of addicted women than to those of women affected by the addictions of others. In society at large, these women's needs are considered unimportant and uninteresting because of the stigma attached to loving an alco-holic or drug addict, a compulsive gambler, or a sexual compulsive. Furthermore, a woman who lives with a compulsive debtor or spender, eating-disordered male, or computer addict is not stigmatized because her problem is invisible.

The premise of this chapter is that women who have significant relationships with addicts of all kinds are inevitably in emotional pain and that the clinician's helping them make cognitive and behavioral changes and get in touch with and work through their feelings is crucial to their functioning and to their emotional well-being.

Scope of the Problem

There is no simple or comprehensive way to assess how many women are living or have lived with addicts or, even more narrowly, with substance abusers. It is difficult to find reliable data on the number of American women affected by addictions, partly because there is widespread disagreement on what constitutes an addiction and partly because the idea that significant others in general, not to mention women in particular, are affected is itself controversial.

From available information on the number of alcoholics and drug abusers, we can infer that there is an enormous population of significant others. According to Dr. Enoch Gordis, director of the National Institute on Alcoholism and Alcohol Abuse (NIAAA, 2000), 10 million children are exposed to alcoholism or alcohol abuse in the family setting in the course of one year, and 28 million children are living with current or former alcohol-abusing or alcohol-dependent adults. A fact sheet from the Substance Abuse and Mental Health Services Administration (2000) reported 113 million American alcohol users in 1998, including 33 million binge drinkers and 10.5 million young people between the ages of twelve and twenty. In addition, 13.6 million Americans were using illicit drugs in the same period, including 9.9 percent of twelve- to seventeen-year-olds. If more than half of Americans are women, and if the greater capacity of women for relationship and connection (Gilligan, 1982; Miller, 1976; Zelvin, 1999) is taken into account, a sizable majority of those suffering as a result of their relationships with addicted partners and family members must be female. Furthermore, the youthful drinkers and drug abusers have mothers or other mostly female caretakers on whom their substance use may have a significant impact.

A literature search online through the National Clearinghouse for Alcohol and Drug Information turned up 177 articles using the keywords *wives/partners/spouses/significant others*—that is, women affected by someone else's alcoholism and drug abuse—compared to 6,594 on substance-abusing or addicted women (National Institute on Alcohol Abuse and Alcoholism, 2000). Of the articles on significant others, only 29 were written in 1996 or later, as opposed to 1,734 on addicted women during the same period. Further, of the 29 articles, only 12 were even marginally relevant to the topic of helping women affected by addictions. Moreover, only 7 recent articles in this group specifically identified daughters of alcoholics as significant others.

A search for literature on women affected by eating disorders also produced limited results, and those were focused mostly on the families of anorexics and bulimics and on testing various hypotheses regarding the role of mothers and other family members in contributing to the development of these disorders. Material on significant others in books on compulsive gambling and sexual addiction will be presented later in this chapter. In general, women with a direct connection to addicts of all kinds are gravely underrepresented in the literature.

Historical Perspectives

Before 1950, wives of alcoholics tended to be viewed popularly as martyrs and saints who were admirable in their commitment to "standing by their man." Clinically, however, they were seen as severe neurotics whose pathology led them to seek out alcoholics to marry and who encouraged their husbands to go on drinking in the service of their secondary gains (Kellermann, 1974; Zelvin, in press). In the 1950s, Al-Anon, a self-help program for the families and friends of alcoholics, evolved out of Alcoholics Anonymous (AA), which had been in existence since 1939. Al-Anon conceptualized the relationship between alcoholics and their loved ones as one of denial and enabling (Kellermann, 1969; Zelvin, 1988). It framed the significant other's attempts to rescue and control as unconscious and inevitable in the context of active alcoholism. Al-Anon both emphasized the need for the affected partner, usually a woman, to take responsibility for her own behavior and, at the same time, acknowledged her pain and suffering in the situation. It gave her practical tools for what it called *detachment with love*, a counterintuitive strengthening of the boundaries between her sense of self or emotional well-being and that of her alcoholic partner. In the early 1980s, the adult children of alcoholics (ACOA) movement advocated for general acknowledgment, understanding, and treatment of the ongoing effects on millions of adults of having grown up in a family with an alcoholic parent. The concept of ACOA issues later expanded to embrace the posttraumatic effects of growing up in families of origin with a variety of dysfunctions. Interest in the gender-specific issues of ACOA women evolved as the relationship between childhood sexual abuse and adult substance abuse, as well as depression, eating disorders, and dissociative disorders, began to be acknowledged.

The concept of codependency, popularized in the 1980s, provided a helpful model for understanding the effects of trying to rescue and control an addicted loved one. At first applied only to the enmeshment of those concerned about a chemically dependent person, it hypothesized that those close to an addict would inevitably fall into an escalating pattern of overinvolvement with the other person and the addiction itself, to the detriment of their own self-care, health, and functioning. A host of characteristics, including excessive caretaking, pathological approval seeking or "people pleasing," and decreased self-esteem, would eventually color all the codependent's relationships.

The ACOA movement quickly began to use *codependent* synonymously with *adult child from a dysfunctional family,* so that those in relationships with addicts were assumed to have grown up in unhealthy family systems. By the 1990s, the term was being generalized almost beyond the point of usefulness to mean any deficits in internal sense of self, or "the tendency to expect external sources of fulfillment and to seek identity and self-worth outside the self" (Zelvin, 1999, p. 15).

Codependency soon became a household word, thanks to the media's growing interest in addictions and recovery, but it was almost immediately challenged by feminists, who balked at the idea of labeling women's capacity to form and maintain relationships as a "disease." They believed that the term codependency fostered blaming the victim of someone else's addiction and pathologizing a woman who was doing her best to survive in a difficult situation. The term was also challenged by some of those who had introduced it: recovering adult children of alcoholics, many of them working in the addiction field, who began to question the wisdom of labeling their characteristic talent for achievement, organization, and leadership as "sick" codependency and workaholism stemming from their overresponsible "family hero" role in their family of origin. Some theorists, to the contrary, have recently begun to consider codependency a form of post-traumatic stress disorder with its roots in childhood (Kellogg, 1990). At the same time, such self-help groups as Al-Anon and Codependents Anonymous (CODA) and treatment facilities based on a twelve-step approach have found the codependency concept useful in relieving the burden of self-blame for not being able to "fix" or "cure" the addict. Many women used their self-identification as codependents as a starting point for disengaging from a pathological connection with a loved one who, because of addiction or other deficits, was not meeting their needs. The concept of codependency helped them build healthy boundaries and a secure sense of self.

Both within the addiction field and in the popular recovery movement, it became obvious that codependency issues were present not only in women who had relationships with addicts but also in women with addictions of their own. The vocabulary of codependency lent itself to those aspects of women's experience that the women's movement had made more visible. These included the sometimes intertwined issues of a distorted reliance on relationship for identity and self-worth; eating disorders, expressed as a pathological relationship to both food and body image; and childhood sexual abuse and domestic violence. In short, women with addictions and women affected by addictions are frequently one and the same.

The Invisible Women Affected by Addictions

The focus on such obvious significant others as wives, partners, lovers, mothers, and daughters of alcoholics and other chemical dependents has been inadequate and has decreased even further in the age of managed care. Even more unfortunately, women in relationships with those who are addicted not to a substance but to a process or behavioral pattern—gambling; debting and spending; sexual pathology; or compulsive overeating, purging, or starving—are virtually invisible. In the twenty-first century, technology-based addictions are newly emerging: compulsive surfing on the Internet; destructive financial activities such as excessive e-trading, a form of compulsive gambling; obsession with compulsive viewing of on-line pornography, a form of sexual addiction; and other compulsive uses of technology to the detriment of the addict's relationships with people and capacity to feel or function. These addictions, observably more common in men, have an impact on millions of women whose emotional needs are yet to be recognized.

When a woman has one addiction herself, such as a dependence on prescription pills, and is affected by another as an addict's caretaker or loved one, it is usually the codependency, not the personal addiction, that becomes invisible. A chemically dependent woman may have been rescuing and seeking approval from other chemical dependents all her life: parents, siblings, partners, colleagues, and friends. A morbidly obese incest survivor is using food addictively to ward off both painful feelings and sexual attention. At the same time, she is living the consequences of having been affected by the substance abuse of a perpetrator who molested her when he was drunk or high. Or a brother who was himself abused by an alcoholic parent might act out against a younger, more helpless sister. A woman may be drawn to alcoholic men because she is replicating not an alcoholic family system but a family with an intergenerational pattern of gambling that generated a similar dynamic: Dad would be intermittently expansive and loving after a big win, then depressed and unavailable when he lost or there was no action, while Mom and the children "walked on eggshells" in response to his changing moods, and the daughter took on a quasimaternal or quasimarital role in response to Dad's immaturity and fecklessness and her mother's powerlessness and rage. Carnes (1992) points out, "Alcoholism and compulsive overeating are frequent partners in the sexual addiction dance. . . . The wife who adds a hundred and fifty pounds as an expression of her rage or as a statement about sexuality is . . . doing something her husband cannot control" (p. 109).

Characteristics of Affected Women

Women affected by addictions have both a degree of commonality and some distinguishing characteristics depending on the addiction and the nature of their relationship to it.

Adult Children: Daughters of Addicted Families

For twenty-eight million children of alcoholics and an uncounted number of children of other kinds of addicts, the damage done by someone else's addiction begins at birth—indeed, shortly after conception in the case of children born with fetal alcohol syndrome to alcoholic mothers. Theorists such as Black (1981) and Wegscheider (1981) have done us a great service by delineating the roles and rules of the so-called dysfunctional family. The traditional gender roles that persist in our culture combines with these unhealthy systems to give us daughters of families with parental or intergenerational addictions who are caretakers, the traditional female version of the "family hero"; passive, self-effacing "lost children"; and "scapegoat" children who act out sexually or fulfill a family pattern of female victimization. One pattern of addictive family behavior is to distract attention from the primary addiction—for example the parent's drug abuse, gambling, or sexual compulsivity—by focusing on a child or children as "not enough." The child internalizes the demand for perfection, believing that if only she could be "enough," the family would magically be healed. For a girl, "not enough" may take the form of not pretty enough, not smart enough, not popular enough, not thin enough, not sexually attractive enough (in some families, not sexually active enough), not good enough, not selfless enough, or not domestic enough. These childhood messages yield women with persistent negative self-perceptions about their bodies, their intelligence, their sexuality, their achievements, and their basic worth.

The "don't feel" rule of dysfunctional families has a particular impact on female children, because women in our culture are seen as the guardians of feeling. If a man from an addicted family has trouble "getting in touch with his feelings," he is seldom considered a failure as a "guy." Women whose feelings are "frozen," in contrast, have a serious deficit in their wholeness as women that transcends traditional versus feminist perspectives. Because women's greatest strengths are relational (Gilligan, 1982; Miller, 1976; Zelvin, 1999), women who did not have good relational role models are at a great disadvantage in coping with the world. Trust, open communication, and honest expression of feelings are not safe in such families. The defenses that girls develop to protect themselves persist into adulthood, when they become increasingly maladaptive. Many of these women use substances, especially chemicals and food, to fill the emptiness where feelings, healthy relationships, and a core sense of self should be. Their own addictions may be secondary to the adverse impact of the parental addiction.

The following case demonstrates the impact of maternal alcoholism on a young woman over the course of her development, even in the presence of sobriety.

Marla

Marla's alcoholic mother, a woman with few female friends who had been physically abused by her mother as a child, got sober when Marla was ten. Previously, Marla had been virtually unsupervised. Now her mother, wanting to be a good parent, took charge of her schedule, checking homework, banning television (to which Marla was addicted), imposing curfews, and reacting strongly to the discovery that Marla had been skipping school frequently. Marla reacted by saying, "I liked her better when she was drinking!" and by acting out with continued truancy, lying, and stealing, until at sixteen she entered residential treatment.

At twenty-eight, Marla had become well informed about chemical dependency and was not a substance abuser. She behaved responsibly at work and had a boyfriend. However, she had serious problems with her body image and was distrustful of women and resistant to developing friendships with them.

Adult Onset or Exacerbation: Lovers, Wives, and Mothers

No matter how healthy a woman's family of origin, living with an addict can elicit or produce pathology in her. Rescue and control, enabling and codependency, poor boundaries and people pleasing (that is, approval seeking)—these are the hallmark symptoms of the woman affected by addictions. In trying to adapt to a situation that becomes progressively more frightening, dangerous, and out of control, she develops responses that cast her in the unattractive roles of victim and martyr. The characteristic denial that accompanies addiction places her in a double bind in which even her perception that something is very wrong is ridiculed and tainted by doubt: *gaslighted*, as gambling treatment professionals call it (Berman & Siegel, 1998), after the famous movie starring Ingrid Bergman. Self-confidence falters, horizons narrow as she tries one strategy after another to control or cure the addict's compulsive behavior: rage, tears, pleading, threats, bargaining, cutting off supplies by pouring liquor down the sink or controlling the checkbook. These futile attempts create an atmosphere of contempt and resentment in the relationship. When the affected woman is the mother of a youthful drug addict, she may seem to be domineering and to be smothering her child, but appearances conceal a pain that is virtually unbearable. When the remedy of letting go and allowing the addict to experience adverse consequences is suggested, it is so counterintuitive that many mothers turn their backs on the possibility of help. "But he's my baby! I can't let them break his legs! They might kill him!" one mother exclaimed when she was advised to apply "tough love" as an alternative to giving her cocaine-abusing son money to pay off his dealers.

In cases in which the addiction is not identified but the mother senses that there is something wrong, it may be difficult to intervene. The following is an example.

A woman goes to a psychologist seeking help for her son, a man in his late thirties who has recently lost his job and is drinking heavily. The psychologist consults an experienced social worker who specializes in addictions, hoping this may prove to be an appropriate referral for the son. The social worker explains that if the man himself is not seeking help, it is not a promising referral. She predicts accurately that if approached by his mother, the man will say that he does not think his drinking is a problem and that, in any case, he cannot afford therapy since he has lost his job. When the psychologist tries to engage the mother in treatment, she responds that it is her son, not she, who needs help.

The options for both clinicians in this case are limited. The social worker has the specialized knowledge to assess the man's drinking problem, offer psychoeducation to the mother, and perhaps motivate one or both of them to seek self-help and treatment. The psychologist has access to the mother and thus the potential for engaging her. If the mother gets help and makes some changes, it may change the family dynamics in such a way that the son becomes more open to intervention. The social worker can use this opportunity to share information about addictions with the psychologist. If the psychologist is open to learning, perhaps even trying some interventions that counter denial and decrease enabling, the two clinicians can form an alliance that may benefit future clients.

Women Affected by Sexual Addiction

Carnes (1992) has broadened our understanding of both sexual addiction and the scope of the problem for women who love a sex addict. He describes the grief the affected woman feels as the relationship is progressively lost to the addiction. In a futile effort to restore the relationship, "co-addicts will [perform] actions which are degrading, self-destructive, or even profound violations of their own values" (p. 92). Prostitutes, surely the most invisible and expendable women in our society, are affected by the degradation and risk of violence imposed by sexually compulsive "johns." Carnes tells us: "a woman who worked in a massage parlor . . . reported . . . a rape of one of the masseuses in the place where she worked. When she went to the police station to examine mug shots of sex offenders, she was stunned to . . . recognize a large number of the pictures—they were her clients. It was shortly after that [that] she entered therapy" (p. 59).

Stressing both the destructiveness and the power of coaddictive love, Carnes cites the case of the mother of a convicted rapist who hired a hit man to kill the prosecutor and judge who convicted and sentenced him to life imprisonment. In another case, Carnes describes a man mandated to treatment for exhibitionism, then to treatment for alcoholism, who eventually admitted to affairs and contacts with prostitutes with financial consequences for his family, and finally admitted to rape. In family treatment because of the alcoholism, the "wife continued a cold and distant hostility. . . . It was not until Bill revealed that he was also a rapist that things changed in the family. The pain was so great for . . . his wife . . . that she too came into therapy" (p. 49). This case demonstrates both the progression of sex addiction and the progression of denial and normalization of addictive behavior in the woman affected by it, as well as the comorbidity of sexual addiction and alcoholism.

Women Affected by Gambling

Compulsive gambling, like sexual addiction, seems to thrive on secrecy that continues into the recovery process. This in turn has an impact on how women are affected. Berman and Siegel (1998) describe its extent: "Being involved with a gambler is like living on an emotional roller coaster that keeps on going. At times you feel as if you are crazy. It can also cause bankruptcy, a lifetime of debt, harassment from people who are owed money, threats from loan sharks, visits to jail, loss of friends, shame, humiliation, fear, homelessness, suicide" (p. 47).

In this particular addiction, the great majority of those seeking recovery have been men, largely in traditional marriages. Berman and Siegel state: "Some Gam-Anon members (they are mostly women) have been in the program since the early 1960s" (p. 165). Denial of the problem manifests as gaslighting, in which the gambler invalidates with lies and accusations the wife's instinct that something is wrong. Enabling includes frequent and escalating financial "bailouts" to rescue the gambler from debt and its consequences. Perhaps the reason for the conventional husband-wife profile frequently seen in compulsive gambling is that marriage and the existence of children inevitably involve a woman in her husband's financial difficulties, and she may even find herself legally responsible for his debts. And in more traditional marriages, in which the wife may have few economic resources of her own, the feelings of panic and being overwhelmed as well as hurt and sad, angry, and betrayed are highly appropriate.

Women Affected by Eating Disorders

For the purposes of this chapter, we will consider eating disorders as a variety of addictive behaviors along a continuum from anorexia (addiction to starving) to bulimia (addiction to purging by vomiting, laxative use, compulsive exercise, or a combination of these) to compulsive overeating with or without obesity and concurrently as a substance addiction to sugar, flour, or any other food category that triggers craving. Eating disorders are unique among the addictions in that they affect mostly women as primary addicts. The most visible woman affected by someone else's eating disorder is usually the mother of an eating-disordered female. Rabinor (1994) observes that the eating disorders literature has continued the "unfortunate tradition" of blaming the mother, with profound consequences for treatment of eating disorders. Rabinor proposes a mother-affirmative reframing of the etiology of eating disorders from a feminist perspective: "Motivated by a desire to remain connected to their mothers, daughters remain unconsciously loyal to their mothers' values and lifestyles. What daughters learn from our patriarchal culture . . . is that their bodies are their most powerful tools. A mother-blaming perspective fails to account for the social context in which a woman's appearance is often the . . . only . . . form of power . . . afforded her. In perfecting her body by dieting, the eating-disordered daughter mirrors her mother's attempts to be powerful. . . . It is a mark of female resilience that . . . mothers do train their daughters to have access to . . . body power" (pp. 276–277).

The mother of an anorexic daughter both fears that her child will die and feels guilty and inadequate in her role as a mother. Medicine, psychology, and popular culture alike tend to confirm this negative view of herself. As Rabinor (1994) points out, a mother's maladaptive messages about her daughter's body may include elements of her own pain about her body and a desire to spare her daughter that pain. In addition, the perfectionism that seems to be a theme in many families with an anorexic daughter may be, among other things, an intergenerational response to family alcoholism or other addictions.

Men with eating disorders are among the least visible of addicts (Jacobson, 2000), and so are the women who love them. The following case illustrates how compulsive overeating can kill and how profoundly a significant other can be affected.

Linda and Lee

When Linda first met Lee, he weighed over three hundred pounds. While they were dating, she felt embarrassed by his appearance and by such incidents as his breaking her bed. She agreed to marry him if he would get help. He lost over one hundred pounds in a well-known weight-loss program before the wedding. Both were convinced that weight was no longer an issue. Within a year, Lee regained all his weight, although he did not overeat at home. Within a few years, Linda had two small children and was feeling helpless, frustrated, and abandoned. Lee was spending more and more money on food and was lying and doctoring the family accounts. By the time she confronted him, he had depleted their bank accounts, destroyed their credit, brought them to the verge of eviction, pawned her engagement ring, cashed in his life insurance policy, and emptied the children's savings accounts. Lee confessed that the money was spent mostly on restaurant food. He was "addicted" to roast beef and would go from restaurant to restaurant. Lee begged Linda not to leave him and promised to get help. He became abstinent in Overeaters Anonymous, Linda went to O-Anon for families, and both entered treatment. Lee lost weight, both became committed to their recovery and the relationship, and they began to recover financially once the huge food expenses were eliminated. However, a year after entering recovery, Lee was diagnosed with colon cancer, a consequence of his long abuse of his body. He died—still abstinent from compulsive overeating—three years later, at age forty, leaving Linda to raise their young children alone on very limited financial resources.

Lesbian Partners and Codependency

From a feminist perspective, it would be easy to blame women's loss of boundaries, self-esteem, and even identity in their relationships with addicted men on the patriarchal toxicity inherent in such relationships. If this were so, lesbian couples would have no codependency issues. In reality, lesbians are overrepresented in the ranks of substance abusers. As many as one in three are believed to have alcohol problems, and twice as many lesbians use tobacco and marijuana as heterosexual women (van Wormer, Wells, & Boes, 2000, p. 127). Inevitably, lesbian women's addictions have an impact on their female partners, whose issues of rescue, control, excessive caretaking, and approval seeking may be compounded by addictions of their own. In turn, a lesbian addict's role in the relationship may be complicated by her own codependency issues, exacerbated by her relational development and socialization as a female. An article on lesbians and chemical dependency acknowledges that there is "a larger than expected proportion of adult children of alcoholics in the lesbian community" (Glaus, 1988, p. 131).

Assessment

Assessment of women affected by addictions is an ongoing process, complicated by several factors. These women are not necessarily the identified patient, but may present as collateral to an addict who is seeking help or whose behavior has brought him to the attention of authorities such as the criminal justice system or an employee assistance program. Women who love an addict may or may not be conscious of the role that the addiction plays in the relationship or family problems. Rarely are they aware of how their behavior has adapted to the addictive situation and how this adaptation is adversely affecting their own lives. If such women come for help, they present with a variety of symptoms: depression, anxiety, problems with weight or body image, a self-diagnosed difficulty with intimacy, sexual dysfunction, or life problems such as being blocked in career or creativity, among a host of others. Not just the skill but also the training of the helping professional who encounters these women will determine whether the impact of living with addiction is ever explored, let alone adequately and differentially diagnosed and effectively treated. In addition, some forms of many of the most devastating addictions, such as compulsive debting or the preoccupation with thinness that underlies bulimia and anorexia, are considered normative in our society.

Assessing Women's Needs

In order to assess a woman's need for help as a consequence of her connection with an addict, interviewers must be familiar with the dynamics of addictive systems and the symptoms of addictions at every stage in their progression. They must also know the characteristics of the emotional and physical disorders that may have emerged or been exacerbated by the stresses of the addictive situation. These may also have taken on a life of their own, so that they must be treated as primary disorders concurrently with any help provided for the woman as an addict's significant other. Because the problem is typically masked by denial—which consists not only of unconscious defenses but also, in many cases, of ignorance and lack of information—and carries social stigma that is internalized as shame, questions must be empathic, nonthreatening, and based on fact. The interviewer must know enough about how addicts and their significant others rationalize and minimize to probe for the question beyond the question. It is important to remember that the significant other's denial is nearly as powerful an unconscious process as the addict's. Women affected by addictions use all sorts of rationalizations and minimizations:

"He doesn't go to casinos anymore; he only plays poker at the club."

"I've told him I won't see him when he's been smoking pot."

"He's cut up most of his credit cards."

"He's not using hard drugs any more."

"He just had a beer or two before he got in the car."

Like addicts themselves, women affected by addictions cling to myths that keep them from the pain of knowing that their choices, as well as their behaviors, have been gravely flawed. How the interviewer frames questions is crucial to accurate assessment. Information must be gathered on the affected woman's family history and her own substance use. In assessing a client whose wife or partner has accompanied him to the interview, the worst possible course is to ask no questions about the significant other's own situation. Leaving the wife, mother, or partner sitting in the waiting room, or viewing her as irrelevant or destructive to the process of engaging the addict, is a clear message that this woman's needs and feelings do not count. It reaffirms her feelings of shame, powerlessness, and worthlessness. Focusing exclusively on the addict's behavior in talking with the affected woman will compound her belief that she is of peripheral importance and that only the addict's recovery matters, no matter how much pain she is in. She will inevitably hear "Your controlling and even your rescuing behavior only enabled the problem" as "You're bad and it's all your fault." The addict, wrestling with deep ambivalence in early recovery—or refusing treatment altogether—may well endorse this view.

A display of knowledgeable empathy during the assessment process goes a long way toward the beginning of a therapeutic alliance with the woman affected by addictions. Frequently, her concerns have been minimized; she herself has been blamed for causing or exacerbating the addictive problem or its consequences; and she has become isolated, fearful, angry, and filled with doubt about her feelings and perceptions. Being approached by someone who not only cares about her feelings and empathizes with her position but also can describe with some accuracy what she has been going through, can seem a miracle of mind reading that provides the first glimmer of hope she has experienced in a long time.

Penny

Penny came to the mental health clinic for what she called a problem with self-confidence. At the intake interview, she said, "I don't know what's wrong with me. When I was younger I wasn't afraid of anything, and I did a lot of adventurous things. I traveled all over Europe alone, I tried hang gliding, I met interesting people just talking to strangers. Now I can't make myself do anything. My life is getting smaller and smaller."

The intake worker, who was experienced in working with women affected by addictions, said, "Are you in a relationship?" Penny said, "Yes, I live with my boyfriend." The worker said, "I may be completely off target here, but does your boyfriend by any chance drink heavily or do drugs?" Penny, amazed, said, "How did you know?"

The assessment must include a therapeutic alliance that begins at the first moment of contact. The woman whose loved one has an addiction needs to hear, "You are important. Loving an addict is painful. Your happiness and your ability to function have been affected. You deserve help whether or not the addict recovers, whether or not you stay with this person." At first, these messages must be conveyed as subtext, because one of the affected woman's symptoms is what Al-Anon calls "having the focus off yourself." She wants to hear that the addict is the important one and that he can be fixed. The assessment process must be intertwined with the engagement process, so that in addition to uncovering the facts and determining in what ways and how severely the woman has been affected, the worker is helping the woman get in touch with *her* anxiety, *her* fear, *her* feelings of loss and abandonment and the grief that they engender.

The assessment process may begin at any point on the continuum of the addict's progressive illness or recovery and also of the affected woman's involvement. The moment when an addict gets help may be the very moment that the wife or mother who has tolerated his behavior for decades abandons the relationship. Change is always frightening, and the woman whose accommodation to the addictive situation has become familiar is defending against terror at the prospect of uncovering painful feelings, having to share not only responsibility but also power and control, and being criticized for her behavior.

Marian called her therapist in a rage after attending an orientation session for family at the rehab her twenty-eight-year-old son had finally agreed to attend. "They said they won't take him," she fumed, "unless I come to family sessions. I won't do it! It's his problem, let them take care of it. I've done enough." Marian had been tolerating, indeed enabling, her son's drug abuse for many years: giving him money, saying nothing when he stole from her, allowing him to come home whenever he didn't have a place to stay.

Ambivalence About Recovery

As the addict recovers and begins to express appropriate needs and feelings, the affected woman finds herself reluctant to give up the power and control that went along with being the sole responsible adult in the relationship. She may be intimidated by the addict's emerging feelings or unwilling to accept them when they conflict with her own needs. Because women are the culture bearers for feelings and relationships, most women think that what they want is for their addicted partner or family member to be able to express feelings and be emotionally present in the relationship. However, when it actually happens, they are frequently dismayed and resentful. It is hard for a woman to be sympathetic when her newly recovering partner expresses negative feelings toward her or ambivalence about the relationship, yet such feelings are common in early recovery.

Treating the Affected Woman

As treatment begins and progresses, the therapist must assess the woman's ability to acknowledge her contribution to the situation—her observing ego, her ability to identify her own shortcomings—and help her self-assess and set goals that balance self-love with the need to change.

Engaging the Affected Woman

Supporting client self-determination and to some extent joining with client resistance are necessary for successful engagement. Yet engagement cannot even start if the woman lacks access to services. This may be problematic, especially if she is responsible for children or other dependents, such as elderly parents. The addict's unavailability, whether because his addiction is active or because he is away for inpatient treatment or spending all his free time at AA meetings, may exacerbate the pressure on the woman to perform responsibly in multiple roles in the family. It is important to approach her caretaker role from a strengths perspective: not "You have to let go your codependency and get to treatment" but "It's wonderful that you're such a giving and responsible person—and let's see if we can figure out a way for you to come to treatment and get some support for yourself as well."

Starting Where the Client Is

Some women are furious at the addict and the situation. The therapist needs to join with their anger, validating their feelings of being unfairly burdened and encouraging them to break the isolation by seeking the support of others who understand. Other women are completely unaware of their own needs, wanting only to "fix" a beloved addict. These women must be told gently that the best way to help an addict is to stop helping; at the same time, their love and loyalty must be praised and validated. It is important to remember that the woman who loves an addict feels simultaneously completely right and completely wrong. The clinician must join with both these feelings to form a therapeutic alliance.

A woman affected by her relationship with an addict is deeply ambivalent about getting help. In general, it is usually women who drag resistant male partners to a therapist, saying, in effect: "I want change—but I don't want to change." For some women who remain in a destructive relationship, including one with an active addict, "throwing the bum out" is not an option because of developmental attachment issues dating from the bond with addicted or unavailable early caretakers (Bartholomew, 1990; Feeney, 1999). In such cases, powerful but unconscious forces within these women prevent them from leaving. If the addict stops using or acting out on his addiction, the problem persists, because the woman has already deeply internalized her resistance to change and her erroneous belief that her own behavior in the relationship is not part of the problem, although she may also believe deeply that she is to blame. In these cases, the therapist must gently disengage her from her death grip on the addict, framing this necessity as supportive to both of them if they wish to feel better, and must help the affected woman self-identify as needing help.

Brown and Lewis (1999) point out that one of the most counterintuitive aspects of the recovery process is that "recovery is organized by the deep acceptance of loss of control. As therapists . . . we are not trying to plug holes or help families regain control. We work to help them widen the holes so the defensive structure, based on the faulty belief in control, can collapse and the new building process of recovery begin" (p. 12).

Choosing Treatment Modalities

When there is a choice of treatment modalities available, the strengths and drawbacks of each kind of treatment must be considered with respect to the individual client. Individual treatment, once a therapeutic alliance is formed, sends the message that the woman is important in her own right and not just in relation to the addict. Ongoing assessment as well as psychoeducation and counseling can take place, and important issues such as addictions in the family of origin, childhood abuse, domestic violence, and eating disorders may be uncovered fairly quickly. Group treatment with other women affected by addictions sends the message that the woman is not alone—that others understand and share her pain, frustration, and confusion, as well as the desire to make the relationship work. Gender-specific women's groups afford a chance to open up, in relative safety, such highly charged topics as sexuality and physical or sexual abuse. Mixed groups of significant others may teach the surprising lesson that addictive systems confound gender roles and that men affected by addictions have similar issues of rescue and control, excessive caretaking, low self-esteem, and people pleasing. Similarly, orientation-specific groups of lesbians affected by addictions provide freedom to explore such lesbian-specific issues as coming out, internalized and external homophobia, and role definition within the relationship. Groups of women, regardless of sexual orientation, may benefit from identifying both the issues common to all women and the issues in addictive relationships that exist for heterosexual and same-sex couples alike. Family treatment is important for establishing that the whole system, not just the adults within it, has been affected by the dynamics of addiction. It also helps families deal with the instabilities that the enormous change of recovery can produce.

Conjoint treatment with the recovering addict may be helpful in arresting destructive behaviors and exploring whether the relationship can and should survive in recovery. However, this work must be carefully timed so that, unless the couple is in crisis, they are not asked to reach conclusions or even let go of their grievances prematurely. Multicouple groups serve to break the isolation in which most couples grapple with the addicted-codependent relationship, and allow participants to hear about feelings similar to those of their partners without becoming defensive.

Education is an essential part of the treatment process. It must include not only information about the course of addictions and recovery but also the dynamics of the addicted family system. Gender-specific information must be included.

When the Addict Is Not Getting Help

Education is more necessary than ever if the addict is still using or acting out, and the affected woman must learn techniques for ensuring physical safety, find appropriate support, and build up the armor of detachment and good boundaries around a core of self. Once initial resistance and denial is overcome, women who have been living with active addiction experience enormous relief when their perception that something is very wrong is validated, and even more when it is confirmed that the addiction is at the core of what is wrong. Women whose preoccupation with the addict has caused them to neglect their own physical and emotional needs must be supported in their attempts to become reacquainted with themselves. How do you feel? What do you want? What do you like? These can be hard questions for the newly recovering significant other. Because the most healthy actions she can take—letting go, detaching, and going about her business regardless of what the addict does—are counterintuitive for a woman in a relationship, her progress may be hampered by guilt. Support not only from helping professionals but also from other women in her situation can give her the courage she needs to embark on this new way of life.

The Role of Self-Help

In the early history of AA, women did not rebel against their adjunctive role until one day in 1951, when, according to twelve-step legend, Lois W., the wife of AA co-founder Bill W., responded to his command to "get a wrap—we're going to a meeting" by throwing a shoe at him. This is the creation myth of Al-Anon, the first twelve-step program for the family and friends of addicts, in this case alcoholics. Today, such programs proliferate: Nar-Anon for those whose loved ones use narcotics; O-Anon and S-Anon for the partners and families of compulsive overeaters and sexual compulsives; Adult Children of Alcoholics (ACOA—ACA on the West Coast), which welcomes all who identify their families as dysfunctional; and Co-dependents Anonymous (CODA) for those whose destructive relationships are not necessarily with addicts but who exhibit the symptoms of poor or absent boundaries, approval seeking, excessive nurture, rescue and control, and low self-esteem. Like AA, these programs are based on the paradox of admitting powerlessness as the first step to accepting help. Like AA, they are frequently misunderstood as "just support groups," "religious," or "blaming the victim." In fact, the twelve steps are a powerful set of tools for healing shame and guilt, building character, and living a life of empowerment and effectiveness (Spiegel & Fewell, in press).

Clinicians need to be familiar with the self-help resources in their community; they will not only refer the client to them but also help her coordinate appropriate participation with her progress in treatment, deal with resistances, and help her integrate twelve-step recovery and treatment into meaningful change. In order to work with resistance, clinicians may need to add a spiritual vocabulary to their existing psychological frame of reference. In communities with high twelve-step consciousness and an abundance of programs and meetings, women may find their way to programs that deal with both the effects of others' addictions and their own addictions or compulsive behaviors. For example, one woman may belong to Al-Anon and Overeaters Anonymous (OA), another to ACOA and Survivors of Incest Anonymous (SIA), yet another to Debtors Anonymous (DA) and CODA. For women who have difficulty asserting themselves, the nonhierarchical structure built into the remarkable traditions of these programs helps them find their voice. For those who have been abused, the structure of a meeting provides safety: "sharing" consists of "I" statements referring to the speaker's own experience; in many meetings, shares are timed; and the "no crosstalk" rule means that the group's only response to each speaker's words is unconditional acceptance. In ACOA, where many members' boundaries have been repeatedly violated, some meetings consider nodding and even laughing a form of forbidden crosstalk. The practices of sponsoring and exchanging phone numbers take a lot of pressure off the clinician with a client who is very needy. And the simple but profound principles of the program offer a highly effective way of framing the process of self-examination and change.

The key concepts in Al-Anon that do not appear in AA are *keeping the focus on yourself* and *detachment with love*. These are particularly important to women in the light of women's relational development and their socialization, even today, to seek approval and provide nurture (Zelvin, 1997). Contrary to claims that the twelve-step approach promotes victimization and self-blame, these concepts encourage a clear sense of self and healthy boundaries and accord well with both feminist and mental health principles of empowerment. ACOA, dealing with the ongoing effects of having lived with addiction as a powerless child, is more about breaking the silence and working through feelings of rage and grief that have never been allowed expression. Clinicians need to be well informed about where they are sending their clients. Some incest survivors, for example, may feel invalidated in Al-Anon when told to let go of the past and take responsibility for the present. These women, among others, may find ACOA liberating.

Gemma reported when she entered treatment that her high-functioning, successful father had abandoned the family when she was ten, leaving her with her alcoholic mother who was by turns violent and depressed. When her therapist introduced her to ACOA, Gemma reveled in the license to express her most tumultuous feelings and hear others doing the same. Later in treatment, it came out that Gemma was a bulimic who used laxatives to purge compulsively eaten food. She tried Overeaters Anonymous, but found it "too tame."

Other adult children, on the contrary, find the freely expressed rage and crying in some ACOA meetings terrifying and all too reminiscent of the chaotic alcoholic or addicted family. Finally, the clinician must be aware of the possibility that women with borderline and histrionic personality disorders may enjoy the drama of ACOA so much that they make raging and crying about their families a way of life, with little genuine interest in healing and moving on.

Treatment Goals

Necessary tasks for the clinician are implicit in the client's short-term and long-term treatment goals.

Short-Term Goals. The first goal of a woman affected by addictions is to achieve understanding of the addiction and how it has affected her. This can be accomplished through education and through both self-help and group treatment with other women in similar situations.

Next, she must become aware of the need to establish or strengthen clear boundaries and a firm sense of self. Cognitive and behavioral work may help her figure out who she is, what she likes, and what she wants. Simultaneously, she must begin to withdraw from her enmeshed overinvolvement with the addict in her life. This is harder and will be an ongoing process. Supporting the love the client feels for the addict and acknowledging the counterintuitive nature of the detachment needed are important tasks for the clinician.

Long-Term Goals. For women in a current relationship with an active or recovering addict, whether to leave or stay may be a burning question. Except in cases of actual or potential violence to the woman or her children, it is usually helpful to reframe this question in terms of process and long-term decision making as the woman examines her options, develops ego strengths, and builds the life skills as well as the emotional skills to succeed at being autonomous, whether in or out of the relationship.

Understanding and resolving family-of-origin issues is another cluster of long-term goals. It is also essential to identify and deal with any addictions the woman herself uncovers during the process. For example, a woman in an alcoholic marriage may disclose her bulimia during the course of treatment. Psychopathology, such as depression or panic disorder, which can be alleviated by medication, may also emerge. The time frame for achieving long-term goals in all these areas must be coordinated with the severity of the problems and the fragility or strength of the individual woman and her degree of commitment. For example, it might take many years of therapy for a woman who was sexually abused as a child to identify the abuse, work through the feelings, deal with any dissociative symptoms that may have resulted from the abuse, and decide whether to forgive or confront the perpetrator or choose some other way of achieving closure. Not only treating pathology but also promoting empowerment are important parts of the clinical task. Recovery may lead to social action as well as to personal fulfillment if helping professionals understand that this is possible and the woman herself wants to move in that direction.

For the prototypical significant other in the prototypical treatment program, concrete goals for the woman client may include connecting with self-help, building self-esteem, and developing a support system within the context of recovery. In reality, clinicians must temper their expectations to the desires and abilities of the individual client.

Ida

Ida was the daughter of one violent alcoholic and the widow of another. She had nine children, of whom the four sons were all alcoholics and drug addicts. Ida's eighty-six-year-old mother, who lived with her, demanded constant attention, often refusing to let the home attendant perform services for her because she preferred to have Ida care for her. Whenever Ida said she had to leave the house to attend her treatment program, the mother would try to coax her not to go, saying it was raining or that it was going to rain. Ida frequently told her therapist after a weekend that she had had a visit from seven or eight of her nineteen grandchildren and that she was "exhausted" from cooking, cleaning, and entertaining them. Although Ida participated in the group for significant others, she did not attend Al-Anon or join in social activities with other women in the group. In the process of ending the group, the clinician suggested that Ida might take the telephone number of Mary, a group member she liked and felt comfortable with, so that they could support each other and spend some time together socially. "That's all right," Ida said, refusing to take Mary's number. "I usually see her in the supermarket."

The clinician in this case had to accept that the client had done well to learn about addictions, change some enabling behaviors, and use those family members who were in recovery as her primary support system, while learning to set limits and assert herself to some extent with her demanding and manipulative mother and the adult children whose addictions were active.

The Tasks of Healing the Adult Child

For the adult child from an addicted family, the concept of the inner child who has been wounded and must be healed provides an effective way of working. This client has four long-term tasks. First, the cognitive task: she must understand the truth of what happened in her family of origin. Second, the dynamic task: she must identify, experience, and work through feelings of grief, pain, and anger that have long been repressed and thus have fueled acting out and self-destructive behaviors. Third, the behavioral task: she must develop new patterns of behavior that are not destructive or self-defeating. And fourth, the spiritual task: she must let go, lay the past to rest, and move forward in her life.

Treatment Resistances and Pitfalls

Both the controlling and nurturing aspects of women's efforts to connect can be interpreted as treatment resistance. The stereotypical wife, mother, or female partner of an addict presents as a controlling, manipulative martyr and victim who believes she is right, knows more than the addiction professionals, and demands that these professionals make the addict shape up and submit to her way of running things. In reality, this woman's need for control is a resistance and a defense against the terror of feeling completely out of control—consciously or unconsciously—in the face of the addiction. The presentation of certainty is a mask for confusion, waning confidence, and self-blame.

The woman who cites domestic duties and demanding family relationships as a reason for being unable to commit fully to treatment or self-help has traditionally been considered resistant. The relational model of women's psychology, while seeing women's capacity for connection and relationship as central to female identity and growth, makes a distinction between destructive relationships and those that are mutual and growth enhancing. Because earlier models of psychological development have tended to see connection as failure to separate—and by extension, failure to be like men in the capacity for independence and autonomy—women's attachments have traditionally been seen as weakness. In the light of the relational model, healthy attachments can be distinguished from destructive ones and a woman's capacity for nurture reframed as a strength (Zelvin, 1999).

In approaches that incorporate the twelve-step model, the concept of spiritual recovery is an important one. The client's resistance may take the form of rejection of "religion" or an inability to connect with spiritual ideas. If clinicians themselves are comfortable with spiritual ideas, they can demystify and reframe these ideas in such a way that the client can relate to them. Conversely, if the client is at home in a spiritual context, whatever form it takes, the therapist can support that as a strength that will make it easier for the client to embrace spiritual recovery—that is, replace negativity and despair with hope and a positive attitude that may well prove self-fulfilling.

Another resistance to recovery is what might be termed the feminist defense: a belief that admitting "powerlessness" over the addiction and making changes in oneself as a way of improving the situation are dangerous for women, who all too often blame themselves for the problems of others and experience themselves as helpless and dependent. The woman affected by addictions must be helped to see that, on the contrary, recovery means no longer expending energy on trying to control the uncontrollable and instead focusing on empowerment within herself and in her life. The paradoxical concept of spiritual powerlessness must be clarified with particular care for the woman who has experienced traumatic helplessness, such as violence and sexual abuse or exploitation. She must be empowered to take full control of the process of healing by choosing when and how she addresses her traumatic history at every stage of treatment.

Sharon

After two years in treatment, Sharon chose to tell her therapist her darkest secret: that she had been molested as a child by three alcoholic uncles, all now dead. The therapist suggested she might want to read *The Courage to Heal* (Bass & Davis, 1994) as a way of learning about other women who had been sexually abused and being told by an authoritative source that what had happened was not her fault. Sharon liked the book and reported that she was reading it a paragraph or two at a time as a way of handling the feelings that uncovering this material brought up. The therapist supported her approach and encouraged her to continue when she felt ready.

Countertransference Issues

The most common source of countertransference is the clinician's unresolved family-of-origin issues. Overresponsible caretakers and family heroes from alcoholic or addicted families are overrepresented in the helping professions. Depending on the family dynamics and how much work a clinician has done on herself, she may overidentify with the affected woman or project onto her client her negative feelings about the overresponsible, controlling caretaker—usually a woman—in her own family. If no work has been done, the clinician may be flooded with old feelings that she had successfully repressed, or she may remain in denial and express the negative countertransference in acting-out behavior. If the clinician is in personal recovery from addiction—and many counselors and other professionals in the chemical dependency field are—it may be difficult to empathize with the significant other who has been adversely affected, especially at the beginning of treatment, when the affected woman may express extreme rage and devastation over the addict's behavior.

For clinicians in private practice, countertransference feelings may arise over such issues as the client's remaining in treatment and her ability to pay the therapist. For clients who are economically dependent on their untreated alcoholic or addicted husbands, progress in treatment may mean leaving their marriage, resulting in financial insecurity and the loss of medical insurance. The client's inability to continue to pay for treatment can evoke the therapist's own abandonment issues and insecurities about failing to sustain the relationship. The therapist can also feel like a "bad mommy" for setting a financial condition on her love for the client, and for feeling angry about losing the revenue of the client's fee.

Conclusion

The range of women affected by addictions and the range of ways they are affected are far broader than generally acknowledged, from prostitutes with sexually abusive fathers and substance-abusing johns to high-achieving business and professional women whose grandfathers were compulsive gamblers or high-functioning alcoholics. Due to a number of factors—including the persistence of sexism in our culture, the high numbers of recovering addicts as helping professionals in the chemical dependency field, and the countertransference issues of clinicians who have not dealt with the addictions in their families of origin—clinicians frequently fail to perceive the woman affected by addictions as a primary person in need of help, apart from her value to her children and her relationship with the addict. The adverse impact of addictions may have begun early in life, when the young daughter of an addict took on a marital, parental, or caretaking role so that the family could function. In relation to a loved person whose addiction is progressing, the affected woman goes through a progression of involuntary and frequently denied changes in behavior and outlook for which "symptoms of the disease" is as good a metaphor as any. Women affected by addictions need to be studied more systematically and served more adequately. Frequently misunderstood and stereotyped, and using controlling and self-defeating behaviors to defend against feeling overwhelmed, helpless, confused, and desperate, women affected by the addictions of their loved ones need and deserve our skill, compassion, and support.

References

Abbott, A. A. (2000). *Alcohol, tobacco, and other drugs: Challenging myths, assessing theories, individualizing interventions.* Washington, DC: NASW Press.

Bartholomew, K. (1990). Avoidance of intimacy: An attachment perspective. *Journal of Social and Personal Relationships, 7,* 147–178.

Bass, E., & Davis, L. (1994). *The courage to heal: A guide for women survivors of child sexual abuse* (3rd ed.). New York: Harper Perennial Library.

Berman, L., & Siegel, M.-E. (1998). *Behind the 8-ball: A recovery guide for the families of gamblers* (Updated ed.). Lincoln, NE: toExcel.

Black, C. (1981). *It will never happen to me.* Denver, CO: MAC.

Brown, S., & Lewis, V. (1999). *The alcoholic family in recovery: A developmental model.* New York: Guilford Press.

Carnes, P. (1992). *Out of the shadows: Understanding sexual addiction* (2nd ed.). Center City, MN: Hazelden.

Feeney, J. A. (1999). Adult romantic relationships and couple relationships. In J. Cassidy & P. R. Shaver (Eds.), *Handbook of attachment: Theory, research, and clinical applications* (pp. 355–377). New York: Guilford Press.

Gilligan, C. (1982). *In a different voice: Psychological theory and women's development.* Cambridge, MA: Harvard University Press.

Glaus, K. O. (1988). Alcoholism, chemical dependency, and the lesbian client. *Women and Therapy, 8*(1/2), 131–144.

Jacobson, S. (2000, November 18). Men aren't immune to eating disorders: Midnight gorging, starving or working out excessively are signs of trouble. *Dallas Morning News.*

Kellermann, J. L. (1969). *Alcoholism: A merry-go-round named denial.* New York: Al-Anon World Service.

Kellermann, J. L. (1974, Fall). Focus on the family. *Alcohol Health and Research World,* pp. 9–11.

Kellogg, T. (1990). *Broken toys, broken dreams: Understanding and healing codependency, compulsive behaviors, and family.* Deerfield Beach, FL: Health Communications.

Miller, J. B. (1976). *Toward a new psychology of women.* Boston: Beacon Press.

National Institute on Alcohol Abuse and Alcoholism. (2000). ETOH database. Available: www.health.org.

Rabinor, J. R. (1994). Mothers, daughters, and eating disorders: Honoring the mother-daughter relationship. In P. Fallon, M. Katzman, & S. C. Wooley (Eds.), *Feminist perspectives on eating disorders* (pp. 272–297). New York: Guilford.

Spiegel, B. R., & Fewell, C. H. (in press). Twelve-step programs as a treatment modality. In S.L.A. Straussner (Ed.), *Clinical work with substance-abusing clients* (2nd ed.). New York: Guilford Press.

Substance Abuse and Mental Health Services Administration. (2000). *National Household Survey on Drug Abuse, 1998.* Available: www.health.org.

van Wormer, K., Wells, J., & Boes, M. (2000). *Social work with lesbians, gays, and bisexuals: A strengths perspective.* Boston: Allyn & Bacon.

Wegscheider, S. (1981). *Another chance: Hope and health for the alcoholic family.* Palo Alto, CA: Science and Behavior Books.

Zelvin, E. (1988). Dependence and denial in coalcoholic women. *Alcoholism Treatment Quarterly, 5*(3/4), 97–115.

Zelvin, E. (1997). Codependency issues of substance abusing women. In S.L.A. Straussner & E. Zelvin (Eds.), *Gender and addictions: Men and women in treatment* (pp. 47–69). Northvale, NJ: Aronson.

Zelvin, E. (1999). Applying relational theory to the treatment of women's addictions. *Affilia: Journal of Women in Social Work, 14*(1), 9–23.

Zelvin, E. (in press). Treating the partners of substance abusers. In S.L.A. Straussner (Ed.), *Clinical work with substance-abusing clients* (2nd ed.). New York: Guilford Press.

PART SIX

TREATMENT APPROACHES AND MODALITIES

CHAPTER TWENTY-THREE

GROUP TREATMENT OF SUBSTANCE-ABUSING WOMEN

Eileen P. Beyer and Karen Carnabucci

Group therapy has a long history as a treatment of choice for substance abuse and dependency. However, gender-specific issues in treating women in groups are rarely addressed in clinician training and supervision. This chapter provides a theoretical framework for the use of groups and discusses the application of group psychotherapy and structured groups for addicted women during different stages of recovery. It includes examples of both cognitive-behavioral and psychodrama groups during early and later recovery processes.

There is much controversy in the field regarding the increasing use of female-only groups and treatment programs instead of mixed-gender treatments, and there is minimal outcome research to support either one (Hodgins, El-Guebaly, & Addington, 1997). This chapter uses the relational model of women's development (Gilligan, 1982) as a basis to explore the benefits and rationale for women-only therapy groups. It also discusses the special issues of group leadership and the need for supervision of leaders of women's groups.

Usefulness of Group Treatment for Addiction

Group treatment is exceptionally versatile. Addiction treatment groups can be adapted to different populations at every stage of recovery and in a multitude of settings. A group experience may begin with the moment of the intervention, when family members and friends gather in a group to recommend treatment to an addicted person (Johnson, 1986), as eloquently described by Betty Ford in her story of recovery (Ford & Chase, 1987), and can continue over the years to meet the different needs of a woman during her recovery process. Groups can be found throughout the continuum of care: in detoxification settings, in primary inpatient treatment, in residential treatment and step-down settings such as halfway houses, in intensive outpatient programs, in couple and family treatment, and as part of relapse prevention and relapse treatment.

Groups can be used for therapeutic purposes to help people make fundamental changes in the way they think, feel, or behave; they also can be used for educational purposes, such as for teaching coping skills (Corey, 1995). These uses are particularly suited to the type of increased awareness and behavioral change necessary to obtain and maintain abstinence from addictive substances. In addition, there are many ways to work with recovering people in supplemental groups that are not actually therapy but provide the opportunity to address important therapeutic needs of individual clients. Adjunctive group activities may include educational lectures, recreational activities, trips to twelve-step meetings, family educational and intervention sessions, drumming circles, parenting classes, and mindfulness meditation groups, to name but a few.

Although there is no question that group treatment is the most preferred modality used in addiction treatment settings, empirical research supporting its effectiveness as the treatment of choice has been limited or equivocal (Flores, 1997). It has been demonstrated, however, that group therapy is at least as effective as individual therapy and has many advantages over individual therapy alone. Group members have the opportunity to benefit from the experiences, insights, and feedback of others. There is the opportunity for identification and validation from other group members that is often lacking in the more hierarchical relationship with an individual therapist, and groups provide social support to those who are isolated from meaningful relationships or are only superficially connected to others (Straussner, 1997). It is commonly believed that the group therapy setting serves as a microcosm of the participant's world, a sample of reality in which her struggles and conflicts are re-created.

Because internal and lifestyle changes are so urgently required to support abstinence, groups provide an especially important function in giving addicted women the opportunity to learn from others and to discuss and practice changes in how they react and respond. By its very nature, group treatment reduces the isolation that is inherent in the downward progression of addiction and helps address the participants' difficulties with connection and self-acceptance by allowing them to identify with others who have similar concerns. It gives recovering people the opportunity to repair their lives and self-concept by working through the guilt and shame that keeps them disconnected from themselves and others and can impair connection to treatment and motivation to change. Through their participation in groups, women can learn how to tolerate and address feelings and to communicate needs and boundaries in healthy ways.

Groups are also popular for their perceived cost-effectiveness. They are typically less expensive to provide and less costly to clients, and they allow for a broader distribution of available therapists. In the age of increasing managed care restrictions on the type and length of treatment, group treatment of addiction has remained the first line of intervention.

History of Group Treatment of Addiction

The physician J. L. Moreno was among the first to recognize the healing power of a group, including the self-help group, in which each person becomes the healing agent of the other without any special training or knowledge other than her own experience. About 1912, while walking the streets of Vienna as a young medical student, Moreno noticed police arresting prostitutes in the city's red-light district. He organized an informal group where the women could talk about their problems. They gradually shifted from talking about their problems with the police to more personal issues, providing emotional support to each other. Looking at the scenario with the eyes of today's clinician, we might imagine that those women may have been addicted, may have been survivors of abuse, and no doubt were also victims of male dominance and lack of financial resources.

This experience contributed to Moreno's preference for working in group rather than individually, which was the style set by Sigmund Freud. Moreno coined the term *group psychotherapy* in 1932 (Blatner, 2000) to recognize this particular form of treatment as he continued to develop psychodrama, a specific method for enacting problematic situations in a group setting. Moreno began working with alcoholics in group settings as early as 1944 (Fuhlrodt, 1990), which converged with the growth of Alcoholics Anonymous (AA). The first twelve-step group started in 1935 after its cofounder Bill Wilson was inspired to create a self-help and mutual-help movement by the earlier Oxford Group Movement, which emphasized self-examination and restitution for harm done (Alcoholics Anonymous, 1957). Treatment centers, many staffed by recovering alcoholics, became established; they adopted the so-called Minnesota model, which supplemented group therapy with twelve-step meetings.

AA, unlike the Oxford Groups, demonstrated the power of a group approach to arrest alcoholism, at a time when most physicians and hospitals had little success with analysis, hypnotism, sedatives, or moral lectures. Unlike the "therapeutic community" model, which was also developing in the nascent treatment of narcotics addiction, AA avoided a confrontational approach and instead emphasized the sharing of common experiences between alcoholics to another (Rogers & McMillin, 1989). It placed a premium on personal disclosure and emphasized the importance of the group as a whole rather than the single individual, who remained anonymous.

Twelve-step groups have continued to demonstrate their efficacy for treating addiction and have become the most recommended adjunct to professional treatment for people dependent on alcohol, drugs, nicotine, and other compulsive behaviors such as gambling, spending, binge eating and restricting, and use of pornography.

Types of Groups and Their Application to Addiction Treatment

According to Corey (1995), there are four different types of therapeutic groups: counseling groups, psychotherapy groups, structured groups, and self-help groups. Although this chapter will focus on the use of group psychotherapy and structured groups to treat addicted women, it is important to understand the distinctions between different types of groups.

Counseling groups have preventive and remedial aims. They focus on discovering internal sources of strength and operate with a specific focus: educational, vocational, social, or personal (Corey, 1995). Counseling groups are for basically well-functioning individuals whose concerns relate primarily to developmental tasks encountered during various stages of life. In contrast, the goals of group psychotherapy are "to correct emotional and behavior disorders that impede one's functioning" and to focus on "remediation, treatment and personality reconstruction" (Corey, 1995, p. 10). In general, psychotherapy groups tend to be more long term in nature than counseling groups.

Addiction treatment groups typically fall into the category of group psychotherapy because of the focus on corrective change in thinking, feeling, and behavior. A primary use of group psychotherapy has been to demonstrate, confront, and alter the addict's defense mechanisms and character dynamics that perpetuate addiction (Flores, 1997). However, typical early recovery groups focus on the present and emphasize behavioral change rather than the development of insight into internal processes. They also tend to be more time limited and more homogeneous in composition than psychotherapy groups.

Group psychotherapy is most often used in the middle and later stages of addiction recovery and is more interactive and dynamic in nature than the more structured groups that are often employed with persons in early recovery. The theoretical foundation of group psychotherapy with addicted populations can have a psycho-dynamic, interpersonal, relational, Gestalt, psychodrama, person-centered, cognitive-behavioral, rational-emotive, or eclectic orientation.

Structured groups focus on a particular theme or population and are typically short term and goal oriented. Information and common experiences are shared in a manner that teaches skills, offers support, and facilitates development of support systems outside the group setting. Many structured groups are based on the learning theory model, which stresses behavioral change through structured exercises and homework assignments. Intensive outpatient groups, which run up to two months, as well as residential groups in a traditional twenty-eight-day rehab or extended care program, often fit this model. These groups usually focus on having the patients share material from assignments given to them by their individual counselors or case managers. Typical assignments may include sharing the consequences of their alcohol and drug abuse, in an effort to promote understanding of the concept of powerlessness (step one of the twelve steps), or identifying their individual relapse triggers so that they can be better prepared to deal with their environment outside of treatment.

The overwhelming acceptance of the disease concept of addiction and need for total abstinence, which has always been promoted by Alcoholics Anonymous, has changed the very philosophy of group psychotherapy for this population. Originally, addictive use of substances was seen as a symptom of intrapsychic conflict and interpersonal dynamics that needed to be brought to conscious awareness and addressed. An addictive personality structure was to blame. Now, addiction is widely viewed as a primary, chronic, and progressive disease, which results in biological, psychological, and social symptoms. If the progression of the disease is arrested through complete abstinence, then the associated biopsychosocial problems often disappear or dramatically improve. Even if coexisting psychological problems exist, abstinence makes their treatment more effective. Therefore, group psychotherapy with addicted persons is less concerned with the detailed analysis of how past experiences influence present behavior, and more concerned with understanding and modifying the present attitudes, moods, and actions that affect the person's ability to remain abstinent and develop and maintain a fulfilling lifestyle in recovery.

Flores (1997) explains the widely held position that group psychotherapy is not intended to be used as a substitute for the abstinence-promoting and social supportive functions of twelve-step recovery groups, which are viewed as being much more effective in achieving these goals. He insists that "group psychotherapy by itself will not keep an alcoholic sober or an addict clean" (p. 43). Group psychotherapy does, however, "offer the recovering person an understanding of the interpersonal and intrapersonal conflicts that interfere with compliance and acceptance of the program as well as the forces that can lead to relapse" (p. 43). In this way, it can speed up and reinforce the twelve-step recovery process.

Usefulness of Group to Meet Women's Relational Needs

The use of specialized group therapy with women is supported by relational (or self-in-relation) theory, which has been identified in recent years as important in regard to the addiction treatment of women (Byington, 1997; Covington, 1999; Covington & Surrey, 1998). Relational theory states that all people have a need for connection with others and that, especially for females, sense of self is grounded in the context of the quality of their relationships. According to Peck (1986, as cited in McManus, Redford, & Hughes, 1997), a woman's self-definition is dependent on the quality and extent of her relationships as well as the era in which she lives. Women's relationship focus and need for connection are viewed as strengths (Jordon, 1994; Miller, 1976) rather than as signs of weakness, lack of self-definition, or dependency. The primary task of healthy psychological and social development for females is to learn to balance their care for others with care for their own needs, to find a way to individuate while remaining connected (Gilligan, 1982, 1990). Relationships are both a source and the goal of development.

Addiction is marked by severe social isolation; the addictive substance or activity becomes the person's primary companion, while human relationships, work, and other personal responsibilities become secondary. Consequently, individual therapy alone may perpetuate isolation, especially for high-functioning women seeking treatment for anxiety or depression (Spiegel & Friedman, 1997). McManus et al. (1997, p. 23) suggest that "group settings might be ideal forums in which to nurture change because each woman can grow in relationship with others" through mutually enhancing exchanges that help them reconnect with their sense of self apart from their primary relationships.

A relational approach to group therapy promotes connections among members that heal emotional wounds and foster psychological growth. Group interactions foster connection or disconnection. The clinician can choose to interpret or process these interactions in group. From a relational perspective, certain healing factors have been identified as essential elements of connection in women's therapy groups: validation, empowerment, self-empathy, and mutuality (Fedele & Harrington, 1990). The group validates women's perceptions, desires, and emotional experiences, especially women's needs for intimacy and connection. Members experience an "empowering connectedness" as they "take in the relational energy, power, and effectiveness of the group" (Fedele & Harrington, 1990, p. 4) as well as recognize their ability to positively affect other members. Self-empathy develops as a woman becomes more connected to her own affect and demonstrates increasing acceptance of herself with less punitive self-images. Self-empathy is fostered through a woman's experience of "emotional resonance with another person's empathy for her" (p. 5) in the group. "Mutuality involves . . . respect for the other person's differentness and uniqueness[,]. . . values enhancement of the other's growth and, most importantly, leaves all participants open to change" (p. 5). Women's groups provide the safe haven to "share and validate memories of painful, nonmutual experiences" and, over time, to "clear away the scar tissue that formed as a consequence of disconnection" (p. 6).

The essential difference between a relational and an interpersonal approach to group is that whereas the goal of the relational approach is remission of "symptoms through movement toward mutually empathic and empowering relationships with others inside and outside the group" (Tantillo, 2000, p. 103), an interpersonal approach focuses on "self-awareness of one's strengths, vulnerabilities, . . . and maladaptive behaviors that produce unwanted responses from others" (p. 103).

McManus, Redford, and Hughes (1997) provide an example of a short-term, structured group format that utilizes the relational model and can be interwoven with traditional addiction treatment topics in early recovery groups for women. The primary goals of their groups were to increase self-esteem and improve relationship skills in an atmosphere that promoted safety and support. These goals were accomplished through six sessions that focused on the following topics: understanding gender role socialization, increasing self-awareness and self-understanding, increasing self-care, understanding healthy relationships, improving communication skills, and integrating skills and applying them in the future. Women participants reported that the groups "helped them to learn to better value and respect themselves" and become "more aware of their strengths" as well as "the importance of self-care" (p. 29). The authors suggested that this type of group may be effective as "an initial group experience for women who are feeling very tentative about participating in a process group" (p. 29). These topics could also be incorporated into the beginning phase of a long-term group for women who have been in mixed-gender treatment in early recovery.

According to McManus et al. (1997), based on the work of Burden and Gottlieb (1987), the following socialized behaviors affect women's interactions in groups:

A woman may forfeit opportunities to meet her own needs by focusing on winning the approval of other group members through "people-pleasing" behaviors.

Through lack of socialization or practice, a woman may be unable to identify her own needs.

A woman may become entrenched in a caretaker role, rescuing other group members and denying them the opportunity to struggle on their own for answers.

Because of personal experience or sex-role stereotypes she may hold, a woman may enter group with a mind-set that devalues the experience or openness of other women.

Because she has discounted her own competencies, a woman may minimize or devalue her ability to contribute to the group.

The way in which these self-defeating behaviors are processed in the group can have a significant impact on a woman's self-esteem and motivation. From the standpoint of the relational model, these behaviors may have served a woman in adaptive ways, as means of maintaining a sense of connection in relationships with persons who did not provide mutual empathy, validation, and empowerment. Thus, rather than just labeling these behaviors as codependency, which may feel pathologizing to the woman, a group therapist using the relational model would empathically explore the antecedents of these behaviors and emphasize how their past adaptive functions now need to be replaced with behaviors that are more effective given the woman's current circumstances and goals.

Tasks of Group According to Stage of Recovery

Just as addiction is recognized as a progressive disease, with specific markers identifying its progression, treatment also needs to be progressive. Recovering women have different treatment needs at different points in their process of change from active addiction into established recovery. The developmental model of addiction and recovery (Brown, 1985) emphasizes the importance of a treatment focus that is stage-specific. In early recovery, the focus is on building the basic foundations of abstinence and providing external supports (Straussner, 1997). In ongoing recovery, the focus shifts to other issues, such as dealing with unhealthy relationships or resolving the effects of past relationship disconnection or trauma (Brown, Lewis, & Liotta, 2000).

In addition to targeting group content and process to stage of recovery, it is also crucial to address issues in ways that are gender specific (Covington & Surrey, 1998). Groups need to be tailored to be sensitive to women's issues in recovery with an interactive process that is most effective in reaching women. The following sections on early and late recovery groups elucidate both stage-specific and gender-specific themes and processes.

Early Recovery Groups

Early phase treatment groups are generally short-term and focused on specific tasks. Treatment typically begins by focusing on the acceptance of addiction and on making a commitment to address it with a plan of care that includes physical, psychological, emotional, relational, and spiritual repair.

It is important to recognize that during the early phase of recovery, substance abusers have some degree of temporary cognitive impairment due to their withdrawal from mind-altering chemicals, which limits the psychological change possible from insight-oriented psychotherapy (Straussner, 1997). Individuals in early recovery are typically anxious, moody, and impulsive; they need support and structure in the group setting in order to settle into the experience and become functional group members. The task focus is on identification of addiction as a primary issue, attaining and maintaining abstinence, and working through resistance to developing external supports.

The group process in early recovery focuses on developing group cohesion through participants' identification with their shared disease and on establishing trust in the group leader and each other. These goals are best accomplished in a homogenous group composed of people in their first few months of sobriety. Individuals who relapse after a period of prior abstinence may benefit from a separate group that addresses the shame and frustration that often accompanies relapse. General themes in early recovery groups include the following:

- Sharing individual accounts of the progression of addiction and identifying shared experiences
- Understanding the relationship between substance abuse and resultant negative consequences
- Exploring how substance use served certain functions, such as self-medication, comfort, escape, and social inclusion, and grieving these lost ways of coping
- Experimenting with new ways of coping and relating within the group and in family and social situations
- Challenging the social isolation, limiting belief patterns, and dysfunctional thinking that maintain addictive patterns of behavior
- Understanding relapse triggers and experimenting with avoidance or with better ways of managing them

Female-specific group themes in early recovery groups include the following:

- Discussing the heightened stigma that addicted women face and how this can negatively affect self-concept, motivation for change, and ability to access and create supportive relationships
- Exploring the external context to help women understand how coexisting issues (for example trauma, sex-role stereotypes, economic dependency, religious values, dependence on the medical model of medication of symptoms) may have fostered or perpetuated her substance abuse
- Exploring how the relationship with the substance became an all-encompassing dependency that betrayed a woman's initial expectations and damaged her identity and relationships with others
- Exploring issues of balancing self-care and the care of others while maintaining essential lifestyle changes in order to sustain recovery
- Discussing how to proactively communicate needs and set boundaries in primary relationships and how to recognize situations, such as domestic violence, in which it may be too dangerous to do so

The group leader gives guidance, focuses on sharing, and models and reinforces appropriate ways to give feedback. The leader creates a supportive holding environment that provides consistent and predictable structure. Such a holding environment is helpful in breaking denial and reducing isolation; as group members begin to experience connection with others, they feel less alone and, often for the first time, are able to openly discuss their experiences with addictive behavior and to share their shameful secrets.

Most addicts in their first months of recovery tend to vacillate between denying and minimizing issues and trying to do too much too soon in an effort to feel fixed or cured. Moreover, women with significant interpersonal trauma or coexisting mental illness often sense strong differences between themselves and the other members of the group. This feeling of differentness can produce isolation and compound the problems of trust. These women may find it hard to trust that they will be received empathically if they begin to share their life stories. The converse is also common. Traumatized women who have not developed a cohesive sense of self and boundaries may want to express their pain at the earliest opportunity, before sufficient relational experience and trust have been developed within the group. Consequently, group members may not know how best to support the woman. Conversely, this woman may interpret group members' ambivalence about how to respond as a lack of empathy, and as a result may feel alienated. On the other hand, if the group expresses feedback that is validating, the woman may mistakenly believe that the hard work is over, that she has successfully purged herself of her pain, and that the empathy she received will be sufficient to repair prior empathic failures. It is therefore very important to socialize female patients with trauma histories, eating disorders, such medical conditions as HIV-AIDS, and other significant coexisting issues to carefully consider what is best for them to share, when, and with whom. There needs to be greater emphasis on empowering women to become aware of and honor their intuition about when they are ready to deal with certain material and in what setting. This empowerment is best worked on in individual therapy that complements the woman's group experience, but it can also be part of the process of establishing group norms.

An excellent example of structured groups for women in early recovery is described in Covington's *Helping Women Recover: A Program for Treating Addiction* (1999). It provides material and handouts for seventeen psychoeducational and discussion-oriented group sessions within four topic modules: self, relationships, sexuality, and spirituality. (See Chapter Three for more detail.)

Later Recovery Groups

Once women's abstinence is secure and they are consistently demonstrating their use of coping skills, the focus of group may be shifted to the here-and-now model of interaction (Yalom, 1985). As Yalom has indicated, therapy groups in many ways represent families, with leaders taking the role of the parents and group members taking roles of siblings. Group can provide a reparative family experience (Vannicelli, 1992) as members unconsciously and consciously work through patterns of behaviors and beliefs that may have originated in their families. Processing relationships from both a here-and-now and a transference perspective can give group members immediate feedback about their patterns of interaction.

This interpersonal-psychodynamic model or use of more sophisticated psychodramatic or experiential techniques can be very useful in open-ended, long-term groups where a multitude of concerns may emerge with women in later stages of recovery. General themes in later recovery groups include the following:

- Continuing discussion of what it means to remain aware of and manage the limitation of addiction while transforming the self and one's relations with others
- Delving into painful feelings from childhood or adult traumas to find resolution and healing
- Exploring family-of-origin conflicts and roles and their representations in behavioral and thinking patterns in the present
- Exploring how interactions with other group members can be used to understand relational patterns and to experiment with new ways of relating

- Translating what is learned in the group to the outside by establishing healthy relationship patterns with partners, children, and other people

Female-specific themes in later recovery groups include the following:

- Exploring continued difficulties in trying to balance self-care and the care of others
- Exploring issues of identity and how it has been, and continues to be, affected by culture, socialization, and family models
- Sharing discovery of new ways of caring for one's body, mind, and spirit, and new ways of relating to others
- Sharing the process of transformation from victim to survivor

Therapy groups for women in later recovery continue to offer a holding environment for ongoing exploration of both painful and pleasurable feelings. The therapist assumes the role of a guide in the exploration, reassuring the woman that her painful feelings can be a sign that she is improving her ability to feel deeply and humanly. The therapist also needs to be alert to any signs of compulsivity (in relationships, sex, or work, for example) that may arise to compensate for the loss of the earlier addictive behavior. As group members begin to demonstrate healthier communication skills, the therapist needs to become less directive. Short-term groups for specific needs, such as parenting skills, couples issues, or meditation (Morell, 1997), may be offered during this later stage of the recovery process.

Gender-Specific and Gender-Separate Groups

The literature suggests a growing trend toward single-sex groups, especially in primary residential treatment, as researchers and clinicians describe differences in male and female behavior and communication (Hodgins et al., 1997). These groups may be *gender-specific* (relating to process and content and addressing coexisting concerns such as eating disorders or sexual abuse). Gender-separate groups may not be gender-specific if the philosophy of care does not distinguish women from men and if the foremost purpose of gender separation is to reduce fraternization.

In traditional addiction treatment settings, "women's voices are often unheard, and their concerns are seldom reflected" because "men's language and interaction patterns usually dominate" (Kauffman, Dore, & Nelson-Zlupko, 1995, p. 358). Kauffman et al. also note that men tend to dominate discussion and time in mixed-group settings, and women may fall into caretaking patterns when men are emotionally distant or emotionally overwhelmed.

Research by Aries (1976) on communication patterns in single- and mixed-gender student groups revealed that in mixed-gender groups, males tended to ask more questions to get information, talked more, controlled the topic more, talked more to the group as a whole (an indication of power), and interrupted more than the females. Overall, males acted more dominant in mixed-gender groups. Females talked more often to males, asked more questions to initiate and encourage conversation, picked up on topics introduced by males, worked at maintaining conversation, provided greater self-disclosure and empathic responses, and made more head nods and eye contact (which denotes interest and receptivity). Aries concluded that mixed-gender groups were of greater benefit to males than females because they allowed men to have more variation in interpersonal style, whereas females demonstrated a more restrictive interpersonal style.

Hodgins et al. (1997) also speculated that there would be a greater focus on emotional and interpersonal issues in female-only groups, whereas male-only groups would have a greater task focus on issues related to substance abuse. Although little research has been conducted on communication and content differences in addiction treatment groups to substantiate these theoretical differences, it is notable that female-only groups are often advocated by addictions therapists, whereas male-only groups typically are not (Hodgins et al., 1997). Hodgins et al. concluded that for women, single-gender groups would "lead to greater engagement, retention and self-disclosure than mixed groups" (p. 810) but that mixed groups would more likely be associated with these benefits for men.

Hodgins et al. (1997) noted that addiction treatment programs "tend to be male dominated both in numbers and style" (p. 810). Kanter (1980) developed a framework for conceptualizing the processes that occur between "dominants" (males) and "tokens" (females) in a variety of group settings. Her review of the literature suggested that in groups in which females were in a token status, the females were more highly visible—which generated more performance pressure—and differences between males and females were exaggerated. Females' attributes were distorted to fit preexisting sex-role stereotypes, and this distortion created role entrapment. It follows that gender composition is an important determinant of interaction patterns in addiction treatment groups and that greater attention should be paid to how cases are assigned to mixed-gender groups to minimize these effects by having more balanced numbers of males and females.

Kauffman et al. (1995) found that women reported greater safety and comfort in single-gender groups, especially in discussing matters of interpersonal relationships, sexual trauma and objectification, motherhood, and life stress. This preference to disclose issues in single-gender groups was first noted by Reed (1985, as cited in Hodgins et al., 1997). Reed also reported that recovering women demonstrated a wider range of behaviors and skills in women-only groups. Because shame and guilt are heightened concerns for women addicts (Gomberg, 1988), privacy and safety are very important in giving women a safe place to discuss and work through these issues.

It is commonly reported that women feel less focused on physical appearance—as well as less sexually objectified—in women's groups. Sexual advances and harassment by men in mixed-gender treatment settings are all too common and can be retraumatizing to addicted women who are likely to have been using chemicals to numb the effects of prior experiences of sexual exploitation and abuse. It also negates their nascent sense of self that is developing in recovery, and their ability to see and value themselves as individuals apart from their sexuality, which is frequently used or exploited in service of the addiction. Men are often distracted or aroused by hearing sexual abuse details from women and are not always able to offer specific needed support. Therefore, "women-only therapy groups provide a safe forum for participants to express anger and frustration about the abusive and harassing behavior to which they were frequently subjected" (Kauffman et al., 1995, p. 360).

The typical argument in favor of mixed-gender treatment in early recovery is that the group is a microcosm of the real world in which females have to learn how to have appropriate boundaries and be assertive in order to negotiate for their needs and to protect themselves. Being in group with men may provide opportunities to have positive interactions with men, perhaps for the first time. However, for the same reasons that inpatient treatment is advocated for those who need some distance from their lifestyle in order to become stable in recovery, it can also be argued that the safety and support of women-only groups are most essential in this early stage of connection to treatment and commitment to recovery.

One negative product of women-only groups that is drawing concern (noted in anecdotal reports to the authors) is escalation of eating-disordered behaviors in groups of women where one or several of the women are diagnosed with an eating disorder, such as anorexia or bulimia. If the eating-disordered patient is dominant or the most popular in the group, then the likelihood of behavioral imitation is increased.

Recovering women often express ambivalence about being in women-only groups because of their past experiences in female relationships or their preconceived notions of what an all-female group or community would be like. Our culture teaches women to value more highly their connection to males because of men's power and hence to devalue female relationships. This tendency may be especially strong for women whose mothers were distant, unprotective, and passive, or controlling and abusive, as well as for those women who had competitive, disappointing relationships with sisters and friends. The intensity of competition and conflict that can emerge in all female groups and therapeutic communities may make it difficult for women with these trust issues to feel safe enough to connect to treatment and focus enough on themselves to become grounded in their sobriety.

Group exchange with other women creates the opportunity for women to work through their issues with women and begin to value their connection to them, which in turn fosters greater understanding and compassion for themselves as women. For the first time, women may experience genuine caring and supportive exchange with other women in an atmosphere that promotes trust and models commitment to working through relationship difficulties with other females. In addition to receiving support and nurture, women are exposed to other women who are "models of power and independent action" (Kauffman et al., 1995, p. 361). Women have the opportunity to be with women who are appropriately responsive and thus may experience healthy reparenting by the group.

Perhaps the biggest justification for women-only groups is that they allow women to focus on their unique experiences as women, such as how shame kept them trapped in addiction, and on their struggles with balancing care of self and others in recovery. They can voice these concerns in a setting that is the most validating. The commonality of experience in women-only groups provides the opportunity to clarify and strengthen the ability to "consolidate ideas, feelings, experiences, and sense of self" (Fedele & Harrington, 1990, p. 3) during critical periods of their development, such as when they are initiating recovery, recuperating from relapse, or facing major life stressors in recovery.

Styles of Group Leadership

The type of group will influence the style of the leadership of the group. Although the therapist's task is always to create and maintain a climate of trust and respect within the group setting, the group leader may be quite active and directive in change-oriented groups, keeping the group on task and gently but effectively confronting group members about their behavior patterns. In more process-oriented groups, the leader may be less directive, allowing group process to flow and giving group members greater responsibility and latitude to bring up issues and topics. The therapist must choose whether a directed, highly structured group or an open, process-oriented group would best serve the needs of the participants (Flores, 1997). Interventions should promote exploration of self, the uncovering of deeply embedded characterological patterns, the loosening of defenses, and the expressing of long-held thoughts and emotions—yet must also be weighed against the need for maintaining emotional safety and homeostasis in order to provide a strong foundation for sobriety.

Leaders serve as role models for women who are struggling to learn how to live without dependence on addictive behaviors and who may not have enjoyed positive relationships with their own mothers or fathers. Leaders are challenged to model resolve, warmth, self-protection, empathy, and a healthy sense of sexuality (Spiegel & Friedman, 1997), as well as to exemplify communication and behavior that are firm without being defensive, demonstrating both flexibility and appropriate limits.

Lovern (1991) recommends that the therapist set up a process of interaction among group members rather than do individual therapy with each patient in front of the group, which is an inefficient use of group therapy and allows for the defense of avoidance to solidify. Like other clinicians, Lovern also suggests that group leaders become alert to unhealthy processes, including the common tendency to rescue or "fix" others in group, especially when painful feelings emerge, and to project family roles on to group members. Through the leader's properly identifying projections and encouraging group members to give direct feedback, speak directly about conflicts, and accompany each other through the pain, the group itself becomes the instrument of healing.

If there is a coleader or a team approach, it is helpful that all leaders use a similar model of therapy and are able to display collaborative relationships that show both cooperation and positive conflict resolution. Coleadership, which is recommended whenever possible (Yalom, 1985), can model examples of healthy decision making, cooperation, and mutual respect even when differences are present. If there are male and female coleaders, it is important to be aware of members' proclivity to respond to the leaders in a sex-role stereotyped fashion. For instance, it has been noted by Butler and Geis (1990, as cited in Hodgins et al., 1997) that "male group leaders receive greater positive responses for their suggestions from group participants than female leaders" (p. 809). This suggests that group members' behaviors are likely to reflect societal mores, which value male input over female. This dynamic must be openly addressed by the group leaders during the group.

It is also the responsibility of the leaders to clearly explain group norms (Vannicelli, 1992) that include guidelines relating to payment, group attendance, and safety (Straussner, 1997). There should be a clear expectation of abstinence and discussion of the difficulties in working toward or maintaining this goal. Highly important is the issue of confidentiality (Straussner, 1997), as many women have engaged in embarrassing and illegal behaviors, such as prostitution, exotic dancing, mistreatment and neglect of children, and drug dealing. The therapist must reassure group members that revelations of past illegal and embarrassing behaviors, as well as current uncomfortable feelings and thoughts, must be kept within the group setting and that any breach of confidentiality will be immediately addressed.

According to McManus et al. (1997), it is important for women leaders to model competency, capacity for egalitarian relationships, openness to change, acceptance of differences, and trust and hope. The prime way to effectively model these concepts and foster the process of reconnection is to develop a here-and-now relationship with group members that is authentic as well as mutually validating and empowering. Well-timed and thoughtful self-disclosure increases the therapist's vulnerability, transparency, and availability, which decreases the inherent power differential in the therapeutic relationship—a crucial issue for substance-abusing women, who often are struggling to overcome the disempowering effects of subordination and traumatic disconnections. If left unaddressed, this power differential may cause female clients to suppress their own experience of power out of deference and hence impair the process of their own empowerment (Fedele & Harrington, 1990). The leader's task is to emphasize "power inside or between members, not power over members" (Tantillo, 2000, p. 105).

The group leader must analyze group members' behaviors, noting each woman's stage in her process of individual change and development of coping skills, as well as determining which defensive and interactional patterns are prominent. The group leader also remains mindful of the stage of development of the group itself: initial, transitional, working through, and final or termination (Corey, 1995). The leader works to strike the delicate balance between a focus on expression of affect and an emphasis on cognition to foster and strengthen new learning.

Parallel Process of Supervision of Women's Therapy Groups

It has been the authors' experience that providing group supervision to female group therapists of all-women groups provides fascinating and useful insights into the gender-specific parallel processes that are likely to occur. There often is a parallel interactive process that occurs between group members and leaders and the clinician-supervisor relationship. The therapy group is a microcosm of the therapeutic community as well as the staff community. A supervision group can be used as a vehicle for staff to increase awareness of parallel process issues, resolve issues among themselves, and discuss ways to intervene in patient therapy groups.

It has also been our experience that in all-female addiction treatment settings, the relationship dynamics on all levels are more intense than in mixed-gender groups. Women expect more empathy, responsiveness, and mutuality from each other than they do from men. Relational disconnections and conflicts often take on greater significance than they would in a mixed community, and they take longer to heal. The heightened expectations of patients and staff contribute to a climate of affective lability in which the community can be exuberant in connection one hour and feel unsafe and broken the next. Therefore, regularly scheduled supervision provides an essential element of emotional outlet for staff and a place to evaluate the therapeutic processes and discuss appropriate stabilization strategies for the community. Using a feminist perspective of supervision, the supervisor acknowledges the impact of the power differential in her relationship and endeavors through self-disclosure and empathic, empowering responses to foster connection with her supervisees, thus modeling the strategies of connection to use with patients as well as with members of the therapy team.

Models of Group Treatment

Just as there are many uses of group in the different stages of recovery, there are different group therapy models. Understanding the theoretical differences between types of groups allows a therapist to best match the type of group to the patient's stage of recovery, given the patient's mental status, style of relating, and recovery experience, and the availability of group modalities. Vannicelli (1992) contrasts what she calls the *stage-of-recovery model* with the *mixed-recovery long-term model,* in which patients join the group generally in the early phases of recovery and attend as long as it is a productive, therapeutic experience for them. She believes that the mixed-length-of-recovery group has appeal because psychological distance from the consequences of substance abuse waxes and wanes over time, and hearing about the experiences of those with differing amounts of sober time can help foster hope. A stage-of-recovery model can best address the issues surrounding addicted women having much higher rates of sexual and physical abuse compared to the general population (Covington, 1999). It is important to integrate what is known about group treatment for the various stages of healing of trauma (Herman, 1992) with standard group models of addiction treatment for women (Covington, 1999).

Although there are, as already noted, many ways to treat women in various types and stages of group, two main approaches are talk therapy, which includes the use of cognitive-behavioral techniques, and experiential groups, exemplified by use of psychodrama or psychodramatic techniques. The use of these two approaches is discussed and illustrated in the next sections.

Cognitive Group Approach

A cognitive therapy approach emphasizes how thinking patterns influence feelings and behaviors. It is highly recommended as a method to foster recovery and prevent relapse in substance abusers (Beck, Wright, Newman, & Liese, 1993). It has been our experience that women are often flooded with feelings and thoughts that make it difficult for them to develop an awareness of thinking patterns that may be self-defeating. In the following example, a cognitive exercise is done in a group to combat self-doubt and self-criticism and to integrate strengths that can serve as resources to motivate continued growth in recovery.

Avis

In this early-stage treatment group for women, participants are slowly beginning to recognize their powerlessness in relation to their drug of choice. The group leader has noticed an emerging theme of low self-esteem among the group members and has planned for a structured session to address these issues using a cognitive-behavioral approach.

The leader takes stiff colored cardboard and writes words in a bold marker that represent individual strengths, such as *courage, honesty,* and *willing to struggle,* on each card. The cardboard signs are then taped on the wall around the room so that they are easily seen.

As group members arrive for the session, the leader is there to greet them. She warms up the group by talking briefly about how addiction overwhelms the individual's sense of goodness, and then asks the group members to close their eyes for a moment to remember a quality that they are proud of within themselves. The participants are then given an opportunity to move around the room and pick the sign that represents the personal quality they like about themselves.

After selecting a sign, each woman returns to her seat and shares with her group the quality that she has chosen for herself. If time permits, other members may share ways they have seen that quality demonstrated by that group member. A second round of sharing may address how each woman can use this strength to reinforce her recovery, as exemplified by Avis, who says, "It's not easy being in recovery, but my willingness to stay in the struggle will help me keep going to meetings even when I'm feeling discouraged."

Sometimes esteem is so depleted that participants may have an especially difficult time claiming their own strengths. In this case, a leader may change the plan to have the member select a sign to give to someone else. The giving (and verbal sharing) may be done in dyads, and this process may be repeated so that women are able to share with several other women or with the group as a whole. As the group concludes, the leader may give an assignment for each woman to keep track of how she uses this strength in daily life and to report back to group at next meeting. Members also may select a less familiar strength that they want to have in their lives and practice using that quality in the interim before the next group.

Psychodrama Group Approach

Psychodrama is an action method that is the root of experiential modalities, which also include a variety of other approaches, such as creative arts therapies (Waller

& Mahony, 1999), work with horses (Loggins, 1998), use of outdoor challenge course groups, mindfulness meditation (Morell, 1997), and the use of rituals and rites of passage.

Psychodrama is a method of role identification and role playing that can be integrated into most forms of group work (Corey, 1995). Blatner (2000) describes a broad range of psychodrama styles used in the addiction field. Some groups focus on discussion and engage in intermittent enactments to address personal issues or work through relationships in the group. In others, the group is primarily a succession of protagonist-centered dramas; group issues are addressed before or after enactments.

What is common to the practice of psychodrama, however, is the concept of a three-phase process within each session: warm-up, action, and sharing. Warm-up can refer to any number of introductory exercises that "warm up" the group to action around a central concern. These introductory exercises may be a simple role play or telling of a vignette. When the drama is concluded, group member sharing takes place, which is the "group psychotherapy" part of the session that allows the participants to connect through mutual experience. The following is an example of a drama that addresses early-stage addiction-related issues.

Josie

Josie, a twenty-year-old woman with a history of marijuana use dating from her early teens and who was using alcohol with increasing frequency, had been referred to a treatment center. With the help of group members, she was beginning to accept not only her problems with substance abuse but also unusual dependence on a drug-addicted boyfriend who attempted to control her use. Cognitively she was able to accept that sobriety would entail the loss of her longest relationship—the one with marijuana—which even preceded the boyfriend. In a psychodrama group session, she was given an opportunity to warm up by verbally identifying three objects that represented this long-term relationship. She recalled a glass bong, a small pipe, and a jar that had held her marijuana.

As the session moved toward action, Josie reversed roles with each of these objects, speaking in first person of its history and importance to her. Returning to her own role in the present day, she was given an opportunity to converse directly with each object, played by an auxiliary, and recall its importance and say farewell to each.

With the therapist acting as her double, or inner voice, suggesting that this relationship was a strong bond—"I have loved you. You've been like my lover!"—Josie readily agreed with a knowing laugh and was able to own that statement verbally.

At the conclusion of the drama, she was directed to create a ritual to destroy these items upon return home.

Psychodrama also can be used effectively to address later-stage addiction-related issues, as exemplified in the case of Laura, who identifies herself as a recovering alcoholic and overeater pursing additional growth. She is an active member in Alcoholics Anonymous and Overeaters Anonymous.

Laura

In this psychodrama group therapy session co-led by male and female therapists, the topic is step one of the twelve steps: "We admitted we were powerless over alcohol and our lives were unmanageable." For the warm-up, the leaders passed around the *Big Book,* asking participants to read from the chapter "How It Works."

To warm up further, participants were asked to close their eyes and think of a time in their lives when they felt out of control due to a particular behavior. They were directed to reverse roles with that earlier self and mingle with the group members, speaking and acting from that perspective.

Then the group was asked to return to the present and reflect in small subgroups on how that experience felt. Each small group picked one member who was "warmed up" and willing to share her story with the larger group. The selected woman told a synopsis of the story that she wished to dramatize in front of the group.

Laura, who tearfully talked about the death of her mother, was selected as protagonist by the large group. She told the group that a few years before, she was newly sober and responsible for caring for her dying mother while her father and siblings drank heavily, making themselves unavailable for help or support.

With the help of group members playing roles, the director first placed Laura's dying mother on the stage area. Then her father and each of her six siblings were introduced, with Laura briefly taking the role of each to demonstrate the essence of each one's attitude: "I don't have time for this," "You're doing such a great job taking care of her," "It's too painful for me to cope with," and so on.

In her own role, Laura surveyed this landscape of unavailable family members. The director gave her the opportunity to verbally express her anger and then her loneliness in the caregiving role. As the director observed Laura facing each family member, she continually asked if Laura was powerless or powerful over others' addictions. Laura was able to clearly state that she was not able to control their drinking and recognized what she had already learned in earlier treatment about her own powerlessness with alcohol, her grief at the loss of connections, as well as her responsibility for her continued recovery.

After the drama concluded, group members were asked to share about their own experiences that paralleled what they had observed in the drama.

Conclusion

Group psychotherapy has long been regarded as the therapy of choice in addiction treatment. Modern clinicians are continuing to explore the best way to deliver group treatment to recovering women, with increased interest in treatment that is sensitive to women, that more fully addresses and appreciates women's needs, attitudes, and ways of relating. At the same time, more attention is being given to the developmental model of addiction and recovery, which goes beyond looking at abstinence as the single goal of treatment.

Although there are many approaches to conducting group, and many styles of doing so, it is important that therapists be fully trained to respond not only to the addiction component of treatment but also to the complex themes of relationship that emerge in a group setting. Women's relationship focus needs to be validated and utilized to foster growth. The philosophy of care that underlies any group addiction treatment should acknowledge the unique aspects of women's addiction and recovery as well as validate women's emotional and relational strengths.

References

Alcoholics Anonymous. (1957). *Alcoholics Anonymous comes of age.* New York: Alcoholics Anonymous World Services.

Aries, E. (1976). Interaction patterns and themes of male, female, and mixed groups. *Small Group Behavior, 7,* 7–18.

Beck, A., Wright, F., Newman, C., & Liese, B. (1993). *Cognitive therapy of substance abuse.* New York: Guilford.

Blatner, A. (2000). *Foundations of psychodrama* (4th ed.). New York: Springer.

Brown, S. (1985). *Treating the alcoholic: A developmental model of recovery.* New York: Wiley.

Brown, S., Lewis, V., & Liotta, A. (2000). *The family guide to recovery: A map for healthy growth.* Oakland, CA: New Harbinger Publications.

Burden, D. S., & Gottlieb, N. (1987). Women's socialization and feminist groups. In C. M. Brody (Ed.), *Women's therapy groups: Paradigms of feminist treatment* (pp. 24–39). New York: Springer.

Butler, D., & Geis, F. (1990). Non-verbal affect responses to male and female leaders: Implications for leadership evaluations. *Journal of Personality and Social Psychology, 58,* 18–59.

Byington, D. B. (1997). Applying relational theory to addiction treatment. In S.L.A. Straussner & E. Zelvin (Eds.), *Gender and addictions: Men and women in treatment* (pp. 31–46). Northvale, NJ: Aronson.

Corey, G. (1995). *Theory and practice of group counseling* (4th ed.). Pacific Grove, CA: Brooks/Cole.

Covington, S. S. (1999). *Helping women recover: A program for treating addiction* (Facilitator's guide). San Francisco: Jossey-Bass.

Covington, S. S., & Surrey, J. L. (1998). The relational model of women's psychological development: Implications for substance abuse. In S. Wilsnack & R. Wilsnack (Eds.), *Gender and alcohol: Individual and social perspectives.* New Brunswick, NJ: Rutgers University Press.

Fedele, N., & Harrington, E. (1990). *Women's groups: How connections heal* (Work in Progress No. 47). Wellesley, MA: Stone Center.

Flores, P. J. (1997). *Group psychotherapy with addicted populations: An integration of twelve-step and psychodynamic theory* (2nd ed.). Binghamton, NY: Haworth Press.

Ford, B., & Chase, C. (1987). *Betty: A glad awakening.* New York: Doubleday.

Fuhlrodt, R. L. (Ed.). (1990). *Psychodrama: Its application to ACOA and substance abuse treatment.* East Rutherford, NJ: Perrin.

Gilligan, C. (1982). *In a different voice: Psychological theory and women's development.* Cambridge, MA: Harvard University Press.

Gilligan, C. (1990). Preface: Teaching Shakespeare's sister: Notes from the underground of female adolescence. In C. Gilligan, N. P. Lyons, & T. J. Hanmer (Eds.), *Making connections: The relational worlds of adolescent girls at Emma Willard School* (pp. 6–29). Cambridge, MA: Harvard University Press.

Gomberg, E.S.L. (1988). Shame and guilt issues among women alcoholics. *Alcoholism Treatment Quarterly, 4*(2), 139–155.

Herman, J. (1992). *Trauma and recovery.* New York: Basic Books.

Hodgins, D., El-Guebaly, N., & Addington, J. (1997). Treatment of substance abusers: Single or mixed gender programs? *Addiction, 92,* 805–812.

Johnson, V. E. (1986). *Intervention: How to help someone who doesn't want help.* Minneapolis: Johnston Institute Books.

Jordon, J. V. (1994). *A relational perspective on self-esteem.* (Working Papers Series No. 70). Wellesley, MA: Stone Center.

Kanter, R. M. (1980). Some effects of proportions on group life: Skewed sex ratios and responses to token women. *American Journal of Sociology, 82,* 965–990.

Kauffman, E., Dore, M. M., & Nelson-Zlupko, L. (1995). The role of women's therapy groups in the treatment of chemical dependence. *American Journal of Orthopsychiatry, 65,* 355–363.

Loggins, S. (1998, June). Equine encounters. *Professional Counselor,* pp. 15–38.

Lovern, J. D. (1991). *Pathways to reality: Ericksonian-inspired treatment approaches to chemical dependency.* New York: Brunner/Mazel.

McManus, P. W., Redford, J. L., & Hughes, R. B. (1997). Connecting to self and others: A structured group for women. *Journal for Specialists in Group Work, 22*(1), 22–30.

Miller, J. B. (1976). *Toward a new psychology of women.* Boston: Beacon Press.

Morell, C. (1997). Women with depression and substance abuse problems. In S.L.A. Straussner & E. Zelvin (Eds.), *Gender and addictions: Men and women in treatment* (pp. 223–242). Northvale, NJ: Aronson.

Peck, T. A. (1986). Women's self-definition in adulthood: From a different model? *Psychology of Women Quarterly, 10,* 274–284.

Reed, B. G. (1985). Drug misuse and dependency in women: The meaning and implications of being considered a special population or minority group. *International Journal of the Addictions, 20,* 13–62.

Rogers, R. L., & McMillin, C. S. (1989). *The healing bond: Treating addictions in groups.* New York: Norton.

Spiegel, B. R., & Friedman, D. D. (1997). High achieving women: Issues in addiction and recovery. In S.L.A. Straussner & E. Zelvin (Eds.), *Gender and addictions: Men and women in treatment* (pp. 151–166). Northvale, NJ: Aronson.

Straussner, S.L.A. (1997). Group treatment with substance-abusing clients: A model of treatment during early phases of outpatient group therapy. *Journal of Chemical Dependency Treatment, 7*(1/2), 67–80.

Tantillo, M. (2000). Short-term relational group therapy for women with bulimia nervosa. *Eating Disorders, 8,* 99–121.

Vannicelli, M. (1992). *Removing the roadblocks: Group psychotherapy with substance abusers and family members.* New York: Guilford Press.

Waller, D., & Mahony, J. (1999). *Treatment of addiction: Current issues for arts therapies.* New York: Routledge.

Yalom, I. D. (1985). *The theory and practice of group psychotherapy* (3rd ed.). New York: Basic Books.

CHAPTER TWENTY-FOUR

WOMEN IN SELF-HELP PROGRAMS

Joyce Schmid

Addiction affects women on many levels: their physiology, thought, behavior, feelings, and worldview. Although everyone experiences addiction in her own way, the fundamental experience is the same: loss of control of behavior. Whether the behavior in question is intake of alcohol or drugs, intoxicated actions, eating, spending, gambling, or focusing on another instead of oneself, loss of control interferes with living a happy life. Addiction reduces the ego to primitive levels; the addict cannot perceive or acknowledge reality, and denial reigns supreme. It creates a terrible isolation, as the addict offers the world a false self that pretends to be in control, while inside, she struggles with a "destructive core story" (Fowler, 1993, p. 115) centering on a pathological belief in the need for self-control and self-reliance. Relationships to other people wither as the relationship with the addictive drug or behavior becomes blindingly important.

For sobriety to occur, these processes must be reversed. Although researchers are investigating the physiology of addiction, physiological interventions are only minimally effective. But thinking, behavior, feelings, and worldview can be addressed. Often, however, an addict cannot address these issues effectively by herself; she needs other people to help her. Self-help groups exist to fill this need.

This chapter takes a brief look at three different types of self-help groups available to addicted women: the twelve-step approach and two of the other groups that have been started in reaction to the twelve-step model. It will then focus on how women interact with a specific, representative twelve-step program (Alcoholics Anonymous) as they progress through the stages of addiction and recovery.

Self-Help: Different Approaches

The term *self-help group* is a misnomer (Brown, 1992, p. viii), perhaps even an oxymoron. Addicts turn for help to other people in a group only when they realize that self-help has failed. Twelve-step programs are formulated around this idea, acknowledging that in order to recover from addiction, the addict must reach toward something or someone outside the self. Other self-help groups, such as Women for Sobriety and Secular Organizations for Sobriety, were started to oppose this notion of the need for help. They stress self-sufficiency instead.

Alcoholics Anonymous and Other Twelve-Step Programs

Alcoholics Anonymous (AA), the prototype twelve-step program, began in 1935. It was based on the experience of two alcoholic men who turned to each other for help in staying sober. Bill Wilson and Dr. Bob Smith, realizing that they could not stop drinking by themselves, began meeting together to talk about their experiences as drunks. They discovered that they were able to achieve sobriety with the help of one another and of their "Higher Power." Wilson had previously tried participating in a nondenominational evangelical movement called the Oxford Group, but had found that its spiritual program and suggested exercises (the forerunners of AA's twelve steps) were not enough. Wilson found that he also needed to share experiences with a fellow alcoholic.

Over time, other twelve-step groups were created on the model of AA in order to deal with other addictions. Narcotics Anonymous, Gamblers Anonymous, Debtors Anonymous, Overeaters Anonymous, as well as Al-Anon, Nar-Anon, and Gam-Anon for families of addicts, are examples of the over two hundred different groups that now are available (Spiegel, 1993). All of the twelve-step programs share the basic tenets of AA: that the addict has lost control and is powerless over the addictive substance or behavior; that something outside the self—a "Higher Power" or "God"—is necessary for recovery and can actually lead to recovery; and that action, not just understanding, is essential (Mäkelä et al., 1996). All of these programs suggest that its members attend peer-led meetings, choose a special guide or sponsor from the membership, and perform twelve exercises, or steps, under the guidance of the sponsor. Often addicts attend more than one program at a time.

Differences among the twelve-step programs program are more peripheral than fundamental. Overeaters Anonymous (OA), for example, invites its members to have a "food sponsor" and to call in their food plans on a daily basis. Debtors Anonymous (DA) encourages members to discuss their finances with two other DA members, called a *pressure group* because they help the addict plan finances and relieve the financial pressure on her. Al-Anon and Sex and Love Addicts Anonymous are designed for people whose addiction is other people. OA and Al-Anon tend to be predominantly female programs. Despite such differences, however, all of these and other twelve-step programs use the twelve steps of AA, minimally modified. They are all based on peer-led meetings, self-disclosure of experiences related to the addiction, nonjudgmental listening, sponsorship, and abstinence.

AA is the most ubiquitous and most frequently studied of the twelve-step programs. It "can be found almost everywhere, almost all the time—in more than 97,000 groups throughout the world" (Alcoholics Anonymous [AA], 1999). Its members maintain sobriety on average for seven years; 47 percent have been sober more than five years (AA, 1999).

Although both men and women worldwide have increasingly used AA as a basis for sobriety, other groups have developed in protest to some of the AA philosophy. Some criticisms of the AA program have a gender basis. Women report discomfort with a male sexist tone to the program, with being outnumbered by men at mixed meetings, or even with the very presence of any men at meetings. Other objections center on the spiritual emphasis in AA and on AA's insistence on the theme of loss of control. In the United States, Women for Sobriety (WFS, founded in 1975), and Secular Organizations for Sobriety (SOS, founded in 1986) were started by people who tried to remedy what they saw as the problems of AA: the gender issue, the "God stuff," and the concept of powerlessness.

The Gender Issue: Women for Sobriety

The male genesis of AA and the sexist social context of the 1930s when it began have left scars on AA and on twelve-step programs in general. AA's Higher Power is conceptualized as a male God. The original AA writings, which constitute the first part of the "Big Book" (AA's basic text), have a sexist tone, although recent additions are more female-friendly. Much of the current AA literature has been written by men (Mäkelä et al., 1996). And although gender bias in staffing volunteer service is absent at the meeting level (such jobs as making coffee, cleaning up, and chairing meetings are equally shared between men and women), "positions in the higher echelons of the AA structure . . . are firmly in the hands of men" (Mäkelä et al., 1996, p. 176).

In addition, women still constitute a minority, if a growing minority, of AA members: 34 percent in 1998 (AA, 1999), up from 22 percent in 1968 (Mäkelä et al., 1996). Among members who are thirty years old and under, an age group making up 11 percent of AA members, the percentage of women is somewhat higher: 38 percent (AA, 1999). The larger percentage of men in AA may be related to the epidemiology of alcoholism, rather than to bias in the AA program. Women are considered to be a minority among alcoholics; cited figures range from 13 percent to 26 percent, depending on the criteria used for the diagnosis (Grant, 1992).

Whatever the cause, the male predominance at meetings can be uncomfortable for some female alcoholics. Coker (1997) and Kaskutas (1994) point out some of the potential difficulties for women in attending mixed-gender groups. Some women may find it harder to speak honestly about themselves in the presence of men. Some women may tend to defer to men, agree, and praise others instead of addressing their own problems, especially where more men than women are present. Women have experienced sexual harassment, such as touching, teasing, or inappropriate comments at meetings, and at times have been treated as sexual objects by men ("thirteenth stepping"). In response to such problems, the number of female-only AA meetings in the United States has grown.

Despite the growing population of women in AA, sociologist Dr. Jean Kirkpatrick believed that the fundamental AA philosophies were wrong for women. She felt that AA's teachings of powerlessness and ego deflation actually exacerbated the normal psychological difficulties of women in a male-dominated society. According to Kirkpatrick, for women to improve their self-esteem and reduce guilt and shame, they need clear affirmations of empowerment and self-reliance. She founded Women for Sobriety (WFS) on this principle. WFS is small in numbers: as of 1991, the entire membership of WFS consisted of only 822 women (Kaskutas, 1994). Although the group's small size makes it a challenge for members to locate meetings to attend, even in metropolitan areas, it also creates an opportunity for valid evaluation of members' response to the WFS philosophy.

AA and WFS have common goals: abstinence from alcohol and personal empowerment. But their assumptions about how to achieve these goals are diametrically opposed. Describing AA, Brown writes, "At the core is paradox: it is precisely the deep acceptance of loss of control—surrender—that forms the foundations for empowerment" (Brown, 1993, p. 140). WFS, in contrast, is based on the belief that women need just the opposite: direct encouragement to believe that they are empowered.

In contrast to the first step in AA, which reads, "We admitted we were powerless over alcohol—that our lives had become unmanageable," the *first affirmation* of WFS is, "I have a drinking problem that once had me" (Kaskutas, 1994). The WFS affirmation is cleverly constructed on a pun on the word *have,* which blends the concept of control with the concept of loss of control. The problem once "had" me, but I "have" it now, interpretable as both "Now I'm in control of it" *and* "I have a problem" (loss of control).

Step two in AA is, "We came to believe that a Power greater than ourselves could restore us to sanity," and later steps continue to offer the idea that the power of the individual to change the self without outside help is limited. In opposition to this, further WFS affirmations come out more firmly as statements that the individual is potentially in full control of the self without outside help. For example: "Happiness is a habit I will develop" (affirmation three); "Problems bother me only to the degree I permit them to" (affirmation four); "I am what I think" (affirmation five); and "I am a competent woman and have much to give life" (affirmation twelve).

Spirituality is not excluded from WFS, as shown in affirmation eight: "The fundamental object of life is emotional and spiritual growth." But WFS affirmations locate power in the individual woman alone ("I"), whereas the steps in AA locate power in a Higher Power, called "God as we understood him," in the context of a group ("We").

It is important to note that AA does *not* teach that the alcoholic is completely powerless over all aspects of her life. According to AA, the alcoholic cannot control her drinking if she drinks. However, AA does not deny that she may have some control over other aspects of her life. The "Serenity Prayer," an AA staple, acknowledges human power while also addressing its limits, in the context of an ultimate Higher Power: "God grant me the serenity to accept the things I cannot change, the courage to change the things I can, and the wisdom to know the difference" (Brown, 1985, p. 210).

Although AA and WFS take fundamentally opposed attitudes toward power, in practice women have been able to make use of both programs at the same time. Analyzing a 1992 survey of the entire membership of WFS, Kaskutas reports that "Women attend WFS because they find it a safe forum for discussing their feelings, especially about women's issues" (1994, p. 190). Over two-thirds of respondents agreed with the statement that coming to WFS kept them sober, but in response to an open-ended question about the benefits of WFS, "Not a single [WFS member] mentioned that what she gets out of WFS is *her sobriety*" (p. 193, italics in original). And, consistent with the WFS philosophy of independence, 60 percent of respondents said they felt they could stay sober without going to WFS meetings! About one-third of the respondents said they also attended AA, many of them calling AA an "insurance policy against relapse." These responses indicate that at least some of the women attending WFS felt that the group was not enough by itself to support their sobriety, and they turned to AA for that support.

Do women need an exclusively female self-help program based on feminist ideas? Clearly, there are differences between male and female addicts. From a political-legal point of view, few would deny that in Western civilization, as in much of the world, women have been a disempowered group, and that the sequelae of this disempowerment still affect women. From a physiological perspective, women are, on average, smaller and have a lower proportion of body water than men, and therefore get more drunk on less alcohol. Partly for this reason, alcoholism progresses more quickly in women once it begins (Blume, 1994). Psychologically, women are more likely to drink to be in relationship with spouse, lover, family, and friends (Coker, 1997) and are more often motivated toward sobriety by family-related issues (Mäkelä et al., 1996). Women are more likely to be drinking to deal with depression and to have been in psychiatric treatment (Coker, 1997). And, in Coker's words, "Alcoholic women suffer lower self esteem, more anxiety, and more guilt about their drinking than men" (p. 274).

But despite these differences, the essential nature of alcoholism is the same for both women and men. In the fourth edition of the *Diagnostic and Statistical Manual of Mental Disorders* (American Psychiatric Association, 1994), five of seven criteria for substance dependence, with no differentiation in regard to gender, involve loss of control. Criteria 1 and 2, tolerance and withdrawal, refer to physiological processes beyond conscious control. Criterion 3, taking a substance in "larger amounts or over a longer period than was intended"; criterion 4, "persistent desire or unsuccessful efforts to cut down or control substance use"; and criterion 7, continuing use "despite knowledge of having a persistent or recurrent physical or psychological problem that is likely to have been caused or exacerbated by the substance" (p. 181)—all refer to behavioral loss of control. Yet the WFS program is based on the belief that admitting powerlessness and focusing on it are detrimental to women! This apparent assumption that women are too fragile to face loss of control and the painful feelings that go with it, whereas men are able to do so, can be seen as yet another incarnation of sexism, with the potential for serious harm to female addicts.

The God Stuff: Secular Organizations for Sobriety

Secular Organizations for Sobriety (SOS), a mixed-gender group, was started in 1986 by James Christopher. According to Chappel and DuPont (1999), SOS has about twenty thousand members and more than two thousand meetings in the United States. Christopher himself got sober in AA, but objected to what he saw as "the emphasis placed on God and more generally on religion" (Connors & Dermen, 1996, p. 283). He started SOS with the aim of having a self-help group something like AA but based on the concept of *sobriety priority* instead of the AA concept of Higher Power. His goal was to emphasize thinking and exclude faith. Although individual groups need not adhere to any particular structure, SOS does suggest a meeting format. One suggested opening is, in part: "Secular Organizations for Sobriety . . . is dedicated to providing a path to sobriety, an alternative to those paths depending upon supernatural or religious beliefs. We respect diversity, welcome healthy skepticism, and encourage rational thinking as well as expression of feelings. We each take responsibility for our individual sobriety on a daily basis. . . . Our focus is on the priority of abstaining from alcohol and other mind-altering drugs. . . At this meeting, we share our experiences, understandings, thoughts and feelings" (Connors & Dermen, 1996, pp. 283–284).

What percentage of SOS is female? Do SOS members tend to use it by itself to maintain sobriety, or, as in WFS, do they also need AA? These questions were addressed in a recent survey of member characteristics and feelings about SOS conducted by Connors and Dermen (1996). Although SOS members cannot be surveyed directly because SOS does not keep a member list, the central office does keep a list of known SOS meeting conveners and those interested in convening meetings. After the 350 names on this list were organized geographically, 200 of them were chosen at random (proportionate to the number of names for each geographical region), and questionnaires were sent to these people. Of these 200 questionnaires, 158 were returned. Although such a small sample probably does not have enough power to describe SOS as a whole, it is likely to consist of people especially enthusiastic about the SOS program, considering that they were interested in starting, or actually did start, new groups. Of the 158 returned questionnaires, 27 percent were from women, suggesting that between a quarter to a third of SOS members are women, a figure comparable to the 34 percent of women in AA. As in WFS, 30 percent of all responders were concurrently attending AA, and over half of the responders said they had been to over one hundred AA meetings. Over half of the responders said that they found AA helpful in maintaining sobriety (Connors & Dermen, 1996). So here again, as in WFS, it appears that a significant number of SOS members felt that they also needed AA and were able to use AA along with SOS, despite the major differences in philosophy between the two programs.

◆ ◆ ◆

Some women find twelve-step programs repugnant and are not able to use them. Sometimes the difficulties are based on a misunderstanding of the twelve-step programs—for example, SOS's view that AA has "supernatural or religious beliefs." Some find difficulties that are based on real characteristics of the program, such as the male bias of its literature and tone and the male majority in its membership. Others are threatened by the prospect of acknowledging loss of control, which is the hallmark of addiction. For addicts who cannot use twelve-step programs for these or other reasons, any self-help group fostering abstinence may be helpful, whatever its approach. Twelve-step programs, however, offer interventions at multiple levels—supportive, cognitive, behavioral, psychological, and spiritual. The addict is encouraged to pick and choose the parts of the program that seem useful, as stated in the slogan, "Take what you like and leave the rest." Twelve-step programs provide a comprehensive basis for sobriety, as will be described in the remainder of this chapter.

AA and the Stages of Recovery

Because AA is the first and largest of the twelve-step programs, this discussion will now focus on AA and how it works for women during the various stages of addiction and recovery: drinking, transition, early recovery, and ongoing recovery (Brown, 1995). For each stage, we will address the alcoholic's relationship to alcohol and then her relationship to AA.

The Drinking Stage

During the drinking stage, the alcoholic woman is drinking to excess. She is having a love affair with alcohol while at the same time losing control of her drinking and her life. At this stage, the woman vehemently rejects the idea of attending AA. An alcoholic in the drinking stage experiences "the need to include more and more alcohol in [her] life without disturbing the central belief in self-control" (Brown, 1995, p. 31). She needs to deny the alcoholism while rationalizing the drinking so that it can continue.

AA describes active addiction as *self-will run riot*, vivid words to describe a massive failure of ego functioning. As pointed out by Spiegel and Mulder (1986), the ego functions of reality testing, regulation and control of instinctual drives, thought processes, and defenses all malfunction as the alcoholic drinks out of control.

The drinking alcoholic experiences a terrible loneliness: she hides a destructive core story behind a false self. The themes of this core story are an "excessive demand for self-reliance" (Fowler, 1993, p. 115), an overwhelming need to control self and others, and a voracious need for alcohol. According to Fowler, "The strain, anxiety, and lack of real intimacy that accompany one's effort to maintain the false self and to live its core story both give rise to and rely upon the use of alcohol as a numbing for pain and as a catalyst for pseudo-spontaneity and intimacy" (p. 115).

The primary emotional attachment of a drinking alcoholic is to alcohol. Caroline Knapp (1996) has written an eloquent autobiography of her alcoholism and named it *Drinking: A Love Story*. Self, friends, job, family, and even children are abandoned for the sake of the addiction, although the alcoholic herself still feels an attachment to them. "I once heard a woman say that as an alcoholic a part of her will always be deeply attracted to alcohol. . . . The attraction doesn't die when you say good-bye to the drink, any more than the pull toward a bad lover dies when you finally walk out the door" (Knapp, 1996, p. 269).

In the drinking stage, with the love affair in full bloom, women are horrified by the idea of AA and see it as the enemy. AA represents both telling the truth about their addiction and giving it up, as well as admitting feelings of deep humiliation that accompany the acknowledgment of loss of control. Many women in the drinking stage who are cajoled, pressured, or forced into attending a meeting will avoid seeing similarities between themselves and the AA members at the meeting and will focus instead on any apparent differences, such as those described next, as reasons to stay away from AA (and continue drinking).

Although women can come to accept differences as they make progress in recovery, some are harder to overcome than others. Race and ethnicity can be foci of division. As one Black woman said, "I wish White people would stay out of our meeting. I don't want to stand up in front of a White meeting and say, 'I'm insecure today because I'm Black, and I need to talk about it.' I need a place to say that" (Hall, 1994, p. 569). Sexual orientation is another potential divide. A lesbian reported that her sponsor cooled toward her upon learning that she was gay (Hall, 1994). Attending homogeneous meetings, especially when first becoming acquainted with AA, may help newcomers to the program feel less alienated.

While the drinking addict is loudly rejecting AA, at a deeper level she may also be noticing positive things, such as kindness, acceptance, humor, and caring. Women in recovery sometimes find that memories of these observations eventually emerge to consciousness and become part of their recovery stories.

The Transition Stage

In transition, a woman is teetering between two worlds: drunk and sober. Her experience of AA depends on which world she inhabits at a given time.

In the transition stage, the still-drinking alcoholic moves away from her attachment to alcohol (the subphase called *drinking transition*), toward abstinence (*recovering transition*) (Brown, 1995). Transition begins when "the disadvantages and problems of drinking begin to outweigh the advantages. The individual begins to doubt the airtight logic that supports the addiction, or is faced with stark evidence [of addiction] that cannot be denied" (Brown, 1995, p. 34). The task of the alcoholic at this stage is to wrench herself away from her primary love object: alcohol. It represents the end of the affair. This is almost impossible to do unless a new attachment can be formed to take its place. In Brown's words, "Individuals do not move from dependence on a substance to no dependence. In fact, there is no such thing as 'no dependence'" (1993, p. 145).

In drinking transition, an alcoholic may clutch all the tighter to the rags and tatters of her denial. She may dislike AA with all her might, and may give many reasonable explanations why she of all people should never be expected to go back. Or, alternatively, she may be willing to attend meetings, begin to identify with a few people, feel positively about the program—and then go home and drink.

Recovering transition is the beginning of abstinence. The alcoholic stops drinking and feels overwhelming emptiness and need, as her world still revolves around the empty space where alcohol has been. At this point, she may turn to AA in despair, ready for connection.

A twelve-step program offers itself as a new object of attachment to replace alcohol and other addictions. NA puts this succinctly in their slogan "Take people, not a hit" (Spiegel, 1993). Straussner and Spiegel (1996) have likened an addict's progress through the twelve steps to the stages of separation-individuation of the human infant as conceptualized by Mahler, Pine, and Bergman (1975). A "symbiotic" attachment to AA during this stage greatly facilitates sobriety, because such attachment can substitute for the substance. Idealization of and dependence on the sponsor and the program are signs that symbiosis is developing. As one recovering woman said of that period in her recovery, "[My sponsors] were the gods, they were my gods through AA and what to do when I got there" (Fowler, 1993, p. 131).

Attachment to the program can occur gradually or suddenly. Joanna experienced a sudden attachment: "Joanna went to [her first] meeting where she sat quietly and left quickly without speaking to anyone. During her third meeting, Joanna heard a woman speaker with whom she strongly identified and experienced a sense of comfort and security for the first time in a long time. She approached the woman who told Joanna to 'keep coming back' and to 'follow the program.' Joanna went home and threw away all her wine bottles; she has never had another drink. . . . Joanna . . . idealized and merged with her friends, her sponsor, and with the program" (Straussner & Spiegel, 1996, pp. 305–306).

Whereas Joanna was able to transfer her primary attachment to AA quickly and without complication, for other women the process of attaching to AA is often more difficult. A history of social oppression or a history of neglect or trauma can impair trust in the organization. And attachments to practicing addicts or other unhealthy people can also be powerful obstacles to attaching to AA.

For those with a history of social oppression, whether it is due to sexual orientation or to racial, ethnic, religious, or socioeconomic factors, the issue of belonging to AA can engender internal conflict (Hall, 1994). Neither joining with those whom the woman experiences as oppressors nor staying separate from them is comfortable. This can present obstacles to joining the AA program, especially in early stages of recovery, as expressed by a lesbian worried about losing her hard-won identity: "AA has that little pamphlet about being gay called, 'So you think you are different?' Well, you are goddam right we are different! I mean we are a group of deeply oppressed people—that's a little different from being heterosexual in this culture. To minimize or trivialize that is dangerous. And I think that is my biggest worry. AA minimizes that difference. No, AA is not safe for lesbians" (Hall, 1994, p. 566). In contrast, another lesbian was concerned about the potential for special groups to overemphasize the differences. She had difficulty with lesbian meetings, feeling that they were less like AA than "a lesbian rap group" (p. 565).

These obstacles to joining are not necessarily insurmountable, however, especially as recovery proceeds. Women who dare to attend meetings often find acceptance based on the common problem of alcoholism and the work of recovery from "people from all walks of life" (Hall, 1994, p. 563).

Early emotional neglect and trauma can also be issues, as the cases of Louisa and Melanie exemplify.

Louisa

Louisa's depressed parents had been unable to give her attention or love or to express emotions. Her father traveled for business all week long and slept and read in his room on weekends. Her mother sat and stared out the window or grimly performed household duties. When Louisa stopped drinking and attended AA after losing a job due to her drinking, she could not bear the love offered by the other people at the meetings. She was humiliated by her own emotionality, but could not prevent herself from crying as she unconsciously compared what she was being offered by strangers at AA to her own parents' neglect of her. She was not able to attend AA, although she did stay sober through her eight-year psychotherapy. Having learned in her therapy to tolerate attention and caring in her life, she became willing to try AA on termination in order to maintain her sobriety.

Melanie

Melanie, who also had a history of trauma in early life, sought individual psychotherapy at an addictions center when her husband threatened to leave her. She attended one AA meeting at the therapist's suggestion, but angrily refused to try a second meeting. She complained of its being a men's program and scoffed at its insistence on powerlessness. She did attend WFS, but continued to drink and to insist that she could control her drinking, which was clearly out of control. Melanie had been raped by her father, and used alcohol to cope with overwhelming anxiety, grief, and rage. Acknowledging her powerlessness over alcohol would also mean facing her powerlessness over the rape. Unable to deal with this, Melanie continued to drink, stopped showing up for her psychotherapy appointments, and was lost to follow-up.

Pathological attachments, particularly to other alcoholics, can also stand in the way of attaching to AA. Susie and Ellen were able to break out of the pull of such attachments and to achieve sobriety in AA.

Susie

Susie had a pathological attachment to an alcoholic husband, an attachment difficult for her to recognize. Susie was her family's "designated alcoholic," while her husband, also an active alcoholic, denied his own alcoholism. He focused on her drinking, forcing her into treatment many times and threatening to leave unless she became abstinent. But her abstinence threatened to pull the covers off his drinking and blow the family to pieces. Susie acknowledged that she was an alcoholic, but resisted going to AA because to recover was to break up her marriage. Then, at one of the treatment centers where her husband had sent her, she met a woman in recovery who took an interest in her and became her sponsor. This woman helped Susie replace her dependency and attachment to her husband and alcohol with a new dependency and attachment to AA, so that Susie could separate from her husband and become sober.

Ellen

Ellen had to struggle with a pathological attachment to her alcoholic mother. Ellen used alcohol to serve different and contradictory psychological functions at the same time. By drinking like her mother, she unconsciously demonstrated her loyalty to her mother. But she also was demonstrating her conviction that she herself was not an alcoholic (only alcoholics have to stop drinking) and that therefore she was different from and better than her mother. Ellen struggled with these issues for years, insisting that she was not an alcoholic while suspecting that she was. As her drinking increased over time, she occasionally tried different AA meetings. She hated them, until she happened upon a group with some very warm, accepting women who actively reached out to her. Identifying with these "sober alcoholic mothers," she was able to reverse the pathological equations in her mind that maintained her drinking. Now she could be an alcoholic, in loyalty and identification with her own alcoholic mother, but at the same time could be sober like her new alcoholic "mothers."

If a new attachment or "symbiosis" can be formed with people in the AA program, and thereby with the program itself, the alcoholic becomes motivated to learn the behaviors that will help her stay sober, much as a child is motivated to imitate and emulate her parents. "Like the mother of the symbiotic child, the Twelve-Step group as a whole, and the sponsor in particular, mediates between the individual and the external world by providing structure and guidance. . . . In essence, the Twelve-Step programs and sponsors lend their observing ego and try to reduce the multiple stimuli impacting on the newly recovering individual" (Straussner & Spiegel, 1996, p. 306).

Junelle describes her experience in transition: "I was so raw, I thought I'd jump out of my skin. I felt a little better at meetings, but at home I just couldn't stand it. I was sober thirty seconds at a time. I'd call my sponsor. She'd say, 'Take a walk around the block and call me back.' I took a walk around the block and called her back."

During this period, ego functions are improving. Recognizing the addiction is a quantum leap in the addict's relationship to reality. The end of drinking allows the brain to perceive and process information more accurately, as well as to inhibit impulsive behavior. If the addict manages to perform the behaviors taught by the program—the behaviors that foster sobriety—and if she can maintain sobriety, eventually she becomes able to interpose thought between impulse and action. In other words, she enters the stage of early recovery.

The Early Recovery Stage

In early recovery, the addict is learning to replace addictive behaviors with recovering behaviors. Often, the addict in early recovery is willing to be connected to AA, having accepted the identity of "alcoholic" and the reality of having lost control. AA provides both a behavioral roadmap for sobriety and fellow travelers along the road.

The stage of early recovery is distinguishable from the recovering transition stage by "a marked reduction in impulses that demand an immediate behavioral response" (Brown, 1995, p. 41). Ego functioning is vastly improved. Out-of-control attempts at instant gratification of impulse are replaced by thinking. The alcoholic is facing the realities of her addiction. Step four of the twelve steps aids in this process, guiding her through a self-inventory of "character defects" and strengths. "This requires enough ego strength to review the drinking years and see how one's sense of reality was distorted" (Spiegel & Mulder, 1986, p. 36).

In early recovery, the transfer of attachment from the drug to AA is proceeding. The AA member feels a sense of belonging and welcome at meetings.

Her identity is shifting: she is an alcoholic among other alcoholics. She may be socializing with other members of AA before and after meetings, and possibly at various AA parties. She talks on the telephone to her sponsor and other AA members. As one woman expressed it, "AA is really great. All these people who are not like you are interested in keeping you sober. They call you. . . . I thought it was beautiful that these strangers that I had nothing in common with would call me and cared about me and would sit with me" (Hall, 1994, p. 564). The unbearable isolation, loneliness, and emptiness of the drinking days are starting to give way as the alcoholic attaches to other people; she is *a part of* rather than *apart from* others.

During this stage, the destructive core story (Fowler, 1993) is changing. The woman no longer has to hide the pain that fueled the drinking, nor the drinking itself. Her excessive demand for self-reliance is no longer necessary, because all can be revealed. The woman is constructing a new autobiography, one that includes the reality of both pain and addiction. She is showing this new story to others on a regular basis, and it is accepted, even applauded, over and over at meetings.

Creating a new self-story provides relief but also can be associated with problems. A common difficulty for the AA woman in early recovery is not with AA but within herself, as she begins to tell the truth about herself and her needs for the first time. Peggy describes her belief that her own recovery would endanger others: "Much of recovery has been a struggle, as I repeatedly resist making positive changes which feel aggressive or damaging to my husband and family at the same time. Anything that will result in a stronger sense of myself also feels hostile to them" (Brown, 1993, p. 149).

And, indeed, sometimes family and friends do feel threatened by the changes made by a recovering woman. She is going to meetings instead of helping with homework. She is exercising or having coffee with recovering friends instead of bringing in the dry cleaning. She is forming new attachments to both men and women outside the family. She has ideas and opinions that she expects people to take seriously. She is behaving very differently, and the people who complained the most loudly about her drinking sometimes wish that they had the old days back. The commercial film *When a Man Loves a Woman* (Touchstone Pictures) eloquently illustrates the stress that a woman's recovery can place on her relationship with her husband. A similarly disruptive process can occur if a woman joins a twelve-step program such as Al-Anon, when it is her husband or other closely related person who is a practicing addict. Relationships in recovery do best when all family members are participating in twelve-step programs, learning the same new principles, behaviors, and vocabularies.

The woman in early recovery is faced with a difficult challenge: the need for a major developmental shift in her thinking. To use Mahler's terms (Straussner &

Spiegel, 1996), the woman now enters the subphase of *differentiation*. She "starts to perceive others more realistically[, and her] idealizing transference slowly dissipates. Members begin to compare more actively the various meetings and become more selective in picking a home group and a sponsor. . . . They become aware of their feelings, begin to label them, and then verbalize them to others" (Straussner & Spiegel, 1996, pp. 306–307).

All of these changes can be frightening. The recovering woman may "revert to the illusion of control with the hope of finding a diversion from or alternative to the responsibilities of self-development" (Brown, 1993, p. 149). She may again seek the person or the substance that will take away the burden and fix her. Although AA specifically recommends against it, sometimes she begins a sexual relationship with someone in the program, which can derail her as she focuses on this relationship instead of on herself and her recovery.

The terror of emerging feelings can be another cause of stasis in recovery, especially where there has been trauma. The terror can be so strong that progress through recovery is halted, as it was for Gina.

Gina

Gina, like many addicts, had been traumatized by events engendered by her own alcoholism. Sober in AA for many years, she had never been able to attempt the fourth step in which she would have evaluated herself in terms of strengths and weaknesses. Many years before, while drunk, Gina had fallen asleep smoking and started a fire in her apartment with her whole family in it. The family had been saved by a fortuitous wrong-number call, which had awakened everyone to a houseful of smoke. She was unable to face this in her recovery. She could not talk or feel about this incident, and so could not resolve her horror, guilt, and shame.

Gina was stuck in the "first tier of recovery" (Brown and Lewis, 1999, p. 73). She did achieve the behavioral changes that maintain abstinence, but trauma prevented her entry into the second tier, which consists of opening up and integrating her feelings and her past as part of herself. This process, which starts with the fourth step inventory, is the hallmark of ongoing recovery.

Ongoing Recovery

The woman in ongoing recovery has internalized the behavioral changes of the earlier stages, so that powerful feelings are much less likely to trigger addictive behaviors. With her ego now strong enough to tolerate a range of emotions, she is able to delve more deeply into exploration of her history and her self, with the purpose of healing traumatic wounds and building a more healthy character. She has a more adult relationship with AA: while still part of the "family," she is also involved in the outside world.

The woman in ongoing recovery is now becoming aware of feelings previously unexpressed, and is learning to articulate them. She no longer needs alcohol to suppress, facilitate, or avoid them. As CK, a thirty-four-year-old recovering woman, states, "It's important to me that I can feel anything. I spent a number of years not feeling, and that's why I drank and why I did drugs, is to not feel. . . . It didn't matter if it was a bad feeling or a good feeling or anything. It was all too strong, or so I thought, for me to take. To me, drinking and doing drugs was a walking deadness, you know, and now it's not" (Fowler, 1993, p. 130). At this point in recovery, the woman can understand an urge to drink as a signal that difficult feelings are present or emerging, and that it need not be a spur to addictive behavior.

From the point of view of ego development (Spiegel & Mulder, 1986), intimacy, trust, and empathy are developing, and the defenses of splitting, grandiosity, and projection are being replaced with "humility, or realistic self knowledge" (p. 39). Thought processes are becoming more symbolic and abstract.

The woman in ongoing recovery is continuing to participate in AA meetings and to see AA friends. "Individuals use the Twelve Steps to question past and present, conscious and unconscious motivation, and to challenge behavior and beliefs" (Brown, 1995, p. 46). The recovering woman is now capable of "constructively critical interactions with the classic text and teachings of AA" (Fowler, 1993, p. 130). She can interpret the "Big Book" herself and can decide how many meetings to attend, adding more at times of stress. She develops a more friend-like relationship with her sponsor, and may sponsor others. She can relate to the program itself and not just to the individuals who happen to be at a meeting. As Julia said, "It was a lousy meeting, just a bunch of old men talking about their drinking days, but I felt calmer when I left."

In ongoing recovery, as Straussner and Spiegel (1996) point out, a woman may need fewer meetings, now that "a stable mental representation of nurturing others and a sense of self-esteem despite numerous unmet needs" (p. 308) have begun to take hold in her mind. When a drinking dream or a desire to drink signals that feelings are becoming especially intense, the person in ongoing recovery takes this as an alert to call her sponsor and to attend extra meetings, as she tries to understand what the feelings are and where they are coming from.

AA is a spiritual program. As defined by Fowler (1993), faith is characterized by the "creation of meaning in one's life" (p. 113), as well as the creation of "core stories that link persons to others who share them, and to an ultimate frame of reference which gives them coherence" (p. 114). In ongoing recovery, the recovering woman has a new core story to replace the destructive one that was at the heart of her addiction. For example, CK says, "I've become a completely different person . . . everything is different. The way that I look at the world is different. The way that I look at life, the way that I look at me. I don't hate myself so much any more" (Fowler, 1993, p. 131).

Misty, who had been told, and had believed, that she had been a bad child "from the start," describes how she is learning to accept herself: "Accepting the good with the bad, you know, character defects with everything. . . . I used to be a person that felt like I had to be the center of attention, and all that, and now I'm learning to just, like, sit back and be there. And just be able to, you know, to be, and not have to earn my place" (Fowler, 1993, p. 127).

Peggy talks about her new spiritual position: "Now I see myself as a small part of a much larger universe, running without my control or authority. I have come to trust and feel safe with my own conception of my higher power" (Brown, 1993, p. 145).

Conclusion

Addiction is a condition characterized by loss of control over behavior. Facing powerlessness is frightening and humiliating. A place of safety and support can make a big difference in allowing this painful process to occur. And so, ever since the founding of Alcoholics Anonymous, the original twelve-step program, addicts have been turning to other addicts for the safety and support necessary to admit their loss of control and deal with the devastation it has caused them. This is the kernel of "self-help," which, paradoxically, means turning to others for help.

Depending on one's experience of others, however, turning to others for help can in itself feel frightening and humiliating. This is true particularly for addicts, who have espoused the destructive core story of self-control and isolation from others. In addition, many female addicts have had bad experiences with men. Women for Sobriety (WFS) was formed on two assumptions: that women, societally disempowered, need a female setting to feel safe and that they should not have to experience additional disempowerment by admitting loss of control. Secular Organizations for Sobriety (SOS), a coed group, was also formed to avoid the sting of dealing with powerlessness. Both of these groups are based on the belief that addicts can and should control themselves, a less humiliating stance than admitting loss of control.

But because addiction is by definition characterized by loss of control, groups that avoid this realization also fail to address the defining characteristic of addiction. To believe that women are too delicate to face their own loss of control over addictive substances and behaviors is to underestimate women. Perhaps because twelve-step groups are willing to confront loss of control directly, they are by far the largest and most available of the self-help groups for addiction.

Looking closely at AA as a model twelve-step program, we see how women are able to make use of it in each stage of addiction and recovery, despite its faults and despite their difficulties with it. Women who are able to use AA stand to experience change on every level of their personalities, change that will support their sobriety. Ego functioning matures as women replace their attachment to alcohol and other substances with an attachment to the program, and then, over time, experience separation and individuation from the program itself. With the help of AA, their destructive core story based on isolation from people and need for alcohol is exchanged for a story allowing authentic connection with others, and ongoing sobriety.

References

Alcoholics Anonymous. (1999). *1998 membership survey.* New York: Alcoholics Anonymous World Services.

American Psychiatric Association. (1994). *Diagnostic and statistical manual of mental disorders* (4th ed.). Washington, DC: Author.

Blume, S. B. (1994). Gender differences in alcohol-related disorders. *Harvard Review of Psychiatry, 2*(1), 7–13.

Brown, S. (1985). *Treating the alcoholic: A developmental model of recovery.* New York: Wiley.

Brown, S. (1992). *Safe passage: Recovery for adult children of alcoholics.* New York: Wiley.

Brown, S. (1993). Therapeutic processes in Alcoholics Anonymous. In B. McCrady & W. Miller (Eds.), *Research on Alcoholics Anonymous* (pp. 137–152). New Brunswick, NJ: Rutgers Center of Alcohol Studies.

Brown, S. (1995). A developmental model of alcoholism and recovery. In S. Brown (Ed.), *Treating alcoholism* (pp. 27–53). San Francisco: Jossey-Bass.

Brown, S., & Lewis, V. (1999). *The alcoholic family in recovery: A developmental model.* New York: Guilford Press.

Chappel, J. N., & DuPont, R. L. (1999, June 22). Twelve step and mutual-help programs for addictive disorders. *Psychiatric Clinics of North America, 22,* 425–446.

Coker, M. (1997). Overcoming sexism in AA: How women cope. In S.L.A. Straussner & E. Zelvin (Eds.), *Gender and addictions: Men and women in treatment* (pp. 263–281). Northvale, NJ: Aronson.

Connors, G. J., & Dermen, K. H. (1996). Characteristics of participants in Secular Organizations for Sobriety (SOS). *American Journal of Drug and Alcohol Abuse, 22,* 281–295.

Fowler, J. S. (1993). Alcoholics Anonymous and faith development. In B. McCrady & W. Miller (Eds.), *Research on Alcoholics Anonymous* (pp. 131–135). New Brunswick, NJ: Rutgers Center of Alcohol Studies.

Grant, B. F. (1992). Prevalence of the proposed DSM-IV alcohol use disorders: United States, 1988. *British Journal of Addiction, 87,* 309–316.

Hall, J. M. (1994). The experiences of lesbians in Alcoholics Anonymous. *Western Journal of Nursing Research, 16,* 556–576.

Kaskutas, L. A. (1994). What do women get out of self-help? Their reasons for attending Women for Sobriety and Alcoholics Anonymous. *Journal of Substance Abuse Treatment, 11,* 185–195.

Knapp, C. (1996). *Drinking: A love story.* New York: Bantam Books.

Mahler, M., Pine, F., & Bergman, H. (1975). *The psychological birth of the human infant.* New York: Basic Books.

Mäkelä, K., Arminen, I., Bloomfield, K., Eisenbach-Stangl, I., Bergmark, K. H., Kurube, N., Mariolini, N., Olafsdóttir, Peterson, J. H., Phillips, M., Rehm, J., Room, R., Rosenqvist, P., Rosovsky, H., Stenius, K., Świątkiewics, G., Woronowicz, B., & Zieliński, A. (1996). *Alcoholics Anonymous as a mutual-help movement: A study in eight societies.* Madison: University of Wisconsin Press.

Spiegel, B. R. (1993). Twelve-step programs as a treatment modality. In S.L.A. Straussner (Ed.), *Clinical work with substance-abusing clients* (pp. 152–168). New York: Guilford Press.

Spiegel, E., & Mulder, E. (1986). The Anonymous program and ego functioning. *Issues in Ego Psychology, 9*(1), 34–42.

Straussner, S.L.A., & Spiegel, B. R. (1996). An analysis of twelve-step programs for substance abusers from a developmental perspective. *Clinical Social Work Journal, 24,* 299–309.

PART SEVEN

EPILOGUE AND RESOURCES

CHAPTER TWENTY-FIVE

EPILOGUE

Shulamith Lala Ashenberg Straussner and Stephanie Brown

The twenty-four chapters in this book have explored the numerous dimensions of women's addictions and a multitude of treatment approaches to addiction problems. The authors identify the growing body of research on women and addictions; they also point out the significant lack of knowledge that still exists. Addicted women continue to experience tremendous stigma, while insurance coverage and treatment resources remain inadequate. Women still face countless major hurdles to seeking help and using it.

Hurdles to treatment utilization and to treatment effectiveness for women include societal, familial, and individual obstacles. Women must cope with male-oriented treatment models, failure to diagnose or misdiagnosis by medical professionals, a lack of knowledge about services, and a lack of comprehensive services to meet their multiple needs. They need safer housing and easier access to treatment and child care. Most important, they need health and mental health professionals who are better trained and more sensitive to women's unique needs. On top of these institutional barriers, women also have to deal with family issues and their own intrapsychic obstacles to change. Women often need to cope with partners who use substances themselves. All women may feel pressure from family and friends not to enter treatment for fear of leaving or losing their children; fear of abuse from or loss of a partner; high levels of shame and guilt resulting from the internalization of society's stigmatization; and lack of self-esteem, hope, and a sense of deserving a better life.

Although social and economic options have improved for many women, the world has also become more complex, with the pace of life faster than ever. Consequently, the desire and the need to escape to a bottle, a pill, a slot machine, a shopping mall or a romantic relationship seem ever more seductive and compelling. Despite the increased recognition of addictions in the lives of millions of women, for many the treatment options have shrunk over the past decade as health benefits have become so "managed" as to effectively disappear. Even those who can afford help may find fewer options now than in the past. Moreover, many women in treatment today suffer from a multitude of psychic traumas. Therapists, limited by managed health care systems and vulnerable to countertransference feelings of helplessness, may question their ability to respond, so some, in frustration, may ask, Why bother?

A strong, consistent finding by all of our authors gives us the answer. While millions of dollars are spent on the latest state-of-the-art addiction research, the authors repeatedly conclude that the core component of any effective treatment approach appears to have changed little over the years: the connection to a caring individual or group, a connection that enables the woman to undo her sense of shame and guilt and that supports her basic sense of self-esteem and worth as a human being.

To be a woman who recovers is a deeply life-changing, transformative experience. Recovery also can be deeply gratifying and life changing. That is why we bother.

Women are all unique individuals with a multitude of diverse experiences, needs, motivations, and wishes. Yet, in treatment and recovery, they come together on the basis of their shared experience, and it is that common bond that gives power and support for their continued recovery and growth.

RESOURCES

Nancy K. Brown and Rita Rhodes

The following resource list includes books, websites, and popular and training videos related to women. A complete and regularly updated master bibliography on women's addictions, which also contains journal articles and other information relevant to women's addiction issues, is available at www.cosw.sc.edu/research/confpresent/index.html/. This website is maintained by the College of Social Work at the University of South Carolina.

Books

Bepko, C. (1991). *Feminism and addiction*. Binghamton, NY: Haworth Press.
Boyd, S. (1999). *Mothers and illicit drugs: Transcending the myths*. Toronto: University of Toronto Press.
Campbell, N. D. (2000). *Using women: Gender, drug policy, and social justice*. New York: Routledge.
Center for Substance Abuse Treatment. (1994). *Practical approaches in the treatment of women who abuse alcohol and other drugs*. Rockville, MD: Department of Health and Human Services.
Dash, L. (1996). *Rosa Lee: A mother and her family in urban America*. New York: Plume.
Evans, K., & Sullivan, J. M. (1995). *Treating addicted survivors of trauma*. New York: Guilford Press.
Finkelstein, N. (1990). *Treatment issues: Women and abuse*. Washington, DC: Coalition on Alcohol and Drug Dependent Women and Their Children.
Finkelstein, N., Duncan, S. A., Derman, L., & Smeltz, J. (1992). *Getting sober, getting well: A treatment guide for caregivers who work with women*. Cambridge, MA: Women's Alcoholism Program of the Cambridge and Somerville Program of Alcoholism Rehabilitation.

Finnegan, D., & Underhill, B. (1996). *Chemical dependency: Women at risk.* New York: Harrington Park Press.

Friedling, M. P. (2000). *Recovering women: Feminisms and the representation of addiction.* Boulder, CO: Westview Press.

Gomberg, E.S.L. (1993). *Women and alcohol use and abuse.* New Jersey: Ablex.

Gomez, L. E. (1997). *Misconceiving mothers: Legislators, prosecutors, and the politics of prenatal drug exposure.* Philadelphia: Temple University Press.

Haack, M. R. (Ed.). (1997). *Drug-dependent mothers and their children: Issues in public policy.* New York: Springer.

Hall, N. L. (1974). *A true story of a drunken mother.* Boston: South End Press.

Howard, J. M., Martin, S. E., Mail, P. D., Hilton, M. E., & Taylor, E. D. (Eds.). (1996). *Women and alcohol: Issues for prevention research* (Research Monograph No. 32). Bethesda, MD: National Institute on Alcohol Abuse and Alcoholism.

Humphries, D. (1999). *Crack mothers: Pregnancy, drugs, and the media.* Columbus: Ohio State University Press.

Hunt, W. A., & Zakhari, S. (Eds.). (1995). *Stress, gender, and alcohol-seeking behavior* (Research Monograph No. 29).Bethesda, MD: National Institute on Alcohol Abuse and Alcoholism.

Inciardi, J., Lockwood, D., & Pottieger, A. (1993). *Women and crack-cocaine.* Old Tappan, NJ: Macmillan.

Jersild, D. (2000). *Happy hours: Alcohol in a woman's life.* New York: Cliff Street Books.

Kandall, S. R. (1999). *Substance and shadow: Women and addiction in the United States.* Cambridge, MA: Harvard University Press.

Kasl, C. D. (1989). *Women, sex, and addiction: A search for love and power.* New York: Harper-Collins.

Ladd-Taylor, M., & Umansky, L. (1998) *"Bad" mothers: The politics of blame in twentieth-century America.* New York: New York University Press.

Mahan, S. (1996). *Crack cocaine, crime, and women: Legal, social, and treatment issues.* Thousand Oaks, CA: Sage.

McGovern, G. (1996). *Terry: My daughter's life-and-death struggle with alcoholism.* New York: Villard Books.

Morrison, M. A. (1988). *White rabbit: A doctor's story of her addiction and recovery.* New York: Crown.

Murphy, S., & Rosenbaum, M. (1999). *Pregnant women on drugs: Combating stereotypes and stigma.* New Brunswick: NJ: Rutgers University Press.

Pagliaro, A. M., & Pagliaro, L. A. (2000). *Substance use among women: A reference and resource guide.* Philadelphia: Brunner/Mazel.

Rahdert, E. R. (Ed.). (1996). *Treatment for drug-exposed women and their children: Advances in research methodology.* Rockville, MD: National Institute on Drug Abuse.

Ratner, M. S. (1993). *Crack pipe as pimp: An ethnographic investigation of sex-for-crack exchanges.* San Francisco: New Lexington Press.

Rosenbaum, M. (1981). *Women on heroin.* New Brunswick, NJ: Rutgers University Press.

Saulnier, C. (1996). *Feminist theories and social work: Approaches and applications.* Binghamton, NY: Haworth Press.

Sherman, B. R. (Ed.). (1998). *Addiction and recovery: Empowering recovery through peer counseling.* Westport, CT: Praeger.

Stevens, S. J., Tortu, S., & Coyle, S. L. (Eds.). (1998). *Women, drug use, and HIV infection.* Binghamton, NY: Haworth Press.

Stevens, S. J., & Wexler, H. K. (Eds.). (1998). *Women and substance abuse: Gender transparency.* Binghamton, NY: Haworth Press.

Straussner, S.L.A., & Zelvin, E. (Eds.). (1997). *Gender and addictions: Men and women in treatment.* Northvale, NJ: Aronson.

Substance Abuse and Mental Health Services Administration. (1997). *Substance use among women in the United States.* Rockville, MD: Office of Applied Studies.

Underhill, B. L., & Finnegan, D. G. (Eds.). (1996). *Chemical dependency: Women at risk.* Binghamton, NY: Haworth Press.

Van Den Bergh, N. (Ed.). (1991). *Feminist perspectives on addictions.* New York: Springer.

Washington, C. L., & Roman, A. B. (Eds.). (1998). *Drug addiction research and the health of women.* Rockville, MD: National Institute on Drug Abuse.

Websites

www.addictionresourceguide.com/   Search for treatment facilities by name, geographical location, type, and special populations served (pregnant women, women, children, gays and lesbians, anorexia or bulimia, PTSD, veterans, and so on). Information about each program includes what percentage of admits last year were women. Provides information about programs for eating disorders.

www.addictionresourceguide.com/listings/wcc.html/   Contact and program information for the Women and Children's Center in Kentwood, MI, a long-term residential chemical dependency treatment program. Allows women to bring children under ten years old to treatment with them.

www.bettyfordcenter.org/   Betty Ford Center. Nationally known treatment program with gender-specific treatment and family treatment programs offered. Check out the Resource Room for a lot of good information.

http://sano.arf.org/women.htm/   Women's Interest Network (Canada). This website has a variety of articles and links to women's health issues.

infoweb.magi.com/~amethyst/   Amethyst Women's Addiction Centre (Canada). This website provides addiction treatment to women that is based on feminist principles.

http://womenstx.homepage.com/   This website makes available the text *Practical Approaches in the Treatment of Women Who Abuse Alcohol and Other Drugs,* a publication of the Substance Abuse and Mental Health Services Administration (SAMHSA).

http://sobrietyhouse.org/steppingstone.htm/   Sobriety House is a treatment program for alcoholic women. Website has good information about women's addiction.

www.womenfdn.org/index.htm/   A Canadian site dedicated to women's addiction. Excellent.

www.womenforsobriety.org/   Women for Sobriety, Inc. A nonprofit organization dedicated to helping women overcome addictions. Works with a "Thirteen Statement" program; establishes self-help groups. Bookstore, writings by Jean Kirkpatrick.

www.lindesmith.org/   Open Society Institute. Policy and research institute. Information on drugs and drug policy; links to Internet resources associated with methadone treatment; full-text writings of the director of the center; search engine available.

www.restoreunity.org/   Restoring Unity to the World. An interesting website with a lot of information for women on a variety of topics, including addiction.

www.alcoholics-anonymous.org/   Alcoholics Anonymous World Services, Inc.

www.al-anon.alateen.org/   Al-Anon/AlaTeen Family Group Headquarters, Inc.

www.health.org/nacoa/kidspage.htm/   National Association for Children of Alcoholics.

www.ca.org/   Cocaine Anonymous World Services.

www.whitehousedrugpolicy.gov/   Office of National Drug Policy and Control.

www.niaaa.nih.gov/   National Institute on Alcohol Abuse and Alcoholism (NIAAA).

www.nida.nih.gov/   National Institute on Drug Abuse (NIDA).

www.health.org/   National Clearinghouse for Alcohol and Drug Information.

/www.dcregistry.com/users/eatingaddictions/index.html/   Eating Addictions Anonymous (EAA). "EAA is a fellowship of men and women recovering from all types of eating and body image addiction. We aren't about diet obsession, food manipulation, or self-hating vanity."

www.samhsa.gov/centers/csat/csat.html/   Center for Substance Abuse Treatment.

http://maxpages.com/gahopeline/Women_Addiction_Recovery/   Support and links for women in recovery from compulsive gambling. Nice site.

www.soberdykes.org/resources.htm/   Support for lesbian women. Nice site.

www.pcc.edu/edserv/ccg/AD/AD_103.htm/   A community college course syllabus on women and addiction.

www.womensjourneys.com/html/computing_online_addiction.html/   A nice site with many links and a self-assessment of Internet addiction.

www.casacolumbia.org/   The National Center on Addiction and Substance Abuse at Columbia University (CASA) is a resource for research on addiction and substance abuse. It provides access to information, research, and commentary on tobacco, alcohol, and drug abuse issues, including prevention, treatment, and cost data.

www.nyu.edu/socialwork/wwwrsw/   A wonderful metasite with almost sixty thousand categorized links of interest to social workers and other professionals. Provides links to many full-text documents, government agencies, and topics related to women. *Updated daily.*

www.nimh.nih.gov/osp/   The Office for Special Populations develops and coordinates research policies and programs to ensure increased emphasis on the mental health needs of women and minority populations.

www.4woman.gov/   National Women's Health Information Center (NWHIC). The NWHIC provides a gateway to the vast array of federal and other women's health information resources. This site can link you to a wide variety of women's health-related material developed by the Department of Health and Human Services, other federal agencies, and private sector resources. The NWHIC also provides a toll-free call center at (800) 994-9662 and TDD at (888) 220-5446.

www4.od.nih.gov/orwh/   The Office of Research on Women's Health serves as the focal point for women's health research at the National Institutes of Health.

www.nida.nih.gov/WHGD/WHGDHome.html/   This is a National Institute on Drug Abuse page on women's health differences (WHGD) in addiction and research.

http://na.basicwebpage.org/   Narcotics Anonymous Online Resources. Directory of local and regional Narcotics Anonymous (NA) meetings and events, online meetings, facts about NA, a message board, FAQ, and NA chat room. Links to other recovery resources.

www.prescriptionanonymous.org/   Get Help for Prescription Addiction. Support for people who have become addicted to prescription drugs.

www.marijuana-anonymous.org/   Marijuana Anonymous. Marijuana Anonymous is a fellowship of men and women who share experiences, strength, and hope with each other.

http://soberrecovery.com/ Recovery Resources Online. Over two thousand resources and links for eating disorders, bipolar disorder, schizophrenia, depression, and alcoholism and addiction. Resources for counseling, therapy, and twelve-step meetings.

www.tui.edu/Research/Resources/Addictions.html/ The Union Institute Resource Engine. A good search engine for getting around the addictions sites.

www.womenfdn.org/ This Women's Addiction Foundation website provides information on substance abuse and eating disorders; women's treatment services; substance abuse and depression, violence, and HIV-AIDS; and substance abuse and older women.

www.women-addiction.com/ This home study program site contains valuable knowledge about women and addiction Internet classes, and counseling and educational services.

www.campbellvalley.com/ Website of a residential treatment program for adolescent girls located outside British Columbia, Canada.

http://smokefreewomen-kids.org Website on women and smoking, primarily targeted to preventing teen girls from smoking. Not a treatment program but informational in nature.

www.renfrew.org/ The Renfrew Center is "a women's mental health center with locations in Philadelphia and Bryn Mawr, PA; Coconut Creek and Miami, Florida; New York City; Southern Connecticut and Northern New Jersey as well as a nationwide referral network." It specializes "in the treatment of eating disorders (anorexia, bulimia and compulsive overeating), trauma, anxiety, depression, substance abuse and other women's issues."

www.newdirectionsforwomen.org/ Women's alcohol and drug treatment center in California.

www.mirasol.net/ Arizona Center for Eating Disorder Recovery.

www.caron.org/ Caron Foundation. Provides gender-specific care for men and women; provides residential and extended-care treatment for men and women.

www.halfwayhouse.net/ Drug and Alcohol Treatment Program for Women Only.

http://newhopemanor.org/ New Hope Manor is a "women's residential substance abuse treatment community located in Barryville, Sullivan County, New York; special tracks for pregnant women, adolescents, criminal justice clients."

Popular Videos

Caron, G. (Producer). (1988). *Clean and Sober.* [Video].
Edwards, B. (Producer). (1962). *Days of Wine and Roses.* [Video].
Mandoki, L. (Director). (1994). *When a Man Loves a Woman.* [Video].
Payne, A. (Director). (1999). *Citizen Ruth.* [Video].
Thomas, B. (Director). (2000). *28 Days.* [Video].
Wilder, B. (Director). (1945). *The Lost Weekend.* [Video].

Educational Videos

A Challenge to Care [Film]. (Available from Vida Health Communications, 6 Bigelow Street, Cambridge, MA 02139).
Straight from the Heart [Film]. (Available from Vida Health Communications, 6 Bigelow Street, Cambridge, MA 02139).

Kennedy, R., & Smith, R. (Producer and Director). *Women of Substance* [Film]. (Available from Women Make Movies, 462 Broadway, New York, NY 10013).

Moyers on Addiction: Changing Lives. (1998). Princeton, NJ: Films for the Humanities and Sciences.

Treatment Issues for Women. (1992). Rockville, MD: National Clearinghouse for Alcohol and Drug Information.

Women: Coming Out of the Shadows. (1991). Boston: Fanlight Productions.

Secret Addictions: Women, Drugs and Alcohol. (1991). Deerfield, IL: MIT/Film & Video.

Women Addicts: The Gender Gap. (1991). Washington, DC: Drug Policy Foundation. (30 min.)

Drugs and Pregnancy: A View from the Street. (1991). Bridgeport, CT: Regional Youth/Adult Substance Abuse Project.

ABOUT THE AUTHORS

PATRICIA ROSE ATTIA, M.S.W., is the vice president of Liberty Behavioral Management Group, where she has established inpatient and outpatient clinical programs for adolescents and adults with psychiatric and chemical dependency problems. She is an adjunct professor at the Wurzweiler School of Social Work, Yeshiva University, where she teaches psychopathology and substance abuse. Attia has written on dual diagnoses and coauthored a chapter on the brief treatment of substance abusers in the forthcoming *Handbook of Brief Treatment* (Aronson). Attia is a Ph.D. candidate at New York University and a guest lecturer at workshops and institutes around the country. TATTIA3921@aol.com

LINDA BARBANEL, M.S.W., C.S.W., is a psychotherapist in private practice in New York City. She is nationally known for her expertise in relationship issues as well as in the psychology of money. She is the author of *Piggy Bank to Credit Card: Teach Your Child the Financial Facts of Life* (Crown, 1994) and *Sex, Money and Power: Smart Ways to Resolve Money Conflicts and Keep Them from Sabotaging Your Closest Relationships* (Macmillan Spectrum Books, 1996). Barbanel writes a monthly advice column for *Woman's Own* magazine, a national publication. She has been quoted in over one thousand national publications and is a frequent guest expert on radio and television shows.

Eileen P. Beyer, Psy.D., CAC, Diplomate specializes in women's issues through her private practice and organizational consulting work. She is the former director of women's services at the Caron Foundation, where she led the development and growth of female-sensitive treatment services within a continuum of care. With a doctorate in clinical psychology and fifteen years of experience as a therapist specializing in the treatment of chemical dependency, Beyer has presented widely on dual-diagnosis issues and the specialized treatment of addicted women. She is coeditor of the second edition of *Managing the Dual Diagnosis Patient: Current Issues and Clinical Approaches* (Haworth Press, 2002), in which she coauthored a chapter on treating women with dual diagnoses. gebeyer@msn.com

Nancy K. Brown, Ph.D., is an assistant professor at the College of Social Work, University of South Carolina. She received her Ph.D. from the University at Albany in New York. Her research focus is primarily on women's addictions and, in particular, on women's high-risk behavior in recovery. Brown's current research examines recovering parents' sense of self-efficacy in substance abuse prevention in their children. Brown spent many years as a practicing social worker in the area of addictions, with a special focus on families, women, and adolescents.

Stephanie Brown, Ph.D., is a clinician, author, teacher, researcher, and consultant in the field of addictions. She is director of the Addictions Institute in Menlo Park, California, where she also maintains a private practice, and is a research associate at the Mental Research Institute in Palo Alto, where she codirects the Family Recovery Project. Brown, who lectures internationally, is the author of four books, including *Treating the Alcoholic* (Wiley, 1985) and *Treating Adult Children of Alcoholics* (Wiley, 1988), and the editor of *Treating Alcoholism* (Jossey-Bass, 1995). She is coauthor of *The Alcoholic Family in Recovery* (Guilford, 1999) and *Treating Alcoholism,* a video series (Jaylen Productions, 1997). Her newest book is *The Family Recovery Guide* (coauthored with Virginia Lewis and Andrew Liotta, New Harbinger, 2000). Brown is the recipient of numerous awards, including the Norman Zinberg Memorial Award from Harvard University (2000) and the Clark Vincent Award from the California Association of Marriage and Family Therapists (2001). sdbrown9@attbi.com

Karen Carnabucci, M.S.S., C.I.C.S.W., L.S.W., CP, PAT, practices and teaches group skills and psychodrama in her private practice in Racine, Wisconsin. She has written on clinical topics for the popular small press in such publications as *Many Voices, Community of Recovery, D&A News,* and *Healing Magazine,* and is the editor of *Psychodrama Network News,* the professional newsletter of the American Society of Group Psychotherapy and Psychodrama. She received her master's degree in clinical social work from the Graduate School of Social Work and Social Research, Bryn Mawr College. karen@companionsinhealing.com

STEPHANIE S. COVINGTON, PH.D., L.C.S.W., is a clinician, author, organizational consultant, and lecturer. Recognized for her pioneering work on women's issues, she specializes in the development and implementation of gender-responsive services. Covington has published numerous articles and books, including *A Woman's Way Through the 12 Steps,* with an accompanying workbook (Hazelden, 1994, 2000); *Awakening Your Sexuality: A Guide for Recovering Women* (Hazelden, 2000); *Leaving the Enchanted Forest: The Path from Relationship Addiction to Intimacy* (with L. Beckett, HarperSanFrancisco, 1988); and a treatment curriculum, *Helping Women Recover: A Program for Treating Addiction* (with a special edition for the criminal justice system, Jossey-Bass, 1999). She is codirector of the Institute for Relational Development and codirector of the Center for Gender and Justice in La Jolla, CA. SSCIRD@aol.com

CATHERINE CRISP, M.S.W., L.M.S.W.-ACP, received her B.A. in sociology from Rutgers University in 1987 and her M.S.W. from the University of Kansas in 1993; she is currently a doctoral candidate at the School of Social Work, University of Texas at Austin. The primary focus of her clinical experience has been on adults with a mental illness, a substance abuse disorder, or both. Other interests include practice with gays and lesbians and the use of technology in practice, research, and education. She is currently working on her dissertation, "Beyond Homophobia: Development and Validation of the Gay Affirmative Practice (GAP) Scale." ccrisp@mail.utexas.edu

JEANNINE CROUSE, C.S.W., D.C.S.W., is a counselor and coordinator of the smoking cessation program at New School University's Student Health Service Center in New York City. She designed the program and implemented it in 1996. Crouse is also a psychotherapist in private practice in New York City. She formerly worked as the coordinator of the dual-diagnosis treatment program and as the clinical manager at Arms Acres Outpatient Chemical Dependency Treatment Program in New York. Jeanninecrouse@aol.com

DIANE RAE DAVIS, PH.D., C.S.W., is an associate professor in the School of Social Work at Eastern Washington University. Davis practiced social work in a variety of settings, including community mental health, residential treatment, juvenile court, and child protective services, prior to receiving her Ph.D. from the University of Texas at Austin in 1991. She is the coauthor of the articles "Making Meaning of Alcoholics Anonymous for Social Workers: Myths, Metaphors, Realities" (with Golie Jansen, *Social Work,* 1998) and "Harm Reduction and Abstinence Based

Recovery: A Dialogue" (with E. Zelvin, *Journal of Social Work Practice in the Addictions*, 2001). She is also the coauthor of the forthcoming book *Addiction Treatment: A Strengths Perspective* (with Katherine van Wormer, Wadsworth Press). ddavis@ewu.edu

A. MEREDITH DEMING, M.S.W., M.P.H., is a recovering addict since 1991 who experienced homelessness for about one year during her active addiction. She is currently a Ph.D. student in the Aging Studies Program, University of South Florida. She has served as the interim executive director of the Community Coalition on Homelessness, Bradenton, Florida, and is a clinical therapist at Healthcare Connections, Tampa. merry1022@aol.com

DIANA M. DINITTO, PH.D., A.C.S.W., L.M.S.W.-ACP is Cullen Trust Centennial Professor in Alcohol Studies and Education and a Distinguished Teaching Professor at the School of Social Work, University of Texas at Austin. She has worked in the detoxification, halfway house, and outpatient substance abuse program of a community mental health center. She is author of *Social Welfare: Politics and Public Policy* (5th ed., Allyn & Bacon, 2000) and coauthor of *Chemical Dependency: A Systems Approach* (2nd ed., Allyn & Bacon, 1998). DiNitto is a board member of the Texas Research Society on Alcoholism, a mentor for AMERSA's Project MAINSTREAM, and a member of the Council on Social Work Education's Commission on Educational Policy. ddinitto@mail.utexas.edu

LAURIE DRABBLE, PH.D., M.S.W., M.P.H., CADC, is an organizational consultant and former executive director of the California Women's Commission on Alcohol and Drug Dependencies. She has developed and delivered numerous training curricula and conference papers on providing culturally competent treatment services for lesbian, gay, bisexual, and transgendered (LGBT) populations and has provided technical assistance in the development of several LGBT-specific substance abuse prevention programs. Drabble has authored numerous publications on LGBT treatment and prevention issues, including her most recent article, "Alcohol, Tobacco and Pharmaceutical Industry Funding: Considerations for Organizations Serving Lesbian, Gay, Bisexual and Transgender Communities," in the *Journal of Gay and Lesbian Social Services*. LADrabble@aol.com

MILENA ESHERICK, M.A., is a Psy.D. candidate at the Wright Institute, Berkeley, California. She has worked in the field of chemical dependency since 1995. Currently she is a supervisor at a residential drug treatment program for adolescents in Oakland. Her research focuses on addiction, eating disorders, and obsessive-compulsive disorder as well as on the treatment of conduct-disordered adolescents. She has a supervised psychotherapy practice in Oakland. mesherick@wrightinst.edu

MURIEL GRAY, PH.D., L.C.S.W., CAC, CEAP, is associate professor at the School of Social Work, University of Maryland Baltimore, where she is chair of the substance abuse specialization. Her thirty-year social work career has included work in a variety of settings—public, nonprofit, and private. She currently counsels individuals who have substance use disorders, and serves as workplace consultant and trainer for a variety of workplaces, employee assistance programs (EAPs), and managed care firms nationwide. She has written numerous professional publications on various aspects of addictions, diversity, and EAP practice. Her most recent book is *Winning at Work: Breaking Free of Personal Traps to Find Success in the New Workplace* (coauthored with Mel Sandler, Davies-Black, 1999). MGRAY@ssw.umaryland.edu

RENEE S. KATZ, PH.D., BCD, is a clinical psychologist in private practice in Seattle, Washington. Formerly with Stanford University's Drug and Alcohol Treatment Center and the Addictions Institute in Menlo Park, Katz is currently continuing education faculty at the University of Washington. Katz publishes, trains, and consults nationally in the areas of grief and complicated bereavement, the addictions, and gerontology. She is the author of *Countertransference and Older Clients* (coauthored with B. Genevay, Sage, 1990).

KERRILY J. KITANO, PH.D., M.S.W., is best known for her program, policy, and research work in HIV-AIDS with Asian and Pacific Islander populations. She received her Ph.D. from the School of Social Welfare, University of California-Berkeley (UCB), in 1997. A two-year postdoctoral fellowship with the Alcohol Research Group through the School of Public Health at UCB signaled a return to the alcohol and substance abuse field, where she started twenty years ago. She is currently research director for a three-year project funded by the Center for Substance Abuse Treatment, "Integrating Spirituality and Healing into Outpatient Programs," through Asian American Recovery Services, Inc., in San Francisco. kerrily@hotmail.com

ROSE FAJARDO LATINO, M.S.W., L.M.S.W.-ACP, LCDC, graduated from the School of Social Work, USF, and the New York School of Psychodynamic Psychotherapy. She is presently a doctoral fellow at the School for Social Work, Smith College, and an adjunct faculty and supervisor at the School of Social Work, University of Texas at Arlington. Latino is the clinical director at the Youth Advocate Programs in Dallas, a unique program for dually diagnosed adolescents that blends an intensive outpatient program with intensive home-based therapy. She is researching the roles of ethnicity, boyfriends, family relationships, and depression as they relate to adolescent girls' substance abuse. Roselatino@aol.com

MELISSA B. LITTLEFIELD, PH.D., is assistant professor at the School of Social Work, University of Maryland Baltimore, where she teaches courses on Racism and Diversity and Social Work Research. Littlefield is a 1999–2002 Maryland Higher Education Commission Henry C. Welcome Fellow. Her research is in the areas of stress and coping among African American women, issues of diversity in social work, and the use of technology in social work education. mlittlef@ssw.umaryland.edu

LIANE J. LOUIE, PH.D., is the clinical director of Asian American Recovery Services, Inc., which serves children, youths, adults, and families in the San Francisco Bay Area. She holds a B.A. from University of California-Santa Cruz, an M.A. from Boston University, and an M.S. and Ph.D. from the Pacific Graduate School of Psychology. Her clinical pre- and postdoctoral experiences include work at the Department of Veterans Affairs, the Kapiolani Counseling Center, and the Kapiolani Child Protection Center, Honolulu. She is committed to addressing Asian and Pacific Islander women and women's issues, working with youths and families, and addiction issues in families. LLouie@aars-inc.org

KAREN MCGOFF-YOST, M.S.W., is a staff social worker in the Spinal Chord Injury Unit of James A. Haley Veterans Administration Hospital. She formerly served as the executive director of the Community Coalition on Homelessness in Tampa. McGoff-Yost holds a B.A. in rehabilitation counseling from the University of Florida and an M.S.W. from USF. shellty@mindspring.com

JUANA MORA, PH.D., is a full professor in the Department of Chicana/o Studies at California State University, Northridge, and an expert on Latina substance abuse treatment and prevention. Mora's current research is on the study of changing drinking practices among Latina women and related lifestyle and cultural influences. She also serves on the editorial boards of several public health and women's studies journals and has served as a grant reviewer and evaluator for the National Institute on Alcohol Abuse and Alcoholism and the National Institute on Drug Abuse, and she coedited a special issue on Latina substance abuse in the *International Journal of the Addictions*. She received the American Council on Education Fellowship offered to leaders in higher education. juana.mora@csun.edu

JANE M. NAKKEN, ED.D., is executive vice president for external relations at the Hazelden Foundation. Her fascination with the process of transformational change began with her clinical work with chemically dependent adolescents. She designed Hazelden's Parent Program, the Women and Children's Recovery Community, and Women Healing conferences held jointly with the Betty Ford Center and the

Caron Foundation. Nakken has served on the faculty of Rutgers University Summer School on Alcohol Studies and the Florida Summer School on Addictions Studies, and consults and lectures internationally. She earned her doctorate in organization change from Pepperdine University, and has sixteen previous publications. jnakken@hazelden.org

LYNN E. O'CONNOR, PH.D., is on the faculty of the Wright Institute, Berkeley, and is its director of evaluation. She conducts research on emotion, psychopathology, addiction, and personality and, in addition, is conducting research on emotions, psychopathology, and subjective well-being in chimpanzees. She has also been involved in psychotherapy research. O'Connor has been a research associate at the Haight Ashbury Free Medical Detoxification Clinic and an evaluator at Walden House, a residential treatment program. She has published in various addiction-focused journals. In addition, O'Connor has conducted research on psychotherapy process and outcome, and has a private psychotherapy and consultation practice in San Francisco. LynnOC@aol.com

SUSAN D. RAEBURN, PH.D., is a clinical psychologist in private practice in Berkeley, and staff psychologist in the addictions program at Kaiser Permanente. After receiving her Ph.D. at the Wright Institute, Berkeley, she interned at Stanford University in behavioral medicine with Dr. Stewart Agras. She continued working at Stanford in both the Behavioral Medicine Clinic and the Alcohol and Drug Treatment Center. While at Stanford, Raeburn coauthored numerous publications on the treatment of eating disorders. She has also published articles on musicians' mental health and is on the editorial board of *Medical Problems of Performing Artists*. SDR510@aol.com

RITA RHODES, PH.D., M.S.W., is an associate professor at the College of Social Work, University of South Carolina. Her research focus is on vulnerable women, with a particular interest in substance abuse and mental health. Rhodes's current research is on the effects of legal intervention on the lives of substance-using pregnant and parenting women. Her practice experience has included work with women in prisons, psychiatric institutions, and shelters. Ritar@gwm.sc.edu

JUDITH E. RUBIN, M.S.S., L.S.W., has been involved with training health care providers for over ten years. She is an instructor at the School of Social Work, San Francisco State University. She is also the clinical consultant to the San Francisco Foster Parent's United Mentors Program. Previously, she directed the Moving Addicted Mothers Ahead (MAMA) project at the Haight Ashbury Free Clinic and helped design and implement the curricula for the UCB Extension Drug and Alcohol Program. She teaches an undergraduate course on treatment issues in addiction at the School of Social Welfare, UCB. jrubin@sfsu.edu

JOYCE SCHMID, PH.D., is a licensed marriage and family therapist in private practice in Menlo Park. She is an associate of the Addictions Institute and has taught classes on addiction at the University of California–Santa Cruz Extension and at the Santa Clara University School of Lifelong Learning. Her publications are on the topic of the alcoholic family and adult children of alcoholics (ACAs). She was on the outpatient staff at the Stanford Alcohol and Drug Treatment Center, where she was coordinator of ACA groups. She earned her Ph.D. at the Pacific Graduate School of Psychology and her B.A. at Harvard University. JoyceGSchmid@aol.com

SHULAMITH LALA ASHENBERG STRAUSSNER, D.S.W., CAS, is a full professor at the Ehrenkranz School of Social Work, New York University, and coordinator of their post-master's program in the treatment of alcohol- and drug-abusing clients. She has been a visiting professor at the School of Social Work, Tel Aviv University, and at Omsk State Pedagogical University in Siberia, Russia. Straussner has numerous publications dealing with substance abuse, occupational social work, and EAPs. Among her eight books are *Ethnocultural Factors in Addictions Treatment* (Guilford Press, 2001), *Gender and Addictions: Men and Women in Treatment* (coedited with E. Zelvin, Aronson, 1997), and *Clinical Work with Substance-Abusing Clients* (Guilford Press, 1993). She is the founding editor of the new *Journal of Social Work Practice in the Addictions* (Haworth Press). She has a special interest in women and addictions, the impact of alcohol and other drugs on families, ethnocultural issues, and couples therapy. Straussner lectures extensively in the United States and abroad and has a private clinical, supervisory, and consulting practice in New York City. sls1@nyu.edu

ANNE L. STROZIER, PH.D., M.S.W., is an associate professor at the School of Social Work, USF, and codirector of the USF Kinship Support Center. Strozier's degrees are in African American studies (M.A.), social work (M.S.W.), and counseling psychology (Ph.D.). She has published in the areas of substance abuse, kinship care, group work, and professional development. She is currently a member of the Alcohol, Tobacco and Other Drugs Steering Committee for the National Association of Social Workers. strozier@chuma1.cas.usf.edu

CAROL TOSONE, PH.D., M.S.W., is an associate professor at the Ehrenkranz School of Social Work, New York University, and a Distinguished Scholar in Social Work in the National Academies of Practice. She is editor of the journal *Psychoanalysis and Psychotherapy*, and also serves on the editorial boards of *Psychoanalytic Social Work and Social Work in Health Care*. She is author of numerous professional articles and has coedited two books: *Love and Attachment: Contemporary Issues and Treatment Considerations* (with Theresa Aiello, Jason Aronson, 1999) and *Doing More with Less: Using Long-Term Skills in Short-Term Treatment* (with Barbara Dane and Alice Wolson, Jason Aronson, 2001). Tosone also serves on the executive board of the New York State Society for Clinical Social Work. carol.tosone@nyu.edu

BRENDA L. UNDERHILL, M.S., CAC, has worked for the past twenty-five years in the field of substance abuse, with a specialty in lesbian-specific services and treatment of women and children. She has authored and edited numerous publications on treatment for women and children, including her most recent book, *Chemical Dependency: Women at Risk* (co-edited with Dana Finnegan, Haworth Press, 1996). Her many lesbian-specific books and articles include *Creating Visibility: Providing Lesbian-Sensitive and Lesbian-Specific Services* (Alcoholism Center for Women, 1993) and "The Pain of Invisibility: Issues for Lesbians" in *Alcohol and Drugs Are Women's Issues* (with S. Ostermann, Women's Action Alliance and Scarecrow Press). Underhill previously served for fourteen years as executive director of the Alcoholism Center for Women in Los Angeles. brenlunder@aol.com

KATHERINE VAN WORMER, PH.D., M.S.S.W., is professor at the Department of Social Work, University of Northern Iowa in Cedar Falls. Previously, she taught criminal justice studies for six years and, after getting her MSSW, practiced substance abuse counseling in Washington State and Norway. She has published over forty articles and book chapters and is the author of *Alcoholism Treatment: A Social Work Perspective* (1995) and *Social Welfare: A World View* (1997), both with Wadsworth; *Social Work with Lesbians, Gays, and Bisexuals: A Strengths Perspective* (2000) and *Women and the Criminal Justice System* (2000), both with Allyn & Bacon; and *Counseling Female Offenders and Victims: A Strengths-Restorative Approach* (Springer, 2001). vanworme@csbs.csbs.uni.edu

CASSANDRA VIETEN, PH.D., a clinical psychologist, is adjunct faculty at the Wright Institute, Berkeley, and an adjunct instructor in the Department of Neurology at the University of California, San Francisco (UCSF). She has extensive experience working in treatment settings with chemically dependent individuals and is coprincipal investigator for the UCSF Family Alcoholism Study, which seeks to find genes involved in alcoholism risk. In addition, she studies the role of personality and emotion regulation in development and recovery from addictions. cassi@itsa.ucsf.edu

NANCY WAITE-O'BRIEN, PH.D., is director of psychological services and professional development at the Betty Ford Center at Eisenhower, Rancho Mirage, California. As the senior staff psychologist, she directs all counseling programs for addictive disease, supervises patient assessments, and guides the clinical staff in the implementation of treatment therapies. She began her association with the Betty Ford Center in 1989 and has played a pivotal role in the design of the center's unique women's program. Waite-O'Brien has twenty years of experience in addiction treatment both in the United States and in the Caribbean. She has taught at Chapman University and coauthored a text on adolescent treatment. She maintains a private practice in the Palm Springs area. nobrien@bettyfordcenter.org

ELIZABETH ZELVIN, C.S.W., CASAC, ACSW, C-CATODSW, has directed treatment programs for substance-abusing women and for homeless alcoholic and drug-addicted clients. She currently practices psychotherapy online, teaches at the Graduate School of Social Service, Fordham University, and serves as special topics editor of the *Journal of Social Work Practice in the Addictions*. She is coeditor of *Gender and Addictions: Men and Women in Treatment* (with S.L.A. Straussner, Aronson, 1997) and has written and lectured extensively on women's addictions, codependency, and couples in recovery. She has also published two books of poetry, *Gifts and Secrets: Poems of the Therapeutic Relationship* and *I Am the Daughter*. LZcybershrink@aol.com LZcyber shrink.com

NAME INDEX

SUBJECT INDEX

A

Abandonment: history of, and provisional personality, 257; issues of, in relationship addiction, 172, 176, 181

Absolute frequency, 120

Abstinence, 37; addiction treatment medications and, 88–89; assessment and, 94; for compulsive gambling, 116–117, 118; for compulsive spending, 194, 195; dual diagnosis women and, 442; for eating disorders, 133–134; moderation *versus*, 89; in recovery, 267; sexual addiction and, 154, 163; in transition stage of recovery, 39–40, 547–549; workplace issues of, 386–389

Abuse, physical. *See* Domestic abuse; Sexual abuse; Trauma

Abusive men. *See* Domestic abuse; Men; Trauma

Abusive relationships, 170–184. *See also* Domestic abuse; Relationship addiction

Acceptance: of agency, 30–32, 34, 49–50; of loss of control, 31–32, 37–38, 40, 41, 46, 49–50, 93, 539, 555–556; of self, 30–31

Acculturation stressors: for Asian and Pacific Islander women, 359–360; for Black women, 317–319; for Latinas, 323–327, 331, 332–335, 336–337, 340

Action gamblers, 101–102

Action stage of change, 441

Active addiction stage, 39, 44–45; Alcoholics Anonymous approach to, 546–547; older women in, 290–291

Acupuncture, 366

Acute stress disorder, 424

Addicere, 267

Addiction: compulsive spending as, 188–189; defined, as developmental process, 36–38; defined, as disease *versus* disorder, 53–54, 94, 519; developmental model of, 26–51; eating disorders as, 132–134; etiology of, 36, 43, 76–82; gender differences in,

35–36, 42–43, 544; meanings of, for women *versus* men, 46–50, 427; multidimensional view of, 53, 54, 62–63; as neglect of self, 57; process of, in developmental model, 43–46; in significant others, women affected by, 487–510; spiral of, 55–56; stages of, in developmental model, 38–42; theories of, 26–51, 53–57; ways of viewing, 43. *See also* Developmental model

Addiction, women's: biological and genetic factors in, 76–79; developmental model of, 26–51; etiology of, 36, 43, 76–82; gender perspectives on, 32, 34–36; historical perspective on, 3–23; psychological predisposing factors in, 80–82; sociocultural predisposing factors in, 79–80; theoretical perspectives on, 26–51, 53–57; women's psychological development and, 57–59. *See also* Alcoholism; Drug abuse; Substance abuse